ASPEN PUBLISHERS

S0-BYV-205

PROPERTY

KEYED TO DUKEMINIER/KRIER/ALEXANDER/SCHILL

SEVENTH EDITION

Calvin Massey

Professor of Law
University of California
Hastings College of the Law

The *Emanuel Law Outlines* Series

Wolters Kluwer
Law & Business

AUSTIN   BOSTON   CHICAGO   NEW YORK   THE NETHERLANDS

Aspen Publishers
Attn: Permissions Department
76 Ninth Avenue, 7th Floor
New York, NY 10011-5201

To contact Customer Care, e-mail customer.service@aspenpublishers.com, call 1-800-234-1660, fax 1-800-901-9075, or mail correspondence to:

Aspen Publishers
Attn: Order Department
PO Box 990
Frederick, MD 21705

Printed in the United States of America.

1 2 3 4 5 6 7 8 9 0

ISBN 978-0-7355-8997-1

Library of Congress Cataloging-in-Publication Data

Massey, Calvin R.
  Property: Keyed to Dukeminier/Krier/Alexander/Schill, seventh edition/Calvin Massey.
      p. cm.—(The Emanuel law outlines series)
  Includes index.
  ISBN 978-0-7355-8997-1
  1.   Property—United States—Outlines, syllabi, etc. I. Property. 7th ed. II. Title.
    KF561. M375 2010
    346.7304—dc22

                                                                2010011713

About Wolters Kluwer Law & Business

Wolters Kluwer Law & Business is a leading provider of research information and workflow solutions in key specialty areas. The strengths of the individual brands of Aspen Publishers, CCH, Kluwer Law International and Loislaw are aligned within Wolters Kluwer Law & Business to provide comprehensive, in-depth solutions and expert-authored content for the legal, professional and education markets.

CCH was founded in 1913 and has served more than four generations of business professionals and their clients. The CCH products in the Wolters Kluwer Law & Business group are highly regarded electronic and print resources for legal, securities, antitrust and trade regulation, government contracting, banking, pension, payroll, employment and labor, and healthcare reimbursement and compliance professionals.

Aspen Publishers is a leading information provider for attorneys, business professionals and law students. Written by preeminent authorities, Aspen products offer analytical and practical information in a range of specialty practice areas from securities law and intellectual property to mergers and acquisitions and pension/benefits. Aspen's trusted legal education resources provide professors and students with high-quality, up-to-date and effective resources for successful instruction and study in all areas of the law.

Kluwer Law International supplies the global business community with comprehensive English-language international legal information. Legal practitioners, corporate counsel and business executives around the world rely on the Kluwer Law International journals, loose-leafs, books and electronic products for authoritative information in many areas of international legal practice.

Loislaw is a premier provider of digitized legal content to small law firm practitioners of various specializations. Loislaw provides attorneys with the ability to quickly and efficiently find the necessary legal information they need, when and where they need it, by facilitating access to primary law as well as state-specific law, records, forms and treatises.

Wolters Kluwer Law & Business, a unit of Wolters Kluwer, is headquartered in New York and Riverwoods, Illinois. Wolters Kluwer is a leading multinational publisher and information services company.

For Ellen

NOTE

This book includes analyses of the facts and holdings of nearly all of the cases treated as principal cases in Dukeminier/Krier/Alexander/Schill, *Property*, Seventh Edition, 2010. The analysis of each Dukeminier/Krier/Alexander/Schill case is preceded by a ★ symbol.

Summary of Contents

Table of Contents ix

Acknowledgments xxix

Preface xxxi

Casebook Correlation Chart xxxiii

Capsule Summary C-1

  1. Conceptual Basics, Possession, and Personal Property. 1

  2. Freehold Estates 29

  3. Future Interests 53

  4. Concurrent Ownership and Marital Interests 85

  5. Leasehold Estates 117

  6. Transfers of Real Property 161

  7. Assuring Good Title to Land 193

  8. Judicial Control of Land Use: Nuisance and Support 215

  9. Servitudes: Land Use Limits Created by Private Bargain 227

10. Public Control of Land Use: Zoning 279

11. Takings: The Power of Eminent Domain and Regulatory Takings 297

Essay Exam Questions 315

Essay Exam Answers 319

Multiple-Choice Questions 329

Answers to Multiple-Choice Questions 341

Table of Cases 351

Subject Matter Index 359

Table of Contents

Acknowledgments xxix
Preface xxxi
Casebook Correlation Chart xxxiii
Capsule Summary C-1

CHAPTER 1

CONCEPTUAL BASICS, POSSESSION, AND PERSONAL PROPERTY

I. **What Is Property?** 1
    A. **Introduction** 1
    B. **Theory** 2
        1. Locke's Labor Theory 2
        2. Other Natural Law Theories 2
        3. Utilitarian Theories 2
        4. Utility and Efficiency 2
        5. Custom 3
    C. **Doctrine** 3

II. **Possession** 3
    A. **Introduction** 3
    B. **Two Meanings of Possession** 4
    C. **Of "Unowned" Things: Discovery, Capture, and Creation** 4
        1. Discovery 4
        2. Capture 4
        3. Creation 7
        4. More on Possession: The Right to Exclude 9
        5. The Right to Destroy 9
    D. **Finders Keepers?** 9
        1. Abandoned Property — General Rule 9
        2. Lost and Mislaid Property — General Rule 10
        3. Equitable Division 13
        4. Statutory Modification 13
    E. **Adverse Possession** 13
        1. Rationales for Adverse Possession 14
        2. Elements of Adverse Possession 14
        3. Extent of the Property Acquired by Adverse Possession 19
        4. Statutory Issues 20
        5. Adverse Possession by Tenants and Co-Owners 21
        6. Adverse Possession of Personal Property 22
        7. Title Acquired by Adverse Possessor 22

     8. Alternatives to Adverse Possession in Boundary Disputes 23

  F. Accession 23

     1. General Rules 23

     2. Mistaken Improver of Real Property 23

III. Personal Property 23

  A. Introduction 23

  B. Bailments 24

     1. Bailors, Bailees, and Third Parties 24

  C. Gifts 24

     1. Intent 24

     2. Delivery 24

     3. Acceptance 26

     4. *Gruen v. Gruen*: An Illustration 27

     Exam Tips on CONCEPTUAL BASICS, POSSESSION, AND PERSONAL PROPERTY 27

Chapter 2

FREEHOLD ESTATES

I. Origins and Taxonomy of Freehold Estates 30

  A. Estates Generally 30

  B. Feudal Tenures 30

     1. Feudal Incidents 31

     2. Feudal Death Tax Avoidance and Statute Quia Emptores 31

  C. A Taxonomy of Freehold Estates 31

II. Fee Simple 32

  A. Introduction 32

  B. Fee Simple Absolute 32

     1. Creation of the Fee Simple Absolute 32

  C. Alienability and Inheritance of the Fee Simple Absolute 33

     1. Alienation 33

     2. Devise 33

     3. Inheritance 33

III. Fee Tail 34

  A. Introduction 34

  B. Origin and Operation of the Fee Tail 34

  C. Elimination of the Fee Tail 34

     1. Fee Tail and Disentailing Conveyance 34

     2. Statutory Conversion to Fee Simple Absolute 35

     3. Statutory Conversion to Fee Simple Subject to Executory Limitation 35

     4. Life Estate and Remainder in Life Tenant's Issue 35

     5. Fee Simple Conditional Created 36
     6. A Modern Equivalent of the Fee Tail 36

IV. Life Estates... 36
  A. **The Nature of a Life Estate** 36
     1. Life Estate *Pur Autre Vie* 37
     2. Defeasible Life Estates 37
     3. Life Estates in a Group or Class of People 37
     4. Ambiguous Grants 37
     5. Transferability and Valuation 38
  B. **The Modern Life Estate**... 39
     1. Judicial Responses to Inflexibility of the Legal Life Estate 39
     2. Legal Life Estates in Personal Property......................... 39
  C. **Waste** 40
     1. Affirmative Waste.. 40
     2. Permissive Waste 41
     3. Ameliorative Waste 41

V. Defeasible Fees... 42
  A. **Introduction** 42
  B. **Fee Simple Determinable**... 42
     1. Words Evidencing Intent to Create Fee Simple Determinable 43
     2. Transferability 43
     3. Abolished in Some States 43
  C. **Fee Simple Subject to Condition Subsequent** 43
     1. Words Evidencing Intent to Create Fee Simple Subject to
       Condition Subsequent 44
     2. Action Necessary to Assert Right of Entry...................... 44
     3. Transferability 44
     4. Preference for Fee Simple Subject to Condition Subsequent 44
  D. **Some Consequences of Classification of Defeasible Fees** 45
     1. Transferability of the Interest Retained by the Grantor 45
     2. Accrual of a Cause of Action for Recovery of Possession 45
     3. Effect Under the Rule Against Perpetuities 46
     4. *Mahrenholz:* An Illustration 46
  E. **Some Problems with Defeasible Fees**............................. 47
     1. Invalid Restraint on Alienation? 47
     2. Defeasible Fee or Covenant?................................... 48
     3. Valuation of the Defeasible Fee and the Associated Future Interest ... 48
  F. **Fee Simple Subject to Executory Limitation** 49

VI. **Restraints on Alienation of Freehold Estates** 50
  A. **Types of Restraints** 50
     1. Forfeiture 50
     2. Disabling 50
     3. Promissory 50

B. Total Restraints on a Fee Interest 50

C. Partial Restraints on a Fee Interest 50

D. Restraints on Life Estates 50

    1. Legal Life Estates 50

    2. Equitable Life Estates 50

       Exam Tips on FREEHOLD ESTATES 51

CHAPTER 3
FUTURE INTERESTS

I.   Introduction 54

II. Future Interests Retained by the Grantor 55

A. Reversion 55

    1. Reversions Are Always Vested 56

    2. Distinguished from Remainder, Possibility of Reverter,
       and Power of Termination 56

B. Possibility of Reverter 56

    1. Transferability 57

    2. Termination 57

    3. Statutory Abolition 57

C. Power of Termination or Right of Entry 57

    1. Transferability 57

    2. Termination 57

    3. Effect of Abolition of Determinable Estates 58

III. Future Interests Created in Grantees 58

A. Remainders 58

    1. Definition 58

    2. Nature of the Estate Held in Remainder 58

    3. Classification of Remainders 58

B. Executory Interests 64

    1. A Note on History 64

    2. Springing Executory Interests 66

    3. Shifting Executory Interests 66

IV. The Proposed *Restatement (Third) of Property* 66

A. Introduction 66

B. Types of Future Interests 66

C. Classification of Future Interests 67

V.   The Trust 67

A. Introduction 67

B. The Basics of the Trust 67

C. Advantages of the Trust 68

    D. **The Spendthrift Trust** 68

VI. **The Marketability Rules** 68

    A. **Introduction** 68

    B. **Destructibility of Contingent Remainders** 69

        1. Effect of Merger 69

        2. Limited Effectiveness of the Rule 69

        3. Modern Replacement of the Rule 70

    C. **The Rule in Shelley's Case** 70

        1. The Rule 70

    D. **The Doctrine of Worthier Title** 71

        1. Statement of the Doctrine 71

        2. Operation of Worthier Title 71

        3. Distinguished from *Shelley's Case* 72

        4. Criticisms of Worthier Title 72

    E. **The Rule Against Perpetuities** 72

        1. Brief Summary of the Rule 73

        2. Vesting 74

        3. Measuring or Validating Lives 75

        4. The Curious Problem of Defeasible Fees 77

        5. Classic Traps for the Unwary 78

        6. Applicability of the Rule Against Perpetuities to Commercial Transactions 79

        7. Reform Doctrines 80

        8. Perpetual Trusts: The End of the Rule? 82

        Exam Tips on FUTURE INTERESTS 83

Chapter 4
CONCURRENT OWNERSHIP AND MARITAL INTERESTS

I. **Forms of Concurrent Ownership** 86

    A. **Introduction** 86

    B. **Tenancy in Common** 86

        1. Nature of Tenancy in Common 86

        2. Presumption of Tenancy in Common 87

        3. Rights to Possession 87

        4. Uneven Shares and Different Estates 87

    C. **Joint Tenancy** 87

        1. Nature of Joint Tenancy 87

        2. The Four Unities of Joint Tenancy 88

        3. Creation of Joint Tenancy 89

        4. Severance of Joint Tenancy 90

        5. Joint Tenancy Bank Accounts 94

    D. **Tenancy by the Entirety** 95

        1. Nature of Tenancy by the Entirety 95

2.   Creation 95
3.   Operation of the Tenancy by the Entirety 96
4.   Termination 98
5.   Personal Property 98

E. **Partnerships and Coparceny** 98
1.   Nature of Partnership Tenancy 98
2.   Nature of Coparceny 98

II. **Rights and Obligations of Concurrent Owners** 98
A. **Introduction** 98
B. **Partition** 99
1.   Partition in Kind 99
2.   Partition by Sale 100
3.   Agreement Not to Partition 100
C. **Rents, Profits, and Possession** 100
1.   Exclusive Possession by One Co-Owner 100
2.   Rents from Third Parties 101
3.   Profits from the Land 102
D. **Accounting for the Costs of Ownership** 102
1.   Mortgage Payments 102
2.   Taxes 102
3.   Repairs 102
4.   Improvements 103
E. **Adverse Possession** 103
F. **Implied Fiduciaries** 103
G.   *Swartzbaugh v. Sampson*: A Case Study 103

III. **Marital Interests** 104
A. **Introduction** 104
B. **The Common Law System** 104
1.   Femes Sole and Femes Covert 104
2.   Husband *Über Alles* 104
3.   Wife's Rights 104
4.   Curtesy 105
C. **The Modern (Mostly Statutory) "Common Law" System** 106
1.   Rights on Divorce 106
2.   Rights on Death 107
3.   Prenuptial Agreements and Spousal Contracts 107
D. **Community Property** 108
1.   Origins and Concept 108
2.   Definition of Community Property 108
3.   Management of Community Property 110
4.   Rights Upon Divorce 111
5.   Rights Upon Death 111
6.   Creditors' Rights 111

E. **"Quasi-Marital" Property: Unmarried Cohabitants** 111
   1. Common Law Marriage 111
   2. Contracts 111
   3. Same-Sex Couples 112

IV. **Condominiums and Cooperatives** 113
  A. **Introduction** 113
  B. **Condominiums** 113
   1. Creatures of Statutes 113
   2. Creation 113
   3. Owners' Association 113
   4. Conveyance and Financing of Units 113
   5. Responsibility for Common Areas 113
   6. No Right to Partition 114
   7. Restrictions on Condominium Conversion 114
  C. **Cooperatives** 114
   1. Financial Operation 114
   2. Transfer Restrictions 114
   3. Limited Liability 114

   Exam Tips on CONCURRENT OWNERSHIP AND MARITAL INTERESTS 114

CHAPTER 5
LEASEHOLD ESTATES

I. **The Nature of Leases** 118
  A. **Origins and Development** 118
  B. **Dual Nature: Estate and Contract** 118
   1. The Traditional View: Estate 118
   2. The Contemporary View: Contract 118
  C. **The General Requirement of a Written Lease** 119
  D. **What Makes It a Lease?** 119

II. **The Types of Leaseholds** 119
  A. **Introduction** 119
  B. **Term of Years** 119
   1. Indeterminate Term 120
   2. Length of the Term 120
  C. **Periodic Tenancy** 120
   1. Notice Necessary to Terminate 121
   2. Fixing the Period of Periodic Tenancies Created by Operation of Law 121
  D. **Tenancy at Will** 122
   1. Distinguished from Leaseholds Unilaterally Terminable 122
   2. Termination 123

E. **Holdovers: Tenancy at Sufferance** 123
    1. What Constitutes Holding Over? 123
    2. Eviction and Damages 124
    3. Election of a New Term 124
    4. Statutory Alterations 126

III. **Delivery of Possession** 126
  A. **Introduction** 126
  B. **Implied Obligation to Deliver Legal Right of Possession** 126
    1. Continuing Obligation 127
    2. Waiver by Tenant 127
  C. **Obligation to Deliver Actual Possession?** 127
    1. The English Rule 127
    2. The American Rule 128
  D. **Tenant Obligation to Take Possession** 129

IV. **Subleases and Assignments** 129
  A. **Introduction** 129
  B. **Assignment** 129
    1. Privity of Estate 130
    2. Privity of Contract 131
    3. Assignor Tenant Liability 132
    4. Multiple Assignments 132
  C. **Subleases** 132
    1. Tenant Default Under the Principal Lease 133
  D. **Distinguishing an Assignment from a Sublease** 133
    1. Parties' Intentions 133
    2. Substance of the Transfer 134
    3. Pitfalls of Error 135
  E. **Lease Provisions Restricting Assignment or Sublease** 135
    1. Strict Construction 135
    2. Limits on Landlord Power to Deny Consent 135
    3. Landlord Waiver 137

V. **Tenant's Obligations** 137
  A. **Introduction** 137
  B. **Pay the Rent** 137
    1. Amount of Rent 137
    2. Accrual 137
  C. **Waste Avoidance** 138
    1. The Duty to Repair 138
    2. The Duty to Avoid Damage 138
  D. **Refrain from Illegal Uses** 138
    1. Landlord Knowledge of Intended Illegal Use 138
    2. Landlord Ignorance of Illegal Use 139

E. Honesty as to Intended Purpose 139
F. Duty Not to Commit Nuisance 139
G. Duties from Express Lease Provisions 139
H. Circumstances Excusing Tenant of Obligations 139
    1. Sole Use Becomes Illegal 139
    2. Primary Use Illegal but Other Uses Permitted 140
    3. Conditional Legality of Use 140
    4. Destruction of the Leasehold Property 140
    5. Loss by Eminent Domain 140
    6. Frustration of Intended Purpose 140

VI. Landlord's Remedies 141
A. Introduction 141
B. Remedies Typically Derived from Lease Provisions 141
    1. Rent Acceleration 141
    2. Security Deposits 141
    3. Liquidated Damages 141
    4. Confession of Judgment 141
C. Remedies Derived from Statute and Common Law 142
    1. Eviction 142
    2. Tenant Abandonment 144
    3. Seizure of the Tenant's Personal Property 146

VII. Landlord's Obligations and Tenant's Remedies 146
A. Introduction 146
B. Quiet Enjoyment 146
    1. Actual Total Eviction 146
    2. Actual Partial Eviction 146
    3. Constructive Eviction 147
C. Warranty of Habitability 149
    1. Implied Warranty of Habitability: General 149
    2. Implied Warranty of Habitability: Rationale 150
    3. Implied Warranty of Habitability: Criticism 150
    4. Scope of the Implied Warranty of Habitability 150
    5. Tenant's Remedies for Landlord Breach of the Implied
        Warranty of Habitability 151
    6. Waiver by Tenant 152
    7. Statutory Codification 152
    8. The Retaliatory Eviction Doctrine 153
D. Tort Liability of Landlords 153
    1. An Aside on Tort Theory 154
    2. Pre-existing Dangerous Conditions 154
    3. Conditions Occurring During the Lease Term 154
    4. Common Areas 154
    5. Landlord Covenant to Repair 155

     6. Statutory or Judicially Created Duty of Landlord to Repair 155
     7. Strict Liability... 155
     8. No Special Rules for Landlords 155
     9. Exculpatory Clauses... 155

VIII. Fixtures 156
  A. Introduction... 156
  B. Fixtures 156
     1. Trade Fixtures 156
  C. Attached Chattels, but Not Fixtures 156

IX. Social Regulations of Leaseholds.. 156
  A. Introduction... 156
  B. Rent Control 156
     1. Criticisms 156
     2. Defenses 157
  C. Anti-Discrimination Statutes 157
     1. 42 USC §1982: The 1866 Civil Rights Act 157
     2. Fair Housing Act 158
     3. Comparison of 42 USC §1982 and Fair Housing Act 158
     4. Proof of Forbidden Discrimination 158
     5. State and Local Laws 158

     Exam Tips on LEASEHOLD ESTATES 159

CHAPTER 6

TRANSFERS OF REAL PROPERTY

I. Contracts of Sale 162
  A. Introduction... 162
     1. Brokers.. 162
     2. Lawyers 163
     3. Mortgage Lenders 163
     4. Closing 163
  B. Statute of Frauds 163
     1. Formal Contract Not Necessary 164
     2. Single Instrument Not Necessary 164
     3. Conditions 164
     4. Electronic Transactions 164
     5. Exceptions to the Statute of Frauds 165
     6. Revocation of Contracts 166
  C. Implied Obligations 166
     1. Good Faith... 166
     2. Time of Closing 166
     3. Marketable Title 167

D. **Default and Remedies** 168
   1. Specific Performance 168
   2. Rescission 169
   3. Damages 169
E. **Duties of Disclosure and Implied Warranties** 171
   1. Duties of Disclosure 171
   2. Implied Warranty of Quality 173
F. **Risk of Loss and Equitable Title** 174
   1. Equitable Title 174
   2. Risk of Loss Goes with Possession 176

II. **Deeds** 176
A. **Formal Requirements and Component Parts** 176
   1. Writing Required 176
   2. Notarial Acknowledgment 176
   3. The Grant 176
B. **Warranties of Title** 177
   1. General Warranty Deed 177
   2. Special Warranty Deed 178
   3. Quitclaim Deed 178
   4. Merger Doctrine 178
   5. Breach of Covenants of Title 179
   6. After-Acquired Title (Estoppel by Deed) 182
C. **Delivery** 183
   1. Presumed Delivery 183
   2. Attempted Delivery at Death 183
   3. Delivery Subject to Oral Condition 184
   4. Commercial Escrows 185
   5. Delivery by Estoppel 185

III. **Financing Devices: Mortgages, Deeds of Trust, and Installment Contracts** 186
A. **Mortgages** 186
   1. The Mortgage Transaction 186
   2. Title or Lien? 188
   3. Sale or Transfer by the Mortgagor 188
   4. Default by Mortgagor 189
B. **Deeds of Trust** 190
   1. How It Works 190
   2. Difference from the Mortgage 190
C. **Installment Sale Contracts** 190
   1. Treated as Contract of Sale 190
   2. Treatment as a Security Device 191
D. **Unfair or Deceptive Lending Practices** 191

   Exam Tips on TRANSFERS OF REAL PROPERTY 192

CHAPTER 7

ASSURING GOOD TITLE TO LAND

I.   **Introduction** 193
      A. **The Problem** 193
          1. The Common Law Answer 194
          2. Modern Answers 194

II.   **Recording Acts and Chain-of-Title Problems** 194
      A. **The Recording System** 194
          1. What the Recorder Does 195
          2. What the Title Searcher Does 195
      B. **Race Acts** 196
      C. **Notice Acts** 196
      D. **Race-Notice Acts** 197
      E. **The Consequences of Recording** 197
          1. The Consequences of Not Recording 197
      F. **When Is an Instrument Recorded?** 198
          1. Instrument Not Indexed 198
          2. "Omnibus" or "Mother Hubbard" Clauses 198
          3. Misspelled Names 199
          4. Ineligible Instrument 199
      G. **Scope of Protection Afforded by Recording Acts** 200
          1. Invalid Conveyance 200
          2. Interests in Land Created by Operation of Law 200
          3. Bona Fide Purchasers 200
          4. Mortgagees 201
          5. Creditors 201
      H. **Notice** 201
          1. Actual Notice 201
          2. Constructive Notice 201
          3. Tract Index: A Solution to Chain of Title Problems? ... 207
      I. **Marketable Title Acts** 207
          1. Validity of Pre-Root Interests 208

III. **Title Registration — The Torrens System** 208
      A. **Introduction** 208
      B. **Adjudication of Title** 208
          1. Scope of the Certificate of Title 208
      C. **Public Records and Title Transfers in the Torrens System** ... 209
          1. Public Records 209
          2. Title Transfers 209
          3. Errors by the Recorder 210
      D. **The Practical Realities of Torrens Registration** 210

      1. Cost 210

      2. Lack of Comprehensiveness 210

      3. Risk of Uncompensated Error 210

  E. **Economic Theory and Torrens Registration** 210

  F. **Possessory Title Registration** 211

IV. **Title Insurance** 211

  A. **Introduction** 211

  B. **Coverage** 211

      1. Duty to Disclose Defects in Title 211

      2. Marketable Title and Encumbrances 212

      3. Exclusions 213

      4. Measure of Damages 213

      Exam Tips on ASSURING GOOD TITLE TO LAND 213

CHAPTER 8

JUDICIAL CONTROL OF LAND USE: NUISANCE AND SUPPORT

I. **The Substance of Nuisance** 216

  A. **The General Principle** 216

  B. **Private Nuisances** 216

      1. Intentional Conduct 216

      2. Unintentional Conduct 218

      3. Substantial Interference 218

  C. **Public Nuisances** 218

      1. Enforcement 219

  D. **Relationship to Trespass** 219

II. **Remedies: Four Views of Nuisance** 220

  A. **Introduction: The Economic Theory of Modern Nuisance Law** 220

      1. Transaction Costs: The Gap Between Theory and Reality 220

      2. Who Gets the Initial Entitlement? 222

      3. Economic and Legal Theory and Remedies 222

  B. **No Nuisance: Continue the Activity** 223

  C. **Nuisance: Enjoin and Abate the Activity** 223

  D. **Nuisance: Pay Damages and Continue the Activity** 224

  E. **Nuisance or Not: Enjoin the Activity but Award Damages**
      to the Enjoined Actor 224

III. **Support Rights** 225

  A. **Introduction** 225

  B. **Lateral Support** 225

      1. Land Itself 225

2. Structures 225

C. **Subjacent Support** 226

*Exam Tips on JUDICIAL CONTROL OF LAND USE: NUISANCE
AND SUPPORT* 226

CHAPTER 9

SERVITUDES: LAND USE LIMITS CREATED BY PRIVATE BARGAIN

I.   **Introduction** 228
     A. **The Concept** 228
     B. **Easements** 228
     C. **Covenants Running with the Land** 229
        1. Real Covenants: Enforceable at Law 229
        2. Equitable Servitudes: Enforceable in Equity 229

II. **Easements** 229
     A. **Introduction** 229
        1. Defined and Distinguished from Fee Simple 229
        2. Types of Easements 230
        3. Profits à Prendre 233
        4. Licenses 233
     B. **Creation of Easements** 235
        1. Easements by Grant 235
        2. Easements by Estoppel 235
        3. Easements by Implication 236
        4. Easements by Prescription 239
     C. **Transfer of Easements** 244
        1. Easements Appurtenant 244
        2. Easements in Gross 244
        3. Profits 245
     D. **Scope of Easements** 245
        1. Parties' Intentions Control 245
        2. How Easement Was Created 245
        3. Change in Location of Easement 247
        4. Enlargement of the Dominant Estate 247
        5. Division of an Easement's Benefit 248
        6. Use or Interference by Servient Estate Owner 249
     E. **Termination of Easements** 250
        1. Expiration 250
        2. Merger 250
        3. Actions of the Easement Holder 250
        4. Cessation of Purpose 251

      5. Actions of the Servient Estate Holder 252
      6. Changed Circumstances in the Surrounding Area 252

III. **Real Covenants** 253
  A. **Introduction** 253
     1. Real Covenants Defined 253
     2. Benefit and Burden 253
     3. "Runs with the Land" 253
     4. Remedy Available: Damages 253
     5. Development of the Real Covenant 254
     6. Covenant, Not Condition 254
     7. Compared to Easements 254
     8. Compared to Equitable Servitudes 254
  B. **Creation of Real Covenants** 255
  C. **Enforceability by or against Successors** 255
     1. Intent 255
     2. Horizontal Privity 255
     3. Vertical Privity 255
     4. Touch and Concern 255
  D. **"Running Elements": Intent** 255
  E. **"Running Elements": Privity of Estate** 255
     1. Horizontal Privity 256
     2. Vertical Privity 257
     3. The Third Restatement's Alternative to Vertical Privity 258
  F. **"Running Elements": Touch and Concern the Land** 259
     1. Essential Meaning of Touch and Concern 260
     2. Negative Covenants 260
     3. Affirmative Covenants 261
     4. Benefit in Gross 263
     5. Burden in Gross 263

IV. **Equitable Servitudes** 263
  A. **Introduction** 263
     1. Differences Between Real Covenants and Equitable Servitudes 263
     2. Origins of the Equitable Servitude 264
  B. **Creation** 264
     1. By Implication from a Common Development Scheme 264
     2. No Implied Covenants 265
  C. **Enforceability by or Against Successors** 266
     1. Intent 266
     2. Privity Not Required 266
     3. Notice 266
     4. Touch and Concern 267
  D. **Identifying the Benefited Land** 267
     1. Land Retained by the Promisee 267
     2. Enforceability by Third Parties 268

V.	**Interpretation of Covenants**	270
	A. **General Rule**	270
	B. **Building Restriction or Use Restriction**	270
	C. **Residential Purposes**	270
	1. Combined Business and Residential Use	270
	2. Group Homes	271
	3. What Constitutes Family?	271
	D. **Racial Restrictions**	271
	E. **Architectural Approval**	272
VI.	**Termination of Real Covenants and Equitable Servitudes**	272
	A. **Duration**	272
	B. **Merger**	272
	C. **Eminent Domain**	272
	D. **Express Waiver or Release**	273
	E. **Expiration of the Covenant**	273
	F. **Doctrines Terminating Equitable Servitudes**	273
	1. Changed Conditions Within the Affected Area	273
	2. Changed Conditions in the Surrounding Area	273
	3. Abandonment	274
	4. Equitable Estoppel	274
	5. Laches	274
	6. Unclean Hands	275
	7. Balance of Hardships	275
	G. **Affirmative Covenants to Pay Money — Perpetual Burden?**	275
VII.	**Common Interest Communities**	276
	A. **Introduction**	276
	B. **Covenants Recorded in the Master Deed**	276
	C. **Covenants Imposed by Homeowners' Associations**	276
	D. **Standard of Review of Actions Taken by Homeowners' Associations**	276
	E. **Cooperative Apartments**	277
	Exam Tips on SERVITUDES: LAND USE LIMITS CREATED BY PRIVATE BARGAIN	277

CHAPTER 10
PUBLIC CONTROL OF LAND USE: ZONING

I.	**Zoning Basics**	280
	A. **Introduction**	280
	B. **General Constitutional Validity**	280
	C. **Statutory Schemes**	280
	1. Cumulative Zoning	280
	2. Mutually Exclusive Zoning	281
	3. Density Zoning	281

II. **Authorization for Zoning** 281
     A. **Enabling Legislation** 281
         1. Defective Enabling Act 281
         2. *Ultra Vires* Local Action 282
     B. **Comprehensive Plan** 282
         1. Legal Status of the Comprehensive Plan 282

III. **Statutory Discretion and Restraint** 283
     A. **Introduction** 283
     B. **Nonconforming Uses** 283
         1. Forced Phase-Out 283
         2. No Expansion 284
         3. Destruction or Abandonment 284
     C. **Administrative Discretion: Variances, Exceptions, Amendments,**
         Spot Zoning and More 284
         1. Variances 284
         2. Exceptional Uses 285
         3. Zoning Amendments and Spot Zoning 286
         4. Floating Zones 287
         5. Conditional Zoning 287
         6. Cluster Zoning 288

IV. **Limits on the Zoning Power** 288
     A. **Introduction** 288
     B. **Zoning for Aesthetic Objectives** 289
         1. Architectural Review 289
         2. Aesthetic Regulation and Free Speech 290
     C. **Zoning that Burdens Religious Exercise** 291
         1. Zoning and the Free Exercise of Religion 291
         2. Zoning and the RLUIPA 292
     D. **Zoning and Environmental Protection** 292
     E. **Zoning Controls of Household Composition** 293
         1. The Fundamental Liberty of Family Association 293
         2. Statutory Limits on Zoning Controls of Household Composition 294
     F. **Exclusionary Zoning** 294
         1. Growth Controls 295

         Exam Tips on PUBLIC CONTROL OF LAND USE: ZONING 296

CHAPTER 11

TAKINGS: THE POWER OF EMINENT DOMAIN AND REGULATORY TAKINGS

I.   **Introduction** 298
     A. **The Eminent Domain Power** 298

    B. **All Property Protected** 298

    C. **Applies to All Governments** 298

    D. **The Purposes of the Takings Clause** 298

        1. Prevent Forcible Redistribution of Property 298

        2. Takings Permitted Only for Public Benefit 298

    E. **The Principal Issues Under the Takings Clause** 298

        1. Public Use 298

        2. Regulatory Takings 298

        3. Compensation 298

    F. **Constitutionally Noncontroversial Takings** 299

II. **The Public Use Requirement** 299

    A. **Constitutional Text** 299

        1. No Takings Except for "Public Use" 299

        2. The Meaning of "Public Use" 300

        3. The Relationship of Public Use and Just Compensation 301

III. **Regulatory Takings: How Much Regulation of Property Is Too Much?** 302

    A. **Introduction** 302

    B. **The *Per Se* Rules** 302

        1. Permanent Dispossession 302

        2. Nuisance Abatement 303

        3. Loss of All Economically Viable Use 304

    C. **Balancing Public Benefits and Private Costs** 305

        1. Origins 305

        2. Contemporary Statement 306

    D. **Exactions: Conditional Burdens** 308

        1. "Essential Nexus" 308

        2. "Rough Proportionality" 309

        3. Summary 310

    E. **Remedies** 310

        1. Injunctive and Declaratory Relief 310

        2. Damages 311

    F. **Academic Theories About Regulatory Takings** 311

        1. Joseph Sax 311

        2. Frank Michelman 311

        3. Bruce Ackerman 312

        4. Richard Epstein 312

        5. Jed Rubenfeld 312

        6. William Fischel 312

    Exam Tips on TAKINGS: THE POWER OF EMINENT DOMAIN
    AND REGULATORY TAKINGS 313

Essay Exam Questions 315

Essay Exam Answers 319

Multiple-Choice Questions 329

Answers to Multiple-Choice Questions 341

Table of Cases 351

Subject Matter Index 359

Acknowledgments

Many people have made this book possible. I express my gratitude to the multitude of Property students I have had the pleasure of teaching. I am grateful to Carol McGeehan, who urged me to write the first edition of this book and shepherded it to a conclusion. I am grateful for the invaluable assistance of Barbara Lasoff in the creation of this edition, and of Peter Skagestad for his very able management of the scheduling, production, and myriad details of ensuring that the final product was timely and of highest quality. Of course, special thanks go to the late Jesse Dukeminier and to James Krier, who created the original splendid Property casebook, as well as to their current additional co-authors, Gregory Alexander and Michael Schill. It's a great pleasure to write a student outline and study aid for such a well-crafted book.

PREFACE

Thank you for choosing this outline to help you understand Property. In writing this book, I have tried to teach on paper. Recognizing that people learn in different ways, I offer some suggestions about the various ways you might use this book.

- You could read the portions of this book that are relevant to your assigned reading after you have read the assigned reading. If you first try to extract the rules and principles from the assigned reading, you will have an opportunity to compare your understanding with mine. To the extent that your assigned reading leaves you confused, this outline may clarify matters.

- You could read the relevant part of this outline before your assigned reading. This will enable you to see quickly what's important in your reading. If you are pressed for time, this may be a better option than the first choice.

- You could read only the outline and skip your assigned reading. This is **not recommended**; you are short-changing yourself if you do this. You are paying a lot of money for a legal education; get the most for your money. There is a reason you have assigned reading. Now, after lecturing you about what you *should* do for your own good, I recognize that there are times when you are in a bind, and you simply don't have time before class to do the reading. In that case, reading the outline is better than nothing. You will have a bare-bones grasp of the issues and principles, and that will help you to derive some value from class. But go back and do the reading.

- You could use the outline as a study aid to help you organize your notes in preparation for the exam. This is a good idea, but it might be wise to supplement the outline with things that are specific to your own Property course. Course coverage in Property varies considerably. This outline covers the field of Property as it is commonly taught, but some professors cover less than this entire book, and some may include special or exotic items not covered much in this book. Be alert to the specific content of your course in using this outline.

- You could use this outline as an organizational guide in preparing your own outline for your own course. If you have the time, preparing your own outline is a great way to understand what you know and what you don't know. When you encounter things you don't know, consult this book and your notes.

This book has a number of tools to help you. The ***Casebook Correlation Chart*** connects the relevant pages of this book with the same topics in the Seventh Edition of Dukeminier, Krier, Alexander, and Schill. The ***Capsule Summary*** condenses the essence of this outline into a very concise format that may serve to refresh your recollection about a much larger set of knowledge. It could be very useful in exam preparation as a last-minute mental review of all you know. The ***Exam Questions*** enable you to gain some sense of what sort of questions you are likely to encounter and give you some practice in thinking through these things before it counts. The ***Exam Tips*** give you some guidance on what sorts of things are commonly asked by professors in exams.

I hope this book is of great help to you. Enjoy Property. If you have ideas for improvement, suggestions, criticisms, or just want to communicate with me, please feel free to send me an e-mail at the address below.

Calvin Massey
Professor of Law
University of California, Hastings College of Law
masseyc@uchastings.edu

Casebook Correlation Chart

Massey: *Property Keyed to Dukeminier/ Krier/Alexander/Schill, Seventh Edition,* The *Emanuel Law Outlines* Series	Dukeminier, Krier, Alexander, & Schill: *Property,* Seventh Edition, © 2010, Aspen Publishers, Inc.
CHAPTER 1 **CONCEPTUAL BASICS, POSSESSION, AND PERSONAL PROPERTY**	
I. What Is Property?	10, 17, 50-52, 65-89, 96
II. Possession	3-96
III. Personal Property	10, 89, 100, 194, 215-216
CHAPTER 2 **FREEHOLD ESTATES**	
I. Origins and Taxonomy of Freehold Estates	183-221
II. Fee Simple	191-198, 201, 223-225, 227, 257, 269, 275
III. Fee Tail	198-201
IV. Life Estates	202-222, 249-259
V. Defeasible Fees	222-249, 876, 257, 291
VI. Restraints on Alienation of Freehold Estates	197, 202-209, 249-250, 275-280, 450-459
CHAPTER 3 **FUTURE INTERESTS**	
I. Introduction	183, 253-254
II. Future Interests Retained by the Grantor	202, 254, 255-256
III. Future Interests Created in Grantees	202, 254, 259-271
IV. The Proposed Restatement Third of Property	888-897, 910-913
V. The Trust	216, 273-280, 614-615, 658
VI. The Marketability Rules	280-316, 557-563
CHAPTER 4 **CONCURRENT OWNERSHIP AND MARITAL INTERESTS**	
I. Forms of Concurrent Ownership	183, 319-322
II. Rights and Obligations of Concurrent Owners	319-416
III. Marital Interests	321, 359-416
IV. Condominiums and Cooperatives	183, 897-899, 912-918
CHAPTER 5 **LEASEHOLD ESTATES**	
I. The Nature of Leases	334-335, 351-355, 357, 419, 428, 430, 492
II. The Types of Leaseholds	184, 222, 419, 421-427
III. Delivery of Possession	438-442
IV. Subleases and Assignments	442-458, 467, 468
V. Tenant's Obligations	441-444
VI. Landlord's Remedies	467-469, 503
VII. Landlord's Obligations and Tenant's Remedies	482-505
VIII. Fixtures	506, 621, 526, 528
IX. Social Regulations of Leaseholds	184, 222, 419, 421-423

Massey: *Property Keyed to Dukeminier/ Krier/Alexander/Schill, Seventh Edition,* The *Emanuel Law Outlines* Series	Dukeminier, Krier, Alexander, & Schill: *Property,* Seventh Edition, © 2010, Aspen Publishers, Inc.
CHAPTER 6 **TRANSFERS OF REAL PROPERTY**	
I. Contracts of Sale	541-573
II. Deeds	585-605
III. Financing Devices Mortgages, Deeds of Trust, and Installment Contracts	616-644
CHAPTER 7 **ASSURING GOOD TITLE TO LAND**	
I. Introduction	645
II. Recording Acts and Chain of Title Problems	648-701
III. Title Registration—The Torrens System	704-709
IV. Title Insurance	520, 714-727
CHAPTER 8 **JUDICIAL CONTROL OF LAND USE: NUISANCE AND SUPPORT**	
I. The Substance of Nuisance	731-739
II. Remedies: Four Views of Nuisance	739-759
III. Support Rights	737-761
CHAPTER 9 **SERVITUDES: LAND USE LIMITS CREATED BY PRIVATE BARGAIN**	
I. Introduction	763
II. Easements	766-845
III. Real Covenants	847-882
IV. Equitable Servitudes	857-920
V. Interpretation of Covenants	847-882
VI. Termination of Real Covenants and Equitable Servitudes	882-896
VII. Common Interest Communities	896-924
CHAPTER 10 **PUBLIC CONTROL OF LAND USE: ZONING**	
I. Zoning Basics	941-944
II. Authorization for Zoning	941-942
III. Statutory Discretion and Restraint	941-942
IV. Limits on the Zoning Power	941-942
CHAPTER 11 **TAKINGS: THE POWER OF EMINENT DOMAIN AND REGULATORY TAKINGS**	
I. Introduction	1061-1062
II. The Public Use Requirement	1065-1079
III. Regulatory Takings: How Much Regulation of Property Is Too Much?	1082-1189

Capsule Summary

This Capsule Summary is intended for review at the end of the semester. Reading it is not a substitute for mastering the material in the outline. Numbers in brackets refer to the pages in the main outline where the topic is discussed.

CHAPTER 1
CONCEPTUAL BASICS, POSSESSION, AND PERSONAL PROPERTY

I. WHAT IS PROPERTY?

A. Introduction: Property is *socially contingent.* Its meaning varies across cultures and, over time, within cultures. At bottom, property is whatever interest in a thing the legal system protects against invasion by others. That definition merely describes a result; it does not explain how we get there. Moreover, property rights are not absolute. Property is relative — it describes the relationship between people with respect to things, not the relationship between persons and things. [1]

B. Theory: The principal theoretical explanations of property are *labor theory, utilitarianism, economic efficiency,* and *custom.* [2-3]

    1. Labor theory: John Locke is the originator of the idea that by mixing your labor with something unowned (e.g., catching a wild fish), you own the resulting mixture of labor and object. [2]

    2. Utilitarianism: David Hume and Jeremy Bentham argued that property was utilitarian — we protect others' possessions as property because we desire the same protection for our possessions. The implicit root of property in this theory is possession. [2]

    3. Economic efficiency: Property is economically efficient. If everything is unowned, or owned communally, under conditions of scarcity people will unduly deplete the resource because the individual gain from depletion is greater than the individual cost. Yet, from the society's perspective, the aggregate gains from depletion are less than the total cost. To an individual, these additional costs are *external.* Property helps to internalize these costs so that individuals make economically efficient judgments. If the Atlantic cod fishery is unowned, individual fishers will take as much cod as they can, since the cost of overfishing is borne by others — external to them. Eventually there will be no more cod, which is pretty much the case today. If each fisher had an individual property interest in the fish, the incentive to overfish would be reduced, to the long-run benefit of the fisher and to the society as a whole. [2-3]

    4. Custom: Property has a customary root. People engaged in a common activity (e.g., whaling or cattle ranching) often develop customs that govern their relationships between themselves and toward their objects of acquisition or husbandry (e.g., whales or cattle). Some customs acquire force of law. [3]

B. Doctrine: Property may be broken up into constituent elements: the right to *use,* the right to *exclusive possession,* and the right to *dispose or transfer.* These elements are important to what constitutes property, but it is not possible to say, for example, that the combination of any two makes property. [3]

II. POSSESSION

A. Introduction: Two meanings of possession: Possession of an object implies its ownership. "Possession" has a dual quality — it can mean the *physical act* of possession, and it can mean the *legal conclusion* that someone is in possession of an object. Usually, the first actual physical possession of an unowned object makes you its owner, but even this must be qualified, because property rights are relative to others. For example, if you trespass upon your neighbor's land to dig up a meteorite you see plunging to Earth you don't own it, even though you had the first physical possession. Caution: "Possession" is often used to describe a conclusion — as by saying that your neighbor had first possession because the unowned meteorite came into his "possession" by landing on his farm. [4]

B. Of "unowned" things: Discovery, capture, and creation: There are several methods of acquiring property rights in unowned things. [4-9]

   1. Discovery: Acquisition by discovery is related to first possession. If you discover a rare shell on an unowned beach, you are simultaneously its discoverer and first possessor. [4]

   2. Capture: Unowned property that is captured (e.g., wild animals, fugitive minerals such as oil and gas) becomes the property of the person effecting the capture. The unowned thing must be actually possessed for it to become property. The niceties of what constitutes actual possession of any given type of unowned thing are largely driven by policy considerations (Will recognition of property rights under these circumstances advance or retard desirable social objectives?) but may sometimes be decided by custom, particularly when those customs embody sound public policies. [4-6]

   3. Creation: Lots of property is acquired by creation — e.g., copyrights, patents, and trademarks. One key issue with respect to intellectual property is the degree of exclusivity the creator ought to have. Cultural expectations shape legal views of the nature and extent of creative property (e.g., the rise within the last half-century of the idea that people have a property interest in their own celebrity, or may patent genetically engineered bacteria, or the debatable proposition that you have a property interest in your discarded bodily tissues). [7-8]

   4. The right to exclude: Possession contains a corollary right: the right to exclude others from possession, but that right is not absolute. When pressing social necessity requires some modification of this principle, an owner may be required to tolerate some unwanted incursions. This is a matter of degree — a permanent denial by the government of an owner's right to exclude others may well be a taking of the property. [9]

   5. The right to destroy: Generally, you may destroy your own property, but the social disutility of doing so leads some to call for limits on this right. [9]

C. Finders keepers? When property is *lost, mislaid,* or *abandoned,* and then is found by another, a problem of relative title emerges. Finders law attempts to restore property to the true owner, reward honest finders, deliver the reasonable expectations of landowners, and discourage trespassers and other wrongdoers. [9-13]

1. **Abandoned property:** When the true owner voluntarily intends to give up ownership of property it is abandoned. Abandoned property is unowned, and the first possessor becomes its owner unless the circumstances of that possession are wrongful (e.g., the finder is a trespasser). [9-10]

2. **Lost and mislaid property:** If your wallet slides out of a hole in your pocket without your knowledge, it is lost; but if you place the wallet down on a counter, intending to put it back in your purse, but forget to do so, it is mislaid. Generally, the finder of lost or mislaid property has a better title to it than anyone else except the true owner, but the owner of the property where the object is found may have a better title than the finder in some circumstances. [10-11]

   a. **Finder v. landowner:** If the object is lost, and the finder is not a trespasser, the finder prevails. If the object is mislaid, the landowner prevails, on the theory that the owner of mislaid property is more apt to retrace her steps to locate where it was misplaced. But even with respect to lost property, the finder loses out to the landowner if the finder is an employee or invitee of the landowner, or the object is embedded in the soil. [11]

3. **Statutory modification:** These rules are often modified by statute, typically by awarding all found property to the finder if, after a reasonable search for the true owner, the true owner cannot be found. [13]

4. **Equitable division:** Some say a fairer solution is to divide the value between claimants with equally legitimate claims. [13]

D. Adverse possession: If a person wrongfully possesses land long enough in a certain manner, the

true owner may be barred from recovering possession by statutes of limitation which prescribe the period within which a suit to recover possession of real property must be brought. Once such an action is barred, the adverse possessor has effectively acquired title. [13-23]

1. **Rationales for adverse possession:** There are three policy rationales for adverse possession. [14]

   a. **Sleeping theory:** If the true owner doesn't care enough to protect his interest in possession, he deserves to lose title.

   b. **Earning theory:** An adverse possessor who takes possession and stays there for the limitations period has probably expended time, energy, and money to make the land productive and so should be rewarded for his efforts, at least when the true owner has not bothered to recover possession.

   c. **Stability theory:** Adverse possession operates to resolve disputed claims of title and possession after there has been a long wrongful occupation with no action to recover possession. Adverse possession promotes efficient resolution of such disputes.

2. **Elements of adverse possession:** For the true owner's claim of possession to be time-barred, the adverse possessor's occupation must meet the following elements. [14-19]

   a. **Actual entry:** The adverse possessor must actually enter and take exclusive possession of the property. Exclusive possession means to exclude the world, except by permission of the possessor.

    b. Open and notorious: The adverse possession must be readily detectable to a true owner by being the type of occupation a true owner would make.

    c. Hostile or under claim of right: There are three different views of hostility.

        i. Good faith: The adverse possessor must actually believe, in good faith, that he is entitled to possess the property.

        ii. Objective: The adverse possessor's acts and statements germane to his occupation objectively appear to be claims of ownership.

        iii. "Aggressive trespass": The adverse possessor must know that his occupation is wrongful but still intend to claim the property.

    d. Continuous: The adverse possessor must continuously occupy for the limitations period. This means that the occupation must be as continuous as a true owner's occupation would be, without voluntary abandonment by the adverse possessor. An adverse possessor may tack his possession onto that of a prior adverse possessor so long as the two adverse possessors are in *privity* — they have voluntarily transferred possession from one to the other. Whenever a true owner transfers title after an adverse possessor has occupied, but before the limitations period has run, the transferee acquires the title subject to the time remaining on the transferor's expiring right to sue to recover possession.

    e. Taxes: A few jurisdictions, mostly in the west, require also that the adverse possessor have paid the property taxes for the requisite limitations period.

3. Color of title: An adverse possessor who enters under a defective deed or some other defective writing that purports to deliver title to the adverse possessor has entered under color of title. Color of title is usually not necessary to establish adverse possession (although some states require it), but an adverse possessor who enters under color of title is deemed to possess all the property described in the deed so long as it is physically contiguous and owned by the person against whom the actual entry was made. [17, 19-20]

4. When the limitations period begins: The statute of limitations starts to run when the adverse possession first begins. If at that moment the owner is legally disabled (typically imprisoned, insane, or under the age of majority), the owner is given an extended period of time (after the disability ends) in which to bring suit. [20-21]

5. By tenants or co-owners: A tenant or one co-owner has a right to possession, so their occupation is not wrongful until and unless there has been a very clear repudiation of the lease (by a tenant) or assertion of exclusive ownership (by a co-owner), at which time possession becomes wrongful, and adverse possession starts.

6. Boundary disputes: Boundary disputes are sometimes resolved by adverse possession, but the doctrines of *agreed boundaries, acquiescence,* and *equitable estoppel* are also employed to resolve these problems.

7. Personal property: Adverse possession was developed to deal with wrongful occupation of real property which, of course, has a fixed location. Adverse possession is not well suited to deal with wrongful occupation of personal property because most personal property is highly portable and easily concealed. A shorter statute of limitations usually applies, and some states have discarded adverse possession altogether, in favor of a rule that triggers the limitations period when the owner first discovers, or reasonably should have discovered, the facts that constitute the cause of action. [22]

D. Accession: Accession occurs when a person *in good faith* adds his labor to the property of another, or when a person *in good faith* mixes his labor and his property with the property of another. Generally, the resulting product is owned by the owner of the original property, unless the value added is substantial, in which case the laborer may keep the mixture if he compensates the owner for his loss. A person who *in good faith* constructs an improvement on the land of another (usually a neighbor) creates in the neighbor an *option* to either (1) *sell the land to the improver at its fair market value (net of the improvement),* or (2) *pay the improver the fair value of the improvement itself.* [23]

III. PERSONAL PROPERTY

A. Bailments: A bailment is a legitimate possession of personal property by someone who is not the owner of the property. The bailor is the owner, and the bailee is the legitimate possessor. [24]

1. **Elements of bailment:** A bailment is created when the bailee has *actual control* of the property and *intends to possess* the property. Parties to a bailment may contractually specify their rights and obligations. In the absence of such a contract, the following rights and obligations govern. [24]

2. **Rights and obligations of bailee:** A bailee has a better right to the property than any third party other than the bailor. Bailees must exercise ordinary care — they are liable for negligence — but older cases hold that a bailee must exercise utmost care over property entrusted for the bailee's benefit, ordinary care over property entrusted for mutual benefit of the bailee and bailor, and minimal care over involuntary bailments and property entrusted for the bailor's benefit. A bailee must, of course, return the property. [24]

3. **Rights and obligations of bailor:** The bailor is entitled to receive the property back and is obligated by contract to pay any contractual charges associated with the bailment. If the bailment is involuntary, the bailor can sue third parties for property damage even if the third party has already paid the bailee, but if the bailment is voluntary, the bailor must look to the bailee, and cannot sue third parties who have already paid the bailee. [24]

B. Gifts: A gift is a voluntary transfer for no consideration. A gift is made when the donor intends to make a gift, the property is delivered to the donee, and the donee accepts the property. [24-27]

1. **Intent:** A donor must intend to transfer title, not just possession. [24]

2. **Delivery:** The subject of the gift must be delivered to the donee. This usually means physical possession, but possession of some property is not easily transportable. Property may be delivered by *deed,* by *symbolic delivery,* or by *constructive delivery.* When actual physical possession is impossible or impractical, the delivery of something symbolic of possession is symbolic delivery. When actual physical possession is possible but impractical, delivery of an object that is the means of obtaining possession (e.g., a safe deposit key) is constructive delivery. [24-26]

3. **Acceptance:** Delivery triggers a presumption of acceptance, which can be rebutted by the donee upon proof of the donee's rejection of the gift. [26-27]

4. Trusts: A trust is created when a person (the settlor) declares his intent to create a trust, transfers property to a trustee to hold in trust for the purposes specified by the settlor, and identifies the beneficiaries of the trust. Gifts to trusts are subject to special rules. While inter vivos gifts are irrevocable, a trust may be either revocable or irrevocable; thus, gifts by a settlor to a revocable trust are revocable at the will of the settlor.

5. Bank accounts: There are special rules to govern the gift of bank accounts.

   a. Power of attorney: A depositor may give another person power of attorney to withdraw funds from the account.

   b. "Pay on death" (POD) accounts: POD accounts are payable on the depositor's death to a named person. These accounts were usually void at common law for want of delivery until death, when a valid will would be required to transfer title, but this rule has been altered by statute in many states.

   c. Totten trusts: A Totten trust is a POD account in the form of a trust, with the depositor as trustee for the death beneficiary but with the sole right to deal with the account during life. It was popular when POD accounts were generally void because the gift to the depositor as trustee was completed during life and thus valid.

   d. Joint tenancy: Two or more people may own a bank account as joint tenants, which creates a right of survivorship, but the joint tenants have equal right to the funds during life, which may not be the depositor's desire.

C. Transfers for value: Bona fide purchasers: Generally, a person may only transfer the title he has, but a bona fide purchaser (BFP) may sometimes acquire a better title than the seller had. A BFP is somebody who pays value, does not know that the seller lacks good title, and has a good faith belief that the seller is a true owner. To acquire a clear title from a vendor without title, it is generally necessary to be a BFP who acquires a negotiable instrument, or purchases an item from a merchant who deals in that type of goods if the property has been entrusted by its owner to the merchant for sale, or purchases from a vendor with voidable title, which results when an owner intends to transfer title but doesn't because the other party (the vendor to the BFP) is guilty of fraud or duress that permits the owner to void the transaction.

CHAPTER 2
FREEHOLD ESTATES

I. ORIGINS AND TAXONOMY OF FREEHOLD ESTATES

An owner of land owns an *estate in land,* not the land itself. Our notions of estates are heavily influenced by their English feudal origins. A possessory estate is the right to possess the land now, as opposed to a future interest, which is a present right to possess the land at some time in the future. Possessory estates are divided into *freehold estates* and *nonfreehold* or *leasehold* estates. There are six basic types of freehold estates: the *fee simple,* the *fee tail,* three forms of *defeasible fees,* and the *life estate.* The most important of these is the fee simple, closely followed by the life estate. The principal difference between each of these types of freehold estates is the *duration of the estate.* [30-32]

II. FEE SIMPLE ABSOLUTE

A fee simple absolute is of perpetual duration. It has no natural end. It is the form of ownership that nonlawyers think of when they think of ownership. [32-34]

A. Creation of the fee simple absolute: At common law, a fee simple absolute was created only by use of words indicating that the estate was capable of indefinite inheritance — "to *A* and her heirs." The words "to *A*" are words of purchase (indicating who owns the estate created), and the words "and her heirs" are words of limitation (indicating the perpetual duration of the estate created). Today, no magic words are required; because a grantor conveys his entire estate unless the grant is to the contrary, a grant "to A" conveys fee simple absolute if that is what the transferor owned. [32-33]

B. Alienability and inheritance of the fee simple absolute: A fee simple absolute is freely alienable, inheritable through intestacy, and can be devised by will. *Inheritance* is a term of art that refers to intestate succession — the succession that occurs by operation of law when a person dies *intestate,* or without a will. If a person dies with a will, his takers under the will are called *devisees;* if a person dies intestate (without a will), his heirs take his property. [33-34]

III. FEE TAIL

The fee tail is virtually extinct, recognized only in a few states. Most of the problems surrounding the fee tail involve how to treat a grant that would at common law have created a fee tail. [34-36]

A. Creation: The fee tail was created by a grant "to A and the heirs of his body." The words "to A" described the owner of the fee tail estate. The words "and the heirs of his body" described the duration of the estate — until all the lineal descendants of *A* have died. A fee tail endures until the bloodline of the initial taker has run out. Because there is a natural end to this estate, every fee tail is followed by a future interest — either a reversion in the grantor or a remainder in somebody else. [34]

B. Elimination of the fee tail: There are five methods by which American states today either destroy the fee tail or permit its destruction. [34-36]

    1. Fee tail and disentailing conveyance: A handful of states continue to recognize the fee tail, but they provide that the holder of a fee tail can destroy it by a conveyance during life. [34]

    2. Statutory conversion to fee simple absolute: Most states statutorily convert anything that would have been a fee tail into a fee simple absolute and simply destroy any remainders or reversions. [35]

    3. Statutory conversion to fee simple subject to executory limitation: Some states convert a purported fee tail into a fee simple, and convert any remainder following the purported fee tail into an executory interest that lapses if the first taker of the fee simple dies without surviving issue, thus leaving the first taker's estate with a fee simple absolute, but if the first taker dies without surviving issue, the executory interest vests in possession as a fee simple absolute. [35]

4. Life estate and remainder in life tenant's issue: A few states convert a purported fee tail into a life estate in the first taker, followed by a remainder in the first taker's issue. This essentially allows the fee tail to persist for one generation only. [35]

5. Fee simple conditional created: Two or three states hold that a purported fee tail is, instead, a fee simple conditional, an estate that predated the fee tail. The fee simple conditional is identical to a fee tail except that if a child is born to the estate holder the estate holder has the power to convey fee simple absolute by an ordinary conveyance. [36]

IV. LIFE ESTATES

A. **The nature of a life estate:** A life estate is a possessory estate that expires on the death of a specified person. A life estate usually endures for the life of the holder of the estate but can be for the life of somebody other than the owner of the life estate, in which case it is called a **life estate *pur autre vie***. A life estate, being of lesser duration than a fee simple absolute, is always followed by either a ***reversion*** in the grantor or a ***remainder*** in a third party. As with any estate, a life estate may be defeasible. A life estate is freely alienable, and its exchange value is dependent on the life expectancy of the person whose life measures the duration of the estate. By reason of the nature of a life estate, only the life estate *pur autre vie* may be inherited or devised. [36-39]

B. **The modern life estate:** Almost all life estates today are ***equitable*** — they consist of a beneficial or economic interest in assets legally owned by a trustee. Legal life estates are rare and a bad idea, because a life estate is simply not as easily marketable as a fee simple absolute. A trustee owns fee simple absolute, albeit for the benefit of the trust beneficiaries, so the trustee can sell trust assets and buy new ones, thus achieving more flexibility and greater economic returns for the trust beneficiaries. [39]

1. **Judicial responses to inflexibility of the legal life estate:** Courts may order sale of the legal life estate and the remainder (which together form fee simple absolute) if such sale is (1) in the best interest of all parties and consistent with the grantor's intent, or (2) necessary to avoid waste. [39-40]

C. **Waste:** When ownership is divided between a life tenant and a remainderman, interests conflict: The life tenant has the economic use of property for life, and the remainderman owns its future economic value. ***Waste*** is the term used to describe actions of the life tenant that ***permanently impair*** the property's value or the interest of the future interest holders. A life tenant is liable to the remainderman for waste. There are three kinds of waste. [40-42]

1. **Affirmative waste:** When a life tenant acts affirmatively to damage land permanently, the life tenant has voluntarily committed waste. [40-41]

2. **Permissive waste:** When a life tenant fails to act reasonably to protect deterioration of the land, permissive or involuntary waste has occurred. [41]

3. **Ameliorative waste:** When the life tenant acts affirmatively to change the principal use of the land, and thereby ***increases the value*** of the land, ***ameliorative waste*** has occurred. Ameliorative waste is actionable only when it is clear that (1) the grantor intended for there to be no change in use, and (2) the property may still reasonably be used in the fashion the grantor intended. [41-42]

V. DEFEASIBLE FEES

Any estate may be defeasible — subject to termination — upon the happening of a specified event. There are three types of defeasible fees simple — the *fee simple determinable,* the *fee simple subject to a condition subsequent,* and the *fee simple subject to an executory limitation.* The basic difference between the first two is that the fee simple determinable *terminates automatically* when the specified event occurs, and the fee simple subject to a condition subsequent *terminates only when the holder of the power of termination exercises it.* The difference between the fee simple subject to an executory limitation and the other two defeasible fees is that the future interest following either of the first two types of defeasible fee is vested in the grantor — the person creating the defeasible fee out of his fee simple absolute — while the future interest in the fee simple subject to an executory limitation is created in a third party. [42-50]

A. Fee simple determinable: This interest is created when the grantor conveys the property only for a limited time — until the specified future event occurs; e.g., "You can have this property only for so long as you farm it." This intent is usually implied from the language of the grant. If the grant is only "for so long as . . . " or only "until . . . " the grantor is thought to have parted with title only provisionally. When a fee simple determinable is carved out of a fee simple absolute, something necessarily is left over. If that leftover is kept by the grantor, it is called a *possibility of reverter.* If it is sent to a third party, it is an *executory interest* and the defeasible fee created is called a *fee simple subject to an executory limitation.* A fee simple determinable is freely transferable in most, but not all, states. It has been abolished in at least two states. [42-43]

B. Fee simple subject to a condition subsequent: This interest is created when the grantor makes an unrestricted grant and then follows it with an attached string; e.g., "Here's your property. Oh, by the way, I want it back if you ever stop farming it." In form, it looks like a grant of a fee simple absolute, except that it is not absolute; it is followed by a condition subsequent. Telltale language includes such usage as "provided, however . . . ," or "but if . . . ," or "but in the event . . . ," or "on condition that . . . " When a fee simple subject to a condition subsequent is carved out of a fee simple absolute, the interest left over is called a *power of termination* or *right of entry* if retained by the grantor. It is an executory interest if created in a third party, and the defeasible fee is then a fee simple subject to an executory limitation. The holder of the power of termination following a fee simple subject to a condition subsequent must take substantial steps to recover possession and title in order to terminate the defeasible fee. When the grant is ambiguous, most courts prefer the fee simple subject to a condition subsequent because it avoids the automatic forfeiture of the fee simple determinable. The fee simple subject to a condition subsequent is freely transferable in most, but not all, states. [43-45]

C. Some consequences of classification of defeasible fees: The type of defeasible fee created may have some significant consequences. [45-47]

1. Transferability of the interest retained by the grantor: At common law, neither a possibility of reverter nor power of termination could be alienated or devised, but were only inheritable. These restrictions still exist in some states, but in most states they may be freely transferred or devised. [45]

2. Accrual of a cause of action for recovery of possession: The statute of limitations for adverse possession begins to run at different times. [45-46]

    a. Determinable fee: Once the limitation occurs, the determinable fee immediately expires. Because continued possession by the holder of the determinable fee is wrongful, the owner's cause of action accrues and the limitations statute starts to run at that moment. This is also true with respect to the fee simple subject to an executory limitation.

    b. Fee simple subject to a condition subsequent: Even though the condition has occurred, continued possession is not wrongful until and unless the holder of the power of termination has exercised it. Unless the limitations statute specifies to the contrary, it starts to run only when the power of termination is exercised. However, the equitable doctrine of laches may cut off the ability of the holder of power of termination to exercise it if she fails to do so for an unduly long time that causes hardship to the possessor of the defeasible fee.

  3. Effect under the Rule Against Perpetuities: A possibility of reverter and a power of termination are each exempt from destruction by the Rule Against Perpetuities because they are vested at the moment of creation, but the analogous executory interests are not vested for perpetuities purposes and will likely be destroyed by the Rule. [46-47]

D. Some problems with defeasible fees: Defeasible fees create some unique problems. [47-49]

  1. Invalid restraint on alienation? Defeasible fees generally restrict the *use* that may be made of the property, and use restrictions inhibit marketability of property. Direct restraints on alienation of property are disfavored because they inhibit economic efficiency and productivity. Thus, a use restriction in a defeasible fee is treated as an invalid restraint on alienation when the use restriction materially affects marketability adversely. [47-48]

  2. Defeasible fee or covenant? A use restriction may be cast as a divesting condition or as a servitude, a covenant limiting use. If the former, the use restriction is enforced by a shift of possession and title from defeasible fee owner to the holder of the future interest; if the latter, the use restriction is enforced by an injunction or an award of damages. Ambiguous grants may be resolved in favor of the servitude. [48]

  3. Valuation of the defeasible fee and the associated future interest: It is difficult to split the value of a fee simple absolute between the defeasible fee holder and the owner of the future interest that will become possessory upon breach of the condition because, unlike a life estate, no actuarial estimate of the duration of the possessory estate is possible. Also, the defeasible fee may not be independently marketable, making valuation of it pure guesswork. [48-49]

E. Fee simple subject to executory limitation: A fee simple subject to executory limitation is a fee simple that is *divested,* or *shifted,* from one transferee to another transferee upon the occurrence of some future event. Both the fee simple determinable and the fee simple subject to condition subsequent involve the creation of a defeasible fee with a future interest retained by the grantor (either a possibility of reverter or right of entry). But the same defeasible fee estates can be created with the future interests transferred to a third party instead of retained by the grantor. When this happens, a fee simple subject to executory limitation is created. When the divesting condition occurs after a fee simple subject to an executory limitation has been created, divestiture of the fee is automatic, and the holder of the executory interest is entitled to immediate possession. [49-50]

VI. RESTRAINTS ON ALIENATION OF FREEHOLD ESTATES

Restraints on alienation of freehold estates are generally void.

A. **Types of restraints:** There are three types of restraints. A restraint may be couched in the form of a *forfeiture* if alienation is attempted, as a *disabling* restraint (no power to convey granted), or as a *promissory* restraint (grantee promises not to alienate). The forfeiture restraint is viewed mostly with skepticism because it is the most draconian. Some restraints on alienation are unenforceable because they violate constitutional law (e.g., racial restrictions on alienation). Each type of restraint must be analyzed individually. [50-51]

B. **Total restraints on a fee interest:** Total restraints are always void because they are thought to promote inefficient allocation of resources. [50]

C. **Partial restraints on a fee interest:** Partial restraints may be valid if they are for a reasonable purpose and limited in duration. [50]

D. **Restraints on life estates:** The validity of restraints on alienability of life estates depend on the type of restraint and the type of life estate to which it is applied. [50-51]

    1. **Legal life estates:** Restraints on alienation of legal life estates are usually void, especially disabling restraints, because they prohibit any transfer. [50]

    2. **Equitable life estates:** Disabling restraints on equitable life estates, in the form of the spendthrift trust, are freely permitted because the property itself — the trust corpus, legally owned by the trustee — is freely alienable, so the spendthrift trust poses no danger to economic efficiency. Objections to the spendthrift trust are mostly based on fear that creditors may be defrauded or on moral distaste. [50-51]

CHAPTER 3
FUTURE INTERESTS

I. INTRODUCTION

A future interest is a legal interest in property that entitles its holder to *possession* at some time in the future. While the holder of a future interest does *not have any right to possession now,* a future interest is a *presently existing* property interest to a *future right to possession.* Future interests may be created in the transferor or the transferee. Future interests created in the transferor are one of three types: a *reversion,* a *possibility of reverter,* or a *right of entry* (also known as a *power of termination*). Future interests created in a transferee may be either a *remainder* or an *executory interest.* A remainder may be either *vested* or *contingent.* A contingent remainder is subject to one or both of two uncertainties: (1) its owner is *unknown* or *cannot be ascertained* or (2) there is a *condition precedent* to ultimate possession (other than the natural expiration of the preceding possessory estate). Executory interests are either *shifting* or *springing.* A shifting executory interest *divests* (cuts off) a vested interest (either a future interest or a presently possessory interest) of another transferee. A springing executory interest divests the grantor's interest at some future time. [54]

II. FUTURE INTERESTS RETAINED BY THE GRANTOR

A. **Reversion:** When a grantor conveys a lesser estate than what he originally owned, a reversion in the grantor is created. Reversions are freely alienable, inheritable, and devisable. Reversions are always vested when created. [55-56]

B. Possibility of reverter: A possibility of reverter is created whenever the grantor conveys his estate upon a ***determinable limitation,*** which is a limit upon the duration of the conveyance, as when the grantor conveys for only "so long as" a given event does not occur or, phrased positively, only "until" the occurrence of a given event. The estate conveyed "determines" or ***expires automatically*** when the limiting event occurs. A possibility of reverter is created only in the grantor, never in a transferee. The analogous interest in a transferee is called an ***executory interest.*** [56-57]

    1. Transferability: At common law, a possibility of reverter could ***only be inherited;*** it could not be transferred *inter vivos* or by will. Today, most (but not all) states permit a possibility of reverter to be freely transferred or devised. [57]

    2. Termination: Because a possibility of reverter is vested when created it cannot be destroyed by the Rule Against Perpetuities, and so can endure forever. Some states have, by statute, provided that a possibility of reverter expires some specified number of years after its creation. A few of those states permit a possibility of reverter to be kept alive for an additional period by recording a notice of its continuation. [57]

    3. Eminent domain: When property in which there is a possibility of reverter is taken by eminent domain, most states give the entire condemnation award to the owner of the fee, but a few require apportionment of the award between the fee and the possibility of reverter.

    4. Abolition: A few states have abolished the possibility of reverter and its correlative possessory estate. In these states, attempts to create a determinable possessory estate will result in a possessory estate subject to a condition subsequent. The possibility of reverter that would otherwise result is turned into a right of entry, also called a ***power of termination.***

C. Power of termination or right of entry: A right of entry (power of termination) is created whenever the grantor conveys his estate subject to a retained right to cut short the transferred interest upon the occurrence of some specified future event. This interest may only be created in the grantor. The analogous interest created in a transferee is called an ***executory interest.*** Issues of transferability, termination, and eminent domain are the same as for the possibility of reverter. [57-58]

III. FUTURE INTERESTS CREATED IN GRANTEES

A. Remainders: A remainder is a future interest created in a grantee that will become possessory (if at all) upon the ***natural expiration*** of the preceding possessory estate. Remainders never divest another interest. A ***vested remainder*** is certain to become possessory. A ***contingent remainder*** has only the possibility of becoming possessory. The term "remainder" identifies the type of future interest, but a remainder is a future interest in some estate, whether it be a fee simple, a fee tail, a life estate, or a term of years. [58-64]

    1. Vested remainders: A remainder is vested if it is created in a known or ascertainable person and ultimate possession is not subject to any condition subsequent. It must necessarily become possessory upon the natural expiration of the preceding estate. [59-62]

        a. Indefeasibly vested remainders: An indefeasibly vested remainder is certain to become and remain possessory. It cannot be divested in whole or in part.

   b. Vested remainders subject to complete divestment: A vested remainder subject to complete divestment is one created in a known or ascertainable person and not subject to any condition *precedent,* but which is subject to a condition *subsequent* that, upon occurrence, will completely divest the remainderman of his interest.

   c. Vested remainders subject to partial divestment: A vested remainder subject to open (also called *partial divestment*) is a remainder created in a class (or group) of people, at least one of whom is known or ascertainable and presently entitled to possession as soon as the preceding estate expires. Because the class of grantees is capable of including others, the class is "open"; thus, the vested remainder is subject to partial divestment in favor of possible new entrants into the open class.

      i. Class-closing rules: A class closes upon the sooner of two events: (1) *physically* — it is no longer possible to have new entrants or (2) under the " *rule of convenience*" — when any member of the class is entitled to take possession. The rule of convenience is a presumption that the grantor intended this consequence and can be rebutted by contrary evidence. When it applies, it causes a class to close around all then living members of the class, whether or not they are all then entitled to possession.

   2. Contingent remainders: A contingent remainder is a remainder created in an unknown or unascertainable person or that has a condition precedent to ultimate possession. The natural expiration of the preceding estate is not a condition precedent. The condition must be expressed. Sometimes the same condition precedent can be used in the alternative (e.g., "to Jane if she marries, but if she never marries, to Elizabeth"). This formulation creates *alternative contingent remainders.* Although the common law did not generally permit contingent remainders to be transferred, that is no longer the case. [62-64]

B. Executory interests: Executory interests are future interests in a grantee that divest either (1) another grantee's possessory or vested future interest (a *"shifting executory interest"*), or (2) the grantor's vested interest at some future time (a *"springing executory interest"*). By nature, the possibility of possession inherent in an executory interest is contingent upon the occurrence of an uncertain future event — the divesting condition. [64-66]

   1. Shifting executory interest: A shifting executory interest divests an interest held by another transferee from the grantor. It cuts short, or divests, that other interest; it "shifts" the interest from one transferee to another. [66]

   2. Springing executory interest: A springing executory interest is a future interest created in a grantee that cuts short the grantor's interest at some future time after the conveyance. It "springs" out of the grantor. [66]

IV. THE TRUST

Future interests are most commonly employed in trusts.

A. The basics of the trust: The central feature of the trust is the division of *legal* ownership from *equitable,* or *beneficial,* ownership. A person (the *trustor* or *settlor*) may transfer property to a *trustee,* who becomes the legal owner and must manage the property for the economic benefit of the trust *beneficiaries,* who have *equitable* ownership. [67-68]

B. Advantages of the trust: A trust enables a person to place assets in the hands of a property manager who can respond to changing conditions by selling assets and acquiring new ones, all for the advantage of the people who may be unknown to the settlor (such as grandchildren yet to be born). The trust combines flexible property management with concentration of assets for the benefit of identified beneficiaries. [68]

V. THE MARKETABILITY RULES

A. Destructibility of contingent remainders: At common law, a contingent remainder in land was destroyed if, at the expiration of the preceding freehold estate, it was still contingent. This rule is virtually extinct today. Its function — increasing the marketability of land — has been supplanted by the Rule Against Perpetuities. It was never very effective, because there were a number of ways to avoid its application. [69-70]

B. The Rule in *Shelley's Case*: This rule dates from the sixteenth century and was designed to stop avoidance of feudal death taxes. That function is of no modern relevance and to the extent that the rule improved the marketability of land its function has been supplanted by the Rule Against Perpetuities. It is virtually extinct today. [70-71]

    1. The rule: If (1) one instrument (2) creates a freehold in real property and (3) a remainder in the freeholder's ***heirs*** (or the heirs of his body), and (4) the freehold estate and the remainder are ***both equitable or both legal,*** then (5) the remainder becomes a remainder in the freeholder. [70-71]

    2. Practical effect: The merger doctrine, by which a possessory estate and the immediately following *vested* future interest are merged into a single possessory estate, caused the destruction of most, but not all, remainders subject to the rule. Like destructibility, the Rule in *Shelley's Case* was riddled with exceptions. [70]

C. The doctrine of worthier title: This doctrine is still observed by some American states. If an ***inter vivos*** conveyance creates ***any future interest*** in the ***heirs of the grantor*** the future interest is ***void.*** The grantor retains a ***reversion*** instead. The doctrine is a rule of construction, raising a rebuttable presumption that the grantor did not intend to create a future interest in her heirs. By contrast, the destructibility rule and the Rule in *Shelley's Case* are rules of law. Worthier title is very broad; it applies to both real and personal property and to any kind of future interest, regardless of the nature of the preceding estate. [71-72]

D. The Rule Against Perpetuities: The Rule Against Perpetuities destroys any future interest that could remain uncertain of ultimate possession after the elapse of a defined period of time from its creation. By destroying interests in property whose ownership is uncertain for a prolonged time, the rule is said to promote free marketability of property and ensure that property is controlled by the living rather than by the desires of people long dead. [72-83]

    1. Brief summary of the rule: A future interest is void unless all uncertainty as to whether it will ultimately become possessory is removed no later than 21 years after the end of some life in being at the creation of the interest. The classic statement of the rule is: "No interest is good unless it must vest, if at all, not later than 21 years after some life in being at the creation of the interest." In its common law form, the rule is concerned with the ***possibility*** of remote vesting, *not* its *probability.* Put another way, the rule is concerned about the mere possibility that uncertainty as to whether the future interest will ultimately become possessory will continue past the permitted period of the rule. [73-74]

a. **Vesting:** The rule is concerned about when future interests *vest in interest* — when uncertainty as to *ultimate possession is removed* — rather than when they actually become possessory, or vest in *possession.* So long as a future interest will timely vest in interest, it does not matter that vesting in possession may occur after the period has expired. A vested interest is certain to become possessory, so no uncertainty attaches to its ownership. With one exception, a vested interest means the same thing for purposes of the Rule Against Perpetuities as it does for purposes of classification of future interests. However, a *vested remainder subject to open is* **not vested for perpetuities purposes** *until the interest of every possible member of the open class is vested.* This rule is but an application of a more general rule that *no interest in any member of a class is good unless the interest of every possible member of the class is good.*

b. **Permitted period of uncertainty:** An interest is good under the rule if it will *certainly vest* or *certainly fail to vest* within (1) 21 years from its creation, or (2) during the life of some person alive at its creation, or (3) upon the death of some person alive at its creation, or (4) within 21 years after the death of some person alive at its creation. To prove validity, you must prove that the interest in question will *vest* or *fail to vest* within this period. If you cannot do so, you will be able to illustrate a possible way in which the uncertainty might persist longer than the perpetuities period, and thus prove that the interest is void.

c. **Future interests to which the rule applies:** The rule applies to all future interests, though future interests indefeasibly vested at creation will always be valid under the rule. The impact of the rule is on contingent interests: contingent remainders, executory interests, and vested remainders subject to divestment.

d. **Validity tested at creation:** The common law rule tests the validity of the interests created at the moment of their creation, even if the actual moment of judicial decision is years later. The common law rule is only concerned about *possibilities,* not about probabilities, nor even about what has actually happened.

2. **Vesting:** An interest is vested for perpetuities purposes when it has *either* become *possessory* (vesting in possession) or has *vested in interest* (the owners are known, existing people and there are no unsatisfied conditions precedent). Some interests only vest in interest at the same time that they vest in possession, but many interests can and do vest in interest well before vesting in possession. An interest that is vested for classification purposes is vested for perpetuities purposes *except for vested remainders subject to open,* because a gift to a *class* of people is **not vested in any member of the class until it is vested in every member of the class.** For this to happen, two things must be true: (1) the *class must be closed,* and (2) *any conditions precedent must be satisfied by* **every** member *of the closed class.* [74-75]

3. **Measuring or validating lives:** To prove validity, you must identify some person (or class of persons) alive on the effective date of the grant whose life (or lives) can serve to validate the interest. If you use a class of persons, the class must be closed on the effective date of the grant in order to be a life in being. If there is any *possibility* that the class could include someone born after the grant, the class is not a life in being. The validating life is almost always someone who is germane to the interests created by the grant. [75-76]

4. **The curious problem of defeasible fees:** A defeasible fee creates a retained interest in the grantor, which interest is vested and thus valid under the rule. But the same fee can be followed by an executory interest instead of a retained interest in the grantor. That executory interest is not vested, and thus subject to the rule. There are three statutory remedies to this inconsistency. [77-78]

   a. **Apply perpetuities to possibilities of reverter or rights of entry:** England applies the rule to possibilities of reverter and rights of entry as well as to executory interests following a defeasible fee.

   b. **Destruction of possibilities of reverter and rights of entry:** Some American states continue to regard the grantor's retained interest (whether a possibility of reverter or right of entry) as vested but destroy it by a statute, independent of the rule, that voids possibilities of reverter or rights of entry some specified number of years after their creation. Some states vary this theme by permitting the grantor to keep the interest alive by periodic recordation of a notice of continuation. In this scheme, executory interests following a defeasible fee remain subject to the rule.

   c. **Destruction of all future interests following defeasible fees:** Some American states exempt from the rule all interests following a defeasible fee (whether retained by the grantor or created in a transferee) but subject them all to a separate statutory rule of destruction. These states also permit the holder of the future interest to keep it alive indefinitely so long as a notice of continuation is recorded within each statutory period.

   d. **Charity-to-charity exemption:** By statute or judicial decision, many states exempt from the rule an executory interest in a charity if the divested interest is also held by a charity.

5. **Classic traps for the unwary:** The classic traps of the rule each result from the rule's insistence on considering *future possibilities,* no matter how outlandish, rather than *probabilities.* [78-79]

   a. **The fertile octogenarian:** The rule presumes that a person of any age, whether male or female, can produce a child.

   b. **The unborn widow:** Without more, "A's widow" refers to the unknown person who answers that description on A's death, not necessarily the person who is A's wife when the instrument is drafted. The rule presumes the *possibility* that aged people might substitute fresh youngsters for their elderly mates — so young that they were not even born at the time of the grant.

6. **Applicability of the Rule Against Perpetuities to commercial transactions:** The rule applies to commercial transactions, such as options to purchase property. Because those options are rarely tied to a natural person (who might serve as a measuring life), to be valid they usually must expire within 21 years of their creation. [79-80]

7. **Reform doctrines:** There are several doctrines that ameliorate the harsh effects of the common law rule. [80-82]

   a. **Wait-and-see:** This statutory reform, adopted in some form by about half the states, evaluates the validity of future interests as events actually unfold, rather than at the time the interests are created: "What-*did*-happen" replaces "what-*might*-happen." The most common form of wait-and-see is to wait for the period permitted by the common law rule, if necessary. This means that you must wait, if necessary, for the expiration of all relevant lives in being at the creation of the grant, plus 21 years. Of course, if the uncertainty is removed before then, there is no need to wait any longer.

　　b. USRAP: The Uniform Statutory Rule Against Perpetuities validates any interest that will vest within 90 years of its creation or if it will timely vest under the common law rule. If, after 90 years, an interest is not vested, it is reformed to vest within the 90-year period of USRAP.

　　c. Construction of the instrument: Many modern courts will construe the instrument creating the future interests in a way that will avoid destruction of future interests by the rule, if that construction is at all plausible.

　　d. Reformation of the instrument: Some modern courts will alter the instrument to make the interests created under it conform to the rule, if such reformation is at all possible.

8. Perpetual Trusts: The end of the rule? In about 23 states, the rule has been expressly rejected or sufficiently modified that it no longer applies as a rule of law. USRAP's 90-year rule is likely to cause the common law rule to perish from neglect. These trends have been hastened by the federal generation-skipping transfer tax, which sharply reduces incentives to use contingent future interests to avoid estate taxation, and which exempts from its application substantial amounts placed in trust. [82-83]

CHAPTER 4
CONCURRENT OWNERSHIP AND MARITAL INTERESTS

I. FORMS OF CONCURRENT OWNERSHIP

Concurrent ownership occurs when the same property is owned by more than one person at the same time.

A. Tenancy in common: Tenants in common own separate, but undivided, interests in the same property. Each tenant in common has a fractional interest in the entire property, and each is entitled to use and possess the property, but none can exclude her fellow owners. A tenancy in common interest may be alienated, devised, or inherited separately from the other tenancy in common interests. By statute or judicial decision, a tenancy in common is the presumed form of co-ownership, rebuttable by clear evidence of intention to create some other form of co-ownership. Property passing by intestacy to two or more heirs is always taken as tenants in common. There is a rebuttable presumption that tenants in common have equal shares. [86-87]

B. Joint tenancy: The distinctive feature of joint tenancy is the *right of survivorship.* Upon the death of a joint tenant, the interest of the deceased joint tenant terminates. Thus, if Blackacre is owned by A and B as joint tenants, upon the death of A Blackacre is owned solely by B. If Blackacre was owned by A, B, and C as joint tenants, upon the death of B Blackacre is owned by A and C as joint tenants. The theory of the joint tenancy is that each joint tenant owns an equal share in all of the property, so when one joint tenant dies, nothing passes to the other joint tenants; the dead joint tenant's interest simply dies with him. [87-95]

1. **The four unities of joint tenancy:** At common law, the interests of joint tenants must be equal in every respect. To create a joint tenancy at common law, four unities must be present: (1) *time,* (2) *title,* (3) *interest,* and (4) *possession.* [88-89]

   a. **Time:** Each joint tenant must acquire his interest at the same time.

   b. **Title:** All joint tenants must receive their interests under the same instrument. At common law it was impossible for a sole owner to convey to himself and another in joint tenancy, since the conveyance to himself was a nullity, but this is typically permitted by statute today.

   c. **Interest:** Each joint tenant must have the identical interest in the property, which means that each joint tenant must have (1) the same share of the undivided whole and (2) the same durational estate. However, it is possible for one fractional interest in property (e.g., two-thirds) to be held by joint tenants, and the remaining fractional interest to be held in tenancy in common, so long as the four unities are met as to the joint tenancy fraction. Thus, A and B can be joint tenants as to a two-thirds interest in Blackacre and tenants in common with C as to the remaining one-third interest.

   d. **Possession:** Upon creation of a joint tenancy each joint tenant must have the same right to possession of the whole property, but after creation joint tenants are free to allocate possession rights as they wish.

2. **Creation of joint tenancy:** Ambiguous grants may not create a joint tenancy. Although the common law presumed that grants created joint tenancy, every American state today presumes that a conveyance to two or more people creates a tenancy in common, unless there is clear evidence of intent to create a joint tenancy. [89-90]

3. **Severance of joint tenancy:** A joint tenant may destroy the joint tenancy at any time by conveyance of the joint tenant's interest. This severs the joint tenancy and creates a tenancy in common in its place. [90-94]

   a. **Unilateral conveyance:** A conveyance by a joint tenant from himself to himself was not effective at common law to sever the joint tenancy, because such a conveyance was an empty act. At common law, you could not convey to yourself what you already owned, but by statute or judicial decision, some American states now permit the unilateral conveyance.

   b. **Mortgage:** States differ as to whether the mortgage by one joint tenant of her interest severs the joint tenancy. Some states follow the *title theory* of mortgages (a *mortgage* is a transfer of title subject to a condition subsequent); other states follow the *lien theory* of mortgages (a mortgage is simply a lien on title). Although under any theory, a mortgage is simply a device to secure payment of a loan, and ought not generally be seen to sever a joint tenancy, some title theory states apply the logic of title theory mechanically to find severance.

   c. **Lease:** Contrary to common law, which viewed leases as a severing conveyance, most jurisdictions today hold that a lease by one joint tenant does not sever the joint tenancy. A corollary to that conclusion is that a lease from one joint tenant endures no longer than the life of the lessor joint tenant, even if the leasehold term purports to be longer.

   d. **Agreement:** A joint tenancy may be severed by a clear agreement to that effect.

e. **Operation of law:** In a few instances, as when one joint tenant murders another, the joint tenancy is severed by operation of law, to avoid unjust enrichment. In case of simultaneous death of joint tenants, one-half of each joint tenant's interest passes as if the other joint tenant had died first, and vice versa.

4. **Joint-tenancy bank accounts:** Joint-tenancy bank accounts may be created for a variety of reasons: (1) to make a *present gift* of an undivided interest in the account, (2) to use survivorship as a *will substitute,* or (3) simply as a *convenience* to permit the other owner to manage the depositor's money. Because of these very different possible intentions, courts try to determine the specific intentions of the depositor. [94-95]

C. **Tenancy by the entirety:** A *tenancy by the entirety* is a variant form of joint tenancy that is only available to a husband and wife. The four unities are required for creation, plus a fifth unity of marriage. [95-98]

1. **Nature of tenancy by the entirety:** There are two important differences from the joint tenancy. [95]

a. **One person:** The common law indulged in the fiction that there was only one owner of a tenancy by the entirety — the fictional marital person — even though it takes two to make a marriage. This fiction has consequences concerning the ability of creditors of one marital partner to seize his or her interest in a tenancy by the entirety.

b. **No severance:** A tenancy by the entirety may not be severed by one tenant acting alone, a rule that makes the right of survivorship indestructible unless both partners join in a conveyance.

2. **Creation:** Most American states that recognize the tenancy by the entirety observe a rebuttable presumption that a conveyance to a husband and wife creates a tenancy by the entirety. [95-96]

3. **Operation of the tenancy by the entirety:** At common law, the husband had exclusive power to control the tenancy by the entirety, except that he could not destroy his wife's survivorship right. Today, each spouse is equal, but there are two ways to achieve equality: (1) endow the wife with equal rights to alienate her possession and survivorship rights, or (2) prevent either spouse from doing so. [96-98]

a. **Equal right to alienate:** The effect of this view is to enable the creditors of either spouse to seize the debtor spouse's possessory interest in a tenancy by the entirety, but not the survivorship interest.

b. **Neither spouse may alienate:** The effect of this view is that the creditors of either spouse may *not* seize the possessory or survivorship interests of the debtor spouse.

c. **Variations on the theme:** A few states permit the creditors of either spouse to seize the *survivorship right* of the debtor spouse but not the possessory right.

d. **Government claims:** The IRS may seize entireties property to satisfy its tax lien against a single spouse. Forfeiture statutes, which permit seizure of property used in criminal activity, often provide an innocent owner defense to forfeiture. When the property subject to forfeiture is owned in tenancy by the entirety, and one spouse is an innocent owner, some division of the property must be made. One solution is to permit the government to seize the criminal spouse's survivorship interest only, leaving the innocent spouse with possession and a survivorship interest.

4. **Termination:** A tenancy by the entirety is terminated by death, divorce, or conveyance by both spouses acting together. [98]

5. **Personal property:** States differ as to whether personal property may be owned in tenancy by the entirety. [98]

D. **Partnerships and coparceny:** Partnerships involve co-ownership of a for-profit business. Partners are personally liable for all the debts of the business. *Coparceny* is an extinct form of ownership in which daughters of a decedent without a male heir took as co-owners. [98]

II. RIGHTS AND OBLIGATIONS OF CONCURRENT OWNERS

A. **Partition:** A joint tenant or a tenant in common may demand partition at any time and for any reason. A tenant by the entirety is not entitled to partition — the effective remedy is divorce. Partition is accomplished by a judicial proceeding resulting in either (1) *physical division* of the property, or (2) *sale and division of the sale proceeds.* [99-100]

1. **Partition in kind:** A physical division of the property is called *partition in kind.* This is the preferred method, but if it is (1) *impossible or very impractical* or (2) *not in the best interest* of **all parties,** a court will order partition by sale. [99-100]

2. **Partition by sale:** This method is actually quite common because it is impractical or impossible physically to divide most property in America today. The property is sold, and the proceeds are divided among the co-owners in proportion to their ownership interests. [100]

3. **Agreement not to partition:** Such agreements are enforceable if they are clear, fair and equitable, and limited to a reasonable period of time. [100]

B. **Rents, profits, and possession:** Absent agreement to the contrary, each co-owner has the right to possess the property, and no co-owner may exclude the others. These contradictory principles invite conflict, which is resolved (in the absence of an agreement) as follows. [100-102]

1. **Exclusive possession by one co-owner:** If exclusive possession is not by agreement the owner in possession has the following obligations to owners not in possession. [100-101]

   a. **Rental value of exclusive possession:** Most jurisdictions hold that the owner in possession has no obligation to pay rent unless (1) the other owners have been *ousted,* or (2) the owner in possession has a *special duty* to the other owners, or (3) there is an agreement to pay rent. *Ouster* is a term of art — it occurs if the owner in possession either (1) *prevents the other owners from possession,* or (2) *denies the other owners' claim to title.* A minority of states hold that the owner in possession is obligated to pay the fair rental value to the other owners whether or not there has been ouster.

2. **Rents from third parties:** A co-owner who receives rents from a third party is obligated to account to his cotenants for those rents and share them pro rata. [101-102]

3. **Profits from the land:** The normal rules regarding possession apply to exclusive possession for farming, animal husbandry, or other agricultural uses, but if a cotenant permanently removes an asset from the land, he must account to his cotenants for this reduction in value. [102]

C. **Accounting for the costs of ownership:** Generally, each cotenant is liable for his proportionate share of the costs of ownership, e.g., mortgage payments, taxes, repairs, and maintenance. [102-103]

1. **Mortgage payments:** A cotenant who pays a disproportionately larger share of mortgage interest or principal may compel his cotenants to reimburse him immediately and, with respect to the disproportionate principal payments, succeeds to the lender's remedies against his co-owners. [102]

2. **Taxes:** Each cotenant is obligated to pay his proportionate share of the taxes, and a cotenant who pays more than his share can recover the excess from his fellow cotenants at any time. [102]

3. **Repairs:** Because a cotenant has no obligation to repair his property, a cotenant who voluntarily repairs the property may not force his cotenants to reimburse him for their share of the repairs, except by deduction from rent due the other owners or upon partition. [102-103]

4. **Improvements:** No co-owner is obliged to improve property. Thus, an improving co-owner may not recover improvement costs from her fellow owners, but upon partition or by way of deduction from rent owed to the other owners, the improving co-owner may recover the ***value added*** by the improvements. [103]

D. **Adverse possession:** In order for one co-owner to occupy adversely to his fellow owners, it is essential that he give the other owners ***absolutely clear and unequivocal notice that he*** **claims exclusive and sole title.** Otherwise, the possession is not wrongful. [103]

E. **Implied fiduciaries:** Generally, cotenants do not owe each other fiduciary duties, unless they are voluntarily assumed. A fiduciary duty is implied in law, however, when one co-owner acts to gain an advantage of *title* over his fellow owners, as when one co-owner purchases the property at a foreclosure sale. [103]

III. MARITAL INTERESTS

A. **The common law system:** The *pure* common law system of marital property is extinct, but aspects of it continue to exist. Upon marriage, a woman lost all legal control over her property to her husband but acquired some inchoate property rights — a right of lifetime support from her husband and a *dower* right. [104-113]

1. **Dower:** Dower was the right given a widow to a life estate in one-third of each and every possessory freehold estate the husband had owned at any point during marriage that was capable of inheritance by children born of the marriage. Once dower attached, it could only be removed by divorce or with the wife's consent. Dower is largely abolished today; its modern analogue is the *spousal elective share*, which guarantees a surviving spouse a specified portion of the decedent spouse's estate. [104-105]

2. **Curtesy:** Curtesy, now abolished, was the common law's sibling to dower. Upon marriage, a husband acquired a life estate in his wife's property, measured by the first to die of husband

or wife, but upon the birth of a child the life estate ripened into one measured by the husband's life alone. [105]

B. The modern (mostly statutory) "common law" system: The common law system of marital property has been altered considerably by statute. [106-108]

    1. Rights on divorce: Most states have some form of *equitable distribution* statute. These statutes define marital property and make that property subject to equitable (usually equal) division. [106-107]

        a. Professional skills and credentials: States split over how to treat the increased earning power one spouse may obtain during marriage (e.g., a professional degree). Some states say it is *not property* and thus not subject to division. Others treat the increased earnings potential as property *subject to equitable division.* Others take a middling course of requiring the benefited spouse to reimburse the contributing spouse for the support supplied.

    2. Rights on death: Today's substitute for dower is the spousal *elective share,* created by statute. The surviving spouse is entitled to elect either the statutory share of the deceased spouse's estate or to take under the deceased spouse's will. Statutory shares differ widely, from as much as one-half to as little as a life estate in one-third. The elective share may be partially avoided by transfers during life to persons other than one's spouse. [107]

    3. Antenuptial agreements and spousal contracts: Common law did not generally enforce agreements made between spouses before marriage that were intended to govern property division upon divorce. Today, many states will enforce such agreements so long as the parties fully disclosed their financial condition and the substance of the agreement is not unconscionable. The enforceability of contracts between spouses after marriage depends on the subject matter. [107-108]

C. Community property: Community property is a civil law institution inherited from French and Spanish colonization of portions of America. The fundamental idea is that a marriage is a partnership of equals, and that the property acquired during marriage by the efforts of either spouse belongs to that marital community. Each spouse has an equal claim to the assets of the marital community. The Uniform Marital Property Act (adopted only by Wisconsin) is, for all practical purposes, a statutory replica of community property. [108-111]

    1. Definition of community property: Community property consists of earnings during marriage of either spouse and all property acquired from such earnings. This excludes *separate property* — property acquired before marriage or, during marriage, by gift, inheritance, or devise. Property can be transmuted from one form to the other only by agreement of both spouses. Courts use a rebuttable presumption that property acquired during marriage is community property. [108-109]

    2. Commingling of separate and community property: Once separate and community property is commingled, it becomes community property unless one spouse can trace the source of some discrete portion to separate property. When a partially paid-for asset is brought to marriage, and the remainder of the purchase is made by community funds, states employ three different approaches. [109-110]

        a. Inception of right: Some states hold that the character of the property is fixed at the inception of legal right to possession.

    b. Time of vesting: Some states hold that the character of the property is determined when title passes.

    c. Pro-rata apportionment: Some states hold that the percentage of the purchase price paid prior to marriage establishes the portion of the property that is separate; the remainder is community property.

  3. Management of community property: Husband and wife have equal management powers. Either spouse can transfer community property, but neither spouse, acting alone, can convey their interest in the community to a stranger. [110-111]

  4. Rights upon divorce: At divorce, each spouse is entitled to half the community property and all of the separate property. [111]

  5. Rights upon death: At death, the half-interest of the deceased spouse in the community property is disposed of according to the deceased spouse's will. It does not automatically go to the surviving spouse. [111]

  6. Creditors' rights: Generally, debts incurred during marriage are presumed to be community obligations, and the community property is subject to seizure to satisfy such debts. [111]

D. "Quasi-marital" property: Unmarried cohabitants: Lots of people live together without marriage. Their property rights depend mostly on whatever agreements they have between themselves as to their shared property. Otherwise, title to property determines ownership. [111]

  1. Common law marriage: Common law conferred marital status on a man and woman who openly lived together as husband and wife, even though they were not ceremonially married. Most states have abandoned common law marriage and, even in jurisdictions recognizing the doctrine, it does not extend to same-sex couples. The American Law Institutes endorses common law marriage for all cohabiting couples, whatever their sex. [111]

  2. Contracts: Unmarried cohabitants may create express contracts to govern their property upon death or termination of the cohabitation. These agreements are generally enforceable, unless they are explicitly founded on illegal consideration. [111-112]

  3. Same-sex couples: Same-sex marriage is permitted only in five states and D.C., but some states provide to same-sex couples the status benefits of marriage under different names. Even then, federal law deprives same-sex couples of the status benefits of marriage available under federal law. Same-sex couples may, however, make contractual arrangements to replicate marital property results as between themselves. [112-113]

IV. CONDOMINIUMS AND COOPERATIVES

A. Condominiums: The condominium consists of fee ownership of an individual unit and a fractional interest as a tenant in common with all other condominium owners of the common areas of the building or development. The condominium is a creature of statute; creation is by compliance with the statute. Each condominium may be sold and financed separately. Each condominium owner is jointly and severally liable for the common areas. No owner can partition the common areas. Condominium owners are members of an association that elects a board of directors, empowered to run the association and make important financial and other decisions about the condominium development. [113-114]

B. Cooperatives: A cooperative apartment building is owned by a corporation. Each apartment "owner" owns shares in the corporation and has a lease to the apartment from the corporation. Thus, each dweller is simultaneously part owner (by virtue of owning shares in the corporate building owner) and a tenant. The corporation's board of directors is elected by its shareholders. Lease rentals are set to recover the operating costs of the building, including insurance, mortgage service, and taxes. Transferability of the corporate stock and the lease are restricted to ensure that transferees are financially capable of discharging the obligations of ownership and tenancy. [114]

CHAPTER 5
LEASEHOLD ESTATES

I. THE NATURE OF LEASES

A. Origins and dual nature: Estate and contract: The lease started out as a nonfreehold estate, probably a device to avoid usury limits. Now it is a hybrid — both a nonfreehold property estate and a contract. A lease is thus simultaneously a conveyance of an estate and a package of bilateral promises. Leases of residential property are more apt to be seen as primarily contracts than commercial leases, but all leases have the dual quality of both property estate and contract. [118-119]

B. The general requirement of a written lease: By the Statute of Frauds, observed in some version in all American states, long-term leases (usually for a year or more) must be in writing to be valid, but if possession is transferred under an invalid oral lease, and rent is tendered and accepted, some form of tenancy has been created by those actions. [119]

C. What makes it a lease? Unlike analogous interests, such as a license or an easement, a lessee has all the rights of possession that the fee owner has. A lessee may recover for invasion of his possession through ejectment, trespass, or nuisance. [119]

II. THE TYPES OF LEASEHOLDS

A. Term of years: A lease for a single, fixed term of any length is a lease for a term of years. A term may be "indeterminate" in the sense that it is not precisely stated, so long as the length of the term can be readily computed by reference to some formula, but if the term is of indefinite duration, a tenancy at will may be created. A term of years may be made defeasible on the occurrence of some uncertain future event. [119-120]

B. Periodic tenancy: A periodic tenancy is a lease for a recurring period of time and continues in existence until either party gives advance notice to the other of termination. Common law required six months' advance notice to terminate a year-to-year tenancy and notice equal to the period for periods of six months or less. These advance-notice requirements have been significantly altered by statute, usually to make the notice period no more than a month. Periodic tenancies may be created by agreement or by operation of law. When created by operation of law, there is often difficulty in deciding what the period is, but the issue is usually resolved by observing how frequently the rent is paid and using that recurring period. [120-122]

C. Tenancy at will: A tenancy at will is a leasehold for no fixed time or period and lasts only as long as both parties desire. It may be terminated at any time by either party. It may be created by agreement or by operation of law. A tenancy for a defined period — either periodic of for a term of years — that is terminable whenever one party wishes is a determinable periodic tenancy or term, but is ***not a tenancy at will.*** A tenancy of uncertain duration that is terminable whenever one party wishes may be a tenancy at will, though many courts regard such a tenancy as a determinable leasehold life estate. [122-123]

D. Holdovers: Tenancy at sufferance: A tenant who stays on in possession after the term has expired is no longer a lawful tenant. The "holdover" is a tenant at sufferance — a legal limbo between the status of trespasser and lawful tenant — until the landlord decides how to treat the holdover. Within a reasonable time, the landlord must elect either (1) to ***evict and recover damages for lost possession,*** or (2) to ***bind the holdover to a new term as a tenant.*** A tenant is a holdover unless the tenant's continued possession after expiration of the term is due to circumstances beyond the tenant's control. If the landlord elects to evict and recover damages, the general measure of damages is the fair market value of possession. If the landlord elects to bind the tenant to a new term, most states treat the new tenancy as a periodic tenancy defined by the rent-payment period. Once made, an election of remedies is irrevocable. A few states provide for a double or treble rent penalty as the exclusive landlord remedy for holdovers. [123-126]

III. DELIVERY OF POSSESSION

A. Implied obligation to deliver legal right of possession: A landlord must deliver to the tenant the legal right to possess the leased premises. This means that the landlord promises that the tenant will not be evicted by somebody with a better title to the premises than the landlord. The tenant can waive this right, either explicitly or by taking possession with knowledge of a paramount title. [126-127]

B. Obligation to deliver actual possession? The English rule (adopted by most American states) imposes on landlords the obligation to deliver actual possession to the tenant. The so-called American rule (but a minority rule in the United States) holds that a landlord is not obliged to deliver actual possession. Under the English rule, a landlord has the right and duty to evict holdovers and is liable to the new tenant for damages for lack of possession. Under the American rule, the burden of evicting a holdover falls entirely on the new tenant. [127-129]

C. Tenant obligation to take possession: A tenant has no obligation to take possession, unless the lease expressly requires a tenant to do so. [129]

IV. SUBLEASES AND ASSIGNMENTS

A. Essential differences: An *assignment* places the assignee in ***privity of estate*** with the landlord, which means that the assignee is personally responsible for performance of those obligations in the assigned lease that "run" with the leasehold estate. A *sublease,* by contrast, does not create privity of estate between the landlord and the subtenant, so the subtenant is liable only to the sublessor for performance of the sublease and has the right to possession only so long as the sublessor is not in default under the master lease. An assignment occurs when the assignor conveys his entire remaining estate to the assignee. A sublease occurs when the original tenant transfers anything less than his entire remaining interest in the leasehold estate. In both cases, however, the assignor or sublessor remains in ***privity of contract*** with the landlord and thus continues to be liable for performance of the original lease, unless the landlord has released the original tenant from his obligations. Neither an assignee nor sublessee is in privity of contract with the landlord unless the assignee or sub-lessee *assumes* the obligations of the original lease. [129-135]

B. Running covenants: A lease covenant runs with the leasehold estate and thus binds the assignee if the promise is *intended to run,* the assignee is in *privity* of estate or contract with the party seeking to enforce the covenant, the substance of the covenant *touches and concerns* the use or enjoyment of the estate, and the assignee has *notice* of the covenant. Personal promises do not run. The covenant to pay rent is the most significant running covenant. [130-131]

C. Lease provisions restricting assignment or sublease: A tenant is free to transfer his leasehold unless the lease restricts that right. Landlords commonly condition assignment or sublease on their consent to the transfer, but landlords may not deny consent for reasons that constitute unlawful discrimination, nor may landlords in commercial leases unreasonably deny consent. The test of "reasonableness" is objective; at the very least, landlords may not deny consent to reap an unrelated commercial advantage. [135-137]

V. TENANT'S OBLIGATIONS

A tenant's obligations are defined by the lease. The principal duties follow, but just about any duty can be imposed by the lease.

A. Pay the rent: This used to be an *independent obligation,* which meant that the tenant had to pay rent, no matter what the landlord failed to do. Most American states today treat this obligation as *dependent* upon the landlord's performance of his obligations, especially with respect to residential leases. The amount of the rent is almost always stipulated; otherwise, it is the reasonable rental value. [137]

B. Waste avoidance: The tenant is obligated to avoid waste. This consists of two components — the *duty to repair* and the *duty to avoid damage.* [138]

    1. The duty to repair: This was a tenant obligation at common law, but most states today have, by statute, made it a landlord obligation in residential leases. Otherwise, it may be apportioned however the parties wish. [138]

    2. The duty to avoid damage: Voluntary acts of the tenant that substantially damage the premises constitute waste. The tenant is liable for such actions. [138]

C. Refrain from illegal uses: A tenant may not use the premises for illegal purposes. If the landlord either intends such use or knows of it, the lease is unenforceable. If a landlord is ignorant of illegal use, he may terminate the lease once he learns of the activity. [138-139]

D. Honesty as to intended purpose: A tenant has a duty not to misrepresent his intentions. Even if the tenant's use is completely legal, but is utterly inconsistent with his representations, the landlord may terminate the lease because of the misrepresentation. [139]

E. Duty not to commit nuisance: A tenant has the duty not to use the premises to commit a nuisance. [139]

F. Duties from express lease provisions: Other duties can be imposed in the lease. [139]

G. Circumstances excusing tenant of obligations: At common law, there were no excuses permitted, but today a tenant is excused from his obligations under a variety of circumstances. The most important ones follow. [139-140]

1. Sole use becomes illegal: If the tenant has bargained for one specific use that later becomes illegal, the tenant is excused from further performance. This excuse is not available if the tenant has not bargained for one specific use (now illegal) and the premises may reasonably be used in a legal manner. [139-140]

2. Destruction of the leasehold property: A tenant may terminate the lease if the premises are destroyed, unless either (1) the destruction was caused by the tenant, or (2) the tenant has agreed in the lease that destruction is no excuse. [140]

3. Loss by eminent domain: A governmental taking of the premises automatically terminates the lease. The tenant is entitled to share in the compensation only to the extent the fair market value of the leasehold exceeds the rent obligation. [140]

4. Frustration of intended purpose: In commercial leases only, a tenant may be excused if (1) *extreme hardship* would result from (2) a third party's *unforeseeable action* that (3) makes the *mutually intended purpose* (4) *virtually impossible* to accomplish. [140]

VI. LANDLORD'S REMEDIES

A. Remedies typically derived from lease provisions: Landlords create many of their remedies in the lease. Some important ones follow. [141]

1. Rent acceleration: A rent-acceleration clause makes the entire remaining rent for the term of the lease immediately payable upon a tenant default under the lease. Usually these clauses give the landlord the option of accelerating rent. [141]

2. Security deposits: The landlord may demand a deposit from the tenant, at the inception of the lease, as security for the tenant's performance of the lease obligations. Especially in residential leases, statutes may govern the landlord's use of the security deposit. [141]

3. Liquidated damages: A lease may provide for liquidated damages. Such clauses are valid if the amount of liquidated damages is reasonably related to the probable damages, but the actual damages are not capable of easy determination. [141]

4. Confession of judgment: These clauses, which stipulate, that upon default, the tenant waives service of process and authorizes a landlord nominee to confess judgment, are widely prohibited by statute and are of doubtful validity even where permitted. [141]

B. Remedies derived from statute and common law: Statutes and common law provide a number of additional remedies, summarized here. [142]

1. Eviction: By statute, a landlord is permitted to terminate the lease and evict the tenant for non-payment of rent and occasionally for breach of other lease covenants. [142-144]

a. Summary proceedings: Unlawful detainer: The usual method of eviction is by a summary judicial proceeding known as *unlawful detainer* or *forcible entry and detainer.* In this proceeding, which is handled expeditiously, the only issue is entitlement to possession.

    b. Ejectment: The common law action for ejectment is also available, but this suit is not a summary proceeding, which means that there is no calendar preference, and the tenant can raise issues that go beyond the right to possession.

    c. Landlord self-help: Some states absolutely forbid self-help, while others permit it so long as the landlord acts peaceably or does not use unreasonable force.

2. Tenant abandonment: A tenant abandonment is an offer to surrender the lease, which the landlord may (1) accept and thus terminate the lease, (2) reject and leave the premises untouched, or (3) reject but retake possession and relet the premises on behalf of the tenant. If the landlord accepts the surrender and terminates, the tenant is liable for unpaid rent up to the moment of termination plus damages created by the abandonment. If the landlord rejects and leaves the premises untouched, the tenant remains liable for the rent. Some jurisdictions require the landlord, even if he rejects surrender, to retake possession and relet the premises to mitigate damages, especially in residential leases. [144-146]

3. Seizure of the tenant's personal property: Common law permitted landlords to seize and hold the tenant's personal property until the tenant cured his default. This right, called *distraint*, is substantially limited by statute today. [146]

VII. LANDLORD'S OBLIGATIONS AND TENANT'S REMEDIES

These landlord obligations and correlative tenant remedies may be rooted in the lease or imposed by law.

A. Quiet enjoyment: A landlord has a duty imposed by law to refrain from the wrongful actual or constructive eviction of the tenant. [146-149]

1. Actual total eviction: A tenant who is wrongfully physically ousted from the entire premises may terminate the lease with no further liability. [146]

2. Actual partial eviction: The traditional rule is that a wrongful eviction from any part of the premises entitles the tenant to abate rent entirely until the tenant is restored to full possession. The modern view is that the tenant should be entitled to a partial rent abatement, reflecting the reasonable value of the lost possession. [146-147]

3. Constructive eviction: If a landlord (not someone else) wrongly interferes with the tenant's use and enjoyment of the premises so substantially that the intended purpose of the tenant's occupation is frustrated, a *constructive eviction* has occurred. The tenant may move out and terminate the lease with no further liability. Before vacating the premises, the tenant must notify the landlord and give him a reasonable chance to fix the problem. Of course, if a tenant vacates, and a court later determines that there was no constructive eviction, the tenant has abandoned. [147-149]

B. Warranty of habitability: The traditional rule is that the landlord makes no warranty that the premises are suitable for the tenant's purposes. The modern trend is to imply into every residential lease a warranty that the premises are habitable. This implied warranty consists of a warranty of habitability at the inception of the lease and a continued obligation to repair as necessary to maintain habitability. The tenant may not waive this warranty. The implied warranty of habitability is often codified by statute. [149-150]

1. **Tenant's remedies for landlord breach of the implied warranty of habitability:** A tenant's remedies for breach of the implied warranty of habitability follow. [151-152]

   a. **Terminate and leave:** In addition, the tenant may recover damages.

   b. **Stay and withhold rent:** If the tenant exercises this remedy, he must deposit rent into an escrow account pending landlord repair of the defects.

   c. **Stay and repair:** The tenant may stay in possession and use a reasonable portion of the rent to make repairs.

   d. **Stay and recover damages:** The tenant may remain in possession and recover damages in the form of a rent abatement or deduction. The measure of damages is either (1) the difference between the warranted value and actual "as is" value, (2) the difference between stated rent and actual "as is" value, or (3) a reduction in stated rent equal to the proportion by which warranted value has been reduced.

   e. **Stay and defend:** The tenant can stay and prove the uninhabitable condition as a complete defense to an eviction action based on tenant failure to pay rent.

   f. **Punitive damages:** When a landlord's breach involves willful, wanton, or fraudulent conduct, a tenant may be entitled to recover punitive damages.

2. **The retaliatory eviction doctrine:** Usually, the landlord's motivation for seeking eviction is irrelevant, but if a landlord seeks eviction in retaliation for a tenant's assertion of the habitability warranty, many jurisdictions will deny eviction. The tenant must prove retaliatory motive, and the remedy is available only to a tenant who is not in default. A landlord may evict after a retaliatory motive has been found only if he can prove an independent good business reason for it; nor may a landlord use indirect methods of eviction, like drastic reductions of services. [153]

C. **Tort liability of landlords:** Modern law places greater duties on landlords to maintain leased premises in a fashion that avoids foreseeable injury to others. This is merely a subset of the tort doctrine of negligence. [153-156]

   1. **Pre-existing dangerous conditions:** At common law, a landlord had no tort liability for pre-existing dangerous conditions unless they were *latent defects* known to the landlord, and the landlord had failed to warn of the defects. [154]

   2. **Conditions occurring during the lease term:** A landlord generally has no liability for injuries resulting from conditions occurring after the tenant has taken possession, unless the landlord has undertaken a duty of repair. [154]

   3. **Common areas:** Landlords are liable for injuries resulting from their negligence with respect to common areas that remain under landlord control. [154]

   4. **Landlord covenant to repair:** The common law rule was that a landlord assumed no duty of care in tort by agreeing to repair leased premises, but this view is rejected by most American jurisdictions today. [155]

   5. **Statutory or judicially created duty of landlord to repair:** Many jurisdictions impose on the landlord a duty to repair, especially in residential leases. [155]

6. **Strict liability:** At one time, California imposed strict liability on landlords for personal injuries resulting from latent defects in leased property. This view has not caught on, and even California has abandoned it. [155]

7. **No special rules for landlords:** About ten states hold landlords to the same duties as anyone else, finding landlords liable when they have failed to act as a reasonable person under the circumstances. [155]

8. **Exculpatory clauses:** These clauses, which purport to relieve the landlord of tort liability he might otherwise have, are generally valid, but some courts refuse to enforce them in residential leases. [155-156]

VIII. FIXTURES

Fixtures (personal property permanently attached to the premises) belong to the landlord, but *trade fixtures* (personal property that is used in carrying on a trade or business) may be removed by the tenant, who retains ownership of them. [156]

IX. SOCIAL REGULATIONS OF LEASEHOLDS

A. **Rent control:** Rent-control laws, usually adopted at the local level, consist of price controls often augmented by limitations on the landlord's ability to evict tenants at the end of the lease term. So long as the landlord is able to earn a reasonable rate of return on his investment, rent-control statutes do not constitute a governmental taking of property without just compensation. [156-157]

B. **Antidiscrimination statutes:** Federal, state, and local laws substantially restrict the landlord's common law right to decide with whom he wishes to deal. These laws prohibit most private acts of racial discrimination in the sale or rental of real property. Probably the most important such statute is the federal Fair Housing Act, which exempts (1) the sale or lease of a single-family house without use of brokers or public advertisements that reveal discriminatory motive, and (2) rentals of residential housing in owner-occupied units of four units or less. [157-159]

CHAPTER 6
TRANSFERS OF REAL PROPERTY

I. CONTRACTS OF SALE

A. **Introduction:** Virtually all nongratuitous transfers of real property involve contracts for sale. [162-163]

1. **Brokers:** Most sales involve a broker. The seller hires a broker (the listing agent) to sell the property on the terms and conditions in the listing agreement. A commission is due when the broker procures a buyer ready, willing, and able to perform on those conditions or others acceptable to the seller. Brokers are fiduciaries. [162-163]

2. **Lawyers:** Lawyers are always valuable — to draft the contract, provide advice concerning the legal effect of the transaction, and examine title — but are often ignored, particularly in residential sales. [163]

3. **Mortgage lenders:** Most transactions involve a mortgage lender, who lends a large portion of the purchase price to the buyer and secures repayment of the loan by taking a mortgage of the property. [163]

4. **Closing:** Real estate sales are a two-step transaction. First, a contract is entered into. Second, a closing occurs, at which the purchase price is exchanged for title. This closing occurs through a third party, an escrow agent, who holds the money and documents and disburses them in accordance with the parties' instructions. [163]

B. **Statute of Frauds:** The Statute of Frauds requires that a contract for sale of real property be in writing and signed by the party against whom it is sought to be enforced. In practice, this means both parties must sign. A formal contract is not necessary, so long as the key terms are present in the writing, which need not consist of a single document. Contracts for sale are usually subject to conditions, and, if the conditions are not carefully spelled out, the entire contract may fail for want of an essential term. [163-166]

1. **Exceptions to the Statute of Frauds:** There are two major exceptions to the Statute of Frauds: *part performance* and *equitable estoppel.* Because each is an equitable doctrine, they are generally available only in a suit seeking specific performance of an otherwise unenforceable contract. [165]

   a. **Part performance:** Every state requires proof of an oral contract. Some states insist that the acts making up part performance be of the sort that would not occur but for the existence of a contract — partial or total payment, taking possession, or making improvements. Many states are content with reasonable reliance on the oral contract. Both buyers and sellers may invoke the doctrine.

   b. **Equitable estoppel:** This familiar doctrine is closely related to the reasonable-reliance branch of part performance. When one party reasonably relies to his detriment upon an oral contract for the sale of property, the other party will be estopped from denying the existence of the contract.

   c. **Electronic transactions:** By statute, electronic transactions are as good as paper, so long as they comprise the entire deal and bear an electronic signature.

2. **Revocation of contracts:** Most (but not all) states do not apply the Statute of Frauds to revocations of a contract for sale of real property. [166]

C. **Implied obligations:** Here are the principal obligations implied in any contract for the sale of realty. [166-168]

1. **Good faith:** Each party is required to act with good faith in discharging the express duties of the contract. [166]

2. **Time of closing:** Performance tendered within a reasonable time after the specified closing date is adequate unless the contract specifies that *time is of the essence* of the bargain. [166]

3. **Marketable title:** The seller has an implied duty to deliver *marketable title* to the buyer — title that a prudent buyer would accept, reasonably free of doubt that there are any rival claimants to title. Marketable title can be delivered by *good record title* or *proof of title through adverse possession.* [167-168]

    a. Defective title: Defects in title must be substantial and likely to injure the buyer to render title unmarketable. A defective link in the chain of title makes title unmarketable. Encumbrances make title unmarketable unless the encumbrance is (1) a beneficial easement known to the buyer, or (2) a restrictive use covenant that does not limit the particular use specified in the sale contract. Zoning restrictions are not encumbrances, but property in violation of existing zoning laws at the time of the contract of sale renders title unmarketable for purposes of an action for specific performance of the contract.

D. Default and remedies: Default occurs when one party has tendered timely performance and demanded timely performance from the other party, and reciprocal performance is not forthcoming. Available remedies include specific performance, damages, or rescission. [168-171]

    1. Specific performance: Because land is unique, damages are inadequate compensation. The equitable remedy of specific performance is available, subject to equitable defenses, to either buyer or seller. However, the emerging trend is to deny sellers specific performance if they are still able to sell the property at a commercially reasonable price. [168-169]

    2. Rescission: This is the polar opposite of specific performance. If the seller breaches, the buyer may rescind, recover any payments made, and depart. If the buyer breaches, the seller may rescind and sell to another party. [169]

    3. Damages: The measure of damages is usually the benefit of the bargain but may sometimes be limited to out-of-pocket losses or defined by contractual liquidated damage provisions. [169-171]

E. Duties of disclosure and implied warranties: Sellers are obligated by law to disclose known defects, and builders impliedly warrant the quality of their construction. [171-174]

    1. Duties of disclosure: The common law rule was that a seller's duty was to refrain from intentional misrepresentation or active concealment of a known defect, unless the seller (1) has a fiduciary duty to the buyer in which case the seller must reveal all known defects, or (2) has created hidden conditions that materially impair property value. The majority rule today is that a *seller must reveal all latent material defects* — defects known to the seller and not easily discoverable by the buyer that materially affect the value or desirability of the property. Some states, by statute, impose specific disclosure obligations on sellers and brokers. [171-173]

    2. Implied warranty of quality: Traditionally, builders were liable for breaches of an express warranty of quality only to those with whom they contracted. Courts today frequently imply a warranty of quality that runs to benefit subsequent purchasers for some reasonable time — a period at least long enough for the latent defects of original construction to become apparent. [173-174]

F. Risk of loss and equitable title: Between the making of a sale contract and the closing, the property may be damaged, or parties may die. [174-176]

    1. Equitable title: The doctrine of *equitable title* (or *equitable conversion*) was the common law's method of dealing with these problems. Equitable title held that equitable ownership of property passed to the buyer at the moment a specifically enforceable contract of sale was made. [174-176]

        a. Application to death of a party: One consequence of equitable title is that for purposes of death of a contracting party, title is treated as having passed at the moment the contract was made. The decedent thus has an interest in real property rather than personal property, which can have consequences under wills or in intestacy.

    b. Application to risk of loss of the property: The traditional and still widely prevailing rule is that equitable title places on the buyer the risk of loss prior to closing. English law gave the seller the proceeds of any insurance, on the theory that rights under an insurance contract were personal. Most American states reject this rule and require that insurance proceeds be credited to the buyer. A few American states place risk of loss on the seller, and some states have enacted statutes that make the risk of loss go with possession.

II. DEEDS

    A. Formal requirements and component parts: The Statute of Frauds requires that a deed be in writing. In order to be recorded, almost all states require that the grantor's signature be acknowledged before a notary. Any words that express an intent to transfer realty will suffice to make the grant, but the grantee must be identified and the property must be clearly described. [176-177]

    B. Warranties of title: A seller's warranties concerning the state of title are expressed in the deed and depend upon the type of deed used. [177-182]

      1. General warranty deed: A general warranty deed contains six covenants of title, each of which is a promise that title is free of the warranted defect, regardless of when the defect arose. [177-178]

        a. Covenant of seisin: The grantor promises that he owns what he is conveying.

        b. Covenant of right to convey: The grantor promises that he has authority to convey the property.

        c. Covenant against encumbrances: The grantor promises that there are no liens or encumbrances upon title other than those excepted in the deed.

        d. Covenant of general warranty: The grantor promises that he will defend against lawful claims of superior title in the property.

        e. Covenant of quiet enjoyment: The grantor promises that the grantee will not be disturbed in possession or enjoyment by someone with a better title.

        f. Covenant of further assurances: The grantor promises to do whatever is reasonably necessary to perfect the conveyed title.

      2. Special warranty deed: This deed contains the same six covenants of title, but the grantor makes these promises only with respect to *defects of title that arose during the time the grantor held title.* [178]

      3. Quitclaim deed: A quitclaim deed contains no warranties of title; rather, it simply conveys whatever the grantor owns. [178]

      4. Merger doctrine: The traditional rule is that any promises in the contract of sale with respect to title are merged into the deed once the buyer accepts the deed. Promises that are collateral to transfer of title are not merged. [178-179]

5. **Breach of covenants of title:** The covenants of title are either *present covenants* or *future covenants.* A present covenant — seisin, right to convey, and encumbrances — is breached, if at all, at the moment the deed is delivered. A future covenant — general warranty, quiet enjoyment, and further assurances — is breached when the grantee is actually or constructively evicted at some time in the future. [179-182]

   a. **Present covenants — seisin, right to convey, and encumbrances:** The benefit of present covenants is generally assignable, though this was not true at common law. The statute of limitations with respect to present covenants begins to run at the moment the deed is delivered.

   b. **Future covenants — general warranty, quiet enjoyment, and further assurances:** These covenants are breached only when the grantee is actually or constructively evicted. Actual eviction is actual dispossession from title or possession. Constructive eviction occurs whenever the grantee's possession is interfered with in any way by someone holding a superior title. The benefit of future covenants runs to later grantees if there is privity of estate between the original grantee and the remote grantee. Privity of estate is satisfied if whatever the original grantor conveyed is conveyed to the remote grantee. Damages for breach of a future covenant are generally limited by the rule that the grantee may not recover more than what the grantor-in-breach received for the property.

6. **After-acquired title (estoppel by deed):** If a grantor conveys property he does not own and later acquires it, this doctrine (also called *estoppel by deed*) holds that the after-acquired title is sent immediately and directly to the original grantee. [182]

C. **Delivery:** A deed must be delivered in order to be effective. Delivery means action demonstrating the grantor's intent to transfer immediately an interest in land to the grantee. Courts presume delivery if there has been (1) physical transfer, (2) notarial acknowledgment, or (3) recording of the deed. [183-186]

1. **Attempted delivery at death:** Attempts to deliver a deed at death are usually ineffective. Exceptions include (1) delivery to an escrow agent under irrevocable instructions to hold until the grantor's death, or (2) where the words of the grant create a springing executory interest upon the grantor's death. [183]

2. **Delivery subject to oral condition:** When deeds are delivered subject to an oral condition, the condition is usually (but not always) disregarded, and the delivery is deemed to be complete and unqualified. [183-184]

3. **Commercial escrows:** Delivery of a deed to a commercial escrow agent under instruction to release it upon payment from the buyer constitutes delivery. Despite this, if a seller conveys his property to a third-party bona fide purchaser (BFP) before the close of escrow, the BFP prevails over the equitable title of the first buyer. The seller is a scoundrel, but as between the innocent buyers the BFP has parted with value, and the first buyer has not yet fully executed the contract. [185]

4. **Delivery by estoppel:** A grantor who lacks intent to deliver a deed will nevertheless be estopped from denying delivery where the deed is either (1) entrusted to a deceitful grantee who uses it to transfer title to an innocent third party, or (2) entrusted to an escrow agent who negligently gives it to the grantee. [185-186]

III. FINANCING DEVICES: MORTGAGES, DEEDS OF TRUST, AND INSTALLMENT CONTRACTS

A. **Mortgages:** A mortgage is a device to secure repayment of a loan, often made to enable a person to acquire real property. The mortgage vests in a lender the power to take the mortgaged property in partial or total satisfaction of the loan debt. In form, the lender makes the loan, and the borrower executes a promissory note (the promise to repay with interest) and a mortgage to secure repayment of the loan. The mortgage gives the lender the power to sell the property and apply the proceeds to the loan if the borrower defaults. The mortgagor has an equitable right to redeem the property (the *equity of redemption*), which can be eliminated by *foreclosure.* Many states have created a separate, independent *statutory right of redemption,* which gives the borrower a specific period of time after foreclosure sale to redeem the property. [186-190]

1. **Types of mortgages:** There are a variety of mortgages. The same property can be used to secure more than one loan, so the most senior mortgage is the first mortgage. A fully amortized mortgage is one that is paid off in equal payments over a fixed term. A balloon mortgage is one that requires a lump-sum payment of principal at maturity. A purchase-money mortgage is one made for a portion of the purchase price. [187-188]

2. **Title or lien?** States differ as to whether a mortgage creates a *lien* on the property or transfers *title* to the property, subject to a condition subsequent requiring retransfer upon payment of the loan. In any case, when title is transferred it is for the limited purpose of securing repayment of the loan. [188]

3. **Sale or transfer by the mortgagor:** A mortgagor may transfer his interest in the mortgaged property. The buyer may *assume the mortgage* or may take *subject to the mortgage.* A buyer who takes subject to a mortgage incurs no personal liability on the mortgage. A buyer who assumes the mortgage becomes personally liable on the mortgage loan. Lenders often impede these transfers by inserting a *"due-on-sale"* clause in the mortgage, which makes the loan immediately due and payable upon any transfer. [188-189]

4. **Default by mortgagor:** In most states, the lender has the option of a suit to collect the debt or to foreclose and sell the mortgaged property to satisfy the debt. If the foreclosure sale proceeds are inadequate to extinguish the debt, the borrower is personally liable for the deficiency. Some states have "antideficiency" statutes that prohibit deficiency judgments, typically with respect to purchase-money mortgage loans for residences. In some states, lenders are obliged to conduct the foreclosure sale in a commercially reasonable manner, such that reasonable efforts are made to realize a fair price. [189-190]

B. **Deeds of trust:** Some states use a deed of trust instead of a mortgage. The borrower conveys the property to a third party as trustee for the lender, for the limited purpose of securing repayment of the loan. The trustee has a power of sale of the property upon default, with an obligation to use the proceeds to pay the debt and return any excess to the borrower. The chief difference from the mortgage is that no judicial foreclosure is required to sell the property, but even this difference has begun to disappear. [190]

C. **Installment sale contracts:** An installment sale contract is, in form, a contract for sale of real property that obligates the purchaser to pay the purchase price in installments and obligates the seller to convey title to the buyer after the purchase price has been fully paid. Because an installment sale contract is economically indistinguishable from a transfer of title followed by a note and purchase-money mortgage, most states treat the installment sale contract as a security device. [190-191]

CHAPTER 7

ASSURING GOOD TITLE TO LAND

I. INTRODUCTION

A. **The problem:** People sometimes convey the same property more than once. The problem that results is to decide which innocent purchaser should prevail. [193-194]

1. **The common law answer:** The common law awarded title to the grantee who took *first in time*. [194]

2. **Modern answers:** Today, the common law approach is the last resort. American states rely primarily on the following methods of resolving conflicting claims to title. [194]

a. **Recording:** A public record of conveyances enables priority to be given to recorded conveyances but still requires some mechanism for sorting out priority between recorded conveyances to the same property.

b. **Registration:** An official registry of land titles makes the registered title dispositive title. By contrast, a recording system merely contains evidence of title.

c. **Title insurance:** Title insurers agree to defend the title they insure and compensate for any defects in title. Title insurance is based upon the recorded title and provides an added measure of security, but it does not establish title.

II. RECORDING ACTS AND CHAIN-OF-TITLE PROBLEMS

A. **The recording system:** A public official, the recorder, maintains a record of real estate transactions presented for recording and indexes those transactions by grantor and grantee, and sometimes by tract. A title searcher is then able to search backward in time through an alphabetical index of grantees to find the transaction by which the present owner received title, and to repeat that process until an adequate root of title is found. Then the searcher looks forward in time through an alphabetical index of grantors to determine whether there were any title transactions made by each owner other than the grant to the next owner. If a tract index is maintained, all of this information is collected in one location. [194-196]

B. **Recording acts:** There are three types of recording acts: a *race* act, a *notice* act, and a *race-notice* act. [196-197]

1. **Race acts:** A race act provides that, as between two grantees to the same property, the *earliest to record* prevails. Thus, there is a race to record. [196]

2. **Notice acts:** A notice act provides that a *later bona fide purchaser without notice of a prior unrecorded grant prevails over the prior grantee, whether or not the later grant is recorded.* [196-197]

3. **Race-notice acts:** A race-notice act provides that *only those later bona fide purchasers who (1) lack notice of a prior unrecorded grant* and *(2) record first* prevail over the first grantee. [197]

C. **The consequences of recording:** Recording provides constructive notice to the world of the grant. In a race or race-notice state, recording cuts off the possibility that either a prior unrecorded purchaser or a later purchaser could prevail. In a notice state, recording prevents a later purchaser from prevailing. [197]

    1. The consequences of not recording: If nobody has recorded, the common law first-in-time rule applies, except in a notice state where the later grantee lacked notice. More importantly, the grantor of an unrecorded conveyance has power to convey good title to someone else. [197-198]

D. When is an instrument recorded: An instrument is recorded when (1) it is eligible to be recorded, and (2) is actually entered in the public records in a manner that complies with the jurisdiction's requirements. [198-200]

    1. Instrument not indexed: The older rule is that an improperly indexed instrument provides constructive notice, on the view that the grantee has done all he can to provide record notice, but the newer view is that it does not provide constructive notice, because even the most diligent searcher will not find it. [198]

    2. "Omnibus" or "Mother Hubbard" clauses: These clauses, inserted in a deed to a single parcel, purport to cover "all other property" of the grantor. Because there is no way a diligent searcher of title to the "other property" will ever find such a clause, tucked away in an apparently unrelated deed, they are usually held to be inadequate to provide notice. [198-199]

    3. Misspelled names: States differ over whether a misspelled name in a recorded instrument gives constructive notice. All states agree that if the misspelling is so significant that it does not even sound like the correct name, there is no constructive notice, but some states regard a misspelling that sounds substantially identical to the correct name as sufficient to give constructive notice. [199]

    4. Ineligible instrument: These are usually instruments that lack a notarial acknowledgment. If the defect is apparent on the face of the instrument, most states treat it as ***not*** recorded, and it does not give constructive notice. If the defect is hidden, most, but not all, states treat it as providing constructive notice. [199-200]

E. Scope of protection afforded by recording acts: The protection provided by recording acts is defined by the act. Recording does not make valid an invalid grant. Recording acts only apply to conveyances and not to interests created by operation of law (e.g., adverse possession or prescriptive or implied easements). [200-201]

    1. Bona fide purchasers: Notice and race-notice acts are intended to protect only bona fide purchasers (BFPs). A BFP gives valuable consideration and lacks notice of any prior unrecorded conveyance. Race acts protect BFPs only to the extent they are first to record. A donee cannot be a BFP, because he gives no consideration. [200-201]

        a. Shelter rule: The protection given a BFP extends to all takers from the BFP, even if that taker knows of a prior unrecorded conveyance. The later taker is "sheltered" by the BFP's status.

    2. Mortgagees: Mortgagees are generally treated as bona fide purchasers, though some states deny BFP status to a mortgagee who takes the mortgage to secure a pre-existing debt. [201]

    3. Creditors: Some recording acts only protect ***purchasers***, a term that excludes creditors unless they purchase at an execution sale. Other recording acts specifically protect "all persons," including creditors. [201]

F. Notice: Notice (which the BFP must lack) may be *actual* or *constructive*. [201-207]

   1. Actual notice: Actual notice is real knowledge. [201]

   2. Constructive notice: Constructive notice may be derived from the record or may be the result of an obligation to make reasonable inquiry. [201-207]

      a. Record notice: Instruments of record are deemed to supply constructive notice to subsequent purchasers, but there can be argument over what constitutes the record.

         i. "Wild deeds" — Outside the chain of title: An instrument made by a total stranger to the record chain of title does not give notice. It is not within the chain of title and could not be expected to be found by a normal and diligent search.

         ii. Expanded chain of title — Deeds from common grantor: States divide over whether a deed from a common grantor to other property, but which imposes a restrictive covenant on the grantor's remaining property, is in the chain of title of the remaining property. States that say to include such deeds in the chain of title impose an enlarged search burden, because title searchers must locate and read all the deeds ever made by every owner of the subject property. States that refuse to expand the chain of title in this way permit title searchers to confine their efforts to the immediate chain of title.

         iii. After-acquired title: Most states say that an instrument made and recorded before the grantor acquires title is inadequate to impart constructive notice, even if the grantor later acquires title. A few hold to the opposite view, thus expanding the concept of the chain of title.

         iv. Deed recorded after grantor has parted with record title: States are about evenly divided. A slight majority hold that the chain of title includes all instruments recorded up to the point the later purchaser acquires title, which means that a title searcher must search the grantor index up to the present for every grantor. The minority reject this rule as too burdensome.

         v. Prior deed recorded after partial payment by later purchaser: Courts divide over the solution to the problem that results when an owner conveys to a purchaser who fails to record the deed, then conveys to a later purchaser lacking notice of the prior conveyance, who makes partial payment before the first purchaser records but then makes the final payments with knowledge of the prior transaction. The traditional solution is *restitution* — give title to the first purchaser on condition that he reimburse the second purchaser for his payments. The alternative answer is *benefit of the bargain* — give title to the second purchaser, but require that all remaining payments (if any) be made to the first purchaser rather than the owner.

      b. Inquiry notice: A person obliged to inquire is constructively notified of facts that would reasonably be revealed by the inquiry. Common circumstances triggering inquiry notice include (1) possession of the property by somebody else, (2) record reference to an unrecorded instrument, (3) deeds from a common grantor, and (4) the character of the neighborhood (at least with respect to the possibility of an implied reciprocal covenant).

   3. Tract index: A solution to chain of title problems? Tract indices would solve many of these problems, but it is expensive to assemble accurate tract records after years of organizing those data by grantor and grantee. [207]

G. **Marketable-title acts:** These acts, adopted by about 20 states, bar all claims of title that predate a specified point in the past — anywhere from at least 22 to 50 or more years ago. Claims that are based on an instrument *older* than the **root of title** — an unbroken good chain of title going back to a point earlier than, say, the 50-year period specified in the act — are forever barred. The effectiveness of marketable title acts is diluted by provisions that either exempt some pre-root interests from the act or permit them to be kept alive by re-recording during the marketable-title-act period. [207-208]

III. TITLE REGISTRATION — THE TORRENS SYSTEM

A. **Introduction:** Title registration is a substitute for recording. The certificate of title is **the** *title*, not just evidence of title. The certificate of title is absolutely binding and definitive ownership. [208]

B. **Operation:** To register title initially it is necessary to join in one judicial proceeding everybody who conceivably claims a title interest in the property. Once that proceeding results in a final determination of title, the title is registered, and a certificate is issued. All interests in title, such as mortgages or easements, are noted as "memorials" on the registered title. The only way thereafter to acquire title is to obtain a new registered title by cancellation of the old certificate and issuance of a new one in the new owner's name. However, registered-title acts often exempt some claims of title from this rule, thus diminishing the effectiveness of the concept. Typical exceptions include claims of governments, claims of persons in actual possession, mineral claims, visible easements, and railroad or utility easements. Also, if a title claimant is not joined in the original proceeding leading to issuance of registered title, her claim is not cut off. Fraud in the procurement of registered title also vitiates it. Title registration is not used much in the United States. It is expensive to initiate and poses some risks of uncompensated loss when the title registrar makes errors. [208-211]

IV. TITLE INSURANCE

This is the most common form of title assurance. Title insurance involves the issuance of an insurance policy by which the insurer warrants that title is as stated in the policy. Title insurance policies contain a number of exclusions, typically such things as off-record liens or interests asserted by persons in possession, boundary disputes, off-record easements or servitudes, and government land-use regulations. The insurer is liable for the difference in value of the property with and without the insured-against defect, up to the maximum limit specified in the policy. [211-213]

CHAPTER **8**

JUDICIAL CONTROL OF LAND USE: NUISANCE AND SUPPORT

I. THE SUBSTANCE OF NUISANCE

A. **The general principle:** No person may use his own land in an **unreasonable manner** that **substantially** lessens another person's **use and enjoyment** of his land. A nuisance may be public or private. A **private nuisance** involves interference with the rights of one or more private landowners. A **public nuisance** involves interference with rights of the entire public. [216]

B. Private nuisances: A private nuisance occurs when there is *substantial interference* with private rights to use and enjoy land, produced by either (1) *intentional and unreasonable conduct,* or (2) *unintentional conduct* that is either *negligent, reckless,* or *inherently dangerous.* [216-218]

1. **Intentional conduct:** Intentional interference occurs when the activity is known by its maker to interfere with another's use of his land. The key focus is on whether the interference is *unreasonable.* There are three views of what is unreasonable. [216-218]

   a. **Balancing: Harm and social utility:** The view of the *Restatement (Second) of Torts* is that an activity is unreasonable if the *gravity of the harm inflicted by the activity outweighs its social utility.* This judgment is highly contextual and may involve weighing of incommensurable values. A nuisance may often be the right thing in the wrong place (e.g., hot tar on the carpet instead of the roof).

   b. **Balancing: Uncompensated harm and ruinous liability:** The *Restatement (Second) of Torts* holds, alternatively, that an intentional activity is unreasonable if it causes *serious harm, and the actor could compensate for that and similar harm without going out of business.* When a defendant would be forced out of business by compensating for the harm he causes, this test concludes that the activity is not unreasonable and thus not a nuisance. Under such circumstances, a court is asked to decide which is worse — uncompensated harm or forcing businesses to close. This test is relevant when the issue is whether a nuisance should continue upon payment of compensation to those harmed; when a plaintiff seeks to enjoin a claimed nuisance, compensation is not a factor, and the general balancing of harm and social utility is applicable.

   c. **Substantial Harm: The liability threshold:** Many courts ignore the balancing tests if *substantial harm* is inflicted; a nuisance exists if the injury it inflicts is severe enough to be above some maximum level of interference that a person can be expected to endure without redress — a "threshold of liability."

2. **Unintentional conduct:** When an actor neither knows nor should know that his action substantially interferes with other people's use and enjoyment of their land, the focus is on whether the activity poses an unreasonable risk of harm to others — either because the actor is careless or the action is inherently dangerous. [218]

3. **Substantial interference:** To constitute a nuisance, the offending use must *substantially* impair use and enjoyment to the average person, not to the specific owner affected. An unusually sensitive person has no augmented power to cry, "Nuisance!" [218]

C. Public nuisances: A public nuisance affects rights held in common by everybody (e.g., to the municipal water supply). A pure public nuisance is rare; usually, a public nuisance is also a private nuisance. The substantive test for public nuisance is the same as for a private nuisance. A private citizen may enforce a public nuisance if he has suffered special injury — some particularized and personalized injury. [128-219]

D. Relationship to trespass: Trespass involves a physical invasion of a person's land — an interference with the *exclusive right to possession.* Nuisance involves an interference with *use and enjoyment* but does not necessarily involve any interference with the exclusive right to possession. However, the two concepts can and do overlap. [219]

II. REMEDIES: FOUR VIEWS OF NUISANCE

A. **Introduction: The economic theory of modern nuisance law:** Nuisance presents a problem of conflicting uses — each user's desired use prevents the other use from occurring. Each use produces externalities — costs that are not imposed on somebody other than the person producing them. While economic theory suggests that it doesn't matter who gets the initial right of use, because the parties will reallocate the right to whoever values it more, *transaction costs* — the costs of moving the right — are not negligible and thus inhibit this efficient transfer. [220-225]

1. **Transaction costs: The gap between theory and reality:** The reality of transaction costs suggests that a legal system concerned with allocative efficiency ought not be indifferent to the initial assignment of a use right. Here are some examples of common transaction costs. [220-221]

   a. **Bilateral monopoly:** When there are only two possible rightholders, the problem is *bilateral monopoly* — only one buyer and one seller. That creates the possibility that the gains from transfer will be frittered away by expensive bargaining, or that one party will obstinately refuse to act in an efficient manner, or that the mutual determination to better the other fellow will prevent an efficient outcome.

   b. **Free riders and holdouts:** When there are numerous parties to the negotiation, the problem is either *free riders* or *holdouts* — people who won't consent, in the hopes of getting something for nothing or in the hopes of extracting an exorbitant payment for their consent.

2. **Who gets the initial entitlement?** The most efficient and economically logical answer is that the *more valuable use* should receive the initial entitlement. Some would give the initial entitlement to the *first user,* on the theory that later users should adapt themselves to existing conditions. Others argue that courts should identify uses that, however efficient or utile, are dangerous to public health or environmental preservation, and award initial entitlement to the competing use. Though inefficient, some argue that the initial use entitlement should be given to the *less valuable use,* on the nakedly redistributionist theory that this will accomplish a forced wealth transfer, thought the merits of such forced transfers are not obvious. [222]

B. **Economic and legal theory and remedies:** In allocating the use right, nuisance law generally pays some attention to the fact of transaction costs. Because any legal right may be protected by a *property rule* (which makes the right immune from forced transfer) or a *liability rule* (which permits the right to be taken away upon payment of damages), there are four possible outcomes to any nuisance suit. [222-225]

1. **No nuisance: Continue the activity:** In this outcome the attacked use is determined not to be a nuisance and thus continues without restraint. The attacked use is protected by a property rule; it will cease only if the plaintiff's use is more valuable and the parties can reach an efficient agreement to shift the right to the plaintiff. [223]

2. **Nuisance: Enjoin and abate the activity:** In this outcome, the attacked use is found to be a nuisance, and its continuation is enjoined. The plaintiff landowner's use is protected by a property rule; the nuisance use will continue only if the nuisance use is more valuable and the parties can reach an efficient agreement to shift the right to the nuisance user. [233]

3. **Nuisance: Pay damages and continue the activity:** In this outcome, the attacked use is found to be a nuisance but is permitted to continue so long as the nuisance maker pays damages to the plaintiff landowner. The plaintiff landowner's use is protected by a liability rule. Courts are likely to employ this remedy when they think that the nuisance use is the more valuable but believe that the transaction costs of shifting the right to the nuisance user would prove to be insuperable. [224]

4. **No nuisance: Enjoin the activity but award damages to the enjoined actor:** In this outcome, whether or not the attacked use is found to be a nuisance, it is enjoined if the complaining landowner pays damages to compensate the attacked user for the discontinuance of the use. The attacked use is protected by a liability rule. Courts employ this remedy when they think that the plaintiffs use is the more valuable, but it is not clear that the attacked use is a nuisance, and transaction costs appear to be an insuperable obstacle to shifting the right from the attacked user to the plaintiff. [224-225]

III. SUPPORT RIGHTS

A. Introduction: Every landowner has the right to both *lateral support* and *subjacent support* of his land. A landowner may not modify his own land in such a way as to deprive his neighbor of either support right. [225]

B. Lateral support: The extent of the duty to maintain lateral support differs with respect to the land itself and structures upon the land. [225]

1. **Land itself:** A landowner is strictly liable for removal of lateral support from the land itself. [225]

2. **Structures:** A landowner is strictly liable for damage to structures resulting from the removal of lateral support if the collapse would have occurred even without the structures; but if the collapse would not have occurred but for the added weight of the structure, a landowner is liable for removal of lateral support only if he was negligent in doing so. [225]

C. Subjacent support: This right becomes an issue only if the surface is owned by one person, and the right to mine underground is owned by another. The underground miner is strictly liable for damages caused to land or structures resulting from withdrawal of subjacent support. [226]

CHAPTER 9

SERVITUDES: LAND USE LIMITS CREATED BY PRIVATE BARGAIN

I. INTRODUCTION

A. The concept: Servitudes are private arrangements concerning the use of land that endure as title and possession of the burdened land passes from the initial contracting party to new owners or possessors. [228]

B. Easements and profits: A servitude that gives a person the right to *use somebody else's land* in a specific and limited manner is either an *easement* or a *profit à prendre.* An easement is a pure use right. A profit à prendre gives the holder the right to take something valuable (e.g., timber) from another's land. [228-229]

C. **Covenants running with the land:** A servitude that consists of a promise that a landowner *will use her own land (or not use her own land)* in a specific way may be either a *real covenant* or an *equitable servitude.* These servitudes are called *real covenants* if damages are sought as the enforcement remedy, and *equitable servitudes* if an injunction is the method of enforcement. [229]

1. **Real covenants: Enforceable at law:** A real covenant is a servitude that meets the somewhat technical requirements to run with the estate in land that was initially burdened by the promise, or benefited by the promise, or both, and is sought to be enforced by recovery of *damages* for breach of the servitude. [229]

2. **Equitable servitudes: Enforceable in equity:** An equitable servitude is a promise the substance of which touches and concerns land usage, that was intended to bind future owners or possessors of the land, is asserted by the lawful possessor of property benefited by the promise, and is sought to be enforced by an *injunction* restraining a subsequent owner or possessor who acquired with notice of the servitude from violating it. [229]

II. EASEMENTS

A. **Introduction:** [229-234]

1. **Defined and distinguished from fee simple:** An easement is the right to *use* another person's land, not to possess it to the exclusion of the world. Almost all easements are *affirmative* — an interest in land that entitles its owner to use another's land. A *negative* easement, though rarely recognized, entitles its owner to restrain the use another makes of his land. Courts employ a rebuttable presumption that an ambiguous grant conveys an easement rather than a freehold. [229-230]

2. **Types of easements:** Easements may be *appurtenant* or *in gross* and also may be *affirmative* or *negative.* [230-232]

   a. **Appurtenant easements:** An easement appurtenant is one that benefits the owner of another parcel of land, rather than conferring a personal benefit. The benefited parcel is the *dominant estate,* and the burdened parcel is the *servient estate.* In cases of ambiguity, courts prefer to find easements to be appurtenant.

   b. **Easements in gross:** An easement in gross benefits its owner personally, and not as an owner of land. That personal right may be transferred if the parties so intended.

   c. **Affirmative easements:** Almost all easements are affirmative. An affirmative easement permits a person to use the servient estate in a specific manner. Affirmative easements can be appurtenant or in gross.

   d. **Negative easements:** A negative easement confers only the right to prevent specified uses of the servient estate. It confers no right to use the servient estate. Very few negative easements exist; the common law recognized only four appurtenant negative easements — for light, for air, for support, and for the continuing flow of an artificial stream. Today, by statute, most states permit the creation of negative easements in gross for purposes of conservation or preservation. Also, if a negative promise does not create a negative easement, it may create a real covenant or equitable servitude.

3. Profits à prendre: A profit à prendre, or profit, is the right to take a natural resource or crop from the land of another. Profits are always in gross and are freely transferable. [233]

4. Licenses: A license is simply permission to enter the licensor's land. Licenses are ubiquitous, may be oral or written, and are revocable at any time unless the licensor makes the license irrevocable, either expressly or by his conduct. The same promise may be seen as a license or an easement in gross; courts prefer to treat the ambiguous promise as a license. Licenses are assignable if the parties so intend, or if the license becomes irrevocable through equitable estoppel. [233-234]

    a. Irrevocable licenses: A license may become irrevocable by *intention,* by *equitable estoppel,* or when *"coupled with an interest."*

        i. Intention: A license is irrevocable if the licensor expressly makes the license irrevocable.

        ii. Equitable estoppel: If a license is granted, and the licensee reasonably relies on it to make substantial improvements to property, equity requires that the licensor be estopped from revoking the license until the reasonable expectations of the relying party have been realized, usually when the value of the improvements has been entirely exhausted. A few states do not recognize these "easements by estoppel," and some states require that some portion of the improvements made in reliance on the representation benefit the party against whom estoppel is sought.

        iii. License "coupled with an interest": When a license is tied together with some other independently legally recognized interest, the license is irrevocable until that other interest is vindicated.

B. Creation of easements: Easements may be created by *grant,* by *estoppel* (an irrevocable license), by *implication* (in two different ways), and by *prescription* (an easement version of adverse possession). [235-244]

    1. Easements by grant: An easement by grant must be in a writing signed by the grantor. [235]

        a. By reservation: A grant that "reserves" an easement from the grant is by reservation. By contrast, an "exception" in a grant excepts from the grant a pre-existing easement. American states today recognize the validity of easements *reserved in favor of the grantor,* but many do not recognize as valid easements *reserved in favor of a third party.* Although this rule makes little sense, only a minority of states have rejected it.

    2. Easements by estoppel: The license made irrevocable by equitable estoppel is the same as an easement by estoppel. Whatever the name, this easement expires when the expectations induced by the representation — typically, the detrimental reliance expenditures — have been fully realized. [235]

    3. Easements by implication: There are two circumstances in which easements are created by implication. [236-239]

        a. Easements implied from prior use: When the following elements are proved, an easement is impliedly created from prior use.

      i. Common owner: A common owner of land must use some part of it for the benefit of the remaining part, and then divide ownership of the "quasi-servient" estate and the "quasi-dominant" estate.

      ii. Reasonable necessity: The prior use must be reasonably necessary for the use and enjoyment of the "quasi-dominant" estate. Some states require that, if the "quasi-dominant" estate is retained by the common owner and creator, the prior use must be "strictly necessary" for the use and enjoyment of the "quasi-dominant" estate.

      iii. Continuous use: The prior use must be continuous.

      iv. Intended continuation: The parties must intend, at division, to continue the use.

      v. Existing use at division: At division, the use must be in existence.

      vi. Apparent use: At division, the use must be apparent, which does not necessarily mean that it is visible.

   b. Easements implied from necessity: An easement is implied from necessity only when an owner divides his property in such a way that one of the resulting parcels is left without access to a public roadway. An easement for right of way between the landlocked parcel and a public road, across the original owner's remaining land, is then implied. The necessity must be present at the time of severance and at the time the easement is asserted. If the necessity is later removed (e.g., by creation of a new public road), the easement implied by necessity terminates.

4. Easements by prescription: Prescription is analogous to adverse possession. Adverse *use* for a sufficient period of time can ripen into an easement by prescription. [239-244]

   a. Elements of prescriptive use: The adverse use must be *actual, open and notorious, continuous,* under an *adverse claim of right,* and *exclusive* for the limitations period applicable to adverse possession.

      i. Prescriptive period: The limitations period applicable to claims of prescriptive use is typically shorter than that applicable to adverse possession.

      ii. Adverse use under a claim of right: The use *must not be permissive.* The objective version of this element is that a neutral, objective observer would conclude that the use is not permissive. The subjective version requires the adverse user to prove that she harbored a good faith belief that she had a right to use the property without permission from the owner.

      iii. Open and notorious use: The use must be readily observable to a true owner.

      iv. Continuous use: The use must be as continuous as a lawful user would make of the putative easement.

      v. Exclusive use: Exclusive use does not typically mean that the adverse user was the *only* user; rather, it means that the adverse user's claim does not depend on somebody else's claim. The adverse user's claim is his own, not part of a public claim. However, some states imply *permission* to use the property if the use is not exclusive to the prescriptive user; this vitiates the hostility, or adverse use, element necessary to establish prescriptive use.

b. **Public prescriptive easements:** Many states permit the public to acquire a prescriptive easement. Other states achieve the same result through implied dedication, custom, or the public trust doctrine. Some states, however, reject all these doctrines.

   i. **Prescriptive easements in favor of the general public:** The general rule is that the public at large can obtain a prescriptive easement in private property so long as the elements of prescriptive use are established.

   ii. **No public prescriptive easements:** There are two reasons why states reject public prescriptive easements: (1) Because the public could not receive a grant of an easement there could not have been such a grant, now lost; hence, no prescriptive easement in the public was possible; or (2) Because an owner's cause of action to prevent wrongful use can only be asserted against specific defendants, the owner's cause of action to stop adverse use can never expire as against the entire public at large.

   iii. **Implied dedication:** This theory is simply a pseudonym for a public prescriptive easement. The idea is that the owner intends to dedicate his property to public use, but the evidence of such intent is entirely inferred.

   iv. **Custom:** To establish a customary right, the public must prove immemorial usage without interruption that is peaceable, reasonable, certain, and consistent with other customs.

   v. **Public trust doctrine:** To vindicate the public trust in ownership of the seashore below the high-tide mark, some states require a limited right of access to the dry sand, privately owned, seashore. Such use rights, when asserted far enough, pose issues of a regulatory taking of private property without compensation.

c. **Prescriptive easements not permitted:** There are two types of easements that may not be acquired by prescription.

   i. **Negative easements:** A negative easement may not be acquired by prescription, because there is no cause of action that is cut off by the statute of limitations.

   ii. **Easements upon public land:** As with adverse possession, it is not possible to obtain a prescriptive easement upon public land.

C. **Transfer of easements:** Transferability of easements depends on the type of easement. [244-245]

   1. **Easements appurtenant:** Easements appurtenant are as freely transferable as the estates to which they are attached. [244]

   2. **Easements in gross:** In general, *commercial easements in gross* are freely transferable, but *noncommercial easements in gross* are transferable only if the parties so intended. [244-245]

   3. **Profits:** Profits have always been freely transferable. [245]

D. **Scope of easements:** Two separate issues are raised by consideration of the scope of an easement: (1) How extensively and intensively may the easement holder use the easement, and (2) To what degree may the servient estate owner use or interfere with the easement? [245-250]

   1. **Parties' intentions control:** The parties' intentions control the scope of any easement, but intentions are not always easy to identify. Other factors, considered below, are thus used to help infer intentions. [245]

2. **How easement was created:** The manner in which an easement is created may indicate something about the parties' intentions. [245-246]

   a. **Easements by grant:** The scope of easements by grant is governed by the express language of the grant, to the extent that disposes of the matter.

   b. **Easements implied from prior use:** The scope of easements implied from prior use is whatever was within the reasonable contemplation of the parties at the time of division.

   c. **Easements implied by necessity:** The scope of an easement implied by necessity is identical to the necessity.

   d. **Easements by prescription:** The scope of prescriptive easements is generally confined to the particular use that produced the easement by prescription.

3. **Change in location of easement:** Easements with a specified location are permanently fixed, unless both parties agree to a change; but some modifications, within that location, may be made if they do not increase the burden on the servient estate. [247]

4. **Enlargement of the dominant estate:** An easement, however created, cannot be used for the benefit of land that is not part of the dominant estate. A landowner who attempts to do so will usually be enjoined, though when the equities favor it, courts may award damages and impose a judicially created servitude on the enlarged dominant estate to ensure that the use of the easement will not impose an unreasonable burden on the servient estate. [247-248]

5. **Division of an easement's benefit:** The benefit of an easement may not be divided if it will produce an unintended increase in the burden on the servient estate. [248-249]

   a. **Appurtenant easement: Division of the dominant estate:** The benefit of an appurtenant estate may be divided into smaller portions so long as the burden on the servient estate is not greater than what the parties initially intended.

   b. **Easements in gross and profits à prendre:** If a profit or easement in gross is shared with the servient estate, it may ***not be divided,*** but if the profit or easement in gross is exclusively held by ***one person,*** it ***may be divided.*** If it is exclusively held by ***several persons*** it ***may be divided,*** but it **must be used as a single unit.** This *"one-stock"* rule is intended to prevent the burden on the servient estate from being materially increased beyond the initial intent. Thus, some courts ignore the one-stock rule and look only at the increased burden.

6. **Use or interference by servient estate owner:** Unless the easement grants to the holder a right of *exclusive use,* the servient estate owner may also reasonably use the easement. In any case, a servient estate owner may not unreasonably interfere with the easement holder's use of the easement. [249-250]

E. **Termination of easements:** An easement may terminate in one of five different ways: (1) *expiration by its terms,* (2) by *merger* of the dominant and servient estates, (3) by *some act of the easement holder,* (4) upon *complete cessation of purpose,* and (5) by *some act of the servient estate owner.* [250-252]

1. **Expiration:** This is self-evident: When the easement says it expires, it does. [250]

2. **Merger:** When title to the dominant estate and servient estate is acquired by one person, the easement is extinguished. [250]

3. **Actions of the easement holder: Release, abandonment, and alteration of the dominant estate:** The easement holder may voluntarily *release* the easement. An easement will be extinguished if its owner manifests a *clear and unequivocal intention to abandon* the easement, but mere lack of use is not sufficient proof of abandonment. If the dominant estate owner so *alters the dominant estate* that the easement may no longer be used, it is extinguished. [250-251]

4. **Cessation of purpose:** Easements end when their purpose is completely extinguished. An easement implied from necessity terminates when the necessity ceases. An easement by estoppel (an irrevocable license) terminates when the benefits of the reliance expenditures have been fully reaped. Acts of third parties that wholly destroy the easement's purpose cause an easement to terminate. The accidental destruction of the servient estate destroys the easement, but this rule only applies to easements in structures and not the ground itself. [251-252]

5. **Actions of the servient estate holder:** If the servient estate owner uses the easement adversely to the easement holder for the prescription period, the easement is extinguished by prescription. In a few states, an easement burdening a structure (not the land) is extinguished if the structure is intentionally destroyed by its owner, because its continued existence is not economically feasible. [252]

III. REAL COVENANTS

A. **Introduction:** [253-254]

1. **Real covenants defined:** A *real covenant* is a contractual promise about land usage that runs with an estate in land so that it binds subsequent owners of that estate. The promise may be affirmative or negative. The promise that forms the substance of a real covenant will benefit some land and burden other land. Either or both the benefit and burden of the promise may run with an estate in land. The remedy available for breach of a real covenant is damages. If an injunction is sought, the identical promise is treated as an *equitable servitude,* and different rules apply to determine whether the benefit or burden of the promise runs to later holders. [253]

2. **Benefit and burden:** The elements necessary to enforce the *burden* of a real covenant against later owners of the burdened estate differ from the elements necessary for a later owner to assert the *benefit* of a real covenant. [253]

3. **"Runs with the Land":** Promises about land use pose ordinary contract issues when the litigants are the original contracting parties; when such promises are sought to be enforced by or against successors to the estates in land that were originally burdened or benefited by the promises, issues of property law emerge because the litigants are not in privity of contract with one another. [253]

4. **Remedy available: Damages:** When the remedy sought for breach is damages, the covenant must be shown to be a real covenant. If an injunction is sought, the covenant must be proven to be an equitable servitude. [253-254]

B. **Creation of real covenants:** A real covenant may only be created in writing and may not be created by implication or prescription. [255]

C. Enforceability by or against successors: [255-263]

   1. Burden running with the estate in land: For the *burden* of a real covenant to run with the estate, the following elements must be proven. [255-263]

      a. Intent: The original parties must have intended the burden to run.

      b. Horizontal privity: The older, but now increasingly disfavored view, is that **horizontal privity** — *privity of estate* between the *original parties* — is required for the burden to run. Horizontal privity of estate is generally satisfied whenever the two original parties either (1) have a *pre-existing mutual interest in each other's estates,* or (2) the real covenant is created in the instrument by which *one owner transfers title to the other owner.*

      c. Vertical privity: Virtually all courts require *privity of estate* between the original promisor and the successor to the burdened estate. Vertical privity of estate is generally satisfied when the successor acquires an estate of *at least the same duration as the original promisor.* The *Restatement (Second) of Property,* (Servitudes) eliminates vertical privity for negative covenants and substitutes new rules for affirmative covenants. Negative covenants apply to all subsequent possessors (both burden and benefit) under the Third *Restatement.*

      d. Touch and concern: The substance of the promise must *touch and concern* the burdened land and, in most cases, the benefited land as well. This means that the promise must affect the use and enjoyment of land, or must affect the advantages and burdens of land ownership. The underlying theory is to identify those promises that are so economically beneficial to land ownership that successor owners might well impose them voluntarily if given the chance to do so. The *Restatement (Second) of Property,* (Servitudes) eliminates touch and concern, focusing instead on the circumstances when covenants ought no longer be enforced.

      e. Notice: The successor to the burdened estate must have notice of the real covenant when she acquires the estate. Notice may be actual or constructive. Notice is most often constructive — the covenant is recorded in the chain of title to the estate.

   2. Benefit running with the estate in land: For the **benefit** of a real covenant to run with the estate, the following elements must be proven. [255-263]

      a. Intent: The original parties must have intended the benefit to run.

      b. Vertical privity: Virtually all courts require *privity of estate* between the original promisor and the successor to the benefited estate, but privity is satisfied so long as the successor acquires *some interest* in the originally benefited estate. Note that *horizontal privity is* **not required** *for the benefit to run.* The *Restatement (Second) of Property,* (Servitudes) eliminates vertical privity altogether for the benefit to run.

      c. Touch and concern: The substance of the promise must *touch and concern* the benefited land. The traditional rule is that "if the benefit is in gross, the burden will not run." This rule is breaking down, partly by statute (to facilitate conservation or historical-preservation covenants, the benefit of which is often held in gross) and partly by judicial decision, but is still the overwhelming majority rule. By contrast, if the burden is in gross, the benefit may still run.

IV. EQUITABLE SERVITUDES

A. **Introduction:** An equitable servitude is a promise about land use that will be enforced in equity (by an injunction) against a successor to the burdened estate who acquired it with notice of the promise. Equitable servitudes are more common than real covenants, because most people prefer to enjoin an offending use rather than simply receive damages for its existence. [263-264]

1. **Differences between real covenants and equitable servitudes:** There are three important differences: (1) the remedy for an equitable servitude is an injunction, not damages, (2) neither vertical nor horizontal privity is needed for either the burden or benefit of an equitable servitude to bind or benefit successors, and (3) an equitable servitude may be created by implication in some states, but a real covenant may never be created by implication. [263-264]

B. **Creation:** Generally, a writing is required to create an equitable servitude, since it is an interest in land, and the Statute of Frauds applies. Some states recognize an exception to this rule, permitting creation of *negative equitable servitudes* by implication from a common development scheme. Other states reject this doctrine and require that all equitable servitudes be created in writing. [264-266]

1. **By Implication from a common development scheme:** If a single landowner develops property by selling off lots subject to an identical servitude (e.g., residential use only) and on the explicit or implicit promise that all the lots in the development will be similarly burdened, some states create an equitable servitude by implication. Of course, if the developer follows through on his promise, there is no need to create an equitable servitude by implication. The equitable servitude thus created must be *reciprocal* (it must cover all lots in the common development) and *negative* (it must restrict use). The development must be of a common and uniform character. An implied equitable servitude only applies to lots conveyed after the beginning of the common scheme. [264-265]

2. **No implied covenants:** Some jurisdictions completely reject creation of equitable servitudes by implication. [265-266]

C. **Enforceability by or against successors:** In order for an equitable servitude to be enforceable by or against successors the original covenant must have been *intended to run to successors,* the successor must *acquire with notice* of the servitude, and the substance of the promise must *touch and concern* the affected property. [266-267]

1. **Intent:** This requirement is the same as for real covenants; the parties must expressly or impliedly intend for the covenant to run. [266]

2. **Privity not required:** Unlike real covenants, neither horizontal nor vertical privity of estate is required for either the burden or benefit of an equitable servitude to run. [266]

3. **Notice:** Notice may be *actual, constructive,* or *inquiry.* [266-267]

   a. **Actual notice:** Actual knowledge of the servitude is actual notice.

   b. **Record notice:** If the covenant is in the recorded chain of title of the property, constructive notice is satisfied. Some states include in the chain of title deeds from a common grantor to grantees other than a direct ancestor of title. This requires title searchers to determine whether any prior grantor conveyed other property under a deed by which he burdened his retained property with a servitude. Most states reject this rule and limit the chain of title (and constructive notice that stems from it) to the direct lineal succession of owners.

   c. **Inquiry notice:** A few courts have ruled that a purchaser has an obligation to inquire about the existence of servitudes if the neighborhood exhibits a common character and there is record evidence of a possible common development scheme.

4. **Touch and concern:** The meaning of *touch and concern* is the same for equitable servitudes and real covenants. The *Restatement (Third) of Property* (Servitudes) substitutes for the touch-and-concern requirement a general rule that all servitudes are initially valid except those that are illegal or unconstitutional, or violate public policy, and permits modification or termination of servitudes when their purpose may no longer be accomplished due to changed circumstances. [267]

D. Identifying the benefited land: Courts identify the benefited land by (1) looking to the parties' intentions and (2) determining whether the land purportedly benefited has actually received a benefit. [267-270]

1. **Land retained by the promisee:** If the party imposing the covenant owns nearby land, it is rebuttably presumed that such land was intended to be benefited. [267]

2. **Enforceability by third parties:** Land owned by a third party — neither a party to the covenant nor a successor to land benefited by the covenant — may sometimes assert the benefit of a covenant if the third party is an intended beneficiary of the covenant. Two fact patterns are common: (1) the intended beneficiary is a ***prior purchaser*** of a lot in a subdivision developed by a common grantor, or (2) the intended beneficiary is a complete ***stranger to the chain of title*** — the beneficiary did not acquire his property from the person who imposed the covenant. Intended beneficiaries are generally, but not always, able to enforce a covenant. [268-270]

   a. **Prior purchasers:** There are three theories by which a prior purchaser of a subdivision lot burdened by covenants may enforce a covenant.

      i. **Through the title chain to the person imposing the covenant:** Some states insist that the prior purchaser and intended beneficiary have acquired title from the person imposing the covenant.

      ii. **Unrestricted third-party beneficiary theory:** Some states permit any intended third-party beneficiary to enforce the benefit of a covenant.

      iii. **By implication from a common scheme:** Even states that do not permit the *creation* of servitudes from implication allow the use of a common scheme of development to *identify the property* **benefited** *by covenants that are* **expressly created.**

   b. **Complete strangers to the title chain descending from the person imposing the covenant:** Covenants are enforceable by the complete stranger only if the stranger to title is an *intended beneficiary,* and the jurisdiction permits *any intended beneficiary* to enforce covenants.

V. INTERPRETATION OF COVENANTS

Courts attempt to implement the parties' intentions, but in cases of ambiguity some judicially created presumptions may apply. Courts prefer to interpret covenants that may restrict either a use or a type of structure to refer to the structure rather than the use. Covenants restricting use to "residential use" create particular problems, because people use their residences for a variety of purposes. Commercial uses are sometimes (but not always) found to violate such covenants. Use as a "group home" (e.g., for the handicapped or juvenile delinquents) does not generally violate a "residential use only" covenant but might violate a "single-family use only" covenant. Racially restrictive covenants are unenforceable, because enforcement of them by courts violates the Constitution and because they are repugnant to public policy. Covenants requiring architectural approval of structures are generally upheld so long as the architectural reviewers act reasonably and in good faith. [270-272]

VI. TERMINATION OF REAL COVENANTS AND EQUITABLE SERVITUDES

A. **Merger:** If title to all of the burdened land and benefited land is united in a single owner, the covenant — whether real covenant or equitable servitude — is extinguished. [272]

B. **Eminent domain:** If the government takes the burdened land for a purpose inconsistent with the restrictive covenant, the covenant is extinguished. Most states require that the owner of the benefited land be compensated for loss of the benefit. [272]

C. **Express waiver or release:** If all holders of the benefit expressly waive or release the benefit of the covenant, it is extinguished. [273]

D. **Expiration of the covenant:** If a covenant has an express expiration date, of course, it expires by its terms. [273]

E. **Doctrines terminating equitable servitudes:** Equitable defenses may be asserted against enforcement of an equitable servitude, but not as against a real covenant. These defenses, when successfully asserted, effectively terminate an equitable servitude. [273]

1. **Changed conditions:** If conditions *within the area affected by the servitude* have so radically and thoroughly changed that the servitude cannot accomplish its purposes, it will be extinguished. If the change occurs in the *area adjacent to, but outside, the area affected by the servitude* the servitude is extinguished only if all of the benefited land has lost the benefit of the servitude. [273-274]

2. **Abandonment:** When a servitude is frequently and persistently violated without enforcement, it may be treated as having been abandoned by the benefit holders. One test of such abandonment is whether the *average person would reasonably conclude that the use restriction has been abandoned.* The competing test is whether the servitude's purpose has been so frustrated that *enforcement would seriously impair the value of burdened properties without producing any substantial benefit.* [274]

3. **Equitable estoppel:** If the party seeking to enforce an equitable servitude has knowingly lied to a defendant ignorant of the true facts, intending to induce, and actually inducing, reliance on the lie, he will be estopped from enforcing the servitude. [274]

4. **Laches:** Unreasonable delay in enforcing an equitable servitude, coupled with some resulting prejudice to the defendant, will bar enforcement. [274]

5. **Unclean hands:** A plaintiff guilty of the same violation of which he complains may not enforce an equitable servitude. [275]

6. **Balance of hardships:** As with all injunctions, a court is free to deny an injunction if the hardship thereby imposed on the enjoined party greatly outweighs the benefits of the injunction. [275]

F. **Affirmative covenants to pay money — Perpetual burden?** Affirmative covenants to pay money may be enforced either by foreclosure or suit to recover the unpaid dues. Equitable defenses may not be available in the latter case, and so the burden of these covenants may be difficult to avoid, particularly if the property is not salable or unwanted as a gift. [275]

VII. COMMON INTEREST COMMUNITIES

America is full of developments that are characterized by restrictive use covenants that purport to govern the behavior of the owners and occupiers in meticulous detail.

A. **Covenants recorded in the master deed:** The recorded covenants in the development's master deed, which burden all the units in the development, can be ridiculously minute. When challenged, some states hold that these restrictions are "clothed with a very strong presumption of validity" and invalidated only when they are arbitrary, violate public policy, or interfere with the exercise of fundamental constitutional right; other states think that such covenants should be generally enforceable unless they are *unreasonable.* [276]

B. **Covenants imposed by homeowners' associations:** Most states are less deferential to covenants imposed by homeowners' associations after the owners have acquired title. Such covenants are valid if *reasonable,* a loose standard that is met by rules that reasonably promote the health, happiness, and peace of mind of the entire community of burdened homeowners. [276-277]

C. **Cooperative apartments:** Because the shareholders and apartment lessees of a cooperative apartment corporation are very financially interdependent, courts are willing to defer to the "business judgment" of the directors of the corporation. [277]

CHAPTER 10

PUBLIC CONTROL OF LAND USE: ZONING

I. ZONING BASICS

A. **Introduction:** Zoning is the use of governmental power to regulate land use. Its purposes are usually to prevent incompatible uses (rather than relying upon nuisance to abate them), to increase property values by minimizing conflicting uses, and to channel development into patterns that are thought to serve larger social goals. [280]

B. **General constitutional validity:** In general, zoning is constitutionally valid. Specific applications may, however, offend a variety of constitutional limits on governmental power. [280]

C. **Statutory schemes:** Zoning of uses can be accomplished by either *cumulative* or *mutually exclusive* zoning. Zoning can also address the density of use. [280-281]

1. **Cumulative zoning:** Land uses are identified and arranged in a spectrum from "highest" to "lowest." Cumulative zoning permits all uses at the zoned level or higher. [280-281]

2. **Mutually exclusive zoning:** By contrast, mutually exclusive zoning permits only the uses designated by the particular zoning classification.

3. **Density zoning:** Zoning laws do not stop with use regulation. Most zoning laws also seek to control the density of occupation within any given use classification.

II. AUTHORIZATION FOR ZONING

A. **Enabling legislation:** Most states reserve to the state government the power to adopt zoning laws, but because almost all zoning is done at the local level, the state must first give municipalities power to zone, through an enabling law. In most states, local government power to zone is derived entirely from the enabling act and must be exercised in conformity with it. [281-282]

1. **Defective enabling act:** An enabling act might be defective if it grants state legislative power to a locality without tying the exercise of that power to some clear standard set forth in the enabling act. This amounts to an unconstitutional delegation of legislative authority.

2. *Ultra vires* **local action:** Local action beyond the authority granted by the enabling act is *ultra vires* and thus void. Frequently litigated issues include *aesthetics, exclusionary zoning,* and *growth controls.*

B. **Comprehensive plan:** Enabling acts require zoning to be done consistently with a "comprehensive plan" of development. The plan itself is not law but, in the absence of any implementing law, local action that violates a comprehensive plan is probably void. [282]

III. STATUTORY DISCRETION AND RESTRAINT

A. **Introduction:** To accommodate change, zoning laws (1) tolerate continuation of nonconforming land uses existing prior to adoption of the zoning law, (2) permit amendment of the law, and (3) confer discretion on public officials in applying the law. These mechanisms invite claims of lawlessness in their administration. [283]

B. **Nonconforming uses:** Even though zoning laws permit continuation of nonconforming uses, most zoning laws confine such uses or force their gradual elimination. [283-284]

1. **Forced phase-out:** A forced phase-out of a nonconforming use is valid if reasonable, and reasonableness depends on the length of the amortization period, the nature of the use, the character and location of the structure, and the effect on the user's business. Absent unusual factors, if the amortization period is long enough to be reasonable, a forced phase-out is valid, although some states hold that all forced phase-outs are void. [283]

2. **No expansion:** Zoning laws typically forbid any expansion of a nonconforming use beyond the precise boundaries of the existing use. [284]

3. **Destruction or abandonment:** Typically, if a nonconforming use is destroyed or abandoned, permission to continue the nonconforming use terminates. [284]

C. **Administrative discretion: Variances, exceptions, amendments, spot zoning and more:** [284-288]

   1. **Variances:** Almost all zoning laws invest a zoning appeals board with the power to permit uses or structures not otherwise in compliance with the law in order to alleviate practical difficulty or *undue hardship* on an owner resulting from problems not of the owner's creation. Undue hardship means, in practice, that the land cannot be used effectively without the variance. [284-285]

   2. **Exceptional uses:** Unlike variances, *exceptional uses* (also called *exceptions,* or *conditional uses,* or *special uses*) are uses that are permitted by the zoning law but might impose material external costs on neighbors, although the standard for the permitted exceptional use is usually something like "compatibility with existing uses," or "in furtherance of public health, safety, and general welfare." [285-286]

   3. **Zoning amendments and spot zoning:** The power to amend zoning acts may be abused by *spot zoning* — a zoning amendment that delivers special private benefits (and no public benefits) to a small, discrete parcel of land and are not in conformity with the comprehensive plan. The prevailing approach is to presume that zoning amendments are valid until the challenger has proven otherwise. Some state courts, however, apply more skeptical review when they perceive the amendment to be essentially adjudicative in character, or when there is no evidence that the amendment was adopted either to: (1) correct a mistake in the existing law, or (2) adapt to a substantial change in conditions affecting land use. [286-287]

   4. **Floating zones:** Some zoning laws provide for *floating zones,* a use designation not attached to any particular land until a landowner seeks to have his land designated as the recipient of the floating classification. [287]

   5. **Conditional zoning:** This involves rezoning in exchange for the grant of a servitude burdening the land that is intended to eliminate or dampen the negative externalities of the proposed use. Critics contend that conditional zoning is (1) spot zoning, (2) an invalid disposal of the police power, (3) *ultra vires,* or (4) a waiver of governmental power to restrict land use, but these objections are usually insufficient when there is a real public benefit in the bargain. [287-288]

   6. **Cluster zoning:** Cluster zoning zones a particular area for a particular use at a specified level of density of occupation, but confers upon zoning administrators the discretion to decide exactly how that use and density will be achieved. [288]

IV. LIMITS ON THE ZONING POWER

A. **Introduction:** Zoning is an exercise of a state's *police power* — the power to act to achieve the people's vision of public welfare, as communicated through their governmental agents — but that power is not unlimited. Exercise by a municipality of zoning power must conform to (1) the U.S. Constitution, (2) valid federal law pre-emptive of the local zoning law, (3) the relevant state constitution, and (4) state law, particularly the state's zoning enabling act and judicial doctrines developed to curb unreasonable and arbitrary exercises of the police power. [288-289]

B. Zoning for aesthetic objectives: The traditional rule was that zoning for aesthetic objectives was beyond the permissible scope of the police power, because beauty is subjective, and thus governments have no warrant to impose their notions of beauty. Today, however, a substantial number of courts have upheld aesthetic land use regulations banning uses that result in *lower property values.* [289-291]

   1. Architectural review: Architectural review typically involves conditioning a land-use permit on (1) the conformity of the proposed structure to the existing character of the neighborhood, and (2) the likelihood that the proposed structure will not cause substantial depreciation of neighboring property values. [289-290]

   2. Aesthetic regulation and free speech: When aesthetic zoning impinges on the constitutional guarantee of free expression, the zoning law may be void. [290-291]

   a. Zoning that is based on the content of speech: Current constitutional law holds that laws that regulate speech based on its *content* are *presumptively void,* valid only when the government proves that they are *necessary* to accomplish a *compelling government objective.* Thus, when zoning restricts users based on the *content* of their speech (e.g., bookstores specializing in political books), the government must justify its *content-based* zoning restriction.

   i. The "secondary effects" exception: If a zoning law discriminates on the basis of speech content but does so to regulate the *secondary effects of speech* — consequences that are **not** *produced by the communicative impact of speech* — the law is presumptively valid and will generally be upheld. Thus, if a zoning law seeks to cluster or disperse bookstores or theaters specializing in pornography in order to control crime that is empirically associated with, but not induced by, pornography (e.g., petty theft), its validity will be assessed under the secondary effects doctrine.

   b. Zoning that is neutral as to the content of speech: Laws that regulate speech in a *content-neutral* fashion are valid if they reasonably serve important government interests and leave open ample alternative channels of communication. Thus, zoning that restricts all bookstores to areas that are zoned commercial is presumptively valid.

C. Zoning and religious exercise: Zoning laws can interfere with the constitutionally protected right of free exercise of religion and with the federal Religious Land Use and Institutionalized Persons Act (RLUIPA). [291-292]

   1. Zoning and the free exercise of religion: Although generally applicable laws that impede religious conduct without the intent to do so are presumptively valid, laws that prohibit acts only when engaged in for religious reasons, or because of the religious belief that they display, are invalid attempts to suppress the free exercise of religion. Thus, a zoning ordinance that prohibits the ritual use of alcoholic beverages in any structure is void. [291-292]

   2. Zoning and the RLUIPA: Under the federal RLUIPA, any individualized application of a land use regulation that constitutes a substantial burden on religious exercise is void unless it can be justified by a compelling governmental interest. [292]

D. Zoning and environmental protection: Changes to zoning laws must conform to applicable state environmental impact–assessment statutes, which usually require an accurate assessment of the impact of the change and a determination that the changes will not pose an unduly negative impact on the physical (or sometimes, the cultural and social) environment. [292-293]

E. **Zoning controls of household composition:** Zoning laws can interfere with important civil liberties concerning living arrangements, liberties protected by the federal and various state constitutions or by federal and state law that is paramount to a local zoning ordinance. [293-294]

   1. **The fundamental liberty of family association:** Zoning laws that substantially interfere with the constitutionally fundamental liberty of people to marry and associate together in traditional family relationships are presumptively void. The government must prove they are necessary to the attainment of a compelling interest in order to overcome the presumption of invalidity. [293-294]

      a. **Unrelated persons: When does "family" begin?** Under the federal Constitution, zoning laws that substantially interfere with the ability of *unrelated persons* (persons not related by blood, marriage, or adoption) to live together are presumed valid and subject only to minimal scrutiny. Some state constitutions provide broader protection of the liberty of unrelated people to live together.

   2. **Statutory limits on zoning controls of household composition:** Federal and state laws prohibit housing discrimination against a variety of people, including those with handicaps. When zoning laws conflict with these statutes, the zoning law is void to the extent of the inconsistency. [294]

F. **Exclusionary zoning:** All zoning is exclusionary in that it seeks to exclude unwanted *uses,* but sometimes zoning is used to exclude unwanted *people,* though perhaps not for constitutionally or statutorily forbidden reasons. The typical case involves zoning for low residential density, with the effect of making it economically impossible for the poor or near-poor to live in the community. Some states have imposed on all communities in the state an affirmative obligation to alter zoning laws to make housing more affordable for all income groups. [294-296]

   1. **Growth controls:** Growth controls, which are either temporary stoppages or permanent limitations on the rate of new entrants, are generally upheld as within the authority conferred by the enabling act and as constitutionally valid exercises of that power, being rationally related to the legitimate state interest of orderly growth. [295-296]

CHAPTER 11

TAKINGS: THE POWER OF EMINENT DOMAIN AND REGULATORY TAKINGS

I. INTRODUCTION

A. **The eminent domain power:** All governments have the power to take private property for public use. The Constitution's "takings" clause requires that "just compensation" be paid for any such taking by any government. All types of property are protected. The takings clause was intended to prevent forcible redistributions (by requiring payment of compensation) and to limit takings to those for some public benefit. The principal issues that arise under the takings clause are (1) whether a taking has occurred, (2) whether a taking is for public use, and (3) whether just compensation has been paid. [298]

B. **Just compensation:** The property owner is entitled to the *fair market value* of the property taken. When only a portion is taken, the owner is entitled to *severance damages* — the difference between the value of the entire parcel before the taking and the value of the parcel the owner is left with after the taking. Fair market value is computed without regard to other collateral effects on the value of the property or on businesses conducted on the property. [298-299]

II. THE PUBLIC-USE REQUIREMENT

The takings clause is interpreted to mean that no taking can occur except for a public use, but the public-use requirement is easily met. So long as a taking is ***rationally related to any conceivable public purpose,*** the public-use requirement is satisfied. This includes takings of private property for transfer to other private owners for redevelopment. [299-302]

III. REGULATORY TAKINGS: HOW MUCH REGULATION OF PROPERTY IS TOO MUCH?

A. Introduction: At some point, government regulation of property becomes so extensive or burdensome that a *de facto* taking occurs, even though the government may deny that a taking has occurred. Regulatory takings are the Court's methodology for locating the point at which regulation ceases to be mere regulation and becomes a taking, requiring just compensation. [302]

B. The *per se* rules: The Court uses three principal categorical rules to help sort out which regulations are or are not takings. One of them identifies a form of regulation that, *per se,* **does *not* constitute a taking.** The other two categorical rules identify when a taking **has occurred.** [302-305]

1. **Permanent dispossession:** When a government regulation ***permanently dispossesses*** an owner of her property, the regulation is a taking. By contrast, a physical *invasion* of property by the government that is *not permanent* and does *not permanently deprive the landowner of the right to exclude others,* is not a *per se* taking, but must be assessed under the balancing process that applies to claims of regulatory takings that cannot be disposed of under the categorical rules. [302-303]

2. **Nuisance abatement:** If a government regulates property to ***abate activities that are common law nuisances,*** there is ***no taking,*** even though the regulations might bar all economically viable uses of the property, because ownership of the property never included the right to inflict nuisances. Nothing has been taken by forbidding what was never lawful. [303-304]

3. **Loss of all economically viable use:** If a government regulation leaves the owner with ***no economically viable use*** of his property, and the regulation does **not *abate a common law nuisance,*** a taking has occurred. This rule poses a problem of identifying the property that is stripped of *all* economically viable use. Application of the rule is easy when the regulation strips the owner of all economically viable use of the *entire* property, but when a regulation operates to deprive the owner of all economically viable use of only *part* of his property, it is likely that the question of whether or not the regulation is a taking will be decided by the balancing tests. This is certainly true when the regulation applies for a limited time. [304-305]

C. Balancing public benefits and private costs: When the per se rules do not resolve the issue of whether a regulation is a taking, courts weigh the public benefits achieved by the regulation against the private costs imposed. A regulation is not a taking if it ***substantially advances a***

legitimate state objective. To determine whether this test has been met, at least the following conditions must exist: (1) ***public benefits from the regulation must outweigh the private costs of the regulation,*** (2) the regulation ***must not be arbitrary,*** and (3) the property owner must be permitted to ***earn a* reasonable return *on investment*** in the property. [305-308]

1. **Contemporary statement: Penn Central:** In the leading modern case, the Court said the balancing test was an *ad hoc* inquiry involving the following factors: (1) the nature of the government regulation, (2) the reasonable "investment-backed" expectations of the property owner, (3) the degree to which the regulation is designed to stop uses that cause "substantial individualized harm" but are not common law nuisances, and (4) the degree to which the regulation enables the government actually to use the property for "uniquely public functions." [306-308]

D. **Exactions: Conditional burdens:** Governments often regulate land use by requiring landowners to obtain a permit for the use (e.g., a building permit). Such regulations become problematic only when the government imposes as a condition to the obtaining of the permit some condition that could not independently be imposed without compensating the landowner. May the state condition the grant of a use permit on the landowner's consent to what would otherwise be an uncompensated taking? There are two dimensions to this problem. [308-310]

1. **"Essential nexus":** Conditions to issuance of use permits must have an ***essential nexus*** to the valid regulatory objective embodied in the permit regulation itself. *A condition that would be a taking, if imposed in isolation, is* ***not a taking*** *when attached as a condition of issuance of a land use permit under an otherwise valid regulation* ***only*** *if the government can prove* that the condition is ***substantially related*** to the ***government's valid regulatory objective.*** [308-309]

2. **"Rough proportionality":** A government may not impose a condition to a land-use permit that is disproportionate to the impact of the proposed use on the activity that the government validly sought to regulate in the first place. Even if a condition that would be a taking if imposed in isolation is valid because it satisfies the ***essential nexus*** test, it *is a taking unless the government proves that the nature and scope of the condition* are ***roughly proportional*** to the impact of the proposed development on matters that the underlying regulation addresses. [309-310]

3. **Summary:** The ***essential nexus*** and ***rough proportionality*** tests are cumulative, not alternatives. If a condition is a taking by itself, the condition *cum* regulation is a taking unless the government can prove (1) the condition is ***substantially related*** to the ***government's valid regulatory objective,*** and (2) the nature and scope of the condition are ***roughly proportional*** to the impact of the proposed development. The logical order of analysis is, first, to establish that the condition would be a taking if imposed independently; second, to prove that such a condition satisfies the essential nexus test and; third, to show that such a condition exacts concessions that are roughly proportional to the development's impact. [310]

E. **Remedies:** Once a regulation is found to be a taking, the affected property owner has several remedies. [310-311]

1. **Injunctive and declaratory relief:** Enforcement of a regulation that is a taking will be enjoined, and the regulation will be declared to be a taking. If the government wishes to proceed with the regulation, it must pay just compensation. [310]

2. **Damages:** Regulations may take effect before they are adjudged to be takings. When this happens, the affected property owner is entitled to damages for the loss of his property during the period when a regulatory taking was in effect. [311]

F. **Academic theories about regulatory takings:** There is a vast academic literature on takings. Sax argues that compensation should be unnecessary when governments regulate as sovereigns but should be required when governments use regulations to achieve ordinary commercial advantages. Sax also thinks that no compensation should be required when a government acts to control external costs of land use. Michelman employs a dense utilitarian calculus to determine when compensation is due. Ackerman employs colloquial, lay understandings of property to conclude that compensation is required when it would be a "bad joke" to claim that the property owner is left with something of value after imposition of the regulation. Epstein argues that regulations that redistribute wealth without conferring some "implicit in-kind" compensation are presumptively takings. Rubinfeld contends that a taking occurs when a regulation enables the government actually to *use* the property in question. Fischel thinks that the legislative process is adequate to protect against overreaching government regulation, except when that process is distorted, and would use heightened judicial review to control the products of distorted legislative processes. [311-313]

CHAPTER 1

CONCEPTUAL BASICS, POSSESSION, AND PERSONAL PROPERTY

ChapterScope ━━━━━━━━━━━━━━━━━━━━━━━━━━━━━━━━━━━

This chapter introduces the concept of property, how it is initially acquired, and the importance of possession to the concept of property, both with respect to real and personal property. Here are the most important points in this chapter.

- Property is socially contingent; its meaning depends on the culture that defines it.

- Property involves the rights and obligations of people in relation to objects, not the study of the objects themselves.

- Property has been justified as an embodiment of one's labor, on utilitarian or efficiency grounds, by custom, or by reference to natural law.

- Possession of an object gives rise to a presumption of ownership. Possession may be actual or constructive (a legal fiction that describes a conclusion).

- Unowned things become property by first possession: discovery, capture, or creation.

- Possession is relative to other people. First possession generally confers property rights superior to later possessors, unless some other supervening public policy dictates the contrary. The law governing claims of possession of found objects — which may be abandoned, lost, or mislaid — is an attempt to mediate between these sometimes conflicting policies.

- Even *wrongful possession* may sometimes ripen into lawful possession, if the circumstances of the possession are indicative of ownership, and the possession endures long enough. This is the law of adverse possession.

- Special rules apply to personal property because it is so easily transferable. Transfers of possession may mean different things in different contexts: A transfer may constitute a bailment, a gift, or a conveyance, depending on intent and circumstance.

━━

I. WHAT IS PROPERTY?

A. Introduction: Property is not absolute. Property is *socially contingent* — its definition will vary from culture to culture and, within cultures, over time. One obvious example is the immoral practice of human slavery. To paraphrase Felix Cohen, if property is what the state does to enforce the private citizen's declaration to the world to keep off without consent, property depends on who the "world" is, or who counts as a "private citizen," or even the identity of the state. "[P]roperty merges by imperceptible degrees into government, contract, force, and value." Cohen, 9 Rut. L. Rev. 357, 374 (1954). Property is whatever interest in a thing — whether tangible or intangible — that is protected against invasion by others by the legal system of the society. That means that the study of property is *not* the study of the relationship of a person to a thing called property, but is the study of the relationship between people with respect to things we call property.

B. Theory: There are as many theories about property as there are theoreticians. Here are a few of the more important ones.

1. Locke's labor theory: John Locke, the seventeenth-century political philosopher, started from the natural law premise that every person owns himself. (But what does that mean? In our society, you can't sell yourself into slavery.) Nevertheless, Locke claimed that because you own your own labor, when you mix that labor with something *unowned by anyone,* you own the resulting mixture. See John Locke, *Two Treatises on Government,* Book II, Ch. V (1690).

Example: Rob Crusoe arrives on a previously unknown island, unclaimed by any political jurisdiction, and proceeds to excavate a colorful rock partially buried in the beach sand. The rock turns out to be a valuable meteorite. Under Locke's labor theory, Crusoe's labor in finding and excavating the meteorite gives him a property right in the meteorite.

2. Other natural law theories: Some theoreticians explain property as a pre-political entitlement, something "natural" and eternally existing. The problem with this view is that conceptions of "natural" property rights vary greatly. Its strength lies in the fact that it is a near universal human trait to link possession of an object with ownership. But this linkage can also be explained by less mystic utilitarian theories.

3. Utilitarian theories: David Hume, the eighteenth-century Scottish philosopher, contended that property was nothing more than self-interested acquiescence in social and legal rules. We accept legal protection for other's property because we desire the same protection for our own. In a world without scarcity, there would be no need for property; you could always get more of whatever was lost or taken from you. But in our real world of scarcity it is important to protect what we possess. Jeremy Bentham popularized Hume's utilitarian explanation, rooting property in the protection of expectations. Note that both Hume's and Bentham's theories rest on the unarticulated premise that the initial possession (which is what is being protected) is legitimate. Locke explained why that was so; Hume and Bentham did not.

4. Utility and efficiency: Economists explain property as an efficient response to scarcity. Efficiency is utilitarian; why waste things? The economic explanation is that *externalities* — costs that are produced by an activity but not borne by the person reaping the benefits of the activity — are *internalized* — borne by their maker. This makes the production of goods needed for human life more efficient. Similarly, few people would undertake costly, time-consuming activities (e.g., growing crops) unless they could be assured that they would keep the benefits of their actions. Recognition of a property right in the crop internalizes the benefits.

Example: Suppose the Centurions, a society of 100 people, subsist by fishing for enormous trout in a lake open to all Centurions. Centurions recognize a captured fish as property but not the free-swimming fish in the lake. The Centurions don't know it, but there are about 1,000 fish in the lake. (Each Centurion thus has a theoretical 1/100 interest in the free-swimming fish, or 10 fish.) If Sam, a Centurion, catches one fish, he has acquired a property right to one fish and continues to have the inchoate, theoretical interest of a 1/100 share in 999 fish. Sam's loss of a theoretical common interest (from 10.0 to 9.99) is more than offset by his acquisition of property in one whole fish, which he can eat. Most of the cost of losing one fish from the lake is borne by others, not Sam. The cost is external to Sam. So long as the subsistence needs of the Centurions and the reproduction rate of the fish remain in balance, there is no need to create a property right to the free-swimming fish, despite the external costs associated with fishing.

But now imagine that Lewis Clark, an explorer and trader, arrives. He offers $5 per fish, a fabulous sum eagerly desired by the Centurions. Each Centurion now has the incentive to catch as many fish as possible, for the costs of the loss will be borne mostly by other Centurions. If Centurions are skillful fishermen, the trout will soon be extinct. This does not do the Centurions any good. In the pursuit of self-interest, the common interest of everyone is destroyed because nobody is bearing that cost. To see why, imagine that the real value of each fish is $20. Although a Centurion loses 20 cents every time he catches a fish (1/100 of $20), he earns $5, for a net increase to his wealth of $4.80. But Centurion society as a whole is poorer by $15 (loss of $20 true value less $5 received).

Even if Centurions see the problem, nobody will quit fishing because there is no assurance that others will cease as well. Centurions probably can't simply agree to stop, because it is probably too difficult to obtain unanimity. Unanimity takes time, and some people will hold out in the hopes of freeloading from others' forbearance from fishing.

Now suppose the Centurions divide the fish into 100 units of ownership of 10 fish each. A Centurion who captures and sells one of his own fish will reap the benefit of Clark's $5 but will also suffer the full loss of the $20 true value of the fish. More importantly, by not fishing, the individual Centurion keeps the full value of the fish, rather than seeing it disappear into his competitor's nets.

5. **Custom:** Some observers point out that property rights often occur by custom, and they note that the customs are intended to maximize aggregate wealth of the customary participants. Whalers, for example, had many customs designed to deal with the uncertain business of capturing giant sea mammals and maximizing the possibility of profit in the enterprise. See generally Robert Ellickson, *Order Without Law: How Neighbors Settle Disputes* (1991). Customs that limit exploitation of common property can also develop, particularly when the common property is so-called **limited access property** — open only to a relatively small number of people, often bounded by kinship, geography, or shared values or occupations. See generally Elinor Ostrom, *Governing the Commons: The Evolution of Institutions for Collective Action* (1990). In 2009, Ostrom received the Nobel Prize in Economics for this work.

C. **Doctrine:** The simplest doctrinal answer to the question of what is property is to say that property is whatever the legal system protects as property. Simple, but useless. Courts tend to break property down into three core elements: the right to exclusive *possession,* the right to exclusive *use,* and the right to *dispose* or *transfer.* But there is no formula by which you can assemble these elements into property. Two atoms of hydrogen and one of oxygen make water, but it is not at all clear that a use right coupled with a disposition right make property. Nevertheless, these are the doctrinal elements of property, and these concepts will pop in and out of your study of property, like the Banks children and their chalked pictures in *Mary Poppins.*

II. POSSESSION

A. **Introduction:** Whatever the best theoretical explanation of property, everybody presumes that possession of an object implies a property right in it. Possession may be "nine points of the law," as the old saying has it, but it isn't all of it. Some people (e.g., thieves) are wrongful possessors. Others (e.g., finders) have property claims that are only *relative* to the claims of others. Sorting these issues out is the objective of this section.

B. Two meanings of possession: The term *possession* means two different things. It describes a *physical act* — by falling down dead drunk at the dinner party, you take *possession* of the floor under you. It also describes a *legal conclusion* — the host of the dinner party is in *possession* of his home when he tosses you out, for purposes of a law that immunizes self-help by "possessors" of property in ousting unwanted visitors. But sometimes physical possession is the fact that produces the legal conclusion of possession that flows from ownership of property. People, including judges, are careless in their usage of this term. Be precise; it clarifies your arguments.

C. Of "unowned" things: Discovery, capture, and creation:

1. Discovery: Not much is undiscovered today, but the idea that property could be acquired by discovery has some modern implications.

★**Example:** In *Johnson v. M'Intosh,* 21 U.S. 543 (1823), the U.S. Supreme Court confronted rival claims for ownership of land in Illinois. Johnson's claim was the last link in a *chain of title* going back to the Piankeshaw, the aboriginal inhabitants of the land. M'Intosh said his title was better because it came from the United States, although *after* the Piankeshaw conveyance to Johnson's predecessor. The Court held for M'Intosh because the Piankeshaw, as Indians, only held *aboriginal title,* a right of occupancy that could be cut off at any moment by the United States, as the successor to the European discoverers of the land. This Eurocentric approach to discovery was supplemented by the idea that the U.S. also derived its ownership by *conquest* of the Piankeshaw. There may not be much land left to discover, but there is still the same amount around to conquer. The fact of conquest as a source of property rights is a reminder of the socially contingent nature of property: Property rights are defined by the society in which they are at issue. Because the Piankeshaw, and those who derived title from the Piankeshaw, were perceived as a conquered society, their rights were declared to be subservient to those of the dominant society. Lest you think only Europeans are capable of this thinking, consider the restructuring of property rights in the wake of Ogotai Khan's invasion of Europe in the thirteenth century, or the practices of indigenous Americans with respect to the persons and possessions of conquered alien tribes.

2. Capture: Wild animals may be one of the few things that are unowned and susceptible to capture.

a. Actual possession: The usual method of acquiring a property right in a wild animal is actually to possess it — dead or alive.

★**Example:** *Pierson v. Post,* 3 Cai. R. 175 (N.Y. 1805), involved rival claims to ownership of a dead fox. For sport, Post chased a fox on common, unowned land — a wild beach. Before Post had wounded or captured the fox, Pierson intervened, killing and taking the fox, although he knew of Post's pursuit. The N.Y. court declared Post did not own the fox until he had physical possession of it. Mere pursuit was not enough. Perhaps pursuit was the labor, but until pursuit produced capture, it wasn't mixed enough with the fox to create property. The result was defended on the ground that a rule of actual possession would promote certainty and peace and would spur people to kill foxes (a public benefit in a society that regarded foxes as vermin rather than as an endangered species). Justice Livingston dissented on two grounds: (1) It was better to adopt the customs of sportsmen to determine ownership of the fox, and (2) Recognition of a property right in wild animals when there is a reasonable likelihood of capture would conduce to more rapid extermination of foxes. Note that behind the doctrinal debate — should ownership depend on actual possession, mortal wounding (making possession a near certainty), or hot pursuit with reasonable likelihood of capture — lies a debate over how law can best effectuate a desired public policy. In 1805, it was a good thing to encourage the killing of foxes, so the doctrinal debate focuses (whether overtly or not) on how best to encourage their destruction.

b. Custom: When should customary rules pertaining to acquisition of ownership establish the legal doctrine? Customary rules often arise to maximize the well-being of the group creating the custom, to ensure that individuals do not grab benefits for themselves that impose net losses on the group as a whole. Individuals conform to customary rules out of self-interest: In the long run, they will be better off, and in the short run, deviation from the customs will result in substantial informal sanctions from the group.

★**Example:** In the Massachusetts Bay whaling community of the nineteenth century, the whalers used "bomb lances" to kill fin-back whales. Each lance was distinctively marked to denote a particular whaler. The whale carcasses sank at death, but as gaseous putrefaction set in, they floated again several days later. When their bodies washed ashore along the perimeter of Massachusetts Bay, word would be sent to Provincetown of the location and the description of the identifying lance. The whaler would then come, remove the animal's oil and blubber, and pay a small salvage fee to the finder. ***Ghen v. Rich,*** 8 F. 159 (D. Mass. 1881), involved a suit by a whaler, Ghen, against Rich, the successor in interest of a finder of a fin-back whale carcass bearing the whaler's distinctive lance. The finder, Ellis, had defied custom by selling the carcass to Rich, who appropriated the whale's oil and blubber. The court held that custom determined ownership because the nature of the fin-back whale industry was that the animals could only be killed without acquiring immediate possession, and that a first-physical-possession rule of ownership would eliminate all incentive to hunt fin-back whales, thus depriving the society of the benefits of a continued supply of whale oil and blubber. Note that while a court could declare that Ghen had "possession" by virtue of killing the whale and leaving it with his distinctive lance imbedded in it, such a statement of doctrine leaves unstated the policy that drives its creation.

c. The importance of policy ends to the nature of property rights: It is a mistake to think that property rights are entirely derived from an intricate set of logical and related rules called legal doctrine. In one sense, that is true, but doctrine is messy because it is driven by instrumental ends that courts seek to serve. Law should serve the human values that are important to the people of the society. As courts try to do this, they tinker with doctrine to serve those policy ends. Generally, property doctrine tries to serve four important values: (1) reward productivity and foster efficiency, (2) create simple, easily enforceable rules, (3) create property rules that are consistent with societal habits and customs, and (4) produce fairness in terms of prevailing cultural expectations of fairness. Sometimes these principles all point to a single resolution; sometimes they point in different directions.

★**Example:** ***Keeble v. Hickeringill,*** 103 Eng. Rep. 1127 (Q.B. 1707). In early eighteenth-century England, landowners created elaborate decoy ponds that were designed to trap large quantities of ducks and other waterfowl to be killed and consumed as food. Keeble maintained such a pond. Hickeringill, his neighbor, frightened the ducks away from Keeble's pond by discharging a shotgun nearby. The English courts ruled that such conduct was actionable, on the theory that Hickeringill was maliciously interfering with Keeble's lawful activity. The court distinguished this case from fair competition, noting that it would be perfectly proper for a schoolmaster to lure students away from another school by offering better instruction but unlawful to frighten them away. The distinction is bottomed on the notion that fair competition improves society (e.g., better schools), while Hickeringill's conduct was a dead-weight drag on societal improvement (e.g., fewer ducks for the table). In a society in which killing wild ducks for food is regarded as inappropriate (e.g., to preserve biodiversity), Hickeringill's conduct might be lawful. It depends on the public policies that law is supposed to serve.

d. **Relative title:** Actual possession isn't everything. One person's claimed property right is almost always good (or not good) only in ***relation*** to others. In *Pierson,* the fox was on unowned land. What if the hunt had occurred on Post's land and Pierson had been a trespasser? Pierson's actual possession of the fox would have given him a property right in it, but only until or unless that right were trumped by Post, invoking his right to exclude others from his real estate. Note that this is a conflict between two different property rules: ***first possession*** and the landowner's ***right to exclude*** others. Post, the landowner, would have a better claim to the fox, not because he was a ***prior possessor*** of the fox, but because he was entitled to deprive trespassers of their game taken from his estate. Similarly, it would have been Pierson's fox if Post had bagged it on Pierson's farm. This assumes that society thinks it's more important to discourage trespass than to reward first possession of unowned objects when the two values collide. The law rarely encourages trespassing, because security of exclusive possession is conducive to peace and order and investment of an owner's resources in that property. Suppose that Post had clobbered the fox, picked up its limp carcass, and slung it across his saddle. If Pierson had yanked it off as he cantered by, Post would have gotten it back, because he would have been a ***prior possessor*** of the single object in dispute. It is ***first*** possession that counts. To see this, suppose Post had trespassed on Morton's land and taken the fox, and that Pierson had come upon Post's land and taken it. As between Post and Pierson, who would have title? Post would win, because even among wrongdoers, the prior possessor prevails. See *Anderson v. Gouldberg,* 51 Minn. 294 (1892).

e. **Escapees and domesticated animals:** When the wild animal escapes, it is unowned. It belongs to the next ***first possessor.*** Domesticated animals aren't wild, so they continue to belong to their prior possessor when they wander off. A wild animal becomes domesticated when, as a matter of fact, it demonstrates a propensity to return "home" (***animus revertendi***). These appear to be simple rules, easily enforced, that comport with cultural expectations. Consider, however, the case of a silver fox, native to Canada but not to Mississippi (where it was confined by its owner-possessor), which escaped and was killed by a hunter. Doctrine says the hunter wins. See *Stephens & Co. v. Albers,* 256 P. 15 (Colo. 1927), so ruling, but should a hunter have a reasonable expectation of acquiring ownership of a wild animal not native to the region? What if the animal were a tiger escaped from a traveling circus? Should fairness, in the form of reasonable expectations, trump other considerations? These are the stuff of policy debates in your Property course. The best approach is to recognize the issues (the policy tensions), assemble arguments to support either outcome, then conclude which set of arguments are most persuasive in light of the culture in which we actually live.

f. Oil and gas: More policy considerations: Because fugitive minerals such as oil and gas appear to be similar to wild animals, courts initially applied legal doctrine pertaining to wild animals. The underlying issue in those cases, however, is really how best to foster productivity by the efficient exploitation of oil and gas. *Barnard v. Monongahela Natural Gas Co.,* 216 Pa. 362 (1907), held that an underground reservoir of oil was open to all drillers, while *Union Gas & Oil v. Fyffe,* 219 Ky. 640 (1927), suggested that overexploitation of the unowned resource might be susceptible to an injunction. The latter view recognizes the "tragedy of the commons," the tendency to over-exploit a common resource because the full costs of the exploitation are not borne by each user, while the former is an uncritical application of the first possession doctrine to circumstances where sound public policy might warrant a different approach. Similarly, the rule in *Hammonds v. Central Kentucky Natural Gas Co.,* 255 Ky. 685 (1934), that natural gas injected into natural underground reservoirs is no longer owned by the injector, is a mechanical application of doctrine with little thought to its policy consequences. The efficiencies of storage of gas in natural underground reservoirs will be inhibited by such a rule, because the injected gas will then be open for capture by anyone who cares to drill into the reservoir. When importing apparently sound legal doctrine from one area to an analogous arena, always pay attention to the public policy considerations that may affect the appropriate notions of property in the new setting. Proper policy conclusions, and the doctrine that derives from them, vary with the circumstances, much as the chameleon changes color with the background.

3. **Creation:** Many intangible property rights are created. A novel is the creation of an inventive and communicative mind. Its property right is the ***copyright*** of the creator — the right to control the reproduction and distribution of the creation. Some creations are also discoveries (e.g., Edison and the incandescent lamp), and the law protects them by ***patent*** and the law of ***trade secrets.*** Courses in ***intellectual property*** deal with these subjects in considerable detail.

   a. **Exclusivity: The problem of imitation:** A key issue is the degree of ***exclusivity*** the property owner has in exploiting the intangible right. Some argue that because information can be used by many people at once (unlike an ear of corn, where the value is in personal consumption to the exclusion of others) the owner ought not to be able to insist on exclusive use. Free availability of information (whether novels or computer software) may make "the public as a whole . . . better off, as long as this freedom to imitate does not destroy the incentive for people to come up with new ideas." Baird, 50 U. Chi. L. Rev. 411, 414 (1983). The law of ***misappropriation*** — the branch of unfair competition law that protects new ideas — tries to answer the question of when imitation is permissible and when it is not because it will destroy the incentive to create.

   ★**Example:** In *International News Service v. Associated Press,* 248 U.S. 215 (1918), the U.S. Supreme Court held it was misappropriation for INS to copy AP's news and release it before AP could. AP expended money and effort to gather the news; the Court thought that INS was attempting to "reap where it has not sown." But later courts have held that skilled imitation of Chanel No. 5 perfume and seasonal fabric designs is not misappropriation. See ***Cheney Brothers v. Doris Silk Corp.,*** 35 F.2d 279 (2d Cir. 1930); *Smith v. Chanel, Inc.,* 402 F.2d 562 (9th Cir. 1968). The conflict is between the inefficiencies produced by a monopoly over creation (higher prices, less accessibility to a desired good) and both the sense of unfairness of allowing copycats to reap what they haven't sown and the fear that, without protection, creators will not create.

b. Personal image as property: Less than a century ago, you would have drawn blank looks if you had spoken about a property right in your personal image, because the idea of a "personal image" was a bit incomprehensible. People in Theodore Roosevelt's era would have understood the concept of personal reputation but would not have considered it capable of assignment during life or transfer at death. Times change. Today, the ability to exploit your image for profit is recognized as a valuable property right because we have created a culture of celebrity in which money can be made from selling image. Witness the ubiquity of clothing emblazoned with the logo of the designer, or the monetary value inherent in a celebrity image such as Madonna, or the congeries of household items associated with Martha Stewart. Note again that, as culture changes, law evolves to protect newly created cultural expectations.

★**Example:** In *White v. Samsung Electronics America*, 989 F.2d 1512 (9th Cir. 1993), the court concluded that Samsung's depiction of a robot clad in blond wig, dress, and jewels posing in front of the Wheel of Fortune infringed Vanna White's common law right of publicity. Judge Kozinski criticized this ruling as "a classic case of overprotection" because it extended the publicity right to preclude even images that might remind the viewer of a celebrity, even though no use was made of her voice, name, likeness, or signature. This overturned the balance between protection of creative endeavors and leaving room for new innovation. Moreover, the decision conflicted with the potential federal copyright exception for parodies of copyrighted material and raised questions of censorship under the free speech guarantee.

c. Your body; your property? To what extent do you have property rights in your own body?

★*Moore v. Regents of the University of California,* 51 Cal. 3d 120 (1990), pits first possession against creation in the context of property claims to body parts. Moore's cancerous spleen was removed and, without either his knowledge or consent, a valuable patented cell line was developed using Moore's unique "hairy leukemia" cells. The California Supreme Court ruled that there was no cause of action for *conversion,* a tort that is the wrongful exercise of ownership rights over the personal property of another. The majority said Moore had no ownership because he never expected to retain possession of the spleen. The court's reasons for refusing to extend conversion to the human waste tissue from surgery were that it would chill medical research, the moral issues involved ought to be left to the politically accountable legislature, and Moore still had available to him claims based on asserted breach of fiduciary duty by his medical care providers. *Moore* poses a conflict between Moore's right of first possession of his body parts (recall Locke's premise that we own ourselves, or at least our labor) and the scientist's right to own the unique cells developed from Moore's voluntarily discarded spleen. In concluding that Moore's spleen was not his property, the court was saying only that Moore didn't own it in the limited sense of having the right to profit from it after he had discarded it. So long as the spleen was in him, it was Moore's exclusively to possess and use. But did he ever have the right to transfer it by sale, as opposed to giving it away? We tolerate a great many limitations on transfer rights by sale; e.g., you can give away your baby, but you can't sell it. (Query: What about the surrogate mother who agrees for money to carry a fetus until birth?) *Moore* reflects the view that body parts ought not to be for sale, but the case is surely not the last word. In a world in which body parts have commercial value, law's task is to mediate the conflict among efficiency (fostering the commercial exchange of body parts and aiding scientific discoveries of broad social value), fairness (Ought body parts go to the highest bidder? Should people be deprived from reaping value from their unique body tissues?), and evolving cultural mores and expectations about commercial profit from one's body. Note, however, that *Moore* does *not* stand for the proposition that, in order to have property, it is necessary to have *all* of the sticks in the property bundle: ***use, possession,*** and ***disposition.***

4. **More on possession: the right to exclude:** The right of possession is usually conceived as containing a corollary right: the right to exclude others from possession. That principle was called into question with respect to intellectual property, where full value can sometimes be reaped even if the right to exclude is taken away, but what about real property? Does (should) the owner of land have an absolute right to exclude others? In *Jacque v. Steenberg Homes, Inc.,* 563 N.W.2d 154 (Wis. 1997), the Wisconsin Supreme Court upheld a landowner's right to bar an unwanted trespasser from moving a mobile home across Jacque's land, declaring that a person has the right to "exclusive enjoyment" of his own land "for any purpose which does not invade the rights of another person." In *State v. Shack,* 58 N.J. 297 (1971), the New Jersey Supreme Court held that Tedesco, a landowner, had no right to bar a poverty agency worker and a legal services lawyer from Tedesco's farm, where they sought to visit a migrant worker who was an employee and tenant of Tedesco. Tedesco's right to exclude ended where the tenant worker's need for reasonable access by visitors began. Rights are relative, said the New Jersey court. Beware of absolutes when confronting the question: What is property?

5. **The right to destroy:** Does the right to dispose of property mean that you have the right to destroy your property? This issue does not frequently arise, because self-interest usually restrains people from destroying their own property, but people sometimes stipulate that certain of their property must be destroyed at their death. Examples include a painter who wants his inferior artwork destroyed, or an author who desires to burn his unfinished manuscripts. A landowner might wish to destroy a building, either to erect something else or to restore the land to its original condition. What property rights do they enjoy? Joseph Sax, in *Playing Darts with a Rembrandt: Public and Private Rights in Cultural Treasures* (1999), argues that such destruction is socially wasteful and ought not be permitted. Lior Strahilevitz, in "The Right To Destroy," 114 Yale. L.J. 781 (2005), argues that a limited right to destroy serves important welfare and expressive interests. Prohibitions upon destruction can also be wasteful and inefficient. When rational people destroy their own property, they must either be expressing something or be calculating the utility of the destroyed property differently from others. The conflict posed is between a notion of property rooted in individual autonomy and one that is grounded in a more collective sense. There are no hard and fast answers here: You must ponder the relevant policies in order to decide which rule is better suited to any particular problem.

D. **Finders keepers?** A property owner continues to own his property even after he loses or misplaces it. But lost property often ends up in the finder's pocket. The finder's claim to the property depends on who the rival claimant is and whether the property was ***lost, mislaid,*** or ***abandoned*** by the true owner. A finder has relative title. The policy objectives in finders' law are to restore property to the true owner, reward honest finders, deliver the reasonable expectations of landowners, discourage trespassers and other wrongdoers, and encourage the productive use of found property.

1. **Abandoned property — General rule:** Abandoned property is property to which the true owner has voluntarily given up any claim of ownership. Generally, a ***finder of abandoned property acquires title,*** but this rule is not invariable. Trespassers are not likely to be rewarded

with the fruits of their wrongful behavior, and owners of land where abandoned property is discovered may sometimes have strong and reasonable expectations of ownership of such abandoned property. Statutes, too, can modify this general rule.

Example: True Owner places his old laptop computer on the sidewalk in front of his house, with a placard that says, "Free—Take Me." True Owner has abandoned his ownership. The first possessor becomes the next True Owner. But if True Owner abandons his laptop computer by placing it under the living room sofa of Neighbor, and Guest then discovers the abandoned computer while searching for his contact lens, it is not so clear that Guest should prevail as against Neighbor. Property is not usually labeled as abandoned. The conclusion of abandonment usually has to be made from circumstantial facts.

Example: True Owner places a bundle of newspapers outside his house for curbside recycling. Absent any relevant statutes, has True Owner abandoned the papers? Almost certainly. His action indicates intent to renounce ownership. If Scavenger takes the papers, he has acquired ownership. Intention to relinquish ownership is critical. A true owner may be prevented from possessing his property but, so long as he never intends to give up his claim of ownership, it remains his.

Example: In 1857, the steamship *Central America* sank in a storm off Cape Hatteras, carrying a large cargo of California gold to the bottom. The insurers paid off and thus acquired ownership of the insured cargo. In 1988, the wreck of the *Central America* was discovered, and part of the cargo recovered. Though 131 years had elapsed, the 4th Circuit ruled that the mere elapse of time was not enough to prove abandonment. *Columbus-America Discovery Group v. Atlantic Mutual Insurance Co.,* 974 F.2d 450 (4th Cir. 1992).

Trespassing finders of abandoned property are denied title unless the trespass is "trivial or merely technical." See *Favorite v. Miller,* 176 Conn. 310 (1978), in which a trespasser found a portion of an equestrian statue of George III, buried in a Connecticut pasture by Loyalists during the American Revolution after rebellious colonists had destroyed the statue. (The true owner of the statue—the British Crown—presumably abandoned its claim by recognizing American independence.)

2. **Lost and mislaid property—General rule:** Generally, *a finder's title is good against the whole world except the true owner, prior finders, and (sometimes) the owner of land where an object is found.* Lost property is just that—it slid out of the hole in your pocket. Mislaid property is property that the true owner placed somewhere with the intention of returning for it, but which cannot now be located—the wallet left on the grocer's counter.

★**Example:** A chimney sweep found a gem in a setting and took it to a jeweler for appraisal. The jeweler's apprentice removed the gem and refused to return it. The sweep was awarded damages, measured by the value of the finest stone that would fit the setting, unless the master produced the stone. *Armory v. Delamirie,* 1 Strange 505 (K.B. 1722).

If the jeweler had been the *true owner* of the gem, the chimney sweep would have lost. Remember, a finder has only relative title.

a. **Prior finders:** Prior finders prevail over later finders.

   Example: True Owner loses his watch, which is found by First Finder. First Finder then loses the watch, which is found by Second Finder. First Finder prevails over Second Finder on the basis of his prior possession. True Owner would, of course, prevail over First Finder. See *Clark v. Maloney,* 3 Harr. 68 (Del. 1840).

The prior possession principle applies even if First Finder had stolen the watch from True Owner. See *Anderson v. Gouldberg,* 51 Minn. 294 (1892); *Payne v. TK Auto Wholesalers,* 911 A.2d 747 (Conn. App. 2006). This is efficient, by avoiding litigation over the circumstances of the finding, and the contrary rule would neither deter thievery nor increase the likelihood of restoring the object to the true owner. The rationales for protecting prior possession, especially when we know there is some unknown true owner, are (1) to encourage finders to make productive use of their finds rather than hide them, and (2) to provide a cheap, easy means of establishing presumptive title.

b. **Finder v. Landowner:** Conflicts frequently arise between a finder and the owner of the land upon which the property was found (often called the owner of the ***locus in quo***). Of course, there is no conflict if the landowner also owns the found object. If the hostess exclaims, "I've lost my wedding ring!" and you find it in your salad, the ring is not yours. But if the true owner is neither the finder nor the landowner, conflict erupts.

   i. **Trespassing finders:** As is true of abandoned property, trespassing finders of lost or mislaid property lose. See *Favorite v. Miller,* supra.

   ii. **Employee finders:** Older cases tend to find that employee finders must surrender the find to their employer if the employee has a contractual duty to report finds.

   Example: A carpenter employed by a hotel was allowed to keep property he found in a hotel guest room he was redecorating, because his carpentry duties did not include reporting found property. The court said the outcome would be reversed if he had been a chambermaid, because "[c]hambermaids frequently find [property] guests have forgotten." *Erickson v. Sinykin,* 223 Minn. 232 (1947).

   Putting aside the (perhaps) sexist subtext of *Erickson,* the rationale is poor. The duty to report makes sense as a way to facilitate restoration of found property to the true owner, but if the true owner is never found, it makes little sense to deprive the honest chambermaid of her find. If reporting the find causes its loss to the finder, diamond rings left on the hotel dresser are likely to disappear silently. The objectives of restoring lost property to the owner and of rewarding honest finders can be achieved by combining a duty to report with award to the finder when the true owner never materializes. For this reason, other cases tend to award found property to the employee finder. See *Hamaker v. Blanchard,* 90 Pa. 377 (1879); *Danielson v. Roberts,* 44 Or. 108 (1904); *Toledo Trust Co. v. Simmons,* 52 Ohio App. 373 (1935).

   iii. **Invitee finders:** Landowners often invite workers and others on to their property for specific and limited purposes. Finding property is almost never one of those purposes. An invitee who finds property in the course of doing what he or she was invited to do must surrender it to the landowner.

   Example: Landowner employed Sharman to clean out the Minster pool. In doing so, Sharman found two gold rings. The rings went to Landowner, who conceded he had been unaware of their existence until the find. Landowner was treated as the ***constructive possessor*** of the rings, a label that is simply a legal conclusion that the landowner should prevail. *South Staffordshire Water Co. v. Sharman,* [1896] 2 Q.B. 44, discussed in ***Hannah v. Peel,*** below.

But why? Leaving the property with the landowner may slightly improve the odds of returning the property to the true owner, and landowners do have expectations of ownership of immobile things on their land. But awarding the find to the landowner undermines the goal of rewarding honest finders. Perhaps the value of the find should be split between finder and landowner.

iv.   **Embedded objects and treasure trove:** When property is embedded in or under the soil, it is awarded to the landowner, on the rationale that the landowner's expectations of owning things in the dirt itself are especially strong.

   Example: A meteorite slammed into Goddard's land and was dug up by Hoagland, an invitee of Elickson, Goddard's tenant in possession. Hoagland sold the meteorite to Winchell. Goddard sued for its return and won, mostly because the meteorite became a part of Earth upon its arrival. *Goddard v. Winchell,* 86 Iowa 71 (1892).

   But when the embedded property is ***treasure trove***—gold, silver, or money buried with the intent of return and recovery—different rules may apply. In England, treasure trove belongs to the Crown—the government. American states have largely rejected the doctrine but split as to whether the find should go to the finder or landowner. Compare *Danielson v. Roberts,* supra, awarding treasure trove to the finder, and *Schley v. Couch,* 155 Tex. 195 (1955), awarding treasure trove to the landowner. Logic suggests that rejection of the treasure trove doctrine means that the normal rules apply.

v.   **Private homes:** Homeowners are awarded objects found in their homes. A homeowner has an especially strong expectation of ownership of objects found inside her home and, to the extent the property was mislaid, the odds of its recovery by the true owner are increased by leaving it with the homeowner. When the homeowner is an absentee owner—not in possession of the home—resolution of the question turns on whether the homeowner was in ***constructive possession*** of the home. If the homeowner is briefly absent—a mere sojourner away from home—she is in constructive possession of objects found in her absence. But what if she never moved in?

   ★**Example:** Major Peel purchased Gwernhaylod House, a country estate in Shropshire, but never moved in. When World War II broke out, the Crown requisitioned Gwernhaylod House to quarter soldiers. Corporal Hannah found a valuable brooch while adjusting his blackout curtain. He reported the find. Two years later, the owner not having appeared, the brooch was turned over to Peel, who then sold it. Hannah demanded the sale proceeds and won. Because Peel had never moved in, he never had constructive possession of Gwernhaylod House's unknown lost contents. ***Hannah v. Peel,*** [1945] 1 K.B. 509.

   Hannah is a case where the "all-or-nothing" approach to ownership seems poorly fitted to the goals of finders' law. Ownership in Peel punishes the honest finder. Ownership in Hannah defeats Peel's reasonable expectation that he owns everything that came with Gwernhaylod House. Perhaps the value of the find should have been split between Hannah and Peel.

vi. Public places: *Lost property* found in public places goes to the *finder. Mislaid property* found in public places goes to the *landowner.* The rationale for this distinction is that the odds of restoring lost property to the true owner are slim, while the true owner of mislaid property may well return to the place where it was mislaid. But true owners often retrace their steps when they lose items, so this rationale is not airtight.

★**Example:** If a wallet is found on a barbershop counter, it was probably placed there by a customer and then forgotten. As mislaid property, it goes to the barbershop owner. *McAvoy v. Medina,* 93 Mass. 548 (1866). But if the wallet is found on the barber's floor, it was probably dropped there unintentionally by a customer. As lost property, it goes to the finder. *Bridges v. Hawksworth,* 21 L.J. (N.S.) 75 (K.B. 1851), discussed in **Hannah v. Peel,** above.

But is it so clear that the wallet on the counter was mislaid? Maybe it fell out as the customer leaned over. And perhaps the wallet on the floor was carefully placed there, or accidentally knocked to the floor from some more secure locale. The lost-mislaid distinction requires courts to surmise from circumstantial evidence. Again, critics argue that the policies of finders' law might be better served by a sharing rule.

3. Equitable division: Because the all-or-nothing approach to found property sometimes results in irreconcilable conflict between the goals of finders' law, some commentators have argued that found property should be shared equitably among the competing claimants, each of whom have a claim as good as the other claimants. See Helmholz, 52 Ford. L. Rev. 313. Though courts have been reluctant to abandon the all-or-nothing approach, an exception was the resolution of the claims to ownership of the baseball that Barry Bonds hit to set a new record for home runs in a single season. Popov, the original brief possessor of the ball, was divested of possession by a wild melee in the stands in which Hayashi emerged as the possessor. Hayashi, however, had not engaged in the violent wrongdoing that had stripped Popov of his possession. Both claimants had claims better than anyone else, and neither claim was better than the other. The California trial court decreed that Popov and Hayashi had equal interests in the ball and must share its value equally.

4. Statutory modification: Some states have enacted statutes modifying these common law rules. A typical approach is to call all found property lost property and award it to the finder after a reasonable search for the true owner has proved unsuccessful. *Hurley v. City of Niagara Falls,* 30 App. Div. 89 (N.Y. 1968), applied New York's statute to award a plumber $4,900 in cash found by him while working in a customer's house.

E. Adverse possession: Virtually all legal causes of action must be brought within the period of time set out in a *statute of limitations.* If the true owner of land fails to start legal proceedings to remove a person who adversely possesses his land within the period of the statute of limitations, the true owner is *forever barred* from removing the adverse possessor. Because there is no other owner, the adverse possessor has taken title to the land and can obtain a judgment to that effect. The adverse possessor acquires whatever title to the property the owner had. This is the doctrine of *adverse possession.* It combines two broad requirements: (1) *expiration of the relevant statute of limitations,* and (2) *adverse possession* during the limitations period. The first requirement is statutory, and its elements are determined by the statute. The second requirement consists of a series of common law elements concerning the nature of the possession that must be proven.

1. **Rationales for adverse possession:** There are three major justifications for adverse possession.

   a. **Sleeping theory:** Slothful owners, who ignore people using their land in brazen violation of legal right, deserve to be penalized. By failing to bring a timely action to recover possession, they create a problem: adjudicating stale claims is very difficult—witnesses die and disappear, memories fade, documents are lost. The slothful owner ought to bear the risk of losing his property if he does not care enough to assert his ownership. Some argue that stripping the slothful owner of title comports with his reasonable expectations. In a sense, use it or lose it.

   b. **Earning theory:** People who use land productively and beneficially for a long time ought to be rewarded. Even though the land is owned by someone else, the actual possessor has invested time and effort in making it productive. After a long enough period, the adverse possessor has earned some interest in the land. When coupled with the sleeping theory, the justice of cutting off the true owner's claim seems even stronger. Psychologically, if not legally, the adverse possessor develops expectations of continued possession, which expectations are met by the doctrine of adverse possession.

   c. **Stability theory:** Adverse possession enables disputes or doubts about land titles to be cleared expeditiously by delivering title to the person who has occupied the land as if she were the owner for a long time without objection.

   Example: O, the true owner of Blackacre, conveys it to A by deed in 1965. A fails to record the deed, so the public land records indicate O as the owner. In 1990, A sells Blackacre to B, who records his deed from A. Then A disappears, along with the unrecorded deed from O to A. In 1997, B agrees to sell Blackacre to C, who balks because the public land records fail to show any deed to A, from whom B obtained title. From the records, O is still the owner. The relevant limitations statute is 20 years. Adverse possession cures the problem. B will be able (at some cost) to establish his ownership and thus convey good title to C.

2. **Elements of adverse possession:** To acquire title by adverse possession, the adverse possessor must prove four elements. The possessor must (1) *actually enter* and take *exclusive possession* that is (2) *open and notorious,* (3) *adverse* or *hostile* to the true owner's interest and under a *claim of right,* and (4) *continuous* for the limitations period. In some places, the possessor must also prove she has paid the property taxes for the limitations period.

   a. **Actual and exclusive possession:** Actual entry means just that—the possessor must actually, physically, take possession of the owner's land. The owner's cause of action *accrues* at that moment, and the clock on the limitations period starts to run at the moment of actual entry. Exclusive possession means that the possessor has *excluded the public and the owner.* It does *not* mean that only one adverse possessor can occupy. A group of people adversely occupying may acquire a shared title—*concurrent ownership*—by adverse possession. Some states define actual possession by statute. For example, a New York law at issue in *Van Valkenburgh v. Lutz,* 304 N.Y. 95 (1952), required adverse possessors occupying without *color of title* (see infra) to prove that they had "substantially enclosed" or "usually cultivated or improved" the property.

   b. **Open and notorious possession:** Occupation must be *open* and *notorious.* This means that the adverse possession must be readily *visible* to any inspector of the property. The idea is that the true owner would know of the occupation if he visited his property. Open and notorious occupation constitutes *notice* to the owner that his rights are being violated. Occupation is open and notorious if it is the type of occupation a true owner would make.

Example: An adverse possessor of a fenced pasture would possess openly and notoriously if he kept horses or cattle in the pasture. An adverse possessor of an urban home would possess openly and notoriously by moving in and coming and going without concealment. An adverse possessor of undeveloped land must do something to leave a visible mark of his control, such as building a cabin, or fencing, or posting a sign announcing his occupancy.

   i. Underground occupation: It is difficult to occupy subsurface locations openly and notoriously. To satisfy the open-and-notorious element in such cases, it is probably necessary to prove that the owner knew of the occupation, or at least knew of the underground space and that it was accessible by outsiders. See *Marengo Cave Co. v. Ross,* 212 Ind. 624 (1937).

   ii. Adverse possession of subsurface minerals: Because an adverse possessor takes whatever title the true owner had, an adverse possessor of the surface acquires title to subsurface minerals if the true owner had title to them. But if the mineral rights were owned by someone other than the surface owner when the adverse possessor occupied the surface, the adverse possessor acquires title only to the surface. In that case, to acquire mineral rights by adverse possession, the possessor would have to remove minerals in a manner that meets each of the elements of adverse possession.

   iii. Boundary disputes: Some jurisdictions hold that encroachments by one neighbor onto the land of another are not open and notorious if the encroachment is of a *small area* and is not*"clearly and self-evidently"* an encroachment. In such situations, the limitations statute does not begin to run until and unless the owner has *actual knowledge* of the encroachment. See *Mannillo v. Gorski,* 54 N.J. 378 (1969).

c. "Hostility" or adverse claim of right: An adverse possessor must occupy the land *without the consent of the owner* and with an *intention to remain.* This element is often called *hostility*, but it does not mean with *malice or ill will*. It simply means that the adverse possessor has *no permission* to be there *and also claims the right to stay* there. "Consent" or "permission" means that the possessor has occupied in some capacity *subordinate* to the owner's title.

Example: Owen, owner of Blackacre, leases it to Charlene. Charlene's entry is consensual; her occupancy is subordinate to Owen's title.

It is relatively easy to decide whether or not the owner has consented to the occupation; but it is difficult to decide whether the possessor claims a right to stay. Courts apply three different tests to this problem. Two are *subjective*—what was the possessor's state of mind? The third is *objective*—what did the possessor do?

   i. Subjective: good faith occupation: Under this test, the adverse possessor must have a *genuine, good faith belief that she owns the occupied property.* Possessors who know that the property they are occupying is not their own can never acquire title by adverse possession in a jurisdiction applying this version of hostility.

Example: True Owner tells Friend that the farm is his. Friend occupies for the limitations period. Friend is not the record owner, because land cannot validly be transferred by oral conveyance, but Friend has acquired title by adverse possession. He genuinely believed the farm was his own. His entry was not consensual, because it was *not subordinate* to the owner's continued claim of title. Rather, True Owner intended to pass title to Friend. See *Newells v. Carter,* 119 A. 62 (Me. 1922).

This test is sometimes criticized as a perversion of the policy objectives and justifications for adverse possession. It rewards the slothful owner, penalizes the productive occupier who lacks a good faith belief of ownership, and does little to promote settlement of clouded land titles. This test is often claimed to be the minority test, but a respected property scholar claims that, in fact, it is the majority view. Squatters and other deliberate trespassers rarely win without a strong equitable case. Helmholz, 61 Wash. U. L.Q. 331 (1983). The good faith view probably persists out of the belief that rewarding deliberate trespassers permits acquisition of title by "larceny."

ii.   **Subjective: Aggressive trespass:** There are a few old cases that appear to require that the occupier *know the property is not his own but intend to claim it nevertheless.*

Example: In 1852, Maine Central Railroad purchased a strip of land from Preble and moved the boundary fence westward to enclose the purchased land. Nobody realized that the fence was actually located to the east of the true boundary land, with the result that Preble openly occupied a triangular portion of the Railroad's land for the statutory period. When the error came to light, Preble claimed title by adverse possession but admitted that he "supposed I was using my own land. I [o]ccupied it on account I thought it was my own land." That admission destroyed Preble's adverse claim of right. The possessor must claim "ownership of land not embraced in his title." He must "claim title to all land within a certain boundary on the face of the earth, whether it shall eventually be found to be the correct one or not." In short, to have an adverse claim of right, the possessor must intend to keep the occupied property regardless of who owns it. *Preble v. Maine Central R.R. Co.*, 85 Me. 260 (1893).

Almost nobody adheres to this view today, because it rewards the most determined of deliberate trespassers.

iii. **Objective: State of mind irrelevant:** Under this test, which is often claimed to be the majority view, the state of mind of the occupier is essentially not relevant. Instead, courts focus on two things: *(1) lack of permission* (in the sense that the occupation is not *subordinate* to the owner's title) and **(2)** whether the *occupier's acts and statements objectively appear to be claims of ownership.* In short, we don't care what you secretly believe, but have you acted like a true owner should?

Example: Refer to the last example, concerning Preble's occupation of Maine Central's property. Preble was not occupying with the permission of Maine Central, but he conducted his occupation as the true owner. He even moved the fence two feet to the west because he thought he was encroaching upon Maine Central's property. To the world's objective eye, Preble appeared to be the true owner. Under this test for adverse claim of right, Preble would prevail.

iv. **Disclaimers of ownership:** If an adverse possessor *disclaims ownership in order to persuade the owner not to sue,* the possessor has stopped being adverse. The adversity element is destroyed, and the limitations clock stops. The conclusion that adversity has ended is a bit fictional—actually, it's just not fair to let the adverse possessor lull the owner into a loss of his rights.

Example: Squatter occupies Blackacre and satisfies all the elements of adverse possession for nine years. The limitations period is ten years. Then Owner discovers Squatter's presence and confronts him. Squatter says, "I'll leave as soon as I can arrange a new place. Just don't sue me." If Squatter stays for another two years, has he acquired title by adverse possession? No. He disclaimed ownership.

But suppose Squatter had said, "Look, I'll buy the place," and offers a price. If negotiations drag on for more than a year has Squatter acquired title? Not necessarily. It depends on how the trier of fact sees the offer. If it was an implicit disclaimer of ownership, Squatter doesn't own Blackacre. But if it was an implicit statement to the effect of, "I own Blackacre, but I'm willing to buy off your spurious claim to avoid litigation," Squatter does indeed now own Blackacre. Delay is risky for true owners.

v. **Boundary disputes:** Often one landowner mistakenly occupies a strip of her neighbor's land in the belief that it is her own. Most courts apply an objective test of hostility to these cases. If the encroaching owner's actions appear to the world to be those of a true owner (e.g., she built a fence), she occupies adversely to her neighbor. A minority applies a variant subjective test, often called the *Maine doctrine* after *Preble v. Maine Central Railroad,* 27 A. 149 (Me. 1893). Under the Maine doctrine the occupier is *not possessing adversely* if she occupied under a *good faith, but mistaken, belief* that the land is hers, but she *would not have occupied if she had known the true facts.* This is not quite the same thing as the subjective good faith test.

Example: If Joe occupies his neighbor Bill's land in the mistaken belief that it is his own, but without concern for whether he is occupying his own or Bill's land, Joe can acquire title by adverse possession under the Maine doctrine. But Joe lacks the subjective good faith belief to establish adversity in those jurisdictions applying subjective good faith.

The Maine doctrine is frequently criticized as perverse. It encourages perjury ("Sure, I would have stayed anyway"), rewards the intentional trespasser but not the honest one, and requires a difficult and contested judgment about what somebody might have done if their state of knowledge had been different. No wonder it's the minority rule.

vi. **Color of title *not* claim of right:** *Claim of right* is the term often used to describe the element of hostility or adversity. It is sometimes confused with *color of title.* Don't make this error! A possessor who enters under *color of title* is one who has a *defective deed or other writing that purports to deliver title to the possessor,* but which the possessor does not know to be invalid. The deed might be improperly executed, or forged, or signed by somebody who doesn't own the land. But note: Possessors who *enter under color of title satisfy the adversity element.* On the other hand, only a few states *require* color of title to satisfy hostility, or adversity. Color of title has other implications concerning how much land the occupier is deemed to have adversely possessed.

d. **Continuous possession:** An adverse possessor must occupy *continuously—without interruption*—during the limitations period. But this does not mean that the adverse possessor must stay on the land for every moment of the ten or 20 years of the limitations period. Rather, it means that the adverse possessor must *occupy the property as continually as would a reasonable and average true owner of the property.* If the possessor ever *abandons* the property—*intentionally* gives up possession with *no intent of returning*—continuity is destroyed. A later return by the possessor triggers a new cause of action in the owner and the start of a fresh limitations period. This element combines the subjectivity of the possessor's state of mind (When he left the property, was it always his intention to return?) with objective appraisal of what the possessor actually did. If the possessor always intended to return, and treated absences as sojourns, and actually occupied the property for as much time as an average true owner would, this element is satisfied.

★ **Example:** Kunto occupied a summer residence under color of title (a defective deed). When Howard, the record owner, sought to eject him, Kunto countered that the limitations period had expired. "Not if you failed to occupy continuously," retorted Howard. "But I was here every summer," replied Kunto. That was good enough. The property was intended for summer occupancy, as were the surrounding properties. A reasonable owner would use the property during the summer and not at other times. *Howard v. Kunto,* 3 Wash. App. 393 (1970).

The key is to decide what the normal use of the property is. If the adverse possessor makes that use, she has likely occupied continuously. But intermittent use that is not sufficient to satisfy continuity may be enough to create a *prescriptive easement*—a right to use another's property for a limited purpose (but not to acquire ownership).

    i. **Tacking—Adverse possessors:** A common problem with continuity is whether one possessor can add—*tack*—the possession of a prior possessor to his own. If *privity of estate* exists between the prior possessor and the present possessor, tacking is permitted. *Privity of estate* means the *voluntary transfer* from the first possessor to the second possessor of *either* an *estate* in the land or *actual possession* of it. (Caution: In the context of servitudes, "privity of estate" has a different meaning.)

        Example: Able adversely entered Blackacre in 1970. The limitations period is 20 years. In 1980, Able gave Baker a deed to Blackacre, and Baker took possession. In 1991, Charles, owner of Blackacre, sues Baker to recover possession. Who wins and why? Baker will win, assuming all the other elements of adverse possession have been met by Able and Baker over the 20-year period. The limitations period started to run in 1970. By the deed to Baker, Able did not transfer an estate in Blackacre (because he had no estate to transfer), but the deed is excellent evidence of a voluntary transfer of actual possession. Privity of estate is present, and Baker is permitted to tack his possession of 11 years onto Able's prior possession of 10 years. The statute of limitations has run. Charles is too late.

        English courts don't require privity for tacking to occur. In England, the sleeping theory alone is sufficient justification for this result. U.S. courts prefer to penalize the slothful owner only when the victor is a deserving possessor.

    ii. **Tacking—Owner:** Tacking follows automatically on the owner's side. Once the statute of limitations has started to run, the cause of action for ejectment (together with its expiring limitations period) goes along with ownership.

        Example: In 1970, Bebe entered Blackacre adversely. In 1975, Jojo, owner of Blackacre, sells it to Hoho. In 1980, Hoho dies and leaves Blackacre by will to Zaza. In 1985, Zaza gives Blackacre to Dada. In 1991, Dada sues to eject Bebe. The limitations period is 20 years. Bebe wins, assuming she meets all the elements of adverse possession. The statute of limitations was triggered in 1970, and the expiring cause of action traveled from Jojo to Hoho to Zaza to Dada.

iii. Ouster: If an adverse possessor is ousted from possession by a third party, the third party may not tack the ousted possessor's period of possession onto his own. Privity is lacking because the transfer was not voluntary. But courts take three different views of what happens if the ousted possessor returns.

- The view most favorable to true owners, which may be the least preferred by American courts, is that the limitations period starts anew with the re-entry. This view treats ousted possessors harshly, ignoring their determined (and successful) effort to regain possession.

- The view most favorable to adverse possessors is that the ouster does not interrupt the continual running of the limitations period. The problem with this view is that it permits the ousted possessor to tack her possession after re-entry onto the third party's possession, but there is no privity to support this conclusion. Courts paper over this flaw by calling the ousting third party a trespasser rather than a possessor, and treating the ousted possessor as being in constructive possession during the third party's occupation.

- An intermediate view, preferred by some academics, is that the ousted possessor can tack her new possession onto her old possession but cannot take credit for occupation by the third party. For the duration of that third party's occupation, the limitations period is *tolled,* or suspended. The effect is that for the possessor to acquire title, she must occupy for the limitations period plus the period of third-party occupation.

e. Payment of taxes: Some states (mostly in the West) require adverse possessors to prove that they have paid the property taxes on the occupied property for the duration of the limitations period. Because tax collectors will usually make the owner aware of a stranger's attempt to tender taxes, this element makes it extremely unlikely that a person can adversely possess without uncommon negligence on the part of the owner or a mutual mistake as to ownership of the property.

3. Extent of the property acquired by adverse possession: Once the adverse possessor has satisfied the elements of adverse possession for the limitations period, she acquires title to the occupied property. But what is the physical extent of the occupied property? The answer depends on whether the adverse possessor entered with or without *color of title*—under a defective deed or other instrument of title but without knowledge of the defect.

a. Entry without color of title: Adverse possessors without color of title acquire *only the land they have actually physically possessed* for the limitations period.

b. Entry under color of title: Adverse possessors who enter under color of title are deemed to possess *all the land described in the defective deed,* so long as it consists of a *single parcel,* and the possessor has occupied a *significant portion* of the parcel. Remember: A possessor lacks color of title if he does not believe, in good faith, that his defective deed is valid.

Example: Echo enters Blackacre, a 100-acre farm, under color of title to Blackacre but actually possesses only 50 acres for the limitations period. Echo is deemed to have *constructively possessed* the remaining 50 acres and will acquire title to all of Blackacre.

The "single parcel" rule is designed to make sure that the owner of each parcel has a chance to protect his or her interest. If there has never been an actual entry against the owner, he or she has no way of knowing of any adverse claim.

Example: Hal gives Barbara a deed to Blackacre, a 100-acre farm, and Whiteacre, an adjacent but separate 70-acre farm. Barbara does not know that Tom owns Blackacre and Mabel owns Whiteacre, but thinks Hal owns both. Tom and Mabel are absentee owners. Barbara enters and actually occupies 50 acres of Blackacre for the limitations period. Barbara will acquire title to all of Blackacre but not to any portion of Whiteacre. Barbara's occupation gave ample notice to Tom of her adverse possession, but Mabel could not reasonably have ever known that Barbara thought she owned Whiteacre.

Constructive possession is never as good as actual possession, so an adverse possessor entering under color of title does not acquire title to land that, while described in the defective deed, is actually occupied by somebody else.

Example: John enters Blackacre, a 100-acre farm owned by Phil, under color of title to Blackacre and actually occupies 60 acres. He would have occupied the remainder but for the fact that Max, a squatter, had already taken possession of those 40 acres. John can only acquire title to the 60 acres he actually occupies.

The same principle applies when the owner is in possession, and an adverse possessor enters a portion of the property under color of title.

Example: Jane, a reclusive artist, owns Mountaintop, a 100-acre tract on which she has built a studio and cabin, occupying one acre. Harry enters Mountaintop under color of title to the entirety of Mountaintop and occupies two acres, building a cabin and woodshed. Harry will eventually acquire title to the two acres he has actually occupied, but nothing more. Harry's actual possession of the two acres is better than Jane's constructive possession of it, but Jane's constructive possession of the 97 acres not actually occupied by either Jane or Harry is better than Harry's constructive possession of it. After all, she is the true owner.

4. **Statutory issues:** Adverse possession law is a blend of statutory and common law. Some of the common statutory issues are discussed here, but each statute is different. Read your applicable statute carefully!

   a. **Length of the limitations period:** Limitations periods vary from statute to statute, from five years to 21 years. States with the shorter periods often require payment of taxes to establish adverse possession.

   b. **When the cause of action accrues:** The owner's cause of action to recover possession accrues (begins) when there is an adverse entry of the land. Once that happens, the clock on the limitations period starts running.

      i. **Disabled owner:** Statutes of limitation typically provide for *tolling* (suspension) of the limitations time clock if the owner is disabled from bringing an action to recover possession *at the time the cause of action accrues.* Statutory disabilities vary but typically include (1) *insanity* or other *unsound mind,* (2) *imprisonment,* or (3) *the condition of being a minor.* Read your statute carefully! A typical statute provides that *if the owner is disabled* **at the time the cause of action accrues,** the owner may bring suit for some specified period *after the disability* **ceases,** even though the normal limitations period has expired.

Example: A statute of limitations on actions to recover possession of land provides that such actions must begin "within 21 years after the cause of action accrues, but if the person entitled to bring such action is imprisoned, of unsound mind, or a minor at the time the cause of action accrues, such person may bring such action after the expiration of 21 years from accrual of the cause of action, so long as the action is commenced within ten years after the end of the disability." If Owner is imprisoned when Possessor enters in 1970, and is released from prison in 1995, Owner has until 2005 to file suit to recover possession.

Remember that the only disabilities that matter are those that *exist at the* **time the cause of action accrues.**

Example: Assume the limitations statute presented in the last example. Bob enters Blackacre, owned by Jill, in 1970. In 1971, Jill is imprisoned for 25 years. Jill's right to bring suit expires in 1991. She was not disabled when the cause of action accrued. Remember also that the cause of action goes along with title when title is transferred.

Example: Assume the limitations statute previously presented. Alan enters Blackacre, owned by Hazel, in 1970. Hazel is a free adult of sound mind. In 1982, Hazel dies, leaving Blackacre by will to her granddaughter Beth, age two. Beth succeeds to Hazel's cause of action. That cause of action will be time-barred in 1991. But Beth will only be 11 years old in 1991. No matter. Hazel was not disabled at the time the cause of action accrued. Beth's adult guardian is responsible for protecting Beth's interests. The guardian should bring suit in Beth's name.

ii. **Lienholders and future interest owners:** Some people are not entitled to file suit to recover possession, so the limitations statute simply doesn't apply to them. No cause of action has accrued. Lienholders (e.g., mortgage lenders) have a claim on the property but no right to possession until and unless there has been a default and foreclosure, so their claims are not destroyed by expiration of the limitations period. Holders of *future interests*—present ownership interests in property of a right to possession at some future time—are also not entitled to possession now. Adverse possession does not cut off their future claim to possession. When the future interest holder becomes entitled to possession, his cause of action accrues, and the limitations period starts running.

Example: Assume the prior limitations statute. Wilma owns a life estate in Blackacre. Jane owns the *remainder*—the right to take possession as soon as Wilma dies. Sam enters and adversely occupies Blackacre in 1970. Wilma does nothing. In 1991, Sam acquires title by adverse possession (consisting of Wilma's life estate). In 1995, Wilma dies. Jane's cause of action now accrues. Jane has until 2016 to bring suit to eject Sam. If she does nothing Sam will acquire yet another title by adverse possession in 2016, consisting of Jane's interest in Blackacre.

5. **Adverse possession by tenants and co-owners:**

   a. **Tenants:** Tenants are not usually capable of adverse possession against their landlords because their entry was permissive—subordinate to the owner's claim of title. They lack hostility, or adversity. Rarely, a tenant will so clearly repudiate the leasehold that she will become an adverse possessor. It takes extraordinarily explicit and clear action on the tenant's part to do this.

   b. Co-owners: One co-owner may not usually adversely possess against her co-owner, because every co-owner has an equal right to possession. A co-owner's possession is not adverse to the claim of ownership of her fellow co-owners. In order to possess adversely against another co-owner, the adverse co-owner must *oust* the other co-owner by *excluding the co-owner from possession* and *claiming sole ownership.*

6. **Adverse possession of personal property:** The law of adverse possession was created to deal with real property, not personal property, but title to personal property can be acquired by adverse possession. A different (often shorter) statute of limitations usually applies. The principal reason that adverse possession is not well suited to personal property is the fact that possession of personal property in the manner of a true owner is not very open and notorious. The traditional answer is that open and notorious possession is satisfied so long as the possessor uses the object in the way the average owner would.

   ★**Example:** Georgia O'Keeffe, the famous artist, had a painting stolen. Years later, it appeared for sale in an art gallery. Snyder, the gallery owner, argued that his predecessor in interest had acquired title by adverse possession. The answer hinges on whether the possessor's exhibition of the painting in his own home was sufficiently open and notorious. But the New Jersey Supreme Court, in *O'Keeffe v. Snyder,* 83 N.J. 478 (1980), ruled that the law of adverse possession ought not apply. Instead, the court ruled that the limitations period for recovery of personal property starts to run at the earlier of (1) when the loss occurs (except where there is fraud or concealment), or (2) when the *owner first discovers, or through reasonable effort should have discovered, the cause of action (including the identity of the possessor).* This turns the focus onto the owner's conduct, rather than the possessor's conduct, and encourages owners to report their losses and undertake reasonable investigation.

7. **Title acquired by adverse possessor:** When adverse possessors acquire title, they acquire a new title. The former owner hasn't transferred his interest; rather, the law has stripped him of his title and created a new one in the adverse possessor. But the new title cannot be any better or greater in scope than the former owner's title. The adverse possessor gets only what the old owner had.

   Example: Oboe owned a *life estate* in Blackacre, meaning he owned it only for the rest of his life. Flute acquired Oboe's title by adverse possession. Though Flute got a new title, it was a title to only a life estate in Blackacre. When Oboe dies, Flute's title to Blackacre dies, too. If Oboe had owned Blackacre in *fee simple absolute* (a title that exists forever, even though owners of that title come and go) but subject to a mortgage lien, Flute would acquire a new title in fee simple absolute but subject to the mortgage lien.

   The adverse possessor's new title cannot be recorded in the public land records, because there is no written record of it. The adverse possessor must bring a suit against the former owner to *quiet title* in the adverse possessor. That judgment can be recorded. While an adverse possessor can transfer his title by deed (the Statute of Frauds requires a writing to transfer a land title), and that deed can be recorded, there will be no evidence in the record of title by adverse possession. The transferee from the adverse possessor receives the adverse possessor's title but still must act to quiet title.

8. Alternatives to adverse possession in boundary disputes: Boundary disputes between neighbors comprise a fair amount of adverse possession cases, and some courts have modified adverse possession doctrine to deal with such disputes. But there are other ways to solve these problems.

    a. Agreed boundaries: Neighbors can always agree on a new boundary, reduce the agreement to writing, and record a conveyance to carry it out. If neighbors *orally agree* on a new boundary when there is *genuine uncertainty about the boundary,* the oral agreement is a binding method of locating the boundary. The law splits hairs here. The oral agreement is not a conveyance, for that would violate the Statute of Frauds, but it has all the effect of a conveyance.

    b. Acquiescence: If one owner acquiesces in a known encroachment for an indefinite but long time, the acquiescence is evidence of an agreed boundary.

    c. Equitable estoppel: If one neighbor does or says things that cause the other neighbor substantially to rely to his detriment on the first neighbor's actions, the first neighbor is estopped from denying his statements or actions.

    Example: Matilda moves into her new house and has a backyard conversation with Lulu, her neighbor, in which Lulu points out a sagging fence as the boundary. "Trust me," she says, "you don't need to do a survey. I know it for a fact." In fact, the fence encroaches on Lulu's property by ten feet. Matilda dispenses with her intended survey and proceeds to rebuild the fence and construct a workshop that partially encroaches on Lulu's property. Lulu then sues for ejectment of the encroachments. Lulu will lose. She will be estopped from denying her statements on which Matilda relied to her substantial detriment.

F. Accession: Accession occurs when a person *in good faith* adds his labor to the property of another, or when a person *in good faith* mixes his labor and his property with the property of another. The issue is who owns the resulting product.

    1. General rules: When only labor is added, the owner of the original property owns the resulting product, unless the value added by the labor is substantial. In that case, the laborer owns the resulting product but must compensate the owner of the original property for the trespass. When labor and new material are mixed with another's original property, the resulting product goes to whichever person supplied the more significant and valuable material. If that is the good faith improver, she must pay for her trespass.

    2. Mistaken improver of real property: The mistaken improver doctrine is a variation of accession that is applied to real property. A person who *in good faith* constructs an improvement on the land of another (usually a neighbor) creates in the neighbor an *option* to either (1) *sell the land to the improver at its fair market value (net of the improvement)* or (2) *pay to the improver the fair value of the improvement itself.*

III. PERSONAL PROPERTY

A. Introduction: Issues concerning personal property are present in many areas of law: e.g., contracts (particularly sales of goods), commercial transactions, and intellectual property. This section deals briefly and selectively with only some personal property issues.

B. Bailments: A *bailment* is a *legitimate possession* of personal property by someone who is ***not the owner*** of the property. The person who owns the property is called the *bailor* and the non-owner in possession is called the *bailee.* Bailments can be created voluntarily or involuntarily.

Example: You leave your watch with the jeweler to be repaired. A voluntary bailment is created. But if you forgetfully leave your car keys on the jeweler's counter when you leave, an involuntary bailment is created.

In order for a bailment to exist, the bailee must have ***actual control*** of the property ***together with intent to possess*** the property.

1. **Bailors, bailees, and third parties:** A bailee has a better claim to the property than any third party and is thus entitled to damages from any third party who wrongfully injures the property, but must turn over the damage proceeds to the bailor. Bailors may recover from a third party for injury to the property if the third party has not already paid the bailee. A bailor of a *voluntary* bailment may not proceed against a third party who has already paid the bailee. The bailor's remedy is to recover from the bailee, his chosen agent. This rule is sometimes called the *Winkfield doctrine* after a case so holding: *The Winkfield,* [1902] P. 42 (1901). The Winkfield doctrine does not apply to an *involuntary* bailment: The *bailor may recover from a third party who has already paid the bailee.* The rationale is that the bailor had no opportunity to select his bailee and thus ought not be bound by whatever settlement or judgment the bailee obtained.

C. Gifts: A gift is a *voluntary transfer* of property for *no consideration.* To accomplish a gift of personal property, the donor must *intend to make a gift,* the property must be *delivered to the donee* (the recipient of the gift), and the donee must *accept* the property. Gifts are commonly divided into gifts *inter vivos* (during life) and gifts *causa mortis* (in contemplation of impending death). A gift is inter vivos if it is made with no knowledge or threat of impending death. Inter vivos gifts are irrevocable. A gift is causa mortis if it is made with knowledge or under threat of immediate death and motivated by that fact. Gifts causa mortis are revocable if the donor recovers from the illness or threat causing the donor to make the gift in contemplation of death, or if the donor dies of some other cause that did not prompt the gift. Courts view gifts causa mortis with some skepticism because the donor is likely to be dead, and the completed gift is a substitute for a will, a form of giving at death that is laden with formalities to be sure that the dead person's wishes are accurately carried out.

1. **Intent:** For a gift to occur, the donor must intend to transfer *title.* If the donor's intent is *merely to transfer possession,* no gift has been accomplished. Evidence on this element is usually circumstantial, unless the donor executes a deed or some other written expression of donative intent.

    a. **Gifts causa mortis:** Recall that gifts causa mortis are revocable if the donor recovers from the threat of death that motivated the gift. The donor's intention is presumed to be to make the gift *only because of impending death.* But if a donor intends the gift to be irrevocable regardless of her impending death, it is not a gift causa mortis (revocable) but is an irrevocable inter vivos gift.

2. **Delivery:** The general rule is that the subject of the gift must be *delivered* to the recipient in order for the gift to be complete. The best form of delivery is *actual physical possession,* but that is not always required. When physical delivery is *impractical* or *impossible,* delivery may be accomplished by *symbolic delivery* or *constructive delivery.*

a. Rationale: Delivery is thought to perform three valuable functions:

- **Making abstraction a reality:** When a donor must part with a cherished possession, the idea of giving becomes real. A donor will part with possession of an object only if she truly wishes to give. As the ancient bromide has it: "Actions speak louder than words."

- **Objective evidence of intent:** Intent is subjective, but delivery is objective. Delivery acts as a secondary check on intent.

- **Objective evidence of acceptance:** Delivery of property is presumptive evidence of acceptance by the donee.

b. Relationship of delivery to intent: To the extent that the element of delivery is easily satisfied by something other than delivery of *actual physical possession*—either *symbolic delivery or constructive delivery*—the element of delivery becomes virtually the same as intent. In both cases, the issue becomes, "What did the donor intend by her acts?"

c. Delivery by deed: Delivery can be accomplished by a *deed of gift* or some other *writing under seal.* Although the law no longer makes much of the distinction between sealed instruments (those that bore a ritual indication of authenticity, as a notarial seal) and unsealed instruments (merely signed by the maker), this distinction persists here. Some courts only recognize sealed instruments as adequate to deliver by writing. But unsealed instruments may accomplish the work of delivery if they are adequate to constitute symbolic or constructive delivery.

d. Symbolic delivery: When actual physical delivery is *impossible* or *impractical,* delivery can be accomplished by delivering some object that is *symbolic of possession.*

Example: Tom, author of a series of hugely successful adventure novels, decides to give to his daughter the copyright in his latest novel, *Last Clear Chance.* He writes the following on his letter paper: "I hereby give my daughter Jane my copyright in *Last Clear Chance.* [signed] Dad." Tom physically gives the paper to his daughter. Jane owns the copyright. It is impossible to physically deliver intangible personal property like a copyright. Tom's writing is symbolic of possession of the intangible right. Cf. *In re Cohn,* 187 App. Div. 392 (N.Y. 1919) (gift of corporate stock). Symbolic delivery is adequate when physical delivery is simply not practical.

Example: Tom decides to give his daughter Jane his concert grand piano, even though she has no room for it in her apartment. He gives to Jane a signed letter: "Dear Jane, I hereby give you my concert grand piano. Come play it whenever you wish and take it away whenever you can. Love, Tom." The letter constitutes symbolic delivery of the piano.

e. Constructive delivery: When actual physical delivery is *possible but impractical,* delivery of some object that is the *means of obtaining possession* of the property constitutes *constructive delivery.*

★**Example:** On his deathbed, Jack gives to Julia all the keys to the household furniture, saying that he intends for her to have everything in the house. Delivery of the keys constitutes constructive delivery of the furniture, because it is impractical to make physical delivery under the circumstances. But delivery of the keys does not constitute constructive delivery of a life insurance policy locked in a bureau drawer, because it was not impractical to deliver the tangible evidence of the life insurance right—the policy itself. *Newman v.*

Bost, 122 N.C. 524 (1898). Constructive delivery cases often raise the problem of whether delivery is an independent element or merely a double check on donative intent.

Example: Phyllis has two keys to her safe deposit box, which is stuffed with valuable stocks, bonds, and jewels. She gives one key to Maude, saying, "Everything in this safe deposit box is yours." Is the gift complete? Cases split on this. Some say that retention of the second key negates constructive delivery because Phyllis did not surrender her control over the box. In essence, this view focuses on doubts about Phyllis's intent. The contrary view—holding that delivery of one of two keys constitutes constructive delivery—focus more on the fact that the key is, literally, the key to possession. Most often, courts look to other factors to decide whether the donor really intended to make a gift. Compare *Hocks v. Jeremiah,* 759 P.2d 312 (Ore. 1988), and *Estate of Abramowitz,* 38 App. Div. 2d 387 (N.Y. 1972) (no delivery; no gift) with *Gilkinson v. Third Ave. R.R. Co.,* 47 App Div. 472 (N.Y. 1900) and *In re Parkhurst's Estate,* 402 Pa. 527 (1961) (constructive delivery; valid gift).

f. **Special problems:** Some delivery problems warrant special mention.

Agents: When donors deliver the property to an agent of the donee, delivery is complete. But sometimes it's not clear whether the third person is an agent of the donor or the donee. If the delivery is to the *donor's agent, there is no delivery* because it is as if the donor had "delivered" the gift to himself. This problem usually comes up when the donor delivers property to his own attorney for the benefit of a donee. The lawyer's client is the donor, but can she also be the agent of the donee? Yes, but courts split on this. This form of delivery is risky at best, and involves courts in the debate over whether delivery is of independent significance or just a redundant test of donative intent.

■ **Delivery on death:** If a donor delivers property to a third party (even a conceded agent of the donee) under instructions to deliver the property to the donee on the death of the donor, there may be *no gift.* The condition attached (death) to ultimate delivery is sometimes seen as an impermissible attempt to avoid the formal requirements for a will, and thus invalid. The preferred (and more modern) view is that the gift is complete upon delivery to the donee's agent, regardless of the condition attached. There are two reasons for this view. First, delivery has been made to the donee through his agent. Second, the attached condition amounts to little more than the creation of a valid *oral trust,* with the donee's agent as trustee.

■ **Choses in action:** The delivery requirements of a *chose in action* (an inchoate legal right) depend on whether the chose in action has assumed tangible form by a writing. Choses in action reduced to a writing (e.g., a promissory note, or an insurance policy) must be delivered in the same way as tangible personal property. To deliver by written assignment it is necessary to show that the assignment is a valid symbolic delivery. Those not reduced to a writing (e.g., a personal injury claim) may always be delivered by a written assignment without the necessity of proving symbolic delivery.

■ **Donee in possession:** When a donee already has possession there is no need to perform the useless act of shifting the property back and forth to prove "delivery." It has been delivered. Once is enough.

3. **Acceptance:** A gift is not complete until it has been accepted by the donee. Delivery triggers a presumption of a completed gift, which presumption can be rebutted by the donee's rejection

of the gift. The presumption of acceptance is strongest when the gift benefits the donee, and virtually nonexistent when the gift is (rarely) of no benefit. A donee's delay in rejecting known unwanted gifts also endangers the donee's ability to claim that there was no acceptance.

4. ***Gruen v. Gruen:* An illustration:** The elements of an inter vivos gift are nicely combined in ***Gruen v. Gruen,*** 68 N.Y.2d 48 (1986), in which Gruen wrote a letter to his son (an undergraduate student at Harvard) telling him that for his 21st birthday he was giving his son a valuable Klimt painting that was displayed in Gruen's home, but that he wished to retain possession for the remainder of his life. The New York Court of Appeals held that the letter constituted a completed and valid gift to Gruen's son of a remainder interest in the painting, a property right that would automatically become possessory upon the elder Gruen's death. Father Gruen retained a life estate in the painting. The elder Gruen manifested his donative intent at the time of the gift because the remainder interest was a *presently existing* property right (even though not one that entitled the younger Gruen to immediate possession). The letter was sufficient to constitute delivery because it "would be illogical for the law to require the donor to part with possession of the painting when that is exactly what he intends to retain." Acceptance of a gift by a donee is essential to a completed, valid gift. While the law presumes acceptance where the other elements of a gift are present, the younger Gruen manifested acceptance by acknowledging the gift to his friends and retaining for 17 years (until the elder Gruen's death) the letter evidencing the gift.

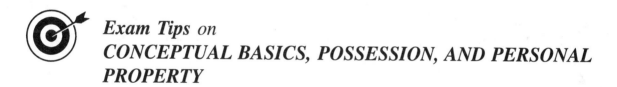

Exam Tips on CONCEPTUAL BASICS, POSSESSION, AND PERSONAL PROPERTY

☞ Finders' law is an easy way to test your ability both to apply common law doctrine and to display your knowledge of how public policies affect doctrine. Answer questions here by invoking the common law doctrine, but *don't neglect to apply sensible policy choices* that ought to affect doctrine. Justify and explain your policy choices; don't be content with a mere recitation of the doctrine and mechanical application of it to the facts.

☞ The resolution of adverse possession issues often depends on what you perceive to be the purposes of adverse possession. Pay attention to the policies justifying adverse possession, emphasize the policy that supports your resolution, and explain why that policy is a good idea and why it dictates the resolution you advance. This is particularly (but certainly not exclusively) true with respect to issues of tacking and the hostility, or claim of right, element.

☞ Adverse possession of personal property can easily be combined with finders' issues. If a person is not entitled to possession as a finder, perhaps he has acquired lawful possession as an adverse possessor. Pay attention to the fact that adverse possession principles (developed for real property) do not work well for personal property; justify the method you apply to assess claims of adverse possession of personal property by reference to the policies that you think are applicable, and explain why those policies should apply.

CHAPTER 2

FREEHOLD ESTATES

ChapterScope _____

This chapter examines the freehold estates — the various ways in which people can own land. Here are the most important points in this chapter.

■ The various freehold estates are contemporary adaptations of medieval ideas about land ownership. Past notions, even when no longer relevant, persist but ought not do so.

■ Estates are rights to present possession of land. An estate in land is a legal construct, something apart from the land itself. Estates are abstract, figments of our legal imagination; land is real and tangible. An estate can, and does, travel from person to person, or change its nature or duration, while the land just sits there, spinning calmly through space.

■ The fee simple absolute is the most important estate. The fee simple absolute is what we normally think of when we think of ownership. A fee simple absolute is capable of enduring forever though, obviously, no single owner of it will last so long.

■ Other estates endure for a lesser time than forever; they are either capable of expiring sooner or will definitely do so.

■ The life estate is a right to possession for the life of some living person, usually (but not always) the owner of the life estate. It is sure to expire because none of us lives forever.

■ There are three defeasible fees, estates that will come to an end upon the occurrence of some specified event.

  ■ A fee simple determinable results when a grantor (owning an estate of longer duration) grants possession only *until* an event occurs, or only for *so long as* something remains true. ("*O to A* so long as Britain remains a constitutional monarchy.") When the defeasible condition occurs, the grantor automatically reacquires possession. The grantor's right to possible future possession is called a ***possibility of reverter.***

  ■ A fee simple subject to condition subsequent results when a grantor (owning an estate of longer duration) grants possession apparently without limitation or condition, but then immediately attaches a condition by which the grantor may retake possession. ("*O to A,* but if Britain should cease to be a constitutional monarchy, *O* may retake possession.") The grantor must act to retake possession when the defeasible condition occurs; thus, the grantor's retained right to possession sometime in the future is called a ***right of re-entry*** or ***power of termination.***

  ■ A fee simple subject to an executory limitation results when either of the above defeasible fees is created *but the right to future possession is transferred to a third party.* ("*O to A* so long as Britain remains a constitutional monarchy and, if not, to *B.*") The third party's right to future possession is called an ***executory interest.***

■ The fee tail is largely extinct; it was designed to endure so long as the first owner has lineal descendants, but whenever the first owner's bloodline should die out, the estate should die. The principal modern issue pertinent to fees tail is what happens when somebody attempts to create one.

■ Restraints on alienation of freehold estates are much discouraged and often invalidated, because such restraints inhibit freedom and efficient allocation of resources.

I. ORIGINS AND TAXONOMY OF FREEHOLD ESTATES

A. Estates generally: A legitimate possessor of land — *real property* — owns an *estate in land* rather than the land itself. A *possessory estate* is a legal right to occupy the land immediately. By contrast, a *future interest* is the right (and sometimes only the possibility) to possess the land at some time in the future. A future interest is a presently existing estate but the estate does not include the right of possession until some future event or events have occurred. Possessory estates are further divided into *freehold estates* (essentially various types of what nonlawyers think is *ownership*) and *nonfreehold* or *leasehold estates* (possession subordinate to the owner's rights of ownership). At early common law, the distinction between freehold and nonfreehold estates was that the freeholder had *seisin,* and the nonfreeholder had *possession but not seisin.* Possessory estates may be of perpetual duration or for some shorter period. The various forms of possessory estates are discussed in this chapter. Our system of estates is derived from the feudal origins of land ownership. While we are long removed from feudal society and, hopefully, your professor is not anxious to test you on your knowledge of feudal law, a brief understanding of the origins will help you make sense of the contemporary concepts.

B. Feudal tenures: When William of Normandy — William the Conqueror — seized the English crown in 1066, he claimed ownership of all the land in England. Then he handed out possession of separate parcels to his henchmen, but with a catch. This possession-with-a-catch was called *seisin.* Each possessor was a tenant of the King, and his continued possession (his *tenure*) depended on his performance of services for the King. The tenant was *seised of the land,* which meant he held possession from the King, his lord, and owed *services to his lord.* These services could be almost anything from the important (e.g., 50 mounted knights to do combat for the King, 100 bushels of corn each year) to the frivolous (e.g., a sprig of holly at the winter solstice). The first tenant (the one holding directly from the King) was the *tenant-in-chief.* The tenant-in-chief could, and often did, transfer all or a part of his possession rights to some lesser chief, who was known as a *tenant in demesne* (pronounced *demean*), and who was obligated to provide services (e.g., ten knights) to the tenant-in-chief, also known as a *mesne lord* (pronounced *mean*), because he was intermediate in the feudal chain of obligation, having a lord above and a tenant below him in the feudal pecking order. This process was called *subinfeudation,* and it could produce a lengthy chain of possession and obligation. Everyone but the King owed duties to some lord. Everyone in the feudal chain also was owed services by his tenants. Those at the bottom only owed services to their lord. Holders of nonfreehold estates (lessees for a term of years) were not seised and owed no feudal duties to the lord from whom their landlord held. (This was because leaseholders were regarded as a bit low and untrustworthy, not because there was something special about leaseholds.) Think of the feudal services as a tax fixed at the time the tenant was *seised in possession* and constant thereafter.

1. **Feudal incidents:** As you can imagine, the value of possession rose as population increased, but the annual services remained constant. This fact made the imposition of *feudal incidents* (essentially death taxes) important, because the lord acquired the tenant's rights (usually possession of the land) — whenever incidents came due. The lord could then either use the property himself or *subinfeudate* — transfer — it anew in exchange for a new package of annual services. The principal incidents were *escheat, forfeiture,* and *wardship and marriage.*

   ■ **Escheat:** If a tenant in possession died without heirs, his tenure ended, and possession returned to the next lord up the feudal ladder.

   ■ **Forfeiture:** If a tenant in possession committed treason against the King or violated his obligations to the lord from whom he held possession, his tenure was forfeited and the next lord up the chain took possession.

   ■ **Wardship and marriage:** If a tenant in possession died leaving an heir who was a minor, the next lord up the chain was entitled to the profits from the land until the heir reached adulthood, and was also entitled to arrange the minor's marriage and receive payment from the family of the minor's prospective spouse for the marriage. (This was before the age of romantic love; marriage was a cold-blooded calculation of financial and social gain.)

2. **Feudal death tax avoidance and statute quia emptores:** To avoid the imposition of incidents, tenants in possession would subinfeudate to their children for nominal services.

   Example: Lord gave possession of Blackacre to Tenant in return for 50 hogs each year. If Tenant dies while his Son is a minor, Lord has possession of Blackacre until Son reaches maturity. But if Tenant had subinfeudated Blackacre to Son for a sprig of mistletoe in midwinter, Lord's incident on Tenant's death would consist of the receipt of a sprig of mistletoe each midwinter.

   Statute Quia Emptores (1290) destroyed this tax avoidance scheme by forbidding any further subinfeudation in fee simple. But the political price for this was recognition of the right of free tenants to transfer, or alienate, their land. A tenant could convey his interest to another in substitution for himself in the feudal chain. This was the beginning of free alienability of land in English law, a critical component of modern property law. Over time, Quia Emptores eliminated most mesne lords, leaving the right of incidents largely held by the King. This fact produced some new tax-avoidance devices by lawyers and freeholders of the fifteenth and sixteenth centuries, another statutory response by the King (in 1536), and the development of new estates, all considered when we study future interests in Chapter 3. By then, however, the feudal economy was all but dead, and the feudal system of tenure, marked by personal obligations, was essentially replaced by the modern view of ownership — private rights of use, possession, and alienability coupled with mostly financial obligations to the state in the form of taxes.

C. **A taxonomy of freehold estates:** When feudal holdings became alienable by free tenants ("free holders"), the modern *freehold estate* began to evolve. There are four basic types of freehold estates: the *fee simple,* the *fee tail,* the *defeasible fees,* and the *life estate.* Each of these has its variations, and all are considered in the rest of this chapter. *Leaseholds* — the *nonfreehold estates* — are considered in Chapter 5. The principal difference between each freehold estate is the *duration of the estate.* Some freehold estates are of finite duration; some may last forever (or at least as long as the legal system that created them). Remember: An estate in land is *not the same* *thing as the land itself.* An estate in land is a legal abstraction — a fictional, imaginary thing that is connected to the land but existing apart from it. An estate in land consists of an important bundle of legal rights and obligations toward others with respect to a particular parcel of Earth. It can move from one person to another, be subdivided in various ways and put back together again, all while the land itself remains unchanged.

II. FEE SIMPLE

A. Introduction: The fee simple is the most common freehold estate. There are two types of fees simple: the *fee simple absolute* and the three forms of *defeasible fees.* The difference between the two types is that the fee simple absolute can endure forever, and the defeasible fees can be terminated upon the happening of some specified future event. The fee simple absolute is considered here. The defeasible fees are discussed in section IV of this chapter.

B. Fee simple absolute: The fee simple absolute is a bit of a misnomer. It is absolute ownership in the sense that its *duration is perpetual.* It may last forever (or at least as long as the legal system). It is probably what you thought of as land ownership before you started law school. It is *not absolute* in the sense that nobody can restrict the owner's use, possession, or alienability of the estate. The state can and does impose such restrictions for perceived public objectives. The question of when such restrictions amount to a taking of the estate is considered in Chapter 11. People (including professors) often speak of a "fee simple" as a shorthand form of the fee simple absolute. But because there are defeasible forms of fee simple, be precise and speak of a fee simple absolute.

1. Creation of the fee simple absolute.

    a. Common law: At common law, the fee simple absolute was created by a grant *"to A and his heirs."* The words to A are *"words of purchase"* — words describing the person or persons who are the takers of the fee simple absolute. The words *"and his heirs"* are *words of limitation* — words *limiting the duration of the estate.* In the early common law, "to A and his heirs'' meant that A was granted an estate that was *capable* of inheritance and, therefore, of *potentially infinite duration.* It did *not* mean that A's heirs (who would not be known because A, being alive, had no heirs) had an interest in the estate.

    Example: In Elizabethan England, if O granted Blackacre to "A and her heirs," a fee simple absolute in A was created. The heirs apparent of A had no interest. If, instead, O granted Blackacre to "the heirs of A," no fee simple absolute was created in Elizabeth I's era. Because no words of limitation were used in the second grant, the "heirs of A" would acquire a life estate — a freehold estate that ends with the life (or lives) of the heirs of A. Of course, until A dies, the "heirs of A" — the takers of the interest created — are unknown. A contingent future interest is created in a set of unknown people — the "heirs of A."

    The words of limitation — *"and her heirs"* — simply meant that because the estate could be inherited, the estate could endure forever. The words *"to A and his heirs"* **created** a perpetual estate, presently held by A. That is a fee simple absolute. Of course, A will not live forever, but his fee simple absolute can endure forever. During A's life, A might convey it to someone else and, if not, after A's death his fee simple absolute will be held by his *devisees* under his *will* or, in the absence of a will, by his *heirs.* Old owners of fees simple absolute wither and die, but their fees simple absolute go on and on. If the grant did not include the words of limitation, only a life estate was created, even though the grantor's intentions might be clear.

Example: William Shakespeare, owner of Blackacre-on-Avon in fee simple absolute, conveys Blackacre-on-Avon in 1610 "to A for eternity." A does not have fee simple absolute. A has a life estate. If William Shakespeare wishes to convey his fee simple absolute to A — as his original conveyance plainly suggests — he must convey it "to A and his heirs."

b. Modern view: In every American jurisdiction today, it is not necessary to use the magic words of limitation — "and his heirs" — to create a fee simple absolute. Either by statutory change or judicial decision, the *usual rule* is that a grantor *conveys his entire estate unless the grant is to the contrary.*

Example: Will Shakespeare, an American contemporary descendant of the bard, owns Blackacre-on-the-Hudson in fee simple absolute. He conveys Blackacre "to A." Fee simple absolute in A is created. Because there is nothing to the contrary in the grant, Will is presumed to have conveyed his entire estate in Blackacre — fee simple absolute — to A.

C. Alienability and inheritance of the fee simple absolute: A fee simple absolute is freely alienable, devisable by will, or inheritable in intestacy (the state of dying without a will).

1. Alienation: An owner of fee simple absolute can convey the entire fee simple absolute to another person. If O conveys his fee simple absolute to A the fee simple absolute continues without interruption. It just has a new owner. An owner can also split his fee simple absolute into lesser estates, but the sum of the estates will add up to a fee simple absolute.

Example: Blackacre is owned by O in fee simple absolute. O conveys Blackacre "to A for her life." By this transaction, O has split his fee simple absolute into two parts: a *life estate* in A and a *reversion,* an estate retained by O. The reversion is a *future interest,* a presently existing estate that entitles its holder, O, to future possession (when A dies and her life estate expires). The sum of the two parts adds up to fee simple absolute. If O later conveys his reversion to A, the reversion and the life estate will be *merged,* and their sum is fee simple absolute in A.

2. Devise: In England, an estate in land could not be devised (transferred by will) until the Statute of Wills in 1540. Until then, an estate could pass at death only to one's heirs. The difference is that one's heirs are prescribed by law (usually children, then the next closely related persons), and devisees can be anybody the testator specifies in his will. Today, an owner of fee simple absolute can send it under his will to whomever he pleases, or split it up into pieces that, when added together, equal fee simple absolute.

3. Inheritance: Lay persons (and many lawyers) often use the term *inheritance* to describe all testamentary transfers, but the strict meaning of the term is limited to transfers of property owned by a person dying *without a will.* This condition, called *intestacy,* is dealt with by statutes that specify the *heirs.* Strictly speaking, a person dying with a will does *not have heirs;* he has *devisees* (of his real property) and *legatees* (of his personal property). Only a person dying intestate has heirs. At early common law, the heirs were the decedent's *issue,* and the rule of *primogeniture* applied: Estates in land went to the decedent's first-born son; daughters inherited only in the absence of sons. The usual statutory scheme today sets aside some portion of the decedent's property for the surviving spouse, and distributes the remainder to the decedent's children. In the absence of a spouse or children, the decedent's parents are heirs. If the decedent leaves no surviving children, spouse, or parents, the heirs are his ***collateral kin*** — brothers, sisters, nieces, nephews, aunts, uncles, and cousins. At some point, these people become so remotely related they are not treated as heirs. If an intestate decedent has ***absolutely no heirs,*** the decedent's property will ***escheat*** to the state.

III. FEE TAIL

A. Introduction: The fee tail is virtually extinct, but its vestigial implications continue to pop up like an unexpected and unwanted guest. Fee tail problems mostly occur, if at all, in connection with the various modern methods of destroying this estate.

B. Origin and operation of the fee tail: Prior to 1285, a conveyance to "A and the heirs of his body" was interpreted by English courts to create a *fee simple conditional,* which meant that A, the estate holder, was empowered to convey fee simple absolute if and when he should sire a child. In 1285, Parliament enacted Statute de Donis, which created the *fee tail,* the purpose of which was to permit the landed nobility to keep their power over land centralized in their families. Statute de Donis accomplished this by creating an estate, the fee tail, that automatically passed from one generation to the next, expiring only when the lineal bloodline ran out. Upon expiration, the estate reverted to the original grantor and through inheritance or devise (because the grantor would then very likely be an ancient skeleton) to the grantor's presently living remote heirs or devisees. The magic words necessary to create a fee tail were "to A *and the heirs of his body*" — meaning his lineal descendants.

Example: O conveys Blackacre "to A and the heirs of his body." A has a fee tail in Blackacre. If A conveys Blackacre "to B and his heirs," B does not have a fee simple absolute. Rather, B has possession of Blackacre only until A's death, at which point A1, A's son, gets possession and the fee tail.

Because a fee tail might expire — the lineal bloodline might die out — every fee tail was followed by either a ***reversion*** in the grantor or a ***remainder*** in a third party. These future interests (reversion or remainder) become possessory estates when the lineal bloodline of the fee tail holder runs out.

C. Elimination of the fee tail: In the United States today, the fee tail has been largely abolished by statute. An attempt to create a fee tail will result in one of the following: (1) a fee tail that can be ended by a simple conveyance, (2) a fee simple absolute, (3) a fee simple subject to an executory limitation, (4) a life estate followed by a remainder in the issue of the life tenant, or (5) a fee simple conditional. Each is discussed below.

1. Fee tail and disentailing conveyance: Four states permit creation of the common law fee tail, but all provide that the fee tail is destroyed by a ***disentailing conveyance*** — an ordinary conveyance of fee simple absolute. This is an exception to the usual rule that a grantor cannot convey more than he owns.

Example: Harold conveys Blackacre to William and the heirs of his body. William has a fee tail. William conveys Blackacre to George and his heirs. George has fee simple absolute. If William wants to keep possession of Blackacre but wishes to own it in fee simple absolute, he must use a ***straw conveyance.*** William would convey Blackacre to his lawyer in fee simple absolute, and the lawyer would immediately reconvey it to William, thus giving William both possession of, and a fee simple absolute in, Blackacre.

2. **Statutory conversion to fee simple absolute:** Many states have, by statute or state constitutional provision, converted the fee tail into a fee simple absolute. Some state statutes declare that an estate that at common law would have been a fee tail is a fee simple. If the creator of the purported fee tail owned fee simple absolute, the grantee would also own fee simple absolute. Other states declare that the fee tail shall not be recognized and that a purported fee tail is a nullity. See, e.g., Texas Const. Art. 1, §26. These states then apply the presumption that a grantor intends to convey the largest estate he owns. Thus, if a grantor owns a fee simple absolute and purports to create a fee tail, he conveys fee simple absolute.

   Example: Bill owns Blackacre in fee simple absolute and conveys it to June and the heirs of her body. June has fee simple absolute, either because a state statute converts the purported fee tail to fee simple absolute or because the purported fee tail is a nullity, and the presumption that Bill intended to convey his entire interest will send his fee simple absolute to June.

3. **Statutory conversion to fee simple subject to executory limitation:** Some states provide that an attempt to create a fee tail will create a fee simple in the first taker under the grant, but if the purported fee tail contains a *remainder,* the purported remainder will be given effect *if and only if* the *first taker dies without surviving issue.* See, e.g., Cal. Civ. Code §§763-764. This statutory method of eliminating a fee tail creates in the first taker a *fee simple subject to an executory limitation.* An executory limitation, or *executory interest,* is a future interest in a transferee from the grantor that becomes possessory by either cutting off another transferee's estate or cutting off the grantor's estate at some future time. See Chapter 3.

   Example: Fred, owner of Blackacre in fee simple absolute, conveys Blackacre to "Emma and the heirs of her body, then to Jane and her heirs." At common law, Emma would have a fee tail, and Jane would have a remainder (which would become possessory when Emma's bloodline expires — indefinite or general failure of issue). But under this statutory scheme, Emma receives a fee simple subject to an executory limitation — the executory interest in Jane. If Emma is survived by Caleb, her son, Emma's successors in interest will own Blackacre in fee simple absolute. Jane will get nothing; her executory interest will lapse or expire. If Emma dies without surviving issue — definite failure of issue — Jane's executory interest will become possessory, and she will own Blackacre in fee simple absolute. Jane's interest is an executory interest because she is a transferee from Fred, and her interest becomes possessory (if at all) by cutting off the fee simple held by Emma. Emma's fee simple doesn't die with her; it either becomes absolute (if she is survived by Caleb) or shifts over to Jane (if Emma dies without surviving issue) and becomes absolute in Jane.

4. **Life estate and remainder in life tenant's issue:** A few states essentially permit a fee tail to persist for one generation, and then convert it into a fee simple absolute. They do this by treating the first holder of the purported fee tail as the owner of a life estate, and recognizing a remainder interest in the issue of the life tenant.

   Example: David conveys Blackacre to Alice and the heirs of her body. Alice has a life estate. Her issue owns a remainder in fee simple absolute. But this remainder is contingent upon Alice having issue. If Alice has a child, Mary, upon Alice's death Mary will own Blackacre in fee simple absolute. If Alice dies childless, the contingent remainder in Alice's issue will fail and David's reversion will become possessory. David or his successors will own Blackacre in fee simple absolute. See, e.g., *Morris v. Albright,* 558 S.W.2d 660 (Mo. 1977).

5. **Fee simple conditional created:** South Carolina and Iowa treat an attempted fee tail as creating a fee simple conditional. These states do not recognize Statute de Donis as part of the common law received from England. The holder of a fee simple conditional has a life estate, but if a child is born to the holder, she may convey fee simple absolute.

   Example: Ernie conveys Blackacre to Susanna "and the heirs of her body." Susanna has a fee simple conditional, and Ernie retains a reversion. If Susanna never has a child, her estate will expire on her death, and Ernie's reversion will become possessory, creating a fee simple absolute in Ernie (or his successor to the reversion). But if Susanna gives birth to Bert, Susanna now has the power to convey a fee simple absolute (destroying Ernie's reversion), but she must make the conveyance in order to create the fee simple absolute.

6. **A modern equivalent of the fee tail:** Despite the virtual elimination of the fee tail, it is possible for a person to create its equivalent in jurisdictions that have abolished the fee tail but that have also abolished the Rule Against Perpetuities. (See Chapter 3.V.E.) The complex Rule Against Perpetuities was designed to destroy interests when uncertainty as to their ownership is prolonged too far into the future. Where the Rule Against Perpetuities does not exist, a grantor may create an interest in all the future issue of the grantee, and that interest will be valid, thus mimicking the fee tail.

   Example: Edmund conveys Blackacre to "Sally for life, then to Sally's issue from time to time living forever." Sally has a life estate, and her issue — children, grandchildren, and further descendants until her bloodline expires — have a contingent remainder. (See Chapter 3.III.A.) The Rule Against Perpetuities would destroy this remainder because the uncertainty of its ownership is prolonged too long — the identity of all of Sally's issue living from time to time may continue to be unresolved centuries from now, but, in its absence, this contingent remainder is valid. Over time, of course, the remainder will be split into smaller and smaller fractions, a problem addressed in Chapter 4. The feudal fee tail avoided this problem by uniting the fee tail with primogeniture.

IV. LIFE ESTATES

A. **The nature of a life estate:** A life estate is, as its name implies, a possessory estate that expires upon the death of a specified person. Usually, the life estate expires upon the death of the life estate holder.

   Example: John, owner of Blackacre in fee simple absolute, grants Blackacre "to Bonnie for life." Bonnie has a life estate that expires on her death. John has a reversion, which will become possessory upon Bonnie's death.

   A life estate is always followed by some future interest — either a *reversion* in the grantor or a *remainder* in a third party. A reversion may only be created in a grantor. A remainder may only be created in a transferee.

   Example: Liz owns Blackacre in fee simple absolute. She conveys Blackacre "to Guy for life." Liz has retained a reversion. If Liz conveyed Blackacre "to Guy for life, then to John and his heirs," Liz would no longer have any interest in Blackacre. Guy would own a life estate, and John would own a remainder.

1. **Life estate *pur autre vie*:** When the duration of a life estate is measured by the life of a person other than the estate holder, it is a ***life estate* pur autre vie** — for the life of another.

   Example: Alison, owner of Tribune Lodge in fee simple absolute, conveys it to Gordon for life. If Gordon then conveys his life estate to Eric, Eric will own a life estate ***measured by Gordon's life*** — a life estate **pur autre vie.** Similarly, if Alison had granted Tribune Lodge to Gordon for "the life of Vincent," Gordon would own a life estate *pur autre vie* — lasting as long as Vincent remains alive.

2. **Defeasible life estates:** Life estates may be defeasible, and the same rules apply to defeasible life estates as to defeasible fees. (See section V of this chapter.)

   Example: Lady Catherine grants Rosings Park "to Rev. Collins for life, so long as he never preaches a sermon." Collins has a determinable life estate, and Lady Catherine has both a possibility of reverter (which will become possessory if Collins preaches a sermon) and a reversion (which will become possessory on Collins's death if he refrains from ever preaching a sermon).

   Example: Lady Catherine grants Rosings Park "to Rev. Collins for life, but if he ever preaches a sermon, Lady Catherine retains the right to enter and retake possession." Collins has a life estate subject to condition subsequent, and Lady Catherine has both a right of entry and a reversion.

   Example: Mrs. Blackett grants Beckfoot to Nancy for life, but if she ever commits an act of piracy, Beckfoot goes to Peggy. Nancy has a life estate subject to an executory limitation in favor of Peggy.

3. **Life estates in a group or class of people:** A life estate may be created in a group of people. The problem with such class interests is that some of the life tenants will die before others, and there is some uncertainty whether the surviving life tenants take the deceased life tenant's share or whether the remainderman or reversion holder is entitled to possession.

   Example: Suppose Elizabeth Taylor were to convey her royalty interest in the film "National Velvet" to "all of my former husbands for their lives, and then to the ASPCA." Assume there are six former husbands, and Eddie, one of them, dies. Most courts rule that Eddie's life interest is absorbed by the remaining five life tenants, rather than permitting the ASPCA to take Eddie's interest. The ASPCA's remainder would not become possessory until all of the former husbands are dead. But if the original grant specified the opposite outcome — "to all of my former husbands for their lives, and upon the death of each one, to the ASPCA" — the ASPCA would be entitled to possession of Eddie's share upon Eddie's death.

4. **Ambiguous grants:** One recurring problem is the ambiguous grant. Courts try to follow the *grantor's intent,* but that is itself often indeterminate. Other factors are often relied upon to decide whether a life estate or some other interest is created.

   ★**Example:** Jessie Lide's handwritten will stated: "I wish Evelyn White to have my home to live in and not to be sold." The Tennessee Supreme Court relied on three Tennessee statutes to presume that Jessie meant to give Evelyn a fee simple absolute, there being no "clear evidence" to the contrary. One statute stated a common presumption that every grant or devise of real estate shall pass the entire interest of the grantor or testator unless there is clear evidence to the contrary. The second statute stated a presumption that a will conveys the entire interest of the testator in the testator's real property unless there is a contrary intention in the will. The third statute created a presumption against partial intestacy, which is what would happen if Jessie Lide's will were read as creating a life estate in Evelyn White, because Lide did not devise the remainder that would then exist; such remainder would pass to her heirs in intestacy. The court treated the "no sale" restriction as an invalid attempt to restrain alienation of a fee simple absolute rather than clear evidence of a life estate. *White v. Brown,* 559 S.W.2d 938 (Tenn. 1977).

★**Example:** Father devises Hollyhock Farm "to Son, so long as he refrains from imbibing any intoxicating liquors." Courts split on whether this creates a fee simple determinable or a determinable life estate. Most courts hold that a fee simple determinable is created, on the theory that Father intended to pass his entire estate save for the limitation. See, e.g. *Lewis v. Searles,* 452 S.W.2d 153 (Mo. 1970) (construing a grant "to Hattie so long as she remains single and unmarried" to be a fee simple determinable). The theory of a determinable life estate is that, because the condition can only be satisfied or broken during Son's life, Father must have intended to give him only a life estate. The problem with this is that it is equally probable (if not more so) that Father hoped the prospect of a fee simple absolute in Son's heirs, devisees, or assigns would be an incentive to Son to stay sober.

5. **Transferability and valuation:** A life estate is freely alienable during life, but the transferee receives the transferor's life estate. The market value of a life estate is thus a fraction of the value of a fee simple absolute. The fraction is determined by multiplying the life expectancy (in years) of the person whose life measures the duration of the estate by the annual value of possession and discounting the product to reflect the fact that payment must be made now to receive value over time.

Example: If the market value of fee simple absolute in Runymede is $100,000, and the life tenant has a life expectancy of five years, the value of the life estate can be computed by determining the annual value of possession (say, 5 percent of $100,000, or $5,000) and multiplying that annual value for the remaining expected duration of the life estate ($5,000 · 5 = $25,000). But that product overstates the "present" value of the life estate — its value today — because the receipt of $5,000 every year for the next 5 years is worth less than $25,000 today. If the $25,000 were invested at 6 percent, compounded annually, it would be worth about $32,400 in 5 years. By inverse reckoning, the right to receive $5,000 per year for the next 5 years (the value of the life estate) is about $21,000.

This valuation procedure is also used whenever a life estate and the remainder are sold in a single package — fee simple absolute — and the sale proceeds must be divided between the life tenant and the remainderman.

Example: In the prior example, if Runymede were sold for $100,000, 21 percent of that sum ($21,000) would go to the life tenant, and 89 percent ($89,000) to the remainderman. The percentages would be more or less reversed if the life tenant had a long life expectancy instead of only 5 years.

This is not always as simple as it seems. Sometimes the life tenant (the owner of the life estate) and the remaindermen disagree about life expectancy and the rate of appreciation of the value of the combined fee simple absolute. When this happens, it is not easy to reach agreement between the life tenant and remaindermen in order to sell a fee simple absolute.

★**Example:** John Weedon devised Oakland Farm to his widow, Anna Plaxico, for life and then to John's grandchildren by a prior marriage. The elderly Anna lived on the farm, which was rising in value because it was in the path of urban development, but earned only about $1,300 annually from farm rents. She wanted to sell the farm and invest the proceeds to increase her income, but the remaindermen were unwilling to do so because they thought that the value of the farm was increasing rapidly and that Anna's life expectancy was shorter than it turned out to be. (She lived for 24 years after the decision in the case.) *Baker v. Weedon,* 262 So.2d. 641 (Miss. 1972). The issue of whether the remaindermen could be forced to join with Anna in selling the farm is discussed in section IV.B.1, below.

B. **The modern life estate:** The *equitable* life estate is a common and important modem estate, but the *legal* life estate is uncommon and a bad idea. An equitable life estate is a property interest, owned for life, in the assets of a trust. A legal life estate is an estate for life in the assets themselves.

Example: Arnie devises Deer Park "to my brother Jack, as trustee, to hold for the benefit of my wife, Elka, for life, then to Lucia and Paul, outright and free of trust." Jack, the *trustee,* has *legal title* to Deer Park in fee simple absolute. Elka, a *beneficiary,* has an *equitable life estate,* and Lucia and Paul, also beneficiaries of the trust, concurrently own a remainder. If Arnie had left Deer Park "to Elka for life, then to Lucia and Paul in fee simple absolute," Elka would have a *legal life estate,* and Lucia and Paul would own the remainder.

A trustee has fiduciary duties to the equitable owners of the trust but, within the limits of those duties, is free to convey the assets in exchange for other assets in order to benefit the equitable owners.

Example: Refer to the prior example. If Elka moves from Deer Park to Palm Beach, making Deer Park useless to her, Jack has power to sell Deer Park and add the proceeds of sale to the trust corpus. A purchaser of Deer Park will receive a fee simple absolute in Deer Park. By contrast, the owner of a legal life estate can only convey her life estate, which may not be very marketable. A purchaser will likely want a fee simple absolute, and that can only be delivered by conveying both the life estate and the remainder (or reversion). If Elka had a legal life estate in Deer Park, she would need the consent of *every remainderman* to convey fee simple absolute in Deer Park. Suppose Paul thinks it is a bad idea for his mother, age 80, to move to Palm Beach. His refusal to sell his remainder would effectively frustrate Elka's plan to substitute Palm Beach for Deer Park because nobody would pay very much for Elka's life estate alone, or even for the combination of Elka's life estate and Lucia's remainder.

Much more flexibility is possible with the equitable life estate than the legal life estate.

Example: Arnie could have made Elka both trustee and holder of an equitable life estate. She could then sell Deer Park as trustee (without having to convince her brother-in-law, Jack, to do so) and use the proceeds to purchase Palm Beach.

1. **Judicial responses to inflexibility of the legal life estate:** There are two principal devices courts use (sparingly) to avoid the effects of the legal life estate.

   a. **Construction:** Courts try to implement the grantor's intent, but if a grant is sufficiently ambiguous, they may interpret it to create a more flexible estate, such as a fee simple absolute.

   b. **Judicial sale:** Courts sometimes order the sale of the life estate and the remainder and either divide the sale proceeds between the life tenant and the remainderman or order the sale proceeds held in trust with the income payable to the life tenant and the trust corpus preserved for the remainderman. This is rarely done. The life tenant and the remainderman can always agree to sell their interests as a package. If they fail to agree, courts are reluctant to impose agreement. Even so, there are two situations where courts might order sale.

  i. **Equitable necessity:** Where it can be proved that *sale is in the best interests of* **all parties** and is the only practical method to effectuate the grantor's intention to provide material comfort for the life tenant and preservation of asset value for the remainderman, a court may invoke its equity powers and order sale of all or part of the property.

  ★**Example:** John Weedon devised Oakland Farm to his wife, Anna, for life, remainder to his grandchildren. Over time, Oakland Farm became valuable for development but produced almost no income to the elderly and impoverished Anna. Anna and the remaindermen could not agree on sale. The Mississippi Supreme Court ruled that sale of *all* of Oakland Farm would not be in the best interest of *all* the parties, but that enough of the property could be sold to provide for Anna's "reasonable needs." But "equity does not warrant . . . sale of all the property since this would unjustly impinge upon the vested rights of the remaindermen" to receive Oakland Farm itself. *Baker v. Weedon,* 262 So. 2d 641 (Miss. 1972). Note that this Solomonic judgment required the trial court to engage in the speculative task of determining Anna's "reasonable needs." How much is enough? Everybody has a different answer.

  Courts may also order sale when the remaindermen are incompetent (e.g., minors, insane) but only when sale is in the best interests of the parties.

  ii. **Waste avoidance:** Courts may also order sale when it is necessary to avoid *waste* — the deterioration or destruction or the underlying property. Again, the idea is that it is in the best interest of all parties to sell the asset before its value is dissipated or destroyed. See, e.g., *Kelly v. Neville,* 136 Miss. 429 (1924).

 2. **Legal life estates in personal property:** While the equitable life estate in personal property — a life interest in the assets of a trust that owns stocks and bonds — a legal life interest in personal property is problematic. Personal property is highly mobile and easily sold. The doctrine of waste is inadequate because the life tenant may sell the asset, spend the proceeds, and be unable to honor a judgment based on waste. By statute, some states convert the owner of a legal life estate in personal property into a trustee. Others subject the legal life tenant to court supervision or require the legal life tenant to post security to ensure against malfeasance.

C. **Waste:** Inherent in a life estate is the idea that the life tenant gets to *use* property for life, thus deriving the economic value of possession (e.g., rents, farm income). This use must be consistent with the fact that the property will be handed over to the remainderman on the life tenant's death. *Waste* is the term used to describe actions of the life tenant that *permanently impair* the property's value or the interest of the future interest holders. Older cases tend to conceptualize waste as derived from the grantor's desire to give the life tenant reasonable use of the land, consistent with its preservation in the same character as when received. Newer cases tend to regard waste as a device to prevent one person from unfairly reaping economic benefits from land possession and imposing economic losses on another person who shares an interest in the land. Waste may be categorized as follows.

 1. **Affirmative waste:** When a life tenant acts affirmatively to damage land permanently, the life tenant has voluntarily committed waste. This is sometimes called *voluntary waste.*

Example: Erma, life tenant in Woodacre, burns the barn, cuts down all the standing mature timber, and removes a large deposit of gravel from Woodacre. Each of these acts constitutes affirmative waste.

2. **Permissive waste:** When a life tenant fails to act reasonably to protect deterioration of the land, *permissive* or *involuntary waste* has occurred.

Example: Ivan, life tenant in Homestead, fails to repair a chronic leaking roof and fails to pay the property taxes on Homestead. Each omission is unreasonable and constitutes permissive waste. See, e.g., *Kimbrough v. Reed,* 130 Idaho 512 (1997)(failure to repair); *McIntyre v. Scarbrough,* 266 Ga. 824 (1996)(failure to pay taxes).

The question of which omissions are unreasonable is dependent on the particular circumstances. The life tenant must "exercise the ordinary care of a prudent man for the preservation and protection" of the property.

3. **Ameliorative waste:** When the life tenant acts affirmatively to change the principal use of the land, and thereby *increases the value* of the land, *ameliorative waste* has occurred. Ameliorative waste is actionable, however, only when it is clear that (1) the grantor intended for there to be no change in use, and (2) the property may still reasonably be used in the fashion the grantor intended.

Example: Adam, owner of Waterside, builds an elaborate complex of tanks, ponds, and buildings comprising a profitable fish farm and hatchery. He devises Waterside "to my son, Abel, for life, then to the University of Eden for use as a fish hatchery and marine biology research facility." Waterside is well suited to these piscine purposes. Abel replaces the fish farm and hatchery complex with a factory, which doubles the value of Waterside. Abel has committed ameliorative waste. It is actionable by the remainderman, University of Eden, because Adam made it clear that he intended Waterside to be preserved as a fish hatchery, and Waterside may still reasonably be used for that purpose.

If the grantor makes clear that he does not intend for the property to be preserved in its original use, ameliorative waste is not actionable.

Example: Suppose Adam had devised Waterside "to my son Abel for life, in order to provide Abel with an opportunity to use Waterside to maximize income, and then to my alma mater, University of Eden." Abel's ameliorative waste would not be actionable, because it is clear that Abel didn't care about preserving its original character.

If the grantor intends that the property be preserved in its original character, but it may no longer reasonably be used in that fashion, ameliorative waste is not actionable.

Example: Otto, founder of a brewery, devises his residence (adjacent to the brewery) to his son, Wilhelm, for life, remainder to his grandchildren. Time passes, and the residence becomes isolated in a sea of industrial facilities. Wilhelm destroys the residence to incorporate the site into the brewery, thereby making the residence site much more valuable. This ameliorative waste is not actionable, because the *changed conditions* render continued use as a residence unreasonable. See *Melms v. Pabst Brewing Co.,* 104 Wis. 7 (1899).

If the grantor fails to specify his intentions, even though ameliorative waste may not support an injunction, damages equal to the value of the destroyed asset may be given.

★**Example:** George Wood devised his interest in the family home to his wife, Catherine, for life, and then to his daughter Patricia Woodrick. The property contained a dilapidated barn, which Catherine proposed to raze. Woodrick objected and claimed that this would constitute waste. Removal of the barn, valued at $3,200, would increase the total value of the property. Because the value of the property would be enhanced rather than diminished, Woodrick's request for an injunction was denied, but she was awarded the value of the barn, $3,200. *Woodrick v. Wood*, 1994 Ohio App. Lexis 2258.

V. DEFEASIBLE FEES

A. **Introduction:** Any estate may be made *defeasible* — subject to termination — upon the happening of some future event. This section considers defeasible fees simple, but the principles discussed here may be used in connection with other estates. The distinction between a fee simple *absolute* and a *defeasible* fee simple is that *no future event can terminate or divest a fee simple absolute,* while a *defeasible* fee simple is *subject to termination or divestment upon the occurrence of a future event.* Of course, the future event may never happen, in which case a defeasible fee endures as long as a fee simple absolute, but all the while the threat of termination hangs, like the sword of Damocles, over the defeasible fee. There are three types of defeasible fees simple: (1) the *fee simple determinable,* (2) the *fee simple subject to condition subsequent,* and (3) the *fee simple subject to an executory limitation.* The fundamental difference between the first two is that the fee simple determinable *terminates automatically* upon the occurrence of the future event, and the fee simple subject to condition subsequent *terminates only when proper action is taken to terminate the estate* following the occurrence of the future event. The fundamental difference between the fee simple subject to an executory limitation and either of the first two types of defeasible fees is that the future interest that cuts short the fee simple subject to an executory limitation is held by a third party (neither the grantor of the interest nor the holder of the fee), while the future interest that cuts short either the fee simple determinable or the fee simple subject to condition subsequent is vested (at least when it is created) in the grantor.

B. **Fee simple determinable:** A fee simple determinable is created when the grantor intends to grant a fee simple *only until a specified future event happens* and uses language in the grant that manifests that intent.

Example: Rick, owner of Blackacre in fee simple absolute, conveys Blackacre "to the Town Library Association for only so long a time as Blackacre is used as a free lending library." Rick has created a fee simple determinable in the Town Library Association. His intent and the words of his grant are clear: Town Library's estate will last only until the moment Blackacre ceases to be used as a free lending library. If the grant had merely said, "to the Town Library Association for the purpose of use as a free lending library," a fee simple determinable *would not* have been created. The Town Library Association would have had a fee simple absolute. Mere expressions of purpose are legally inconsequential surplusage.

Because a fee simple determinable is less than a fee simple absolute, a grantor of a determinable fee (who owned a fee simple absolute before the grant) necessarily retains an interest. That retained interest is called a *possibility of reverter.* Note: The retained interest is *not* a reversion, and it is *not* a reverter; it is a *possibility of reverter.*

Example: In the prior example, Rick would retain a possibility of reverter in Blackacre. Rick did not have to expressly mention its creation, because it was created by operation of law — the fact that he conveyed a fee simple determinable, an estate of less duration than his fee absolute, means that he did not convey his entire interest. Once the possessory estate Rick conveyed terminates, the interest Rick retained must become possessory, and that interest will be a fee simple absolute. Put another way, Rick has divided his fee simple absolute into a presently possessory estate (called a *fee simple determinable*) and a future interest (called a *possibility of reverter*), and the two pieces added together equal his original fee simple absolute. The arithmetic of estates is simple but inexorable. Of course, in the grant, Rick could expressly retain his possibility of reverter, but he does not need to do so in order to create one.

1. **Words evidencing intent to create fee simple determinable:** Some "magic words" still matter when courts decide whether or not a fee simple determinable has been created. Usages like *so long as, until, during,* or *while* are indicative of a grant for a limited duration, and thus are likely to be construed as creating a fee simple determinable. This conclusion will be bolstered if the grantor also expressly retains a possibility of reverter or uses other words indicating an intention to create an automatic return of possession in fee simple absolute.

   ★**Example:** Tom, owner of Blackacre in fee simple absolute, conveys Blackacre "to Swank Yacht Club only for so long as Blackacre is used as the SYC clubhouse and, if not so used, the estate granted hereby shall automatically terminate, and all right, title, and interest in Blackacre shall revert to grantor." A grant for a limited duration is clear, and the nature of the grant is equally clear, even though Tom never described the granted estate as a fee simple determinable or the retained interest as a possibility of reverter. See, e.g., *Mahrenholz v. County Board of School Trustees,* 93 Ill. App. 3d 366 (1981).

2. **Transferability:** A fee simple determinable is a freely transferable estate, but the nature of the estate stays the same. The transferee takes the estate subject to the limitation that makes it defeasible.

3. **Abolished in some states:** At least two states, California and Kentucky, have abolished the fee simple determinable. An estate that would be a fee simple determinable is, instead, a fee simple subject to condition subsequent.

C. **Fee simple subject to condition subsequent:** A fee simple subject to condition subsequent is created when the words of a grant support the conclusion that the grantor intends to convey a fee simple "absolute," but has attached a string to the grant so that if a specified future event happens (the *condition subsequent* to the grant), the grantor may pull the string and get his fee simple absolute back. Conceptually, the grantor has conveyed his fee simple forever but has added (almost as an afterthought) a condition that will enable him to get it back. By contrast, the theory of the fee simple determinable is that the grantor has conveyed his fee simple only for a limited period. It is somewhat like the difference between a loan of your computer to a friend for a week (analogous to a fee simple determinable) and a gift to your friend of your computer, but if she ever plays computer games on it, you have the right to take it back (analogous to a fee simple subject to condition subsequent).

Example: Orville, owner of Blackacre in fee simple absolute, conveys Blackacre "to Battered Women's Shelter; provided, however, that if Blackacre should ever be used for any purpose other than sheltering abused women, grantor may enter and retake possession of and title to Blackacre." Orville has indicated an intent to part with his entire estate in Blackacre ("to Battered Women's Shelter"). By itself, that would give BWS a fee simple absolute. But Orville added a proviso ("if Blackacre should ever be used . . .") and appended to that proviso a retained power ("grantor may enter and retake possession of and title to Blackacre") that is utterly inconsistent with the preliminary conclusion that Orville conveyed a fee simple absolute. Orville has conveyed a fee simple subject to condition subsequent.

As with the fee simple determinable, because the grantor has parted with less than a fee simple absolute, the grantor necessarily retains an interest. The interest retained by the grantor when a fee simple subject to condition subsequent is created is called a *right of entry* or *power of termination.* Unlike the possibility of reverter, which automatically becomes a possessory interest upon occurrence of the future event, a holder of a right of entry (power of termination) must *actually exercise the power to terminate* the fee simple subject to condition subsequent in order for that defeasible fee to come to an end. The holder of a right of entry has the *option to terminate* the fee simple subject to condition subsequent.

Example: In the last example, if the Battered Women's Shelter started to use Blackacre as an amusement park instead of a shelter for abused women, the condition subsequent would have occurred. But the Shelter's estate in Blackacre would not end *until and unless* Orville takes affirmative action to retake possession and thus terminate the Shelter's estate.

1. **Words evidencing intent to create fee simple subject to condition subsequent:** If the words used in the grant indicate an intention to convey the grantor's entire estate, coupled with a conditional right to take it back, courts will construe the grant as creating a fee simple subject to condition subsequent. Phrases suggesting this intent include *provided, however, but if,* and *on condition that.* The key is whether the grant evidences intent to pass title completely, save only for a right to take it back.

2. **Action necessary to assert right of entry:** To exercise a right of entry, the holder must take substantial steps to recover possession and title. The holder of a right of entry need not actually physically enter and retake possession, but must do more than merely proclaim his intention to retake possession. Filing suit to recover possession is surely good enough. A letter demanding possession is debatable; whether it is enough to constitute exercise of the right of entry may depend on other added facts.

   Example: Bruce conveys fee simple in Blackacre to Ian, subject to the condition subsequent that "no hunting shall ever occur on Blackacre." Bruce writes Ian as follows: "I hear you have been shooting deer on Blackacre. If true, this is to let you know I hereby exercise my right of entry." If Bruce does nothing further for five years, this is probably not enough to constitute exercise of the right of entry. But if Bruce follows up that letter with an investigation that proves conclusively that Ian had shot 40 deer on Blackacre, turns over these facts to the relevant government authorities, posts signs at the edge of Blackacre stating, "No Hunting," signed "Bruce, Owner," and retains a lawyer to advise him, his efforts probably amount to exercise of the right of entry.

3. **Transferability:** Like the fee simple determinable, the fee simple subject to condition subsequent is freely transferable during life, is inheritable, and may be devised by will. Of course, once the limiting condition has occurred, and the right of entry exercised, there is no estate left to be transferred.

4. **Preference for fee simple subject to condition subsequent:** It is often difficult to determine which defeasible fee has been created. In ambiguous cases, courts prefer to find fee simple subject to condition subsequent. The reason for this preference is that fee simple determinable produces *automatic forfeiture* of title and possession, while the fee simple subject to condition

subsequent makes *forfeiture an option* of the holder of the right of entry. In general, courts try to avoid forfeiture of title because it is harsh, depriving a fee holder of the considerable reliance interest she has developed by possession of the land.

Example: Simon, owner of fee simple absolute in Blackacre, conveys Blackacre "to Alicia and her heirs so long as Blackacre is left forever wild, but if it is not, then grantor has the right to enter and retake possession and title." This confused grant suggests that the grantor intended to pass title for only a limited time ("so long as") but also indicates reservation of the future interest connected to a condition subsequent ("but if . . . then . . . right to enter and retake possession and title"). Most courts will resolve this mess in favor of the condition subsequent in order to avoid the harsh consequence of automatic forfeiture of Alicia's estate.

Sometimes courts will rely on extrinsic evidence — evidence wholly apart from the grant itself — to decide which defeasible fee has been created. This usually occurs where the consequences of automatic forfeiture are especially severe.

Example: Larry, who holds fee simple absolute in Blackacre, a large but idle wheat ranch, conveys it "to Lynn so long as within one year from today she places Blackacre into agricultural production and harvests a crop of wheat in an amount of not less than 50 bushels per acre." Lynn invests a very large sum to bring Blackacre back into cultivation (buying machinery, seed, and other tools of the farming trade; hiring people; making contractual commitments), and she is about to harvest her wheat crop ten months later when a freak hailstorm wipes out the crop. A sympathetic Larry writes Lynn that she has another year to fulfill the terms of the original deed. Larry then dies and his heir, Madeline, sues to eject Lynn, contending that Lynn owned fee simple determinable in Blackacre, that the limitation had occurred and, consequently, title had automatically reverted to Larry and descended to Madeline as Larry's heir. What result?

Although the grant seems clearly to create fee simple determinable, many courts will look to the extrinsic evidence (the freak hailstorm, Larry's extension of time, the substantial expenditures of Lynn) to conclude that Lynn had a fee simple subject to condition subsequent and that Larry, holding a right of entry, could and did waive his right for the extended period. Lynn may well prevail.

D. **Some consequences of classification of defeasible fees:** Classification of a defeasible estate as a fee simple determinable or as a fee simple subject to condition subsequent can have significant legal consequences. Some of these are introduced here.

1. **Transferability of the interest retained by the grantor:** At early common law, neither a possibility of reverter nor a right of entry could be alienated or devised. They could only be inherited. This was because they were not regarded as estates — a presently existing property right — but something more gossamer — a mere possibility. Today, most states permit a possibility of reverter and a right of entry to be alienated, devised, or inherited. But some states only permit possibilities of reverter to be freely transferable. And other states extinguish possibilities of reverter if the holder attempts to transfer them. See 2A Powell, *The Law of Real Property* ¶275[2]-275[3] (Rev. ed. 1992).

2. **Accrual of a cause of action for recovery of possession:** Because a possibility of reverter is automatic, once the limitation has occurred, the holder of the possibility of reverter has a right to possession. A cause of action accrues at that moment against the person in possession of the

property. The possessor, who used to occupy under a fee simple determinable, is now an adverse possessor. If suit is not instituted timely, a new title by adverse possession may result.

Example: Ron holds a possibility of reverter in Blackacre, and Caroline holds a fee simple determinable in Blackacre. In 1980, the limitation occurs. Ron does nothing about it until 1991, when he files suit to eject Caroline, who has remained continuously in possession. The state has a ten-year statute of limitations for actions to recover possession of real property. Assuming Caroline can prove the elements of her adverse possession, she now has fee simple absolute in Blackacre, via adverse possession.

But the cause of action for recovery of possession does not accrue the moment the limitation occurs if the title is fee simple subject to condition subsequent. Because the holder of the right of entry must take affirmative action to exercise the right of entry, the cause of action accrues when the right of entry is exercised.

Example: Refer to the last example. If Ron held a right of entry, and Caroline a fee simple subject to condition subsequent, Ron's cause of action for recovery of possession accrued in 1991, when he first took action to recover Blackacre, thus exercising his right of entry. Ron's suit would be timely, and Caroline would likely be ejected.

This stark difference in result has been softened somewhat by various doctrines. Some states apply the equitable doctrine of *laches* — undue delay in asserting one's rights — to bar the assertion of stale claims.

Example: Refer to the last example. Even though Ron's cause of action for recovery of possession accrued in 1991 (for purposes of the statute of limitations), a court applying the laches doctrine might well conclude that Ron's delay in exercising his right of entry was undue, producing inequitable consequences to Caroline. The equitable doctrine of laches — not the statute of limitations — might bar Ron's recovery of Blackacre.

Some states have statutorily or judicially altered their rules concerning accrual of causes of action to recover possession of real property to remove this anomaly. In such states, the cause of action would accrue the moment the limitation occurs, regardless of whether the retained future interest is a possibility of reverter or a right of entry.

3. **Effect under the Rule Against Perpetuities:** The Rule Against Perpetuities is a tricky doctrine designed to foster alienability and marketability of property. Under the rule, when uncertainty concerning ownership of a future interest persists too long the future interest will be destroyed. The details are best left for Chapter 3; however, a possibility of reverter and a right of entry are each exempt from the rule. But if the very same interest is created in a third party (not the grantor), and thus called an *executory interest,* it is subject to the rule and will most likely be invalid. Moreover, the consequences of a destroyed executory interest are quite different, depending on whether the void executory interest was akin to a possibility of reverter or a right of entry. In general, a void executory interest akin to a right of entry will leave the holder of the defeasible fee with a fee simple absolute, and a void executory interest akin to a possibility of reverter will leave the holder of the defeasible fee with a fee simple determinable and the original grantor (or his heirs) with a possibility of reverter.

4. **Mahrenholz: an illustration:** Many of the foregoing principles are illustrated by *Mahrenholz v. County Board of School Trustees,* 93 Ill. App. 3d 366 (1981). W.E. and Jennie Hutton had conveyed an acre or so of their farm to the school district under an ambiguous grant ("this land

to be used for school purpose only; otherwise to revert to Grantors''), and the school district built the Hutton School on the land. Later the Huttons conveyed their farm and whatever interest they had in the Hutton School land to the Jacqmains, who then conveyed the same interests to Mahrenholz. Under Illinois law, however, neither a possibility of reverter nor a right of entry may be conveyed during life or pass by will; such interests may only be inherited. Thus, in 1969, when Jennie Hutton, W.E. Hutton's widow, died, her interest in the Hutton School land was inherited by her son Harry Hutton. The school district stopped holding classes in the Hutton School in 1973 but used the building for storage. In 1977, Harry Hutton conveyed to Mahrenholz his interest in the Hutton School land. Mahrenholz then sought to quiet title to the Hutton School land in his name. If the original grant created a fee simple determinable in the school district and a possibility of reverter in the Huttons (which is what the court concluded, based on conflicting Illinois precedent), and if the cessation of classes in the Hutton School in 1973 terminated the fee simple determinable (an issue the court remanded to the trial court), then Harry owned a fee simple absolute in the Hutton School when he conveyed his interest in the Hutton School to Mahrenholz, and Mahrenholz should prevail. This is because a possibility of reverter *automatically becomes possessory* upon breach of the condition. But if the original grant had created a fee simple subject to condition subsequent in the school board, and a right of entry in the Huttons, and even if the ending of classes in the Hutton School was a breach of the condition, Harry would only have owned a right of entry in the Hutton School when he conveyed his interest to Mahrenholz (because Harry never took any action to reclaim possession of the Hutton School after breach by the school board), and under Illinois law, a right of entry cannot be conveyed, only inherited, so the school board should prevail. *Mahrenholz* vividly illustrates the fundamental difference between the fee simple determinable and the fee simple subject to condition subsequent: A fee simple determinable comes to an *automatic* end upon breach of the condition, while a fee simple subject to condition subsequent comes to an end *only when the holder of the right of entry asserts his right to recover possession.* Note that the Illinois rule preventing transfer of a possibility of reverter or right of entry by conveyance or will is not commonly followed in America today.

E. Some problems with defeasible fees: Among the issues presented by creation of the defeasible fees and their associated future interests are the following.

1. Invalid restraint on alienation? All defeasible fees restrict the use that may be made of the property. As discussed in section VI, below, restraints on alienation of property are disfavored because they inhibit economic efficiency and productivity; such restraints prevent resources from being reallocated by the market into the hands of a person who values them most highly and who will presumably make productive use of them. When does a use restriction embodied in a defeasible fee become so onerous that it amounts to an invalid restraint on alienation? The general answer is: when the use restriction materially affects marketability adversely.

★**Example:** Toscano gave to the Odd Fellows Lodge a lot adjacent to its existing building. By the deed, he restricted its use to the Odd Fellows Lodge only, and stipulated that in the event of a "sale or transfer" of the property or a failure by the Odd Fellows to use the property, title would revert to Toscano. In *Mountain Brow Lodge No. 82, Independent Order of Odd Fellows v. Toscano,* 257 Cal. App. 2d 22 (1968), a California appellate court voided the no-sale-or-transfer restriction as an invalid restraint on alienation but upheld the use restriction, on the theory that because Toscano meant to convey a determinable fee to the Odd Fellows rather than merely restrict alienability, the use restriction was valid. This is mechanical reasoning that fails to get at the real issues. Does the use restriction embodied in a defeasible fee materially inhibit marketability? Would invalidation of such use restrictions, thus converting defeasible fees into fees simple absolute, materially discourage charitable gifts? Do the social and economic benefits of the use restriction embodied in a defeasible fee outweigh the costs imposed by the restriction?

2. **Defeasible fee or covenant?** A use restriction might be seen as the limitation or condition in a defeasible fee (e.g., "so long as Blackacre is used for residential purposes only") or as a covenant enforceable by a suit seeking either damages for its breach or an injunction preventing violation of the promise. Creation and enforcement of use covenants — generically termed *servitudes* — is considered in detail in Chapter 6. Note here that if language is ambiguous, a court might interpret a use restriction imposed by a grantor as creating a servitude rather than a defeasible fee. The consequence of the difference is in the remedy for breach of the use restriction. If the restriction is a defeasible fee, the remedy is forfeiture — taking title away from the owner of the defeasible fee and sending it to the owner of the future interest; but if the restriction is a servitude, the remedy is either damages or an injunction, not loss of possession and ownership.

   Example: Suppose Toscano had conveyed his property "to the Mountain Brow No. 82 Lodge of the Odd Fellows on the stipulation that the property shall always be used for Lodge purposes." This "stipulation" might be read as surplusage, giving the Lodge a fee simple absolute, or as covenant — a promise made by Lodge by its acceptance of the deed — which might be enforceable by an injunction or damages, or as creating a defeasible fee. Which interpretation is best depends primarily on which result is most consistent with Toscano's intent and the policies applicable to creation and enforcement of such a use restriction. Don't overlook the varied interpretations that can be given to an ambiguous use restriction.

3. **Valuation of the defeasible fee and the associated future interest:** Placing a separate value on a defeasible fee and its associated future interest is harder than the analogous problem of valuing a life estate separately from its associated remainder. In the case of a life estate, the problem is confined by the fact that the estate will expire on someone's death (usually the life tenant), and we can use actuarial techniques to measure that probable life span. The condition that might terminate a defeasible fee is not so limited, and thus the valuation problem becomes vastly more complicated.

   ★**Example:** Harry Ink conveyed land to the city of Canton, Ohio, so long as it was used for a public park. The State of Ohio took most of the park by eminent domain to construct a highway, and a suit arose between the city of Canton and the Ink family, owners of Harry Ink's possibility of reverter, regarding how the condemnation proceeds should be divided. In ***Ink v. City of Canton***, 4 Ohio St. 2d 51 (1965), the Ohio Supreme Court ruled that the Ink family, as owners of the possibility of reverter in the condemned land, should receive that portion of the total proceeds that exceeded the value of the land *as a public park*. There are problems here. (1) How is a park to be valued? There is no exchange value; public parks are not bought and sold as public parks. There is a replacement value, but because land is unique, it is difficult to be sure what that value is. (2) Because the city did not voluntarily cease its park use, should the value of the possibility of reverter be discounted by the probability that the city would have violated the limitation voluntarily? The *Restatement of Property* says that unless violation is imminent or probable independent of eminent domain, condemnation proceeds should go entirely to the defeasible fee owner. (3) Because the city's determinable fee was a gift to it, would award of the entire proceeds to the city deter charitable giving and deliver a windfall to the city? The court did not consider whether Harry Ink's original objective — endowing Canton with a public park — might better be served by awarding the entire proceeds to the city, subject to an order to use them to acquire replacement park land and attaching the possibility of reverter to that substituted land. Note that the *Restatement* view does not apply when the government initiating condemnation is also the owner of the defeasible fee, because to do so would permit the owner of the defeasible fee to create unilaterally a fee simple absolute in itself without compensation. See *City of Palm Springs v. Living Desert Reserve,* 70 Cal. App. 4th 613 (1999).

F. Fee simple subject to executory limitation: A fee simple subject to executory limitation is a fee simple that is *divested,* or *shifted,* from one transferee to another transferee upon the occurrence of some future event. Both the fee simple determinable and the fee simple subject to condition subsequent involve the creation of a defeasible fee with a future interest retained by the grantor (either a possibility of reverter or right of entry). But the same defeasible fee estates can be created with the future interests transferred to a third party instead of retained by the grantor. When this happens, a fee simple subject to executory limitation is created. If a grantor uses the words necessary to create a fee simple determinable but, *instead of retaining the possibility of reverter the grantor transfers that interest to a third party,* the interest created in the third party is called an **executory interest,** and the interest created in the immediate transferee is a *fee simple subject to executory limitation.* If a grantor uses the words necessary to create a fee simple subject to condition subsequent but, *instead of retaining the corollary right of entry the grantor transfers that interest to a third party,* the interest created in the third party is called an **executory interest,** and the interest created in the immediate transferee is a *fee simple subject to executory limitation.* Prevailing doctrine says that a fee simple subject to executory limitation is *automatically divested* in favor of the executory interest, no matter whether the divesting condition is phrased in the form of a determinable fee or a fee simple subject to condition subsequent.

Example: Joe, owner of Blackacre in fee simple absolute, conveys Blackacre "to Emily and her heirs for so long as Blackacre is cultivated annually and, if not, to Paula and her heirs." Joe has used words indicating his intent to convey Blackacre for a limited time — "so long as Blackacre is cultivated annually." If the grant had stopped there, Joe would have created a fee simple determinable and retained a possibility of reverter. But the grant sends what would have been Joe's possibility of reverter to Paula. Emily has a fee simple subject to executory limitation, and Paula has an executory interest. Similarly, suppose that Phil, who holds fee simple absolute in Whiteacre, conveys it "to Michelle and her heirs; provided that no banana trees shall ever be planted on Whiteacre, and if so, to Bob and his heirs." Without the last clause, this would have created a fee simple subject to condition subsequent in Michelle and a right of entry retained by Phil, but the added clause turns Michelle's estate into a fee simple subject to executory limitation and creates an executory interest in Bob. In both cases, the executory interest automatically becomes possessory if the divesting condition occurs.

Somewhat inexplicably, these differences in the language of the grant have real consequences when the grantor retains the future interest (a possibility of reverter automatically becomes possessory; a right of entry does not), but have no legal consequences when the future interest is created in a third party (all executory interests automatically become possessory upon breach). Perhaps the assumption is that the creator of the interests wants to endow the third-party executory interest holder with automatic possession in all circumstances, but what if the creator explicitly says otherwise?

Example: A1 conveys Blackacre to Mary "for residential use only, and if not so used, Sigmund shall have the right to retake possession." If A1's intentions are the lodestar of interpretation, shouldn't a court treat Sigmund's executory interest as divesting Mary only when and if Sigmund manifests his intention to do so? The traditional answer is that Sigmund's executory interest automatically becomes possessory. What policy is served by such a rule? Simple administration, perhaps, but surely the policy of honoring a grantor's intentions is poorly served.

VI. RESTRAINTS ON ALIENATION OF FREEHOLD ESTATES

A. **Types of restraints:** Attempts to prevent alienation of a freehold estate are generally void. These restraints are of three types.

   1. **Forfeiture:** A forfeiture restraint purports to cause forfeiture of the estate if alienation is attempted, as when Will conveys The Farm "to Margy, but if she should ever attempt to transfer it in any fashion, to the Modern Language Association."

   2. **Disabling:** A disabling restraint purports to disable the owner by depriving him of any power to transfer the estate, as when Will conveys The Farm "to Margy, but no further transfer by Margy of any interest in The Farm shall be valid."

   3. **Promissory:** A promissory restraint purports to extract a promise from the transferee that she will not alienate the property, as when Will conveys The Farm "to Margy, and Margy promises that she will never transfer any interest in The Farm."

B. **Total restraints on a fee interest:** No matter what type of restraint is used, a *total restraint on alienation* of a fee interest is *void.* The reason for this rule is mostly economic efficiency. Restraints on alienation prevent property from moving into the hands of the person who would use it most productively.

C. **Partial restraints on a fee interest:** Some partial restrictions on alienation of a fee interest are valid, but most are void. The general rule is that a restraint on alienation that is *for a reasonable purpose* and *limited in duration* is *valid.*

D. **Restraints on life estates:** Restraints on alienability of life estates are more readily upheld, but validity depends on the type of restraint and the type of life estate to which it is applied.

   1. **Legal life estates:** A life estate is theoretically alienable, but not readily marketable by itself. Thus, the practical effect of a restraint on alienation of a life estate is to prevent gift of the estate or creditor seizure of it. These are considerable impediments to economic efficiency and, in the form of a disabling restraint, operate totally to bar alienability, so courts almost always void disabling restraints on alienation. Forfeiture or promissory restraints pose no less a roadblock to economic efficiency, but courts sometimes uphold them on the ground that, unlike the disabling restraint, these restraints can be released.

   2. **Equitable life estates:** Disabling restraints on equitable life estates are freely permitted. Such a restraint is called a *spendthrift trust,* because it is usually created in a trust designed to provide a spendthrift relative with an income but prevent him from his folly by denying him power to pledge the trust assets as security for a loan or otherwise use it to tempt creditors to extend credit to the spendthrift beneficiary.

Example: Decedent devises $75,000 in trust and instructs the trustees to pay the income from the fund "to my brother Charles W. Adams during his natural life, . . . free from the interference or control of his creditors, my intention being that the use of said income shall not be anticipated by assignment." This is a valid spendthrift trust. No payments may be made to Charles's creditors to discharge his debts. Of course, once payments are made directly to Charles, creditors may seize the funds disbursed. *Broadway National Bank v. Adams,* 133 Mass. 170 (1882).

The validity of spendthrift trusts is defended on the ground that the property itself — the trust corpus, legally owned by the trustee — is freely alienable, so the spendthrift trust poses no danger to economic efficiency. Moreover, creditors are not defrauded, because they can determine before extending credit whether the borrower's source of wealth is available to repay the debt.

Objection to spendthrift trusts is mostly moral: "[I]t is not the function of the law to join the futile effort to save the foolish and the vicious from the consequences of their own vice and folly . . . [S]pendthrift trusts . . . form a privileged class, . . . an aristocracy, though certainly the most contemptible aristocracy with which a country was ever cursed." John Chipman Gray, *Restraints on the Alienation of Property* 247 (2d ed. 1895).

Exam Tips *on*
FREEHOLD ESTATES

☞ Freehold estates are elementary building blocks in the property lawyer's conceptual toy chest.

☞ These issues are almost always combined with something else, usually future interests, perpetuities, or concurrent ownership, or all three, or any combination.

☞ The differences between the defeasible estates are mostly a matter of linguistic expression and characterization, but if there is additional evidence that suggests the intention of the grantor to create one or the other type of interest, use that evidence. Grantor's intention should be of paramount concern. Pay attention to the consequences between the two types of defeasible fees.

☞ Know how these estates are created, and know what to do when you spot a purported fee tail.

☞ Make sure you understand that the essential difference between these various freehold estates is in their duration. Only the fee simple absolute endures forever. Think of these estates as a series of nesting boxes or eggs — the fee simple absolute is the largest box, encompassing all others. Smaller estates can be carved out of larger estates, and only your imagination (or that of your professor) is the limit.

☞ Life estates, which are sure to end, pose particular possibilities of conflict between the life tenant and the remainderman. Waste is the doctrine to mediate that conflict. Be alert to issues of waste that can crop up whenever you confront a life estate.

CHAPTER 3

FUTURE INTERESTS

ChapterScope

This chapter examines future interests — the various *presently existing* property interests that consist of a right to *future possession* — and the rules limiting their validity, primarily the rule against perpetuities. Here are the important points in this chapter.

■ Future interests are created when an owner of a possessory estate grants a lesser possessory estate to someone, thus necessarily creating a future right to possession when the lesser estate expires.

■ Future interests may be created in the grantor, in which case they are either a reversion, a possibility of reverter, or a right of re-entry (also called a *power of termination*), or in third-party transferees, in which case they are called either a *remainder* or an *executory interest*.

■ Future interests may be vested or contingent. A contingent future interest is a right of possession that depends upon the satisfactory resolution of some uncertainty or uncertainties. A vested future interest is certain to become possessory at some future time. Illogically, some future interests are called *vested interests* even though there may be an unresolved uncertainty. The principal examples are the possibility of reverter, the right of re-entry, and vested remainders subject to partial or complete divestment.

■ Remainders are future interests that become possessory after the natural expiration of the prior possessory estate. Remainders almost always follow a life estate. Remainders are classified as *vested* or *contingent*.

■ A contingent remainder is either owned by an unascertainable person ("to the President of the United States in 2020"), or possession is made dependent upon satisfaction of some express condition precedent ("to A if A shall have become a judge"), or both ("to the President in 2020 if the President is a woman"). The natural expiration of the prior estate is not an express condition precedent.

■ A vested remainder may be indefeasibly vested, vested subject to partial divestment, or vested subject to complete divestment.

■ An indefeasibly vested remainder is certain to become possessory at some point in the future; it may not be destroyed.

■ A vested remainder subject to partial divestment is a remainder held by a known or ascertainable person who has satisfied all conditions precedent to possession, but who is a member of a class of people who own the remainder, not all of whom are known or have yet satisfied the conditions precedent. A grant of a future interest following a life estate "to the children of A who reach age 21" creates a vested remainder subject to partial divestment in A1, the 22-year-old child of A.

■ A vested remainder subject to complete divestment is a remainder held by a known or ascertainable person who has satisfied all conditions precedent to possession, but whose remainder is subject to being taken away, or divested, if some subsequent event occurs. If

O conveys Blackacre "to A for life, then to B, but if B should become a lawyer, to C," B has a vested remainder subject to complete divestment, and C has an executory interest.

■ Executory interests are future interests created in a transferee that will cut short, or divest, another transferee's possession or vested future interest. All executory interests are contingent.

■ The principal modern rule to limit the validity of uncertain future interests is the rule against perpetuities. This rule is designed to destroy future interests that allow uncertainty about ownership to persist too long, because uncertainty of ownership inhibits marketability of property, and because there is thought to be a point beyond which the wishes of dead owners of property ought not to govern the present.

■ The rule against perpetuities destroys any future interest that cannot be proven will either vest, or fail to vest, no later than 21 years after the end of some relevant life in existence at the moment the future interest becomes effective. It is a rule of law, applies regardless of a grantor's intentions, and considers only possibilities (however outlandish), not probabilities. Unless you can prove that the uncertainty of ownership will be removed, one way or the other, within the rule's period, the future interest is void.

■ Modern doctrines reform or temper the rule, but these doctrines are not universally accepted. The principal doctrines are "wait-and-see," by which a court waits to see what actually happens rather than indulging in fanciful possibilities, reform, or construction of the instrument creating the future interest to accomplish compliance with the rule, and the Uniform Statutory Rule Against Perpetuities, which waits for 90 years and then reforms future interests still contingent to make them then vest.

I.   INTRODUCTION

Future interests are legal interests in property that are ***not possessory*** but ***are capable of becoming possessory*** at some time in the future. A future interest is a ***presently existing*** property interest, but it confers only a ***future right to possession.***

Example: Philip, owner of Drippy Trees in fee simple absolute, conveys Drippy Trees to Ethel for her life, then to Muriel and her heirs. Ethel has a life estate — a presently possessory interest — and Muriel owns a ***remainder*** — a future interest. Muriel's remainder is in existence now, but it will not become possessory until the expiration of Ethel's life estate. There are five types of future interests. Three of these — the ***reversion,*** the ***possibility of reverter,*** and the ***right of entry*** (or ***power of termination***) — are the future interests ***retained by the grantor.*** The remaining two — the ***remainder*** and the ***executory interest*** — are future interests ***created in a transferee.*** Remainders are either ***contingent*** or ***vested.*** A contingent interest is subject to one or both of two uncertainties: It is either granted to an ***unknown person*** or there is some ***condition precedent*** to the future right to possession (other than the natural expiration of the preceding possessory estate). Contingent and vested remainders are fully explored in section III.A, below. Executory interests are future interests that ***divest*** (cut off) either (1) *another transferee's possessory or future interest* (a ***shifting executory interest***) or (2) *the grantor's interest at some future time* (a ***springing executory interest***). Executory interests are discussed in section III.B, below.

II. FUTURE INTERESTS RETAINED BY THE GRANTOR

A. Reversion: The reversion is the future interest that is created when the grantor conveys a *lesser estate* than that he originally owned. A reversion is freely alienable during life and may be devised or inherited.

Example: Barry, owner of Blackacre in fee simple absolute, conveys Blackacre to Scott for life. Barry has conveyed a life estate, which is less than a fee simple absolute. When Scott dies, the life estate will end, and somebody will then be entitled to possession. That "somebody" is the owner of the *reversion* that Barry necessarily retained (even without mentioning it in the grant), because he conveyed less than his own estate, fee simple absolute. Barry might still own the reversion when Scott dies, or he might have conveyed it, or it might have passed via Barry's will (if he predeceases Scott), or through intestate succession.

A reversion is created automatically, by operation of law, whenever the grantor conveys less than his entire interest in the property. It need not be expressly retained. A person need not own a fee simple absolute to convey a lesser estate and create a reversion. *The conveyance of any estate that is less than the original estate owned by the grantor will create a reversion.*

Example: Barry, owner of Blackacre in fee simple absolute, conveys Blackacre to Scott for life. If Scott leases Blackacre to Elmer for one year, Scott retains a reversion in Blackacre, which will become possessory upon expiration of the lease (assuming Scott remains alive). If Scott conveys Blackacre to Elmer for Elmer's life, Scott has also retained a reversion. Elmer has a life estate in a life estate *pur autre vie* — measured by Scott's life. If Elmer dies before Scott, his life estate expires, and Scott's reversion becomes possessory. If Scott dies before Elmer, Scott's life estate ends, and that terminates Elmer's life estate *pur autre vie,* which makes Barry's reversion possessory.

A reversion is *not necessarily certain* to become possessory in the future. In the prior example, Scott's reversion would never become possessory if he were to die before Elmer, but would if Elmer were to die first.

Example: Lewis, owner of Blackacre in fee simple absolute, conveys Blackacre to Mary for life, then to Alice and her heirs if she survives Mary. Lewis has retained a reversion, but it will never become possessory if Alice does, in fact, survive Mary. Alice has a *contingent remainder:* A condition precedent to possession is that Alice must survive Mary. If she does, her remainder becomes a possessory estate — fee simple absolute. Lewis's reversion is then destroyed, because Alice at that point would own Lewis's entire original estate in Blackacre. Similarly, if Alice does not survive Mary, her remainder will be destroyed, because the contingency never occurred, and Lewis's reversion will become possessory.

A reversion is *not created* when the grantor conveys to one person part of his estate and simultaneously conveys the rest of his estate to another person.

Example: Jonathan, owner of fee simple absolute in Blackacre, conveys Blackacre to Eleanor for life, then to Roberta and her heirs. Jonathan *has not* retained a reversion. Eleanor has a presently possessory life estate (which is, of course, a lesser estate than Jonathan's fee simple absolute), but Roberta has a *vested remainder in fee simple absolute.* Roberta is a known person, and there is no condition precedent to her taking possession upon the natural expiration of Eleanor's life estate. Roberta's vested remainder is in fee simple absolute because the grant makes clear that it is to

"Roberta and her heirs." Jonathan has conveyed his entire interest in Blackacre — part of it in the form of a presently possessory estate, and the rest of it in the form of a future interest.

Note that a person has *not conveyed their entire interest* when they convey a lesser present possessory estate followed by a *contingent remainder* in fee simple absolute.

Example: Suppose Jonathan, in the last example, had conveyed Blackacre to Eleanor for life, then to Roberta and her heirs if she should survive Eleanor. Now Roberta has a *contingent remainder in fee simple absolute.* While Roberta is a known person, we do not know whether the express condition precedent to her possession — survival of Eleanor — will or will not occur. Jonathan has retained a reversion.

1. **Reversions are always vested:** Even though not all reversions will certainly become possessory, all reversions are *vested interests.* Normally, for a future interest to be a vested interest, it must be created in a known person and must not be subject to a condition precedent. Reversions are vested because they are created in the person who owned the entire estate at the moment of creation; because the grantor has not parted with all that he owned, his retained interest is regarded as vested, even though his future right to possession is uncertain. This is important because, being vested at creation, it is *not subject to destruction by the Rule Against Perpetuities.*

2. **Distinguished from remainder, possibility of reverter, and power of termination:** A remainder looks very much like a reversion but is created in a *transferee,* not retained by the grantor. A possibility of reverter is retained by the grantor, but is the future interest created when the grantor conveys a *determinable* version of the *same estate he owns.* A power of termination (or right of re-entry) is also retained by the grantor, but is the future interest created when the grantor conveys his estate subject to a condition subsequent.

B. **Possibility of reverter:** A possibility of reverter is created whenever the grantor conveys the same *quantity* of estate that he originally had, but conveys it with a *determinable limitation* attached and retains the right to future possession if and when the determinable limitation occurs. That future interest in the grantor is a possibility of reverter.

Example: Bill conveys Blackacre to Pete so long as it is used as a warehouse. Pete has fee simple determinable. Bill has retained a possibility of reverter.

Though the possibility of reverter is usually created when the grantor conveys fee simple determinable, it can be created by the conveyance of any determinable estate.

Example: Orca, owner of a life estate in Blackacre, conveys Blackacre to Sal so long as Blackacre is devoted to agricultural use. Orca has conveyed her life estate to Sal — an estate of the same quantity she originally had — but with an attached determinable limitation. If, during Orca's life, Sal uses Blackacre for any purpose other than agricultural, Orca's possibility of reverter will become immediately possessory. If Sal farms Blackacre until Orca's death, Orca's life estate will come to its natural end, and the holder of the reversion or remainder (whichever was created simultaneously with Orca's life estate) will be entitled to possession. In that event, Orca's possibility of reverter will expire with her life estate.

Another way to remember this is to link together the possibility of reverter and determinable estates. Whenever a determinable estate is created, the grantor retains a possibility of reverter, *unless the grantor simultaneously creates in a third party what would be a possibility of reverter if retained by the grantor.*

Example: April, owner of Fleur-de-Lis in fee simple absolute, conveys Fleur-de-Lis to May so long as Fleur-de-Lis is used solely as a single-family residence and, if not, to June and her heirs. April has conveyed fee simple determinable to May and has created in June a future interest that would be a possibility of reverter if April had retained it. But because it is created in a transferee — June — it is an *executory interest.* Put another way, a possibility of reverter can *never be created in a grantee.*

1. **Transferability:** Common law did not permit transfer of a possibility of reverter inter vivos or by will, but only by inheritance. Today, most states permit a possibility of reverter to be alienated inter vivos, devised, or inherited.

2. **Termination:** Both the possibility of reverter and the right of entry (see section II.C, below) can endure forever, because (1) the triggering limitation may never occur, and (2) both future interests are vested at creation and so are immune from destruction under the Rule Against Perpetuities. Some jurisdictions have enacted statutes that terminate the possibility of reverter and right of entry after some fixed period, typically 30 years. Other statutes provide for termination after 30 years unless the interest is re-recorded within that period (thus evidencing a fresh desire to maintain the limitation). See, e.g., Cal. Civ. Code §885.010 et seq. This type of statute permits a possibility of reverter to remain in existence in perpetuity, so long as it is re-recorded every 30 years. A third approach is England's, which has made these interests subject to destruction under the Rule Against Perpetuities.

3. **Statutory abolition:** In those few states that have abolished determinable estates by statute, the possibility of reverter, its corollary future interest, has also been abolished.

C. **Power of termination or right of entry:** A power of termination (or right of entry) is created whenever the grantor retains the power to cut short the conveyed estate before its natural termination.

   Example: Hilda conveys Driftwood Farm "to Olga and her heirs, but if Driftwood Farm should cease to be used for pasturing horses, Hilda may terminate the conveyed estate and retake possession." Olga has a fee simple subject to condition subsequent, and Hilda has retained a power of termination (right of entry).

   Like the possibility of reverter, a power of termination may only be created in the grantor. The analogous interest created in a grantee is an executory interest.

   Example: Hilda conveys Driftwood Farm "to Olga and her heirs, but if Driftwood Farm should cease to be used for pasturing horses, to Gertrude and her heirs, who may terminate the conveyed estate and retake possession." Olga has a fee simple subject to an executory limitation, Gertrude has an executory interest, and Hilda has retained nothing.

   1. **Transferability:** Like the possibility of reverter, at common law a power of termination (right of entry) was neither alienable inter vivos nor devisable by will. It could only be inherited. Jurisdictions today split over whether to follow the common law rule or to permit free alienability. A very few jurisdictions hold that the mere *attempt* to alienate a power of termination destroys it, freeing the possessory estate of the condition subsequent.

   2. **Termination:** This issue is discussed in section II.B.2, above.

3. **Effect of abolition of determinable estates:** In those few jurisdictions that have abolished determinable estates (and, thus, the corresponding future interest — a possibility of reverter), what would have been a possibility of reverter is converted by operation of law into a power of termination.

III.   FUTURE INTERESTS CREATED IN GRANTEES

A. Remainders:

1. **Definition:** A remainder is a future interest created in a *grantee* that *will become possessory (if it ever becomes possessory)* upon the *natural expiration of the preceding possessory estate.* The parenthetical clause is in the prior sentence because some remainders are *certain to become possessory,* and others have *only the possibility of becoming possessory.* But all remainders *never divest* another estate. The *only* way a remainder becomes possessory is the natural expiration of the prior estate.

   Example: Olga conveys Blackacre to Nicholas for life, then to Alexandra and her heirs. Alexandra has a remainder. It is certain to become possessory upon Nicholas's death, which is the *natural expiration* of Nicholas's life estate.

   Example: Olga conveys Blackacre to Nicholas for life, then to Alexandra and her heirs if Alexandra survives Nicholas. Alexandra has a remainder. It is not certain to become possessory (Alexandra must outlive Nicholas), but it is capable of becoming possessory, and the only way it can become possessory is to succeed the natural expiration of Nicholas's life estate.

   Example: Olga conveys Blackacre to Nicholas for life, but if Alexandra should win the Nobel Prize for Literature, to Alexandra and her heirs. Alexandra does *not* have a remainder. Her future interest will become possessory, if at all, by *divesting* Nicholas of his life estate, or Olga of her fee simple (if Alexandra wins a Nobel Prize after Nicholas's death, because then Olga's reversion would become possessory). Alexandra has an *executory interest.*

2. **Nature of the estate held in remainder:** The term *remainder* simply identifies the type of *future interest* it is. A remainder is a future interest in some estate — fee simple, fee tail, life estate, or a term of years. It can be any estate. Be precise, and identify both the future interest and the possessory estate.

   Example: Heinrich conveys Blackacre to Dieter for life, then to Erwin for five years, then to Helmut for life, then to Wilhelm and the heirs of his body, then to Olga and her heirs. Erwin has a remainder for a term of years. Helmut has a remainder for life. Wilhelm has a remainder in fee tail (if fee tail is permitted). Olga has a remainder in fee simple absolute.

3. **Classification of remainders:** Remainders are classified as *vested* or *contingent.* The purpose of distinguishing between the two is to identify those remainders that are of uncertain ownership or ultimate possession. Persistent uncertainties of these sorts make property difficult or impossible to alienate. Common law devised a number of "marketability rules" designed to destroy contingent remainders (and other contingent future interests) if the contingency persists for too long. See section VI, below.

   a. **Classification method:** To classify future interests, you must classify each interest created by a grant *in the order of creation.* Examine the first interest created. Is it presently possessory or a future interest? If it is a future interest, what kind is it? If it is a remainder, is the interest created in a known person? If so, is ultimate possession subject to any condition precedent? If not, you have a vested remainder. Do this again for each subsequent interest in the grant.

Example: Roger conveys Holly Farm to Susan for life, then to Dorothea and her heirs if she has published a novel, but if not, to Nancy's then-living children and their heirs. The first interest created is a presently possessory life estate, held by Susan. The next interest, Dorothea's, is a future interest. It is a future interest because it is not now possessory. It is a remainder because it will become possessory, if at all, upon the natural expiration of Susan's life estate. It is a contingent remainder because, although Dorothea is a known person, there is no certainty that Dorothea will have satisfied the condition precedent to possession — publication of a novel. Dorothea has a contingent remainder in fee simple absolute. The last interest, in Nancy's then-living children, is also a remainder because it will become possessory, if at all, upon the natural expiration of Susan's life estate. It is a contingent remainder for two reasons: (1) the class of grantees — Nancy's then-living children — is unknown and cannot possibly be known until Susan's death, and (2) there is a condition precedent to possession — that Nancy's children survive Susan. Nancy's then-living children have a contingent remainder in fee simple absolute. Roger has retained a reversion.

b. Vested remainders: A remainder is vested if it is created in a known person, and possession is not subject to any condition subsequent. As a result, a vested remainder ***must necessarily become possessory*** whenever the prior possessory estate expires.

Example: Oscar conveys Arrowsmith to Margot for life, then to Connie and her heirs. Connie's remainder is vested because she is a known person and there is no condition precedent to her possession. Whenever Margot dies, Connie (or her legal successor) is ready to take possession of Arrowsmith.

The natural expiration of the preceding estate is ***not*** a condition precedent.

Example: In the prior example, Connie will not receive possession of Arrowsmith until Margot dies, but Margot's death is not a condition precedent to possession because her death simply marks the natural expiration of her life estate. By contrast, if Oscar had conveyed Arrowsmith "to Margot for life, then to Connie and her heirs if Connie survives Margot," there would be a condition precedent to Connie's possession — surviving Margot. Connie would hold a contingent remainder. These look like the same thing, but they are not: In the first example, if Connie dies before Margot, Connie's vested remainder passes to her assignee, devisee, or heir (call him Hector); but in the second example if Connie dies before Margot, Connie's contingent remainder is destroyed, and Hector receives nothing. Because Connie's death means that she can never satisfy the condition precedent, her contingent remainder dies with her. It has ***lapsed.*** Vested remainders are not uniform. There are three types of vested remainders: ***indefeasibly vested remainders, vested remainders subject to complete divestment,*** and ***vested remainders subject to open (or partial divestment).***

i. Indefeasibly vested remainders: An indefeasibly vested remainder is ***certain to*** become ***and*** remain ***possessory.*** Nothing will prevent possession from happening eventually, and once possession occurs, it will last forever.

Example: Dahlia conveys Laurel Hill to Pietro for life, then to Arturo and his heirs. Arturo has an indefeasibly vested remainder in fee simple absolute. Arturo (or his legal successor) is certain to obtain possession following expiration of Pietro's life estate, and once he has possession Arturo cannot be divested of his possession (except, of course, by operation of law, as by eminent domain). He has a fee simple absolute.

Despite the "certain to become and remain possessory" rule, an indefeasibly vested remainder is subject to the qualification that any estate can expire naturally, and that expiration might occur while the interest is still in its future interest form. In such cases, the indefeasibly vested remainder is not divested; it has simply expired in accordance with its natural or inherent limits.

Example: Bridget conveys Falcon Perch to Sam for life, then to Miles for life, then to Joel and his heirs. Miles has an indefeasibly vested remainder in a life estate, but if Miles should die before Sam, his life estate will terminate naturally, even though he never enjoyed possession. Miles's interest is not divested by Joel, it simply came to its natural end, and Joel, owner of an indefeasibly vested remainder in fee simple absolute, will take possession upon Sam's death. An analogy may help. A caterpillar is genetically certain to become a butterfly, but if it dies while still a caterpillar, its genetic nature is unaltered; it simply came to an untimely end before it could ever take wing.

ii. **Vested remainders subject to complete divestment:** A vested remainder subject to complete divestment is a remainder created in a known person and not subject to any condition precedent, but it is *subject to a condition* **subsequent** that, if it occurs, will *completely divest* the remainderman of his interest.

Example: Keith conveys Blackacre to Edgar for life, then to Eve and her heirs, but if Adam should ever return from Vietnam, to Adam and his heirs. Eve has a vested remainder subject to complete divestment. Adam has an executory interest. Eve is a known person, and there is no condition *precedent* to her possession. If Edgar dies today, Eve will be entitled to possession. But both Eve's remainder and her possession, should it occur, may be taken away from her if Adam ever returns from Vietnam. Note that if Edgar dies before Adam returns from Vietnam, Eve will possess a fee simple subject to an executory limitation. Adam's executory interest will continue until his death. If Adam never returns from Vietnam, his executory interest will lapse at his death. Note that, as drafted, Edgar's life estate is also subject to an executory limitation in favor of Adam. If Keith wishes to convey to Edgar a life estate not subject to executory limitation, he must make that intent clear in the grant.

Vested remainders subject to complete divestment are still **vested**, and they may be transferred inter vivos, devised, or inherited. Note, however, that a vested remainder subject to complete divestment can be created in such a way that it cannot be passed on at death.

Example: Frieda conveys Round Top to Dan for life, then to James and his heirs, but if James does not survive Dan, to Robert and his heirs. James's vested remainder is subject to complete divestment by Robert's executory interest. Because the divesting condition subsequent is James's failure to survive Dan, James could never pass his remainder at his death. If James dies before Dan, his vested remainder is divested in favor of Robert. If Dan dies before James, James acquires possession, and the divesting condition subsequent can never occur. In that event, James will pass his fee simple absolute at death, not a remainder.

iii. **Vested remainders subject to open or partial divestment:** A vested remainder subject to open (or partial divestment) is a remainder created in a *class* (or group) of grantees, at least one of whom is presently existing and entitled to possession as soon as the preceding estate expires, but which is capable of expansion to include as yet unknown people. It is called *subject to open* because the class is left open for the entry of new members.

Example: Robin devises Orange Hall "to my husband, Harold, for life, then to such of my children who have graduated from law school." Robin has created a remainder in a class — her children who have graduated from law school. If, at the moment of creation, Robin has three children — Tom, Dick, and Harry — but none has graduated from law school, the remainder is contingent. At the moment that Tom graduates from law school, Tom will acquire a vested remainder, but it is subject to open (or partial divestment) because it is possible that Dick or Harry, or both, will graduate from law school. If Dick does graduate from law school, Tom's vested remainder will be partially divested in favor of Dick. Tom and Dick must share possession of Orange Hall. If Harry also graduates from law school, the remainder held by Tom and Dick is further diluted. But then the remainder shared by Tom, Dick, and Harry is indefeasibly vested because Robin is dead and can have no more children, and all of her children have satisfied the condition precedent. The class is closed at that moment. Note that the classification of the future interest created by Robin will change as future events dictate. Future interests are dynamic, not static.

Remember: Vested remainders subject to open are *vested.* Even though they are subject to dilution, the interest will survive its holder.

Example: In the prior example, if Tom had graduated from law school, thus acquiring a vested remainder subject to open, and then died from the stress, his vested remainder would pass under his will or by intestate succession.

A vested remainder can be subject to *both* partial *and* complete *divestment.*

Example: Peter devises Blackacre "to William for life, then to Catherine's children and their heirs, but if Ivan returns from Turkey, to Ivan and his heirs." At Peter's death, Catherine is living and has two children, Anna and Russell. The class of Catherine's children has a vested remainder subject to partial and complete divestment. Catherine may have another child and, if so, that child would enter the class, partially divesting Anna and Russell. Ivan, holder of an executory interest, may return from Turkey at any time, thus completely divesting Anna, Russell, and any new members of the class of Catherine's children.

iv. **Class gifts:** Whenever a grant creates an interest in a group of people, it is a *class gift.* The group can be any ascertainable body of people, but is most often a family group; e.g., "to my children," or "to my surviving nieces and nephews," or "to my grandchildren who have reached age 21." A class is *open* if it is possible for new people to enter it, and is closed if new entrants are *not possible.*

v. **Class-closing rules:** A class closes when either of two events occurs: (1) it is *no longer physiologically possible to have new entrants,* or (2) if the *"rule of convenience"* applies. The rule of convenience is an interpretive rule, not a rule of law, and states in essence that a class closes if *any member of the class is entitled to* **immediate possession** and that result is consistent with the intent of the grantor making the class gift. See also section VI.E.3.b, below.

Example: Physiologically closed: Arthur devises Hilltop "to Maggie for life, then to my children and their heirs." Arthur is survived by two children, Mordred and Cedric. Arthur has created an indefeasibly vested remainder in the class of his children. It is indefeasibly vested because the class of Arthur's children is physiologically closed — Arthur is dead and can have no more children. Mordred and Cedric compose the entire class; nobody else can enter.

Example: Rule of convenience: George devises Blackacre "to my wife, Liz, for life, then immediately to my grandchildren and their heirs." George is survived by Liz and one child, Betty. Betty has two children, Charles and Diana. Charles and Diana, George's grandchildren, hold a vested remainder subject to open. When Liz dies, they will be entitled to immediate possession. The rule of convenience probably applies, because the term *immediately* in the grant appears to suggest George's intent that the class of his grandchildren be determined as soon as Liz dies, and under the rule of convenience, the class of George's grandchildren closes at that moment. If Betty later gives birth to Anne, this third grandchild of George's is born too late to share in the class gift.

Caveat: Medical technology now permits posthumous conception of children, and courts have yet to resolve definitively whether the possibility of such children causes a class of children to remain open after its ordinary physiological closure. Cf. *Woodward v. Commissioner of Social Security,* 435 Mass. 536 (2002), in which the Massachusetts Supreme Judicial Court ruled that twins posthumously conceived and born two years after their father's death were his intestate successors if (1) he was genetically related to them, and (2) he had affirmatively consented during life to posthumous conception and support of the children. The court noted that the state's interest in orderly administration of estates might permit it to impose a limitations period. See also Cal. Probate Code §6453(b)(3), which provides that paternity may be established by clear and convincing evidence where it was impossible during life for a father to acknowledge paternity.

c. **Contingent remainders:** A contingent remainder is a remainder created in an ***unknown person*** or that has a ***condition precedent*** to ultimate possession.

Example: Unknown persons: Martha conveys Blackacre to Kevin for life, then to Ellen's children. Ellen is 12 years old and has no children. Ellen's nonexistent children have a contingent remainder. Martha has retained a reversion.

Example: Unknown persons: Martha conveys Blackacre to Kevin for life, then to Kevin's heirs. Kevin's heirs are not known until Kevin dies, so the class of Kevin's heirs has a contingent remainder. Recall that the term ***heirs*** refers to those people who inherit by intestate succession. Again, Martha has retained a reversion.

Example: Condition precedent: Martha conveys Blackacre to Kevin for life, then to Ellen if she graduates from Princeton. Ellen is 12 years old and in the sixth grade. Ellen has a contingent remainder; she must graduate from Princeton in order to be entitled to possession. Martha has retained a reversion.

Contingent remainders have no certainty of becoming possessory, but that is also true of vested remainders subject to complete divestment. Don't make the error of thinking that certainty of ultimate possession is the dividing line between vested and contingent remainders. Note also that a contingent remainder in fee simple will *always* leave a reversion in the grantor.

i. **Conditions *precedent:*** A condition precedent must be expressed in the grant. Neither the natural expiration of the prior estate nor precatory language in the grant constitutes a condition precedent.

Example: Condition precedent: Harry conveys Elderfield to Annie for life, then to Eileen if she graduates from Harvard. The condition of graduation from Harvard is expressed in the grant and is a condition precedent to Eileen's possession.

Example: Condition precedent: Jose conveys Soledad to Rose for life, then to William if he survives Rose. The condition of survival is expressed in the grant as a condition precedent to William's possession.

Example: Not a condition precedent: Jose conveys Soledad to Rose for life, then to William. William (or his legal successor) has no right to possession until the natural expiration of Rose's life estate, but that is inherent in the estates conveyed by Jose. William has a vested remainder.

Example: Not a condition precedent: Jose conveys Soledad to Rose for life, and in the event of Rose's death, to William. Though couched as a condition, the language "and in the event of Rose's death" is wholly precatory. It adds nothing; it merely describes the natural expiration of Rose's life estate.

ii. **Recognizing the difference between a condition *precedent* and a condition *subsequent:*** The difference between a vested remainder subject to complete divestment upon the occurrence of some condition subsequent and a contingent remainder subject to a condition precedent can be very subtle. You must pay careful attention to the language of the grant. If the condition is made an integral part of the grant in remainder, it is a contingent remainder. But if the grant uses words to create a vested interest, and then proceeds to add a divesting condition, it is a vested remainder subject to partial or complete divestment.

Example: Vested remainder: Phil conveys Seabreeze to Jane for life, then to Emily, but if Emily ever goes to Canada, to Evan. Emily has a vested remainder subject to complete divestment upon the occurrence of the condition subsequent — Emily going to Canada. Evan has an executory interest. Because Phil has created a vested remainder in fee simple, he has not retained a reversion.

Example: Alternative contingent remainders: Phil conveys Seabreeze to Jane for life, then to Emily if she has never gone to Canada, but if she has ever gone to Canada, to Evan. Now Emily has a contingent remainder because the condition — never going to Canada — is expressed as an integral part of the grant in remainder to her. Evan also has a contingent remainder because the same condition is repeated as an integral part of the grant to Evan. These are *alternative contingent remainders.* Because contingent remainders are created, Phil has retained a reversion. Phil's reversion will only become possessory in the unlikely event that Jane's life estate will terminate prior to her death, perhaps by forfeiture for drug dealing or disclaimer of the life estate. Phil's intentions are identical in both examples, but quite different consequences flow from the choice of language.

In cases of hopeless ambiguity, the law prefers a vested remainder to a contingent remainder.

iii. Alienability:
With a few exceptions, common law did not permit alienability of contingent interests, but today nearly every jurisdiction permits alienability of contingent interests. Of course, if the contingency is survival, the interest cannot pass by will or intestate succession, and if the contingency results from the fact that the holder is unknown (perhaps not born), there is no owner to convey it, so as a practical matter it is not alienable.

B. Executory interests:
Executory interests are future interests in a grantee that divest either (1) another grantee's possessory or future interest (a *shifting executory interest*), or (2) the grantor's interest at some future time (a *springing executory interest*).

1. A note on history:
Executory interests resulted from Henry VIII's desire to eliminate the *use,* an early form of the trust, in order to stop death tax avoidance by means of the use. In order to provide the economic benefits of land to another, a feudal grantor might *enfeoff* (convey possession of a freehold estate) to another person, to hold "for the use and benefit" of a third party. The law courts did not recognize the use, but the equity courts (with power only to act upon a person) would command the *feoffee* to use to administer the land in accordance with the instructions in the use.

Example: John, a sea captain, enfeoffs Blackacre to his brother, Robert, for the use and benefit of John's wife, Elizabeth, and her children. The chancellor in equity would force Robert, on pain of imprisonment, to administer Blackacre for the benefit of Elizabeth and her children. The use provided a number of advantages in Tudor England.

Example: Common law required conveyances of realty to occur by *livery of seisin,* a formality in which the seller physically handed the buyer a clod of earth or a twig from the property, while both were on the property. No doubt, this was annoying and often inconvenient, so lawyers began to convey property by *deed,* in which the buyer would pay valuable consideration for the property. The law courts refused to recognize a deed because there had been no transfer of seisin, but the chancellor in equity would order the seller to hold seisin for the use of the buyer. Equitable title was every bit as good as legal title.

Lawyers and landowners quickly recognized other advantages of flexibility provided by the use. Common law forbade the creation of interests springing out of the grantor at some future time, because the ritual of livery of seisin could not be performed in advance. For equally rigid reasons, the common law also forbade creation of interests shifting ownership of freehold estates from one grantee to another. Each of these arrangements could be accomplished through the use.

Example — Springing use: In Tudor England, Basil wishes to marry his daughter Sybil to Norbert, which is satisfactory to Norbert so long as Basil supplies Blackacre as her dowry. Norbert is unwilling to wed Sybil, however, unless he can have iron-clad assurance that the dowry will exist, and Basil is unwilling to endow Sybil with Blackacre unless he is certain that Norbert will go through with the marriage. (Poor Sybil is not consulted, and romantic love forms no part of these arrangements between these deeply skeptical men.) To solve the problem, Basil conveys Blackacre "to Orlando for the use of Basil, and upon the marriage of Norbert and my daughter Sybil, for the use of Sybil." This enables Basil to provide a dowry to Sybil, but only upon her marriage, and simultaneously to satisfy Norbert's family that the dowry would really be there when the marriage vows were pledged.

Example — Shifting use: Basil conveys Oak Park "to Orlando for the use of my son, John, but if my son Roger, who went off with John Cabot, should ever return from the Western Ocean, for the use of Roger." This enables Basil to provide for the contingency of Roger's return while still providing for his other son.

Perhaps the most exciting advantage of the use to wealthy landowners was that it afforded a method to avoid the feudal incidents, or death taxes. Recall that these death taxes fell due whenever a freeholder died, and seisin descended to his heirs. The use enabled seisin to stay frozen in the hands of the trustee (the feoffee to use) forever, thus avoiding death taxes.

Example: Basil conveys Blackacre to Alvin, Bertrand, Charles, and David, jointly, to hold for the use of Basil's first son, then to the first son's first son, then to the first son's first son's first son, then . . . and so forth. Seisin stays in the hands of the four feoffees, so no death taxes ever become due. If Alvin and Bertrand die, it would be prudent for Charles and David to convey, jointly, to themselves and some younger persons (say, Edward and Frank) to keep seisin frozen in the trustees. This process could go on forever, subject to the limits imposed by the Rule Against Perpetuities.

a. **The statute of uses:** The corpulent, self-indulgent, and profligate Henry VIII resolved to end this tax avoidance and did so by forcing the ***Statute of Uses*** (1535, effective 1536) upon an unwilling Parliament. The Statute of Uses simply converted the beneficial interests in uses to legal interests. Because the Statute of Uses "executed" the use, the term ***executory interest*** eventually was bestowed on those future interests that would have been beneficial interests in a springing use or a shifting use prior to its adoption.

   Example: After 1536, Sybil, in the earlier example of a springing use, would have a legal interest in Blackacre — an executory interest before her marriage to Norbert and a fee simple absolute afterward.

   Example: After 1536, Roger, in the earlier example of a shifting use, would have a legal interest in Oak Park — an executory interest before his return from the Western Ocean, and a fee simple absolute afterward.

   For a time after enactment of the Statute of Uses, it was necessary to "raise a use" in order for the statute to execute it into a legal interest. This is no longer necessary; any deed or will can create an executory interest.

   i. **How the trust survived the Statute of Uses:** The Statute of Uses was held by the courts not to apply to so-called ***active trusts***, where the trustee was charged with a duty to manage the property for the beneficiary rather than merely protecting it and conveying it whenever the beneficiary directed. Also, the courts held that a "use-on-a-use" was not affected by the statute. Thus, after 1536, a conveyance "to *X* for the use of *A* for the use of *B*" resulted in the creation of a legal estate in *A* (because the first use was executed by the Statute of Uses) for the benefit of *B*. Finally, the Statute of Uses did not apply to personal property, so conveyances of money or securities in trust could continue to be created. These exceptions permitted the modern trust to develop. See section IV, below.

2. **Springing executory interests:** A springing executory interest is a future interest created in a grantee that *divests the grantor* at some future time after the conveyance. Thus, it "springs" out of the grantor.

Example: Professor Dweeb, a teacher of property law, conveys Blackacre to the first student in his property class who becomes a judge. This unknown student has a springing executory interest.

Example: Alice conveys Carter Hall to Ben for life, then to Stephen if he shall give Ben a proper funeral. Stephen has a springing executory interest, not a contingent remainder. It is not possible for Stephen to give Ben a proper funeral (or any funeral, for that matter) until at least some time has elapsed following the expiration of Ben's life estate. During that interval, possession has reverted to Alice (or her legal successor to her reversion). Thus, when Stephen delivers the proper funeral for Ben, possession will spring out of Alice or her legal successor.

3. **Shifting executory interests:** A shifting executory interest is a future interest in a grantee that *divests another grantee* upon the occurrence of some condition. By such divestiture, the shifting executory interest *cuts short* the preceding estate prior to its natural expiration.

Example: Ron conveys Waterfront to Alex, but if Sarah should ever be released from prison, to Sarah. Sarah has a shifting executory interest that will divest Alex, another grantee, by cutting short his fee simple subject to an executory limitation if and when Sarah is released from prison.

Example: Woody conveys Rose Arbor to Tammy for life, then to Esther, but if Esther does not survive Tammy, then to Arlo. Arlo has a shifting executory interest that will divest Esther, another grantee, of her vested remainder in fee simple subject to an executory limitation if Esther does not survive Tammy.

IV. THE PROPOSED *RESTATEMENT (THIRD) OF PROPERTY*

A. **Introduction.** The *Restatement (Third) of Property* proposes changes in this classification system. These changes are touted as simplifications. Even if the *Restatement (Third)* is fully adopted by the American Law Institute, it will have no legal effect. The American Law Institute is a purely advisory body of lawyers, judges, and academics. Nevertheless, the ALI's Restatements have an effect on the future development of law.

B. **Types of Future Interests.** The *Restatement (Third)* would label all future interests simply as *future interests,* whether they are *possibilities of reverter, rights of entry (powers of termination), remainders, reversions, or executory interests.*

Example: Mary conveys Hidden Farm to the city of Santa Claus, "so long as it used as a children's farm and zoological garden, and if used for any other purpose to revert to Mary and her heirs." Under the *Restatement (Third),* the city has a fee simple *defeasible,* and Mary has a future interest.

Example: Thomas conveys Swampland to "Jerry for life, then to Sam if Sam becomes a judge." Sam's contingent remainder and Thomas's reversion are each treated by the *Restatement (Third)* as a future interest.

C. **Classification of Future Interests.** The *Restatement (Third)* would treat all future interests that are not certain to become possessory as contingent future interests. It would abolish the distinctions among future interests that are contingent, indefeasibly vested, vested subject to complete divestment, and vested subject to partial divestment (or "subject to open"). It would also stipulate that either a vested or contingent future interest can be subject to open.

Example: Mary's future interest in Hidden Farm (see above) is contingent because it is not certain to become possessory.

Example: Each of Thomas and Sam's future interests in Swampland (see above) are contingent future interests because each is not certain to become possessory.

Example: Molly conveys Richland to "Harry for life, then to Elspeth, but if Elspeth predeceases Harry, to return to Molly." Elspeth's vested remainder subject to complete divestment is treated by the *Restatement (Third)* as contingent, because it is not certain that Elspeth will survive Harry and be entitled to possession. Molly's vested reversion subject to complete divestment is treated by the *Restatement (Third)* as contingent, because it is not certain that Harry will outlive Elspeth, the condition that must happen for Molly to be entitled to possession.

Example: Molly conveys Richland to "Harry for life, then to Elspeth, but if Elspeth predeceases Harry, to Margaret." As in the prior example, Elspeth's vested remainder subject to complete divestment is treated by the *Restatement (Third)* as contingent, because it is not certain that Elspeth will survive Harry and be entitled to possession. Margaret's executory interest (which would become an indefeasibly vested remainder should Elspeth die before Harry) is treated as a contingent future interest, because Harry might outlive Elspeth.

V. THE TRUST

A. **Introduction:** Future interests are most commonly employed in trusts, so it is useful to understand the general architecture of the trust and the advantages it affords.

B. **The basics of the trust:** The central feature of the trust is the division of *legal* ownership from *equitable* ownership (or, as it sometimes called, *beneficial* ownership). A person (called the *trustor* or *settlor*) may transfer legal title of his assets to a *trustee,* who becomes the legal owner of the assets, but who is charged with the responsibility to manage those assets (in accord with the terms of the trust and relevant legal standards pertaining to the fiduciary duties of trustees) for the economic benefit of the trust **beneficiaries**, who have **equitable** ownership of the assets.

Example: Evelyn conveys Blackacre, which she owns in fee simple absolute, to Isabel in trust to pay the income for life to Sophie, and then to pay the principal to Sophie's children who survive her. Isabel, the trustee, now owns a legal fee simple absolute in Blackacre. Sophie has an equitable life estate in the trust assets (which consist of Blackacre at the moment) and Sophie's children have an equitable contingent remainder in the trust assets. Isabel, as trustee, may convey fee simple absolute in Blackacre to Steven in return for $500,000, which sum is now the trust's assets.

Sophie and her children continue to have their equitable interests in these assets. Isabel could spend the $500,000 to acquire a portfolio of blue-chip corporate stocks, and so on. None of the transfers alters the nature of the equitable interests held by Sophie and her children; only the composition of the trust assets is altered.

C. **Advantages of the trust:** A trust enables a person to place assets in the hands of a property manager who can respond to changing conditions by selling assets and acquiring new ones, all for the advantage of the people who may be unknown to the settlor (such as grandchildren yet to be born). There is thus combined great flexibility in property management and concentration of assets for the benefit of the identified beneficiaries for some distance into the future, often well past the lifetime of the settlor. Of course, trusts may be used for many purposes other than transmission of wealth through ever-wider family generational lines while keeping the asset management concentrated and flexible.

D. **The spendthrift trust.** The common law prohibited restraints on alienation of otherwise absolute grants of legal ownership of property, but American courts have held that this prohibition does not apply to equitable, or beneficial, interests in property. Because trust beneficiaries have only an equitable interest in the trust corpus, a trust settler may provide that a beneficiary's interest may not be alienated by him. This means that creditors of the beneficiary may not reach the trust assets in which the beneficiary has an equitable interest to satisfy the beneficiary's debts.

★**Example:** By his will, Decedent creates a funded trust for the benefit of his brother Charles, and the terms of the trust stipulate that the trustee is to make payments of the income from the fund to Charles "free from the interference or control of his creditors, my intention being that the use of said income shall not be anticipated by assignment." Charles's creditors sought to satisfy their claims from the trust income. The Massachusetts Supreme Judicial Court, in a leading case on the point, ruled that Decedent's intentions should be honored because there was no public policy against the practice. Creditors would not be misled because they could determine in advance whether the beneficiary had any right to the income before its receipt by him, and decide whether to extend credit on the basis of this information. ***Broadway National Bank v. Adams***, 133 Mass. 170 (1882).

This rule has been criticized as obnoxious because it permits a person to "have an estate to live on, but not an estate to pay his debts with." ***Tillinghast v. Bradford,*** 5. R.I 205 (1858), and as "undemocratic" because it permits "the most contemptible aristocracy with which a country was ever cursed." John Chipman Gray, *Restraints on the Alienation of Property* (2d ed. 1895).

VI. THE MARKETABILITY RULES

A. **Introduction:** Common law judges devised a number of rules to increase the marketability of land by eliminating uncertainties of title that inhibited alienability. These rules are considered here. Three doctrines — ***destructibility of contingent remainders,*** the ***Rule in Shelley's Case,*** and the ***doctrine of worthier title*** — are mostly abandoned today, although enough jurisdictions cling to them to make it worthwhile to study them briefly. The principal modern marketability rule is the ***Rule Against Perpetuities.***

B. Destructibility of contingent remainders: At common law, a *contingent remainder in land was destroyed if, at the expiration of the preceding freehold estate, it was still contingent.* To become possessory, a contingent remainder had to vest at or prior to the termination of the prior freehold estate.

Example: Roger conveys Baskerville Hall to Arthur for life, then to Holmes if he should be knighted. Holmes has a contingent remainder; his possession of Baskerville Hall is subject to the condition precedent that he receive a knighthood. If Holmes is knighted by the King before Arthur dies, his remainder will become vested because the condition precedent will have been satisfied. Upon Arthur's death, Sir Holmes would take Baskerville Hall in fee simple absolute. But if Holmes has not been knighted before Arthur's death, his contingent remainder would be destroyed, leaving Roger's reversion as the possessory interest in Baskerville Hall in fee simple absolute.

The rule was created when seisin was still important. The holder of seisin was responsible for the feudal obligations. Because seisin could not be passed from an expiring freehold estate to a contingent remainderman — a person who could not hold seisin — the contingent remainder must be eliminated, because seisin must go somewhere. There could be no gaps in seisin. Because seisin is irrelevant to the modern world, this rationale is utterly useless today. The amazing thing is that about a quarter of American states have not explicitly abolished this rule. The issue is rarely litigated, and when it is, courts appear to use good judgment and eliminate the rule as part of the common law. See, e.g., *Johnson v. Amstutz,* 101 N.M. 94 (1984).

1. **Effect of merger:** The rule had a significant impact on contingent remainders following a life estate because it applied at the ***natural termination*** and at the ***artificial termination*** of a life estate. A life estate could terminate early — before the death of the life tenant — by forfeiture or merger. Forfeiture occurred if the life tenant committed treason or tortiously attempted to convey a fee simple. Merger occurred if the same person held the present possessory freehold estate (the life estate) and the ***next vested estate,*** in which event the two titles would merge to form one possessory fee simple. Note that if a life estate were followed by a contingent remainder, the next *vested* estate would be a reversion. The merger doctrine enabled conspiracies by the life tenant and the holder of the reversion to destroy the intervening contingent remainder.

    Example: William conveys Bayberry Hall to Alfred for life, then to Hortense if she survives Alfred. Hortense has a contingent remainder. Suppose that William dies before Alfred, and his reversion is inherited by his greedy son Cecil. If Cecil can persuade Alfred to convey his life estate to him, Cecil will own both the possessory freehold estate and the ***next vested estate*** (the reversion). The merger doctrine extinguishes the life estate prematurely and, because Hortense has not yet satisfied the contingency of surviving Alfred, her remainder is destroyed. Cecil owns Bayberry Hall in fee simple absolute.

2. **Limited effectiveness of the rule:** The destructibility rule had lots of loopholes, so it wasn't very effective. Because vested remainders were exempt, the inclusion of a vested remainder before a contingent remainder would block the merger doctrine. Executory interests are not remainders, and so the rule did not apply to them, despite the fact that they are contingent interests. This was logical in the world of seisin, because an executory interest posed no possibility of any gap in seisin. Seisin would either spring from the grantor to the holder of the executory interest or shift from one seised freeholder to another. Because a leasehold is considered personal property, a leaseholder could not hold seisin. Thus, a contingent interest

following a term of years was treated as an executory interest, not a remainder (because it does not follow a freehold estate) and was exempt from the destructibility rule. Finally, contingent equitable remainders were unaffected by the rule, because the trustee held legal title and was thus seised for the duration of the trust. Thus, real property could be placed in trust, held there until the contingency was satisfied, and then distributed.

3. **Modern replacement of the rule:** All the work performed by the destructibility rule can be, and is, performed by the Rule Against Perpetuities. See section V.E, below. The *Restatement (Third)* declares that the destructibility rule is no longer good law, a view that, if not true, should be true.

C. **The Rule in *Shelley's Case:*** This rule, which takes its name from *Wolfe v. Shelley (Shelley's Case),* 1 Co. Rep. 93b, 76 Eng. Rep. 206 (1581), was originally intended to prevent avoidance of the feudal incidents (death taxes). After the abolition of feudal incidents in the mid-seventeenth century, the rule survived because it improved marketability of land. That function, however, is fully performed by the Rule Against Perpetuities. The Rule in Shelley's Case has been virtually abolished. In those few states where it survives, it usually applies only to grants made prior to elimination of the rule.

1. **The rule:** If (1) ***one instrument*** (2) creates a ***freehold in real property*** and (3) a ***remainder in the freeholder's*** heirs *(**or heirs of the freeholder's body**),* and (4) the freehold estate and the remainder are **both** *equitable* **or both** *legal,* then (5) the remainder becomes a remainder in the freeholder.

   Example: Warren conveys Blackacre to Smith for life, then to Smith's heirs. In this ***single instrument,*** Warren has created a life estate in Smith and a purported contingent remainder in Smith's heirs. The Rule in Shelley's Case converts the remainder in Smith's heirs into a remainder in Smith. That is all the Rule in Shelley's Case does. The ***merger doctrine*** operates independently but inexorably to give Smith a fee simple absolute in Blackacre, thus making Blackacre easily alienable by Smith rather than only after his death.

   a. **Freehold estate:** Given the virtual extinction of the fee tail, the only freehold estate that can be followed by a remainder is a life estate. As a practical matter, a Rule in Shelley's Case problem will only occur if the freehold estate is a life estate.

   b. **Remainder only:** The Rule in Shelley's Case only applies to remainders, not to executory interests, but the rule does apply to the rare case of a life estate and a remainder combined within an executory interest.

   Example: Amy conveys Blackacre to Hazel so long as motor vehicles never enter Blackacre and, if so, to Florette for life, then to Florette's heirs. The shifting executory interest is split into a life estate in Florette and a remainder in Florette's heirs. The Rule in Shelley's Case applies, giving Florette the entire shifting executory interest.

   c. **Heirs:** The common law judges who created the rule had in mind a special meaning of the term *heirs.* They did *not* mean the *specific persons who would inherit,* for in their time that was usually only one person, the decedent's eldest son. Rather, they meant the term to describe an *indefinite line of succession* of heirs: the class of people, *over time,* who would be heirs in each successive generation. This means that if the remainder is phrased to describe **only** *the specific* **immediate** *heirs of the freeholder,* the Rule does *not* apply.

Example: Eric conveys Blackacre to Rich for life, then to "Rich's heirs, his children." Though the grant reads, to "Rich's heirs" it adds language — "his children" — that makes it plain that the term *heirs* does *not* refer to an *indefinite* line of succession but only to Rich's *immediate heirs.* The Rule in Shelley's Case does not apply. Even so, some confused American courts have applied the rule in similar circumstances.

    d. Both estates legal, or both equitable: Remember that the rule does *not* apply if one of the two estates is equitable and the other is legal.

D. The doctrine of worthier title:

  1. Statement of the doctrine: If an *inter vivos* conveyance creates **any *future interest*** in the **heirs *of the* grantor,** the future interest is **void.** Instead, the ***grantor*** retains a ***reversion.***

    Example: Lewis conveys Tucker Hall to "my son Scott for life, then to my heirs." Lewis has purportedly created a future interest — a vested remainder — in Lewis's heirs. The doctrine of worthier title voids this interest. Lewis is necessarily left with a reversion, which may be conveyed by him during his life, devised, or inherited by his heirs.

    A very few courts have applied this doctrine to testamentary gifts, but mostly it applies to inter vivos conveyances. In its modern form, the doctrine is a ***rule of construction*** — it raises a ***rebuttable presumption*** that the grantor did not intend to create a future interest in her heirs. The rationale for this presumption is that a ***living grantor*** is not likely deliberately to create a future interest in his ***heirs,*** but is far more likely to make that decision as part of his will. Worthier title preserves that option ***unless the grantor clearly intended otherwise.*** Note, by contrast, that the Rule in Shelley's Case and the rule of destructibility of contingent remainders are ***rules of law.*** This old common law rule was originally formulated to curb avoidance of feudal death taxes (by causing real property to descend by inheritance rather than pass inter vivos) but persisted because it also improved alienability of land. Worthier title is still observed in some American states.

  2. Operation of worthier title: The scope of the worthier title doctrine is very broad. It applies to both ***real and personal property*** and to ***any kind of future interest.*** It applies ***regardless of the nature of the preceding estate*** and ***regardless of intervening future interests*** in people who are not the grantor's heirs.

    a. Heirs of the grantor: Worthier title applies to future interests in the ***heirs*** of the grantor, so long as it appears that the term ***heirs*** is used to mean ***indefinite succession*** rather than specific people (who are likely to be the prospective immediate heirs of the grantor).

      Example: James conveyed 37 acres to Nate for life, and if Nate "should die leaving no lawful heir from his body, then the land . . . shall revert back to James . . . or to his lawful heirs." The Virginia Supreme Court ruled that worthier title applied to create a reversion in James rather than a remainder in his heirs, because this language did not "signify anything other than its normal and technical meaning of indefinite succession as determined at the death of the grantor." But if James had said, "The land shall pass to my children," or "to my issue," or even "to my heirs as determined when Nate dies," worthier title would not apply because of these references to ***immediate and specific heirs.*** *Braswell v. Braswell,* 195 Va. 971 (1954).

b. Trust revocation: Worthier title can become an issue when a person establishes an irrevocable trust for the benefit of himself and his heirs but has a change of heart and seeks to revoke it.

Example: Maude conveys property irrevocably to Opus in trust for the benefit of Maude for life, then to Maude's heirs. An irrevocable trust can be terminated only if all the beneficial interest holders consent. Maude owns all those interests (and so can terminate this trust) if worthier title applies, because the remainder in Maude's heirs is void, leaving instead a reversion in Maude. But if Maude left persuasive evidence that she *intended* to create a remainder in her heirs, she is out of luck. Remember that the modern version of worthier title is a rebuttable presumption that Maude retained the reversion instead of creating the remainder in her heirs. See, e.g., *Hatch v. Riggs National Bank,* 361 F.2d 559 (D.C. Cir. 1966). This problem is common enough that some states that have abolished worthier title have, by statute, retained the principle that the settlor of a trust may terminate it if she owns all the interests except for a remainder in her heirs. See, e.g., N.Y. Estates, Powers & Trusts Law §6-5.9.

3. Distinguished from *Shelley's Case:* The Rule in Shelley's Case involves the grant of a future interest to the heirs of the life *tenant,* while worthier title involves the grant of a future interest to the ***grantor's heirs.*** The Rule in Shelley's Case is completely independent of worthier title. Abolition of the Rule in Shelley's Case has no effect on worthier title.

Example: Ben conveys Wolfwood to Terry for life, then to Terry's heirs if they are Roman Catholic, otherwise to Ben's heirs. If both Shelley's Case and worthier title apply, the contingent remainder in Terry's heirs is converted by Shelley's Case into a contingent remainder in Terry, and the alternative contingent remainder in Ben's heirs is converted by worthier title into a reversion in Ben. If Shelley's Case is abolished, but not worthier title, Terry's heirs hold a contingent remainder and Ben has a reversion. If Shelley's Case applies, but not worthier title, Terry holds a contingent remainder, and Ben's heirs have an alternative contingent remainder.

4. Criticisms of worthier title: It is charged that the doctrine breeds litigation because the presumption can be overcome by sufficient evidence that the grantor really meant what he apparently said. It is also claimed that worthier title is a death tax trap because the grantor may think he has parted with all interest in property during his life, but in fact has retained a reversion that is part of his taxable estate. Finally, some critics doubt the assumption that a person is unlikely to wish to give his heirs a future interest in his property. The legendary Professor Richard Powell's rejoinder was to note that while stability was more important than either outcome, worthier title's presumptive reversion "would be less likely to run counter to the real desires of settlors and would help to keep trusts readily revocable and property more easily alienable." 3 R.B. Powell, *Real Property* ¶269 (1952).

E. The Rule Against Perpetuities: After the Statute of Uses, lawyers began to employ shifting executory interests to tie up ownership of property for very long periods into the future. The marketability rules considered so far mostly applied to remainders and not to executory interests. A rule was needed that would apply to ***all contingent future interests*** to prevent uncertainty about future ownership and possession from continuing so far into the future that land would become inalienable. Beginning with the *Duke of Norfolk's Case,* 3 Ch. Cas. 1, 22 Eng. Rep. 931 (1681), that rule is the Rule Against Perpetuities.

1. **Brief summary of the rule:** The classic statement is that by John Chipman Gray:*"No interest is good unless it must vest, if at all, not later than twenty-one years after some life in being at the creation of the interest."* J.C. Gray, *The Rule Against Perpetuities* 191 (4th ed. 1942).

   a. **Vesting:** The Rule is designed to eliminate **uncertainty about ownership** that persists too long. If an interest is **certain to vest** or **certain not to vest** within the permitted period, it is good. But if there is **any possibility,** *no matter how unlikely,* that vesting could occur after expiration of the permitted, period the interest is void. See section VI.E.2, below.

   b. **Permitted period of uncertainty:** An interest is good under the Rule if it will **certainly vest** or **certainly fail to vest** within (1) 21 years from its creation, or (2) during the life of some person **alive at its creation,** or (3) upon the death of some person **alive at its creation,** or (4) within 21 years after the death of some person **alive at its creation.** Thus, the Rule requires you to identify some person, **living on the effective date of the grant,** whose life can serve as the **measuring life** (or **validating life**) for the interest in question. That person, who could consist of a class or group of persons, is always a person whose life is germane to the grant — a person who can affect vesting of the interest. If an effective measuring (or validating) life cannot be identified, the interest is void. See section VI.E.3, below.

   c. **Future interests to which the Rule applies:** The Rule applies to all **contingent** future interests (**executory interests, contingent remainders,** and **vested remainders subject to open**) except for interests **created in the grantor (reversions, possibilities of reverter, and rights of entry).** These latter interests are regarded as vested at the moment of creation, because they represent a **retained portion** of the grantor's estate. The contingency concerning future possession is thus permitted to persist forever. Note that when these latter interests are created in a grantee (and so are executory interests), they are subject to the Rule. See section VI.E.4, below.

   d. **Validity tested at creation:** The validity of future interests under the Rule is tested *when they are created.* This means that, in order to prove validity (or invalidity), you must conjure up *what* **might** *happen* in the future. The Rule boils down to proof. If you can prove that the future interest in question is **certain** *to vest or fail to vest* within the permitted period, the interest is valid. If you can prove *any* **single** *scenario, no matter how* **improbable** *of actual occurrence,* in which uncertainty of vesting will continue until after expiration of the permitted period, the interest is void.

   Example: On July 15, 1997, Alice dies and devises Blackacre "to Barry's first child to graduate from college." Barry's only child, Ted, is a senior at Columbia. The validity of this springing executory interest is tested at the moment of its creation — July 15, 1997. It is void. It is **possible** (though unlikely) that (1) Ted will die tomorrow, before graduating from college, (2) Barry will have another child, Mary, born in 1998, (3) Barry will die immediately after Mary is born, and (4) Mary will graduate from Yale 23 years later. The only conceivable validating lives are Barry and Ted. The hypothetical Mary's hypothetical graduation **could occur** more than 21 years after the expiration of all conceivable measuring (or validating) lives.

   For an interest to be valid, it must be proven that the interest will **necessarily vest or fail to vest** within the permitted period.

   Example: Martha devises Blackacre "to my husband William for life, then to my children for their lives, then to my grandchildren then living." At Martha's death she has two children, Thomas and Louise. The life estate in William is presently possessory. The remainder to Martha's children is vested at its creation (because there is no condition precedent and the class of Martha's children closes at her death around Thomas and Louise), so the Rule does not apply to it. The remainder in Martha's grandchildren who survive both Thomas and Louise is contingent, but that contingency will be eliminated the instant that both Thomas and Louise are dead. At that moment, the remainder will *certainly vest* (there will be surviving grandchildren) *or certainly fail to vest* (there will be no surviving grandchildren). Because both Thomas and Louise are lives in being at the creation of the interest, this interest will *certainly vest or fail to vest* at the expiration of the second of two lives in being. The interest is valid.

2. **Vesting:** With one major exception (see section VI.E.2.a, below), an interest is vested for perpetuities purposes when it has *either* become *possessory* (referred to as *vesting in possession*) or has *vested in interest* (the owners are known, existing people and there are no unsatisfied conditions precedent). Some interests (e.g., an executory interest following or divesting a defeasible fee) can only vest in interest at the same time that they vest in possession. But many interests can and do vest in interest well before vesting in possession. An interest that is vested for classification purposes is vested for perpetuities purposes *except for vested remainders subject to open (or partial divestment).* The reason is that, for purposes of the Rule Against Perpetuities, a gift to a *class* of people is **not vested in any member of the class until it is vested in every member of the class.** For this to happen, two things must be true: (1) the *class must be closed* and (2) *any conditions precedent must be satisfied by* every **member** *of the closed class.*

    Example: In 1997, Olaf devises Blackacre "to my daughter Karen for life, then to Karen's children for their lives, then to Karen's grandchildren." Olaf is survived by Karen, her two children, Victor and Alexa, and Karen's sole grandchild, Natalie. Karen's life estate is possessory and thus not subject to the Rule. Victor and Alexa have a vested remainder subject to partial divestment, as Karen may have more children. While this remainder is *vested for classification purposes,* it is **not** *vested for perpetuities purposes.* The class of Karen's children will not close until Karen dies, but because Karen is a life in being at Olaf's death (the effective date of the grant), the remainder is certain to vest in every member of the class of Karen's children no later than the end of Karen's life, and so it is valid. Similarly, Natalie's vested remainder subject to open is vested for classification purposes but not for perpetuities purposes. The uncertainty about the identity of Karen's grandchildren will not be removed until the class of Karen's grandchildren is closed, and that will happen only when Karen and all of her children are dead. There is no certainty that the class of Karen's grandchildren will close at Karen's death or within 21 years after her death. (Victor might have a child 22 years after Karen's death.)

    While the death of Karen's children will close the class of Karen's grandchildren, the class of Karen's children is not a life in being, because that class is not closed. (There could be another child born to Karen after Olaf's death, and unless *every possible member* of a class is alive at the time the interests become effective, the class is not a life in being.) Thus, none of the lives of Karen, Victor, or Alexa provides sufficient certainty to serve as a validating life, and the remainder in Karen's grandchildren is void in its entirety. The following scenario *might happen:* (1) Karen has another child, Tony, in 1999; (2) Karen, Victor, Alexa, and Natalie all die in a plane crash in 2000; (3) Tony has a child, Ava, in 2026. At that point — 2026, or 26 years after the death of all the relevant lives who could have served as measuring (or validating) lives — Ava would have a vested remainder subject to open. (Tony could have more children.) It is too late. Note that Natalie's remainder interest is destroyed in 1997, simply because of this chain of unlikely possibilities.

3. **Measuring or validating lives:** The concept of the measuring or validating life is crucial to the Rule Against Perpetuities. To validate future interests under the Rule, you must prove that the interest is *certain to vest* or *fail to vest* within the lifetime of one or more people alive when the grant becomes effective, or within 21 years after the death of that person or persons. This person serves as the measuring or validating life. This person will be found among the relatively small number of people whose lives are *relevant* to the interest in question — they *can affect vesting of the interest in question.*

    Example: Orville devises Cliff House to Tina for life, then to Tina's children who reach age 21. The contingent remainder in Tina's adult children is valid because (1) the uncertainty as to the identity of "Tina's children" will be resolved at Tina's death, and (2) the uncertainty as to which, if any, of Tina's children will reach age 21 will be resolved no later than 21 years after Tina's death. (Tina might die in childbirth.) Tina, a life in being when Orville died, is clearly relevant (she can affect the vesting of the remainder), and her life will serve to prove the validity of the remainder.

    The measuring or validating life is not always mentioned in the grant.

    Example: Erwin, an orphan, devises Holmescroft "to my nieces who reach age 21." Erwin is survived by two sisters and five nieces, who range in age from three to 15. The springing executory interest in the nieces is good because the class of Erwin's siblings (not mentioned in Erwin's grant) can serve as validating or measuring lives. Because Erwin's parents are dead, the class of Erwin's siblings is closed; all possible members of that class are lives in being. The contingency in the executory interest (the identity of Erwin's nieces and which of them will reach age 21) will be resolved no later than 21 years after the death of both of Erwin's sisters. Different lives may be used to validate different interests.

    Example: A1 conveys Blackacre to Bill for life, then to Bill's widow for life, then to Connie if she is then alive but, if not, to Connie's heirs. The contingent remainder in Bill's widow is good because we will know her identity when Bill dies. (Bill is the validating life.) The contingent remainder in Connie is good because it will vest or fail during (or at the end of) Connie's life. Either Connie will outlive Bill's widow (and her remainder will vest during Connie's life) or Connie will die before Bill's widow dies (and Connie's remainder will fail to vest). Connie is the validating life for her contingent remainder. The alternative contingent remainder in Connie's heirs is good because it will vest or fail no later than upon the death of Connie. If Connie outlives Bill's widow, the contingent remainder in Connie's heirs will lapse (and thus fail to vest); if Connie predeceases Bill's widow, the contingent remainder in Connie's heirs will be indefeasibly vested because we will know the identity of Connie's heirs, and there will be no condition precedent to their taking possession after Bill's widow dies. Connie is the validating life for the contingent remainder in her heirs.

    A person is a life in being if *in utero* at the effective date of the grant. Common law considered (and still does) a person born within nine or ten months of the effective date of the grant to be a life in being at the effective date.

    a. **Class of persons as measuring lives:** It is possible to use a group or class of people as measuring or validating lives, but *every possible member of the class must be alive at the* *effective date of the grant.* In other words, the **class must be closed at the effective date of the grant** for a class of persons to be effective as validating lives. See section VI.E.2, above.

Example: If Erwin, in the prior example, had been survived by his parents as well as his two sisters and five nieces, the springing executory interest in the nieces would be void. The class of Erwin's siblings is **not closed** (Erwin's parents may have another child) and thus may not be used to validate the executory interest in the nieces. Here's what **might** happen: (1) Erwin's parents have another child, Zelda; (2) Erwin's parents, both of his older sisters, and all five nieces are killed in an avalanche; (3) Zelda, the sole survivor, has a child, Zoe, who reaches age 21. Only then would Zoe's remainder vest, for that is the moment the condition precedent is satisfied, but that moment is over 21 years since Erwin's death, or that of his parents, the two most relevant lives in being at Erwin's death.

Occasionally, lawyers make a large number of people artificially relevant to the grant for purposes of creating a large class of lives in being. This works only if the class is sufficiently small that it will be practical to know when the perpetuities period has expired. See *Restatement (Third) of Property,* Wills and Other Donative Transfers §27.1, comment d (2008).

Example: Rocco conveys Sweetbrier to Maribelle for life, then to Maribelle's children after the last person now alive in the City of Los Angeles has died. The springing executory interest in Maribelle's children is void because it is simply not possible to know when this event will occur.

Example: Viscount Leverhulme devises gobs of property in trust to be distributed to a class of beneficiaries when all descendants of Queen Victoria living at the time of his death have died. An English chancery court upheld this artificial class of lives in being even though there were "at least 134" members of the class, and the court admitted that there were "certain difficulties in ascertaining exactly how many of Queen Victoria's descendants were living" on the date of the viscount's death, to say nothing of the problem of determining when this class would expire. *Cooper v. Leverhulme,* 2 All.E.R. 274 (Ch. 1943).

b. **Class closing rules and the Rule of Convenience:** Ordinarily, a class closes when every possible member of the class has been identified. The class of A's children is closed upon A's death, for example, because all of A's possible children will be known at that moment. See section VI.E.2, above. The **Rule of Convenience,** however, holds that a class closes artificially when *any one member* of the class is entitled to present possession (or present distribution from a trust). The rule of convenience is a rule of construction and will be ignored if the grantor provides adequate evidence that he or she does not wish it to be applied. See also III.A.3.b.v, above.

Example: Victor devises Hardacre to "such of Adele's children who reach age 25." At Victor's death, Adele has two children, Bart (age 26) and Cynthia (age 22). Bart is entitled to possession immediately, so, under the Rule of Convenience, the class will close and consists of Bart and Cynthia (who holds an executory interest that will become possessory and partially divest Bart if and when she reaches age 25). Note that the Rule of Convenience saves this class gift from destruction under the Rule Against Perpetuities. Without the Rule of Convenience, the class of Adele's children would remain open until her death. Adele could have a third child, Mortimer, two years after Victor's death, and then Adele, Bart, and

Cynthia could all die in a mass accident, leaving Mortimer alive. Because Mortimer's interest could vest later than 21 years after the death of all relevant lives in being at Victor's death, the entire class gift would be void. The rule of convenience avoids this result by closing the class prematurely around Bart and Adele, who serve as the validating lives for their interests. Should Mortimer arrive later, he does not share in the devise from Victor.

4. **The curious problem of defeasible fees:** Recall that a defeasible fee is followed by either a possibility of reverter or right of entry (if retained by the grantor) or by an executory interest (if transferred to a grantee). Executory interests are subject to the Rule, but neither a possibility of reverter nor a right of entry is subject to the Rule. Thus, the ***identical contingency*** can last forever if preserved by a possibility of reverter or right of entry but may well be destroyed by the Rule if created in a grantee as an executory interest. That is curious enough, but even more curious is the fact that, due to the differing grammatical construction of a fee simple determinable, as opposed to a fee simple subject to condition subsequent, the estate left after destruction of the executory interest will differ.

Example: Executory interest following determinable fee: Thomas conveys Thimbleberry to Edward and his heirs so long as Thimbleberry is never fenced, then to Paul and his heirs. The executory interest in Paul is void because you cannot prove that it will necessarily vest or fail to vest within 21 years after any life in being at the time of Thomas's conveyance. The condition of "no fences" may not be broken for generations, if ever. Paul's executory interest is erased. It is as if the grant stopped at "fenced," with the final clause expunged. *The effect of this removal is to leave Edward with a fee simple determinable.* The law then operates to create a possibility of reverter in Thomas. Note that Thomas could avoid this result by first conveying a fee simple determinable to Edward, then conveying separately his possibility of reverter to Paul.

Example: Executory interest following a fee simple subject to a condition subsequent: Thomas conveys Thimbleberry to Edward and his heirs, but if Thimbleberry is ever fenced, then to Paul and his heirs. As in the prior example, the executory interest in Paul is void because you cannot prove that it will necessarily vest or fail to vest within 21 years after any life in being at the time of Thomas's conveyance. Paul's executory interest is erased, so that the grant stops at "Edward and his heirs," with the final clauses expunged. *The effect of this removal is to leave Edward with a fee simple absolute.* Again, Thomas could avoid this result by first conveying a fee simple subject to condition subsequent to Edward, then conveying separately his right of entry to Paul, assuming that local law permits rights of entry to be conveyed inter vivos. This dramatic difference in result is hard to justify, as is the difference in result between a possibility of reverter or right of entry, on the one hand, and the analogous executory interest on the other. This common law result has been modified in some jurisdictions, but modification schemes differ.

a. **Apply the Rule Against Perpetuities to possibilities of reverter or rights of entry:** By statute, this change has been adopted in England but has not been widely adopted in the United States. This approach eliminates the preferential treatment under the Rule accorded possibilities of reverter and rights of entry but does nothing to alter the different estates that result from destruction of the future interest following a defeasible fee.

b. **Statutory destruction of possibilities of reverter and rights of entry:** A number of American states have enacted statutes that automatically destroy possibilities of reverter and rights of entry a specific number of years after creation, usually 30 years. See, e.g.,

Mass. Ann. Laws c.184A, §7. Some of these statutes permit a possibility of reverter or right of entry to be preserved for an additional period if notice of that intention is recorded prior to expiration of the initial period. These interests continue to be exempt from the Rule Against Perpetuities. The statutory destruction rule performs the work of the Rule and, in practice, can be harsher than the Rule Against Perpetuities.

    c. Statutory destruction of all future interests following defeasible fees: Some states have enacted statutes that automatically destroy possibilities of reverter, rights of entry, *and executory interests following a defeasible fee* a specific number of years after creation, usually 30 years. These statutes typically permit a possibility of reverter, right of entry, or analogous executory interest to be preserved for an additional period if notice of that intention is recorded prior to expiration of the initial period. This process of preservation can go on forever, so long as somebody cares enough to record the notice of intent to preserve every 30 years. See, e.g., Cal. Civ. Code §§885.010-.030. In this scheme, all of these interests are exempt from the Rule Against Perpetuities, but the statutory destruction rule will accomplish that job once the holder of the interest fails to keep it alive. Though conceivable, no jurisdiction exempts possibilities of reverter, rights of entry, and the analogous executory interests from the Rule Against Perpetuities *without subjecting them to some statutory rule of destruction.*

    d. Charity-to-charity exemption: By statute, and sometimes by judicial decision, an executory interest following a defeasible fee is exempt from the Rule Against Perpetuities *if the defeasible fee* **and** *the following executory interest are* **both** *owned by charities.* The justification for this rule is to foster and preserve charitable giving.

    Example: Ellen conveys Thornhedge to Whitman College so long as it is used for educational purposes, and if not, to the National Trust for Historic Preservation. Whitman College has a fee simple subject to an executory limitation, and the National Trust has an executory interest. This executory interest would normally be destroyed by the Rule Against Perpetuities, but because **both** Whitman College and the National Trust are charities, the executory interest in the National Trust is exempt from the Rule.

5. Classic traps for the unwary: This section discusses two of the classic traps of the Rule Against Perpetuities. Each results from the Rule's insistence on considering *future possibilities,* no matter how outlandish, rather than *probabilities.*

    a. The fertile octogenarian: The Rule presumes that a person of any age, whether male or female, can produce a child. This presumption can lead to some harsh results.

    Example: Edward devises Blackacre to Mary, but if and when Mary ceases to have any lineal descendants, to the children then living of John and Elizabeth. At the time of Edward's death, Mary is 65 years old, John and Elizabeth are each 80 years of age, and John and Elizabeth have two children, Amos and Obadiah, each in his fifties. Mary has a fee simple subject to an executory limitation in favor of the open class of John and Elizabeth's children. The executory interest in John and Elizabeth's children is void. Though biologically well-nigh impossible, the common law Rule Against Perpetuities assumes that Mary and Elizabeth are each capable of conception and childbirth. Mary could have a child, Zoë, and then die. John and Elizabeth could have a third child, Isaac, and then each die. Amos and Obadiah could then die. Finally, more than 21 years after all these deaths, Zoë could die with no lineal descendants. At that point, the executory interest in Isaac and the successors in interest to Amos and Obadiah would vest, but it would be too late — more than 21 years after the expiration of any relevant life in being at the time of Edward's death. This conclusion results from imagining the possibility of fertile octogenarians and the like. Of course, people can adopt children at any age. (This example is a variation on the facts of the classic case, *Jee v. Audley*, 1 Cox 324, 29 Eng. Rep. 1186 (Ch. 1787).)

b. The unborn widow: This is another classic. Without more, a bare reference to "*A*'s widow" is construed to refer to the unknown person who answers that description on *A*'s death, not necessarily the person who is *A*'s wife when the instrument is drafted. The Rule presumes the possibility that aged men and women might substitute fresh youngsters for the elderly mates — so young that they were not even born at the time of the grant.

Example: William devises Mosswood to "my son, Charles, for life, then to his widow for life, then to his children then living." At William's death, Charles is 40, married to Diana, age 35. Charles has a possessory life estate. The remainder to "his widow" is contingent because we cannot know the identity of this person until Charles's death. This contingent remainder is valid under the Rule Against Perpetuities because the uncertainty concerning her identity will be removed at Charles's death: Charles serves as a validating or measuring life. The contingent remainder in Charles's children is void, however, because the uncertainty as to which, if any, of Charles's children will survive Charles's widow will not be removed until the death of that person. It may be Diana, a life in being, but *it is possible that may be someone not alive when William dies.* Diana may die, or Charles may divorce her and, as an 80-year-old man, might marry Lolita, age 16, a person born 24 years after William's death. The "class" of "Charles's widow" is open at William's death and, even though it is a class of one, it may be composed of a person not alive when the executory interest is created. So, "Charles's widow" is ineffective as a validating life.

6. **Applicability of the Rule Against Perpetuities to commercial transactions:** Although frequently criticized, the Rule applies to commercial option agreements with respect to real property. The optionee has an equitable interest in the property, consisting of a specifically enforceable right to purchase on the terms of the agreement.

★**Example:** *The Symphony Space, Inc. v. Pergola Properties, Inc.:* In 1978 Broadwest Realty sold a building in Manhattan to Symphony Space for much less than its real value, in return for which Broadwest leased much of the building for a nominal rent and obtained an option to purchase the building, exercisable any time until July 2003. The value of the building increased significantly, and Pergola Properties, the assignee of Broadwest's interests in the building, exercised the option in 1987. Symphony Space contended that the option violated the Rule, and the New York Court of Appeals agreed. Because corporations were involved (and corporations have no natural life span), the period during which the option must either vest or fail was the naked 21-year period. Although the Rule was never designed to curb lengthy uncertainty of ownership produced by commercial options, the court concluded that the Rule's policy of fostering alienability in order to enhance productive use of resources was advanced by applying the Rule to commercial options. Because of the option, Symphony Space had no incentive to improve the building. Moreover, the option's existence foreclosed sale to someone other than the optionee who might make a better use of the land. The court refused to construe the option to comply with the Rule because it was apparent from the option agreement that the parties intended it to last for longer than 21 years. The court refused to apply the "wait-and-see" doctrine (see the next section) because New York's legislature had not adopted wait-and-see.

Symphony Space v. Pergola Properties, 88 N.Y. 2d 466 (1996), is representative of the common law approach to commercial options.

The Uniform Statutory Rule Against Perpetuities (USRAP), adopted in some form or another in over 20 states, exempts options and other commercial transactions from the Rule, although one USRAP jurisdiction, Indiana, has construed the exemption to mean that options remain subject to the otherwise displaced common law Rule. The *Restatement (Third) of Property* (Servitudes) also exempts options from the Rule but subjects them to generally applicable principles voiding unreasonable restraints on alienation. Some courts avoid applying the Rule to options by implying into the option agreement a proviso that the option must be exercised, if at all, within 21 years of its creation. See, e.g., *Robroy Land Co. v. Prather,* 95 Wash. 2d 66 (1980).

7. **Reform doctrines:** The common law Rule Against Perpetuities has been reformed in over half the American states by adoption of ***wait-and-see*** statutes. Many jurisdictions also attempt to save interests by **construction of the grant,** if possible, and some are willing to engage in ***reformation of the grant*** in order to save interests created by it from destruction.

   a. **Wait-and-see:** As the name implies, this statutory reform evaluates the validity of future interests under the Rule Against Perpetuities ***as events unfold,*** not at the time of creation of the interests. The focus under wait-and-see is on ***what actually happens,*** not on ***what might happen.*** The common law Rule has the virtue of supplying a quick answer to the question of validity of future interests, albeit sometimes at the expense of common sense. Wait-and-see avoids that expense, but at the cost of years of uncertainty while we wait to see what actually happens. Wait-and-see comes in two essential forms, with a few permutations on each.

      i. **Wait-and-see for the common law period:** About two-thirds of the non-USRAP wait-and-see states wait for the period permitted by the common law Rule Against Perpetuities. This means that you must still determine the appropriate measuring or validating life for the interest in question, ***even if it won't work to validate the interest under the common law Rule,*** and then wait for that life (or lives) to expire plus 21 years.

          Example: Chuck devises Converse Hall to Taylor for life, then to Taylor's children for their lives, then to Taylor's grandchildren. At Chuck's death, Taylor has two children, Agnes and Ethel, and one grandchild, Sean. Under the common law Rule, the contingent remainder in Taylor's children is good because their identities will be fully known upon Taylor's death (the class will close), and Taylor is a life in being. But the contingent remainder in Taylor's grandchildren is void because their identity will not be known until all of Taylor's children are dead, and the class of Taylor's children, being open at Chuck's death, cannot serve as a validating life because all possible members of the ***class*** are not lives in being. Under wait-and-see for the common law period, we wait for the following lives to end: Taylor, Agnes, Ethel, and, if necessary, Sean. All of these people were lives in being at Chuck's death. If Taylor never has any more children, the remainder in Taylor's grandchildren will be completely vested when both Agnes and Ethel are dead, and it will be good. If Taylor has an after-born child, Cedric, the remainder in Taylor's grandchildren will not vest when both Agnes and Ethel are dead, because the class of Taylor's grandchildren is not yet closed. We would continue to wait for Sean's death. If Sean dies before Cedric, we will wait for 21 years more. If Cedric is still alive at that point, the class of Taylor's grandchildren is still open, and the contingent remainder in the grandchildren is void. If Cedric predeceases Sean or dies within 21 years after Sean's death, the class of Taylor's grandchildren closes, and the contingent remainder is vested within the permitted perpetuities period.

ii. **USRAP: Wait-and-see for 90 years:** The Uniform Statutory Rule Against Perpetuities (USRAP) provides for waiting for a maximum of 90 years after the creation of the interest to see whether it has vested. This avoids the necessity of locating the lives that measure the common law perpetuities period, but may (in some cases) permit uncertainty to persist for a longer period than under wait-and-see for the common law period. If, at the end of the 90-year wait, an interest is still not vested or lapsed, USRAP commands that the contingent interest be judicially reformed to vest within the 90-year period and conform as closely as possible to the grantor's intent.

Example: In the prior example, we would simply wait for 90 years after Chuck's death to see whether all of Taylor's children had died, thus closing the class of Taylor's grandchildren and causing the remainder in Taylor's grandchildren to vest (or fail, in the absence of any grandchildren). If, at the end of that 90-year period, Taylor's after-born son Cedric were still alive, thus keeping open the class of Taylor's grandchildren, USRAP would require a court to reform Chuck's will so that the interest in Taylor's grandchildren would be vested within the 90-year period. This would probably mean that the class of Taylor's grandchildren would be closed at the 90-year mark, thus excluding from the class any grandchildren of Taylor born after that moment. Under USRAP, an interest is good if it is valid *either* under the common law Rule Against Perpetuities *or* under the wait-and-see-for-90-years approach.

b. **Construction of the instrument:** Most modern courts will construe an instrument to save future interests from destruction by the Rule, if possible to do so without plainly violating the grantor's intent.

Example: Edward devises Blackacre to Mary, but if and when Mary dies without issue, to the children then living of John and Elizabeth. At the time of Edward's death, Mary is 65 years old, John and Elizabeth are each 80 years of age, and John and Elizabeth have two children, Amos and Obadiah, each in his fifties. Mary has a fee simple subject to an executory limitation in favor of the open class of John and Elizabeth's children. A modern court would likely construe the phrase "dies without issue" to refer to Mary's death without children, rather than the extinction of Mary's imaginary bloodline generations hence. This construction would validate the executory interest in John and Elizabeth's children because Mary would serve as the validating life. A modern court would also be likely to construe the phrase "children then living of John and Elizabeth" to mean Amos and Obadiah, thus excluding some fanciful child born to the octogenarian couple. This latter construction, by itself and without the former construction, would also save the executory interest because it would close the class of John and Elizabeth's children around their two now-living children, who must also be living when Mary's bloodline expires, even if that occurs generations later. Amos and Obadiah could serve as the validating lives because the divesting condition (expiration of Mary's bloodline) would necessarily occur or fail to occur within the joint lives of Amos and Obadiah.

c. **Reformation of the instrument:** Some modern courts apply the *cy pres* **doctrine** to reform a grant to make it comply with the Rule Against Perpetuities. *Cy pres* is a doctrine of wills and trusts (usually applied with respect to gifts to charities) that permits courts to revise the grantor's instrument to get as close as possible to the grantor's intentions when the grantor's actual intentions are impossible to accomplish. Eight non-USRAP states specify that all or some violations will be reformed. Under USRAP (adopted by 24 states), violations after 90 years of wait-and-see will be reformed.

> **Example:** Harry conveys Woodlot to Angela for life, then to Angela's children who reach age 30. The contingent remainder is void under the common law Rule because Harry and Angela's now-living children might all die, and Angela might have another after-born child and die in childbirth. The after-born child could satisfy the contingency 30 years after the expiration of Angela's life, and Angela is the only possible relevant measuring or validating life. Reform by *cy pres* would rewrite Harry's conveyance to read, "to Angela's children who reach age 21." Now the remainder is good because even the hypothetical after-born child born at Angela's death would necessarily satisfy (or fail to satisfy) the contingency no later than 21 years after Angela's death. Under USRAP, there would be no necessity to reform because the after-born child would necessarily satisfy the age contingency or fail to do so within the 90-year wait-and-see period.

8. **Perpetual trusts: The end of the Rule?** Over twenty states have either repealed the Rule in its entirety or made it inapplicable to interests in trusts (which is where almost all future interests are created). Washington permits trusts to endure for 150 years, Florida allows 360 years, and Utah and Wyoming permit trusts to last for 1,000 years. This movement has its origins in federal tax law. A rich person, *T*, could create a trust at his death that would pay the income from the trust principal to his child *A* for her life, then to pay the income to *A*'s children for their lives, and then to pay the principal out free of trust to *A*'s grandchildren. With an appropriate saving clause, this trust would comply with the Rule. Until 1986, an estate tax would be paid by T's estate on the amount transferred into the trust, but no estate taxes would be paid at the deaths of *A* or *A*'s children because those persons owned no interest in the trust at their death. (They only had a life estate, which expired at their death; in tax parlance, they did not own a "transmissible interest.") The next estate tax would be due only upon the deaths of *A*'s grandchildren. Thus, estate taxes could be avoided for two generations with respect to the amounts placed in trust. In 1986, Congress enacted a "generation-skipping transfer tax" (GST) that applies in lieu of estate taxes whenever wealth is transferred by means of a life estate that avoids the estate tax by skipping a generation, as would the trust described above. The GST rate is the highest rate under the estate tax. If that is all Congress had done, the GST might have served as a practical brake on the creation of dynastic trusts, making the Rule a bit redundant. But Congress also provided that a person could transfer up to $3.5 million in a trust that would be exempt from the GST. At the end of 2010, many estate taxation rules will revert to those existing in 2000, so Congress is considering revision of estate taxation. These rules may change in the future. Because the urge to avoid taxes is basic to human nature, states began to compete to attract these "GST exempt" trusts, and the surest way to do so was to eliminate the Rule, thus permitting such trusts to endure forever without the burden of any estate or generation-skipping taxes. Of course, Congress could eliminate the GST exemption or eliminate the estate tax and GST altogether, either of which would remove the incentives for creating perpetual trusts.

Another factor that may hasten the end of the common law Rule is the widespread adoption of USRAP. USRAP permits contingent interests to endure for 90 years and reforms those that remain contingent at that time. Although USRAP permits the common law period to be used as an alternative to the 90-year period, it is quite possible that, if USRAP becomes universal, after a century of reliance upon the 90-year period the common law Rule will be largely forgotten by lawyers and judges, a relic much like the Rule in Shelley's Case.

The rise of perpetual trusts and the uncertain future of the Rule illustrate the conflict in American law concerning dead-hand control of property. One view is that the property belongs to the decedent, and he should be entitled to do with it what he wishes, regardless of the practical or policy consequences. The other view is that property should be controlled by the living. For centuries, the Rule has been the compromise between these principles.

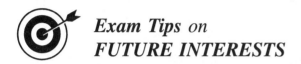

Exam Tips on
FUTURE INTERESTS

☛ This is fertile examination ground. Pay attention to how much time your professor devotes to this area. If this is taught in detail, it will almost surely be an examination subject. Future interests are rarely examined without combining the issues with the Rule Against Perpetuities. The question will require you to classify accurately the various interests created, then determine whether any of them is invalid under the Rule Against Perpetuities (or any of the other moribund marketability doctrines, such as *Shelley's Case,* or worthier title, if your professor thinks those are of much significance). You must analyze each future interest created in turn to decide whether it is valid or not. Be alert to the consequences of destruction — once a future interest is destroyed, that may require you to reclassify the prior interest. Remember to apply the reform doctrines if any of them applies, unless your professor has stipulated that your analysis should focus on the common law Rule Against Perpetuities.

☛ When analyzing perpetuities problems, classify first. After you have identified the uncertainty or uncertainties, ask yourself when they will be resolved. To do this, you will need to locate that moment in relation to someone's life, someone who can serve as a validating life because they were alive when the interest became effective. Many uncertainties will be resolved upon the death of someone; if that person is alive when the future interest becomes effective, the interest is good. If you cannot prove validity, you must prove invalidity by illustrating some possible way in which the uncertainty will be prolonged beyond the perpetuities period. In concocting such a scenario, be imaginative; usually you will have to invent some person or persons born after the interest became effective (thus not eligible to serve as a validating life), kill off all the people who could serve as validating lives, and then illustrate how the uncertainty will persist during the life of the hypothetical after-born, or at least until some point longer than 21 years after the end of all possible validating lives.

☛ Make sure you understand the classic pitfalls of the common law Rule Against Perpetuities — the unborn widow, the fertile octogenarian — because some version of these traps is likely to occur.

CHAPTER 4

CONCURRENT OWNERSHIP AND MARITAL INTERESTS

ChapterScope ━━━━━━━━━━━━━━━━━━━━━━━━━━━━━━━━

This chapter examines various forms of concurrent ownership of property, marital property interests, and the rights and obligations of co-owners. Here are the most important points in this chapter.

- All types of property may be owned simultaneously by multiple people, a condition that invites conflict among co-owners. While co-owners are generally free to specify the terms of their relationship, law must provide some default rules that mediate conflict.

- The principal forms of concurrent ownership are **tenancy in common, joint tenancy, and tenancy by the entirety.**

  - Tenancy in common is the modern default position. Unless a grant indicates a contrary intention, tenancy in common results from a grant to two or more persons. Tenants in common own separate, but undivided, interests in the whole of the property.

  - Joint tenancy differs from tenancy in common in that each joint tenant has an undivided interest in a single unit. The consequence is that each joint tenant has a right of survivorship — when a joint tenant dies, his or her interest dies with him, and the remaining joint tenant or tenants own it all. When there are two joint tenants, this is an effective way to avoid probate.

    - At common law, a joint tenancy was possible only if the joint tenants had *unity of interest, time, title, and possession*. These requirements have been relaxed by statute. A corollary to the four unities was that the destruction of any unity severed the joint tenancy, producing a tenancy in common instead. Today, a conveyance by one joint tenant will sever the joint tenancy.

    - Tenancy by the entirety is a form of joint tenancy limited to married couples, but unlike the joint tenancy, the survivorship right is indestructible — it may not be destroyed by the unilateral act of a single owner.

- Two different forms of marital property exist: *Community property and separate property*.

  - Community property, a civil law institution recognized in nine states, treats all property acquired during marriage (except gifts and inheritances) as owned by the marital community. Each marital partner has an equal interest in the property of the marital community.

  - Separate property, the form of marital property recognized by the common law, holds that property acquired during marriage is owned by the marital partner who acquired it. This "his-is-his" and "hers-is-hers" rule is tempered at divorce by equitable distribution laws that require courts to ignore title to achieve equity in property division, and at death by spousal elective share statutes that permit a surviving spouse to take some portion of the deceased spouse's property, even if the deceased spouse's will is to the contrary.

■ Unmarried cohabitants may agree to share property but cannot by agreement acquire any of the status benefits of marriage. In eleven states, same-sex partners may obtain some or all of the status benefits of marriage by civil ceremony.

■ Every co-owner, except tenants by the entirety, has the right at any time to demand partition of the property. Divorce is the effective method of partition for tenants by the entirety.

    ■ Partition is in-kind (physical division) unless that is impracticable or would not be in the best interests of *all* co-owners, in which case partition is by sale and division of the sale proceeds.

■ Each co-owner is entitled to possession of the whole, but when one co-owner actually possesses the entire property, courts disagree over whether the tenant-in-possession must pay fair rent to the tenants not in possession.

    ■ Most courts hold that unless the tenant-in-possession has ousted the other tenants, there is no duty to pay rent. Ouster consists of either refusing a co-owner's demand to share possession or unequivocally denying that one's co-owner is really an owner.

    ■ Some courts hold that a co-owner in sole possession has an obligation to pay fair rent to the other co-owners regardless of whether there has been ouster.

■ Co-owners must account to each other for the rents they have received from third parties. Co-owners are liable to each other for their proportionate share of the costs of ownership, but not for improvements. An improving co-owner can recover the value added by the improvement only upon partition or sale.

■ Condominiums and cooperative apartment corporations are unique forms of co-ownership. Condominium owners have title to their unit and own the common areas of the development as tenants in common. Cooperative apartment owners actually own shares in the corporation that owns the building, and they lease their apartments from the corporation, thus making the shareholder-tenants extremely financially interdependent.

I. FORMS OF CONCURRENT OWNERSHIP

  A. Introduction: When the same interest in property is owned by more than one person at the same time there is *concurrent ownership.* There are at least five forms of concurrent ownership recognized by the common law, only three of which are studied in the typical property course: *tenancy in common, joint tenancy,* and *tenancy by the entirety.* Of the remaining two, *co-parceny* is extinct in the United States, and *tenancy in partnership* is usually covered in courses on business associations. This chapter also covers marital interests, only some of which are forms of concurrent ownership.

  B. Tenancy in common:

    1. Nature of tenancy in common: Tenants in common own *separate but undivided* interests in the same interest in property. Conceptually, each tenant in common owns the entire property but must necessarily share that ownership with the other tenants in common. Two people who own a sailboat as tenants in common each own a fraction of the entire boat, and they are each entitled to sail it, but they cannot prevent the other from doing so. Much of the law of concurrent ownership is designed to mediate the friction that can arise from co-ownership of the same article. A tenancy-in-common interest may be alienated, devised, or inherited separately from the other tenancy-in-common interests. Unlike the joint tenancy, there are *no survivorship rights* among tenants in common.

Example: Tim conveys Roundhouse to Ezra and Geraldo, as tenants in common. If Ezra conveys his interest in Roundhouse to Newt, Geraldo and Newt are tenants in common. If Geraldo dies, devising his interest in Roundhouse to Maxine, Newt and Maxine are tenants in common.

2. **Presumption of tenancy in common:** By statute or judicial decision, a conveyance of real property to two or more persons who are not married to each other is *presumed to convey a tenancy in common.* That presumption is rebuttable. The best evidence rebutting it is a clear statement in the conveyance of the alternative form of co-ownership (e.g., joint tenancy). Property that passes by intestate succession to two or more heirs is always taken as a tenancy in common.

3. **Rights to possession:** Each tenant in common is entitled to possess the entire property. In practice, this means that a tenant in common can possess the entire property if *no other cotenant objects.* Tenants in common may, and often do, regulate their rights to the property by agreement among themselves. But if they do not, and disagreement erupts, their rights and obligations are governed by "default" rules of law. See section II, below.

4. **Uneven shares and different estates:** Tenants in common may own *unequal shares* and *different estates.*

Example: Able, Baker, and Cassie own Blackacre, in equal shares, as tenants in common. Able conveys his interest to Baker. Baker and Cassie are still tenants in common, but Baker has a two-thirds share, and Cassie a one-third share. Cassie conveys her interest in Blackacre to Sophie for life, then to Andrea and her heirs. Baker is now a tenant in common with Sophie (as to possession) and with Andrea (as to her remainder).

There is a rebuttable presumption that tenants in common have equal shares in the property. The best evidence rebutting this presumption is a clear statement in the conveyance creating the tenancy in common (e.g., "O conveys a two-thirds share to A, and a one-third share to B, as tenants in common"), but evidence extrinsic to the conveyance (e.g., relative contributions of purchase cost or carrying costs) is germane to this issue.

C. Joint tenancy:

1. **Nature of joint tenancy:** Joint tenants own an undivided share in the same interest in either real or personal property, but the surviving joint tenant owns the entire estate. This *right of survivorship* is the hallmark of joint tenancy, setting it apart from tenancy in common. Any number of people may be joint tenants. Upon the death of one joint tenant, the share held by the remaining joint tenants increases proportionately.

Example: Alan, Betty, and Charles own equal undivided interests in Blackacre as joint tenants. Alan dies, leaving all his property by will to David. Betty and Charles now own equal undivided interests in Blackacre. Alan's will is ineffective to transfer his interest in Blackacre because the nature of joint tenancy is that his interest expires at his death. Charles then dies intestate, leaving Emmy as his heir. Betty now owns the entirety of Blackacre by herself. Charles's estate has no interest in Blackacre. When a joint tenant dies, his *entire interest* dies with him.

A joint tenancy may only be created by an inter vivos conveyance or a will. Property acquired by multiple heirs through intestate succession is taken as tenants in common.

a. **The theory of joint tenancy:** Common law conceived of joint tenants as bound together as a single owner. The common law's expression for this unwieldy concept was to say that each joint tenant owned the property *per my et per tout* — by the moiety (the half) and the whole. This summed up the inherent duality of the joint tenancy — multiple people own an equal interest in the entirety of the property. Each joint tenant owns it all. Thus, when a joint tenant dies, his interest dies, because he was a mere participant with others in a single ownership entity. The dead joint tenant simply drops out of the ownership unit. No interest in property passes to the survivors, because they already own the entire property. There is just one fewer member of the ownership consortium. Significant consequences flow from the idea that no interest passes at death: (1) A *joint tenancy is not subject to probate,* an expensive, cumbersome, time-consuming judicial procedure to transfer a decedent's property; and (2) Creditors of a joint tenant must seize and sell the debtor's joint tenancy interests during the debtor's life because the joint tenant debtor's interest disappears at his death.

2. **The four unities of joint tenancy:** From the theory of the joint tenancy, common law judges derived the principle that the *interests of joint tenants must be equal in every respect.* Hence, the *four unities* of joint tenancy: *all joint tenants* must take their interests: (1) at the *same time,* (2) under the *same instrument,* (3) with the *same interests,* and (4) with the *same right to possession of the entire property.* At common law, a joint tenancy *could not be created without the four unities being satisfied.* If the four unities were not satisfied, a tenancy in common resulted. This is still the law in many states, but many states have relaxed the rule to permit creation of a joint tenancy whenever there is sufficiently clear intention that a joint tenancy was intended.

   a. **Time:** The joint tenants must receive their interests at the same moment in time.

      Example: Oliver conveys Blackacre to "my son, Michael, and to my daughter, Eliza, if and when they marry, as joint tenants." This springing executory interest vests in interest and possession as each of Michael and Eliza marry. Obviously, they cannot marry each other and, unless they happen to marry in an exquisitely timed double ceremony, their respective interests in Blackacre will vest at different times. When Michael marries Jane and, a year later, Eliza marries Roger, Eliza and Michael will own Blackacre as tenants in common, not as joint tenants.

   b. **Title:** All joint tenants must receive their interests under the same instrument: a deed, a will, or a decree quieting title by joint adverse possession.

      Example: Edward was the sole owner of Bower Cottage prior to his marriage to Andrea. As a marriage present, Edward conveyed Bower Cottage "to Andrea and Edward, as joint tenants." At common law, this did *not* create a joint tenancy, because Edward's interest in Bower Cottage was created by a prior instrument. The deed from Edward to Edward and Andrea was construed as a nullity insofar as it purported to transfer Edward's interest, but did operate to convey half of Edward's interest to Andrea. Common law did not recognize transfers from oneself to oneself. Thus, Edward and Andrea would be tenants in common.

      This example, which occurred with some frequency, proved to be a bothersome annoyance. The solution at common law was for Edward to convey to his lawyer (or some other trusted friend), who would promptly convey back to Edward and Andrea, as joint tenants. This "straw man" conveyance met the four-unities requirement but was cumbersome and, in essence, an empty formality. As a result, many states today have, by statute, provided that a person may create a joint tenancy by a conveyance from himself to himself and another, as joint tenants. Under such a statute, Edward, in the example, would have created a joint tenancy between himself and Andrea. See ***Riddle v. Harmon,*** 102 Cal. App. 3d 524 (1980), discussed in section I.C.4, below.

    c. Interest: Each joint tenant must have the identical interest in the property. This means two things: (1) each joint tenant must have the same share of the undivided whole, and (2) each joint tenant must have the same durational estate.

        Example — Same share: George conveys "a two-thirds interest in Whitewall to Andrew, and a one-third interest in Whitewall to Bruce, as joint tenants." Andrew and Bruce take as tenants in common because the unity of equal interest is not present.

        Example — Same durational estate: George conveys Whitewall to Andrew and his heirs, and to Bruce and his heirs so long as Whitewall's library remains intact, as joint tenants. Bruce and Andrew are tenants in common because Andrew has a fee simple absolute, and Bruce has a fee simple determinable (George retaining a possibility of reverter as to half of Whitewall). But this requirement does ***not*** preclude holding a portion of an estate in joint tenancy and another portion in tenancy in common.

        Example Olivia conveys "a half interest in Tinderbox to Amy and Ben, as joint tenants, and a quarter interest in Tinderbox to Cameron, as a tenant in common." After this conveyance, Amy and Ben own an undivided interest as to half of Tinderbox in joint tenancy; Cameron owns a quarter undivided interest as a tenant in common, and Olivia continues to own a quarter undivided interest as a tenant in common. If Ben dies, Amy will be the sole owner of an undivided half interest in Tinderbox, as a tenant in common with Cameron and Olivia. ***Remember:*** The joint tenancy is considered a single ownership entity, so throughout this scenario the joint tenancy owned an undivided half interest in Tinderbox as a tenant in common with Cameron and Olivia. When Ben dies, Amy simply owns the entire interest formerly held by the joint tenancy, but the relationship of tenancy in common with respect to the other interests is not altered.

    d. Possession: At creation of the joint tenancy, each joint tenant must have the right to possession of the whole property. After creation, joint tenants may agree among themselves to divide possession, or to deliver exclusive possession to one joint tenant. So long as the arrangement is consensual, it amounts to a voluntary waiver of a joint tenant's legal right to possess the whole. Generally, the law is willing to enforce the voluntary agreements of co-owners concerning their co-ownership.

3. Creation of joint tenancy: Common law presumed that any conveyance or devise to two or more persons (other than husband and wife) was in joint tenancy. This simplified the performance of feudal obligations, because only one entity — the joint tenancy — owed those obligations. Because we don't live in a world of feudal obligations, every American jurisdiction has reversed the presumption. Today, a tenancy in common is presumed, unless there is clear evidence of joint tenancy. At common law, husbands and wives were presumed to take as tenants by the entirety. Today, husbands and wives are presumed to take either as tenants by the entirety or as joint tenants.

a. **Evidence sufficient to create joint tenancy:** The modern presumption of tenancy in common can be overcome only by a clearly expressed intention in the grant itself. The best expression is "to A and B, as joint tenants with right of survivorship," although Michigan and Kentucky regard this clear expression as creating a joint life estate in A and B, with a contingent remainder in the survivor. See *Albro v. Allen,* 434 Mich. 271 (1990); *Sanderson v. Saxon,* 834 S.W.2d 676 (Ky. 1992). The significance of the Michigan and Kentucky view is that the survivorship right cannot be destroyed by a joint tenant through a conveyance to a third party that severs the joint tenancy.

b. **Evidence insufficient to create joint tenancy:** The following common expressions are dangerous. Some courts regard them as adequate to create a joint tenancy; others do not.

   Example: "To *A* and *B* as joint tenants." This is ordinarily adequate to create a joint tenancy, but some states hold that failure to include the phrase "with right of survivorship" renders this usage inadequate to create a joint tenancy. But note that inclusion of that phrase in Michigan and Kentucky creates a joint life estate with contingent remainder in the survivor.

   Example: "To *A* and *B* jointly." This is problematic, because the term *jointly* is often used colloquially to refer to any form of co-ownership.

   Example: "To *A* and *B,* joined together." This probably produces a tenancy in common, because the term *joined together* is not a term of art, and is probably a lay reference to co-ownership.

   Example: "To *A* and *B* as joint tenants, then to the survivor and her heirs." This is hopelessly ambiguous; a mixed message. The phrase "joint tenants" is clear enough, but when followed by the express conveyance of an interest "to the survivor and her heirs," the inference is reasonable that the grantor intended to create a remainder in the survivor. On the other hand, the "survivor and her heirs" language could be taken to mean nothing more than an empty restatement of the legal effect of a joint tenancy. This usage may result in a joint tenancy but is probably more apt to create a joint life estate or tenancy in common in *A* and *B,* followed by a remainder in the survivor. The latter result prevents either *A* or *B* from destroying the survivorship right by an inter vivos conveyance.

4. **Severance of joint tenancy:** A joint tenant may destroy the joint tenancy at any time by severing the joint tenancy, usually by conveyance. A tenancy in common results. Because the "four unities" were necessary to create a joint tenancy at common law, the destruction of any one of those unities would operate to sever the joint tenancy. That rule is still alive, but many courts today prefer to rely on evidence of the intention of the conveying party.

   a. **Conveyance:** If a joint tenant conveys his interest to a third party or to another joint tenancy, the joint tenancy is severed *as to that interest.*

      Example: Tom, Dick, and Harry are joint tenants. If Tom conveys his interest to Bill, the joint tenancy is severed *as to that interest.* Bill owns a one-third undivided interest as a tenant in common with Dick and Harry. Dick and Harry continue to be joint tenants with respect to their interests. If Dick then dies, Bill and Harry will be tenants in common, with Harry holding two-thirds, and Bill one-third. If Tom had conveyed his interest to Harry, instead of to Bill, Harry would own a one-third interest (the interest acquired from Tom) as a tenant in common with Dick, and a one-third interest in joint tenancy with Dick. If Harry then died, Dick would own a two-thirds interest as a tenant in common with Harry's heirs or devisees.

A conveyance includes a contract to convey that is specifically enforceable, because the buyer under such a contract has equitable title to the property. Severance occurs at the moment such a contract is made.

★i.   **Unilateral severance: Conveyance to self:** Common law regarded a conveyance of an interest held by a person to himself as an empty act, devoid of legal effect. Thus, to convert a joint tenancy into a tenancy in common, the joint tenant would have to employ a straw man, to whom the severing conveyance would be made and from whom a reconveyance would be made. In *Riddle v. Harmon,* 102 Cal. App. 3d 524 (1980), the California Court of Appeal held that Frances Riddle could validly sever the joint tenancy with her husband, Jack, by a conveyance from herself as joint tenant to herself as tenant in common with Jack. Frances's deed made plain that her intent was to sever the joint tenancy; the reasons for refusal to recognize a conveyance from self to self were archaic and rooted in livery of seisin; many other, but more complex, ways to unilaterally sever a joint tenancy existed; and by statute, California had already permitted *creation* of a joint tenancy by a conveyance from "*A* to *A* and *B,* as joint tenants." *Riddle v. Harmon* takes a realistic view of severance and elevates the intent of the grantor to prominence. Note, however, the possibilities of some injustice occurring: (1) Jack probably never knew that the joint tenancy was severed; as a result, his interest would pass at his death through intestacy or the residual clause of his will (dispositions that he might not have made had he known he owned a tenancy in common); and (2) An unscrupulous hypothetical Frances could sever the joint tenancy by executing a deed, not recording it, and telling a trusted, but equally unscrupulous, beneficiary of her will of the deed's existence, but then wait to see whether Jack dies first, at which point the severing deed would secretly be destroyed; if Frances were to die first, her devisee would produce the deed. California dealt with this dark possibility by requiring such conveyances to be recorded.

b. **Mortgage:** Jurisdictions differ as to whether a joint tenancy is severed by the act of one joint tenant mortgaging his interest. Resolution of this issue traditionally depended upon whether the jurisdiction adhered to the *lien theory* or the *title theory* of mortgages, but that distinction has mostly broken down for this purpose.

   i.   **Title theory of mortgages:** The title theory holds that a mortgage effects a transfer of legal title, subject to an equitable right of the mortgagor (the borrower) to reclaim title by paying off the loan secured by the mortgage *(equity of redemption).* This was the common law theory of mortgages. As a result, a mortgage by one joint tenant had the effect of severing a joint tenancy because the unity of interest is destroyed. The joint tenancy could not be restored by redemption, because the unities of time and title would not be present. After the mortgage, the former joint tenants would become tenants in common, and there would be, of course, no right of survivorship. See, e.g., *Stewart v. AmSouth Mortgage Co., Inc.,* 679 So. 2d 247 (Ala. App. 1995). This result has often been criticized as inconsistent with the intentions of the mortgagor (who likely never considered, or even knew of, the magic four unities of the common law). Many (but by no means all) jurisdictions today modify the title theory to treat the title held by the mortgagee (the lender) as one held only for purposes of securing the loan, a view that effectively makes a title theory state into a lien theory state for purposes of resolving this issue of severance. See, e.g., ***Harms v. Sprague,*** 105 Ill. 2d 215 (1984); *Brant v. Hargrove,* 129 Ariz. 475 (1981); *Hamel v. Gootkin,* 202 Cal. App. 2d 27 (1962).

ii. **Lien theory of mortgages:** The lien theory of mortgages holds that the mortgagee (lender) only has a lien against the property (an inchoate right to seize title if the loan is not paid). On this view, a mortgage by one joint tenant makes no alteration to title and thus does ***not*** sever the joint tenancy. But another problem crops up, one that divides lien theory states (and title theory states that treat mortgages as liens for this purpose): Upon death of the mortgaging joint tenant while the loan is unpaid, does the surviving joint tenant have an interest that is ***wholly unencumbered by mortgage,*** or an interest that is ***burdened by the mortgage?*** The prevailing answer is that the surviving joint tenant takes free and clear of the mortgage.

★**Example:** John and William Harms owned a farm as joint tenants. John mortgaged his interest to Carl and Mary Simmons in order to secure a loan made by them to John's friend, Charles Sprague. Later, John died while the loan was unpaid. In ***Harms v. Sprague,*** 105 Ill. 2d 215 (1984), the Illinois Supreme Court held that (1) there was no severance, and (2) William owned the farm entirely free of the mortgage to Carl and Mary Simmons. The court reasoned that the mortgage burdened only John's interest and that because John's interest died with him, leaving only the previously unencumbered interest of William as the surviving title, the mortgage had died with John. Accord: *People v. Nogarr,* 164 Cal. App. 2d 591 (1958); *Ogilvie v. Idaho Bank & Trust Co.,* 99 Ida. 361 (1978); *Irvin L. Young Foundation, Inc. v. Damrell,* 511 A.2d 1069 (Me. 1986).

The majority view, exemplified by ***Harms v, Sprague,*** is criticized on the ground that it penalizes the unsophisticated lender (because a savvy lender will never lend to a single joint tenant on the strength of the joint tenancy interest as security for payment of the loan) and delivers a windfall to the surviving joint tenant. Consider the opposite result.

Example: Suppose that after John's death William took John's interest in the farm subject to the mortgage to Carl and Mary Simmons. This result would fully preserve William's survivorship rights and still preserve the Simmons' expectation that a half interest in the farm would continue to secure payment of their loan to Charles. After all, John always had the right to mortgage his interest, or even convey it outright (which would destroy William's survivorship right), so it does not seem unfair to William to allow him to take John's interest subject to the burden John placed upon it. Cf. Wis. Statutes §700.24.

c. **Lease:** At common law, if one joint tenant leased his interest the joint tenancy was severed. The unity of interest was destroyed, because the leasing joint tenant retained only a reversion in the property. The lease, however, was valid. Most jurisdictions today do ***not*** regard a joint tenancy as severed by one joint tenant's lease of his interest. The survivorship right continues but, as with mortgages, the problem is presented of whether the lease survives the death of the leasing joint tenant. Most jurisdictions say, "No."

Example: Johnson and Tenhet were joint tenants. Without Tenhet's knowledge or consent, Johnson leased the entire parcel to Boswell for 10 years, then died three months later. Tenhet demanded that Boswell vacate. He refused, relying on his lease. The California

Supreme Court held that (1) the lease did not sever the joint tenancy, and (2) the lease expired on the death of Johnson, the lessor. See *Tenhet v. Boswell,* 18 Cal. 3d 150 (1976).

As a practical matter, the *Tenhet v. Boswell* view requires a prospective lessee either (1) to examine title to be sure that the lessor is not a joint tenant, or (2) to insist that all joint tenants join in the lease. The opposite view, which rejects the idea that the lease expires with the lessor, allows the surviving joint tenant to take subject to the possessory interest of the lessee.

d. Agreement: A joint tenancy can be severed by agreement, so long as the intention is clearly manifested. This usually occurs in the context of marital dissolution.

Example: Betty and Aaron owned their residence as joint tenants. When they divorced, they agreed that the house would be sold, and the proceeds evenly divided between Betty and Aaron, when (1) Betty remarried, or (2) their youngest child reached age 21, or (3) they agreed to sell. Before any of those events occurred, Betty died, and Aaron claimed to own the entire house by virtue of the right of survivorship. The Colorado Supreme Court ruled that the agreement severed the joint tenancy because it clearly "evince[d] the intent to no longer hold the property in joint tenancy." Thus, because Betty was a tenant in common, her half interest in the property passed to her children instead of to her ex-husband. See *Mann v. Bradley,* 188 Colo. 392 (1975). See also *Sondin v. Bernstein,* 126 111. App. 3d 703 (1984).

An agreement to sever can be inferred from the manner in which the parties deal with the property. See, e.g., *Thomas v. Johnson,* 12 Ill. App. 3d 302 (1973); *Mamalis v. Bornovas,* 112 N.H. 423 (1972); *Wardlow v. Pozzi,* 170 Cal. App. 2d 208 (1959). But this is dangerous; in order to preserve certainty in land titles, many courts will not find severance based on agreement unless that agreement is absolutely clear. See, e.g., *Estate of Violi,* 65 N.Y.2d 392 (1985). However, an agreement to permit one joint tenant to have exclusive possession of the property does not destroy a joint tenancy (even though it destroys the unity of possession), absent additional and specific evidence of intent to sever. See *Porter v. Porter,* 472 So. 2d 630 (Ala. 1985); *Tindall v. Yeats,* 392 Ill. 502 (1946). Perhaps the intentions of the parties should always govern.

e. Operation of law: Most severance issues begin with some voluntary act of a joint tenant that immediately implicates the four unities and thus, joint tenancy. But there are two recognized instances in which the law operates to sever a joint tenancy even in the absence of these voluntary acts.

    i. Criminal homicide: If one joint tenant kills another joint tenant with criminal culpability, the usual result is severance of the joint tenancy by operation of law, thus turning the interests into tenancy in common. This can occur by statute, or by judicial conclusion that criminal homicide is "inconsistent with the continued existence of the joint tenancy" because it would benefit the wrongdoer. *Duncan v. Vassaur,* 550 P.2d 929 (Okla. 1976). Accord: Uniform Probate Code §2-803.

    ii. Simultaneous death: Under section 4 of the Uniform Simultaneous Death Act, applicable in most states, the simultaneous death of joint tenants (e.g., a plane crash) results in a division of the joint tenancy into separate shares unless there is clear and convincing evidence that one person survived the other by 120 hours or a governing instrument (e.g., a will) provides otherwise.

f. Theoretical possibilities: Whenever one joint tenant transfers an interest that is a lesser estate than that which he holds (e.g., a joint tenant in fee simple absolute leases, mortgages, or conveys a life estate of his interest), there are four possible outcomes that courts could reach. Which outcome is theoretically preferable might depend on the evidence of the grantor's intent, the other joint tenants' reasonable expectations, and the reasonableness of the consequences to third parties.

Example — Severance: Thelma and Louise are joint tenants in fee simple absolute of Blackacre. Thelma leases her interest to Jack. If the lease severs the joint tenancy, Jack and Louise are tenants in common for the duration of the leasehold; thereafter Louise and Thelma are tenants in common.

Example — No Severance, No Encumbrance: If Thelma's lease to Jack does not sever the joint tenancy, what happens if Thelma dies before the leasehold expires? The *Tenhet v. Boswell* answer was that Jack's interest expired on Thelma's death, and Louise took Blackacre free of Jack's interest.

Example — No Severance, Encumbrance: If Thelma's lease to Jack does not sever the joint tenancy, and Thelma dies before the leasehold expires, another possible outcome is that Jack and Louise become tenants in common for the duration of Jack's lease; thereafter Louise is the sole owner of Blackacre. If Louise should die before Thelma, Thelma is the sole owner of Blackacre, subject to Jack's leasehold.

Example — Temporary Severance: Finally, Thelma's lease to Jack could sever the joint tenancy temporarily, during the life of the lease. If Thelma dies before Louise but during the term of the lease, Louise and Jack become tenants in common for the duration of the lease; thereafter Louise is a tenant in common with Thelma's estate. If Louise dies before Thelma during the lease period, Thelma is a tenant in common with Louise's estate, subject to Jack's interest. If both Thelma and Louise survive Jack's leasehold, the joint tenancy between them is restored.

5. Joint tenancy bank accounts: Litigation frequently results when a bank account is established in joint tenancy, because there are a variety of reasons for creating such an account. A depositor might wish to make a *present gift* of an undivided interest in the account ("It's yours and mine together from now on"), or might wish to use the survivorship aspect as a *will substitute* — a "payable on death" or *POD account* ("It's mine until I die, and then it's yours"), or might wish to use joint ownership as a *convenience* to permit the other owner to manage the depositor's money, much like giving a person power of attorney ("It's mine, but you can have access to it to pay my bills"). Because there is the possibility of very different intentions, courts do not automatically honor the putative survivorship rights but seek to ascertain the specific intentions of the depositor.

Example: Otto, a widower, opens a joint bank account with Ally, his niece, telling her, "I want your name on this account so if I get sick you can get the money for me." No present gift was intended; this was a convenience account. *Franklin v. Anna Natl. Bank of Anna,* 140 Ill. App. 3d 533 (1986). See also *Allen v. Gordon,* 429 So. 2d 369 (Fla. App. 1983).

Example: Otto adds Ally to the signature card giving access to his safe deposit box, which contains $328,000 in cash and securities. The safe deposit box lease agreement stipulates that the contents of the box are owned in joint tenancy. Despite this, the lack of an additional specific written statement by Otto that he intended to make a present gift of the contents to Ally negated the lease agreement's stipulation of joint tenancy. The significant value of the contents influenced the result. As value increases, probably more and better evidence of a present gift is needed to prove joint tenancy. See *Newton County v. Davison,* 289 Ark. 109 (1986).

Generally, creditors of one joint tenant can reach only the portion of a joint tenancy bank account that equals the debtor's contribution to the account, but the burden of proving the proportion of contributions is on the joint depositors, on the theory that these facts are more likely to be known by the depositors than the creditor. See *Maloy v. Stuttgart Memorial Hospital,* 316 Ark. 447 (1994).

D. Tenancy by the entirety:

1. **Nature of tenancy by the entirety:** A tenancy by the entirety is a *form of joint ownership available only to a husband and wife.* Like the joint tenancy, each tenant by the entirety has a right of survivorship. In essence, this is the common law's special joint tenancy for marital partners. The usual four unities of joint tenancy are required for its creation, plus the requirement of marriage between the tenants. There are, however, significant differences from the joint tenancy. About half the states recognize tenancy by the entirety. Hawaii and New Jersey permit creation of the tenancy by the entirety between same-sex partners who are not permitted to marry each other.

    a. **One person:** The common law presumed that, upon marriage, a husband and wife merged into *one legal person.* The woman lost her legal identity and became the legal ward of her husband. Before marriage, she was a *feme sole;* after marriage she was a *feme covert.* From the common law's perspective, marriage produced one person — the husband. Of course, we do not observe this disabling condition of married women today, but states that recognize tenancy by the entirety still observe the fiction that the tenancy by the entirety is owned by one person, with consequences that are discussed in the remainder of this section.

    b. **No severance:** One key attribute of the tenancy by the entirety is that it *cannot be severed.* Unlike the joint tenancy, neither tenant acting alone can destroy the tenancy by the entirety. Thus, neither tenant may obtain partition (see II.B, below), nor can either spouse, acting alone, convey the entire estate. The right of survivorship is indestructible so long as the marriage remains intact.

2. **Creation:** At common law, a conveyance to a husband and wife necessarily created a tenancy by the entirety. Because they were one person, legally speaking, they could share a tenancy in common or joint tenancy. It was all or nothing, and the "all" was tenancy by the entirety. No American jurisdiction observes this rule today. A husband and wife may own property as joint tenants, tenants in common, or as tenants by the entirety. Some states recognize the civil law institution of the "marital community" as the owner of property, and in these *community property* states, a husband and wife compose a marital community that owns most property acquired by them during marriage. See III.C, below. Tenancies by the entirety are not recognized in the community property states.

    a. **Presumptions concerning creation:** Most states that recognize tenancies by the entirety observe a *rebuttable presumption* that a conveyance to a husband and wife creates a tenancy by the entirety. A minority of states recognizing the tenancy by the entirety presume (unless rebutted) that the ambiguous grant to a husband and wife creates a tenancy in common. Another minority of states recognizing tenancy by the entirety employ a rebuttable presumption that the ambiguous grant to a husband and wife creates a joint tenancy.

   b. **Failed attempts:** An attempt to create a tenancy by the entirety in unmarried persons will fail everywhere. Most states treat this failed attempt as creating a tenancy in common, though a few hold that it creates a joint tenancy because a joint tenancy is closer to a tenancy by the entirety than a tenancy in common. Much may depend on the parties' intentions.

3. **Operation of the tenancy by the entirety:** The modern tenancy by the entirety functions differently from its common law predecessor.

   a. **Common law:** The common law fiction that marriage produced one person, embodied by the husband, made the husband the master of the tenancy by the entirety. The husband had the right to exclusive possession as well as his survivorship right. Both of those rights could be alienated by the husband inter vivos, and so could be seized by the husband's creditors. The wife had only her survivorship right, which could not be alienated by her without her husband's consent (and thus could not be seized by her creditors).

      Example: Harry and Wanda own Blackacre as tenants by the entirety. If Bank, Harry's creditor, seizes and acquires Harry's interest in Blackacre, Bank is entitled to exclusive possession of Blackacre during Harry's life. If Wanda predeceases Harry, Blackacre is owned solely by Bank. If Harry predeceases Wanda, Blackacre is owned solely by Wanda, and Bank has no further interest. Wanda's creditors, however, may not seize her interest in Blackacre.

      The pure common law tenancy by the entirety no longer exists in the United States.

   b. **Modern operation of the tenancy by the entirety:** The modern tenancy by the entirety treats both spouses as equals. The principal source of this change has been the Married Women's Property Acts, adopted by every state in the mid-nineteenth century in order to eliminate the legal disabilities placed on married women by the common law. They did so by restoring to a married woman her separate legal identity, which the common law had taken away from her on the occasion of her marriage. Courts then interpreted these acts, as applied to a tenancy by the entirety, to equalize the interests of husband and wife in the tenancy. But this could be done in one of two ways: Either (1) the *woman acquired equal rights with the man to alienate her possession and survivorship rights,* or (2) *neither spouse was permitted to alienate their possession and survivorship rights.*

      i. **Equal right to alienate:** Perhaps a half-dozen states (including Alaska, Oregon, New York, and New Jersey) provide that either spouse may alienate their possession or survivorship rights in a tenancy by the entirety. The principal effect of this version of equality, which gives the wife the same rights the husband had at common law, is to *enable her creditors to seize her possessory interest* in the tenancy but not the survivorship right. At common law, the husband's possessory interest, of course, was always subject to seizure by his creditors.

         Example: Todd and Heidi own Blackacre in tenancy by the entirety. Todd is indebted to Loanshark, who seizes Todd's interest in Blackacre in satisfaction of the debt. Loanshark and Heidi are now equally entitled to possession. Heidi continues to have her indestructible survivorship right, and Loanshark now owns Todd's survivorship rights. Note that this estate, owned concurrently by two unmarried people, is functionally identical to a tenancy in common with the added twist of indestructible survivorship rights.

ii. **Neither spouse may alienate:** The majority of states recognizing tenancy by the entirety provide that neither spouse may alienate their possession or survivorship rights in a tenancy by the entirety. The principal effect of this version of equality, which places the husband on the same footing as the wife at common law with respect to a tenancy by the entirety, is that it *prevents the creditors of either spouse from seizure of their interest* in the tenancy.

★**Example:** Kokichi Endo inflicted personal injuries on Masako and Helen Sawada by his negligent operation of an auto. Kokichi owned a home in tenancy by the entirety with his wife, Ume. After the auto accident, but before the Sawadas brought suit, Kokichi and Ume conveyed their home to their sons. This conveyance would be a fraud on Kokichi's creditors, including the Sawadas, if Kokichi's creditors were entitled to seize his interest in the tenancy by the entirety to satisfy their claims. In *Sawada v. Endo,* 57 Hawaii 608 (1977), the Hawaii Supreme Court held that property held in tenancy by the entirety may not be subjected to claims of creditors against only one spouse. The rationale for this view was partly the fiction of one person (the estate is owned by the marital couple, not the constituent partners), partly the view that contract creditors have ample opportunity to insist on both spouses pledging the property as security for extensions of credit, and partly the view that tort creditors of a single spouse ought not be permitted to seize a portion of the family residence with dangerous consequences to the innocent spouse. Given a conflict between creditors and the family unit, the Hawaii court preferred protection of the family unit.

iii. **Variations on the theme:** A few states recognizing tenancy by the entirety hold that creditors can seize the *survivorship right* of a spouse but *not the possessory rights* of either spouse. See., e.g., *Covington v. Murray,* 220 Tenn. 265 (1967); *Hoffman v. Newell,* 249 Ky. 270 (1932).

Example: Creditor obtains a judgment lien against Henry, owner with Willa of Blackacre in tenancy by the entirety. While both Willa and Henry are alive, Creditor has no right to possession. If Willa predeceases Henry, Creditor may enforce the lien on Blackacre, owned now entirely by Henry. If Henry predeceases Willa, Creditor's lien is extinguished with respect to Blackacre. If Henry and Willa divorce, or if Henry and Willa join together to convey Blackacre, Creditor can enforce the lien against Henry's share of Blackacre, because the tenancy by the entirety would have terminated.

iv. **Federal government claims:** There are a variety of ways in which the federal government can become a creditor of a person who owns property in tenancy by the entirety. If the government's claim is by way of a tax lien, the government may seize the debtor spouse's interest as if it were a tenancy in common, regardless of the state law rules with respect to creditors' claims. Federal tax law displaces contrary state law. See *United States v. Craft,* 535 U.S. 274 (2002). If the government seeks civil forfeiture of property that has been used in criminal transactions (e.g., illegal drug dealing), *United States v. 1500 Lincoln Avenue,* 949 F.2d 73 (3d Cir. 1991), held that the government could only seize the debtor spouse's survivorship interest (rather than all or none of the property), because that compromise would best accomplish the twin goals of forfeiture of the guilty spouse's interest and protection of the interest of the innocent spouse. But if the property subject to civil forfeiture has itself not been used in the criminal transaction, at least one circuit has ruled that the government's interest in forfeiture is not sufficient to outweigh the innocent spouse's interest in retaining her property without the government becoming her co-owner. See *United States v. Lee*, 232 F.3d 556 (7th Cir. 2000).

    v. Bankruptcy: After *Craft*, some creditors claimed that filing a federal bankruptcy petition by a single spouse operates to sever the debtor spouse's interest in any property held in tenancy by the entirety, thus rendering the debtor spouse's share subject to creditors' claims in bankruptcy. This position seems to be untenable with respect to bankruptcy debtors who elect the state law exemptions in bankruptcy, as 11 U.S.C. §522(b)(3)(B), enacted after *Craft* was decided, provides that "an individual debtor may exempt from property of the estate . . . any interest" the debtor may have in property owned "as a tenant by the entirety . . . to the extent that such interest as a tenant by the entirety . . . is exempt from process under applicable nonbankruptcy law." Bankruptcy law thus appears to incorporate explicitly state law rules regarding creditors' claims in bankruptcy.

  4. Termination: A tenancy by the entirety is terminated by (1) death of a spouse, (2) divorce, or (3) joint action of both spouses to convey the property held in tenancy by the entirety. Upon divorce, most states convert a tenancy by the entirety into a tenancy in common, but a few inexplicably convert it into a joint tenancy.

  5. Personal property: Common law did not recognize a tenancy by the entirety in personal property because the husband, upon marriage, became the sole owner of his wife's personal property. Today, most states that recognize tenancy by the entirety permit tenancies by the entirety in most forms of personal property. Some forms of personal property (e.g., deposit accounts) are not susceptible to tenancy by the entirety, because it is impossible to maintain inviolate survivorship rights when either spouse can withdraw the deposited property at any time.

E. Partnerships and coparceny:

  1. Nature of partnership tenancy: Tenancy in partnership is inextricably connected to the rights and obligation of business partners. The property is owned by the partnership, and each partner has an interest in the property via their partnership interest. The details of partnership are covered in courses in business associations.

  2. Nature of coparceny: Coparceny is extinct. The English common law system of primogeniture made the first-born son the sole heir. If a decedent had no sons, his daughters inherited as coparcenors, an estate that was a bit like tenancy in common. Because primogeniture never took root in America, coparceny never had occasion to develop. Good riddance.

II. RIGHTS AND OBLIGATIONS OF CONCURRENT OWNERS

A. Introduction: In general, the rights and obligations of co-owners are the same regardless of the type of concurrent ownership. The exceptions, of course, are the rights and duties ***inherent in the***

type of concurrent ownership, e.g., the right of survivorship that forms part of the joint tenancy, and tenancy by the entirety. Those exceptional issues have been discussed in section I, above.

B. Partition: A joint tenant or a tenant in common may demand ***partition*** of the property at any time and for any reason, or for no reason at all. A tenant by the entirety may not demand partition — the effective remedy is divorce. Absent agreement among the parties, partition is accomplished by a suit in equity. The court will order ***either*** (1) ***physical division*** of the property, or (2) ***sale and division of the sale proceeds.*** Any other claims among the parties (e.g., for an accounting or for rent — see II.C and D, below) will also be resolved in the same proceeding.

  1. Partition in kind: Physical division of the property (called ***partition in kind***) is the preferred method. Courts will order partition in kind unless a party can prove either (1) that physical partition is ***impossible*** or ***extremely impractical,*** or (2) that physical partition *is* ***not in the best interest of all*** **parties.** See, e.g., ***Delfino v. Vealencis,*** 181 Conn. 533 (1980). Evidence germane to the "best interest" prong includes the economic costs (or gain) involved in physical partition, but also the more subjective costs imposed on a tenant in possession by ordering partition by sale. Compare the following examples.

  ★**Example:** Helen Vealencis owned 20.5 acres in Bristol, Connecticut, as a tenant in common with Angelo and William Delfino. Helen lived on a portion of the property and operated a garbage-hauling business from there. The Delfinos wished to develop the property into single-family residences and so demanded partition by sale even though the property was capable of partition in kind. Although the evidence suggested that the total value of the property would be maximized by sale and development, the Connecticut Supreme Court held that it was not in the best interest of ***all parties*** (including Helen) to sell the entire property. The value to Helen of continued possession (secured by physical partition) was sufficient to convince the court that partition in kind should be ordered. ***Delfino v. Vealencis,*** 181 Conn. 533 (1980).

  Example: Karl Hendrickson and his twin sons lived on and farmed a 160-acre farm, in which they owned a one-third interest as tenants in common with the Baumans, a group of relatives who owned fractional shares ranging from one-twelfth to two-ninths. The Baumans sought and obtained partition by sale under a statute authorizing partition by sale if physical partition could not be accomplished without "great prejudice to the owners." The South Dakota Supreme Court gave little weight to the value of continued possession to Karl and his sons, relying almost entirely on the conclusion that division of the farm into parcels ranging in size from 13.33 acres to 53.33 acres would "materially depreciate its value, both as to salability and . . . use for agricultural purposes." The court did not even consider the possibility that the Baumans could unite to sell their 106.67-acre block after physical partition. *Johnson v. Hendrickson,* 71 S.D. 392 (1946).

  When implementing partition in kind, courts strive to divide property so that the value of each divided parcel (as a fraction of the value of the entire property) is equal to the ownership share of the recipient. If not, the recipient of the disproportionately valuable parcel is obligated to pay *owelty* — enough cash to the other tenant(s) to equalize values.

  Example: Ed and Louise own Blackacre as tenants in common. Louise has a two-thirds interest; Ed owns a one-third interest. The value of Blackacre is $120,000. If, after partition in kind, Ed's parcel is worth $50,000, and Louise's is worth $70,000, Ed will owe Louise $10,000 cash to equalize their proportionate shares.

Some states extend owelty to its logical extreme: If partition in kind is impractical, and sale will not protect the interests of all parties, one party may be awarded the entire property, subject to an obligation to pay the other owners their fair market value of their lost interests. See, e.g., *Zimmerman v. Marsh*, 365 S.C. 383 (2005).

2. **Partition by sale:** Even though partition by sale is not favored by courts, it is probably the most common method of partition. This is because it is impractical or impossible physically to divide most real property in America: houses, condominiums, office buildings, warehouses, and retail stores. Rural undeveloped land is the most likely candidate for physical division. After a partition by sale, the net proceeds are divided among the co-owners in proportion to their ownership interests. In the absence of express evidence in title of unequal shares, courts employ a rebuttable presumption that each co-owner is entitled to an equal share of the proceeds.

3. **Agreement not to partition:** Though courts often say that "partition between cotenants is an absolute right," an agreement between cotenants not to partition is *enforceable* if (1) it *clearly manifests the parties' intent not to partition,* and (2) its *duration is limited to a reasonable period of time.*

   Example: Marion and Alexandra, husband and wife, separated and entered into an agreement by which they promised not to "do or permit anything [to be done] to defeat the common tenancy" of Marion and Alexandra in certain properties for the remainder of their joint lives. A New Jersey appellate court found this to be a sufficiently clear expression of their intent not to partition. Its duration was reasonably limited because it would expire upon the death of either party, and both Marion and Alexandra were of "advanced age" (apparently about 60 when they entered into the agreement). *Michalski v. Michalski,* 50 N.J. Super. 454 (1958).

   Because partition is inherently equitable, a nonpartition agreement (even if otherwise enforceable) will be enforced only if it is "fair and equitable." Changed circumstances are especially relevant to this inquiry.

   Example: In their 1949 nonpartition agreement, Marion and Alexandra promised to treat each other "with kindness and respect" and agreed that they would continue to reside together in their home. By 1951, they were not living together in the home and had embarked on a continuous bout of civil and criminal litigation against each other. In 1958, a New Jersey appellate court ruled that "the circumstances have so changed that it would be inequitable to deny partition. The intent of the parties has been entirely destroyed." *Michalski v. Michalski,* 50 N.J. Super. 454 (1958).

C. **Rents, profits, and possession:** Each co-owner has the right to possess the entire property, and no co-owner may exclude his fellow co-owners. If co-owners cannot agree on how they share possession, the "default" rules discussed here apply.

1. **Exclusive possession by one co-owner:** Because each co-owner has a right to possess all of the property, exclusive possession by one co-owner is presumptively valid. If it is pursuant to agreement of all co-owners it is conclusively valid. If not by agreement, the cotenant in exclusive possession has the following obligations to his cotenants.

   a. **Rental value of exclusive possession:** Jurisdictions split on the question of whether the cotenant in exclusive possession is liable to his cotenants for their share of the fair rental value of his exclusive possession. Here are the two views on this question.

i. **No liability absent ouster or special duty:** The *majority rule* is that a cotenant in exclusive possession has no liability for her share of the rental value of possession unless:

(1) the other cotenants have been *ousted,* or (2) the cotenant in possession owes a *fiduciary duty* to the other cotenants, or (3) the cotenant in possession has *agreed to pay rent.* This rule is premised on the fact that each cotenant is entitled to possession. The exceptions reflect instances in which the cotenant in possession has voluntarily assumed a duty to his cotenants (by agreement to pay rent or by acting as a fiduciary) or has prevented his cotenants from exercising their equal right to possession (*ouster*). The corollary to this rule is that the cotenant validly in exclusive possession is obligated to pay the "carrying costs" of the property (e.g., mortgage payments, taxes, utilities, maintenance) up to the fair rental value of the property. Any excess costs must be shared ratably by all cotenants. *Ouster* occurs if the tenant in exclusive possession *either:* (1) actually *prevents or bars physical entry by a cotenant,* or (2) *denies the cotenant's claim to title.* The former can occur by such things as changing the locks; the latter can occur by express statements denying that the cotenant out of possession has any valid claim of ownership of the property.

★**Example:** Spiller and Mackereth owned a commercial building as tenants in common. Spiller took possession of the entire building and used it as a warehouse. Mackereth demanded that he vacate half the building or pay rent. Spiller did nothing, and Mackereth sued for the rental value of half the building. In *Spiller v. Mackereth,* 334 So. 2d 859 (Ala. 1976), the Alabama Supreme Court reversed an award of rent, reasoning that Spiller had neither denied that Mackereth was an owner of the building nor prevented Mackereth from actually moving in and taking possession. Mackereth's demand that Spiller vacate or pay rent was insufficient to trigger ouster; she needed to prove that she "actually sought to occupy the building but was prevented from moving in by Spiller."

ii. **Liability for rent:** The *minority rule* is that the cotenant in exclusive possession is liable to cotenants out of possession for their share of the fair rental value of the occupied premises, *unless there has been an agreement among the parties to excuse the tenant in possession from this obligation.* On this view, there is no need to show ouster, or agreement to pay rent, or the presence of a fiduciary obligation to the cotenants out of possession. Instead, the burden is on the cotenant in possession to prove the existence of an agreement excusing him from the obligation to pay rent. This rule is designed to induce agreements among the parties by placing the burden on the tenant in possession (the one who is gaining the economic value of occupancy) to pay or prove an agreement not to pay. But this rule also undercuts the general principle that a cotenant is entitled to possess the whole.

2. **Rents from third parties:** A cotenant who receives rents on the property from a third party is obligated to account to his cotenants for those rents. If the rents or other income received by a cotenant are greater than the cotenant's share, he is obligated to pay the excess to the other cotenants.

Example: Anne and Clarke own Blackacre as equal cotenants. A portion of Blackacre is rented to Ajax for $500/month, and the remainder is rented to Hector for $700/month. If Clarke receives Hector's rent, and Anne receives the rent from Ajax, both must account to each other for the rents they received, and Clarke must pay $100/month to Anne.

This duty to account is a continuing one and may be enforced at any time during the cotenancy, upon partition, or within the period of the statute of limitations following expiration of the cotenancy.

3. **Profits from the land:** The normal rules regarding possession apply to exclusive possession for farming, animal husbandry, or other agricultural uses, but if a cotenant permanently removes an asset from the land, he must account to his cotenants for this reduction in value. If minerals are removed, the cotenant must pay to the other cotenants their proportionate share of the value of the removed minerals. Other natural resources, like standing timber, may be removed by a cotenant without payment to other cotenants so long as the cotenant does not cut more than her share of the total timber. Some states require the consent of all cotenants to the cutting of timber.

D. **Accounting for the costs of ownership:** Subject to the exceptions set forth in II.C, above, and others discussed here, each cotenant is liable for his proportionate share of the costs of ownership — mostly mortgage payments, taxes, repairs, and maintenance.

1. **Mortgage payments:** Mortgage payments consist of *principal* and *interest.* A cotenant's payment of a disproportionate share of these items is treated differently.

   a. **Interest:** Each cotenant is obligated to pay his proportionate share of mortgage interest. A cotenant who pays more than his share can force the other cotenants to reimburse him for their share immediately, upon partition, or within the limitations period following the end of the cotenancy.

   b. **Principal:** Each cotenant is obligated to pay his proportionate share of the mortgage principal, but the cotenant who pays more than his share of the mortgage principal has additional remedies. The paying cotenant succeeds to the mortgagee's (lender's) rights, called *subrogation.* The paying cotenant can enforce all the rights and powers of the mortgagee against his cotenants who fail to pay their share of the principal, including foreclosure sale.

2. **Taxes:** Each cotenant is obligated to pay his proportionate share of the taxes, and a cotenant who pays more than his share can recover the excess from his fellow cotenants at any time during the tenancy, upon partition, or within the limitations period after cessation of cotenancy.

3. **Repairs:** A cotenant has no obligation to repair his property. If he wishes to let it fall into ruin, that is his choice. The law will not generally compel prudent and responsible behavior toward one's own affairs. Accordingly, a cotenant who voluntarily repairs the property generally may not force his cotenants to reimburse him for their share of the repairs, but a few jurisdictions permit such recovery if the repairing cotenant has first given notice to the other cotenants. Despite the general rule, the repairing cotenant can recover his excess repair costs in two situations.

   a. **Accounting for rents:** If a repairing cotenant is under a duty to account to his fellow cotenants for rent (whether received from third parties or for the reasonable rental value of exclusive occupancy), the repairing cotenant may deduct from the rents due the other cotenants their share of the repair costs incurred by the repairing cotenant.

b. Partition: Upon partition, a repairing cotenant is entitled to be reimbursed for the repair costs in excess of her share. If partition is by sale, this will occur by a cash reimbursement from the sale proceeds before pro rata distribution to all cotenants. If partition is in kind, the repairing cotenant will receive either cash reimbursement from the other cotenants before physical division or a larger parcel, representing reimbursement in kind.

4. Improvements: No cotenant has a duty to improve property. Indeed, cotenants may disagree about what constitutes an improvement, or what improvements are optimal. Accordingly, an improving cotenant may not recover from her fellow cotenants their pro rata share of the cost of the improvements. Upon partition, or if the improving cotenant is under a duty to account to cotenants for rent, the improving cotenant is entitled to *recover only the* **value added** *by the* *improvement,* **not the cost** *of the improvement.* If the improvement adds no value, there is no recovery. If the value added is less than the cost of the improvement, the improver is only entitled to her fellow cotenants' share of the added value.

E. Adverse possession: Cotenants can occupy adversely to their fellow cotenants, but it takes more than mere possession to do so, because every cotenant is entitled to be in possession. A cotenant must give his cotenants *absolutely clear and unequivocal notice that he* **claims exclusive and sole title** in order for adverse possession to begin. Nothing less will do.

F. Implied fiduciaries: In general, cotenants have no fiduciary duties to each other. A cotenant can, of course, voluntarily assume such a duty, and a fiduciary duty will be implied when one cotenant acts to gain an advantage of *title* over his fellow cotenants.

Example: Bert and Ernie own Blackacre as cotenants. They fail to pay the property taxes, and Blackacre is sold by the government at a tax foreclosure sale. Bert buys Blackacre at that sale for a fraction of its fair market value. Bert is not the sole owner of Blackacre. He will be held to a fiduciary obligation toward Ernie, and Ernie has the right to pay his share of the purchase price to Bert in order to redeem his cotenancy. See, e.g., *Massey v. Prothero,* 664 P.2d 1176 (Utah 1983). The same principle applies to mortgage foreclosure sales. See, e.g., *Barr v. Eason,* 292 Ark. 106 (1987).

★**G. Swartzbaugh v. Sampson: A case study:** This case provides an illuminating study of the options available to a cotenant who is unhappy with the actions of her fellow cotenant. John and Lola Swartzbaugh owned in joint tenancy a 60-acre walnut orchard. John leased four acres to Sam Sampson, a boxing promoter, who constructed a boxing pavilion on the site. Lola did not join in the lease; indeed, she objected vehemently to the boxing pavilion. Lola sought to cancel the lease made by John, and in *Swartzbaugh v. Sampson,* 11 Cal. App. 2d 451 (1936), the California Court of Appeal denied her claim, reasoning that a lease by a single joint tenant to a third party "is not a nullity but is a valid . . . contract in so far as the interest of the lessor in the joint property is concerned."

Consider the possibilities open to Lola Swartzbaugh after this ruling, keeping in mind that her objective is to eliminate the presence of Sam and his objectionable pugilists: (1) She could appear at the pavilion and demand that Sam let her into possession. He would probably invite her in to watch the fights and, if he did not, she would simply have triggered ouster, thus causing Sam to be liable to her for half the fair rental value of the premises. In that event, Sam's ability to deduct the rent paid Lola from what he had agreed to pay John might depend on how clearly Sam understood he was leasing only John's interest. If he knew that to be the case (which seems to be so), he would not be entitled to any deduction. (2) Lola could acquiesce in the lease and demand and receive half the rents received by John from Sam. (3) Lola could partition the leasehold, which would probably result in a partition by sale (because it would be impossible to physically divide the pavilion). But who would buy the leasehold, and for how much? In any case, the proceeds of sale would be used first to reimburse Sam for his "improvement." (Is it an improvement? Should the value of the destroyed walnut trees be deducted from the value of the improvement?) The balance of the proceeds would be divided between Sam and Lola, leaving the buyer with a leasehold and the obligation to pay rent to John. (4) Lola could hope for John's death, which would terminate Sam's leasehold because Sam had leased only John's interest, and John's interest would expire at his death. (He owned the land as a joint tenant with Lola.) None of these options is particularly desirable in terms of removing Sam, and the last is more of a bitter and cynical hope than an option.

III. MARITAL INTERESTS

A. Introduction: Many of the property issues involved in the law governing the property of married people are covered in other courses dealing with marital dissolution, family, and related issues. These issues are discussed here only to the extent relevant to a first-year property course.

B. The common law system: The pure common law system of marital property no longer exists in any relevant jurisdiction, but knowledge of its structure will help you in understanding the many current versions of marital property.

1. Femes sole and femes covert: A single woman (a *feme sole*) had power to use, dispose, and possess her own property. While that sounds axiomatic, a married woman (a *feme covert*) had almost none of those rights. Common law said husband and wife were one, but the husband was the One. The very wealthy avoided the severity of these rules through the creation of elaborate marriage settlements, usually involving trusts, which were designed to enable a married woman to control her property through a compliant trustee.

2. Husband über alles: With the marriage vow, the common law bestowed *jure uxoris* on the husband: the right to possess, use, or convey all of his wife's property, except her clothes and jewelry, for the duration of the marriage. Even her earnings were his. In the hands of an honorable and capable husband in a happy marriage, *jure uxoris* preserved or increased the value of the wife's property. In the hands of a rogue, *jure uxoris* was license to steal. Like the dodo, *jure uxoris* is extinct.

3. Wife's rights: A wife had no legal control of her property but had some inchoate property rights:

a. Support: A wife had the right of *support* from her husband. Thus, in the event of divorce, the husband was obliged to continue support by paying *alimony* to her.

b. Dower: On death of her husband, a wife had the *right of dower.* Dower was the right to a *life estate* in one-third of each and every *possessory freehold estate* the husband enjoyed at *any point during the marriage* which was *capable of inheritance by children born of the marriage.* This was a valuable right for a widow of a wealthy landowner or freeholding tradesman in seventeenth-or eighteenth-century England but was useless to those without land ownership.

i. Each freehold ever possessed: The dower right attached to every freehold the husband possessed that was capable of inheritance by children of the marriage. Thus, dower did *not* attach to the husband's life estates, leaseholds, personal property, equitable interests, future interests, or any possessory freehold held in tenancy by the entirety with the wife or in joint tenancy, whether with the wife or a third party. The common law's gift to the bride was a dower right in all the inheritable freeholds her husband possessed at the moment of the ceremony, *and* to every additional such freehold he possessed in the future during their marriage. But, as seen from the list of property to which dower did not attach, it was an easy matter for a husband to acquire property in a manner that avoided dower.

ii. **Scope and release of dower:** The inchoate dower right, once attached, could only be removed by divorce or with the wife's consent.

Example: During George I's reign, Harry owns Blackacre in fee simple while married to Molly. Harry mortgages Blackacre, then defaults on the mortgage, and Bank buys it at foreclosure sale. Bank conveys Blackacre to Zelmo. Harry dies. Molly is entitled to a life estate in one-third of Blackacre. Zelmo must turn over to Molly possession of one-third of Blackacre or one-third of the rents and profits from Blackacre.

Example: Suppose Harry paid off the mortgage, then conveyed Blackacre to Arnie without Molly signing anything. Upon Harry's death, Molly is entitled to dower in Blackacre because she never released her dower.

Example: Molly and Harry divorce. Molly's inchoate dower rights are irrevocably extinguished. But if Molly and Harry simply separate and remain legally married, Molly's inchoate dower rights are unaffected.

iii. **Operation of dower:** A physical third of all properties subject to dower that were capable of physical division was set aside for the wife's life estate. If a property was not susceptible to division, the wife received a third of the rents or profits from the land for the remainder of her life.

iv. **Defeasible fees:** Most jurisdictions hold that a dower interest in a defeasible fee ends if the limiting condition occurs, reasoning that the dower interest is derived from the husband's title, which was defeasible. A few reject this logic and hold that dower is indefeasible, a conclusion permitting a widow to flout limiting conditions during her lifetime. In most states, the issue will not arise, because dower is no longer recognized.

v. **Abolition:** Fewer than ten states continue to observe dower. In most states, dower has been abolished by statute, usually replaced by an analogous right usually known as the *spousal elective share,* which entitles a surviving spouse to take a specified portion of the decedent's probate estate even if the decedent spouse left a lesser share by will to the surviving spouse. See section III.C.2, below. Some states that observe dower have made the widow's share more generous: a fee simple interest in one-third or even one-half of dower lands.

4. **Curtesy:** Common law gave a husband who survived his wife a right similar to dower, called *curtesy.* Curtesy attached to *all possessory interests in land* of the wife, *including equitable possessory interests.* Thus, while the marriage settlement trust avoided *jure uxoris,* it did not evade curtesy. But curtesy only attached if *issue were born to the marriage.* Once a child was born, even if it later died, curtesy attached. Curtesy no longer exists in the United States.

C. The modern (mostly statutory) "common law" system: Every common law marital property jurisdiction (as distinguished from community property states; see III.D, below) has altered the common law system substantially. Statutes vary considerably, but set forth below are the major themes of these statutory alterations.

1. **Rights on divorce:** Almost every jurisdiction has adopted some form of an ***equitable distribution*** statute, designed to produce an equitable (usually equal) division of the marital property subject to the statute. Differences occur, however, in the way the states define what marital property is subject to equitable distribution. Some include *all property owned by either spouse,* whenever and however acquired; others limit equitable distribution to *property acquired during marriage,* no matter how; and some limit equitable distribution to *property acquired by the earnings of the marital partners.* Some kinds of personal property, like clothing and jewelry, are often exempted.

    a. **Professional skills and credentials:** One major issue is whether professional degrees and skills acquired during marriage are subject to equitable distribution. What happens when one spouse supports another while he or she obtains a professional degree or some similar enhancement of earnings power? Courts divide three ways.

        i. **Not property:** Some states hold that professional degrees and skills are not property, but simply personal accomplishments that may or may not produce property, and thus not subject to equitable distribution.

            ★**Example:** After Dennis and Anne Graham married, Anne continued to work as an airline flight attendant, and Dennis mostly pursued his education, earning a B.S. and an M.B.A. Shortly after he had embarked on his business career, the marriage foundered. A Colorado trial court awarded Anne about $33,000, representing 40 percent of the estimated future earnings value inherent in Dennis's M.B.A. In ***In re Marriage of Graham,*** 190 Colo. 429 (1978), the Colorado Supreme Court reversed, concluding that Dennis's M.B.A. was not "property" because it could not be transferred or inherited but was simply "an intellectual achievement." Granted that, why weren't the increased earnings of Dennis attributable to his "intellectual achievement" property?

        ii. **Property subject to equitable distribution:** Other states, particularly New York, treat professional degrees and enhanced professional skills as property subject to equitable distribution.

            ★**Example:** After a 17-year marriage, Frederica von Stade, the celebrated opera diva, and her husband divorced. At the beginning of the marriage to her voice teacher, von Stade was young and unknown, performing minor roles with New York's Metropolitan Opera. By the time the marriage ended, she was an opera superstar, earning over $600,000 annually. A New York trial court ruled that the "enhanced value" of her career and her celebrity status were not marital property subject to equitable distribution, but in ***Elkus v. Elkus,*** 169 App. Div. 2d 134 (1991), New York's appellate court reversed, ruling that the contributions to her career and *career potential* made by her husband (in the form of voice instruction and domestic duties) entitled him to share in the increased earnings power acquired by von Stade during their marriage. See also *O'Brien v. O'Brien,* 66 N.Y.2d 576 (1985) (increased earnings power attributable to medical degree acquired during marriage). Note that because professional degrees and skills cannot be divided and conveyed, the New York position requires the degree holder to pay a lump sum now or a portion of future earnings to satisfy equitable distribution.

    iii. Restitution: Some states take the middling course of requiring the degree-enhanced spouse to reimburse the supporting spouse for the financial support (***"reimbursement alimony"***). See, e.g., *Mahoney v. Mahoney,* 91 N.J. 488 (1982).

2. Rights on death: In place of dower, most states give the surviving spouse the right to receive in fee simple a fraction (anywhere from one-quarter to one-half) of all property owned by the deceased spouse at his or her death. This is called an ***elective share*** because a surviving spouse may elect this share or to take under the deceased spouse's will, ***but can't have both.*** Some states recognizing dower give a surviving spouse the further election of whether to take dower or a statutory elective share. In a few states, the spousal elective share is much like dower, being as little as a life estate in one-third of the decedent spouse's probate estate. One common law state, Georgia, has no elective share.

    a. Difference between dower and elective share: The elective share applies to **all property *of the deceased spouse* owned at his or her death.** Thus, the elective share is broader than dower ("***all*** property," not just freehold realty) and narrower ("only property owned at spouse's death").

    b. Avoidance of the elective share: A spouse sometimes tries to avoid the elective share by transferring all his property to a trust, retaining an income interest for life, and vesting a remainder in someone other than the spouse.

    Example: Oscar, married to Hilda, conveys all his property to his brother Sam, as trustee, under directions to pay to Oscar for life the income and such principal as necessary to support Oscar, then to distribute the principal outright and free of trust to Minnie, Oscar's paramour. (Oscar's will, which disposes of only the incidental property of Oscar that was not placed in trust, leaves everything to Minnie.)

    This works in all states to defeat the elective share if the trust is irrevocable and created *before* the marriage. It works in many states to defeat the elective share if the trust is irrevocable and created *after* the marriage (because the settlor spouse owns no property at death), but is more problematic if the trust is revocable. Some states treat a revocable trust just like an irrevocable one, so long as the assets are conveyed to the trust prior to death. Others refuse to recognize a revocable trust for this purpose, and some refuse to recognize the trust if the settlor's intent was to defeat the elective share. Still other states focus on how much real control the settlor retained over the trust assets — the more control retained, the more likely that the surviving spouse's elective share will reach the trust assets.

3. Prenuptial agreements and spousal contracts

    a. Prenuptial agreements: Agreements made between prospective spouses prior to marriage purporting to govern property division upon divorce were not generally enforceable at common law. Jurisdictions today split on their validity. The emerging standard is that such agreements are enforceable if (1) the parties' assets and earnings power have been fully revealed to each other, and (2) the substantive terms of the agreement are not unconscionable. See, e.g., Uniform Marital Property Act §10(g); Uniform Premarital Agreement Act §6.

b. Spousal contracts: In community property states, spouses may agree to transmute separate property into community property and to divide community property into separate property. It is an open question, however, whether agreements between spouses in a common law state to hold their property as community property will be enforced. In some states, a contract between spouses by which one spouse agrees to care for another in return for property to be received at the death of the invalid spouse is not enforceable for want of consideration, because spouses are obliged to care for one another. See, e.g., *Borelli v. Brusseau,* 12 Cal. App. 4th 647 (1993).

D. Community property:

1. **Origins and concept:** The civil law of Spain and France recognizes marriage as creating a "marital community" of husband and wife, and treats that community, rather than its constituent members, as the owner of most property acquired during marriage. The fundamental premise of community property is that each spouse is an equal partner in marriage, and that each spouse has an equal claim to the material possessions that are derived from the efforts of either spouse during marriage. By contrast, the pure common law system presumed that the wife was and should be economically dependent on her husband, and imposed a correlative obligation of lifetime support on the husband. The modern common law system is far more equitable and produces results that often are not dramatically different from community property. Community property came to America through French and Spanish colonization and was absorbed into the United States along with formerly French or Spanish territory. Arizona, California, Idaho, Louisiana, Nevada, New Mexico, Texas, and Washington are the only states recognizing community property. This discussion of community property is cursory, adequate for the survey course in property but not detailed enough for a separate course in community property.

   a. **Uniform Marital Property Act:** The Uniform Marital Property Act (UMPA), proposed in 1983, is based on community law principles and, for all practical purposes, is a community property regime. Wisconsin is the only state to have adopted the UMPA. The UMPA defines *marital property* to include all property acquired during marriage except through gift, devise, or inheritance. Everything else is *individual property.*

2. **Definition of community property:** American community property systems define community property as the **earnings during marriage** of either spouse and **all property acquired from such earnings.** This definition *excludes* property acquired *before marriage* or acquired during marriage *by gift, devise, or inheritance.* Such property is **separate property** and is owned solely by that spouse. The character of property — separate or community — may *not be changed except by* agreement of **both spouses.** When it is difficult to determine the character of property, courts apply a **rebuttable presumption** *that the property is* **community property.**

   a. **Tracing, not title:** Once property becomes community in character, it retains that character even if it is exchanged for other property and *regardless of its title.* If its original source can be *traced to community property,* it is community property, absent agreement of both spouses to change its character.

      Example: Irene, married to Al, lives in a community property state. She deposits one of her paychecks in a deposit account owned solely by Irene. She then uses the money in the deposit account to purchase a painting, which she trades for a vacation home, taking title in her name alone. Because the source of this chain of assets — deposit account to painting to second home — was Irene's earnings during marriage, each of these assets is community property. Title in Irene's name doesn't matter if the property's source can be traced to community funds. The vacation home is community property, and Al has an equal interest in it.

b. Commingling of separate and community property: The tracing rule applies to commingled property as well. If the sources of commingled property can be identified accurately as separate or community funds, the commingled property will be divided into separate and community portions. If it is ***impossible to trace*** the sources of commingled funds, the entire property will be ***presumed to be community property.*** In the absence of accurate records, commingled property will, in practice, become community property. A variation on this principle occurs when a partially paid-for asset is brought to a marriage, and the remainder of the purchase price is paid with community funds. There are three approaches to this problem.

   i. Inception of right: This approach (followed by Texas) holds that the character of the property is determined at the inception of the legal right to the property.

   ii. Time of vesting: This approach holds that the character of the property is determined when title passes.

   iii. Pro-rata apportionment: This approach (followed by California and Washington) holds that the percentage of the purchase price paid prior to marriage establishes the portion of the property that is separate, and the percentage of the purchase price paid with community funds establishes the community interest in the property.

   Example: Al enters into an installment sale contract to purchase a building lot for $45,000. He pays a total of $15,000 under the contract, then marries Jane. The remaining $30,000 is paid with the combined earnings of Al and Jane, at which point Al and Jane divorce. The lot is worth $120,000. Who owns the lot?

   ■ In Texas, an ***inception of right*** state, the lot is Al's separate property (because Al acquired a contract right in the property before marriage), but the community is entitled to return of $30,000 plus interest (but Al is entitled to half this sum). Ignoring interest, Jane gets $15,000; Al gets $105,000. See *McCurdy v. McCurdy,* 372 S.W.2d 381 (Tex. Civ. App. 1963).

   ■ In a ***time of vesting*** state, the lot is community property because title did not pass until the payments were completely made. Al and Jane each get $60,000 out of the lot.

   ■ In California or Washington, ***pro-rata apportionment*** states, one-third of the lot is Al's separate property, and two-thirds is community property. Al's share is $80,000 (consisting of $40,000 separate property and his equal $40,000 share of the community property). Jane's share is $40,000, one-half of the community's two-thirds interest in the lot. See, e.g., *Estate of Gulstine,* 166 Wash. 325 (1932).

c. Agreement transmuting the character of property: So long as both spouses are fully informed about the consequences of their actions, an agreement to transmute community property into separate property or separate property into community property will be enforced.

d. Income from separate property: The general rule is that income earned from separate property retains its character as separate property. Three states (Texas, Louisiana, and Idaho) hold that income earned from separate property is community property.

e. Pensions: Vested pension rights are community property because they are the fruits of earnings. The status of nonvested pension rights is less clear. California and Nevada treat such rights as community property. See *In re Marriage of Brown,* 15 Cal. 3d 838 (1976); *Gemma v. Gemma,* 105 Nev. 458 (1989).

f. Personal injury damages: The portion of personal injury damage awards that is compensation for ***pain and suffering*** is ***separate property,*** but the portion that is compensation for ***lost earnings*** is ***community property.*** See, e.g., *Rogers v. Yellowstone Park Co.,* 97 Idaho 14 (1974).

g. Increased value of separate property from community efforts: A spouse may devote time and energy to the management of his or her separate property. The community is entitled to share in the value added to the separate property by those efforts. The amount of the community's share depends on whether the increased value of the separate property is primarily attributable to the ***spouse's personal effort*** or to the ***capital investment.*** If the spouse's personal effort produced the increased value, the increment is community property (after deduction of a fair rate return on the separate capital investment).

Example: Hugo owned an art gallery and then married Alice. Hugo's capital investment in the gallery at the time of marriage was $100,000. During the marriage, the art gallery prospered because of Hugo's unerring eye for art that would be highly in demand. As a result, when Hugo and Alice divorced after 10 years of marriage, the gallery was worth $500,000. The increment ($400,000) is due primarily to Hugo's personal efforts, but first Hugo must receive a reasonable rate of return on his separate capital investment of $100,000. Assume 6 percent annually is a reasonable rate of return. Ignoring compounding, Hugo would be entitled to receive (as his separate property) 6 percent of $100,000 (or $6,000) multiplied by 10 years ($60,000). The remainder of the increment ($340,000) is community property (of which Hugo and Alice are each entitled to half).

If the increased value is due to the capital investment, the community's share is simply the value of the spouse's services; the remainder is separate property.

Example: Suppose that when Hugo married Alice, he also had a $100,000 portfolio of stocks and bonds. Hugo hired Lou to manage the portfolio, paying Lou from his separate property. Hugo took no active role in managing the portfolio. Ten years later, when Hugo and Alice divorce, the portfolio is worth $500,000. The community's share of this increase is the value of Hugo's services, which appears to be practically nil. Call it $10,000, of which half belongs to Hugo. The remainder of the increment ($390,000) is Hugo's separate property.

Some courts hold that the community is entitled to share in the increased value of separate property attributable to inflation in the proportion that the community has contributed to acquisition cost. See, e.g., *In re Marriage of Elam,* 97 Wn. 2d 811 (1982).

3. Management of community property: Husband and wife have equal management powers. Either spouse, acting alone, may sell, lease, or otherwise deal with community property. Of course, neither spouse acting alone may convey their ***interest in the community*** to a stranger.

And, as a practical matter, both spouses will be required to join in a conveyance of real property held as community property. However, the **equal management rule** permits either spouse to invest or otherwise deal with deposit or investment accounts. Each spouse has a fiduciary duty toward the other spouse in the management of community affairs. States differ with respect to gifts: some hold that gifts of community property may not be made by a single spouse, others hold that only gifts defrauding a spouse may be set aside, and still others hold that either spouse may make "reasonable" gifts from community funds. The exception to the equal management rule is that each spouse is the sole manager of any business carried on by the spouse, even if the business itself is a community asset.

4. **Rights upon divorce:** At divorce, each spouse is entitled to half of the community property and, of course, all of their separate property.

5. **Rights upon death:** Upon death of one spouse, the one-half interest of the decedent spouse in the community property is disposed of according to the decedent spouse's will. In the absence of a will, it descends by intestate succession.

    Example: Donald, married to Marla and residing in a community property state, dies, devising all his property to Babette. Babette takes a half interest, as a tenant in common with Marla, in all the former community property. If Donald died intestate, survived by Marla and Zoe, their child, Zoe would take Donald's half interest in the former community property, as a tenant in common with Marla.

6. **Creditors' rights:** In general, debts incurred during marriage are presumed to be community obligations, and the community's assets are liable for their satisfaction. Debts incurred by a spouse prior to marriage are separate obligations, and only that spouse's separate property is exposed to the creditor. The extent to which separate creditors may reach community property is in disarray.

E. **"Quasi-marital" property: Unmarried cohabitants**

1. **Common law marriage:** Common law recognized a de facto marriage between a man and woman if they were cohabitants, agreed between themselves to be husband and wife, and thereafter represented to the public that they were husband and wife. The status thus acquired was indistinguishable from ceremonial marriage. Common law marriage is still recognized in only 11 states and Washington, D.C. Section 6.02 of the American Law Institute's Principles of Family Dissolution endorses a common law marriage approach to the problem of any cohabiting couple, whether of the same or opposite sexes. So long as they share a primary residence and exhibit other traits of a couple sharing life together, upon separation during life their property will be divided under marital property principles.

2. **Contracts:** Unmarried cohabitants may create *express contracts* to govern their property upon death or termination of the relationship in a fashion similar to that delivered by law to married couples. Such agreements are generally enforceable. See, e.g., *Cook v. Cook,* 142 Ariz. 573 (1984). This extends to contracts *implied from the parties' conduct.* See, e.g., *Marvin v. Marvin,* 18 Cal. 3d 660 (1976). *Marvin* involved an unmarried heterosexual couple, but the principle has been applied to same-sex couples. See *Whorton v. Dillingham,* 202 Cal. App. 3d 447 (1988). The *Marvin* rule is not invariable. In *Hewitt v. Hewitt,* 77 Ill. 2d 49 (1979), Illinois refused to enforce such contracts (whether express or implied) on the ground that they were an attempt to create by contract the doctrine of common law marriage, which had been eliminated by statute: "The policy of the Act gives the State a strong continuing interest in the institution

of marriage and prevents the marriage relation from becoming in effect a private contract terminable at will . . . [P]ublic policy disfavors private contractual alternatives to marriage." New York recognizes only express contracts. See *Morone v. Morone,* 50 N.Y.2d 481 (1980).

★3. **Same-sex couples:** Even where enforceable, a contract cannot create the status benefits of marriage, such as the right to spousal benefits under social security, or the right to file a joint tax return, or the right to take the marital deduction for federal estate tax purposes, or the right to inherit from one's spouse. The rights and obligations of the marital state are entirely dependent on legislation. In ***Varnum v. Brien***, 763 N.W.2d 862 (Iowa 2009), the Iowa Supreme Court relied on the Iowa Constitution's equal protection clause to strike down Iowa's limitation of marriage to opposite-sex couples. The Iowa court applied so-called intermediate scrutiny, in which the challenged classification is presumed to be void unless the state can prove that it is "substantially related to an important state interest." The state asserted five interests: promoting and protecting the traditional concept of marriage, conserving scarce resources that are expended upon marital status, promoting procreation, promoting child-rearing by a mother and father, and promoting stable opposite-sex marriages as cradles in which to raise and nurture children. The court found the first interest to be circular and thus unimportant, and found the remaining interests, even if important, to be insufficiently related to the interest.

Other courts have reached different views. The California Supreme Court ruled that governmental sexual orientation classifications are subject to strict scrutiny, in which the government must prove that its classification is necessary to achieve a compelling objective. The Massachusetts Supreme Judicial Court struck down the state's ban on same-sex marriage under minimal, or rational-basis, scrutiny, in which the challenged classification is presumed to be valid, and the challenger must prove that the government either lacks any conceivable legitimate interest for the classification or that the classification is not rationally related to such a legitimate interest. By contrast, the New York Court of Appeals and the Washington Supreme Court upheld bans on same-sex marriage under minimal, or rational-basis, scrutiny. The California court ruling was reversed by a constitutional amendment; as of November 2009, thirty-one states have rejected same-sex marriage by vote of the people. Only Iowa, Massachusetts, Connecticut, Vermont, and New Hampshire recognize same-sex marriage.

a. **Marriage substitutes:** Several states provide substitutes for marriage. California and Washington confer on registered **domestic partners** (a term that includes same-sex and opposite-sex couples) all the status benefits and obligations of marriage. Hawaii and New Jersey have more limited substitutes. Hawaii permits same-sex couples to register as "reciprocal beneficiaries," a status that confers inheritance rights upon the survivor. New Jersey permits same-sex and opposite-sex domestic partners age 62 or older to register as such and obtain certain health care and retirement benefits but not inheritance rights. Maine permits domestic partners to have inheritance rights that mimic marriage and power to control disposition of a deceased partner's remains.

b. **DOMA and interstate migration:** The federal Defense of Marriage Act (DOMA) provides that marriage is limited to opposite-sex partners, thus depriving same-sex married partners of various federal tax and welfare benefits. DOMA also stipulates that no state must recognize a same-sex marriage that is valid in the state in which it was contracted. While some 35 states have acted to prohibit recognition of such marriages, DOMA does not compel any state to do so. Apart from recognition of Massachusetts same-sex marriages, a number of related questions remain unanswered. May a Massachusetts same-sex married couple acquire property as tenants by the entirety in a state that does not recognize their marriage? If such a couple moves to a state that does not recognize their marriage, how may they dissolve their union?

    c. What determines sex? States are divided over the knotty question of whether sex is chromosomally determined at birth, or whether sex is a matter of outward genital appearance. The issue is most acute with respect to post-operative transsexuals but can also affect people with a variety of intersex disorders. One of the most common is Klinefelter Syndrome, in which a person is born with the combination of XXY chromosomes. Some of these people have "androgen insensitivity syndrome" or "gonadal dysgenesis," conditions that produce external female genitalia. In a state that determines sex on the basis of chromosomal alignment, is such a person male or female?

IV. CONDOMINIUMS AND COOPERATIVES

    A. Introduction: Strictly speaking, neither condominiums nor cooperatives are true forms of concurrent ownership, but they combine sole ownership with concurrent ownership in unique ways.

    B. Condominiums: The condominium consists of (1) fee ownership (or long-term leasehold) of an individual unit (usually defined to include the interior perimeter surfaces of the unit) and related auxiliary space (e.g., parking or storage spaces), and (2) a fractional or percentage tenancy in common interest with all other condominium owners of the common areas (e.g., walls, roof, foundation, grounds, stairs, elevators).

    1. Creatures of statutes: Every state has enacted legislation governing the creation and administration of condominiums. These statutes vary. The description here is a typical composite.

    2. Creation: The owner wishing to establish a condominium development usually does so by recording a master deed or declaration stating that intent.

    3. Owner's association: Once the condominium units are sold the owners are members of an association empowered to elect a board of directors to run the association, usually by hiring a manager or making important decisions about repair, maintenance, or improvement of common areas, and promulgating rules for the use of owners' units and common areas. These rules can be very restrictive (e.g., no pets, no laundry lines, no loud noise, no prickly plants) but are generally enforceable if they are reasonable. See, e.g., ***Nahrstedt v. Lakeside Village Condominium Association,*** 8 Cal. 4th 361 (1994), discussed in section VII.B of Chapter 9.

    4. Conveyance and financing of units: Because each condominium unit is a separate freehold estate, each unit is conveyed by deed (like any other real property). Purchase of condominiums is conducted like any other realty transaction, in that the buyer is likely to obtain a loan secured by a mortgage on the borrower's individual unit.

    5. Responsibility for common areas: Pursuant to condominium by-laws, each condominium owner is responsible for his or her proportionate share of the cost of maintaining or improving common areas. Owners are also jointly and severally liable for injuries resulting from failure to maintain the common areas adequately.

6. **No right to partition:** Even though each owner is a tenant in common with respect to the common areas, the governing statutes deny to owners any right to partition this tenancy in common.

7. **Restrictions on condominium conversion:** Many municipalities have legislated to limit the ability of owners of rental housing to convert such units to condominiums. These laws are designed to preserve rental housing, but probably serve more to drive up the price of condominiums. Nonetheless, such ordinances are usually valid exercises of municipal authority.

C. **Cooperatives:** A cooperative apartment building is owned by a corporation. To acquire an apartment, one must purchase the capital shares of the corporation that represent the value of the apartment, and enter into a lease with the corporation for occupancy of the apartment. Each cooperative apartment owner is part owner (by virtue of owning shares in the corporate building owner) and tenant (by virtue of the lease).

1. **Financial operation:** The corporation will, of course, have a board of directors elected by the tenant-shareholders. Lease rentals are set to reflect the operational costs of the building. Because the corporation is the sole owner of the freehold, any mortgage loan will be the corporation's obligation, but a proportionate share of the mortgage expenses will be passed on to each tenant under the leases. Mortgage lenders insist on clauses in each lease subordinating the tenant's interest to that of the mortgage lender. The effect of these clauses is that, in the event of default and foreclosure, the mortgage lender is entitled to occupancy of the entire building, and the tenants have no further occupancy right or ownership interest.

2. **Transfer restrictions:** Given the high interdependence of tenant-shareholders, restrictions are typically placed on transfer of both stock and lease in order to be sure that any transferee is financially and otherwise capable of discharging the obligations of ownership and tenancy. These restrictions are typically valid. New York goes so far as to hold that consent to transfer may be withheld for any reason, though most jurisdictions hold that consent may not be withheld unreasonably.

3. **Limited liability:** Because the corporation is the sole owner of the building, any tort liability accruing from ownership is the corporation's responsibility. The liability of tenant-shareholders is limited to their capital investment in the corporation.

Exam Tips *on*
CONCURRENT OWNERSHIP AND MARITAL INTERESTS

☛ One easy issue to include in an exam is an ambiguous conveyance that may be one of several different types of co-ownership. Be attentive to any facts that may indicate the intent of the grantees. This issue can easily be combined with a later conveyance by one co-owner, thus producing multiple possibilities of resulting ownership. Cover all bases.

☞ Whenever you spot co-owners, there are multiple rights and responsibilities of the co-owners. Check them all to see which are relevant to your problem Also consider the possibilities for future action. Partition is always an option.

☞ Marital property issues crop up whenever you have married couples. Pay attention to whether the state is a community or separate property state. Be alert to the problems that can occur when couples migrate from one type of state to the other. Property is not a course in family law, but be sensitive to the emphasis your professor places on these issues; there is enough material in Dukeminier and Krier to create marital property issues.

☞ What counts as property for purposes of division of marital property at divorce varies from state to state. This is often governed by statute, so be particularly attentive to statutes that may be included in your exam.

CHAPTER 5

CHAPTER 5

LEASEHOLD ESTATES

ChapterScope

This chapter examines leaseholds, including their nature and the duties and obligations of landlords and tenants. Here are the most important points in this chapter.

■ The legal conception of leases has been transformed. While a leasehold is a property interest, it is also a contract, and contract notions of dependent covenants play a large role in regulating the relations of landlords and tenants, particularly in residential leases.

■ There are three types of true leaseholds.

- The *term of years* is a leasehold for any single, fixed period of time.

- The *periodic tenancy* is a leasehold for a fixed period of time that automatically renews for the same period unless either party has given adequate advance notice of termination. The month-to-month tenancy is the most prevalent such leasehold.

- The *tenancy at will* is a leasehold that may be terminated at any moment by either party.

■ When a tenant stays in possession after the term expires, the tenant is an unlawful possessor. The landlord has the option of treating the tenant as a trespasser or of renewing the leasehold, but some states by statute limit the landlord's remedy to double or triple rent plus other damages.

■ A landlord must deliver the *legal right to possession* to the tenant at the beginning of the term. A few states hold that a landlord must also deliver *actual physical possession* to the tenant. Tenants generally have no obligation to take possession.

■ Unless the lease is to the contrary, a tenant may assign or sublease his interest.

- A *sublease* occurs when the tenant and sublessor intends to create a new tenancy carved out of his own, and that intention is almost always found when the tenant and sublessor retains a reversion in the master lease. The consequence of a sublease is that the sublessor remains in privity of estate and privity of contract with the landlord, while the subtenant is in privity of estate and contract with only the sublessor.

- An *assignment* occurs when the tenant and assignee intends to and does transfer his entire leasehold to another person. After assignment, the assignor remains in privity of contract with the landlord (unless released by the landlord) but is no longer in privity of estate; the assignee is in privity of estate with the landlord but not privity of contract (unless the assignee has assumed the lease obligations).

■ While leases commonly restrict the ability to assign or sublease, in commercial leases some courts rule that the landlord may not unreasonably withhold consent.

■ A tenant's duties are imposed either by lease or by law. The principal duties are the duty to pay rent, to avoid waste, and to refrain from illegal uses.

■ Landlord remedies for tenant breach are derived from the lease or by law. The principal remedy is summary action to recover possession. Upon abandonment by the tenant, a landlord has the option of accepting the surrender and terminating the lease, reletting for the tenant's account, or simply collecting rent, but some states impose on the landlord an obligation to mitigate damages by seeking to relet abandoned residential premises.

■ The important obligations of landlords, mostly imposed by law, are not to interfere with a tenant's quiet enjoyment and, in residential leases in some states, to maintain the premises in habitable condition. Failure to do so enables the tenant to withhold rent or to terminate the lease. Landlords may not evict tenants in retaliation for their assertion of legal rights. An array of federal and state statutes forbid many types of discrimination in the sale or rental of housing.

I. THE NATURE OF LEASES

A. **Origins and development:** Common law treated the leasehold as a nonfreehold estate. Some say that this was due to the lease's origin as a device to avoid canon law — church law — restrictions against charging interest.

Example: In 1350, Rodrigo, needing money, might borrow a sum of money from Walter, a money lender. But Walter could not charge interest, because church law (backed by the Crown) forbade interest. Walter would receive in exchange for the loan Rodrigo's promise to repay the principal on a future date and possession of some of Rodrigo's land for a term of years. The length of the term would be set to permit Walter to earn enough profits and rents from the land to produce a satisfactory interest rate on the loan.

Because money lenders were thought to be unscrupulous and untrustworthy (consider Shakespeare's portrayal of Shylock in *The Merchant of Venice*), the money lender was not a fit person to perform feudal obligations and was not permitted to hold seisin. Thus, the estate acquired by the money lender (a term of years) was treated as a nonfreehold estate. The lender only had possession; the owner never parted with title.

B. **Dual nature: Estate and contract:** The leasehold is an evolving hybrid. It started out as a personal contract, then sometime in the sixteenth century, courts began to treat it as more akin to an estate in land. In this century, courts have come to regard the lease (especially the residential lease) as mostly contract. A lease has both aspects: It is a conveyance of a possessory estate in land and it is a contract. This duality affects the way courts decide the rights and obligations of landlords and tenants.

1. **The traditional view: Estate:** In this view, a lease is a conveyance of an estate in land. The tenant has purchased possession of an estate for a term. The responsibility for maintaining the property and the risk of its destruction is upon the tenant. The landlord's obligation is to deliver possession. The tenant has the obligation to pay rent no matter what, because rent is the price for possession and nothing more. The landlord has the right to retake possession only if the tenant defaults in paying the rent. This view is not entirely a relic of the past, but almost no jurisdiction construes a lease exclusively in this manner.

2. **The contemporary view: Contract:** In this view, a lease is just another package of bilateral promises that are mutually dependent. If the landlord fails to perform a promise (e.g., to provide access to tennis courts and a swimming pool), the tenant may refuse to perform his

promises (e.g., pay rent). The estate view treats these promises as completely independent; the tenant must pay the rent no matter how many promises the landlord breaks. The tenant's remedy is to sue the landlord for damages. Today, courts are apt to treat residential leases as contracts in most respects, but they are less quick to do so with respect to commercial leases. Even in residential leases, the leasehold has a property aspect as well as a contractual one. Leases are legal hybrids — they are *estates* and *contracts.*

C. **The general requirement of a written lease:** The original Statute of Frauds (enacted in 1677, during Charles II's reign) required all leases for a period of more than three years to be in writing in order to be valid. By statute, most American states have made the requirement of a writing apply to all leases except "short-term" ones, usually defined as those for a year or less. An oral lease for longer than the short-term period is void and unenforceable, but if the tenant takes possession anyway, a *tenancy at will* is created. See II.D, below. Once the tenant pays rent, and it is accepted, a *periodic tenancy* is created, though jurisdictions differ as to the length of the period. See II.C.2, below.

D. **What makes it a lease?** Sometimes it is difficult to tell whether a transaction has created a leasehold or some other interest, like an *easement, license,* or *profit à prendre.* Easements and licenses are rights to use the land of another, although they differ in some important respects. (See Chapter 9.) A profit à prendre is the right to take away something fixed to the land of another, such as the right to cut and remove timber, or the right to gather wild blackberries. None of these interests is *possessory,* in the sense that they give the holder the right to exclusive possession of the property. The lease, by contrast, gives the leaseholder the right to exclusive possession for the duration of the term, so long as the tenant performs the lease obligations. A lessee has all the legal rights of a possessor and may sue others for invasion of his possessory interest, via *ejectment* (to oust the wrongful possessor), *trespass* (to recover damages for physical invasion of the property), or *nuisance* (to recover damages or to abate nonphysical interference with a possessor's use and enjoyment of property). The easement holder, licensee, or profit holder lacks these powers because they do not have a possessory interest in property.

Example: Landowner executes a "lease" giving Oil Corp. the "right to drill for oil within two years and, if oil is discovered, to remove it from the property via pipeline or trucks passing across the property." Though called a lease, this is either a fee simple determinable (terminated when either drilling is not timely commenced or oil production ceases) or a profit à prendre (the right to pump oil) coupled with an easement (the right of access to remove oil). States differ on this point, but none considers this a leasehold, no matter what the parties call it.

Example: Helen, tired after a day's travel, checks into a hotel and rents a room. No lease is created; Helen holds a license to occupy the room overnight. The hotel does not even give Helen exclusive possession; maids can and do enter her room. But if Helen rented the room on a weekly or monthly basis, a lease might well be created, given the longer duration and the consequent heightened expectation of possession.

II. THE TYPES OF LEASEHOLDS

A. **Introduction:** There are four types of leasehold estates.

B. **Term of years:** The *term of years* is a lease for a *single, fixed term* of any length. The term must either be set out clearly in the lease (e.g., "for five years, ending on July 1, 2002") or by reference to a formula that will produce a fixed calendar date for the beginning and ending of the leasehold. Though called a "term of years," it can be of any length — a month, six months, ten years — so long as the period is fixed.

Example: On July 1, Rosemary leases Salmon House to Don "from today until the end of the current salmon fishing season." If local law provides that the salmon season ends on October 31, a term of years has been created, beginning 12:01 a.m., July 1 and ending at 11:59 P.M. on October 30.

A term of years may be defeasible, either ***determinable*** or ***subject to condition subsequent.***

Example: If Rosemary added to the lease with Don the phrase "so long as Don uses Salmon House as a salmon smokehouse," a ***determinable term of years*** would be created. If the added phrase was "but if Don shall stop using Salmon House as a salmon smokehouse, Rosemary may terminate the lease and retake possession," a ***term of years subject to condition subsequent*** would be created.

1. **Indeterminate term:** Sometimes a lease is for an indeterminate term, as "for the duration of the war." These leases are puzzlers, because at the time, nobody knows when the war will end. Courts adhering to the letter of the common law find these leases to create a tenancy at will (terminable by either party), because the ending date cannot be precisely determined. See, e.g., *National Bellas Hess, Inc. v. Kalis,* 191 F.2d 739 (8th Cir. 1951) (applying Missouri law). Other courts reason that the parties intended to create a term of years because they used an event that neither of them could influence, thus indicating that they wished the leasehold to endure until that future date. See, e.g., *Smith's Transfer & Storage Co. v. Hawkins,* 50 A.2d 267 (D.C. 1946).

   Example: Bob leases Fairhaven to Kathy "from today until Halley's Comet next appears visible to the naked human eye on Earth." Is this a tenancy for years? There might be some dispute about the exact termination date — when is the first moment that Halley's Comet will become visible? — but we can reliably predict that Halley's Comet will appear in 2062. The better conclusion is to call this a term of years, because it seems clear that the parties intended to create a single, fixed term ending in 2062.

2. **Length of the term:** Common law permitted a term of years of any length, but some states have enacted statutes restricting the length of a leasehold term.

C. **Periodic tenancy:** A ***periodic tenancy*** is a leasehold for a ***recurring period of time,*** such as month to month or year to year. A periodic tenancy continues in existence until either the landlord or tenant gives ***advance notice*** to the other party of termination of the lease. Common law required at least six months' advance notice to terminate a year-to-year tenancy, and notice equal to the length of the period (but not more than six months) for periods of less than a year (e.g., a month's advance notice to terminate a month-to-month tenancy). A periodic tenancy is created by the ***parties' intentions*** or by ***operation of law.***

Example: Otis leases Blackacre to Terry "from year to year, beginning on January 1, 1990." A periodic tenancy — from year to year — is created by the clearly expressed intentions of the parties.

Example: Otis leases Blackacre to Terry "for an annual rent of $12,000, payable in monthly installments of $1,000." This creates a periodic tenancy, but the period — month to month or year to year — is none too clear. Common law treated this as year to year, reasoning that a statement of "annual rent" set the period of the tenancy as a year and that monthly payments were a mere "convenience." Without any more evidence as to the parties' intentions, most contemporary courts would treat this as a year-to-year tenancy, especially in a nonresidential lease.

Example: On January 1, 1996, Otis leases Blackacre to Terry from year to year. Terry gives Otis timely notice of termination as of December 31, 1996, but Terry remains in possession on January 1, 1997. Terry is a "holdover," or a tenant at sufferance, and Otis may elect to treat Terry as having renewed his tenancy for another year. This is a new periodic tenancy created by operation of law. See II.E, below.

Example: Otis leases Blackacre to Terry for 100 years, rent payable in monthly installments of $1,000. State law invalidates leases for a term of more than 60 years. Terry takes possession and pays the rent monthly for five years, when Otis decides he made a bad deal and notifies Terry that the lease is terminated in 60 days. All courts will treat this as a periodic tenancy, but they will differ as to whether it is year to year or month to month. (See II.C.2, below.) By operation of law, Terry's occupancy under a void lease created at least a tenancy at will and, also by operation of law, the tender and acceptance of rental payments transformed the leasehold into a periodic tenancy.

1. **Notice necessary to terminate**

   a. **Common law:** Six months' advance notice is necessary to terminate a year-to-year tenancy, and notice equal to the length of the period (but not more than six months) is necessary for periods of less than a year. Notice is only effective as of the ***end of the period.***

      Example: Olivia leases Blackacre to Tom "from year to year, beginning on January 1, 1995, for an annual rent of $12,000." Tom takes possession and, on July 10, 1995, notifies Olivia that he is terminating the lease "at the end of the year." Tom moves out on December 31, 1995. On January 15, 1996, Olivia notifies Tom that his notice was defective, that the periodic tenancy has been renewed, and that he is liable for $12,000 rent for 1996. What are Tom's obligations to Olivia, if any? The notice was defective in order to terminate on December 31, 1995. To do so, Tom must have notified Olivia no later than July 1. At common law, Tom is liable for another $12,000 in rent. Some jurisdictions (and the *Restatement (Second) of Property,* §1.5, comment f) treat Tom's notice as effective six months after it was given, or January 10, 1996. In that case, Tom is liable for about $330 in rent. A few states treat a defective notice as no notice at all, so the periodic tenancy will continue until and unless Tom gives proper notice.

   b. **Statutory changes:** Many states have legislated on this subject, typically by reducing the notice period to a single month. A few states (e.g., California, Civ. Code §1946) stipulate that notice is effective one month after it is given, regardless of whether that date happens to coincide with the end of a period.

   c. **Modification by agreement:** The parties may shorten or eliminate notice times, but they cannot agree to make them longer than allowed by law.

2. **Fixing the period of periodic tenancies created by operation of law:** The problem is deciding what the period is when a tenant has taken possession under a void lease, usually an oral long-term lease that is void under the Statute of Frauds, but has paid rent, which has been accepted. All courts agree that a periodic tenancy results, but there are three different views as to the period.

   a. **Year to year:** Most courts conclude that a year-to-year tenancy results, reasoning that this is closest to what the parties intended.

Example: Josie orally agrees to lease Seaside to David for a five-year period, rent to be $1,000 per month. David takes possession and pays the rent for six months, then decides that he doesn't like Seaside. He tells Josie he is moving out, does so, and immediately stops paying rent. Assume that the state in which Seaside is located regards year-to-year tenancies as terminated six months after notice is given. The parties intended a term of five years; the periodic tenancy that is closest to their intent is a year-to-year tenancy. David is liable for six months rent.

   b. **Period measured by the rent calculation in the void lease:** Some courts measure the period by the way the rent is calculated or stated in the void lease.

   Example: Refer to the prior example. Suppose David and Josie orally agreed that the rent was "to be $1,000 per month." Because the rent was stated in monthly terms, a month-to-month tenancy was created. David is liable, at most, for a month's rent.

   c. **Period measured by the way rent is paid:** Finally, some courts measure the period by the way the rent is *actually paid.*

   Example: Suppose Josie and David had signed a written lease, under which Josie leased Seaside to David "for a term of 70 years for a rent of $840,000, payable (solely for the convenience of the parties) in monthly installments of $1,000 each." The state in which Seaside is located prohibits leases of longer than 60 years. David takes possession and pays the rent for two years. On June 15, Josie notifies him that she is terminating the lease "effective as soon as the law allows." When must David move out? In jurisdictions that measure the period of the periodic tenancy resulting from operation of law by the way rent is actually paid, a month-to-month tenancy has resulted. David must vacate Seaside no later than July 31, unless Seaside's state follows the California rule (see II.C.1.b, above), in which case, David must vacate no later than July 15.

D. **Tenancy at will:** A *tenancy at will* is a leasehold for no fixed time or period. It lasts as long as *both* parties desire. Termination is bilateral — *either* party may terminate it at any time — or by operation of law. It may arise by agreement, though this is uncommon because of the lack of security of the tenure, or by operation of law, usually upon the failure of some other leasehold or intended leasehold.

   1. **Distinguished from leaseholds unilaterally terminable:** A unilaterally terminable leasehold — only one party has the right to terminate — *cannot be a tenancy at will.* It is a determinable tenancy.

   Example: Jim leases Acorn Farm to Pam "for two years, but Pam may terminate sooner if she wishes." A determinable term of years is created. If Jim had leased Acorn Farm to Pam "from year to year, but Pam may terminate whenever she wishes," a determinable periodic tenancy would have been created. Pam need not give *advance* notice to terminate, but Jim must do so. A problem occurs when a lease is both determinable and for an *uncertain duration.* If Patrick leases a barn to Kathy "for so long as Kathy desires," what tenancy is created? There are two answers: The older one is that a tenancy at will is created; the more modern (and better) answer is that a determinable leasehold life estate is created.

   ★**Example — Modern view:** Robert Donovan leased a house to Lou Gerrish for $100 per month from May 1, 1977, until Lou decided to terminate. Robert then died, and David Garner, Robert's executor, notified Lou that he was terminating the lease. In order to carry out the parties' intentions, the New York Court of Appeals construed this to create a determinable leasehold life estate. Lou alone held the power to terminate the lease before his death. ***Garner v. Gerrish,*** 63 N.Y.2d 575 (1984). See also *Thompson v. Baxter,* 107 Minn. 122 (1909) (finding a determinable life estate on similar facts).

Example — Older view: Frye leased a house to O'Reilly for "so long as you please for $40 per month." After several years, Frye notified O'Reilly that the lease was terminated. Because the lease term was of indefinite duration, and tenancies at will are of indefinite duration, the Massachusetts Supreme Judicial Court reasoned that it must be a tenancy at will and so implied a power to terminate on the part of Frye. Little attention was paid to the intentions or expectations of the parties. *O'Reilly v. Frye,* 263 Mass. 318 (1928).

2. Termination

   a. By the parties: Because one principal feature of the tenancy at will is that it can be terminated by either party, the question here is whether a party has so acted. A landlord terminates by giving notice. A tenant terminates either by giving notice or by abandoning the property. Advance notice was not necessary at common law, but many states today require some notice (usually a month), and some require only the landlord to give notice.

   b. By operation of law: If either party dies, if the tenant attempts to assign his tenancy, or if the landlord conveys his interest in the property, a tenancy at will is terminated by operation of law. Most states require notice of termination to be given under these circumstances, so the tenancy may continue if both parties desire and, in any case, will last until the end of the required notice period.

E. Holdovers: Tenancy at sufferance: Tenants sometimes "hold over" — remain in possession after their right to do so has expired. When this happens, a ***tenancy at sufferance*** is created. A tenancy at sufferance is a legal limbo — the tenant has no right to be there, but he is not automatically treated as a trespasser either (mostly to avoid triggering adverse possession). For this reason, a tenancy at sufferance is not a true tenancy. The landlord has not consented to the tenant's occupation. A tenancy at sufferance only lasts until the landlord exercises one of two options the law makes available: (1) ***eviction*** and ***recovery of damages for the lost possession,*** or (2) ***binding the tenant to a new term.*** The landlord must exercise one of these options within a reasonable time.

1. What constitutes holding over? At common law, a tenant held over if she stayed for the merest tick of the clock past the old term. Excuses, however compelling, were simply not accepted.

Example: Two days before Halloween, Meg, age 89, breaks her hip while moving her household goods out of The Lawn, a cottage she has rented for a year's term, ending October 31. Her son, Ron, continues to move her goods out and care for his elderly mother. But the result is that Meg has not fully vacated The Lawn until noon on November 1. At common law, Meg is a holdover tenant. The landlord may elect to bind Meg to another one-year term.

The common law ameliorated this harsh rule by grafting onto it the principle that a holdover must be ***voluntary.***

Example: Tenant stays on because her physician advised her that she is too ill to move. She vacates as soon as she is sufficiently recovered to move. No holdover tenancy resulted because her continued occupancy was involuntary. *Herter v. Mullen,* 159 N.Y. 28 (1899). From this principle, the prevailing modern doctrine has evolved: There is **no holdover** so long as the **tenant's continued possession is the product of circumstances beyond the tenant's control.**

On this view, the holdover tenancy is created when the tenant fails to vacate as soon as possible under the exigent circumstances. Modern doctrine would not treat Meg, in the first example, as a holdover tenant. A few courts go even further and find no holdover tenancy even without extenuating circumstances, so long as the tenant's action causes no hardship to the landlord.

Example: Hirschfield's leasehold to his Chicago apartment expired on September 30. He started moving on September 27. By the night of September 30, the only items remaining were the beds and some carpets. Hirschfield's family slept in the apartment that night and removed these last items the following morning. By 10 a.m. the landlord had elected to renew the lease for another year. The Illinois Appellate Court found no tenancy at sufferance, reasoning that Hirschfield's acts could not have caused a reasonable landlord to assume that Hirschfield intended to stay for another term, nor did his acts significantly damage the landlord. In this connection, the court relied on the fact that the lease stipulated that Hirschfield would be liable for double rent for "the actual time of his occupancy" after midnight on September 30. The landlord got a few hours of double rent, not the right to renew for another year. *Commonwealth Building Corp. v. Hirschfield,* 307 Ill. App. 533 (1940).

2. **Eviction and damages:** A landlord may evict the holdover tenant and recover damages, measured by the reasonable value of the use of the property for the holdover period.

   a. **Eviction:** Every state provides an expeditious (usually summary) procedure for eviction and recovery of possession. Some states permit the landlord to use **reasonable self-help** to evict holdovers and recover possession.

   b. **Damages for wrongful possession:** A landlord who opts for eviction may also recover damages for the period of wrongful occupancy. The common law measure of these damages is the fair market value of the occupied premises, plus any special damages (e.g., physical injury to the premises). The original rent is presumptive evidence of the fair market value, but that presumption may be rebutted if there is convincing evidence that the fair market value is greater or lesser than the original rent.

3. **Election of a new term:** If a landlord elects to bind the holdover tenant to a new term, a number of issues occur, dealt with in the succeeding subsections. Although permitting the landlord to bind the tenant to a new term may seem harsh, the usual rationale for this rule is that it deters holdovers, and deterrence of holdovers is for the benefit of tenants generally, because a new tenant places a great deal of reliance on the old tenant's timely departure. Nobody wants to sleep in the moving van while waiting for the old tenant to move out.

   a. **Nature of the new leasehold:** Most states treat the new tenancy as a periodic tenancy. Some treat the new tenancy as a term of years for a maximum of one year. A very few regard the new tenancy as a tenancy at will, with the tenant liable only for the fair market value of the premises. See, e.g., *Townsend v. Singleton,* 257 S.C. 1 (1971) (interpreting a statute abrogating the common law of holdover tenancies).

   b. **Length of the new term:** Whether a periodic tenancy or a term of years results, courts divide over how to determine the length of the new term. Some states determine the new term's length by the **way the rent is stated (reserved) in the old lease.**

Example: Allan holds over, and Max, his landlord, elects to renew. The old lease was a term of years for three years, with rent stated as $10,000 per year. In a jurisdiction using the old stated rent as the measuring rod for the new term, Allan's new term is one year. While some states use the ***original term*** as the measure of the new term, none will permit the term to be longer than one year. In those states, Allan's new term would also be one year.

c. **Provisions of the new leasehold:** The provisions of the old lease (except for length or anything else inconsistent with the new relationship) apply to the new leasehold. If the landlord notifies the tenant of his election to renew at a higher rent, and the tenant makes no objection, the tenant is liable for the higher rent.

Example: Selk took possession under a lease for 70 days at a total rent of $1.00. Forty-seven days after the lease had expired, the landlord notified Selk that his continued occupancy would cost $300 per month rent. Selk never replied to this letter or to a later, similar one, but remained in possession for 23 months after his original term ended. A Florida appellate court ruled that the rent for the new periodic tenancy was $300 per month. Selk's failure to object to the new rent constituted his implicit agreement to pay the higher rent. *David Properties, Inc. v. Selk,* 151 So. 2d 334 (Fla. App. 1963).

d. **What constitutes election?** The easy case is when a landlord clearly states his election of a remedy. Once the landlord has done so, the ***election is irrevocable*** — the landlord ***cannot change his mind.*** But the landlord's election of a remedy can be inferred from his actions.

Example: C & P leased property to Smith for a five-year term, ending February 7, 1969. Before expiration of that term, C & P and Smith discussed a short-term extension of the term to accommodate Smith's relocation. Smith wrote a letter to C & P confirming his understanding of an oral extension. On Feb. 6, C & P replied by letter, denying any such extension and demanding that Smith vacate on schedule. Smith stayed on and tendered a rent check for one month, which C & P cashed, and then vacated after giving sufficient notice to terminate the new periodic tenancy. At that point, C & P declared that he was electing to renew the old tenancy for a term of years. C & P's February 6 letter constituted his election "to terminate the lease and to treat [Smith] as [a] trespasser." C & P's subsequent acceptance of the tendered rent created a new periodic tenancy. *Crechale & Polles, Inc. v. Smith,* 295 So. 2d 275 (Miss. 1974).

Example: Forester leased an apartment to Kilbourne for a term of years. After expiration of the term, Kilbourne held over for two more years. During that time, Kilbourne tendered rent on a monthly basis, but Forester never accepted it. Forester sent Kilbourne many letters demanding that she vacate but never did anything more to enforce the demand. Finally, Forester brought suit to recover possession. A Missouri appellate court rejected Kilbourne's contention that, by laches and acquiescence, Forester had elected to treat her as a tenant for a new term. However dilatory Forester had been, he had at least been consistent in never accepting Kilbourne's tendered rent, and had never otherwise manifested an intention to recognize Kilbourne as a tenant for a new term. It is the landlord's intention that counts. *Kilbourne v. Forester,* 464 S.W.2d 770 (Mo. App. 1970).

e. **When must the landlord elect the remedy?** The landlord must make his election within a ***reasonable time,*** but there are not many decided cases on the question of what period is reasonable. *Kilbourne v. Forester* implicitly found two years to be a reasonable time, but that is surely at the outer edges of reasonableness. If the landlord fails to act within a reasonable time, whatever it is, the tenant's status is unclear. Some of the few cases addressing the issue treat the tenant as a periodic tenant, others treat the tenant as a trespasser, and still others conclude that a tenancy at will is created. The periodic tenancy conclusion punishes the landlord for his sloth; the trespasser conclusion gives no reward to the wrongful occupier but starts the adverse possession clock; and the tenancy at will is a pragmatic compromise. See 1 *American Law of Property* §3.33.

4. **Statutory alterations:** The common law of holdovers has been altered by statutes, mostly designed to limit the landlord's common law remedies. These statutes take a variety of forms. Some states require that holdover tenants of farm land must be permitted to remain for six months to even a year, in order to enable the tenant to harvest crops. See, e.g., *Estate of Thompson v. O'Tool,* 175 N.W.2d 598 (Iowa 1970). Some statutes prescribe the nature of the new tenancy resulting from landlord election to bind the tenant to a new term, and others provide for penalties for the **willful holdover.** The Uniform Residential Landlord & Tenant Act (URLTA), §4.301(c), provides that a willful holdover may be liable for treble damages or three months' rent, whichever is greater, plus the landlord's reasonable attorney's fees. Some states have statutes that subject holdover tenants to liability for double or triple rent. These statutes are usually expressly or impliedly limited to the willful holdover tenant, but some states have adopted the double-damage remedy as the exclusive remedy for any holdover. See, e.g., *Mississippi State Dept. of Public Welfare v. Howie,* 449 So. 2d 772 (Miss. 1984), which held that Mississippi's double-rent statute was the sole remedy for "a tenant's holdover. The common law rule has been abrogated . . . and may [not] be used to impose the renewal of an expired lease."

III. DELIVERY OF POSSESSION

A. **Introduction:** Delivery of possession is the essence of a leasehold. All agree that the landlord has an implied-in-law obligation to deliver to the tenant the **legal right to possession,** but states are divided on the subsidiary question of whether a landlord has an implied obligation to deliver **actual physical possession** at the beginning of the lease term. Everyone agrees that there is no implied-in-law obligation of the tenant actually to take possession or to use the premises for any particular purpose. These matters are discussed below.

B. **Implied obligation to deliver legal right of possession:** A landlord is obligated to deliver to the tenant the **legal right** to possess the leased premises. If a third party has a better claim to possession than the landlord, the landlord will not be able to deliver to the tenant the legal right to possess.

Example: Buck, in adverse possession of Blackacre for five years (the limitations statute is ten years), leases Blackacre to Buster. Soon after Buster takes possession of Blackacre, Sophie, the true owner, sues Buster for ejectment and evicts him. Buck has breached his implied obligation to deliver to Buster the legal right to possession.

The obligation to deliver the legal right to possession consists of two promises, implied in law, by the landlord:

- The landlord has the ***power to demise*** — the power to grant to the lessee the interest he purportedly grants under the lease. In the prior example, Buck would have violated this promise the moment the lease was made, because he had no legal right to possession.

- The landlord promises that the tenant will have the ***quiet enjoyment*** of possession — meaning that the landlord promises that the tenant will not be evicted by somebody with a legally better title to the property than the landlord. In the prior example, Buck breached this promise when Sophie, the true owner, evicted Buster.

1. **Continuing obligation:** The obligation to deliver legal right to possession is a continuing one, as the quiet enjoyment promise makes clear. If, at any time during the tenant's possession, someone with ***paramount title*** — a better legal claim to the property than the landlord — interferes with the tenant's possession, the landlord has failed to deliver his promise of legal right to possession.

   Example: Richard owns and leases Charter House to Serena. Prior to the lease, Richard had borrowed money from OmniBank, giving OmniBank a mortgage on Charter House to secure repayment. OmniBank has a paramount title, but so long as Richard is not in default on the loan, there will be no interference with Serena's right of possession. But if Richard defaults, OmniBank forecloses on the mortgage and evicts Serena, Richard has breached his continuing obligation to deliver legal right of possession. See *Ganz v. Clark,* 252 N.Y. 99 (1929); *Standard Live Stock Co. v. Pentz,* 204 Cal. 618 (1928).

2. **Waiver by tenant:** A tenant may ***waive*** this obligation ***expressly,*** or by virtue of the ***tenant's knowledge*** *at the time he enters into the lease* that there is a paramount title. If the tenant is ignorant of the paramount title and takes possession, he has not waived the landlord's obligation, but he has no remedy until and unless the holder of paramount title interferes with his actual possession. By contrast, if the tenant does not know of the paramount title when he signs the lease, but learns of it before he takes possession, the tenant is entitled to repudiate the lease without penalty.

C. **Obligation to deliver actual possession?** The problem here is another facet of a tenant holdover. Does the landlord have an obligation implied in law to deliver ***actual possession*** to the new tenant at the beginning of the term? If he does, the burden of removing the holdover tenant is borne entirely by the landlord, and the landlord is liable to the new tenant for damages resulting from delay in placing him in possession. If he does not, the burden of ousting the holdover falls on the new tenant.

★**Example:** Dusch leased premises to Hannan for a 15-year term, beginning on January 1, 1928. When that date arrived, the old tenant had not moved out, and Hannan was unable to take actual physical possession. The lease contained no explicit term obligating Dusch to deliver physical possession to Hannan at commencement of the lease term. Hannan sought damages attributable to Dusch's violation of an alleged implied-in-law obligation to deliver physical possession. In ***Hannan v. Dusch,*** 154 Va. 356 (1930), the Virginia Supreme Court sustained Dusch's demurrer, reasoning that a landlord's obligation was to deliver the *legal right to possession* to the new tenant, not actual physical possession. This rule is often termed the ***American rule***; the obligation to deliver actual physical possession is usually called the ***English rule***.

1. **The English rule:** Under this view (said to be the majority view of American states), the ***landlord has an implied-in-law obligation to deliver actual possession*** to the tenant on the first

day of the lease term. See, e.g., *Coe v. Clay,* 130 Eng. Rep. 113 (1829); *Jinks v. Edwards,* 11 Exch. 775 (1856); *Adrian v. Rabinowitz,* 116 N.J.L. 586 (1936); *Herpolsheimer v. Christopher,* 76 Neb. 352 (1907); *King v. Reynolds,* 67 Ala. 229 (1880). The rationale for the English rule is that the lessee "expects to enjoy the property, not a mere chance of a lawsuit." Also, the landlord (especially a large one) is probably more efficient at ousting the holdover because he is likely to be more familiar with eviction procedures. Finally, a landlord is more apt to know when a holdover problem is likely to occur and can thus avoid the problem by refraining from a lease in advance of vacation.

   a. **Tenant remedies:** The tenant may either: (1) *terminate the lease,* find other premises, and recover *damages* pertinent to this exercise in musical chairs, or (2) *adhere to the lease, withhold rent* for the period he is out of possession, and *recover damages* related to the lost possession. If the tenant affirms the lease, the measure of damages is the excess of fair market value over the agreed rental for the period of lost possession, plus special damages (e.g., storage costs, temporary quarters). Special damages may, but usually do not, include lost profits. Lost profit claims must be supported by especially clear proof. If the tenant terminates the lease, his damages are measured by the excess of the replacement rent over the agreed rent (assuming equivalent premises) for the lease term, plus special damages (e.g., storage costs, transaction costs associated with the replacement leasehold).

   b. **Partial possession:** If the tenant is deprived of only part of the leased premises, the tenant is entitled only to abate a proportionate share of the rent for the period of lost possession. Do not confuse this with the independent phenomena of a landlord's partial eviction of a tenant in possession, which may give the tenant the right to suspend rent entirely, depending on the jurisdiction. See VI.B, below.

   c. **Waiver:** Some jurisdictions applying the English rule permit the parties to waive this obligation in the lease. See, e.g., *Restatement (Second) of Property*, §6.2. Other English rule jurisdictions do not permit waiver. See, e.g., URLTA §1.403. Because leases are also contracts, some jurisdictions that otherwise permit waiver might find a particular purported waiver to be unenforceable as unconscionable (e.g., the waiver is in microscopic type on page 10 of a 15-page lease).

2. **The American rule:** Under this approach, which is the minority rule in the United States, the landlord has no implied obligation to deliver actual possession. The tenant has the legal right to possession; obtaining actual possession is up to the tenant. See *Hannan v. Dusch,* 154 Va. 356 (1930); *Snider v. Deban,* 249 Mass. 59 (1924); *Gazzolo v. Chambers,* 73 Ill. 75 (1874). Justifications offered for this rule are: (1) The landlord is not responsible for wrongful possessors after the tenant takes possession, so he should not be responsible for those existing at the dawn of the lease term, (2) the lease delivers to the tenant the landlord's possessory rights, so the wrongful possession interferes only with the tenant's rights, and (3) the tenant could have bargained for an express promise of the landlord to deliver actual possession.

   a. **Tenant's remedies:** The tenant has the same rights against the holdover tenant that the landlord would have had, absent the new lease. The incoming tenant can treat the holdover as a trespasser and evict and recover damages, or the incoming tenant can renew the holdover for a new term, receiving the rent from the holdover. See II.E, above. These may not be satisfactory remedies to most incoming tenants, especially in residential leases.

b. Landlord's remedies: The logic of the American rule suggests that the landlord should have no remedies against the holdover tenant, but American-rule jurisdictions frequently ignore logic and permit the landlord to elect one of the customary remedies. There is some practical sense in this, because an incoming tenant in an American-rule jurisdiction, disgusted with what law serves up to him, is simply apt to disappear.

c. Modification by agreement: In American-rule jurisdictions, the parties are free to create an express obligation on the landlord's part to deliver actual possession. Indeed, one of the rationales for the American rule is that parties may do so. It is obviously a good idea for tenants in American-rule jurisdictions to insist on such an express promise from the landlord.

D. Tenant obligation to take possession: Tenants have no obligation to take possession or to use the leasehold for a particular purpose, ***unless the lease obligates them to do so.*** Absent such an express promise, the tenant is free to leave the leased space vacant, although he is still obliged to pay the rent. Sometimes this situation may constitute an abandonment of the leasehold by the tenant, with the consequences discussed in V.C, below. This issue can become important where the rent is simply a stated percentage of the tenant's sales at the leased premises.

Example: Byron, owner of a parcel located next to an exit from an interstate highway, leases it to Major Brand Gas, a national refiner and retailer of gasoline, for a term of 15 years at a rent of 3 cents per gallon of gasoline sold at the premises. If Major Brand Gas never occupies the parcel, Byron will be an enormous loser. Byron would be extremely foolish to sign such a lease without explicit promises from Major Brand to build a first-class gasoline station, occupy it, and use its best efforts to sell as much gasoline as possible. Cf. *Mercury Investment Co. v. F. W. Woolworth Co.,* 706 P.2d 523 (1985).

IV. SUBLEASES AND ASSIGNMENTS

A. Introduction: An *assignment* of a leasehold places the assignee in *privity of estate* with the landlord, meaning that the assignee and landlord are liable to each other for performance of the lease obligations that "run" with the leasehold estate; i.e., carry over from one estate holder to the next. (See IV.B.1.a, below). An assignment of the *landlord's reversion* similarly places the assignee and the tenant in privity of estate. Assignment, by itself, does not destroy *privity of* contract, which means that the contractual duties created by a lease continue to be personal obligations of the original parties to the lease even after assignment. By contrast, a *sublease* by the tenant does **not** *create privity of estate* between the landlord and the subtenant. *The subtenant is liable only to the tenant for the sublease obligations, and the subtenant has no claim against the landlord for failure to perform his lease obligations. There is generally no privity of contract, either, because only the tenant and subtenant have a contractual relationship.* Consequently, the critical issue usually is to decide whether any given transfer of a leasehold is an assignment or a sublease.

B. Assignment: An assignment is the ***transfer of the party's*** **entire interest** ***under the lease.*** If a tenant retains any interest, it is a sublease. See IV.C, below. The methods of deciding whether any given transfer is an assignment or sublease are discussed in Section IV.D, below. Unless the lease prohibits or conditions assignment, either the landlord or the tenant may freely assign the reversion or leasehold, respectively, that they hold. Most leases either prohibit assignment by the tenant or require the tenant to obtain the landlord's consent.

1. **Privity of estate:** An assignment places the assignee in privity of estate with the other original party. Privity of estate is rooted in the idea that leaseholds are an estate in land.

   Example: Lord leases Blackacre to Tenant, who assigns the leasehold to Newcomer. Lord and Newcomer are now in privity of estate with respect to Blackacre; Lord and Newcomer have the relationship of landlord and tenant.

   The consequence of being in privity of estate is that the assignee is obligated to perform all the lease covenants that "run with the estate." See IV.B.1.a, below. Perhaps the most important lease promise that runs with the estate is the promise to pay rent.

   Example: The lease between Lord and Tenant provided that Tenant would pay $1,000 per month rent. This promise runs with the estate. Because Newcomer is in privity of estate with respect to Blackacre, Newcomer must perform the promise and pay the rent.

   a. **Promises that run with the leasehold estate:** For a promise to run with the leasehold estate, and thus be enforceable against assignees, the following elements must be present:

      i. **Intent:** The original parties to the lease must intend that the promise bind assignees.

      ii. **Privity:** The assignee must be in *either* privity of estate *or* privity of contract with the party enforcing the promise or against whom the promise is sought to be enforced.

      iii. **"Touch and concern":** The promise must "touch and concern" the assigned estate — either the leasehold (when the tenant assigns) or the reversion (when the landlord assigns). A promise "touches and concerns" an estate when its performance (or nonperformance) is integrally connected with the *use or enjoyment* of the estate. Any promise has both a *benefit* and a *burden*. For an assignee to enforce a promise or to have a promise enforced against her, it must be shown that the benefit of the promise, or the burden of the promise, respectively, touches and concerns the assignee's estate.

         Example: L1 leases Blackacre to T1, who promises to keep the fences mended. If L1 assigns her reversion to L2, L2 must prove that the benefit of this promise touches and concerns L2's reversion in order to enforce it against T1. If T1 assigns his leasehold to T2, L1 must show that the burden of the promise touches and concerns T2's leasehold in order to enforce it against T2. If L2 seeks to enforce it against T2, L2 must demonstrate that both burden and benefit touch and concern the leasehold and reversion, respectively.

         Most of the contentious issues revolve around "touch and concern." Usually, both the benefit and burden of a promise will either touch or concern the relevant estates, or neither will. But sometimes a landlord (or tenant) will extract a promise that benefits other property of the landlord (or tenant), and not the reversion (or leasehold).

         Example: Landlord leases Blackacre to Tenant, and Tenant promises not to build a fast-food restaurant on Blackacre. Landlord operates Quik Fat, a fast-food restaurant located on Whiteacre, a neighboring property. Tenant's leasehold is burdened, but Landlord's reversion is not benefited. Rather, the benefit resides in Whiteacre, Landlord's neighboring property.

   b. **Personal promises don't run:** A personal promise does not run with the estate, but the promisor remains obligated to perform it even after assignment, unless he is released from the obligation. See IV.B.2.a, below.

Example: Landlord leases Blackacre to Tenant, and Tenant promises to walk Landlord's dog daily. Tenant then assigns her leasehold to Katt, who refuses to walk the dog. The promise is personal to Tenant and does not burden the leasehold (because it does not "touch or concern" the leasehold) and so cannot be enforced against Katt. However, Landlord can enforce the promise against Tenant, even after the assignment.

2. **Privity of contract:** Remember that a lease is also a contract. An assignment does not, by itself, destroy the binding effect of contractual promises as personal obligations.

Example: Lord leases Blackacre to Tenant, who assigns the leasehold to Newcomer, who fails to pay the rent. Lord may sue Newcomer because Newcomer is in *privity of estate* with Lord, but Lord *may also sue Tenant,* because Tenant and Lord remain in *privity of contract* with each other. Of course, Lord can only recover once, but Lord has two pockets out of which to satisfy his judgment.

   a. **Release and novation:** To destroy privity of contract it is necessary for the landlord and original tenant to agree to release each other from their contractual promises. A landlord's consent to an assignment and acceptance of rent from the tenant's assignee *does not constitute a release.* There must be clear evidence of a landlord's intent to release, usually found in some explicit agreement. This *express release,* when coupled with a promise by the assignee to *assume performance* of the lease obligations, is called a *novation.*

   Example: If Newcomer had expressly agreed to assume the obligations of Tenant in the lease, and Lord had expressly agreed to release Tenant from his obligation to perform those promises, a novation would have occurred. Tenant would no longer be in privity of contract with Lord. Thus, because the assignment placed Newcomer in privity of estate with Lord (in substitution of Tenant), Tenant would have no liability to Lord.

   b. **Assumption:** Assumption of performance of the lease obligations can occur without release, a condition that places both the original tenant and the assignee in privity of contract.

   Example: Suppose the instrument of assignment between Tenant and Newcomer contained an explicit consent by Lord to the assignment and an express assumption of the lease obligations by Newcomer. Now both Tenant and Newcomer would be in privity of contract. Tenant remains in privity under the original lease because there has been no release. Newcomer and Lord forged a new contractual relationship, the terms of which are embodied in the lease, by their bilateral promises — Lord's consent to the assignment, and Newcomer's promise of assumption.

   In states that recognize the contract notion of *third-party beneficiary,* an assignee can become in privity of contract with the landlord by an *express assumption* of the lease obligations.

   Example: Suppose that the instrument of assignment by which Tenant assigned his leasehold to Newcomer recited that "Newcomer assumes the obligation to perform all of Tenant's duties under the lease." Lord is the third-party beneficiary of this promise, and thus Lord and Newcomer are in privity of contract.

   Once privity of contract is created by assumption, it remains until and unless the contractual obligations are released.

Example: Newcomer assumes Tenant's lease obligations to Lord and performs them diligently. Then Newcomer assigns the lease to Thrifty, who is now in privity of estate (but not privity of contract) with Lord, because Thrifty does not assume the lease obligations. Thrifty performs, then assigns the lease to Deadbeat, who defaults. Absent any releases, Newcomer and Tenant are both liable for Deadbeat's default, because they are in privity of contract with Lord. Thrifty has no liability: his privity of estate ended with the assignment to Deadbeat, and he was never in privity of contract. See, e.g., *First American Natl. Bank of Nashville v. Chicken System of America, Inc.,* 616 S.W.2d 156 (Tenn. 1980).

Assumption will *not be implied from the mere fact of assignment,* or from the fact that the instrument of assignment recites that the assignment is "subject to the lease" or "subject to the obligations and covenants of the lease." See 1 *American Law of Property* §3.61. An express assumption is needed. Once in privity of contract, the assuming tenant remains in privity until released.

3. **Assignor tenant liability:** When a tenant assigns his leasehold and *is not released from the contract,* he remains liable to the landlord. Upon default, the landlord is free to sue either or both of the original tenant and assignee. If the landlord recovers from the assignor tenant, the assignor tenant is *subrogated* — succeeds to — the landlord's claims as against the defaulting assignee tenant, and the assignor tenant will be entitled to recover from the assignee tenant any amount he pays to landlord on behalf of the assignee's default.

    Example: Tenant assigns his leasehold in Blackacre to Newcomer. Newcomer fails to pay rent for six months. Lord sues Tenant and recovers $6,000. Tenant is subrogated to Lord's status as a creditor of Newcomer, which means that Tenant can now pursue Lord's claim against Newcomer and recover the $6,000.

4. **Multiple assignments:** When a leasehold is assigned several times, things may appear more complicated, but the general rules outlined still apply. Keep in mind the following: An assignee in *privity of contract* with the landlord remains liable for the default of subsequent assignees, however remote, unless there has been a release. An assignee in *privity of estate* with the landlord is liable only for the default that occurs *during the period in which there is privity of estate.* An assignor who has not been released remains in *privity of contract* with the landlord and is liable for the default of any assignee.

    Example: Tenant assigns to Newcomer, who assigns to Thrifty, who assigns to Deadbeat. Newcomer commits no default, Thrifty defaults on one month's rent of $1,000, and Deadbeat defaults on five months' rent. Tenant is liable to Lord for all the defaults ($6,000) because he is in privity of contract and has not been released, but Tenant is entitled by subrogation to recover $1,000 from Thrifty and $5,000 from Deadbeat. Newcomer has no liability, because he was never in privity of contract, and no default occurred during his period of privity of estate. Thrifty is liable to Lord for $1,000 because he was only in privity of estate, and $1,000 is the measure of his default during that period of privity. For the same reasons, Deadbeat is liable to Lord for $5,000.

C. **Subleases:** A *sublease* occurs when the lessee transfers *anything less than his entire interest in the leasehold,* thereby retaining a *reversion.* A minority of states treat the retention of a *right of entry* as sufficient to create a sublease. See IV.D, below. Absent a prohibition in the principal lease, a tenant is free to sublease at will, although many leases prohibit subletting, or condition a sublease upon the landlord's approval.

Example: Owner leases Blackacre to Lessee for a term of four years under a lease that says nothing about subletting. A year later, Lessee transfers possession to Subb for a year. A sublease between Lessee and Subb is created, with Lessee as the sublessor, and Subb as the sublessee.

A sublessee has *neither privity of contract nor privity of estate* with the principal lessor. A sublessor remains in both privity of contract and privity of estate with his landlord. The sublessor and sublessee are in privity of contract and privity of estate with respect to their new contract — the sublease.

Example: Owner leased Blackacre to Lessee for a rent of $1,000 per month. Lessee subleased Blackacre to Subb for a rent of $1,500 per month. Lessee remains in privity of estate and privity of contract with Owner. Subb is in neither relationship with Owner, but Subb is in privity of contract and privity of estate with Lessee, with respect to the separate sublease contract. The result is that Owner is entitled to receive $1,000 per month from Lessee and, under the sublease, Lessee is entitled to receive $1,500 per month from Subb.

The fact that the subtenant has no personal liability to the landlord under the principal lease has its negative qualities from the subtenant's perspective.

1. **Tenant default under the principal lease:** If the principal tenant/sublessor defaults on the principal lease, the landlord is entitled to terminate the principal lease. Because the sublease is merely a lease of whatever leasehold the principal tenant had, and that leasehold is now over, the subtenant has no further right of possession.

   Example: Suppose that Lessee subleases Blackacre to Subb for one year for a rent of $18,000, payable in advance. Lessee collects the $18,000, Subb takes possession, and Lessee fails to pay any rent to Owner under the principal lease. Two months later, Owner exercises his right under the principal lease to terminate that lease. Subb has no further right of possession, despite having paid Lessee the year's rental in advance. Subb's remedy is a lawsuit against Lessee for breach of the sublease.

   To prevent such disastrous outcomes, subtenants often insist on paying the tenant/sublessor's rental obligation directly to the landlord of the principal lease, and remitting any excess between the principal lease obligation and the sublease rental to the sublessor.

D. **Distinguishing an assignment from a sublease:** Courts claim to use two methods to determine whether any given transfer is a sublease or assignment: (1) examining the *substance* of the transaction *to determine whether the tenant has transferred her entire interest in the leasehold*, and (2) examining the *intentions of the parties.*

1. **Parties' intentions:** The problem with intentions is that the parties often do not appreciate the legal significance of the two modes — assignment and sublease — and so lack any real intention. Sometimes courts rely on the words the parties use to characterize the transfer, but the words are insignificant if the parties don't understand the legal consequences. If they do appreciate the legal significance, the substance will probably support their intentions, making reliance on labels unnecessary.

   ★**Example:** In June 1960, Ernst leased some land to Rogers for 53 weeks under a lease that required Ernst's consent to any assignment or sublease. Rogers took possession, built a "GoCart" track on the premises, and then in July 1960 agreed to sell the business to Conditt. In August 1960, Ernst and Rogers signed an agreement by which the term of the lease was extended to July 31, 1962, and Ernst consented to the "subletting" of the premises to Conditt upon the "express condition" that Rogers would remain personally liable for performance of the lease. Rogers signed a statement on the same agreement by which he "sublet the premises" to Conditt, and Conditt signed yet another statement on the document, by which he "accepted" the "foregoing subletting of the premises." Conditt ceased rent payments in November 1960 and, after the extended term expired, Ernst sued Conditt for the unpaid rent on the theory that the lease had been assigned from Rogers to Conditt, and thus Conditt was in privity of estate with Ernst. Conditt denied liability to Ernst because the August 1960 document characterized the transaction as a sublease. In ***Ernst v. Conditt,*** 54 Tenn. App. 328 (1964), a Tennessee appeals court applied the principle that the parties' intentions control this question, and concluded that the parties intended an assignment. The evidence that the court relied on to reach this decision about intentions, however, was much the same as would be used under the common law test of substance: Rogers parted with his entire interest in the lease; Conditt acquired every iota of Rogers's interest and paid the rent directly to Ernst.

Example: Jaber transferred his leasehold to Miller under an instrument entitled "assignment" but which expressly reserved in Jaber the right to re-enter if the "assignee" were to default. Rent payments were made by the assignee, Miller, to Jaber. The Arkansas Supreme Court mostly ignored the substance of the parties' dealings in professing to ascertain their intentions, but found those intentions exclusively in their chosen nomenclature: "assignment." *Jaber v. Miller,* 219 Ark. 59 (1951).

Courts relying on intentions do look beyond labels, though. If the transfer is for an increased rent, a sublease is usually indicated. If the transfer is for a lump sum, assignment is the usual inference. If the transferee expressly assumes the lease obligations, an assignment is the inferred intention.

2. **Substance of the transfer:** Courts that examine the substance of the transfer may well parse the labels the parties place on the transfer but are more likely to examine whether the transferring tenant has reserved a sufficient interest in the leasehold to constitute a sublease.

   a. **Reversion:** The common law rule was that the transfer was an assignment ***unless*** the tenant retained a reversion, no matter how brief its duration.

   Example: Tenant transfers the "remainder of the term of my leasehold, 40 years, except for the very last second of the term." This is enough of a reversion at common law — one second! — to qualify as a sublease.

   b. **Right of re-entry:** A right of re-entry is simply the right to retake possession if the transferee defaults. At common law, this right, which was not a reversion and lacked any certain duration, was not an estate and thus not enough to create a sublease.

   Example: Tenant transfers the "remainder of the term of my leasehold, 40 years, but reserves the right to re-enter and retake possession in the event of any default by transferee." The common law view was that Tenant had transferred her entire interest in the leasehold, and thus an assignment had occurred.

   A significant minority of American states treat the retention by the tenant of a right of re-entry, when coupled with a transfer of the remainder of the term, as sufficient to create a sublease. See, e.g., *Dunlap v. Bullard,* 131 Mass. 161 (1881); *Davis v. Vidal,* 105 Tex. 444 (1912); *Hartman Ranch Co. v. Associated Oil Co.,* 10 Cal.2d 232 (1937). This view is also endorsed by the *Restatement (Second) of Property,* §15.1, comment i.

3. Pitfalls of error: Two common misadventures result from erroneously thinking an assignment is a sublease.

   a. Double rent: A transferee who thinks he has a sublease (but actually has an assignment) and pays the rent to the tenant/sublessor will find that he is liable for the same rent to the landlord (assuming the tenant/sublessor pockets the rent). The transferee may recover the sums paid to the tenant/sublessor if he is solvent. Fortunately, this condition will not persist for long, as the landlord will not likely let too many months go by with unpaid rent.

   b. Merger: A tenant who "subleases" for the entire remainder of his term (at a handsome profit) will find that he is denied that profit if he fails to retain a reversion or a right of re-entry, assuming that retained right is enough to create a sublease. The transfer is an assignment, and the "subtenant's" occupation places him in privity of estate with the landlord, thus extinguishing through merger the intervening purported subleasehold. See *Webb v. Russell,* 3 Term Rep. 393, 100 Eng. Rep. 639 (1789); *Smiley v. Van Winkle,* 6 Cal. 605 (1856).

E. Lease provisions restricting assignment or sublease: Unless a lease expressly limits or prohibits assignment or sublease, a tenant is free to transfer the leasehold by either method. However, most leases do contain such restrictions.

   1. Strict construction: Because restrictions on assignment or sublease hinder alienability, they are narrowly construed by courts, but are generally valid.

   Example: L leases Blackacre to T, under a lease prohibiting "any assignment by T," T is free to sublease. If L leases to T under a lease prohibiting "any sublease by T," T is free to assign the leasehold.

   Express restrictions only apply to *voluntary inter vivos* transfers.

   Example: L leases Blackacre to T, under a lease prohibiting "any transfer, whether by assignment or sublease." If T dies, devising the unexpired leasehold to his daughter, D, the covenant has no effect. The result is the same if T dies intestate, and D takes the leasehold by intestate succession.

   Of course, even when an express restriction does apply, the landlord may consent to a transfer.

   2. Limits on landlord power to deny consent: Common law permitted a landlord to deny consent to a transfer *for any reason, or for no reason at all.* That view is under attack.

   a. Anti-discrimination laws: Anti-discrimination statutes (see IX.C, below) limit landlord ability to reject prospective tenants, including assignees or sublessees.

   b. Implied obligation of reasonableness: A number of states have implied a landlord obligation to *act reasonably when denying consent to a transfer,* a position endorsed by the *Restatement (Second) of Property*, §15.2, and adopted by statute in some states. This obligation is typically limited to *commercial leases only.*

   ★**Example:** Ernest Pestana, Inc. was the lessor of 14,000 square feet of hangar space at the San Jose municipal airport, under a master lease that required his consent to any assignment or sublease of the leasehold. Bixler, the tenant, agreed to sell his entire airplane maintenance business to Kendall, including assignment to Kendall of Bixler's leasehold. Kendall was financially stronger and richer than Bixler and was willing to assume the leasehold obligations. Nevertheless, Ernest Pestana, Inc., refused to consent to the assignment unless the rent was increased and "other more onerous terms" were imposed. Kendall sued Ernest Pestana, Inc., claiming that its refusal to consent to assignment was unreasonable and an unlawful restraint on alienation. In *Kendall v. Ernest Pestana, Inc.,* 40 Cal. 3d 488 (1985), the California Supreme Court held that in a commercial lease a landlord may withhold consent to transfer only when the landlord has a *commercially reasonable objection* to the transfer. See also *Newman v. Hinky-Dinky Omaha Lincoln, Inc.,* 229 Neb. 382 (1988).

However, these jurisdictions typically uphold flat bans on transfers (see, e.g., Calif. Civ. Code §1995.230), and some even uphold lease provisions that *explicitly* give the landlord the right to deny consent arbitrarily. See, e.g., *Julian v. Christopher,* 320 Md. 1 (1990). Moreover, so long as freely negotiated, "termination and recapture" clauses are permissible. Such a clause requires the tenant to notify the landlord of the identity of an intended transferee and the terms of the proposed transfer, gives the landlord the right to then terminate the lease and enter into a new lease with the intended transferee, and explicitly stipulates that any profit that results belongs to the landlord, not the tenant. See, e.g., *Carma Dev. v. Marathon Dev. California, Inc.,* 2 Cal. 4th 342 (1992). Yet, despite this trend toward an implied obligation of reasonableness, some states have rejected it and reaffirmed the traditional common law doctrine. See, e.g., *Merchants Row Corp. v. Merchants Row, Inc.,* 412 Mass. 204 (1992); *First Federal Sav. Bank v. Key Markets, Inc.,* 559 N.E.2d 600 (Ind. 1990). The rationale for the emerging view is the perception that increased alienability is a practical necessity in our restless society. The rationale for judicial rejection of an implied obligation of reasonableness is that legislatures ought to make this essentially social judgment, and that commercial lessees particularly are usually able to protect themselves in lease negotiations. In residential lease settings, courts have been especially reluctant to hold landlords to the obligation of reasonableness, partly out of fear of a flood of litigation. See, e.g., *Slavin v. Rent Control Bd. of Brookline,* 406 Mass. 458 (1990).

c. **What's reasonable?** Courts apply an *objective* test to this question. Landlords may reject transferees of doubtful financial strength or if the transferee's proposed use is not suitable in light of other commercial uses of this or similar property, but they may not reject transferees to secure a commercial advantage or because the transferee's proposed use is ethically offensive to the landlord though otherwise reasonable.

Example: Harry, an enormous landlord, rejects Ted, a transferee, because Ted was a tenant in another building owned by Harry, and Harry desired to retain Ted as a tenant. Harry and Ted were at a stalemate in negotiations over a new lease, and Harry's rejection of Ted as a transferee was designed to pressure Ted into accepting Harry's terms. Harry's rejection was not reasonable. See *Krieger v. Helmsley-Spear, Inc.,* 62 N.J. 423 (1973).

Example: Landlord, a religious organization that abhors abortion as a tenet of the faith, refuses to consent to a transfer to a birth control and abortion counseling center, although the center was financially responsible, and its use was otherwise suitable. Landlord's rejection was not *commercially* reasonable. See *American Book Co. v. Yeshiva Univ. Dev. Found.,* 59 Misc. 2d 31, 297 N.Y.S.2d 156 (1969).

Example: Miller, a landlord, demanded a fee from Giordano, his tenant, as the price for Miller's consent to transfer of the lease. While the lease permitted landlord to withhold his consent to transfers, it did not mention a fee as the price for that consent. The fee demand was unreasonable. See *Giordano v. Miller*, 288 App. Div. 2d 181, 733 N.Y.S.2d 94 (2001).

   d. What's a transfer? Courts are split on the question of whether a corporate lessee's merger with another corporation constitutes a transfer. Courts are also split on the question of whether the sale of a large block of the outstanding capital stock of a corporate lessee constitutes a transfer of the lease. A reasonableness standard would probably limit refusals to consent to situations where the financial strength of the lessee is materially impaired by the change in corporate structure or share ownership.

   3. Landlord waiver: A landlord may waive lease restrictions on transfer, either expressly or by implication, usually as a result of knowing acceptance of rent from an assignee. An old common law rule, originating in *Dumpor's Case*, 4 Coke 119b, 76 Eng. Rep. 1110 (1578), holds that *once the landlord has expressly waived a transfer restriction, the restriction is destroyed* **unless he specifically reserves the right to bar future transfers.** Though heavily criticized as nonsensical, and rejected by the *Restatement (Second) of Property*, §16.1, this rule is still followed by many American jurisdictions. The rule in *Dumpor's Case* is easily avoided, though, by either (1) an express declaration by the landlord, at the time of transfer, that waiver is *limited to this transfer only,* or (2) an express statement in the lease that transfer restrictions bind the *tenant's assignees,* thus preserving the transfer restrictions as to future assignees.

V. TENANT'S OBLIGATIONS

  A. Introduction: A tenant's obligations are defined by the lease, but in the absence of an express lease provision, the law presumes the existence of certain duties. The nature of these duties reflects the hybrid nature of leaseholds — both an estate and a contract.

  B. Pay the rent: This is the principal obligation. At common law, it was an *independent obligation,* meaning that the tenant had to pay rent regardless of the landlord's breach of any of his obligations. This view reflected the conception of a leasehold as an estate, and the rent as the payment for the estate. In most American jurisdictions today, the rent obligation is *dependent* on the landlord's performance of his lease obligations, reflecting the modern conception of the lease as a contract. Upon landlord breach in these jurisdictions, a tenant may terminate and vacate, withhold rent, or abate a portion of the rent. See VII, below. The right to receive the rent is normally part of the landlord's reversion but can be separately assigned or retained upon any transfer of the reversion.

   1. Amount of rent: The rent amount is virtually always stipulated in the lease but, if not, the tenant must pay the *reasonable rental value* for the occupied property. This same rule applies if the lease is void for some reason, such as noncompliance with applicable housing and building codes.

   2. Accrual: Unless the lease says otherwise, rent is due on the last day of the term (e.g., at the end of the month in a periodic tenancy from month to month; on the last day of the term in a tenancy for a term of years). Many states have, by statute, changed this rule to provide for apportionment of rent when a lease is terminated in mid-term. A handful of states hold that, for any purpose, rent is apportioned daily throughout the term. See *Restatement (Second) of Property*, §12.1.

C. **Waste avoidance:** Given the limited duration of a leasehold estate, the common law imposed on tenants the duty to avoid waste. The duty to avoid permissive, or involuntary, waste (see Chapter 2, V.D.2) is addressed in the ***duty to repair.*** The duty to avoid affirmative, or voluntary, waste (see Chapter 2, V.D.1) is addressed in the ***duty to avoid damage.***

   1. **The duty to repair:** Common law required a tenant to keep the premises in good repair, ***ordinary wear and tear excepted,*** but imposed no obligation to make extraordinary or substantial repairs. The common law duty may be altered by agreement in the lease, and many states have modified it by imposing a duty to repair on the landlord, either by statute or an implied-in-law warranty of habitability on the part of the landlord. See VI.C, below.

      a. **Alteration by agreement:** The common law rule allows ordinary deterioration of the premises because the landlord has no repair obligation and the tenant's duty is limited. Thus, leases typically address responsibility for repairing ordinary wear and tear. Except when the result is unconscionable or where prohibited by law (see VII.C, below), the parties may agree to impose the repair obligation however they wish. A typical lease might impose on the landlord the duty to make exterior or structural repairs, with the tenant obligated to make all remaining repairs.

         i. **"General repair" clauses:** A "general repair" clause obligates either tenant or landlord to make all repairs necessary to preserve the property in the same condition as it was at the outset of the lease term. A tenant who is bound by an unqualified general repair clause is traditionally obligated to make ***any and all repairs,*** even including the ***duty to rebuild*** after complete destruction of the premises by acts not of the tenant's fault (e.g., flood, earthquake, hurricane, war, riot). See, e.g., *Chambers v. North River Line,* 179 N.C. 199 (1920); *Armstrong v. Maybee,* 17 Wash. 24 (1897). The same rule applies to a landlord bound by an unqualified general repair clause. This rule is eroding: By statute, some states have eliminated the tenant duty to rebuild, and judicial decisions are undermining its vitality. See, e.g., *Washington Hydroculture, Inc. v. Payne,* 96 Wash. 2d 322 (1981).

   2. **The duty to avoid damage:** Affirmative acts of the tenant that ***substantially damage*** the premises constitute affirmative (voluntary) waste, and are breaches of this duty. To constitute waste, the damage must change the appearance, function, or utility of the property, and be "extraordinary in scope and effect, or unusual in expenditure." *Pross v. Excelsior Cleaning & Dyeing Co.,* 179 N.Y.S. 176 (1919).

      Example: Tenant replaced a defective ceiling and added a light fixture and switch, a closet, and a window frame. These changes were not waste, even though the ceiling replacement was substandard. *Rumiche Corp. v. Eisenreich,* 40 N.Y.2d 174 (1976).

      Although common law courts held that ameliorative waste violated the duty to avoid damage, most courts today reach the opposite conclusion, so long as there is no long-term economic loss inflicted on the landlord.

D. **Refrain from illegal uses:** Tenants may not devote the leasehold premises to illegal uses. At common law, the landlord's remedy and the tenant's continued right to occupation depended on whether the landlord knew of the intended illegal use at the time the leasehold was created.

   1. **Landlord knowledge of intended illegal use:** If the landlord actually intended the tenant to make illegal use, or if the landlord simply knew of the tenant's intention to make illegal use,

the lease was ***unenforceable at common law.*** While the landlord could not recover rent, he could recover possession because there was no valid leasehold created. This is still good law, with the added wrinkle that the landlord may not even recover possession if eviction constitutes unlawful retaliation. See VII.C, below. See, e.g., *Brown v. Southall Realty Co.,* 237 A.2d 834 (D.C. App. 1968); *Restatement (Second) of Property*, §9.1.

2. **Landlord ignorance of illegal use:** At common law, if the landlord was ignorant of the tenant's illegal use, the lease remained ***enforceable.*** Absent an express provision in the lease, the landlord could not terminate but could only enjoin the illegal use and obtain damages. The preferred view today is to permit the landlord to terminate the lease if she acts while the illegal use is ongoing or within a short time of its cessation. See *Restatement (Second) of Property*, §12.5.

E. **Honesty as to intended purpose:** As with all transactions, a tenant has a duty not to misrepresent his intentions. Even if the tenant's use is completely legal, but is utterly inconsistent with his representations, the landlord may terminate the lease because of the misrepresentation.

Example: Landlord leases space to Tenant, on the strength of Tenant's representation that no toxic chemicals will be used on the property. After occupation, Tenant uses the property for stripping chrome plating from metal parts. To do so, Tenant uses a variety of legal, but toxic, chemicals and takes care to employ and dispose of them in compliance with all applicable laws. Landlord may terminate the lease because of the misrepresentation.

F. **Duty not to commit nuisance:** Any possessor of land, including a tenant, has the obligation not to commit a nuisance — a nontrespass interference with the use and enjoyment by others of their property. Reasonable noise or other activity that is bothersome to other tenants in an apartment building does not constitute nuisance. Landlords often insert express covenants against noise or other disturbance, but these covenants are construed to prohibit only ***unreasonable noise or disturbance,*** so they add little to the common law duty not to commit nuisance. On nuisance generally, see Chapter 8.

G. **Duties from express lease provisions:** The lease may impose just about any duty imaginable on a tenant, so long as the duty is not illegal or unconscionable and does not otherwise violate public policy. Read the lease carefully!

H. **Circumstances excusing tenant of obligations:** The common law did not admit of any such excuses. The tenant had purchased a leasehold estate, and any act of a third party preventing the tenant from enjoying the estate was his problem. The tenant still had to perform all of his leasehold obligations, including rent payment.

Example: Tenant leases Blackacre, a large country home, for a term of years. Civil war breaks out during the term, and one side destroys Blackacre. Tough luck; the tenant still must pay rent. See, e.g., *Paradine v. Jane,* 82 Eng. Rep. 897 (1647).

Modern law has softened this harsh doctrine by recognizing a number of such excuses, summarized here.

1. **Sole use becomes illegal:** If the tenant has bargained for one specific use, which later becomes illegal, the tenant is excused.

Example: Landlord and Tenant agree that the leasehold property will be used solely for a brewery. Prohibition arrives. The intended use is now illegal. Tenant is excused from the lease. *Brunswick-Balke Collender Co. v. Seattle Brewing & Malting Co.,* 98 Wash. 12 (1917); *Restatement (Second) of Property,* §9.2.

2. **Primary use illegal but other uses permitted:** If the tenant has not bargained for a specific use, but the tenant's actual use is now illegal, and the premises may *reasonably* be used for another purpose by the tenant, the tenant is *not excused. Restatement (Second) of Property,* §9.2.

3. **Conditional legality of use:** If the *sole intended use* may be continued only by *obtaining a governmental permit* (typically a conditional use permit or zoning variance), jurisdictions split on whether the tenant or the landlord is obliged to apply for the permit, though most place the burden on the tenant. See, e.g., *Warshawsky v. American Automotive Products Co.,* 12 Ill. App. 2d 178 (1956). All jurisdictions excuse the tenant if the permit is denied.

4. **Destruction of the leasehold property:** Destruction of the property, even by causes outside the tenant's control, was no excuse at common law. This is not true today, unless a tenant foolishly undertakes such an obligation pursuant to an express lease provision. See V.C.1.a.i, above. By statute, most states permit a tenant to terminate whether the premises are destroyed or rendered unusable for their intended purpose, unless the destruction is due to tenant negligence or intentional misconduct. See, e.g., *Albert M. Greenfield & Co., Inc. v. Kolea,* 475 Pa. 351 (1976); *Restatement (Second) of Property,* §5.4.; URLTA §4.106.

5. **Loss by eminent domain:** When governments take leased property by exercising their power of eminent domain, the leasehold is automatically terminated. The very idea of a government taking is to seize all private interests in the property. The government must fairly compensate owners of the interests taken, though, so the tenant is entitled to just compensation for the value of the remainder of the leasehold. For eminent domain generally, see Chapter 11.

   a. **Amount of compensation:** Governments provide a lump-sum payment for *all* the interests taken, so there must be an apportionment of the award between the landlord and the tenant. The tenant is entitled to the fair market value of the remainder of the leasehold minus the rent obligation for that period. A tenant will receive nothing unless he holds an advantageous lease — the fair market value exceeds the rental obligation. A tenant may sometimes receive damages reflecting the cost of relocation or of damage to items, like fixtures, that are not taken by the government but must be severed from the taken leasehold ("severance damages").

6. **Frustration of intended purpose:** In a *commercial lease only,* a tenant may be excused if (1) *extreme hardship* would result from (2) some third party's *unforeseeable* action (usually a government) that (3) makes the *mutually intended purpose of the leasehold* (4) *virtually impossible* to accomplish. This is *very difficult to prove.* This concept is *not* the same thing as the contract doctrine of impossibility of performance — performance is possible, but accomplishment of the intended purpose is not.

VI. LANDLORD'S REMEDIES

A. Introduction: There are a variety of remedies available to a landlord to deal with a tenant's default under the lease. Some are the product of a lease provision, others are provided by statute, and still others are old common law remedies.

B. Remedies typically derived from lease provisions: As the remedies discussed in this section illustrate, a landlord can augment his remedies by a well-drafted lease.

    1. Rent acceleration: A rent acceleration clause makes the rent for the entire balance of the term immediately payable (if the landlord so elects) upon a tenant default under the lease. Because the parties were free to prepay rent for the entire term at the outset, courts find nothing infirm about a rent-acceleration clause. See, e.g. *Restatement (Second) of Property*, §12.1. If a landlord elects to accelerate rent, she may not terminate the lease. By accelerating rent, the landlord has chosen to enforce an immediate sale of the balance of the lease term. A landlord may not sell the remainder of the term and then take it away from the tenant. For the same reason, a landlord who retakes possession after tenant abandonment may not then elect to accelerate rent.

        a. Prepaid rent: If a tenant prepays rent (e.g., pays the last month's rent at inception of the lease), the landlord is entitled to retain the prepaid rent if the tenant terminates without justification before expiration of the lease term. The rationale for this rule is the same as that justifying rent acceleration.

    2. Security deposits: Almost every lease contains a security deposit clause, under which the tenant deposits a sum of money as security for her performance of the tenant's lease obligations. The landlord is indebted to the tenant and must return the deposit at expiration of the leasehold, less any charges attributable to tenant default, and provide an accounting of the deposit amount. Some states require, by statute, that security deposits bear interest, or be placed in trust or escrow accounts. Other statutes penalize landlords for failure to provide an accounting. Some states make tenants a preferred class of creditor in the event of landlord insolvency.

    3. Liquidated damages: A lease may provide for liquidated damages, but such clauses are not always valid. Generally, the amount of liquidated damages must be reasonably related to the probable amount of damages suffered by the landlord upon tenant default, but those damages must not be capable of easy determination. This validity rule is, of course, a bit of a "Catch 22." A security deposit may be retained as *liquidated damages* only if this test can be met. Lease clauses that provide for increased rent (e.g., double rent) upon default (as well as acceleration) are of doubtful validity. The increased rent is, in effect, a liquidated damage clause, and it is unlikely that the probable damages (even if not readily ascertainable) are reasonably related to the increased amount of accelerated rent.

    4. Confession of judgment: Leases sometimes provide that, upon default, the tenant agrees to waive personal service of process and authorizes someone (perhaps anybody, perhaps a landlord nominee) to confess judgment against him. This permits the landlord to reduce his claim to judgment quickly, cheaply, and *without notice to the tenant,* who may well have some defense, because lease covenants are mostly dependent today. Confession-of-judgment clauses have been widely prohibited by statute and are of doubtful validity even where apparently permitted. See, e.g., URLTA §1.403.

C. **Remedies derived from statute and common law:** Most common law remedies have been codified by statute and altered in that codification. Accordingly, this section treats them as a package.

1. **Eviction:** Because lease covenants were regarded as independent, the common law did not permit a landlord to terminate the lease and evict the tenant upon default, even for nonpayment of rent. The landlord could only sue for the unpaid rent. Today, because lease covenants are generally regarded as dependent, statutes permit a landlord to terminate the lease and evict the tenant for nonpayment of rent, but usually not for breach of most other lease covenants. As a result, most leases contain express provisions permitting the landlord to terminate the lease upon tenant *default of any lease obligation.* Of course, even at early common law, the landlord had the power to evict the holdover tenant — the tenant who remained unlawfully after expiration of the term.

   a. **Procedural prerequisites for eviction after tenant default:** If the lease provides only that the landlord *may terminate* upon tenant default, the landlord has retained a *right of re-entry* which must be properly exercised before the landlord becomes entitled to possession and may evict. If, instead, the lease provides that it terminates automatically after the landlord notifies the tenant of termination following tenant default, the lease is *determinable,* and the landlord is entitled to immediate possession, thus hastening eviction. As explained below, this distinction has been partially eroded by statute.

      i. **Right of re-entry:** To perfect the right to eviction, the landlord must notify the tenant of the default and permit the tenant a *reasonable time to cure the default.* See *Restatement (Second) of Property,* §13.1. In some states, the landlord may not be entitled to proceed judicially by a summary proceeding, where the only issue is entitlement to possession. See VI.C.1.b, below. Many states have, by statute, made summary proceedings available to landlords regardless of whether the forfeiture provision in the lease is determinable or confers a right of re-entry.

      ii. **Determinable:** If the lease is determinable, the landlord is immediately entitled to possession and may proceed judicially by a summary proceeding.

   b. **Summary proceedings: Unlawful detainer:** The most expeditious judicial eviction remedy is the summary proceeding known variously as *unlawful detainer* or *forcible entry and detainer.* This remedy is created by statute, and every American state has enacted such a statute.

      i. **Notice to quit:** Under a typical statute, the landlord is required to give the tenant minimal notice before filing suit (called *notice to quit,* and often no more than three days). The substance of a notice to quit is that the landlord will terminate the lease and file suit for unlawful detainer if the default (usually nonpayment of rent) is not cured within three days.

      ii. **Unlawful detainer procedures:** Unlawful detainer suits are entitled to a calendar preference on the court's docket and are speedily concluded. The only issue that is permitted to be contested is *entitlement to possession.* Thus, the landlord must prove that the lease has been validly terminated and that he is now entitled to possession. This means that the landlord will usually have to prove the fact of tenant default and proper notice to quit. Tenants may defend only on grounds that, if proven, would give the tenant a continued right to possession.

Example: A residential tenant in an unlawful detainer action may defend on the ground that the landlord has violated his implied-in-law obligation to provide habitable premises, on the theory that breach of this obligation abates the rent obligation and that, because no rent is due, the landlord is not entitled to possession. *Jack Spring, Inc. v. Little,* 50 Ill.2d 351 (1972). On the landlord's implied warranty of habitability, see VII.C, below.

Depending on the state, a jury trial may be available and sometimes may be constitutionally required. See *Pernell v. Southall Realty,* 416 U.S. 363 (1974). Appeals are usually allowed, although a stay of execution of judgment may be conditioned upon posting of adequate security.

c. **Ejectment:** Ejectment was the traditional common law remedy and is still available. It is not used much because it is not a summary proceeding and thus is not entitled to any calendar preference. Moreover, a tenant in an ejectment action is entitled to plead and prove any affirmative defense or counterclaim she may have, and can implead third parties.

d. **Landlord self-help:** At common law a landlord was entitled to use ***reasonable force*** to oust the tenant himself, but American jurisdictions are badly splintered on this remedy.

   i. **No self-help:** A slender minority of states absolutely forbid self-help. In these states, a tenant may recover personal and property damages if ousted nonjudicially by the landlord. See, e.g., *Kassan v. Stout,* 9 Cal. 3d 39 (1973). In these jurisdictions, lease provisions giving the landlord the right to use self-help upon tenant default and termination are void. See, e.g., *Jordan v. Talbot,* 55 Cal. 2d 597 (1961). The *Restatement (Third) of Property* endorses the *Jordan v. Talbot* view.

   ★**Example:** Wiley leased premises to Berg for use as a restaurant, under a lease that required Berg to obtain written permission from Wiley to alter the structure, obligated Berg to operate her restaurant lawfully, and gave Wiley the right to retake possession upon default. Berg's restaurant was cited for health code violations, and Berg began to remodel the premises without Wiley's written permission. Wiley notified Berg that if the lease violations were not corrected in two weeks he would retake possession. Fifteen days later, the violations having gone uncorrected, Wiley entered the premises and changed the locks. Berg sued Wiley for damages consisting of property damage and lost profits and was awarded $34,500 by a jury. The trial court ruled that Wiley's self-help repossession was "wrongful as a matter of law." In ***Berg v. Wiley,*** 264 N.W.2d 145 (Minn. 1978), the Minnesota Supreme Court affirmed that ruling, declaring that "the only lawful means to dispossess a tenant who has not abandoned nor voluntarily surrendered but who claims possession adversely to a landlord's claim of breach of a written lease is by resort to judicial process." The rationale for this "modem rule" is that self-help always carries with it the risk of violence or other breach of the peace. The common law response was that peaceful self-help was valid, but self-help that involved breach of the peace was wrongful. The landlord assumed the risk of breach of the peace by engaging in self-help.

   ii. **Reasonably forceful self-help:** At the opposite end of the spectrum are those states that permit landlords to use reasonable force to oust the tenant. See, e.g., *Shorter v. Shelton,* 183 Va. 819 (1945); *Gower v. Waters,* 125 Me. 223 (1926).

    iii. Peaceable self-help: The common law rule, still observed in many jurisdictions, limits self-help to peaceful ouster. See, e.g., *Rucker v. Wynn,* 212 Ga. App. 69 (1994), involving a commercial lease that explicitly permitted the landlord to exercise self-help upon tenant default. However, some of these jurisdictions define force so broadly that practically no ouster will be considered peaceful, making these states virtually indistinguishable in practice from those that prohibit self-help.

    iv. Self-help: Good idea? Defenders of self-help make two points: 1) Landlords will pass on the cost of judicial repossession proceedings to tenants who comply with lease terms, and 2) self-help results in no reporting of the action to credit bureaus nor creation of public records, the existence of which materially impede the defaulting tenant in a search for replacement premises. See, e.g., Strahilevitz, 102 Nw. L. Rev. 1667 (2008). Self-help is also at issue in the context of charitable temporary housing shelters (e.g., for homeless persons or battered women). In this context, the issue is whether the relationship ought to be viewed as landlord and tenant. Courts split on this matter.

2. Tenant abandonment: If a tenant abandons the leasehold premises in the midst of a valid lease term, the tenant is regarded as having offered to **surrender** the lease. Traditionally, the landlord has one of three options: (1) accept the offered surrender and **terminate the lease,** (2) reject the surrender by **leaving the premises untouched,** thus preserving the landlord's entitlement to rent as it comes due for the remainder of the term, or (3) **retake possession and relet the premises** for the benefit of the tenant. Today, the neatness of these options has broken down: Some jurisdictions prohibit the second option (at least for residential leases), thus forcing the landlord into the first or third options in order to discharge a **duty to mitigate damages.** Some states regard the third option (when undertaken voluntarily and under some circumstances) as effecting a surrender.

    a. Termination: If the landlord elects to terminate the lease after tenant abandonment, the tenant is treated as having surrendered the lease. Tenant obligations cease at the moment of termination and surrender, not the moment of abandonment. Similarly, if the landlord elects to terminate, termination becomes the landlord's exclusive remedy. The tenant's liability for unpaid rent accrues to the moment of termination plus damages created by the abandonment.

        i. Damages: Most of the damage caused by abandonment consists of the transactional costs of finding a new tenant, plus whatever shortfall exists between the lease rentals for the remainder of the surrendered lease and the fair market value of that remainder. At common law, the landlord was not entitled to damages resulting from abandonment because the common law regarded the rent obligation as nonexistent until it came due under the lease. This rule is still followed in some jurisdictions. See, e.g., *Jordan v. Nickell,* 253 S.W.2d 237 (Ky. 1952). Other states apply the contract doctrine of anticipatory repudiation to leases (because leases are contracts as well as estates) and permit the landlord to recover damages when the tenant has made it clear that he is not only abandoning but denies any further lease obligations. See, e.g., *Kanter v. Safran,* 68 So. 2d 553 (Fla. 1953). Damages recoverable from anticipatory repudiation are limited to a period in which such damages can be "reasonably forecast." See, e.g., *Hawkinson v. Johnston,* 122 F.2d 724 (8th Cir. 1941), in which such damages were limited to a ten-year period even though there were 67 years left in the lease term.

b. Leave the premises untouched: Because a lease is also an estate, the *traditional, but now minority, view* is that the tenant is free to abandon his unpaid-for property but is still liable for the payments if the landlord elects to leave the premises undisturbed. This rule rejects the idea that the landlord has a duty to mitigate the damages resulting from tenant abandonment. See, e.g., *Restatement (Second) of Property*, §12.1(3). See, e.g., *Holy Properties v. Kenneth Cole Productions, Inc.,* 87 N.Y.2d 130 (1995). The justifications for this rule vary: (1) The tenant is in breach, and he should not be able to impose duties on the landlord by his misconduct, (2) The tenant bought possession for a term, and if he wishes to throw money away by not using his purchase, that is his problem, not the landlord's, (3) A duty to relet an abandoned apartment might deprive the landlord of marginal rents by diverting prospective tenants of a vacant, but not abandoned, apartment to an abandoned one, and (4) the contrary rule encourages abandonment. In *Holy Properties,* the New York Court of Appeals thought that commercial expectations about governing law was reason to adhere to this long-held common law principle, regardless of any logical defects it may have.

c. Retake and relet for the tenant: A landlord may retake possession and relet the premises for the tenant's account either ***voluntarily*** or pursuant to a ***duty to mitigate damages*** imposed by law.

    i. Voluntary action: If a landlord voluntarily retakes possession and relets on the tenant's account, he must be careful to avoid action that implies acceptance of the offered surrender. In some states, acceptance of surrender is implied by reletting unless the tenant has consented to the reletting. Other states conclude that reletting without notice to the tenant constitutes acceptance of surrender. Still other states regard acceptance of surrender as determined by the landlord's intent, and treat the landlord's acts simply as evidence bearing upon his intent. Virtually all states regard reletting for a term longer than the abandoned term as acceptance of surrender. The importance to the landlord of avoiding acceptance of surrender is that, absent surrender, the rental obligation remains intact. If surrender occurs, the rental obligation ceases, although the landlord might still be able to recover damages equal to the shortfall between the original lease rentals and the relet rentals. See, e.g., *Lennon v. U.S. Theatre Corp.,* 920 F.2d 996 (D.C. Cir. 1990).

    ii. Duty to mitigate damages: Most states now hold that a landlord is not free to do nothing after tenant abandonment, but should be ***held to a duty to mitigate damages caused by the tenant's abandonment.*** See, e.g., *United States Natl. Bank of Oregon v. Homeland, Inc.,* 291 Ore. 374 (1981).

    ★**Example:** Kridel leased an apartment from Sommer for a two-year term, beginning May 1, 1972. On May 19, 1972, Kridel wrote Sommer that his impending marriage would not occur and that as a result, he had neither a need for the apartment nor the funds to pay the rent. He explicitly offered to surrender the lease and agreed to forfeit the two months' rent he had prepaid. Sommer did not reply and refused to show the apartment to prospective tenants who were ready, willing, and able to rent it. On September 1, 1973, Sommer finally rented the apartment and sought damages for unpaid rent from Kridel for the period May 1972 through August 1973. In ***Sommer v. Kridel,*** 74 N.J. 446 (1977), the New Jersey Supreme Court overruled the prior common law rule and held that a landlord had a duty to mitigate damages once a tenant has abandoned. This rule promotes use of scarce housing resources and avoids deadweight losses. In *Sommer,* the New Jersey court imposed the burden of proof on the landlord to show that he had exercised reasonable diligence to relet the apartment and that in doing so he had treated the abandoned apartment as one of his vacant stock. That may be the minority rule. Compare *Austin Hill Country Realty, Inc. v. Palisades Plaza, Inc.,* 948 S.W. 2d 293 (Tex. 1997) (burden of proof of mitigation or its absence on tenant) with *Snyder v. Ambrose,* 266 Ill. App. 3d 163 (1994) (burden of proof on landlord).

These jurisdictions divide on the question of whether this landlord option should be abolished for *all leases* or only for *residential leases.* Most of these states limit abolition to residential leases. But see *McGuire v. City of Jersey City,* 125 N.J. 310 (1991). Another issue is whether the duty to mitigate is mandatory or subject to waiver in the lease itself. A "no-mitigation" clause in a commercial lease has been upheld where there was no "inequality of bargaining power" and public policy did not forbid such clauses. *Sylva Shops Limited Partnership v. Hibbard,* 175 N.C. App. 423 (2006).

3. **Seizure of the tenant's personal property:** If a tenant failed to pay the rent, the common law entitled the landlord to seize the tenant's personal property in the leased premises and to hold it until the tenant cured the default. This was called *distress* or *distraint.* Some states have abolished distress completely; others have substituted a more limited right, usually requiring the landlord not to breach the peace and sometimes forbidding landlord self-help altogether. See *Restatement (Second) of Property*, §12.1, statutory note.

   a. **Liens on personal property:** One related remedy, provided by statute, is a lien in favor of the landlord against the tenant's personal property on the leased premises, in order to secure performance of the tenant's obligations. The landlord has no right to seize these goods by himself and must file suit to enforce the lien.

VII. LANDLORD'S OBLIGATIONS AND TENANT'S REMEDIES

A. **Introduction:** The landlord's obligations considered here are either implied or imposed by operation of law. These and other obligations can also be imposed by agreement in the lease. The tenant's remedies for breach of these obligations are considered in the context of each obligation.

B. **Quiet enjoyment:** Every tenant has the right to *quiet enjoyment* of the leased premises. A landlord may explicitly promise the tenant quiet enjoyment, but it doesn't matter much, because this obligation is also implied in law. One aspect of this obligation — the landlord's obligation to deliver to the tenant the legal right to possession of the premises — was considered in III.B, above. Another aspect of this obligation is considered here: the *duty of the landlord to refrain from wrongful* **actual** *or* **constructive** *eviction* of the tenant. Unlike other lease obligations, common law made the tenant's duty to pay rent conditional upon the landlord's performance of this obligation.

1. **Actual total eviction:** A tenant who has been *totally ousted from physical possession* of the leased premises — whether by the landlord or by someone with better title than the landlord — no longer is obligated to pay rent and may elect to terminate the lease.

2. **Actual partial eviction:** The traditional rule is that actual physical ouster of the tenant from *any part of the premises* relieves the tenant of the obligation to pay *any rent at all* until and unless the tenant is restored to possession of the entire leasehold property. This is true even if the tenant remains in possession of the rest of the property.

Example: Landlord permits a brick wall to encroach upon Tenant's leased property, ousting Tenant of a small strip of land. Tenant's rent obligation is suspended until the wall is removed, restoring him to full possession. *Smith v. McEnany,* 170 Mass. 26 (1897).

The preferred view of academics is to permit only ***partial abatement*** of rent in cases of actual partial eviction and to give the tenant the further option of termination or suit for damages. *Restatement (Second) of Property,* §6.1.

    a. By a third party under paramount title: If actual partial eviction occurs by a third party holding paramount title, the tenant's rent obligation is only ***partially abated.*** This makes sense only because of recording acts (see Chapter 6) that effectively define paramount title as a claim of which the tenant has actual or constructive knowledge. If the tenant knew about the better title, or with reasonable diligence should have known about it, the landlord ought not be punished for the tenant's assumption of a known risk.

3. Constructive eviction: If the landlord ***substantially interferes*** with the tenant's use and enjoyment of the leased property — so much so that the intended purposes of the tenant's occupation is frustrated — a ***constructive eviction*** has occurred. Eviction is constructive, rather than actual, because the tenant has ***not been physically ousted;*** instead, the utility of physical possession has been virtually destroyed. The tenant may terminate the lease and move out, and thereafter he will be excused from any further lease obligations.

Example: If the owner of a high-rise office building promises, but fails, to provide heat, air conditioning, or elevator service after normal working hours, a constructive eviction has occurred, not a partial actual eviction. See, e.g., *Charles E. Burt, Inc. v. Seven Grand Corp.,* 340 Mass. 124 (1959); *Barash v. Penn. Terminal Real Estate Corp.,* 26 N.Y.2d 77 (1970). There are three elements to constructive eviction: (1) ***wrongful act or failure of the landlord,*** (2) ***substantial and material deprivation of the tenant's beneficial use and enjoyment of the premises,*** and (3) ***complete vacation of the premises*** by the tenant.

    a. Landlord's wrongful action: The *landlord* must act wrongfully, ***not a third party.*** If the alleged wrongful act is the landlord's failure to act, the landlord must be under a duty to act.

        Example: Landlord refuses to provide heat on weekends, even though the lease expressly obligates Landlord to provide heat "at all times." Landlord is under a duty to act; his failure to act is wrongful.

        If a third party causes the interference, it is usually not constructive eviction. This is normally true even if the third party is another tenant. "The general, but not universal, rule . . . is that a landlord is not chargeable because one tenant is causing annoyance to another, even where the annoying conduct would be a breach of the landlord's covenant of quiet enjoyment if the landlord were the miscreant." *Blackett v. Olanoff,* 371 Mass. 714 (1977). However, a landlord is responsible for tenant actions that constitute a ***nuisance*** or which occur in ***common areas*** under the control of the landlord. Some courts have held that actions of a tenant may be attributable to the landlord if the landlord could control them, and the "disturbing condition was the natural and probable consequence" of landlord action.

        Example: Landlord maintained a residential apartment building and then leased adjacent space to Nightclub, under a lease that obligated Nightclub to conduct operations so as not to disturb the residential tenants. Nightclub's entertainment was so loud and prolonged that residential tenants could not sleep and even had difficulty conversing within their apartments. Because Landlord retained the power to control Nightclub's conduct, and introduced the problem, and the result was a natural and probable consequence of Landlord's action, Nightclub's action was deemed to be Landlord's. *Blackett v. Olanoff,* 371 Mass. 714 (1977).

Example: Tenant leased space in a shopping mall to sell patio furniture. Landlord promised Tenant that it would take action to abate the "[l]oud music, screams, shouts and yells" from Body Electric, an adjacent workout salon. The interference "caused walls to vibrate" and prevented normal business operations. Landlord's failure to act on his promise was wrongful, and it was no defense that Tenant had agreed in the lease that Landlord would neither be liable for its failure to perform its obligations nor for actions of other tenants. *Barton v. Mitchell Co.,* 507 So. 2d 148 (Fla. App. 1987).

Some courts go so far as to reason that because the landlord has the *power* to control his tenants, he has a *duty* to control them in order to preserve the quiet enjoyment to which tenants are entitled. See *Bocchini v. Gorn Management Co.,* 69 Md. App. 1 (1986).

b. **Substantial interference with tenant use and enjoyment:** The rule is easy to state: The tenant must be so "essentially deprived of the beneficial enjoyment of the leased premises [that] they are rendered unsuitable for occupancy for the purposes for which they are leased." *Barton v. Mitchell Co.* Application is more difficult. Courts try to be objective, taking into account the duration and severity of the interference, its foreseeability, and the ease or difficulty of abatement.

★**Example:** Cooper leased office space on the bottom floor of a building. Landlord maintained an adjacent driveway in such a manner that after every rainstorm Cooper's space would be inundated with water running off the driveway. The problem waxed and waned but eventually became so repeated and severe that she could not conduct normal business at the premises and had to rent space in a hotel for a sales meeting. Cooper was sufficiently deprived of her use and enjoyment of the premises to constitute constructive eviction. A single flooding would probably not have been sufficient. Cooper did not waive her claim of constructive eviction by remaining in possession for an unreasonably long time, because after each flooding incident she was assured by the landlord's agent that the problem would be corrected, and the landlord did attempt to fix the problem, albeit unsuccessfully. *Reste Realty Corp. v. Cooper,* 53 N.J. 444 (1969). Cooper did not know of the problem before signing the lease. If she had known, she would have been deemed to have waived any constructive eviction claim arising from that problem.

c. **Complete vacation of the premises:** A tenant may not remain in possession and still press a constructive eviction claim. The tenant must completely vacate the premises within a reasonable time after the interference. A "reasonable time" depends on all the circumstances.

★**Example:** In *Reste Realty Corp. v. Cooper,* the tenant remained in possession through a succession of floods but was led to believe that the problem might be corrected. She left for good after the last big flood, and it was apparent that the problem would not be fixed. That was reasonable.

However, if the tenant moves out, and a court later determines that there was no constructive eviction, the tenant has abandoned the leasehold and is very likely liable for unpaid rent or damages from anticipatory repudiation. See VI.C.2, above. One solution is to permit the tenant to bring an action for declaratory relief, prior to vacating the premises, to establish whether it would be constructive eviction if the tenant actually vacates. Cf. *Charles E. Burt, Inc. v. Seven Grand Corp.,* 340 Mass. 124 (1959) (dicta). Another solution is the *Restatement* position that a tenant ought to have the option of vacation and termination (at the tenant's risk that there is no constructive eviction) or remain in possession and receive damages or rent abatement or both. *Restatement (Second) of Property,* §6.1.

    d. Tenant remedies after vacation: The tenant's rent liability stops, and the lease is terminated upon justified vacation of the premises. The tenant is also entitled to recover damages caused by the constructive eviction.

    e. Dependent covenants as an alternative: When the landlord's breach is significant, but not enough to constitute constructive eviction, a few courts invoke the doctrine of dependent covenants, which permits the tenant to vacate and be excused from his obligation to pay rent. See *Wesson v. Leone Enterprises, Inc.*, 437 Mass. 708 (2002). Other courts have ruled that lesser landlord breaches permit the tenant to stay in possession and seek damages equal to the diminished value of the leasehold due to the breach. See *Echo Consulting Services, Inc. v. North Conway Bank*, 140 N.H. 566 (1995).

C. Warranty of habitability: The traditional rule is that a landlord has no implied obligation to warrant that property is suitable for the intended purposes of the tenant, so long as the tenant "has a reasonable opportunity of examining the property and judging for himself as to its qualities." *Anderson Drive-In Theatre v. Kirkpatrick,* 123 Ind. App. 388 (1953); *Blackwell v. Del Bosco*, 191 Colo. 344 (1976); *Murphy v. Hendrix*, 500 So. 2d 8 (Ala. 1986). Under the traditional view, a landlord has such an obligation only if he expressly makes such a warranty; otherwise, "the rule of caveat emptor applies." *Id.* This rule has partially broken down, but even where the warranty is implied, it may not extend to all residential leases. Typical exceptions include single-family homes, agricultural leases, and very short-term or long-term leases. Most jurisdictions do not extend the warranty to commercial leases.

    1. Implied warranty of habitability: General: The modern trend is to imply into most residential leases a warranty of habitability, but this is still a minority view. The majority rule is typified by *Miles v. Shauntee,* 664 S.W.2d 512 (Ky. 1983), in which the Kentucky Supreme Court rejected the idea that a warranty could be implied by the existence of housing codes: "It is for the legislature to create rights and duties nonexistent under the common law . . . No implied warranty of habitability exists under Kentucky law." The *Restatement* phrases this emerging duty as a warranty of suitability for residential use. *Restatement (Second) of Property,* §5.1. Under either label, it is really an implied-in-law obligation of the landlord to provide premises that are fit for human inhabitation, both at the inception of the lease and continuing throughout the lease term. This obligation consists of ***two separate obligations:*** (1) An "implied warranty of habitability" that properly refers to the warranty implied at ***inception of the lease,*** and (2) an implied ***continuing duty of repair.*** Neither courts nor commentators make this distinction with any regularity; in practice, both are lumped together as the implied warranty of habitability.

        a. Illegal lease: A lease of premises that the landlord knows is not habitable and in violation of local housing codes at the inception of the lease is an illegal, unenforceable lease, the result of which is that the tenant is a tenant at sufferance, and the landlord may only recover the "reasonable" rental value of the premises. See *Brown v. Southall Realty Co.,* 237 A.2d

834 (D.C. 1968). By contrast, a lease of property that degenerates during the term into an uninhabitable condition is valid though in breach of the implied warranty of habitability.

2. **Implied warranty of habitability: Rationale:** The implied warranty of habitability is defended on several grounds: (1) implied warranties of quality and fitness are a commonplace feature of contract law and, because leases are contracts, should be a feature of landlord-tenant law; (2) urban tenants lack the skills necessary to repair uninhabitable premises and the judgment necessary to detect such premises; (3) an implied warranty of habitability is necessary to redress the unequal bargaining power of rich landlords and poor tenants; and (4) an implied warranty will encourage compliance with local housing codes.

★**Example:** Hilder rented an apartment in Rutland, Vermont, from St. Peter. The apartment was filthy, lacked a locking front door, had plumbing that leaked water through the walls and ceilings (causing chunks of plaster to fall onto a child's crib), had inoperable electrical outlets and switches, and had a broken buried sewer line that produced raw sewage in the basement, which emitted intolerable odors and caused an inoperable toilet that remained clogged with feces and other waste even after repeated flushing with pails of water. In *Hilder v. St. Peter,* 144 Vt. 150 (1984), the Vermont Supreme Court held that these conditions resulted in breach of the implied warranty of habitability. See also *Javins v. First Natl. Realty Corp.,* 428 F.2d 1071 (D.C. Cir. 1970).

3. **Implied warranty of habitability: Criticism:** The implied warranty is often criticized on economic grounds. If implied warranties achieve their intended effect by forcing landlords to improve the condition of leased premises, the result will be to reduce the supply of low-income housing and raise its price. See Richard Posner, *Economic Analysis of the Law*, §16.6 (4th ed., 1992), for a complete demonstration of this conclusion. The standard remedy for breach of the implied warranty of habitability is to abate the rent obligation, but "[f]rom the standpoint of protecting poor people [this] is particularly pernicious." *Id.* It raises landlords' costs (thus increasing rental rates in times of low vacancy) and reduces the supply of rental housing because landlords have an additional incentive either to withdraw from the market by converting their property to some other use (e.g. commercial or conversion to condominiums) or to improve the housing to the point that it is no longer affordable by the poor. The entire movement toward implied warranties of habitability has been marked by a belief that it aids the poor, but critics contend that this may be another example of the road to Hell being paved with good intentions.

4. **Scope of the implied warranty of habitability:** The implied warranty is generally limited to residential leases, but there are a few cases applying it to small-scale commercial tenants. See, e.g., *Davidow v. Inwood North Professional Group,* 747 S.W. 2d 373 (Tex. 1988). The measure of "habitability" is usually the standards set by the local housing code, because the acknowledged objective of proponents of the implied warranty is to spur compliance with such codes. However, minor violations of housing codes that do not immediately affect habitability do not trigger the landlord's implied duty to repair the premises. Nor is the landlord in breach until he has been *notified of the uninhabitable condition and given a reasonable opportunity to correct the problem.*

★**Example:** After Hilder had rented her Vermont apartment from St. Peter, she repeatedly drew its manifold defects to the attention of St. Peter, but he did nothing to correct the problems, which persisted for at least nine months. *Hilder v. St. Peter,* 144 Vt. 150 (1984). See also *King v. Moorehead,* 495 S.W. 2d 65 (Mo. App. 1973).

5. **Tenant's remedies for landlord breach of the implied warranty of habitability:** Upon breach, and after notice to the landlord, the tenant's rent obligation is suspended, and the tenant has the following remedies.

   a. **Terminate and leave:** The tenant may terminate the lease, vacate the premises, and recover damages (usually relocation costs plus the excess of replacement rentals over the lease rentals for the balance of the term).

   b. **Stay and withhold rent:** The tenant may remain in possession and withhold rent, pending landlord correction of the defects. The *Restatement (Second) of Property*, §11.3, provides that a tenant must notify the landlord of exercise of this remedy and deposit rent into an escrow account.

   c. **Stay and repair:** The tenant may remain in possession and use a reasonable amount of the rent to make repairs sufficient to bring the premises into habitable condition. *Marini v. Ireland,* 56 N.J. 130 (1970). Some states have codified this remedy in statutory "repair and deduct" provisions that specify how much rent may be used for repair purposes and how frequently this remedy may be invoked. See, e.g., Cal. Civ. Code §1942.

   d. **Stay and recover damages:** The tenant may remain in possession and recover *damages in the form of a rent abatement or deduction* plus, in some jurisdictions, damages for *discomfort and annoyance*. See, e.g., *Hilder v. St. Peter,* 144 Vt. 150 (1984). There are three different measures of the amount of damages in the form of a rent deduction.

      i. **Value as warranted:** The tenant is entitled to the difference between the value of the premises *as warranted* (i.e., in habitable condition) and the value of the premises *as is* (i.e., in uninhabitable condition), up to the amount of the stated rent. The stated rent is rebuttably presumed to be the value as warranted. In essence, this method causes the stated rent to be reduced to actual value, which may be zero. This seems to be the prevailing method. See, e.g., *Hilder v. St. Peter,* 144 Vt. 150 (1984); *Berzito v. Gambino,* 63 N.J. 460 (1973).

      Example: George leases an uninhabitable apartment to Amy for $150 a month. Amy proves that the value of the apartment, if it were habitable, is $200 a month, rebutting the presumption that stated rent equals value as warranted. The apartment's value "as is" is $100 a month. Amy is entitled to the difference between the last two values, or $100 a month, deducted from the stated rent of $150 a month, leaving Amy with a rent obligation of $50 a month. If the value "as warranted" had been $275 a month, Amy's damages would have been $175 a month, or more than the stated rent, but Amy would be entitled only to a complete abatement of rent.

      ii. **Value as-is:** The tenant is entitled to the difference between the *stated rent* and the *actual fair value* of the premises in their uninhabitable condition. See, e.g., *Kline v. Burns,* 111 N.H. 87 (1971). If the stated rent accurately reflects the fair value of the premises in their dilapidated state, damages are nil. Of course, in that situation, the tenant is not paying for more than he receives.

      Example: George leases the same dilapidated apartment to Amy for $150 a month, and its actual value is $100 a month. Amy is entitled to damages in the form of a rent reduction of $50 a month, leaving her with a rent obligation of $100 a month. If the actual value of the apartment in its sorry state was $150 a month, Amy would not have been damaged.

    iii. Proportionate reduction: The tenant's rent obligation is reduced to a percentage of the stated rent. The percentage is determined as follows: (1) compute the fair market value of the premises *as warranted* (habitable); (2) compute the value *as is* (uninhabitable); (3) compute the percentage relationship of actual value to warranted value; and (4) apply that percentage to the stated rent. The *Restatement (Second) of Property*, §11.1 adopts this method.

    Example: George leases the same substandard apartment to Amy for $150 a month. Its value as warranted (habitable) is $200 a month, and its value as is (uninhabitable) is $100 a month, or 50 percent of the habitable value. Amy is entitled to damages in the form of a rent reduction of 50 percent of the stated rent, or $75 a month, leaving her with a rent obligation of $75 a month.

e. Stay and defend: The tenant can remain in possession and plead and prove the landlord's breach of the implied warranty as a *complete defense* to an eviction action *based on the tenant's failure to pay rent.* This is a complete defense because, after breach and notice to the landlord of the breach, there is *no further rent obligation.* See, e.g., *Hilder v. St. Peter,* 144 Vt. 150 (1984). *Note:* If the landlord is seeking to evict the tenant because the term has expired and the tenant is a holdover, this is *not a defense.* It is a defense only to a landlord's claim of possession founded on failure to pay rent.

f. Punitive damages: In circumstances involving willful, wanton, and fraudulent conduct on the part of the landlord, a tenant may be entitled to recover punitive damages.

    ★**Example:** St. Peter, the landlord in *Hilder v. St. Peter,* falsely told Hilder that he would refund her security deposit if she would clean the apartment (which she did), and that he would furnish the heat even though the electrical furnace was wired through Hilder's electric meter (for which she was responsible to the utility). St. Peter also promised to fix the many defects but did absolutely nothing. The Vermont Supreme Court concluded that "[w]hen a landlord, after receiving notice of a defect, fails to repair the facility that is essential to the health and safety of his or her tenant, an award of punitive damages is proper." *Hilder v. St Peter,* 144 Vt. 150 (1984).

6. Waiver by tenant: Courts almost uniformly hold that a tenant may not waive the landlord's obligation to provide habitable premises. Some courts hold that the implied warranty of habitability may not be waived under any circumstances. See *Hilder v. St. Peter,* 144 Vt. 150 (1984). The *Restatement (Second) of Property*, §5.6, permits waiver of the landlord's obligations only to the extent such waiver is neither unconscionable nor against public policy. See also *P.H. Investment v. Oliver*, 818 P.2d 1018 (Utah 1991). The URLTA, §2.104, permits a limited imposition of a duty to repair on the tenant, but not elimination of the landlord's implied obligation to comply with housing codes.

7. Statutory codification: A number of states have enacted statutes that codify these rules, usually with some modifications that increase the breadth of tenant remedies. See, e.g., URLTA §2.104 (imposing specific landlord duties), §4.103 ("repair and deduct" remedy), §4.104 (permitting the tenant to obtain emergency services, such as heat, light, and even substitute housing by deducting its cost from rent), and §4.105 (permitting the tenant to offset her expenses incurred against landlord rent claims in summary eviction proceedings).

8. **The retaliatory eviction doctrine:** The traditional rule was that, so long as a landlord is entitled to possession, the landlord's **motivation** for evicting the tenant is **irrelevant.** Today, most jurisdictions hold that a landlord may not evict a tenant, even if he is otherwise entitled to do so, if the landlord seeks to evict the tenant in **retaliation** for the tenant's reporting of housing code violations to government authorities. See, e.g., *Dickhut v. Norton,* 45 Wis. 2d 389 (1970); *Edwards v. Habib,* 397 F.2d 687 (D.C. Cir. 1968). This position is often codified by statute. See, e.g., URLTA §5.101; *Restatement (Second) of Property*, §§14.8, 14.9 and commentary thereto. The URLTA extends the retaliatory eviction doctrine to instances of tenant invocation of the implied warranty of habitability, and it is likely that this position will be adopted by courts even in non-URLTA jurisdictions. At least one state, New Jersey, has moved beyond retaliatory eviction to provide that a landlord may "evict a tenant at the end of the lease term only for "good cause." Rabin, 69 Corn. L. Rev. 517, 534-35, citing N.J. Stat. Ann. §2A:18-61.1.

a. **Rationale:** The rationale for the retaliatory eviction doctrine is that, without it, landlords will simply refuse to renew periodic tenancies (usually month to month) of tenants who have been so bold as to report substandard condition to government enforcement officials. To ensure the effective operation of housing codes, it is argued, landlords must be prevented from retaliating against tenants who report these violations of law.

b. **Proof of retaliatory motive:** The tenant has the burden of proving retaliatory motivation. By statute, some states provide that retaliatory motive is presumed if the landlord terminates the lease, raises rent, or decreases services within some period (typically 90 to 180 days) after the tenant has complained of housing code violations. In those states, the landlord has the burden of proving that his motive is not retaliatory. One alternative approach is to permit the landlord to evict after repairs have been made (action likely initiated by tenant complaint), but to impose on the landlord the burden of proving that he afforded the tenant a "reasonable opportunity to procure other housing." *Building Monitoring Systems, Inc. v. Paxton,* 905 P.2d 1215 (Utah 1995).

c. **Available only to tenant not in default:** The retaliatory eviction defense is available only to a tenant **not in default.** Recall that a tenant who is withholding rent after landlord breach of the implied warranty of habitability is not in default.

d. **Eviction after retaliatory motive found:** A landlord who has been found to have sought a retaliatory eviction is not forever barred from eviction. If the landlord can later prove that there are good business reasons for eviction, he is entitled to evict.

e. **Indirect eviction.** A landlord may not seek to evict a tenant **indirectly** in retaliation for the tenant's reporting of housing code violations. Indirect eviction can take a variety of forms but typically consists of draconian reductions in service (e.g., a utility cutoff) or dramatic increases in rent that are designed to drive the tenant away. Such actions are treated as a form of retaliatory eviction.

D. **Tort liability of landlords:** This issue is a specialized application of the ordinary tort doctrine of negligence. Negligence is conduct that deviates from the standard of care — what a reasonable person would do in similar circumstances. Every person has a duty to use ordinary care to avoid foreseeable harm to others. Except for a few exceptions, the common law provided that landlords had no duty to make the leased premises safe for tenants or their guests. The tenant took the property as it was. If there were dangerous aspects to the premises that could be expected to injure others (e.g., a beam protruding into a dark doorway at head height), the tenant had the duty to correct the condition and was liable to others for injury caused by his failure to do so. Today, the duty of landlords to maintain leased premises in a fashion that avoids foreseeable injury to others is increasing. This section deals with this phenomenon but does not attempt to deal with all facets of the law of negligence. Your torts course is the place for that.

1. **An aside on tort theory:** The law of torts developed on the principle of *fault* — people ought to be held responsible for their individual failures but nothing more. In the latter half of the twentieth century, American courts began to conceive of tort law as a device to ***share the cost of personal injury.*** Accordingly, the fault principle has been eroded (e.g., strict liability torts). In this area, a minority of courts seem willing to impose greater duties (and ultimately tort liabilities) on landlords because they believe that the (sometimes) extremely high cost of personal injury judgments will be borne by all tenants as a class through higher liability insurance premiums paid by landlords and passed on in higher rents. This rests on two assumptions: (1) liability insurance is endlessly available in sufficient amounts to share the costs of accidents widely, and (2) personal injury awards will fairly reflect the fault of tortfeasors and the true value of the injuries suffered. These assumptions may not be accurate in a world where tort law is no longer based entirely on fault. Nevertheless, expansion of duties and consequent tort liability continues.

2. **Pre-existing dangerous conditions:** The common law recognized the following exceptions to the general rule that a landlord had no tort liability to the tenant or his guests for dangerous conditions existing on the leased premises at the inception of the lease.

   a. **Latent defects:** Because only the landlord would know (if anyone would) of a concealed defect, common law imposed on the landlord a duty to warn the tenant of their existence and the specifics of the defects. If the landlord did so, and the tenant occupied anyway, the landlord had no liability to either the tenant or his guests. The tenant assumed the risk and acquired a duty to correct the condition.

   b. **Public use:** A landlord is liable to the public for injuries occasioned by a defect ***existing at inception of the lease*** which is ***known to the landlord,*** if the premises are ***intended for use by members of the public,*** the landlord ***knows or should know that the tenant will probably not correct the defect*** before admitting the public, and the landlord has ***failed to use ordinary care to correct the defect.*** The term ***public use*** usually means use by any members of the public, though some courts interpret this more narrowly, confining it to cases where a great many members of the public are invited (e.g., a theater).

3. **Conditions occurring during the lease term:** A landlord generally has no liability for dangerous conditions that occur after the tenant has taken possession. A landlord can voluntarily assume such a duty, though, by undertaking repairs. If the repairs do not comport with the duty of ordinary care and skill, the landlord will be liable for resulting injuries.

4. **Common areas:** A landlord has a duty to exercise reasonable care over common areas that remain under his control. This duty extends to taking reasonable precautions to prevent criminal activity by third parties that injures tenants. See, e.g., *Kline v. 1500 Mass. Ave. Apt. Corp.,* 439 F.2d 477 (1970).

5. **Landlord covenant to repair:** The common law rule was that a landlord assumed no tort duty of care by agreeing to repair leased premises. This view is rejected by most American jurisdictions today, as well as by the *Restatement (Second) of Torts*, §357, and the *Restatement (Second) of Property*, §17.5.

6. **Statutory or judicially created duty of landlord to repair:** Landlords may be under a duty to repair that flows from a statute, like a housing code or a codified version of the implied warranty of habitability, or by virtue of a judicially created implied warranty of habitability. Failure to conform to a ***statutory duty*** may be treated as ***negligence* per se** or merely as ***evidence of negligence.*** Failure to make repairs sufficient to cure breach of the implied warranty of habitability may result in tort liability if the landlord was negligent in correcting the defect — if he knew, or should have known, of the problem and failed to correct it within a reasonable time. See, e.g., *Dwyer v. Skyline Apartments, Inc.,* 123 N.J. Super 48, *aff'd* 63 N.J. 577 (1973).

7. **Strict liability:** California adopted, and then rejected, a rule of strict liability for personal injuries resulting from latent defects in leased property. See *Becker v. IRM Corp.,* 38 Cal. 3d 454 (1985), overturned by *Peterson v. Superior Court (Paribas),* 10 Cal. 4th 1185 (1995). An Indiana appellate court has hinted that the now-rejected California rule of strict liability might apply in the case of "professional landlords." See *Johnson v. Scandia Associates, Inc.,* 641 N.E.2d 51 (Ind. App. 1994). Louisiana has a statutory rule of strict liability for defects in existence at inception of the lease term. Otherwise, no other jurisdiction seems to have followed California's experiment in strict liability.

8. **No special rules for landlords:** Perhaps fewer than ten American jurisdictions have rejected the categorical rules summarized above in favor of a rule that treats landlords like everybody else. In this approach, a landlord is liable to the tenant or third parties for injuries occurring on the leased premises if the landlord fails to "act as a reasonable person under all the circumstances." *Sargent v. Ross,* 113 N.H. 388 (1973); *Joiner v. Haley,* 777 So. 2d 50 (Miss. Ct. App. 2000). The common law categories are treated as factors to be taken into consideration but are not used as rigid rules to define liability. See *Pagelsdorf v. Safeco Insurance Co.,* 91 Wis.2d 734 (1979).

9. **Exculpatory clauses:** An exculpatory clause in a lease is an attempt to relieve the landlord of any liability he might otherwise have to the tenant for personal injuries or property damage caused by defective conditions in the leased premises or common areas. Exculpatory clauses are generally ***valid,*** but some courts refuse to enforce them in ***residential leases,*** either because of supposed unequal bargaining power or because they are thought to increase the risk of personal injury. See, e.g., *Henrioulle v. Marin Ventures, Inc.,* 20 Cal. 3d 512 (1978); *Cardona v. Eden Realty Co.,* 118 N.J. Super. 381 (1972); *Cappaert v. Junker,* 413 So. 2d 378 (Miss. 1982); *McCutcheon v. United Homes Corp.,* 79 Wash. 2d 443 (1971). But see *O'Callaghan v. Waller & Beckwith Realty Co.,* 15 Ill. 2d 436 (1958) (upholding an exculpatory clause on the theory that landlords lack monopoly power). A later case decided by Illinois's intermediate appeals court, *Strauch v. Charles Apartments Co.,* 1 Ill. App. 3d 57 (1971), holds that exculpatory clauses are not automatically valid, but that the tenant has an opportunity to prove sufficiently unequal bargaining power to void the clause. Some states have voided exculpatory clauses by statute, usually with respect to residential leases but sometimes including commercial leases, too. See *Restatement (Second) of Property*, §17.3, statutory note. URLTA

§1.403 voids exculpatory clauses in residential eases only. Except where voided by statute, exculpatory clauses are virtually always valid in commercial leases.

VIII. FIXTURES

A. **Introduction:** Tenants often attach personal property — *chattels* — to the leasehold premises. Who owns the chattels upon termination of the lease — landlord or tenant?

B. **Fixtures:** Fixtures belong to the landlord. Common law defined a fixture as any chattel *permanently affixed* to the leased property, a definition that merely shifted the focus to defining "permanent" and "affixed." The modem approach is to define "fixture" by examining the *tenant's intent* through such objective measures as how it is attached, what sort of chattel it is, and the damage that removal would cause. The last factor — *removal damage* — is often dispositive; if the removal damage is not substantial, the chattel is not likely to be a fixture.

Example: Tenant removed a large pipe organ at the end of the lease term. To do so, tenant removed and restored part of a brick wall to the building. The damage was *not irreparable,* and after restoration (at tenant expense), the premises were in substantially their original condition. The Washington Supreme Court ruled that the pipe organ was not a fixture. *Ballard v. Alaska Theater Co.,* 93 Wash. 655 (1916).

1. **Trade fixtures:** Despite the general rule, a tenant is permitted to remove and retain ownership of trade fixtures — attached items of personal property used in carrying on a trade or business, broadly defined.

   Example: Tenant, a bookseller, bolts bookshelves to the wall and floor for display of the inventory. Though the shelves are as "permanently affixed" as is practical, courts regard them as trade fixtures and permit their removal at the end of the lease term.

C. **Attached chattels, but not fixtures:** If a tenant attaches a chattel to the property, but it is *not a fixture* (e.g., a bookcase secured to the wall to prevent earthquake damage), it belongs to the tenant *unless the tenant leaves it behind at the end of the lease term.* Such chattels belong to the landlord because the tenant has effectively abandoned them.

IX. SOCIAL REGULATIONS OF LEASEHOLDS

A. **Introduction:** Many of the issues discussed so far in this chapter involve "social regulation" of leaseholds, but this section deals with two particular areas of regulation that are avowedly for the accomplishment of larger social objectives.

B. **Rent control:** Rent control laws have been adopted in many places, usually at the local level. Rent control consists of price controls (set at below-market rates), usually augmented by limitations on a landlord's ability to evict tenants at the end of the lease term (thus curbing the landlord's ability to lease to a new tenant at market rates).

1. **Criticisms:** Rent control is often criticized as an unconstitutional taking of property without just compensation and as economically inefficient.

   a. **Taking:** Some argue that rent control amounts to a governmental seizure of the landlord's reversion followed by its transfer to the tenant in place, coupled with an obligation delegated to the tenant to compensate the landlord for the seizure at a below-market rate. See Richard Epstein, *Takings* (1985). By this reasoning, rent control laws ought to be violations of the constitutional requirement that private property may not be taken for public use without payment of just compensation, but the U.S. Supreme Court has rejected that argument. See *Pennell v. City of San Jose,* 485 U.S. 1 (1988). But if the permitted rents are set so low that the landlord is deprived of a *reasonable rate of return on his investment,* a taking has occurred. See generally Chapter 11.

    b. Economic inefficiency: Rent controls and other similar limits placed on landlords are often criticized on the economic ground that they produce an inefficient allocation of housing resources.

      ★**Example:** Chicago enacted an ordinance that codified the implied warranty of habitability, required interest payments on tenant security deposits, and permitted tenants to deduct the cost of minor repairs from rent and to withhold rent in an amount equal to the damages inflicted by a landlord's violation of a lease term. In ***Chicago Board of Realtors, Inc. v. City of Chicago,*** 819 F.2d 732 (7th Cir. 1987), the ordinance was upheld against a constitutional attack, but Judges Posner and Easterbrook, two premier advocates of economic analysis in law, concurred separately, expressing the policy view that such requirements benefit in-place tenants at the expense of would-be tenants, provide an incentive for landlords to skimp on maintenance, deter the construction of new rental housing, benefit landlords in neighboring jurisdictions that lack rent controls or similar regulations, and produce an inefficient allocation of residential living space.

  2. Defenses: Defenders of rent control usually deny the validity of the efficiency arguments (even though virtually all economists agree that rent control produces inefficient resource allocation) or contend that other factors are more important than efficiency. These other factors are often said to be keeping economically vulnerable (usually elderly or poor) tenants in place with a relatively fixed portion of their income going to housing, but the effect of rent control is rarely, if ever, this confined.

C. Anti-discrimination statutes: The common law gave unlimited freedom to a property owner to decide to whom he wished to sell or lease his property. Today, that freedom is circumscribed by federal, state, and local statutes that prohibit discrimination in the *sale* or *rental* of real property on the basis of race, sex, ethnicity, national origin, age, religion, and, under some state and local laws, sexual orientation. The major federal statutes are considered here.

  1. 42 U.S.C. §1982: The 1866 Civil Rights Act: During Reconstruction, the 1866 Civil Rights Act was enacted, providing in part that "All citizens of the United States shall have the same right . . . as is enjoyed by white citizens . . . to inherit, purchase, lease, sell, hold, and convey real and personal property." This provision is now codified at 42 U.S.C. §1982. Its intent was to place newly emancipated black Americans on the same footing as white Americans with respect to property rights. In *Jones v. Alfred H. Mayer Co.,* 392 U.S. 409 (1968), the Supreme Court held that this provision applied to private conduct as well as state action, and that Congress had power under §2 of the Thirteenth Amendment to regulate this private behavior. Thus, 42 U.S.C. §1982 *prohibits private discrimination on the basis of race or ethnicity with respect to sales or rentals of real property.* Violators are subject to injunction and liable for damages.

2. **Fair Housing Act:** Title VIII of the 1968 Civil Rights Act is the Fair Housing Act, 42 U.S.C. §§3601–3619, 3631. In its original form, it prohibited private discrimination in the sale or rental of residential housing on the basis of race, color, religion, or national origin. It has since been amended to forbid discrimination against people with handicaps, people with children (except in "seniors only" developments), and on the basis of sex. The definition of *handicap* includes a physical or mental impairment that "substantially limits [at least one] major life activit[y]," but specifically excludes drug addiction or cross-dressing. This handicap definition is not as broad as that under the Americans with Disabilities Act of 1991.

   a. **Exemptions:** There are several important exemptions to the discrimination ban of the Fair Housing Act.

      i. **Sale or lease by owner of a single-family dwelling:** A person who does not own more than three single-family residences may discriminate on otherwise forbidden grounds in the sale or lease of his single-family residence so long as he neither uses a broker nor advertises in a manner that reveals his discriminatory intent. See 42 U.S.C. §3603(b)(l).

      ii. **Owner-occupied rental housing of four units or less:** In the debates concerning adoption of the Fair Housing Act, certain members of Congress worried about the application of the law to "Mrs. Murphy's boardinghouse" — small owner-occupied rental housing. Out of concern that these situations might be sufficiently intimate to implicate free association rights, Congress adopted this exemption, which permits a landlord to discriminate on otherwise forbidden grounds in the rental of residential housing so long as the landlord is an owner and occupant of the house or apartment building and it consists of four units or less. See 42 U.S.C. §3603(b)(2). However, such a person may not advertise in a manner that reveals his discriminatory intent. See 42 U.S.C. §3603(b)(1).

   b. **Remedies:** Violators are subject to injunction, compensatory, and punitive damages. Jurisdiction over Fair Housing Act claims is vested in the federal courts.

3. **Comparison of 42 U.S.C. §1982 and Fair Housing Act:** The Fair Housing Act forbids discrimination on more grounds, but it only applies to residential housing, and it admits of some exemptions. 42 U.S.C. §1982 applies to all types of property but only forbids private racial or ethnic discrimination, and has no exemptions to the transactions to which it applies.

4. **Proof of forbidden discrimination:** Under either 42 U.S.C. §1982 or the Fair Housing Act, a presumptive case of forbidden discrimination is made out if the landlord's or seller's practices produce a forbidden *discriminatory effect.* The burden then shifts to the landlord or seller to prove that he was not, in fact, motivated by forbidden grounds. This is mostly a matter of offering convincing alternative reasons for rejection and benign explanations for the discriminatory effect. If, however, a forbidden ground is even one of many motivations, prohibited discrimination is proven.

5. **State and local laws:** There are a variety of state and local laws that address discrimination in the sale or rental of real property. Most apply to residential property. While the forbidden grounds of discrimination vary, almost all forbid discrimination on the basis of race, ethnicity, or national origin; most include religion and sex; and some add age, marital status, having children, or physical handicap to the forbidden categories. A few include sexual orientation.

These statutes differ widely in their enforcement mechanisms (some involve administrative complaint and investigation; others permit private lawsuits directly against alleged violators) and available remedies.

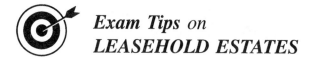

Exam Tips on
LEASEHOLD ESTATES

☛ An ambiguous lease invites issues of characterization (periodic, at will, or term of years), and these issues can be easily combined with a holdover problem in which the landlord makes an election to renew. You will have to decide what the initial lease was in order to decide what type of lease was created by the landlord's election.

☛ Issues of transfer of a leasehold are very attractive test candidates. Many consequences flow from whether the lessee's transfer accomplishes an assignment or a sublease. Be certain you understand the differences between privity of contract and privity of estate, and be able to apply those differences to a fact pattern filled with multiple transfers. Be alert to the possibility of a landlord's unreasonable refusal to consent to transfer. Not all states impose an obligation of reasonableness on landlords, and almost none does so with respect to residential leases. If you are imposing such an obligation where courts usually do not, you must make a good policy argument for your conclusion.

☛ Residential leases raise a number of possible issues. If the facts pose an issue of landlord self-help in recovering possession, be prepared to argue the policy merits of permitting or preventing self-help. If the tenant has abandoned before the end of the term, pay attention to facts that indicate the nature of the landlord's election, and don't forget that the modern trend (though by no means universally accepted) is to impose a duty on the landlord to mitigate damages. Landlord breach of the implied warranty of habitability raises a number of possible remedies on the part of the tenant. Pay attention to facts that suggest which remedy might be of most advantage to the tenant. Remember that quiet enjoyment must involve some breach of a landlord duty; this can be tricky when the interference comes from another tenant. Look for facts suggesting that the landlord has a duty to control such tenant behavior. This problem might also involve a nuisance issue or a question of tort liability of a landlord.

CHAPTER 6

TRANSFERS OF REAL PROPERTY

ChapterScope

This chapter examines transfers of real property, including the contract of sale, the deed by which title is transferred, and the financing devices that enable the sale to occur. Here are the most important points in this chapter.

- To be enforceable, a contract to convey real property must be in writing and signed by the party against whom it is sought to be enforced. Exceptions occur when there has been part performance and when equitable estoppel applies.

- Implied in any contract to sell real property is an obligation of good faith and timely performance, as well as an obligation to deliver marketable title. In order for a defect in title to make title unmarketable, it must be substantial and likely to injure the buyer. Such defects include recorded encumbrances but not zoning restrictions unless the property actually violates them.

- Remedies for default of a contract of sale include specific performance, rescission, or damages.

- Sellers may not intentionally misrepresent the property, and they must disclose all seller-created conditions that materially impair value and are not likely to be discovered by an ordinarily prudent buyer. The trend is to require sellers to disclose all latent defects known to the seller — defects that materially impair value and could not be discovered by a reasonably prudent buyer. Builders are generally held to make an implied warranty of quality.

- Deeds must be in writing and signed by the grantor. To be recorded, the grantor's signature must be acknowledged before a notary, and that fact must be memorialized on the deed by a notarial seal and signature. A deed must contain an adequate description of the grantee and the property conveyed.

- Deeds may be a general warranty deed, a special warranty deed, or a quitclaim deed. The difference inheres in the scope of the warranties of title made by the grantor.

  - A general warranty deed contains six warranties of title, three of which are promises about present conditions, and three of which are promises about future action. In substance, the present covenants are that the seller both owns the property and has the right to convey it, and there are no encumbrances except those disclosed. The future covenants are that the seller will defend the buyer's title against lawful claims of superior title, the buyer will not be disturbed by such claims, and the seller will do whatever is reasonably necessary to perfect title.

  - A special warranty deed contains the same six warranties, but only as to the time the seller owned the property.

  - A quitclaim deed contains no warranties of title at all, but is effective to transfer whatever interest the seller happens to have in the subject property.

- To be effective, a deed must be delivered to the grantee. This often becomes a problem when a grantor executes a deed with the intention that it become effective at his death.

■ Purchase of real estate is usually financed in large part by a commercial loan of much of the purchase price to the buyer. The lender secures repayment of that loan by either a mortgage of, or deed of trust to, the property. A ***mortgage*** is a lien on the property that can produce a transfer of title upon the borrower's default. A ***deed of trust*** is a transfer of title of the property to a trustee for the purpose of conveying it to the lender if the borrower defaults, or back to the borrower if he does not default. In practice, both devices are treated as liens until title is transferred after borrower default.

■ Sometimes sellers lend the buyer a portion of the purchase price by taking the buyer's note. Sellers may secure payment of the note by taking a mortgage or deed of trust, but sometimes they use an installment sale contract, under which title is not transferred until the buyer has paid the entire price. When a buyer defaults under such a contract, virtually every state treats the contract as functionally identical to a mortgage or deed of trust and requires the seller to act as would any other mortgage lender.

■ Mortgages usually involve a foreclosure sale, at which the property is sold to pay off the unpaid balance of the loan. Deeds of trust usually involve a private sale for the same purpose. Under either mechanism, the borrower usually has some statutorily defined period of time in which to redeem his property following sale, unless that right has been cut off by judicial decision. Some states impose on lenders the obligation to act in a commercially reasonable fashion when conducting a foreclosure sale or private sale, in order to realize fair value for the property.

I. CONTRACTS OF SALE

A. Introduction: All arm's length transfers for consideration will involve a contract for the sale of the land involved. Much of the law pertaining to that contract is the domain of your contracts course. This discussion focuses on aspects of the contract for sale that are peculiar to the fact that land is the subject matter.

1. **Brokers:** Brokers are ubiquitous. Very few transfers of houses occur without the involvement of one or more brokers, and many transfers of commercial real estate involve a broker. In the typical arrangement, a seller hires a broker (the ***listing agent***) to sell the property on terms and for a commission specified in the ***listing agreement.*** In most states, the commission is earned when the broker has produced a buyer ***ready, willing, and able*** to purchase on the terms of the listing agreement or other terms acceptable to the seller. Unless the listing agreement provides otherwise, most courts find that the broker is entitled to his commission if the deal fails regardless of seller's or buyer's default. The minority view is that if the deal falls through because the ***seller defaults*** or the ***seller refuses to sell on the terms of the listing agreement,*** the broker is entitled to the commission anyway; but if the ***buyer defaults,*** no commission is earned.

    a. **Brokers' fiduciary duties:** A listing agent is the seller's agent and owes to the seller all of the fiduciary duties that come with an agency relationship. Reduced to the essentials, the broker must put his principal's interests ahead of his own and exercise diligence to obtain the best result.

    ★**Example:** Six siblings lacking knowledge of real estate transactions retained a broker to sell the Connecticut property they had inherited. The broker enlisted the services of another broker to assist in marketing the property. Less than 24 hours after the signing of a listing agreement, in which the property was offered for sale for $125,000, the defendant broker offered to purchase the property for $115,000. The broker's offer was accepted. Six days after the closing, the broker resold the property for $160,000, making a profit of $45,000 on a cash investment of $111,500. In *Licari v. Blackwelder*, 539 A.2d 609 (Conn. App. 1988), a damage award of $45,000 against the broker was upheld. The broker had withheld from his client the fact that he was negotiating the sale of the property to a third party even before he purchased it; failed to exercise his best efforts to obtain the best price for his client; and misrepresented other facts.

Because the listing broker shares the commission with other brokers who are working with buyers, the ostensible buyer's broker is actually a subagent of the listing agent; thus, while the buyer may think "his" agent is representing him, in fact, the broker is representing the seller. Some states require disclosure of this fact. Although true buyers' brokers have begun to exist, such brokers have no contractual right to share the listing agent's commission, thus presenting economic obstacles to the proliferation of buyers' brokers.

2. **Lawyers:** Most residential sale transactions are done via a standard, preprinted contract, with critical terms (e.g., price, financing, closing costs) to be supplied by the parties. Often brokers fill in these gaps, and lawyers are not involved. Brokers must be careful not to do much more than "fill in the blanks" lest they be deemed to be practicing law. Of course, the choices made or advised by brokers have large legal consequences. Buyers and sellers are well advised to consult lawyers in the making of the contract, but most don't. In some states, lawyers are engaged to prepare a *title abstract* — a history of the chain of title — and an opinion as to the state of title that would pass from seller to buyer. In other states, title insurance companies perform this chore and ensure that the buyer receives good title. See Chapter 7. In more sophisticated transactions, lawyers will draft the sales contract, draft the deed, examine title or obtain title insurance, and oversee the closing.

3. **Mortgage lenders:** Very few people buy real property without borrowing a substantial portion of the purchase price. Key portions of any sales contract deal with the seller's existing and the buyer's proposed mortgage. The mortgage lender is usually a third party, but sometimes the seller will become a mortgage lender by agreeing to receive a portion of the purchase price in the form of the buyer's promissory note secured by a mortgage to the property. See III, below.

4. **Closing:** Real estate sales are two-step transactions. The nature of a real estate sales transaction is that some time will elapse between execution of the sales contract and the closing — the actual exchange of title and purchase price. Time is needed for the buyer to arrange financing, for a proper examination of title, and for various inspections and other acts to occur as called for under the sale contract or as required by law. Closings are usually conducted through an independent *escrow agent*. The critical items are deposited into escrow — the executed deed, the purchase price, the mortgage (if any) executed by the buyer. The escrow agent makes various adjustments of the purchase price to reflect pro rata apportionment of taxes and other prepaid expenses, and then disburses a portion of the purchase price to extinguish the seller's old mortgage, records the deed and buyer's new mortgage, and finally delivers the balance of the purchase price to the seller.

B. **Statute of Frauds:** The Statute of Frauds, adopted in some form by every state, requires that, unless there is some exception available, a contract for the sale of land *must be in writing* and *must be signed by the party against whom it is sought to be enforced.* Because both parties wish to enforce the agreement, if necessary, against the other, this means in practice that *both parties must sign the contract for sale.*

1. **Formal contract not necessary:** A binding contract can be quite informal. So long as the key terms are present — price, description of the property, and the parties' signatures — an enforceable contract may exist. Parol evidence — evidence extrinsic to the document — is permissible to remove ambiguities.

   Example: George agrees to sell his beach house to Martha for $100,000. On a cocktail napkin, George writes, "My Malibu beach house to Martha for $100,000 as soon as practical. [signed] George." Martha writes, "OK. [signed] Martha." This contract is sufficient. As they part, George and Martha orally agree to close the transaction 90 days later. Parol evidence concerning this oral clarification of the closing date is admissible to clear up the contractual ambiguity of what is "as soon as practical."

2. **Single instrument not necessary:** The contract need not consist of a single document, so long as the multiple writings are consistent, embody the essential terms (price, parties, and property description), and are signed by the parties.

   Example: Martha sees her friend George in a bar and passes George a note: "George, will you sell me your Malibu beach house for $100,000 cash? Martha." George passes a separate note back to Martha: "Martha, I wouldn't sell my beach house to anybody but you, and I'm happy to take $100,000 cash for it. George." The two notes, taken together, constitute an enforceable contract. See, e.g., *Ward v. Mattuschek,* 134 Mont. 307 (1958).

3. **Conditions:** Real estate sale contracts often make the buyer's obligation subject to financing conditions — that the buyer obtain loans in an amount sufficient to meet the purchase price and on terms acceptable to the buyer — or some other condition (e.g., the property is acceptable to the buyer's structural expert, or the issuance of a building permit to enable the buyer to build an intended structure). Financing conditions are usually spelled out carefully and precisely. If not, two problems can occur. If the financing conditions are vague, and there is no parol evidence to clarify the ambiguity, the contract may be void for want of an essential term. If the financing conditions are "to the buyer's satisfaction," an obligation is implied on the part of the buyer to use reasonable efforts to obtain the necessary financing on commercially reasonable terms. Failure to do so will result in buyer's default. The same obligation of good faith is implied with respect to other conditions that are "to the buyer's satisfaction."

4. **Electronic transactions:** The ubiquity of the Internet caused Congress to enact the "E-sign Act," which provides that an electronic contract is as fully enforceable as its paper equivalent. The E-sign Act defines an electronic signature as any electronic "sound, symbol, or process" that is "attached to, or logically associated with" the putative contract and is created with "intent to sign." Some courts find an exchange of e-mails adequate to form a contract for the sale of realty, so long as their substance covers all the requisite points necessary to establish the contract. Other courts and some commentators are more wary. They fear that the cautionary and memorializing functions of traditional written contracts will be undermined by giving effect to electronic contracts. The virtue of the paper deal is that it takes longer, and that fact gives all sides more time to contemplate the significance of their actions. Also, the prospect of forged electronic contracts may be significantly greater. Are these objections weighty enough to reconsider E-sign?

5. Exceptions to the Statute of Frauds: There are two major exceptions to the Statute of Frauds — *part performance* and *equitable estoppel.* Each is an *equitable doctrine* and thus is generally available only when a buyer seeks *specific performance* of an otherwise unenforceable contract of sale.

   a. Part performance: The elements necessary to establish part performance vary among the states. Every state requires proof of an oral contract. The differences occur with respect to the additional elements.

   i. Unequivocal evidence of contract: Some states insist that the acts constituting part performance be of the sort that would not occur but for the existence of a contract — often labeled as actions of *unequivocal reference to a contract.* These acts consist of *payment of all or a part of the purchase price,* taking *possession,* and making *improvements.* None of these things would likely be done if there were not a contract. Some states require all of these elements in order to establish part performance, but others are satisfied if possession alone is proven.

   ii. Reasonable reliance: The modern trend is to require proof of (1) an *oral contract* and (2) *reasonable reliance* on the contract — enough reliance that it would be inequitable to deny specific performance.

   ★**Example — Reliance:** Mrs. Green orally agreed to sell Hickey a building lot for $15,000 and accepted, but did not deposit, Hickey's check for part payment. Hickey then sold his house, expecting to build a new house on the lot. Mrs. Green refused to complete the sale. In ***Hickey v. Green,*** 14 Mass. App. Ct. 671 (1982), the Massachusetts Appeals Court held that Hickey's reliance was reasonable and that equity required specific performance of the oral sale contract.

   Example — No reliance: Ireton orally agreed to sell his farm to Walker for $30,000. Although a written contract was discussed, none was prepared. When Walker asked for a written contract, Ireton assured Walker that he was honest and that none was needed. Walker gave Ireton a $50 check as part payment, and Ireton accepted but did not cash the check. Walker then sold his own farm without ever mentioning to Ireton his intention to do so. Ireton then refused to convey, and, in *Walker v. Ireton,* 221 Kan. 314 (1977), the Kansas Supreme Court ruled for Ireton. Walker's sale of his own farm was not reasonable reliance on the oral contract because the parties had neither discussed that action nor was it foreseeable by Ireton.

   iii. Enforceable by seller: The part performance doctrine is a two-way street, available to buyers and sellers. In most states, a seller may invoke the part performance doctrine to compel specific performance by the buyer, if the buyer's acts are sufficient to constitute part performance and the buyer has acted to diminish the value of the property in the hands of the seller. A few states do not require any proof of diminished value. In those states, the principle of mutuality reigns — if the buyer can compel specific performance, mutuality of remedies requires that the seller have the same opportunity.

   b. Equitable estoppel: The familiar doctrine of equitable estoppel may be used to enforce an oral sale contract if the seller has caused the buyer reasonably to rely significantly to his detriment upon the seller's oral agreement to sell. This is not much different from the reasonable reliance branch of part performance.

Example: Cities Service orally agreed to sell Newman two building lots and to convey title when "construction was well under way." Cities Service reaffirmed this promise to Newman's construction lender, inducing a $5,000 loan to Newman. After the foundation was constructed, Newman ran out of money and assigned his contract to Baliles. Cities Service refused to convey, and the Tennessee Supreme Court ruled that Cities Service was equitably estopped from asserting the Statute of Frauds as a defense. *Baliles v. Cities Service Co.,* 578 S.W.2d 621 (Tenn. 1979).

Example: Ireton orally agreed to sell his farm to Walker and, when Walker asked for a written contract to evidence the deal, Ireton told Walker that he was honest and that no written contract of sale for the farm was necessary. Should that statement, coupled with Walker's later sale of his own farm, be sufficient to trigger equitable estoppel? In *Walker v. Ireton,* 221 Kan. 314 (1977), the Kansas Supreme Court thought that Walker's reliance, in the form of selling his own farm, was "purely collateral" and thus found equitable estoppel inapplicable.

6. Revocation of contracts: Most states do not apply the Statute of Frauds to revocation of a contract for sale of realty. Thus, if both parties agree orally to revoke a contract, the oral agreement is sufficient to do so. A few states reason that the original contract vested equitable title in the buyer and that a revocation amounts to a transfer of title back to the seller. In those states, the Statute of Frauds applies to revocations.

C. Implied obligations: There are a number of obligations implicit in every contract for the sale of realty. The principal ones are considered here.

1. Good faith: Each party is required to act with good faith in discharging the express duties of the contract. This has particular force when the obligation to complete the transaction is expressly conditioned upon future events that are subject to influence by the parties. These conditions often refer to the buyer's obtaining financing, or public approval of an intended use, or the buyer's satisfaction with some unknown aspect of the property. A party must exert reasonable efforts to discharge such conditions. Failure to do so will result in default. See, e.g., *Bushmiller v. Schiller,* 35 Md. App. 1 (1977).

Example: Buyer agrees to purchase Blackacre "if Blackacre yields a well for potable water of at least ten gallons per minute." Buyer makes no effort to determine whether Blackacre has any ground water. Buyer will be in default if he fails to complete the purchase. By contrast, if Buyer drills a well in the location recommended by a professional well driller, but it only yields three gallons per minute, Buyer has used reasonable efforts. Buyer need not drill in another location and may refuse to close without incurring liability.

2. Time of closing: Most contracts state a date for the closing — the completion of the transaction. But if the closing does not occur on the specified date, it still may be enforced in equity if full performance is tendered within a reasonable time after the closing date. Courts reason that a particular closing date is not an essential term on the contract. To avoid this lingering uncertainty, sale contracts often stipulate that *time is of the essence* of the agreement. By expressly making the time of performance an essential term of the agreement, a party able and willing to perform on the closing date is relieved of any future obligations under the sale contract if the other party fails to perform on the required closing date. On the other hand, if some unforeseen event occurs that makes timely closing impossible, such a clause may be more harmful than helpful.

3. **Marketable title:** Every contract for sale of realty contains an implied duty of the seller to deliver *marketable title* to the buyer. This obligation can be expressly disclaimed by agreement between buyer and seller. Marketable title is a title a prudent buyer would accept, one reasonably free of doubt that there is any other rival to title or any portion of it. Any defect in title must be *substantial* and likely to result in injury to the buyer.

   a. **Proof of marketable title:** A seller can deliver marketable title by either (1) producing *good record title* — a recorded chain of title, showing an unbroken transfer of title from some original root of title in the past to the seller, with no recorded encumbrances (e.g., mortgages, easements, or servitudes), or (2) proving *title by adverse possession* — either through a successful quiet title action or evidence sufficient to establish that the rival claim to title would not succeed if asserted and "that there is no real likelihood that any claim will ever be asserted." A careful buyer may well insist on a contractual term obligating the seller to deliver *good record title,* thus depriving the seller of the ability to deliver marketable title by proof of adverse possession.

      i. **Root of title:** To deliver good record title, it is usually *not necessary* to trace the chain of title back to the original possessor of the property. About 20 states have *marketable title acts,* which provide that a deed at some distance in the past (typically, older than 20, 30, or 40 years) is a *root of title,* and cuts off any claims to title founded on earlier instruments. See Chapter 7. Even in states without marketable title acts, good record title may be produced by a title search that goes back to the point that is deemed acceptable under local practice. The rationale is that a search of the records for the preceding 80 years, for example, is adequate to reveal virtually all present claims to title and, if there is any claim founded on some earlier instrument, it is likely barred by the statute of limitations. Even though this might not always be so, the risk of such claims is so low that the courts regard the record title thus produced as "marketable." This risk to the buyer may be even further reduced or eliminated by title insurance (see Chapter 7) or reliance on the seller's warranties of title in the deed. See section II.C, below.

   b. **Defective title:** To be unmarketable, the defect in title must be *substantial* and likely to injure the buyer. Defective title does not always prevent the transaction from taking place. Buyers can, and often do, waive certain defects (e.g., easements, or a mortgage that can be assumed by the buyer), and other defects can be removed prior to or at the closing (e.g., an existing mortgage may be paid off by the sale proceeds so that the buyer receives unencumbered marketable title). Common defects in title are discussed in this section.

      i. **Defective chain of title:** The chain of title may have a faulty or nonexistent link. If a deed describes the wrong land, for instance, it is a faulty link. If there is no record evidence of a deed from B to C in a chain of title purportedly from A to B to C to D, the nonexistent link makes D's title unmarketable. Because a chain is only as good as its weakest link, such defects make title unmarketable unless there is adequate proof of adverse possession sufficient to create a new, valid, and marketable title. See, e.g., *Conklin v. Davi,* 76 N.J. 468 (1978).

      ii. **Encumbrances:** Generally, an encumbrance makes title unmarketable. An encumbrance is a burden on the title, such as mortgages, judgment liens, easements, or covenants.

★**Example:** Bower and Lohmeyer entered into a written agreement by which Bower agreed to sell, and Lohmeyer agreed to purchase a one-story wood-frame house in Emporia, Kansas. The lot was burdened by a covenant requiring all residences constructed on the land to be two stories tall. In *Lohmeyer v. Bower,* 170 Kan. 442 (1951), the Kansas Supreme Court opined that the mere *existence* of a covenant restricting use is an encumbrance making title unmarketable. Only because Lohmeyer had agreed to take title "subject to all encumbrances of record" did the mere existence of the covenant not make title unmarketable; however, Lohmeyer had not agreed to accept *existing* violations of the covenant. Those existing violations made title unmarketable. There are two exceptions to the general rule. (1) An easement that *benefits the property* (e.g., a utility easement) is regarded by some courts as *not an encumbrance* so long as the easement is *known to the buyer* before entry into the contract. (2) Covenants restricting use are encumbrances, but some courts treat them as not making title unmarketable *if the sale contract specifies a particular use that is permitted by the restrictive covenants.* The rationale for the second exception is that the buyer has bargained for a specific use, not all possible lawful uses.

iii. **Zoning restrictions:** Use limits imposed by public authority through zoning laws are not regarded as encumbrances upon title. The rationale is that all property is subject to the lawful regulation of public authority, and that all land titles implicitly incorporate such use limits. However, if the existing use of the property violates a zoning ordinance, the title will be held unmarketable on the theory that the buyer could not possibly have intended to purchase a violation of law and consequent liability.

★**Example:** In the prior example, an Emporia zoning ordinance prohibited the location of any frame structure within three feet of any lot line. The house that Lohmeyer had agreed to buy from Bower was located 18 inches from one lot line. In *Lohmeyer v. Bower,* 170 Kan. 442 (1951), the Kansas Supreme Court held that the mere existence of the zoning law did not constitute an encumbrance making title unmarketable but that the present and continuing violation of the ordinance sufficiently exposed Lohmeyer "to the hazard of litigation" to make the title unmarketable.

D. **Default and remedies:** Default occurs when one party has tendered performance in time and demanded timely performance from the other party, and reciprocal performance is not forthcoming. Remedies for breach are *damages, rescission,* and *specific performance.* The plaintiff may choose the remedy.

1. **Specific performance:** Because land is unique, damages are thought to be inadequate compensation for breach, but because specific performance is an equitable remedy, the defendant may assert the usual equitable defenses (e.g., if specific performance would work an undue hardship upon the defendant, it will be denied).

a. **Sought by buyer:** Buyers are generally able to demand specific performance. If the seller's title is defective (e.g., an easement), and the buyer still wants the property, the buyer is entitled to an abatement of the price to reflect the diminution in value attributable to the defect.

b. **Sought by seller:** Sellers have traditionally been able to demand specific performance from the buyer, but the emerging trend is to deny sellers specific performance if they are still able to sell the property at a commercially reasonable price. A seller entitled to specific performance will be required to reduce the price if there is an ***insubstantial defect in title.*** Of course, if the title defect is substantial, the title is not marketable, and the seller would not be entitled to specific performance.

    c. Equitable conversion: If a contract for the sale of realty is specifically enforceable, the doctrine of equitable conversion operates to treat the buyer as the equitable owner from the moment the contract becomes effective, even if title passes later, as it almost always will. Traditionally, this meant that the risk of casualty loss (e.g., fire, earthquake) was on the buyer from that moment forward. See, e.g., *Paine v. Meller,* 31 Eng. Rep. 1088 (Ch. 1801). The traditional view, while still probably the majority view, is being eroded. The Uniform Vendor and Purchaser Act puts the risk of loss on the party in possession until title has passed. Other states place the risk on the seller if the loss is substantial and central to the contract. Of course, the parties should explicitly agree who bears the risk of loss until title passes, and they should express that agreement clearly in the sale contract. See section I.F, below, for a fuller discussion.

2. Rescission: The polar opposite of specific performance is rescission. If the seller breaches, the buyer may elect to rescind, recover his partial payments already made, and "walk away" from the deal. If the buyer breaches, the seller may elect to rescind the contract and sell the property to another party. The rescission right does not ripen until the closing date, however, because either party has until then to tender performance. An attempted rescission prior to the closing date is not only ineffective but is a breach of the contract.

3. Damages: If the plaintiff does not want (or cannot obtain) specific performance, she may obtain money damages. The measure of damages is usually the ***benefit of the bargain,*** but one frequently employed alternative for the buyer's breach is ***retention of the buyer's deposit.*** Under some circumstances, damages are limited to recovery of ***money out of pocket,*** and damages may be defined by the contract's ***liquidated damages*** provisions.

    a. Benefit of the bargain: This measure of damages gives the aggrieved party the difference between the contract price and the fair market value of the property at the time of breach.

        Example (seller's breach): Seller agrees to sell Blackacre for $50,000 but refuses to convey at the closing date because she is aware that, in the interim, the value of Blackacre has risen to $90,000. Buyer is entitled to $40,000 damages — the value of which she is deprived by Seller's breach. Buyer thus gets the benefit of the bargain as of the date of breach. It would not reduce the damages if Seller were to sell the property later to another party for $80,000. The value of the bargain to Buyer on the date Buyer was entitled to it was $40,000.

        ★**Example (buyer's breach):** Mr. and Mrs. Lee entered into a contract to purchase Jones's home for $610,000 and then unjustifiably refused to perform. Jones later sold the house for $540,000 and sought to collect the $70,000 difference from the Lees. The trial court awarded Jones that amount as damages, together with another $87,000 in punitive damages and special damages for certain out-of-pocket expenses made by Jones in reliance upon the pending sale. In ***Jones v. Lee***, 971 P.2d 858 (N.M. App. 1998), the award of special and punitive damages was upheld, but the award of compensatory damages was vacated, and the case was remanded to determine whether the fair market value of the house on the date of the Lees' breach had declined to $540,000. The New Mexico appellate court instructed the trial court that, in making that determination, the later sale for a lesser price "may be considered evidence of the market value at the time of breach'' and should be considered with all other relevant evidence on that point. Note that, even if no compensatory damages were proven, the Lees remained liable for the out-of-pocket losses incurred by Jones and for punitive damages because of the Lees' ''wanton, utterly reckless'' actions ''in utter disregard of their contractual obligations.''

b. **Deposit retention:** The venerable common law rule is that a seller may elect to retain the entire deposit made by the buyer in the event of the buyer's breach, even if the deposit exceeds the actual damages to the seller. This rule has been criticized as unfair and inefficient. It is unfair because it gives the seller a windfall. It is inefficient because it deters efficient breaches — those that would be more economically beneficial than performance — by making the cost of the breach to the breaching party greater than the loss to the victim. See Richard Posner, *Economic Analysis of the Law* §4.10. Accordingly, a minority of courts limit retention of the buyer's deposit to the actual damages incurred by the seller, unless the parties have agreed to retention as liquidated damages.

★**Example:** Mr. and Mrs. Pirnie agreed to purchase the Kutzins' house and deposited $36,000 toward the purchase price. The contract contained no liquidated damages provision. After the Pirnies unjustifiably failed to perform, the Kutzins sought to retain the entire deposit. A trial court ordered the Kutzins to return about half the deposit, but a New Jersey appellate court reversed that decision, applying the common law rule. In *Kutzin v. Pirnie*, 591 A.2d 932 (N.J. 1991), the New Jersey Supreme Court abandoned the common law rule and adopted the rule in the *Restatement (Second) of Contracts* §374(1) that the party in breach is entitled to restitution of any portion of his deposit that is ''in excess of the loss he has caused by his own breach.'' Principles of unjust enrichment and economic efficiency dictated the result. The court placed the burden of proof upon the party in breach and stressed that the rule was limited to realty sale contracts that did not dispose of the deposit as liquidated damages.

c. **Out of pocket:** This rule is primarily designed to limit the exposure of the seller who breaches innocently — whose breach is in good faith. About half the states limit damages awarded against a seller who has breached in good faith to the actual money that the buyer has expended in reliance on the contract, which means that the buyer is able to recover any part payments, expenditures on experts (e.g., engineers, lawyers, title insurers), and interest and fees incurred with respect to loans obtained in connection with the prospective purchase. The other half of the states make the good faith seller in breach liable for the entire benefit of the bargain.

Example: Seller agrees to sell Blackacre for $50,000 but cannot deliver marketable title due to a title defect previously unknown to Seller. At the closing date, Blackacre is worth $90,000. Buyer has paid $5,000 to Seller and has incurred another $5,000 in lawyers' fees, appraisals, loan fees, and title examination costs. Seller's default is not the product of bad faith. In an *out-of-pocket* state, Buyer is entitled to $10,000 damages. In a *full-benefit-of-the-bargain* state, Buyer will be able to recover $40,000 damages.

d. **Liquidated damages:** Sellers typically protect themselves against a buyer's breach by stipulating in the contract that the buyer's deposit may be retained as *liquidated damages* in the event of buyer's breach. Such provisions are enforceable so long as there is some *reasonable relationship* between the deposit amount and the actual damages suffered by the seller.

Example: Seller and Buyer agree to transfer Blackacre for $50,000, and Buyer gives Seller a deposit of $5,000, which the contract recites may be retained by Seller as liquidated damages if Buyer should breach. Buyer breaches. Seller will assert that his actual damages consist of (1) the added cost of reselling the property (e.g., advertising and promotion), (2) the delay in consummating another sale and consequent reduction in the present value of a later sale at the same price (or, phrased differently, the loss of interest on the sale proceeds until the later sale is completed), (3) the uncertainty that any replacement sale will actually be for that price or better, (4) the loss of other prospective buyers, and (5) any expenditures made in reasonable reliance on Buyer's performance. Seller will probably be able to keep the $5,000 deposit as liquidated damages.

Example: Seller and Buyer enter into an ***installment sale contract*** for Blackacre, under which Buyer takes possession and pays Seller monthly installments of the $50,000 purchase price. Seller promises to deliver title after the entire purchase price has been paid. The contract recites that Seller may keep all payments as liquidated damages in the event of Buyer's breach. Buyer pays a total of $49,000 and then breaches. Almost no state will permit Seller to keep the $49,000 as liquidated damages. The installment sale contract will be treated as a mortgage (see section III, below), or Seller will be required to refund to Buyer all payments in excess of Seller's actual damages. Otherwise, Seller gets $49,000 from Buyer and continued ownership of Blackacre.

E. Duties of disclosure and implied warranties: This section deals with the duties imposed by law on sellers to disclose known defects, and the warranty, implied by operation of law, of quality in the construction of buildings. Warranties of title, which may be contained in the deed, are covered in section II, below.

1. Duties of disclosure: The traditional common law rule is that, absent a fiduciary relationship, a seller has no duty to disclose known defects in the property. The seller's duty was to refrain from ***intentional misrepresentation*** — the outright lie about the property's condition (e.g., the seller says "the roof is watertight" when he knows it leaks like a sieve) or ***active concealment*** of a known defect (e.g., the construction of a fake heating system to conceal the building's lack of a furnace). This rule of *caveat emptor* was justified on the theory that buyers ought to use diligence and care to examine the property for themselves. *Caveat emptor* has been largely abandoned today.

a. Fiduciary relationships: Even under *caveat emptor*, if the parties were in a fiduciary relationship — a relationship in which one party is dependent upon and reposes special trust in the other — the fiduciary was obligated to reveal all defects known to him. This duty arises from the fiduciary's obligation to place the other party's interests ahead of his own.

b. Disclosure of seller-created conditions: The narrowest departure from *caveat emptor* is the rule that a seller is obligated to disclose conditions that (1) are ***created by the seller,*** (2) ***materially impair property value,*** and (3) are ***not likely to be discovered by a reasonably prudent buyer using due care.***

★**Example:** Ackley owned a home in Nyack, New York, and repeatedly publicized various abnormal phenomena ("spectral apparitions") that had occurred in the house, encouraging the reputation of the house as haunted by ghosts. Stambovsky agreed to buy the house and then learned "to his horror" that the house "was widely reputed to be possessed by poltergeists." He promptly sought to rescind the contract. In ***Stambovsky v. Ackley,*** 169 App. Div. 2d 254 (N.Y. 1991), a New York appellate court concluded that *caveat emptor* did not apply: The seller had promoted the property's reputation as haunted, and that reputation was not likely to be discovered by a reasonably prudent buyer ("the most meticulous inspection . . . would not reveal the presence of poltergeists . . . or unearth the property's ghoulish reputation . . ."). The court concluded, without discussion of the evidence, that the haunted reputation of the house "materially impair[ed] the value of the contract."

c. **Disclosure of latent material defects:** The emerging majority rule today is that a seller must reveal all ***latent material defects.*** A latent material defect is a defect that (1) ***materially affects the value or desirability*** of the property, (2) is ***known to the seller*** (or only accessible to the seller), and (3) is ***neither known to or "within the reach of the diligent attention and observations of the buyer."***

★**Example:** The Davises purchased Johnson's house, moved in, and learned within a few days that water leaked in around the windows and from the ceiling in two rooms. The Davises sued to rescind. In ***Johnson v. Davis,*** 480 So. 2d 625 (Fla. 1985), the Florida Supreme Court ruled for the Davises on two separate grounds. First, because Johnson had told the Davises that "the roof was sound," Johnson was liable for his fraud. Second, and quite apart from the fraud, the court concluded that Johnson was obligated to disclose any facts known to him, or accessible only by him, that materially affected the value or desirability of the property and were either unknown to the buyer or could not be learned by a diligent search.

See also *Lingsch v. Savage,* 213 Cal. App. 2d 729 (1963) and *Posner v. Davis,* 76 Ill. App. 3d 638 (1979). While courts may differ as to whether the test of materiality is ***objective*** (would the ***reasonable person*** think the defect was important?) or ***subjective*** (did the defect affect value or desirability to ***this particular buyer?***), a seller who fails to disclose all latent material defects has committed ***fraudulent concealment.*** The buyer may elect either damages or rescission. *Nystrom v. Cabada,* 652 So. 2d 1266 (Fla. App. 1995). The range of latent defects is quite broad. See *Reed v. King,* 145 Cal. App. 3d 261 (1983) (seller's failure to reveal the fact that the house had been the site of a decade-old multiple murder was actionable). Note particularly that under some statutes, a seller is obligated to reveal the existence of environmental toxins known to be located on nearby property. See, e.g., *Strawn v. Canuso,* 140 N.J. 43 (1995); *Haberstick v. Gundaker Real Estate, Inc.,* 921 S.W.2d 104 (Mo. App. 1966).

d. **Statutory disclosure obligations:** Some states have enacted statutes that require sellers to disclose a number of specified conditions. See, e.g., Cal. Civil Code §1102.6, which obligates sellers to reveal structural or soil defects, hazardous materials, underground tanks, alterations made without permits, encroachments, or neighborhood noise problems or other nuisances. This extensive disclosure obligation requires sellers to reveal the presence of annoying neighbors and possibly even barking dogs or crying infants. See, e.g., *Shapiro v. Sutherland,* 64 Cal. App. 4th 1534 (1998). California has gone from "buyer beware" to "seller tell all."

e. **Broker's disclosure obligations:** Some states impose upon the seller's broker the same disclosure duties that are imposed upon the seller. See, e.g., *McEneaney v. Chestnut Hill Realty Corp.,* 38 Mass. App. Ct. 573 (1995); *Easton v. Strassburger,* 152 Cal. App. 3d 90 (1984); Cal. Civ. Code, §2079.16.

f. Post-closing survival of causes of action for nondisclosure: The common law doctrine of merger held that, upon passage of title, all warranties in the sale contract were merged into the deed, and that the buyer could then sue only on the warranties contained in the deed, if any. (On deed warranties, see section II, below.) This doctrine is now riddled with exceptions, the principal ones being that claims for fraud and actions based on promises collateral to the contract survive. The concept of a promise collateral to the contract can be expansive. See, e.g., *Davis v. Tazewell Place Associates,* 254 Va. 257 (1997) (promise to construct residence in "good and workmanlike manner" found to be collateral to sale of the land on which the construction was to occur).

g. "As is" sales: If the sale contract stipulates that the buyer takes the property "as is," the seller is generally relieved of disclosure obligations for defects that are reasonably discoverable, absent fraud. See *Burgess v. French*, 100 Ark. App. 51 (2007); *Snyder v. Lovercheck*, 992 P.2d 1079 (Wyo. 1999).

2. Implied warranty of quality: The traditional rule was that a builder had no liability to anyone for his poor workmanship unless he had given an ***express warranty*** of quality. In time, a builder's warranty of quality was implied into the contract between builder and owner, but the builder's liability for economic loss resulting from breach of this warranty was limited to those with whom he was in ***privity of contract*** — the ***immediate purchaser*** of the structure from the builder, or the owner with whom the builder contracted. Recovery in tort for the builder's negligence was generally unavailable, because the loss was wholly economic — damage to neither property nor person. See, e.g., *Sensenbrenner v. Rust, Orling & Neale,* 236 Va. 419 (1988). In recent years, most jurisdictions have abandoned the traditional rules and now imply a warranty of quality by the builder of a new home, that may be enforced by subsequent purchasers of the structure.

★**Example:** Dagenais built a garage for owners of property, who then sold the property to the Lempkes. Shortly after the Lempkes took possession, they noticed severe structural problems with the roof of the garage. After some fruitless attempts to persuade Dagenais to repair the garage, the Lempkes sued Dagenais for negligence and breach of an implied warranty of quality. The trial court dismissed the complaint, but the New Hampshire Supreme Court, in ***Lempke v. Dagenais,*** 130 N.H. 782 (1988), reversed as to the implied warranty claim. The court concluded that when a builder sells his structures, a warranty of workmanlike quality is implied by law and runs for the benefit of subsequent purchasers with respect to *latent* defects that become apparent after the remote purchaser has acquired title, and which could not have been discovered prior to the remote purchaser's acquisition. The court thought that abandonment of privity of contract was appropriate because, in our mobile society, defects often manifest themselves after a structure has changed hands; remote buyers are entitled to rely on a builder's skill even if they have not contracted with him; and as the builder already owes this duty to his immediate vendee, an extension of this duty to others for a reasonable time does not unduly enlarge his liability.

a. No disclaimer: Courts generally agree that the implied warranty of quality in favor of subsequent purchasers may not be disclaimed, but are divided about the rationale for that result. Some say it is grounded in tort law's implementation of public policies — protecting innocent buyers of houses from shoddy work, imposing the risk of loss on the builder (the party most able to avoid the loss by building with care), and encouraging the creation of a sound housing stock. See, e.g., *LaSara Grain v. First Natl. Bank of Mercedes,* 673 S.W.2d

558 (Tex. 1984). Other courts contend that the warranty is based on contract, but because the builder has created a defective product that will inevitably harm others beyond the initial buyer, they have ignored privity of contract as a barrier to its enforcement. See, e.g., *Redarowicz v. Ohlendorf*, 92 Ill. 2d 171 (1982). In theory, if the implied warranty is rooted in tort, it should be incapable of disclaimer, but if founded upon contract, its scope and existence ought to be limited by the bargain struck. Courts, however, pay no attention to theory here and generally are reluctant to permit disclaimer, perhaps because they have begun to agree that the warranty of workmanlike quality is implied by law to effect the public policies of placing the loss on the party best able to avoid it and to protect consumers from shoddy work they are ill-equipped to detect. See *Lempke v. Dagenais,* 130 N.H. 782 (1988).

     b. Limitations period: Courts permit subsequent purchasers to bring suit against the original builder for a *"reasonable time"* — usually a period long enough for latent defects of the original construction to become apparent. Some states have enacted statutory limitations periods. See, e.g., Cal. Code Civ. Proc., §337.15 (ten years). The Uniform Land Transactions Act, §2-521, provides for a six-year limitations period commencing with the initial sale, but no state has adopted it.

     c. Subsequent owner's liability: The owner of a home who is not the builder has no liability based on the implied warranty of quality. Only the original builder is liable on that theory, but a seller may be liable for breach of a duty to disclose a known defect.

F. Risk of loss and equitable title: During the time between making of the contract for sale and the closing, various bad things can happen — the property can be destroyed or damaged, or one or both of the parties may die. The common law reacted to these possibilities by creating the notion of *equitable title* (or *equitable conversion,* as it is often called).

     1. Equitable title: This doctrine holds that equitable ownership of the subject property passes to the buyer at the moment the contract of sale is made. Of course, the seller remains the legal owner until the closing, but for purposes of equity the buyer is treated as the owner. The seller's legal title is analogous to the legal title held by mortgage lenders in states that treat the mortgage as a transfer of legal title: It is retained as security for the buyer's payment of the purchase price. Because the doctrine is equitable, courts apply it in order to deliver fair results. The touchstone for its application is often whether it is necessary to carry out the parties' intentions or to avoid a palpable injustice. Note that only equitable title is passed to the buyer; unless the contract of sale permits the buyer to take possession prior to the closing, the buyer, as equitable owner, has no right to possession. If the contract does permit the buyer to take possession, the buyer is obligated to avoid waste of the property, for that would impair the value of the seller's retained legal title. Equitable title does not apply to contracts giving the buyer an option to purchase until and unless the option is exercised.

         a. Application to death of a party: One important effect of equitable title is that, for purposes of the seller's or buyer's death before closing, the parties are treated as having transferred the real property by entry into the contract. This means that a seller who dies after contracting, but before closing, leaves an estate that owns personal property — a contract right — and not real property. If the buyer dies before closing, the buyer's estate includes the real property.

Example: Opus, owner of Blackacre, enters into a valid contract to sell Blackacre to Baggins for $100,000. Before the closing, Opus dies. His will devises his real property to Bertha and his personal property to Camellia. At his death, Opus's interest in Blackacre is deemed to be personal property, which passes to Camellia. If Baggins performs, Camellia will receive the sale proceeds. If Baggins should default, and equitable title should return to Opus's estate, Camellia will still receive Blackacre. At Opus's death, his interest in Blackacre is personal property; the later conversion of that interest into real property occurs after Opus's, death so Blackacre represents the proceeds of the personal property. The character of Opus's property at his death is what matters. Similarly, if Baggins dies before the closing, his interest in Blackacre passes under his will as real property. Of course, Baggins's estate must perform at the closing for that real property to become tangible.

b. **Application to risk of loss of the property:** English law used the doctrine of equitable title to place on the buyer the risk of loss of the property from causes not attributable to either buyer or seller (e.g., fire, earthquake, storm damage). See *Paine v. Meller,* 6 Ves. 349, 31 Eng. Rep. 1088 (Ch. 1801). Most American states follow this rule, which requires the buyer to perform at the closing despite the loss. Of course, the seller must tender timely performance to perfect his choice of seeking either damages (measured by the diminution of value produced by the loss) or specific performance should the buyer default.

   i. **Entitlement to insurance proceeds:** The old English rule was that the seller was entitled to insurance proceeds, even though the buyer had the risk of loss, because the insurance policy was regarded as a personal contract right of the seller. If the buyer wanted insurance protection, he would have to secure his own. Most American states reject this rule and require the seller to credit the insurance proceeds against the purchase price in an action for specific performance or, in an action for damages, reduce the damage award by the insurance proceeds. The rationale is that the seller is maintaining insurance as much for the benefit of the buyer as himself, and thus holds the proceeds in **constructive trust** for the buyer. See, e.g., *Bryant v. Willison Real Estate Co.,* 350 S.E.2d 748 (W.Va. 1986); *Heinzman v. Howard,* 366 N.W.2d 500 (S.D. 1985). It is always a good idea, however, for the buyer either to (1) procure his own insurance, or (2) insert a provision in the sale contract requiring the seller to keep the property insured for the benefit of the buyer. A buyer who procures his own insurance keeps the proceeds even if risk of loss is on the seller, because it is quite clear that the buyer's insurance is obtained solely to protect the buyer's interest. No constructive trust is created.

   ii. **Minority rule:** The minority of American courts place the risk of loss on the seller, despite the doctrine of equitable title, on the theory that an intact structure was an essential part of the bargain. See, e.g., *Caulfield v. Improved Risk Mutuals, Inc.,* 66 N.Y.2d 793 (1985). Thus, if the loss is substantial, it falls entirely on the seller, and the buyer may not be forced to perform. If the loss is insignificant, the buyer may still be forced to perform, but is entitled to an abatement of the purchase price to reflect the lost value, usually measured by the insurance proceeds received by the seller. The minority rule is thus effectively the same as the majority rule in cases of **insubstantial insured loss.** The minority rule is different only in cases of **substantial loss.** In minority jurisdictions, the buyer may **not be forced to perform;** in the majority of states, the buyer **must perform or incur liability,** though the buyer will receive **credit for the seller's insurance proceeds.**

2. **Risk of loss goes with possession:** Many states have enacted statutes that make the risk of loss go with possession. See, e.g., Cal. Civ. Code, §1662. Thus, despite equitable title, if the seller remains in possession he assumes risk of loss. Buyers in these jurisdictions acquire risk of loss prior to closing only if they take possession or assume that risk under the sale contract.

II. DEEDS

A. **Formal requirements and component parts:** A deed is the usual method by which title to realty is transferred. This section addresses the formal requirements for a valid deed and the elements of the instrument.

1. **Writing required:** The Statute of Frauds requires a writing signed by the grantor in order to transfer an interest in land. A deed signed by the grantor is the usual method of compliance, but other writings will suffice. Because the grantor is the only party bound by the deed (as distinguished from the contract of sale), only the grantor needs to sign the deed.

2. **Notarial acknowledgment:** A notarial acknowledgment is the act of a notary public attesting to the fact of the grantor's signature and to the identity of the grantor. A deed is valid without acknowledgment, but virtually all deeds are acknowledged because notarial acknowledgment is almost universally required for recording the deed in the public land records.

3. **The grant:** The first clause in a deed is the *granting clause,* which recites the parties, the words making the grant, the consideration, and the description of the property.

   a. **Words making the grant:** Any expression of an intent to effect a transfer of realty will accomplish the grant. No "magic words" are required.

   b. **Description of the grantee:** Ordinarily, the grantee is described clearly and specifically, but a grantee can be described without reference to a specific person, so long as the description is sufficient to identify an actual person. Otherwise, the deed may not be valid, either because of uncertainty as to ownership or inability to deliver the deed to a nonexistent grantee.

   Example: A deed to "the first-born son of Diana, Princess of Wales" is sufficient to describe William. A deed to "the eldest daughter of Diana, Princess of Wales" is invalid because no such person exists or ever will exist.

      i. **No grantee named:** While the traditional rule has been that a deed that mentions no grantee is void, most American states today hold that the *intended grantee* has *implicit authority,* as the *agent of the grantor,* to fill in the intended grantee's name at *any later time.* Without a grantee, the deed is a legal cipher, but once the intended grantee's name is inserted, it becomes effective. See, e.g., *Board of Education v. Hughes,* 118 Minn. 404 (1912).

   c. **Consideration:** While consideration is *not necessary* to convey land, deeds often recite the *fact of consideration* rather than the actual amount of the consideration. Thus, the granting clause often states, "for ten dollars and other good and valuable consideration" in order to establish that the buyer is a *bona fide purchaser for value* (which gives the grantee the protection of the recording acts; see Chapter 7) and simultaneously keeps the actual purchase price out of the public records.

d. Description of the land: The property conveyed may be described in any fashion that clearly and precisely identifies the parcel. Common forms of description include *metes and bounds* (a surveyor's description of the length and direction of the boundaries), reference to a *recorded survey map* or other survey, and *street and number.* So long as the description contains enough to identify the land, an ambiguous description will suffice if extrinsic evidence will clarify the ambiguity. If there is no ambiguity in the description, extrinsic evidence is not permitted to contradict the deed except to establish a mutual mistake in the description.

   i. Rules of construction: If a property description is internally inconsistent, plainly mistaken, or incomplete, courts strive to *determine the intentions of the parties.* If there are no better clues to intent, courts employ a hierarchy of rules to sort out these problems. In descending order of preference and reliability, these are as follows: (1) *original survey markers,* (2) *natural monuments* (e.g., trees), (3) *artificial monuments* (e.g., structures), (4) *maps,* (5) *courses of direction* (e.g., "a line running ENE" or "a line 90 degrees to the left of the baseline"), (6) *distances,* (7) *common names* (e.g., "McDonald's Farm"), and (8) *quantity* (e.g., 140 acres).

   Example: The deed description reads as follows: "Brigham's Farm, being that tract of 40 acres encompassed by a line beginning at an iron survey marker topped with a brass ball, located 10 feet due north of Highway 1, going east 1,000 feet to an old fir tree with a circumference of 25 feet, turning northerly 82 degrees and running for 1,220 feet to a wood rail fence marked on the USGS topographical map for the region, following the rail fence in a westerly direction for 1,750 feet to Bishop's Creek, then southerly along the bank of Bishop's Creek for 1,072 feet to the intersection with an undeveloped road platted on county survey map No. 872, as recorded in the county records, then southeasterly 420 feet to the point of origin." In trying to make sense of this description, we would first prefer the original iron survey marker even if it were not 10 feet due north of Highway 1, then we would prefer the old fir tree (even if it were more or less than 1,000 feet from the survey stake), then we would prefer the 82-degree course change to the 1,220 foot distance in order to reach the rail fence. If the fence were located in some place different from that marked on the USGS topographical map, we would prefer its actual location to its mapped location. Again, we would prefer the meandering fence line to Bishop's Creek rather than the described distance, and the natural course of the creek to the described distance along the creek. We would also prefer the mapped location of the undeveloped road to the asserted distance to it. Finally, as a last recourse, we would prefer "Brigham's Farm" over the described quantity of 40 acres. See, e.g., *Riley v. Griffin,* 16 Ga. 141 (1854).

B. Warranties of title: A seller's warranties concerning the state of the title conveyed are expressly contained, if at all, in the deed. No warranties are implied. There are three types of deeds: the *general warranty* deed, the *special warranty* deed, and the *quitclaim* deed. The general and special warranty deeds contain covenants that warrant the state of title; the quitclaim deed does not.

1. General warranty deed: The general warranty deed usually contains six covenants concerning title. Each covenant is a promise that the title is absolutely free of the warranted defect, regardless of whether the defect arose before or during the time the grantor had title.

Occasionally, a general warranty deed will contain fewer than these six covenants. Some states have enacted statutes that provide that use of terms of conveyance in a deed (e.g., ***grant, sell, convey***) carries with them the six general warranties of title. Such deeds are sometimes referred to as ***statutory warranty*** deeds; they are simply statutory forms of a general warranty deed.

    a. Covenant of seisin: The grantor promises that he owns what he is conveying by deed.

    b. Covenant of right to convey: The grantor warrants that he has the power or authority to convey the property.

    c. Covenant against encumbrances: The grantor warrants that there are no liens, mortgages, easements, covenants restricting use, or other encumbrances upon title to the property other than those specifically excepted in the deed.

    d. Covenant of general warranty: The grantor warrants that he will defend against ***lawful claims*** of a ***superior title*** and will compensate the grantee for any loss suffered by the successful assertion of a superior title.

    e. Covenant of quiet enjoyment: The grantor warrants that the grantee will not be disturbed in his possession or enjoyment of the property by someone's successful assertion of a superior title to the property. This covenant is functionally identical to the covenant of general warranty and, for that reason, is frequently omitted from general warranty deeds.

    f. Covenant of further assurances: The grantor promises to do whatever else is reasonably necessary to perfect the conveyed title, if it turns out to be imperfect. This covenant is also frequently dropped from general warranty deeds, perhaps because of the open-ended obligation imposed on the seller, or because it adds little to the first four covenants, or because the doctrine of after-acquired title (see section II.B.6, below) has made this covenant redundant.

2. Special warranty deed: A special warranty deed contains the same six (or fewer) covenants of the general warranty deed. The only difference is that the grantor warrants against defects of title that arose ***during the grantor's time of holding title.*** Defects arising ***before the grantor's ownership*** are not covered. The grantor warrants, in essence, only that he has not created or suffered a defect to occur during his ownership period.

3. Quitclaim deed: A quitclaim deed contains no warranties of title whatsoever, but operates to convey to the grantee whatever interest in the property the grantor may own. If the grantor owns the Brooklyn Bridge, a quitclaim deed is sufficient to transfer ownership; but if the grantor owns no interest whatsoever in the Brooklyn Bridge, nothing is transferred by a quitclaim deed, nor is the grantor liable for breach of any covenants of title because none was made. The usual function of a quitclaim deed is to remove apparent and uncontested defects in title without resort to litigation.

4. Merger doctrine: The traditional rule is that any promises in the contract of sale ***with respect to title*** are "merged" into the deed once the buyer accepts the deed. This means that the buyer can only sue for breach of the deed covenants of title and may not rely on the contract of sale's provisions with respect to title. The justification for this rule is that buyer's acceptance of the deed is conclusive evidence that the buyer was satisfied that the deed fully conformed to the seller's obligations under the sale contract with respect to title. If the buyer was not satisfied that the deed conformed to the contract, he should not have accepted the deed. The merger doctrine does not extinguish those portions of the sales contract that are ***independent of or collateral to the transfer of title,*** such as seller's promise to remove all rubbish from the premises. The merger doctrine is under attack, and courts are apt to find a great many provisions of the sales contract to be independent of, or collateral to, transfer of title. The Uniform Land Transactions Act, §1-309, eliminates the merger doctrine and permits all provisions of the sales contract to remain alive and enforceable by the buyer after acceptance of a deed.

5. **Breach of covenants of title:** Covenants of title may be divided into ***present covenants*** and ***future covenants.*** A present covenant is breached, if at all, at the moment the deed is delivered. A future covenant is breached when the grantee is actually or constructively evicted at some time in the future.

   a. **Present covenants — Seisin, right to convey, and encumbrances:** These are representations of currently existing facts. Either the grantor owns the property or he does not; he has the right to convey or he does not; title is burdened by an encumbrance or it is not. The covenant is either breached when made (because it was not true) or can never be breached (because the facts were as promised at that moment in time).

      i. **Breach of covenant of seisin:** This covenant is broken if the grantor doesn't own what he purports to convey, regardless of whether he is aware of the defect or not. The covenant is broken even if the grantee knows that the grantor does not own the interest purportedly conveyed. If title is totally defective (or so defective that the grantee is left with good title only to an unusable parcel), the grantee is entitled to a return of his purchase price but must reconvey the right to possession to the grantor. If title partially fails, the grantee is entitled to recover that portion of the purchase price that is equal to the value of the failed title and must reconvey his possessory right.

      ii. **Breach of covenant of right to convey:** This covenant is broken if the grantor lacks the power or authority to convey the interest (e.g., the grantor is a trustee who is barred by the trust instrument from transferring title), whether or not he is aware of the limits on his authority to convey. Grantee's knowledge of the grantor's lack of authority to convey is not usually a defense to suit on this covenant. The measure of damages for breach is the same as for breach of the covenant of seisin.

      iii. **Breach of covenant against encumbrances:** This covenant is breached if the title is encumbered (other than as expressly excepted in the deed) at the time of delivery of the deed, whether or not the grantor is aware of the encumbrance. In most states, the grantee's knowledge of the encumbrance does not excuse or obviate breach, but a minority of states hold that the grantee's knowledge (actual or constructive) of an ***open and visible*** encumbrance (such as an easement) prevents breach. See, e.g., *Leach v. Gunnarson,* 290 Ore. 31 (1980). The prevailing rule is that violations of governmental land-use regulations that are not known to the seller, and have not become the subject of government enforcement, are not encumbrances.

      ★**Example:** DiLoreto owned property abutting a tidal marsh. He constructed a bulkhead, filled a portion of the marsh, built a house, and sold it to Anzellotti by quitclaim deed. Two years later, Anzellotti conveyed the property to Frimberger under a general warranty deed. When Frimberger sought to repair the bulkhead, he learned that a significant portion of the lot unlawfully encroached on protected wetlands. Rather than seeking a variance from the use regulation, Frimberger sued Anzellotti on the covenant against encumbrances. In *Frimberger v. Anzellotti,* 25 Conn. App. 401 (1991), the Connecticut intermediate appeals court held that "latent violations of [governmental] land use regulations that do not appear on the land records, that are unknown to the seller . . . , as to which . . . no official action to compel compliance [has been taken] at the time the deed was executed, and that have not ripened into an interest that can be recorded . . . do not constitute an encumbrance." Recall that in *Lohmeyer v. Bower,* the Kansas courts held that a present violation of zoning laws made title unmarketable and entitled the buyer to rescind the sale contract. The different result here is arguably justified by the difference between an executory agreement and a fully executed one. In the executory agreement (e.g., *Lohmeyer*), permitting the buyer to rescind enables the seller to minimize loss by finding another buyer willing to take the defective title (perhaps at a reduced price), but in the fully executed contract (e.g., *Frimberger*), the damages imposed on the seller are under the buyer's control. (Perhaps Frimberger would conform to the use regulations in a particularly expensive way, calculated to enhance value to Frimberger.) The *Frimberger* rule is not universally applied. See *Bianchi v. Lorenz,* 166 Vt. 555 (1997), in which the Vermont Supreme Court held that any significant violation of a government land-use regulation, the existence of which could be determined by inspecting government records, constituted an encumbrance.

The measure of damages for breach depends on whether the encumbrance is removable by the grantee. If the *grantee can remove the encumbrance* (e.g., by paying off a mortgage or lien), the grantee is entitled to recover what he expended to remove the encumbrance. If the grantee fails to remove a removable encumbrance, he will not receive damages unless he proves actual damage by selling the property for less than its unencumbered market value. If the encumbrance is *not removable unilaterally by the grantee* (e.g., an easement or use covenant), damages are measured by the difference between the unencumbered and encumbered fair market value at the time of the conveyance.

iv. **Statute of limitations:** Because breach of present covenants occurs, if at all, at the moment the covenant is given, the statute of limitations begins to run at that moment. The length of these statutes varies but is usually three to six years. Of course, the buyer ought to know about breach almost immediately.

v. **Assignment of present covenants:** The still-prevailing majority rule in America is that a present covenant is for the benefit of the immediate grantee and that, if breached when made, the grantee has a *chose in action* — the claim against the grantor — that is *not impliedly assigned* if the grantee conveys to a remote grantee. This rule is rooted in the now-outmoded view that choses in action are not assignable. But because we permit assignment of choses in action today, there is no good reason to bar implicit assignment of the chose in action to the remote purchaser — the person who needs the benefit. Some states recognize this logic and hold, as do English courts, that a transfer to a remote grantee implicitly operates to assign the grantee's chose in action to the remote grantee.

★**Example:** Connelly acquired title to 80 acres at a foreclosure sale, then conveyed the property by general warranty deed to Dixon, who in turn conveyed by special warranty deed to Hansen & Gregerson. The foreclosure sale was invalid, so Connelly never owned the 80 acres and thus breached the covenant of seisin given to Dixon, but because Dixon had conveyed by special warranty deed, he had not breached the covenant of seisin he gave to Hansen & Gregerson. H&G sued Connelly on the covenant of seisin he had given Dixon, H&G's vendor. In *Rockafellor v. Gray,* 194 Iowa 1280 (1922), the Iowa Supreme Court ruled that Dixon's chose in action was impliedly assigned to H&G by the conveyance to H&G.

b. Future covenants — General warranty, quiet enjoyment, and further assurances: These are representations as to future events, guaranteeing the grantee's security of title in the future. They are breached only when the grantee is actually or constructively evicted, which always occurs some time after the transfer. Actual eviction is, of course, actual dispossession from title or possession. Constructive eviction occurs whenever the grantee's possession is interfered with in any way by someone holding a superior title.

★**Example:** Bost conveyed 80 acres to Brown under a general warranty deed containing no exceptions, even though Bost only owned one-third of the mineral rights. After the statute of limitations on the present covenants had expired, Brown agreed to sell the mineral rights to Consolidated Coal for $6,000 but was forced to accept only $2,000 once it was learned that Brown owned only a third of the mineral rights. In *Brown v. Lober,* 75 Ill. 2d 547 (1979), the Illinois Supreme Court ruled that Brown had not been constructively evicted, because "the mere existence of a paramount title does not constitute a breach of the covenant" of quiet enjoyment. If the owner of the other two-thirds of the mineral rights had started mining coal under Brown's land, Brown would have been actually evicted. If, in order to prevent a real and manifest threat of such mining, Brown had purchased the other two-thirds of the mineral rights from the owner, Brown would have been constructively evicted, but if Brown had purchased the other two-thirds of the mineral rights without such a threat, it probably would not have constituted constructive eviction.

  i. Breach of future covenants: The future covenants are breached only when the grantee's possession has been disturbed by someone holding a superior title. That can occur years after the original transfer and, as in *Brown v. Lober,* after the statute of limitations has barred suit on the present covenants.

  ii. Benefit runs with the estate: If there is *privity of estate* between the *original grantor* and the *remote grantee,* the benefit of a future covenant given to the original grantee runs with the estate conveyed to the remote grantee. For this purpose, *privity of estate* means that the original grantor conveyed *either* title *or* possession, and the same interest was conveyed to the remote grantee. If the original grantor has **neither** *title nor possession* (e.g., the original grantor was a brazen fraud with no interest in the subject property), there is no estate created with which the covenant can run. This rule, though logical, insulates wrongdoers from liability to remote grantees; thus, it is not surprising that some courts have invented an "estate" held by the original grantor and passed on to the remote grantee, usually the mere possibility that the original grantor might later acquire an interest that would be passed on to the remote grantee under the doctrine of after-acquired title.

  iii. Extent of the obligation to defend: The covenant of general warranty obliges the grantor to defend against **lawful** *superior claims of title* but imposes no obligation to defend against the spurious claim of paramount title. Because it is impossible to know one from the other with certainty prior to litigation, the effect is to require the *grantee* to defend. In the event the third party's claim of paramount title is lawful, the grantee will be able to recover the costs of defense plus damages. But if the third party's claim is defeated, the costs of the victory are borne entirely by the grantee, because the claim was not lawful. If the grantor is notified of the claim and asked to defend, the grantor will be bound by the result, whether he defends or not. Otherwise, the litigation between the grantee and the third party does not bind the grantor.

c. **General limit on damages for breach:** The overwhelming majority rule is that the grantee may not recover more than what the grantor-in-breach received for the property. This is problematic under several circumstances.

   i. **Suit by original grantee:** When the original grantee has expended considerable sums to improve the property, or the property value has increased markedly due to extrinsic factors, the grantee will not be able to obtain the benefit of the bargain but is limited to a return of his purchase price. On the other hand, without the basic damage limitation, grantors would face the specter of potentially ruinous open-ended liability. Prejudgment interest on the damages is often awarded, but courts split over whether the interest should accrue from the date of the promise or the date of eviction. Courts holding to the former view argue that, because the grantee might be liable to the paramount for the grantee's wrongful occupation, interest is fair compensation for that potential liability. Courts holding to the latter view argue that, unless such a claim for rent is actually made, it would be a windfall to the grantee to award interest for the time the grantee is in possession. Some courts refuse to award damages to the grantee if the transfer was a gift.

   ii. **Suit by remote grantee:** Nearly all courts agree that if the remote grantee has paid *more* for the property than the original grantor received, the remote grantee is subject to the general damage limit and will only recover what the original grantor received. See, e.g., *Rockafellor v. Gray,* 194 Iowa 1280 (1922). But if the remote grantee paid *less* for the property, courts differ on whether the remote grantee should recover (1) what the original grantor received, (2) what the remote grantee paid, or (3) actual damages up to the amount received by the original grantor.

6. **After-acquired title (estoppel by deed):** If a grantor conveys an interest in property that he does not own, and later acquires the unowned interest, this doctrine operates to send that after-acquired title directly and immediately to the grantee or his successors in interest. The grantor is estopped from denying the scope of the original deed. Put another way, the grantor's original deed carries an implied promise that he will convey the missing pieces of title should he later acquire them. Though originally limited to warranty deeds, this doctrine now applies to quitclaim deeds conveying fee simple absolute, on the theory that the doctrine operates to effectuate the parties' probable intent.

Example: Schwenn gave her mineral rights to oil-producing property to her daughter. Then she conveyed the property (with no exception or reservation of the mineral rights) to Kaye. Once litigation threatened, Schwenn asked her daughter to reconvey the mineral rights to her, and the daughter did so. At that moment, Schwenn's after-acquired title to the mineral rights was vested in Kaye. Schwenn was estopped from denying the validity and scope of her original deed to Kaye. *Schwenn v. Kaye,* 155 Cal. App. 3d 949 (1984).

C. **Delivery:** A deed must be delivered by the grantor in order to be effective to transfer an interest in land. *Delivery* means that the grantor has said or done things that demonstrate the *grantor's* **intent to transfer immediately** *an interest in land to the grantee.* Delivery does *not necessarily require* the physical act of handing over the paper deed to the grantee. The key is the *grantor's intent.* If a grantor hands a deed to the purported grantee and says, "You are to hold on to this until I'm dead, and only then will it be effective," there has been no delivery. If the grantor executes and records a deed to the grantee, vacates the property, tells others that he has "given the farm" to the grantee, but neither informs grantee nor physically hands the deed to grantee, delivery has nevertheless occurred. Delivery problems do not usually occur in commercial transfers; usually they crop up when gifts are involved.

1. **Presumed delivery:** Courts employ a *rebuttable presumption* that delivery has occurred under any of the following circumstances: (1) *physical transfer to the grantee,* (2) *notarial acknowledgment* of the deed, or (3) *recording* of the deed. Courts also employ a *rebuttable presumption* that no delivery has occurred if the grantor retains physical custody of the deed.

   ★**Example:** Maurice Sweeney, estranged from his wife Maria, wished to ensure that, upon his death, his brother John, rather than Maria, would take Maurice's farm and tavern. Maurice executed and recorded a deed of the property to John, and John executed a deed of the property to Maurice, which was not recorded. Both deeds were prepared at the same time by the town clerk, who gave the originals to Maurice. Later, Maurice gave both deeds to John. When Maurice died, Maria contended that the unrecorded, but fully executed, deed from John to Maurice had been delivered to Maurice and operated to vest title in Maurice. Accordingly, she claimed her elective share in Maurice's estate, including the farm and tavern. John asserted that there had been no delivery, because he had never intended to deliver the deed to Maurice or, in the alternative, that there was an oral condition attached to the delivery — that the deed be effective only in the event John died before Maurice. In *Sweeney v. Sweeney,* 126 Conn. 391 (1940), the Connecticut Supreme Court of Errors ruled that, because the John-to-Maurice deed had been manually delivered to Maurice, there arose a presumption of delivery that was not rebutted by the fact that the motivation of John and Maurice was to defeat Maria's elective share by ensuring that title to the farm was in John at Maurice's death, but to cause title to return to Maurice if and only if John were to die before Maurice.

2. **Attempted delivery at death:** An attempt to deliver a deed at the death of the grantor is almost always ineffective. If the grantor intends that the deed become effective only upon his death, the deed is void unless it can be admitted as a will, and this is not usually the case, because the formalities required for making a will are often lacking in the execution of a deed. If the grantor intended the deed to be effective during his life, the grantor's death does not destroy the delivery already accomplished by that intent.

   ★**Example:** Harold and Mildred Rosengrant, a childless elderly couple in failing health, owned a farm in Oklahoma that they wished to convey to their nephew, Jay Rosengrant, effective at their death. Harold and Mildred went to a local bank, where they executed a deed of the farm to Jay, which they handed to Jay, and Jay then handed the deed to the banker for safekeeping. Harold instructed the banker to keep the deed until he and Mildred had died, then to give it to Jay so that he could record the deed. The banker put the deed in an envelope marked, "J.W. Rosengrant or Harold H. Rosengrant" and kept it in the bank's vault. After Harold and Mildred's deaths, Jay Rosengrant retrieved the deed from the bank and recorded it. An Oklahoma trial court canceled the deed and, in *Rosengrant v. Rosengrant,* 629 P.2d 800 (Okla.

App. 1981), the Oklahoma court of appeals affirmed, reasoning that the deed was never delivered during Harold and Mildred's lifetime because there was never any intent to give "outright ownership at the time of the delivery." The court made much of the fact that, under the bank's policies, the deed could have been taken at any time by Harold, but the court found the parties' extraordinarily clear intentions to be of lesser moment.

a. **Exception — Irrevocable escrow:** If a grantor executes a deed in favor of grantor and hands it over to an escrow agent with *irrevocable* instructions (either *written* or *oral*) to hold it until the grantor's death, delivery has occurred. The rationale is that the escrow agent is the agent of *both the grantor and the* **grantee.** Delivery to the grantee's agent is delivery to the grantee. But if the escrow is *revocable,* the escrow agent is deemed to be only the grantor's agent, so no delivery has occurred. It is sometimes said that delivery has not occurred because the deed is not yet out of the grantor's control. This rule is often criticized on the ground that a grantor can validly accomplish the same end by simply transferring the property into a revocable trust, with the grantor as both trustee and beneficiary for life, and the grantee as beneficiary upon the grantor's death.

b. **Uncertain exception — Express conditions:** A deed may contain an express provision that makes transfer of possession conditional upon the grantor's death (e.g., "to A, effective upon my death" or "to A if A survives me"). These conditional grants can be interpreted to mean either that the deed has passed a *springing executory interest* to the grantee or that *no delivery has occurred* — the deed is a nullity until the subsequent condition (the grantor's death) occurs. By the latter construction, the deed would be of no effect unless it could qualify as a will. By the former construction, the grantee received a valid springing executory interest that became possessory upon the grantor's death. Courts are badly divided on this issue, and there is no safe general answer. The academic answer is that the deed should be given effect as making a transfer of a springing executory interest, because the deed is adequate by itself to indicate the grantor's intentions at death. There is little reason to be worried that, by giving effect to the deed, the grantor's wishes concerning disposition of his property upon death are not being carried out. Presumably the grantor appreciated the significance of the deed when he signed it, and there is no need to rely on evidence other than the deed itself to carry out the grantor's wishes.

   i. **Grant of life estate distinguished:** Of course, a grantor can convey by deed a life estate to himself and a remainder in another grantee. Such grants are valid and not problematic, so long as they are clear. The effect of a grant from O "to A, effective on my death" and a grant from O "to O for life, then to A" may be functionally identical, but only the latter clearly creates a life estate. The former style is uncertain. While it may be valid as a *springing executory interest*, many courts will conclude that it is void for want of delivery — the present intention to transfer an interest in the subject land.

3. **Delivery subject to oral condition:** The usual response to delivery of a deed subject to an oral condition is to disregard the oral condition and treat the delivery as complete and unqualified, but this rule is not invariable.

★**Example — Unenforceable condition:** Refer back to *Sweeney v. Sweeney,* 126 Conn. 391 (1940), section II.C.1, above. John Sweeney claimed that the John-to-Maurice deed was delivered to Maurice subject to an oral condition — that delivery be effective only if John predeceased Maurice — and that because that condition had not occurred, there was no valid delivery. Connecticut's highest court rejected this contention, noting that because the delivery had been made directly to the grantee (Maurice), rather than to a neutral escrow agent, the condition was unenforceable.

Example — Enforceable condition: Facing the prospect of hazardous military duty, Husband delivered a deed to Wife with oral instructions that if he were killed, she should record the deed, but if he were to return, she must return the deed to him for destruction. Husband returned from the mission, but Wife refused to return the deed, perhaps due to other marital difficulties. In *Chillemi v. Chillemi,* 197 Md. 257 (1951), Maryland's highest court enforced the oral condition and voided the deed. The court styled as "primitive formalism" the "ancient rule" that physical transfer of a deed to the grantee, subject to an oral condition of later effectiveness, is a completed delivery. In the Maryland court's view, "conditional delivery is purely a question of intention, and it is immaterial whether the [deed], pending satisfaction of the condition, is in the hands of the grantor, the grantee, or a third person."

4. **Commercial escrows:** Most real estate transfers involve a commercial escrow. Usually, the seller gives the escrow holder specific written instructions that define the escrow agent's authority to hand over the deed to the buyer. The transfer of a deed into escrow along with written instructions is a completed delivery. Delivery is also completed when the deed is given to the escrow holder under oral instructions *if there is a written sale contract.* But without a written sales contract, an escrow agent holding a deed under oral instructions is deemed to be the seller's agent only, and the seller is empowered to revoke the escrow at any time. The power to revoke undermines the claim that the seller had an intention to pass title at the moment the deed was placed into the escrow agent's hands. Also, the oral instructions may well be silent on the essential issue of price. Despite these objections, a few states regard delivery as completed when the deed is placed in escrow under oral instructions.

   a. **Equitable title:** Although legal title passes only when the deed is handed over to the grantee out of escrow, equitable title passes to the grantee once delivery is completed to the escrow agent. This is more usually called the ***relation-back doctrine*** — the essential idea is that the buyer's title, once acquired out of escrow, will "relate back" to the moment the deed was delivered into escrow. This fiction enables courts to ignore the effect of the grantor's death or incapacity after deposit into escrow, or a creditor's attempted seizure of the property after the deed is delivered into escrow. From that moment on, the buyer has equitable title.

      i. **Exception — Bona fide purchasers:** If a seller double-crosses his buyer after depositing a deed into escrow, by conveying a deed to a ***bona fide purchaser*** (a person who pays real consideration and has no knowledge of the pending escrow), the bona fide purchaser (holder of legal title) prevails over the first grantee's equitable title. As between two innocents, the loser is the one who has yet to rely completely upon the seller's duplicity.

5. **Delivery by estoppel:** Even if a grantor does not intend to deliver a deed, he will be estopped from denying delivery under two principal circumstances.

   a. **Entrustment to a deceitful grantee:** If the grantor gives a deed to a grantee with no intent to transfer title, but the grantee uses the deed to convey to a third-party bona fide purchaser, the grantor will be estopped from denying delivery.

Example: Damian gives Agnes a deed to Blackacre, telling her, "Look it over and think about it, for this is what I propose to do if you will marry my son, Mordred." Instead of marrying Mordred, Agnes records the deed and promptly sells Blackacre to Myrtle, who pays good value and is utterly ignorant of the circumstances under which Agnes obtained the deed from Damian. Damian will be estopped from denying delivery to Agnes. Damian had more opportunity than Myrtle to avoid the problem (he could have simply told Agnes of his planned marital gift), so the loss should fall on him. Of course, he may have recourse against Agnes.

   b. Entrustment to a negligent escrow agent: If the grantor gives a deed to an escrow agent, but the grantee obtains it wrongfully, using it to sell the property to a bona fide purchaser, courts are split on whether the grantor is estopped from denying delivery.

   i. Rationale for estoppel: The grantor chose his escrow agent, so he ought to shoulder the consequences of a poor choice. The grantor could have picked a more careful or honest agent. The grantor is more culpable than the bona fide purchaser, so the grantor should lose.

   ii. Rationale for no estoppel: The grantor didn't intend delivery, so he ought not be prevented from denying delivery. The problem with this view is that it does not really address the underlying issue — of two innocents, which should bear the loss? The usual answer to this question is that it should fall on the party who had the better ability to prevent the loss in the first place. To say that the grantor didn't intend delivery does not address this problem. However, courts holding to this view will estop the grantor if the grantor knew about the grantee's wrongful possession and did nothing about it. In a sense, these courts are saying that they will not hold the grantor's agent's conduct against him, but will hold the grantor responsible for his own conduct.

III. FINANCING DEVICES: MORTGAGES, DEEDS OF TRUST, AND INSTALLMENT CONTRACTS

A. Mortgages: Loans secured by mortgages are the principal device enabling people to acquire real property. Very few people are able or willing to pay the entire purchase price in cash. Instead, they borrow a significant portion of the purchase price from a lender on terms that require them to repay the loan with interest via monthly payments made over an extended period of time (frequently 30 years). To secure repayment of the loan, the lender will require the borrower to give the lender a mortgage on the property. The mortgage empowers the lender to sell the property in the event of the borrower's default on the loan, and to apply the sale proceeds to repayment of the loan. Any proceeds left over go to the borrower. Generally, if the sale proceeds do not eliminate the loan, the borrower remains liable for the deficiency. This discussion of mortgages is only the tip of the mortgage law iceberg; there are a great many state variations on the general principles outlined here, but this outline will enable you to understand mortgages in the context of a first-year property course.

   1. The mortgage transaction: The term "mortgage" is often used loosely to refer to the entire transaction, which consists of two distinct elements: the ***loan*** and the ***mortgage.*** The loan is evidenced by a ***promissory note,*** a personal promise to repay the loan on the terms contained in the note. The mortgage is evidenced by a document called a ***mortgage;*** it is a ***security***

agreement between the parties, by which the borrower gives the lender the right to sell the property if the borrower defaults on the loan and to apply the sale proceeds toward reduction of the loan. The mortgage is usually recorded in the public land records, thus giving notice of the lender's security interest in the property. In some places, the note and the mortgage are combined into a single instrument, but they still perform separate functions. The borrower is often called the *mortgagor;* the lender is the *mortgagee.*

a. **Development of the mortgage:** The mortgage began as a conveyance. Lenders would require the borrower to convey the property to the lender in fee simple subject to a condition subsequent (e.g., "Borrower conveys Blackacre to Lender, but if Borrower pays £1,000 to Lender on Christmas Day, 1643, Lender will reconvey Blackacre to Borrower"). The law courts rigidly enforced this provision. If Borrower tendered £1,000 on Boxing Day (Dec. 26), 1643, it was too late; Blackacre was irrevocably Lender's.

   i. **Equity of redemption:** The equity courts began to rule that the borrower had an equitable right to redeem the property at any time after the due date. This *equity of redemption,* unlimited in time, was a constant cloud on title that made the property effectively inalienable. To remove the blot, lenders then brought suit in the law courts to *foreclose equity of redemption* — by obtaining a court order to extinguish the equitable right of redemption and sell the property free of that cloud to a new purchaser. Today's mortgage foreclosure is similar — the equity of redemption is extinguished, the property is ordered sold, the sale proceeds are applied to the loan, and any excess is given to the borrower. Note carefully that the foreclosure sale cuts off *only* this *judicially created equity of redemption.*

   ii. **Statutory right of redemption:** About 20 states have created a separate, independent *statutory right of redemption,* which gives the borrower a defined period of time (anywhere from a few months to a year or two) *after the foreclosure sale* in which the borrower can redeem the property from the purchaser at the foreclosure sale.

b. **Types of mortgages:** Although all mortgages have the same general characteristics, there are some terms of art used to describe mortgages with different features. The principal types follow.

   i. **First and second mortgages:** The same property can be used to secure more than one loan. The first mortgage is the mortgage that is given first in time. The second mortgage is given next in time. Sometimes these are referred to as *senior mortgages* or *junior mortgages*. The second mortgage is taken subject to the rights of the senior mortgage. Upon foreclosure, the holder of a second mortgage is entitled to share in the sale proceeds only after the first mortgage has been fully satisfied.

   ii. **Fully amortized mortgage:** A fully amortized mortgage loan is one in which the principal is retired over the life of the loan so that the monthly payments are constant (if the interest rate is fixed for the life of the loan) or vary with interest rates (if the interest rate is adjustable by formula during the life of the loan). Most residential mortgage loans in the United States are fully amortized.

   iii. **Balloon payment mortgage:** Some mortgage loans provide for very small payments of principal during the life of the loan (or none at all). While such loans reduce the monthly payment, they require payment of the entire principal balance on the due date.

Because few borrowers are likely to have cash on hand to make that payment, a balloon payment mortgage has the practical effect of forcing the borrower to obtain a new mortgage loan to retire the old one.

    iv. **Purchase money mortgage:** A mortgage loan made for a portion of the purchase price is a purchase money mortgage.

2. **Title or lien?** States take different views of whether the mortgagee (the lender) has **title** to the mortgaged property or only a **lien** upon that property. The title theory predominates in the east, and the lien theory is favored by western states. The difference is no longer of much practical consequence, because title theory states treat the lender's title as for security purposes only, thus making it virtually indistinguishable from a lien. The only difference lies in who is entitled to possession. In some title theory states, the mortgagee is entitled to possession; in other title theory states, the mortgagor is entitled to possession until default and the mortgagee is entitled to possession thereafter. In lien theory states, the mortgagor is entitled to possession until foreclosure. In title theory states, a lender has enhanced ability to recover possession after default fairly quickly (by suit for ejectment or judicial appointment of a receiver).

3. **Sale or transfer by the mortgagor:** A mortgagor is always free to transfer his **equity** — his interest in the property. **Equity** is the term used to describe the value of the borrower's interest in the property — the difference between market value and the principal balance of the loan secured by the mortgage. The term originated as a shorthand expression for the interest protected by the equity courts in the early days of mortgages. A buyer of the mortgagor's interest can acquire the interest **subject to the mortgage** or can **assume the mortgage.**

    a. **Acquisition subject to the mortgage:** By taking title subject to the mortgage, the buyer incurs **no personal liability on the mortgage.** In the event of default, the mortgagee can foreclose and sell the property, but if the foreclosure sale proceeds do not extinguish the debt, the lender has no further recourse against the owner who has acquired title subject to the mortgage. The lender can, however, obtain a personal judgment against the original mortgagor for the deficiency, except to the extent that states prohibit deficiency judgments.

    b. **Assumption of the mortgage:** If a new buyer assumes an existing mortgage, he becomes **personally liable for the mortgage loan.** The lender can obtain a deficiency judgment against the assuming buyer as well as the original mortgagee (unless the lender has released the original mortgagee).

    c. **Due-on-sale clauses:** Lenders dislike transfer of the mortgagor's interest, whether by assumption or by taking subject to the mortgage, because it is against their financial interest. In periods of declining interest rates, buyers will not likely assume or take subject to an existing fixed-rate mortgage, because they can obtain a new mortgage at lower rates. But in periods of rising interest rates, buyers will be anxious to assume or take subject to an existing fixed-rate mortgage at a lower-than-current-market rate. Lenders, of course, would prefer that the buyer obtain a new mortgage at a higher rate. Lenders also say they are concerned that the new buyer might be less creditworthy, but that argument is mostly bogus because the original mortgagor remains personally liable, and the property is the principal security for the loan. To prevent assumption of, or a sale subject to, a mortgage, lenders insert a **due-on-sale clause** into the mortgage and loan. This provision permits the lender to demand immediate payment of the outstanding principal balance of the loan in the event the mortgagor sells his interest. In the 1970s, some states, particularly California, invalidated due-on-sale clauses. Lenders reacted by obtaining federal law, which preempts state law, making due-on-sale clauses enforceable. See, e.g., *Fidelity Fed. Sav. & Loan Assn. v. De La Cuesta,* 458 U.S. 141 (1982).

4. **Default by mortgagor:** In most states, the lender has the option of a suit to collect the debt or to foreclose and effect a sale of the property to satisfy the debt. A few states require the lender first to foreclose and sell before seeking to enforce the debt personally by obtaining a deficiency judgment. The availability and utility of deficiency judgments are often limited by statute.

   a. **Anti-deficiency statutes:** Some states prohibit deficiency judgments on purchase money mortgage loans for residences. These statutes reflect a legislative bias in favor of homeowners. One variation is to permit a deficiency judgment only for the amount by which the debt exceeds a judicially determined fair market value for the property.

   b. **Statutory right of redemption:** The statutory right of redemption after foreclosure typically permits redemption by paying the *foreclosure sale price* rather than the *mortgage debt.* This is a strong inducement to the mortgagee, who is often the only bidder at a foreclosure sale, to bid the amount of the mortgage debt. Otherwise, the mortgagee might buy the property for a trifling fraction of the mortgage debt and seek to collect the remainder through a deficiency judgment. In some states, the mortgagor in default may stay in possession until the expiration of the statutory redemption period.

   c. **Inadequate sale price at foreclosure:** The fact that the sale price at foreclosure is inadequate, in the sense that it is less than fair market value, will not by itself void the foreclosure sale. The usual rule is that the sale price will stand unless it is so far below market value that it "shocks the conscience," or fraud or other overbearing unfairness is present. Some states go further, however, and impose on the mortgagee a fiduciary duty to act in a commercially reasonable manner in conducting a foreclosure, such that reasonable efforts are made to realize a fair price.

   ★**Example:** The Murphys refinanced their home in 1980, executing a promissory note secured by a first mortgage in favor of Financial Development Corp. FDC then sold the mortgage to Colonial Deposit. By September of 1981, the Murphys were seven months in arrears on their mortgage payments, and the lender gave notice of its intent to foreclose. Although the Murphys then paid the overdue mortgage payments, they failed to pay additional costs which had come due as a result of the foreclosure notice. The lenders scheduled a foreclosure sale for December 15, 1981, which occurred on that day. Present at the foreclosure sale were the Murphys, a lawyer retained by the lender to conduct the sale, and a representative of the lender. The lender made the only bid, $27,000, which was roughly the amount owed to the lender by the Murphys. Two days later, the lender sold the Murphys' home to a realtor for $38,000. The Murphys sued to set aside the foreclosure sale; a trial court refused to set aside the subsequent sale to the realtor because he was a bona fide purchaser for value but did award the Murphys $27,000 damages, an amount equal to the difference between the foreclosure sale price and the market value of the home, and legal fees due to the lender's bad faith. In *Murphy v. Financial Development Corp.,* 126 N.H. 536 (1985), the New Hampshire Supreme Court ruled that the lender was a fiduciary in conducting a foreclosure sale, and thus owed a duty of good faith and due diligence to exert commercially reasonable efforts to obtain a fair and reasonable price, but the court ruled that the lender did not act in bad faith. The lender did not advertise or use any other commercially reasonable methods to generate interest in the property. The New Hampshire Supreme Court also ruled that the trial court had erred in its determination of damages: Rather than finding damages to be the difference between foreclosure price and *fair market value,* damages are the difference between foreclosure price and a *fair price.* A fair price may be less than fair market value because fair market value can be expected to be realized in a voluntary exchange with plenty of opportunity to shop for buyers; in a forced sale, some diminution in price is reasonable. But the key point is that the lender must act diligently to generate a fair price.

B. Deeds of trust: The deed of trust is used in many states as the form of mortgage.

   1. **How it works:** The borrower conveys the real property to a third party as ***trustee*** for the lender, for the limited purpose of securing repayment of the debt. The trustee is often a nominee of the lender (e.g., the lender's lawyer, employee, or affiliated corporation). The deed of trust gives the trustee the power to sell the property upon default (the ***power of sale***), to use the proceeds to pay off the debt, and return any excess to the borrower.

   2. **Difference from the mortgage:** Traditionally, judicial foreclosure was required to enforce a mortgage, which meant bringing suit and conducting a judicially supervised sale, a time-consuming and costly process. A power of sale vested in a trustee, by contrast, is relatively quick and cheap. In some states, the mortgagee may not be given a power of sale; in other states, a mortgagee may exercise the power of sale if the mortgage gives the mortgagee that power. Under a deed of trust, the sale is conducted by the third-party trustee at the lender's request, which is virtually identical to the procedure under a mortgage with power of sale vested in the mortgagee. Some states treat deficiency judgments or redemption differently, depending on whether a deed of trust or mortgage is the security instrument.

C. Installment sale contracts: The installment sale contract is, in form, merely a contract of sale for real property obligating the purchaser to pay the purchase price in installments and obligating the seller to deliver title to the buyer after the purchase price has been paid in full. Economically, the transaction is indistinguishable from delivery of a deed to the buyer in exchange for a note and purchase money mortgage to secure the purchase price.

Example: Vendor, owner of Blackacre, agrees to sell Blackacre to Vendee for $133,333, under an installment sale contract by which Vendee takes possession and agrees to pay the purchase price at the rate of $1,111 per month for ten years, and Vendor agrees to deliver a deed to Vendee when the purchase price is fully paid. This is economically identical to a transaction by which Vendor deeds Blackacre to Vendee now, and receives from Vendee a note for $100,000, bearing interest at 6 percent per year, requiring Vendee to make monthly payments of $1,111 for ten years (at which time the debt will be extinguished), secured by a mortgage.

   1. **Treated as contract of sale:** The original reason for the installment sale contract was the seller's desire to avoid the procedural difficulties of extinguishing a mortgagor's equity of redemption. If a buyer under an installment sale contract defaulted, the seller could summarily evict the buyer upon default and, perhaps, keep all or a large part of the partially paid purchase price as damages. See, e.g., *Jensen v. Schreck,* 275 N.W.2d 374 (Iowa 1979). Because the seller retained legal title until the buyer had fully performed, buyer's default served to excuse any further performance on the seller's part. This result was very much like the old *"strict foreclosure,"* by which the equity of redemption was irrevocably cut off. See, e.g., *Harris v. Griffin,* 109 Ore. App. 253 (1991).

2. Treatment as a security device: The modern trend of courts is to treat installment sale contracts as security devices. There are two good reasons for this view: (1) the installment sale contract is economically indistinguishable from a mortgage, and (2) it is inequitable to permit a buyer to lose his equity of redemption under circumstances where an identically situated mortgagor would not. Nowadays, a court is likely to require judicial foreclosure of an installment sale contract, permit the seller to retain payments only to the extent of the reasonable rental value of the property, and perhaps give the buyer an equitable right to cure his default and resume payments (analogous to the mortgagor's equity of redemption).

★**Example:** Buyer agreed to purchase Seller's home under an installment sale contract for $15,000. The contract required Buyer to pay the $15,000 over 15 years at 5 percent interest on the unpaid balance, in monthly installments of $118.62, for a total of payments of about $21,350. The contract provided that if Buyer were to default and fail to cure the default for 30 days, Seller could terminate the contract, take possession, and retain all payments paid. Eight years into the contract, Buyer defaulted, having paid about half the purchase price. Seller sought to eject Buyer, and a New York trial court granted summary judgment to Seller. In ***Bean v. Walker,*** 95 App. Div. 2d 70 (1983), a New York intermediate appeals court reversed, holding that the principle of equitable title or equitable conversion applied, causing title to vest in the buyer at the moment the contract was executed, placing the buyer in the same position as a mortgagor. See also *Parise v. Citizens Natl. Bank,* 438 So. 2d 1020 (Fla. App. 1983); *Skendzel v. Marshall,* 301 N.E.2d 641 (Ind. 1973); *Union Bond & Trust Co. v. Blue Creek Redwood Co.,* 128 F. Supp. 709 (N.D. Cal. 1955).

D. Unfair or deceptive lending practices: Mortgage lending used to be a local activity, in which the lender retained the mortgage and serviced the loan. With the advent of securitized mortgages (in which mortgages are sold from the originating lender to a third party, who packages a small portion of that loan with many other such loan slivers in a collateralized debt obligation that is then sold to global investors), mortgage lending lost its original character. Mortgages originated with brokers, who located a lender, who then sold the resulting loan and mortgage to entities that repackaged it as a security. Thus, the originating lenders cared very little about the ability of the borrower to repay the loan. The purchasers of the loans, who packaged them into securities, did not care about the borrower's ability to repay the loan because they bundled them with more credit-worthy loans to dilute the risk of default. Purchasers of the securities did not worry about repayment because they thought that risk was minimal due to the blended nature of the security. But when the housing bubble collapsed in 2007, and defaults became widespread, attention was focused on these practices. Borrowers and regulatory agencies claimed that some mortgage-lending practices were unfair and deceptive.

★**Example:** Fremont Investment made mortgage loans to borrowers through mortgage brokers. Fremont offered adjustable-rate loans, in which the initial interest rate was very low but adjusted upward sharply after two years or so. Fremont made loans to people whose debt-to-income ratio was as high as 50 percent, a ratio computed without regard to the higher monthly cost of the loans once the introductory interest rates were phased out. Fremont also loaned 100 percent of the (often inflated) purchase cost of the homes pledged as security. Accordingly, there was little realistic expectation that these loans could be paid. A trial court enjoined Fremont and its successors from foreclosure upon the pledged properties because it found that these practices were unfair and deceptive. In ***Commonwealth v. Fremont Investment and Loan,*** 452 Mass. 733 (2008), the Massachusetts Supreme Judicial Court affirmed the trial court's injunction.

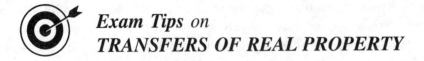

Exam Tips *on*
TRANSFERS OF REAL PROPERTY

☛ Note your professor's interests and inclinations. A lot of this area is contract law imported into property. If your professor is fond of this material, it is more likely to be tested. If your professor treats it in cursory fashion, don't ignore it, but it may be of lesser importance in his or her pedagogical calculation.

☛ Contracts of sale involve issues of enforcement and choice of remedies. Remember the implied duties imposed on sellers here; watch out for facts suggesting a lack of marketable title, or breach of a duty to disclose.

☛ Deed warranties are fruitful areas of testing. Pay attention to the type of deed and the facts that will indicate which, if any, covenants may be violated. Make sure you have a good understanding of the method by which damages for violation of deed covenants are determined.

☛ The law pertinent to real estate finance is a bit of a specialty, but if your professor covers this material, watch out for an exam question. Good candidates include an installment sale contract in which the buyer has defaulted, and foreclosure or private sale at which the lender arguably fails to act in a commercially reasonable manner.

CHAPTER 7

ASSURING GOOD TITLE TO LAND

ChapterScope ━━━

This chapter examines the problem of how current owners can obtain assurance that they actually have good title to the land they purchase. Included is discussion of how problems occur, often by multiple purchasers of the same land from the same seller, and the mechanisms of resolving these competing claims—recording acts, marketable title acts, title insurance, and registered title. Here are the most important points in this chapter.

- In cases of conflicting claims to the same property, the common law preferred the earliest claimant in time. That rule has been largely displaced by recording acts, which operate to give priority to those claimants who comply with the terms of the acts.

  - Recording acts are based on the fact that every county in America maintains a public record of title transactions in real estate, usually organized and indexed alphabetically by grantors and grantees, in which any title transaction may be recorded. There are three types of recording acts: *Race, Notice,* and *Race-Notice*.

    - Race statutes give priority to the title claimant who first records his deed.

    - Notice statutes give priority to the bona fide purchaser who lacks notice of a prior unrecorded claim.

    - Race-Notice statutes give priority to the bona fide purchaser who lacks notice of a prior unrecorded claim only if the bona fide purchaser records first.

- Marketable-title acts function as a statute of limitations to cut off old claims of title. The acts bar assertion of title claims that are not in the chain of title within some specified period of time prior to the present, but there are many exceptions to the limitations bar of marketable-title acts.

- Registered title substitutes a registration system for the prevailing notice system. Under registered title, the title is exactly what is registered in the registry, and nothing can impeach that title. It delivers certainty, but if the registered title is in error, the results can be devastating. Registered title is not popular in the United States.

- Title insurance is the most widely used method of providing meaningful assurances of good title.

- A well-funded title insurer issues a policy of title insurance to the owner, promising to insure that title is as stated in the policy, and stands ready to reimburse the insured for any title defects, up to the policy limits.

━━

I. INTRODUCTION

A. **The problem:** To paraphrase James Madison, if men were angels there would be no need for methods to assure good title to land. But humans are often rogues, and sometimes they convey the same property more than once. The rogue grantor may be universally condemned, but the remaining problem is to decide which purchaser from the rogue is to prevail.

Example: Rogue, owner of Blackacre, conveys it to Angel on January 1 for $50,000. On January 10, before Angel has taken possession, Rogue conveys Blackacre to Beatrice for $50,000. Beatrice is ignorant of the prior conveyance to Angel. Rogue is, of course, a scoundrel, but let us suppose he has disappeared with his $100,000 and so cannot be forced to disgorge his ill-gotten gain. As to the innocents — Angel or Beatrice — who should prevail?

1. **The common law answer:** The common law used the *first-in-time* principle to award title to Angel. She was the first grantee and, at that moment, Rogue conveyed his interest in Blackacre. Rogue had no interest in Blackacre to convey to Beatrice, so she was the loser. To protect grantees, the common law relied heavily on the warranties of title contained in a general or special warranty deed (see Chapter 6, section II.B), but these were of little use if Rogue had skipped off with his loot.

2. **Modern answers:** Because the common law method was crude, uncertain, and harsh, Americans quickly devised better methods of assuring good title. A brief summary of these methods follows.

   a. **Recording:** The first innovation was *recording.* A recording act creates a system for placing conveyances in a public record, and then stipulates who has priority in the event of conflict. A deed is valid without recording, but an unrecorded deed is likely to lose out to a recorded deed if both deeds are from the same grantor to the same property. In the example, neither Angel nor Beatrice has recorded, so the recording act does not apply until one or both records. There are three different types of recording acts, and the answer may vary. See section II, below.

   b. **Registration:** A later method, and one not much used in the United States, is to create an official registry of land titles. This system is different from recording of conveyances in that the *registry is the title,* and the public records simply contain *evidence of title.* From the example above, Rogue's registered title, in a registry system, would be replaced by a new registration in Angel. Beatrice would probably never part with the purchase price because of the inability to register title in her name. See section III, below.

   c. **Title insurance:** A ubiquitous method for obtaining practical assurance of good title is to obtain *title insurance.* For a fee, a title insurer agrees to *defend title* and to *compensate for the loss of the insured title to the claim of a paramount owner.* So long as the title insurer remains solvent, this is good enough for most buyers. The title insurer, of course, carefully examines title before issuing its title insurance policy, and will refuse to insure if it finds any defects in title. But a title insurer will not generally insure title unless the purchaser's deed is recorded and the insurer is satisfied that no rival claimant can have a better title. In the example, because neither Angel nor Beatrice has recorded, it is not likely that either could find an insurer willing to provide title insurance without specifically excepting from its coverage any unrecorded prior conveyances.

II. RECORDING ACTS AND CHAIN-OF-TITLE PROBLEMS

A. **The recording system:** A public official in each county, often called the *county recorder,* maintains a record of the transactions affecting real estate located in the county, but that record is only as complete as what is presented to the recorder for filing. Any instrument affecting realty may be filed and recorded so long as it meets the formal requirements for recording (usually notarial acknowledgment). The most common instruments that are recorded are deeds and mortgages, but such things as judgment liens, tax liens, installment sale contracts, and leases can be and often are recorded.

1. **What the recorder does:** The recorder's job is mostly ministerial. The recorder accepts instruments for filing by stamping the date and time of filing on them, then photocopying them and placing the copy in an official record. The original is returned to the person who presented it for filing. Then the recorder *indexes the instrument* by noting a description of the instrument in an index maintained to facilitate location of the instrument. Just as a searcher for a library book must consult a catalog of books by author, subject, or title, the searcher of title records must consult the recorder's index. There are two types of indices.

    a. **Grantor-grantee index:** By far the most common type of index is the grantor-grantee index. An alphabetical record of all grantors and all grantees, by surname, is maintained in separate volumes. The typical entry will contain the date, the name of the grantor (or grantee, as appropriate), the other party to the transaction, a brief description of the property and the instrument, and a citation to the precise location in the public records of a complete copy of the instrument.

        Example: On July 2, 1988, Harry Simpson conveyed 123 Elm Street to Agnes Darby. Here is how that transaction might appear in the grantor index of the county:

        SIMPSON, Harry to Darby, Agnes. 7/2/88. General warranty deed to 123 Elm Street, recorded in Book 484, Page 1186.

        And here is how that transaction might appear in the grantee index of the county:

        DARBY, Agnes from Simpson, Harry. 7/2/88. General warranty deed to 123 Elm Street, recorded in Book 484, Page 1186.

    b. **Tract index:** A few jurisdictions maintain a tract index, in which every transaction pertaining to a particular parcel is entered in one location, instead of chronologically by grantor and grantee. Tract indexes are most common where property has been platted by map into various blocks and lots within blocks.

        Example: Here is how the transaction in the last example might be indexed in a tract index:

        TRACT: BLOCK 39, Lot 2 (123 Elm Street). 7/2/88, General warranty deed from Harry Simpson to Agnes Darby, recorded in Book 484, Page 1186.

2. **What the title searcher does:** A title searcher's objective is to identify all the *past* title transactions pertinent to a particular parcel, in order to determine the *present* state of title. This is a simple job if the jurisdiction maintains a tract index; the title searcher finds the page describing all title transactions pertinent to the parcel. The process is more complicated if a grantor-grantee index is involved. The searcher begins by looking back in time through the grantee index to find the transaction by which the present owner acquired title, then searches the grantee index further back to find the transaction by which the present owner's grantor acquired title. This process continues until an adequate root of title has been found (usually a title transaction far enough back in time to cut off any prior claims by a statute of limitations).

Then the searcher will turn to the grantor index and search forward in time, beginning with the initial grantor, to see if any owner ever conveyed her interest prior to the grant that appears to make up the chain of title traced backward in time. In most jurisdictions, the searcher need only search forward from the time the grantor acquired title to the point when the grantor transferred title to the next owner in the chain. But in a few jurisdictions, it is necessary to search forward to the present for every grantor.

Example: In 1890, Arthur conveyed Blackacre to Smith. In 1910, Smith granted Wilson an easement appurtenant for right of way over Blackacre. In 1920, Smith conveyed Blackacre to Rogers. Rogers conveyed Blackacre to Candiotti in 1950. Candiotti conveyed it to Alvarez in 1980. In 1990, Alvarez granted Trustco a mortgage upon Blackacre. Your client, Barker, wishes to purchase Blackacre. To determine the state of title, you would search the grantee index, under Alvarez, from the present time back to 1980, when you would find the deed from Candiotti to Alvarez. Then you would search the grantee index under Candiotti back to 1950, when you would find the deed from Rogers. Then you would search the grantee index under Rogers back to 1920, when you would find the Smith conveyance. Ditto back to 1890, when you would find the Arthur conveyance. Assume that a conveyance more than 80 years old is an adequate root of title; that makes the Arthur-to-Smith conveyance of 1890 the root of title. Then you will search forward from 1890 in the grantor index under Smith. You will first find the 1910 easement grant to Wilson, then the 1920 conveyance to Rogers. You will search the grantor index under Rogers until you find the 1950 conveyance to Candiotti. You will then search under Candiotti from 1950 until 1980, when you find the conveyance to Alvarez. A final search forward under Alvarez from 1980 will reveal the mortgage to Trustco in 1990. You now know that Alvarez has good title to Blackacre, subject to an easement for right of way in favor of the present owner of Wilson's property and a mortgage to Trustco.

   a. Legal obligations of the title searcher: Any title searcher is obligated to exercise reasonable diligence in performing the search. A searcher is liable for a negligent search that results in damage to the buyer if the search results are provided to the buyer. This is true even if the search is performed for the seller, because the buyer is universally treated as the third-party beneficiary of the search, and it is obviously foreseeable that a buyer might rely on any such search.

B. Race acts: A race act provides that, as between two grantees to the same property, the *earliest to record* prevails. Hence there is a race to record first. Under a race act, it does not matter that the first person to record had notice of a prior unrecorded conveyance. The reason for ignoring such notice is that making the record dispositive obviates the need to rely on extrinsic evidence about notice, which may be controverted and unreliable. But most jurisdictions regard the equitable cost of the race statute as too high, because it permits a later grantee to prevail over a known earlier grantee so long as the later grantee is quicker to record.

Example: On January 15, Rogue, owner of Blackacre, conveys for value to Prof. Scatterbrain, who absent-mindedly leaves the deed on his desk for a month, before recording it on February 15. Prof. Sly, Scatterbrain's colleague, sees the deed on Scatterbrain's desk, reads it, and observes that it is not yet recorded. On January 30, Prof. Sly pays value to Rogue for Blackacre and receives a deed from Rogue, which Prof. Sly records on February 1. As between Sly and Scatterbrain, Sly prevails because he recorded first. Sly's knowledge of Scatterbrain's prior purchase is irrelevant.

C. Notice acts: Notice acts address the inequity of permitting a later purchaser to prevail over an earlier purchaser when the later purchaser knows of the prior purchase. They do so by providing that a *subsequent bona fide purchaser* **without notice of a prior unrecorded transfer** prevails over the prior purchaser who has failed to record. And this is true *even if the subsequent purchaser has not recorded.* Here is a simplified example of a notice statute: "No conveyance is valid against a subsequent bona fide purchaser who has no notice of the conveyance, unless the conveyance is recorded." About half of American states have notice acts.

Example: On January 15, Able conveys Blackacre to Hector, who fails to record the deed. On February 15, Able conveys Blackacre to Artemis for $100,000. Artemis is ignorant of the January conveyance to Hector. Artemis prevails over Hector, regardless of who might first record his deed. The critical facts are that, at the moment Able conveyed to Artemis for value, (1) Artemis lacked notice of the prior conveyance to Hector, and (2) Hector had not recorded his deed (which would have given constructive notice to Artemis).

D. Race-notice acts: A race-notice act protects a more limited class of subsequent bona fide purchasers who lack notice of the prior conveyance: It protects only those subsequent bona fide purchasers who lack notice and who *record before the prior purchaser.* Here is a simplified example of a race-notice statute: "No conveyance is valid against a subsequent bona fide purchaser who has no notice of the conveyance and who has recorded his conveyance first." The supposed virtues of a race-notice act, as compared to a notice act, are (1) encouraging recording, and (2) eliminating disputes over which of two conveyances was first delivered. The first rationale is probably true but weak, and the second addresses a largely imaginary problem. Even so, these arguments are persuasive enough to have caused about half of American states to enact race-notice acts.

Example: On June 1, Bilbo conveys Blackacre to Jane, who does not record. On July 1, Bilbo conveys Blackacre to Sally for $100,000. Sally is ignorant of the prior conveyance to Jane. On July 15 Jane, records her deed. On July 20, Sally records her deed. Jane prevails over Sally because, even though Sally lacked notice of the conveyance to Jane, Jane recorded before Sally.

E. The consequences of recording: Recording provides constructive notice to the world of a conveyance. Even if a later purchaser fails to consult the record, he is charged with knowledge of its contents. In a race or race-notice jurisdiction, recordation cuts off the possibility that either a prior unrecorded purchaser or a later purchaser could prevail. In a notice jurisdiction, recordation provides constructive notice, thus preventing later purchasers from prevailing.

1. The consequences of not recording: There are two important consequences to failure to record.

   a. Common law rule applies: If nobody has recorded, the common law principle of "first-in-time" continues to apply, except in a notice jurisdiction when the subsequent bona fide purchaser lacks notice.

   b. Grantor can convey good title to a later purchaser: More ominous to purchasers is the fact that, without recordation, the grantor is left with the power to convey good title to a later purchaser. Of course, the grantor who does this is often a scoundrel and may well be liable to the losing first purchaser for the proceeds received from the second purchaser.

   Example: Olivia, the record owner of Blackacre, conveys Blackacre to Brewster, who fails to record. Then Olivia conveys Blackacre to Abigail for $100,000. Abigail, who is ignorant of the conveyance to Brewster, then records. In all three types of jurisdictions, Abigail will prevail. Had Brewster recorded before the sale to Abigail, Brewster would have prevailed everywhere. Brewster may be able to recover from Olivia the $100,000 she received from

Abigail, on the theory that Olivia holds those proceeds in a constructive trust for Brewster, but Brewster could have avoided the whole mess by prompt recordation. Always record promptly.

F.   When is an instrument recorded?   To be recorded, an instrument must be eligible for recording and must be entered in the records in a manner that complies with the jurisdiction's requirements. Virtually anything that affects title to or an interest in real property may be recorded. Most states require that an instrument may not be recorded without a notarial acknowledgment. To obtain a notarial acknowledgment, the grantor must prove his identity to a notary and sign the document with the notary as witness. Some states require or permit witnesses to perform the function of the notary. The problem is that recorders, being human, are not infallible. The following are the common instances of instruments appearing in the record that are wholly are partially unrecorded.

1. **Instrument not indexed:** This recorder's error is to fail to index an instrument or to index it so improperly that it cannot be found by a diligent searcher using the standard search methods. Jurisdictions split on the proper resolution of this problem. The older rule is that "a purchaser is charged with constructive notice of a record even though there is no official index which will direct him to [the particular instrument]." 4 *Amer. Law of Prop.* §17.25 (1952). On this theory, the purchaser has done all he can do by tendering an eligible instrument to the recorder for recording. See, e.g., *Haner v. Bruce,* 146 Vt. 262 (1985). However, the diligent searcher cannot find the unindexed instrument. Because constructive notice from the record is founded on the assumption that a searcher can find it if he looks, the newer rule is that the unindexed or improperly indexed instrument ought not provide constructive notice. See, e.g., *Dyar v. Martinez,* 147 Cal. App. 4th 1240 (2007), *Hochstein v. Romero,* 219 Cal. App. 3d 447 (1990).

2. **"Omnibus" or "Mother Hubbard" clauses:** A variation on the improperly indexed instrument is an instrument that accurately describes one parcel, Blackacre, and also includes "all other land owned by the grantor in the county." These omnibus clauses are sometimes called "Mother Hubbard" clauses, because they "sweep the cupboard bare." The recorder can only record this instrument by reference to Blackacre, because it is an unreasonable burden on the recorder to search the records to identify all the other property owned by the grantor. Omnibus clauses are void as against later purchasers of the grantor's property (other than Blackacre) because a diligent searcher of the index (with respect to a parcel other than Blackacre) will never locate any reference to the omnibus clause.

★**Example:** Grace Owens owned interests in eight oil and gas leases in Coffey County, Kansas. She assigned to International Tours her interest in those leases under an assignment that specifically described each of the seven different parcels and included an omnibus clause that assigned to Tours Owens's interest "in all oil and gas leases in Coffey County, Kansas" owned by Owens, "whether or not [such leases] are specifically enumerated" in the assignment. The Kufahl lease, in which Owens had an interest, was not specifically described. Four years after Tours recorded the assignment, Owens assigned her interest in the Kufahl lease to Burris, who had checked the public records and had obtained an abstract of title from a professional title searcher. Neither search revealed the existence of the omnibus clause in the Owens-to-Tours assignment. Kansas has a notice statute. In ***Luthi v. Evans,*** 223 Kan. 622 (1978), the Kansas Supreme Court held that the omnibus clause in the Owens-to-Tours assignment did not give constructive notice to later purchasers of Owens's interest in the Kufahl lease. Burris prevailed, taking the Kufahl lease free of Tours's interest because it was not reasonable to expect a title searcher to locate and read every other conveyance ever made to Owens at any time conferring an interest in an oil and gas lease in Coffey County, Kansas. That would be a monumental task, greatly increasing the time and expense of title searches, which Kansas's recording act did not contemplate.

3. **Misspelled names:** Jurisdictions divide over whether a misspelled name in a recorded instrument gives constructive notice. All jurisdictions agree that if the misspelling is so significant that it does not even sound like the correct name, there is no constructive notice. Thus, "Kirk" for "Church" is inadequate, even though both names refer to a house of worship. The problem that divides jurisdictions is whether the misspelling that sounds like the correct name supplies constructive notice. The doctrine of *idem sonans* holds that a misspelling that sounds substantially identical to the correct name gives constructive notice. See 4 *Amer. Law of Prop.* §17.18, which adopts *idem sonans* so long as the misspelling begins with the same letter as the correct spelling. However useful *idem sonans* may be to establishing identity in other contexts, it is **not** *the prevailing rule* with respect to the issue of constructive notice from the real estate records.

★**Example:** Orr obtained a judgment against Elliott, but Orr's lawyer prepared the judgment by spelling Elliott's name as "Elliot." An abstract of the judgment, listing the judgment debtor as "Elliot" or "Eliot," was recorded in Orange County, California, and indexed under those two names only. Elliott later conveyed property subject to the judgment lien to Byers, and Orr sought to foreclose his lien against the parcel acquired by Byers from Elliott. In ***Orr v. Byers,*** 198 Cal. App. 3d 666 (1988), the California intermediate appeals court held that *idem sonans* did not apply in California, and thus that the recorded abstract did not give constructive notice of Orr's lien. Byers prevailed, but if he had had *actual notice* of Orr's lien, he would have lost. The court reasoned that *idem sonans* would place an unreasonable burden on title searchers, especially given the uncertain contours of the doctrine in a highly multicultural society. Also, the problem can be more easily avoided by those who prepare instruments for recording.

4. **Ineligible instrument:** The usual ineligible instrument is an unacknowledged instrument that nevertheless appears on the record through the recorder's oversight. Because such an instrument is not eligible for recording, it is treated as unrecorded and thus does **not give constructive notice** of its contents. A subsequent purchaser will prevail unless she has **actual notice** of the prior conveyance or is under a duty to inquire, and that inquiry would reveal the prior conveyance.

   a. **Defect not apparent on the face of the instrument:** Jurisdictions split on whether constructive notice is imparted by an apparently recorded instrument that is ineligible for recording due to some defect **not apparent** from the instrument itself. The majority rule is that an instrument with a defect on its face does **not** give constructive notice, but an instrument with a hidden defect **does impart** constructive notice. See, e.g., *Metropolitan Natl. Bank v. United States,* 901 F. 2d 1297 (5th Cir. 1990); *Mills v. Damson Oil Co.,* 437 So. 2d 1005 (Miss. 1983). Because even the most diligent searcher of the records could not possibly have any inkling of a hidden defect, it makes little sense to rule that the instrument is not recorded and thus imparts no constructive notice, but some states do just that.

   ★**Example:** Caroline Messersmith and her nephew Frederick owned land in North Dakota as equal tenants in common. Caroline conveyed to Frederick her interest under a deed that Frederick did not record, probably because the parties intended the deed to be a will substitute. Caroline, still in possession, conveyed a half interest in the mineral rights to Smith under a deed that Smith then took to a notary, who then spoke to Caroline by phone to ask whether the signature on the deed in front of the notary was hers. Upon being assured that the signature was Caroline's, the notary affixed his notarial seal and acknowledgment, but this notarial acknowledgment was void because Caroline was not physically present to be certain that the document in front of the notary was in fact the deed she signed and not some other instrument. (It's possible that Smith could have forged her signature to a different deed, which he then presented to the notary.) Smith then conveyed his mineral interest to Seale, who claimed to have no notice of Frederick's interest in the land. Only then did Smith record the Caroline-to-Smith deed; on the same day, the Smith-to-Seale deed was recorded. Six weeks later, Frederick recorded his Caroline-to-Frederick deed and then brought suit to quiet title in his name. A trial court ruled that, because Seale was a bona fide purchaser who lacked notice of the Caroline-to-Frederick deed, and who recorded his deed from Smith and the Caroline-to-Smith deed before Frederick recorded, Seale should prevail under North Dakota's race-notice statute. On appeal, the North Dakota Supreme Court, in ***Messersmith v. Smith,*** 60 N.W. 2d 276 (N.D. 1953), reversed, holding that no subsequent instrument in the chain of title passing through the secretly defective instrument is validly recorded. Given that the defect could not possibly be known to anyone carefully scrutinizing the record, it is hard to see what purpose was served by the ruling. Notarial acknowledgments are intended to prevent forgery, but there was no allegation of forgery and, absent that, the record should speak for itself.

G. Scope of protection afforded by recording acts: The protection afforded by a recording act is defined by the statute, as interpreted by the courts of the jurisdiction. Read the recording act carefully!

   1. Invalid conveyance: Although recordation creates a presumption of validity, if in fact the instrument was invalid (e.g., it was forged or never delivered), recordation does not make it valid.

   2. Interests in land created by operation of law: Recording acts only apply to ***conveyances*** (e.g., deeds, mortgages, grants, contracts) and ***liens*** created by operation of law (e.g., judgments). They do ***not apply to*** interests ***created by operation of law,*** such as adverse possession, prescriptive easements, or implied easements. Even though such interests are not of record, they are still valid and enforceable against subsequent purchasers.

   3. Bona fide purchasers: Notice and race-notice recording acts are intended to protect the ***bona fide purchaser*** of property. A bona fide purchaser is one who gives ***valuable consideration*** to purchase the property and is ***without notice*** of a prior unrecorded conveyance. Race acts protect bona fide purchasers only to the extent they are the first to record. Obviously, a ***donee does* not receive protection,** because a donee has not given value.

      a. Shelter rule: The protection given a bona fide purchaser under a recording act extends to all takers from the bona fide purchaser, even if such a taker knows of a prior unrecorded conveyance. This "shelter rule" is necessary to give the bona fide purchaser the full value of his purchase in reliance on the records. Part of that value is the ability to transfer good title to others.

      Example: Ovid conveys to Alan, who does not record. Ovid then conveys to Barbara, a bona fide purchaser (BFP), who does record. Barbara then conveys to Charles, who knows all about the Ovid-to-Alan deed. Barbara will prevail over Alan in all three types of jurisdictions. In a notice or race-notice jurisdiction, Charles's knowledge of Alan's deed is irrelevant only because he is a taker from Barbara, a bona fide purchaser. Charles is "sheltered" by his vendor's status as a BFP.

4. **Mortgagees:** Mortgagees are generally treated as bona fide purchasers, either because the statute specifically includes them or because courts have interpreted the phrase *bona fide purchaser* to include them. But this only applies to the mortgagee who actually gives value (e.g., the loan proceeds) in return for the mortgage. In most states, a mortgagee who receives a mortgage to secure a *pre-existing debt* without some detrimental change in its position (e.g., a reduction in the interest rate) has not acquired the mortgage for value and so is not a bona fide purchaser. See, e.g., *Gabel v. Drewrys Ltd., U.S.A., Inc.,* 68 So. 2d 372 (Fla. 1953). The contrary view is taken by the Uniform Simplification of Land Transfers Act, §§1-201(31) and 3-202.

5. **Creditors:** The status of creditors depends on the language of the act.

   a. **No protection:** If a recording act protects only "purchasers," a creditor is protected only if he should purchase the owner's interest at a judicial sale resulting from a successful lawsuit to collect the debt.

   b. **Specific protection:** If a recording act specifically protects "creditors" or "all persons," a creditor will receive protection without the necessity of a purchase at a judicial sale, but the scope of that protection is often limited by courts to *judgment creditors* or *lien creditors.* The rationale is that creditors do not generally rely on the state of the public land records in extending unsecured credit, but a creditor who has reduced a claim to judgment or lien intends to seize and sell the debtor's property. The judgment or lien creditor has an interest in the state of the record in order to know what his priority is with respect to the debtor's property.

H. **Notice:** To be protected under a notice or race-notice statute, a purchaser must be without *actual or constructive notice* of any prior unrecorded interests at the time the purchaser pays the consideration.

1. **Actual notice:** Actual notice is real, actual knowledge of the prior unrecorded transaction. Evidence beyond the record is necessary to prove actual notice.

2. **Constructive notice:** There are two forms of constructive notice: *record notice* and *inquiry notice.*

   a. **Record notice:** The entire world, specifically including a subsequent grantee, is charged with constructive notice of the contents of the record. If an instrument is validly recorded, every subsequent grantee has constructive notice of it, and so cannot be a bona fide purchaser. However, there can be argument over what constitutes the record, thus supplying constructive notice to subsequent purchasers.

      i. **"Wild deeds" — Outside the chain of title:** If a complete stranger to the record chain of title records a conveyance (a "wild deed"), the conveyance does not give constructive notice, because it is not within the chain of title.

         ★**Example:** In Minnesota, a race-notice state, Hoerger conveyed a lot to Duryea & Wilson (D&W), who did not record. D&W then conveyed the lot to Board of Education, who did record, after which Hoerger conveyed the same lot to Hughes, who lacked notice of the conveyance from Hoerger to D&W. Hughes recorded. In ***Board of Education of Minneapolis v. Hughes,*** 118 Minn. 404 (1912), the Minnesota Supreme Court decided that Hughes prevailed over the Board of Education because the conveyance from D&W to the Board of Education was outside the chain of title and did not impart constructive notice. At the time Hughes purchased from Hoerger, a diligent title search would reveal Hoerger to be the record owner. Even though the deed from D&W to the Board of Education was recorded first, it would appear to be a deed made by a complete stranger to the chain of title. Because the Hoerger-to-D&W link in the chain was not recorded, a diligent searcher would never find the D&W-to-Board conveyance. See also *Zimmer v. Sundell,* 237 Wis. 270 (1941).

ii. **Expanded chain of title — Deeds from common grantor:** Reciprocal implied covenants restricting land use may be implied by a developer's conveyance of property subject to express covenants burdening the developer's retained land (see Chapter 9), but such a covenant does not appear in the chain of title of the retained land, if it is conveyed without the implied covenant being made express. Does a deed by a developer to Lot 1, which imposes a use restriction on Lot 1 and all other lots retained by the developer (including Lot 2), impart constructive notice of the covenant to a later purchaser of Lot 2 from the developer? Note that the use restriction does not appear in the developer's deed to Lot 2. Jurisdictions split on this issue. Most conclude that the burden on title searchers to locate and read all deeds out from a common grantor is unreasonable. See, e.g., *Buffalo Academy of the Sacred Heart v. Boehm Bros., Inc.,* 267 N.Y. 242 (1935). A few states conclude that purchasers of property from a common grantor have constructive notice of the contents of all deeds out from a common grantor, thus imposing the practical burden of searching all deeds out from a common grantor.

★**Example:** Gilmore, a developer and subdivider, conveyed a lot to Guillette under a recorded deed that restricted the lot's use to a single-family residence, and recited that "the same restrictions are hereby imposed on each of [the] lots now owned by seller." This was effective to impose the single-family residence use restriction on all of Gilmore's remaining lots. Later, Gilmore conveyed a restricted lot to Daly under a recorded deed that made no mention of any restrictions. Daly obtained a building permit to construct 36 apartment units on the lot. Other owners of lots in the development (all of whom obtained title from Gilmore) sought to enjoin Daly from violating the single-family residence use restriction. In ***Guillette v. Daly Dry Wall, Inc.,*** 367 Mass. 355 (1975), the Massachusetts Supreme Judicial Court held that Daly had acquired the lot with constructive notice of the restriction even though the restriction was not in the chain of title from Gilmore to Daly. The ***Guillette*** rule requires a purchaser to expand his search of title to include all conveyances made by the grantor of other adjacent property he owned, in order to be certain that the grantor did not burden his remaining property with a use restriction contained in a deed to a third party. Jurisdictions rejecting this rule reason that this search burden is not reasonable.

iii. **After-acquired title:** Suppose a grantor conveys title without having title, but then later acquires title. Under the after-acquired-title doctrine (see Chapter 6), the title "shoots through" the grantor to the grantee. But suppose the grantor conveys title twice, once before acquiring it and once afterward to a person without actual notice of the prior conveyance, and both conveyances are immediately recorded. Does the first conveyance, made at a time when the grantor has never been a grantee (and thus will not be found in the usual backwards-in-time search by grantees) impart constructive notice? Or should a title searcher be obligated to search a period earlier in time than the grantor acquired title, on the possibility that the grantor conveyed away his title before he ever got it? The majority rule is that the first conveyance does ***not impart constructive notice*** because it is not reasonable to expect title searchers to search the records for the time period prior to the grantor's acquisition of title on the off chance that the grantor might have conveyed his title before he received title.

Example: The United States owned a tract of land that Lowery occupied under a statutory right of temporary possession, a latter-day version of the Homestead Act under which Lowery could ultimately acquire title if he performed certain acts of improvement over a specified time period. While Lowery was in possession, but before he had any title to the land, Lowery conveyed his interest in the tract to Horvath, who recorded the deed. Later, after the United States had conveyed its title in the land to Lowery (and Lowery had recorded the deed from the United States), Lowery conveyed the same property to Sabo, who recorded his deed. In *Sabo v. Horvath,* 559 P.2d 1038 (Alaska 1976), it was held that Sabo prevailed over Horvath, because Horvath's deed was outside the chain of title. A diligent title searcher would go back in time until he found the conveyance from the United States to Lowery in the grantee index, and would then search the grantor index (under Lowery) forward in time to see if Lowery had made any other conveyances, but could not reasonably be expected to search the grantor index ***before Lowery had title.***

A few old cases apply after-acquired-title doctrine uncritically and hold that title searchers must examine the grantor index before the time each record owner acquired title in order to see whether the owner conveyed title before he acquired it. See, e.g., *Tefft v. Munson,* 57 N.Y. 97 (1874); *Ayer v. Philadelphia & Boston Face Brick Co.,* 159 Mass. 84 (1893). By requiring a more extensive search, these cases expand the scope of the chain of title, and such expanded searches are expensive, especially if the chain of title is long.

iv. **Deed recorded after grantor has parted with record title:** Must a title searcher search the grantor index forward past the point that the record discloses he has already parted with title? If the first recorded conveyance is to a bona fide purchaser (BFP), and the shelter rule applies, there will be no need to do so, but if the first recorded conveyance is ***not*** to a BFP (perhaps it is to a donee or a purchaser with actual notice of a prior unrecorded conveyance), the question becomes more complicated. Jurisdictions split on this issue.

Example: Ovoid, owner of Blackacre, conveys to Alice, who fails to record. Then Ovoid conveys Blackacre to Ben, who knows of the Ovoid-to-Alice conveyance. Ben records his deed. Alice then records her deed from Ovoid. As between Alice and Ben, Alice will prevail because Ben is not a BFP without notice. But then Ben conveys to Charles, who pays value and is ignorant of the Ovoid-to-Alice conveyance. Charles records. Who prevails, Alice or Charles? The answer depends on whether the Ovoid-to-Alice deed, although recorded later than the Ovoid-to-Ben deed, gives constructive notice to Charles, a later BFP. About half the states rule in favor of Alice, holding that the chain of title includes all instruments of record up to the moment the subsequent purchaser acquires title, even though they may be recorded after a grantor has first parted with record title. In these jurisdictions, a diligent title searcher must shoulder the huge burden of searching the grantor index forward to the present for each person who ever owned the property. See, e.g., *Woods v. Garnett,* 72 Miss. 78 (1894); *Westbrook v. Gleason,* 79 N.Y. 23 (1879); *Mahoney v. Middleton,* 41 Cal. 41 (1871); *Angle v. Slayton,* 102 N.M. 521 (1985). The other half of the states would rule in favor of Charles, reasoning that a title searcher should be excused from further search forward in time after he finds a recorded conveyance of title from the grantor to another person. Thus, once a searcher has found the Ovoid-to-Ben deed, he need not search any further forward in time. In these jurisdictions, the Ovoid-to-Alice deed is outside the chain of title and provides no constructive notice. See, e.g., *Morse v. Curtis,* 140 Mass. 112 (1885); *Day v. Clark,* 25 Vt. 397(1853).

v.   **Prior deed recorded after partial payment by later purchaser:** Courts are much vexed over the following problem: Owner conveys to Prior Purchaser, who fails to record the deed; Owner then conveys to Later Buyer (who lacks notice of the prior conveyance) under a contract calling for a down payment and subsequent payments; Later Buyer records his deed but before making the final payment learns of the prior conveyance. Who should prevail: Prior Purchaser, because Later Buyer was on notice of the prior claim before he fully paid (depriving Later Buyer of BFP status) or Later Buyer, because he lacked notice at the time he entered into the transaction? The traditional answer is to prefer Prior Purchaser and employ *restitution* as the remedy: Give the property to Prior Purchaser on condition that he reimburse Later Buyer for the payments made by him. The alternative answer is to give Later Buyer the ***benefit of the bargain:*** Award the property to Later Buyer but require that the remaining payments be made to Prior Purchaser rather than Owner.

★**Example — Restitution:** Jacula conveyed a lot to Daniels and in the contract of sale gave Daniels a right of first refusal to purchase another parcel contiguous to the first lot (the "Contiguous Parcel"). The contract was not recorded. Later, Jacula conveyed the Contiguous Parcel to Zografos for $60,000, under an installment sale contract calling for a $10,000 down payment and later installments. Zagrofos paid Jacula another $30,000 before learning of Daniels's prior claim, made the final payment of $20,000, and then received and recorded a deed. Daniels sought and received specific performance of his purchase option. In ***Daniels v. Anderson,*** 162 Ill. 2d 47 (1994), the Illinois Supreme Court affirmed, reasoning that Zografos was protected by his lack of notice only for the payments made before he received notice, and concluding that an award of the property to Daniels with a requirement that Daniels reimburse Zografos for the total of his payments to Jacula was the best method to deal with the mischief caused by Jacula.

★**Example — Restitution:** Thomas and his son Charles owned a house as equal tenants in common. Thomas then conveyed his interest in the house to Mary, his daughter. A week later, Thomas conveyed the same interest to Charles in return for $1,000 and Charles's promise to care for Thomas for the remainder of his life. Charles, who was unaware of the prior deed to Mary, recorded his deed. A few months later, Mary recorded her deed. Charles cared for Thomas until Thomas's death. Mary claimed a half interest based on her prior deed; Charles claimed to be a subsequent purchaser without notice of Mary's prior claim. In ***Alexander v. Andrews,*** 135 W. Va. 403 (1951), the West Virginia Supreme Court held that Charles was protected only to the extent of the $1,000 he paid before Mary recorded. The value of his care of Thomas after Mary's recording was expended with constructive notice of Mary's claim.

★**Example — Benefit of the bargain:** The Lewises agreed to purchase a house from Shipley for $2.3 million. Before the closing, Fontana Films filed for recording a *lis pendens* on the house. A *lis pendens* is a notice of pending litigation in which the plaintiff claims an ownership interest in the subject property; once duly recorded, it is a lien on title, and any subsequent purchaser takes subject to the plaintiff's claim. On February 28, 1992, the Lewises paid Shipley $350,000 down, gave Shipley their note for $1,950,000, and received and recorded a deed. On February 29, 1992, the *lis pendens* was indexed, the magic moment of recording in California; from then on, it constituted constructive notice. (Note that, because California is a race-notice state, Fontana lost its priority to the Lewises because they recorded first without notice.) In March 1992, the Lewises paid Shipley the balance due on their note and then spent another $1 million or so on renovations. (This is Southern California.) Only in September 1993, when Fontana Films served them with summons and complaint, did the Lewises acquire *actual notice* of Fontana's claim, but, of course, they had *constructive notice* of Fontana's claim since February 29, 1992. The Lewises sued to remove the *lis pendens* and quiet title in their names. A trial court denied this relief but, in *Lewis v. Superior Court,* 30 Cal. App. 4th 1850 (1994), the California intermediate appeals court reversed. Limiting an 1895 California Supreme Court opinion applying the traditional rule to its specific facts, the court of appeal thought that the Lewises should get the benefit of their bargain for four reasons: (1) The traditional rule is inconsistent with modern expectations of a buyer who makes part payment and binds himself irrevocably to pay the rest of the purchase price; (2) the Lewises lacked actual notice throughout the saga, and application of the traditional rule to constructive notice "penalizes a completely innocent purchaser for simply living up to his payment obligations"; (3) equity requires that the wrongdoer's interests be sacrificed first and, although the court did not say so, as among the trio involved in *Lewis,* inasmuch as Shipley had been paid, the loss should fall on the party best able to avoid it — Fontana, because it could have recorded its *lis pendens* in timely fashion so that it would have been of record when the Lewises closed their deal with Shipley; and (4) the traditional rule provides an anomalous and unwarranted benefit to cash buyers (or those who finance their purchase with third-party lenders rather than by installment sale or purchase money mortgages from the seller).

b. **Inquiry notice:** In most states, a subsequent purchaser has an obligation to make reasonable inquiries and is charged with knowledge of what those reasonable inquiries would reveal. The following subsections explore some of the circumstances that trigger a duty to inquire.

  i. **Record reference to an unrecorded instrument:** If a recorded instrument refers expressly to an unrecorded instrument, a purchaser is under an obligation in many states to inquire about the substance of the unrecorded instrument to which the record refers.

  ★**Example:** In 1922, Susan Harper conveyed her Georgia farm to Maude Harper for life, remainder to Maude's children. The deed was mislaid and thus not recorded. In 1928,

Susan having died, Susan's children executed and delivered a quitclaim deed to Maude by which they conveyed any interest they might have in the farm to Maude. The 1928 deed, which contained a recital that it was "to take the place of the deed made and executed by Mrs. Susan Harper during her lifetime," was duly recorded. In 1933, Maude executed a deed of trust of the farm to Ella Thornton to secure a $50 loan. Thornton foreclosed after default and received a sheriff's deed, recorded in 1936. Through a succession of recorded conveyances from Thornton, title to the farm was vested in 1955 in the Paradises. In 1957, the mislaid 1922 deed was found and recorded. Upon Maude's death in 1972, her children sued to recover possession. A trial court ruled for the Paradises, but in *Harper v. Paradise,* 233 Ga. 194 (1974), the Georgia Supreme Court reversed. Paradise could not rely on a Georgia statute protecting the title of innocent purchasers from heirs or apparent heirs who lack actual notice of prior claims, because the recitals in the 1928 deed made specific reference to an unrecorded 1922 deed, thus negating the inference that otherwise would exist that the makers of the 1928 deed were conveying their inherited interest. Adverse possession was unavailing for the Paradises because their entry was against Maude, and all Maude owned was a life estate; thus, the limitations period did not begin to run until Maude's death in 1972. Although the 1928 deed, upon which the Paradises' title was founded, was recorded before the 1922 deed, upon which Maude's children based their claim, Georgia is a race-notice state, and the court concluded that the recitals in the 1928 deed placed a duty upon subsequent purchasers to inquire of Maude to determine the details of the unrecorded deed referred to in the 1928 deed. Thus, the Paradises had constructive notice of the prior claim when they acquired title and so lost.

This rule is not universally followed, especially when the issue is whether a subsequent taker should be charged with inquiry notice by a recorded memorandum of a lease that does not set forth the specifics of the lease. Compare *Mister Donut of America, Inc. v. Kemp,* 368 Mass. 220 (1975) (inquiry notice, subsequent taker charged with constructive notice of lease contents), with *Howard D. Johnson Co. v. Parkside Dev. Corp.,* 169 Ind. App. 379 (1976) (no inquiry notice and thus no constructive notice of the lease contents).

ii. **Possession:** Most states impose a duty to inquire of whoever is in possession of the subject property.

★**Example:** Choctaw Partnership, a developer, built a condominium complex financed by construction loans secured by a recorded mortgage, later assigned to Eglin National Bank. Then Choctaw sold Unit 111 to Waldorff under a contract of sale that was unrecorded, but sufficient to vest in Waldorff equitable title to Unit 111. Waldorff moved in and occupied Unit 111 for 11/2 years, then moved out but kept furnishings in the unit and asserted exclusive possessory rights to the unit. Choctaw borrowed additional money from Eglin, secured by a recorded mortgage to a number of condominium units, including Unit 111. Then Choctaw, which owed Waldorff money, executed and delivered a deed to Unit 111 in return for Waldorff's cancellation of the debt. Waldorff recorded the deed. Choctaw then defaulted on its notes to Eglin, and Eglin sought to foreclose on Unit 111. The trial court ruled that Eglin's prior recorded mortgage liens had priority over Waldorff's interest, but in *Waldorff Insurance & Bonding, Inc. v. Eglin Natl. Bank,* 453 So. 2d 1383 (Fla. App. 1984), the Florida intermediate appeals court reversed. Because Waldorff was in possession, Eglin was on inquiry notice that Waldorff might have a prior unrecorded claim. Even though Waldorff, as the party in possession, in theory might be the party who could avoid the problem by recording, it is unlikely that the contract of sale was notarized and capable of recording. Sellers under installment sale contracts dislike making such contracts recordable because they wish to avoid any clouds on title until the purchase price is fully paid.

If inquiry would reveal that the possessor occupies under an unrecorded conveyance from the record owner, the subsequent purchaser has constructive notice of the claim by virtue of this doctrine of inquiry notice. See, e.g., *Miller v. Green,* 264 Wis. 159 (1953) (inquiry notice of a prior unrecorded contract of sale to a farm predicated upon the later buyer's knowledge of the prior purchaser's acts of fertilizing and plowing the farm in November, time when only owners are apt to be working their land). There are various permutations on the inquiry notice theme: Some states limit the obligation to inquire to instances where the possession is by a stranger to the record title; others limit inquiry to instances where the later purchaser has actual knowledge of the existence of a possessor.

   iii. **Character of neighborhood:** As discussed in Chapter 9, reciprocal implied covenants restricting land use may also be implied by a uniform development scheme undertaken by a common owner/developer of property. In states that recognize implied reciprocal covenants from a common scheme, a purchaser is under a duty to inquire about the deeds out from a common grantor, deeds that may establish the common scheme, if the character of the neighborhood suggests such a common scheme. The leading case is *Sanborn v. McLean,* 233 Mich. 227 (1925).

   iv. **Immediate grantee of a quitclaim deed:** A few jurisdictions hold that a conveyance by quitclaim deed is inherently suspect because it raises doubts about the grantor's belief in the validity of his own title. Thus, the immediate grantee of a quitclaim deed is obligated to inquire into the actual state of the grantor's title and cannot simply rely on the public records. But this is ***not the majority rule;*** in most states, the mere fact that a conveyance is by quitclaim deed does not trigger inquiry notice. See 6A Powell, *The Law of Real Property*, ¶905[1][B] (rev. ed. 1992).

3. **Tract index: A solution to chain-of-title problems?** Grantor-grantee indexes, which are by far the most common form of index to public land records in the United States, spawn a variety of problems with the chain of title, which have been discussed above. Many of these problems will not occur with a tract index, but most jurisdictions do not maintain tract indexes, and it would be very expensive to find and index, by tract, all of the prior transactions currently indexed by grantor and grantee.

I. **Marketable-title acts:** Marketable-title acts are the principal legislative response to the fact that, like all human systems, the recording system is imperfect. Eighteen states have adopted marketable-title acts, which are designed to limit the relevant chain of title to some specified period of recent history — from 22 to 50 years in the past. If a chain of title can be traced back to a root of title older than the period prescribed by the marketable-title act (say, 40 years) most claims based on some older instrument are barred by the statute, unless they are incorporated into a later instrument recorded during the marketable-title period.

Example: Blackacre is located in a state with a 40-year marketable title act. In 1953, Elvis, the record owner of Blackacre, conveyed to Frank an easement for parking on Blackacre, which Frank recorded. George purchased Blackacre from Elvis via a deed recorded in 1955. In 1964, George conveyed and recorded an easement for cable television access to Cablecorp. The present record owner is Lottie, who purchased from George via a deed recorded in 1970. The deed from Elvis to George is the root of title, because it is more than 40 years old. If the state's act makes no exception for older claims, the easement in Frank is extinguished by the marketable title act, but the easement in favor of Cablecorp is valid because it is of record within the past 40 years. Note that, in 2010, the root of title will be updated to the George-to-Lottie deed in 1970, and that will eliminate the easement in favor of Cablecorp, which dates from 1964. This presumes also that none of the post-1953 deeds refers to Frank's parking easement and that none of the post-1964 deeds refers to the Cablecorp easement.

1. **Validity of pre-root interests:** Unless the act makes a specific exception for pre-root interests, pre-root interests are only valid if (1) they are referred to in the root of title itself or some post-root recorded instrument, or (2) they are recorded anew during the marketable-title-act period. In the preceding example, Frank and Cablecorp could keep their easements alive by re-recording them every 40 years.

   a. **Statutory exceptions:** The interests excepted from marketable-title acts vary. Most statutes except most easements, claims of the current possessor, restrictive covenants, and, sometimes, mineral rights. These exceptions undercut the utility of marketable-title acts.

III. TITLE REGISTRATION—THE TORRENS SYSTEM

A. **Introduction:** Title registration is a substitute for recording. Instead of recording evidence of title, which is what a recording system does, a registration system makes a certificate of title the exclusive and definitive title. Title registration was invented in Australia in 1858 by Sir Richard Torrens, whose name is commonly used to describe the system. For a registration system to work, there must first be a final and conclusive determination of ownership, binding on all the world. This requires a court proceeding to cut off all rival claims. Then the definitive title is registered and indexed in a tract index. When ownership changes, the certificate of title is canceled, and a new one issued. The Torrens system is widely used in England, Canada, Australia, and New Zealand. Title registration is an option in 11 American states but is not much used.

B. **Adjudication of title:** To implement title registration, it is necessary to adjudicate title, in order to cut off all possible rival claims. The owner must bring an *in rem* action that is functionally identical to a quiet title action. Notice must be given to all persons who might have any conceivable claim to title or an interest in the property. At the conclusion of this proceeding, the court will issue a certificate of title that declares the definitive title to the property. It will state the owner and itemize as "memorials" all encumbrances upon the property (e.g., mortgages, easements, covenants, and liens).

   1. **Scope of the certificate of title:** The certificate of title *is title.* It is binding on the entire world and cuts off all interests not included as memorials on the certificate, except for those discussed in this section. Otherwise, the certificate as registered in the public records is conclusive title. It is thus not possible to acquire title by adverse possession against a registered title. However, the exceptions that follow are significant and undercut the utility of title registration.

a. **Federal government claims:** States lack the power to adjudicate claims of the federal government unless the federal government consents to such adjudication. Thus, a certificate of title does not eliminate federal tax liens or any other interest that might be claimed by the federal government.

b. **Statutory exceptions:** Most of the American Torrens statutes except from the certificate of title mineral claims, visible easements, utility or railroad easements, public thoroughfares, and interests or claims of state or local governments or persons in actual possession. These exceptions make the certificate of title a lot less definitive and conclusive than it purports to be.

c. **Defective notice in initial adjudication:** If a person with an interest in the property does not receive constitutionally acceptable notice of the initial title adjudication proceeding, the certificate of title that results is not effective to bar the person's interest. The Due Process Clause of the Fourteenth Amendment requires that governments give people adequate notice and opportunity to be heard before taking their property away.

d. **Fraud:** If fraud or deceit is employed to procure the initial certificate of title, it can be set aside by the true owner or, alternatively, the registered owner will be held to hold in constructive trust for the true owner. It is not clear whether the true owner could obtain the same remedies against a bona fide purchaser of registered title from the initial and deceitful "owner." If the initial certificate of title is validly obtained, subsequent fraud that results in a new certificate upon which a bona fide purchaser relies is not sufficient to cancel the title held by the BFP.

   Example: Arnold adjudicates title to Blackacre and obtains a certificate of title. Then Arnold gives his copy of his certificate to his brother, Bill, who forges Arnold's signature to obtain a new registered title in Bill's name. Then Bill sells Blackacre for value to Jane, who knows nothing of Bill's forgery. Jane has a valid registered title that cannot be upset by Arnold.

e. **Not bona fide purchaser:** Courts in many Torrens jurisdictions have preserved the rule that a person who takes with notice of some off-record claim or interest takes subject to that claim. Thus, a purchaser of registered title who actually knows of some interest not included as a memorial on the registered title is often held to take subject to that interest. See, e.g., *Butler v. Haley Greystone Corp.,* 347 Mass. 478 (1964).

C. Public records and title transfers in the Torrens system

1. **Public records:** Once a registered title has been adjudicated, the official certificate of title is given to the recorder for preservation, and a copy is given to the owner. The recorder will then maintain a tract index of registered titles and will enter in it the certificate of title. A title searcher simply finds the property in the tract index and reads the certificate of title. If any memorials are noted on the certificate (e.g., mortgages), the searcher will then look up the mortgage instrument to read it fully.

2. **Title transfers:** The holder of registered title may transfer title by surrendering his certificate, together with a deed or other instrument conveying title, to the recorder. The recorder will then cancel the old registered title and issue a new one in the name of the purchaser. If a holder of registered title mortgages the property, the mortgage is simply added as a memorial. If the mortgage is then paid off, the memorial is removed.

3. **Errors by the recorder:** Because the registered title *is title,* errors by the recorder are especially significant. If, for example, the recorder fails to include a mortgage as a memorial on the certificate of title, the mortgage is extinguished. Or, if the recorder means to register title to Blackacre in Jones but actually registers title to Blackacre in Smith, Blackacre is owned by Smith, not Jones. This is a serious flaw; Torrens systems deal with this by providing for compensation to those who lose their interests due to recorder error, but the funds provided for compensation "are often absurdly small in comparison to . . . potential liability." Nelson, Stoebuck, and Whitman, *Contemporary Property,* 1004 (1996). Moreover, governments use their sovereign immunity to avoid liability except to the extent of these meager compensation funds. Understandably, this glaring flaw has been a strong inhibition to acceptance of Torrens registration.

D. **The practical realities of Torrens registration:** Torrens registration has not caught on in the United States, for three good reasons: initial cost, lack of comprehensiveness, and the risk of uncompensated recorder error.

1. **Cost:** The initial cost of title adjudication is high, and most of its benefits are reaped in the form of lower costs of transferring title. There is little incentive for the first owner to incur costs for the benefit of later owners. A developer, however, might find it advantageous to register title for an entire subdivision, in order to minimize the title transfer costs as the subdivided lots are sold, and because the initial cost can be spread over the entire subdivision.

2. **Lack of comprehensiveness:** The exceptions that riddle the purported global effect of a certificate of title further dampen the incentive to incur the cost of obtaining a certificate that is not as conclusive as it is supposed to be.

3. **Risk of uncompensated error:** This problem could be corrected by governmental assumption of liability for all recorder errors, but it is probably politically and practically impossible for financially hard-pressed state and local governments to do so.

E. **Economic theory and Torrens registration:** Under Torrens registration, the possessor of the registered title prevails as against a claimant to title, however meritorious the claim might be in the absence of Torrens registration. Under the recording system, a meritorious claimant prevails against the possessor. This is of consequence if possessors attach a subjective value to their property, such that they value continued possession more than its market value to prospective purchasers. Many possessors (especially of residences) do attach subjective value to their homes. Under these conditions, Torrens is better at accomplishing "exchange efficiency" — ensuring that the property ends up in the hands of the party who values it more highly — *if transaction costs of reassigning the right are high.*

Example: Arthur owns Blackacre and would not part with title for less than $100,000. Nobody else would pay more than $70,000 for Blackacre. Arthur's subjective value of Blackacre is $30,000. Bertha, a meritorious claimant to Blackacre, would happily sell Blackacre for $70,000 (its market value) once she secures possession. Under the recording system, Bertha would prevail, and Arthur would appear to lose his subjective value. Because Arthur values Blackacre more highly than Bertha, he would presumably pay Bertha a price somewhere between $70,000 and $100,000 to retain possession. Only if transaction costs exceed $30,000 (the total potential gains from trade) would the reassignment of the right back to Arthur not occur. Under the Torrens system, Arthur would prevail and reap the full subjective value of $30,000. If transactions costs are higher than the subjective value, Torrens produces an "exchange-efficient" outcome. If not,

Torrens simply ensures that possessors of registered title reap all the gains, thus essentially distributing income to Torrens holders from meritorious claimants.

Another measure of efficiency is "development efficiency," or the maximization of incentives for socially productive use of land. In theory, because Torrens ensures that there will no claimants, the risk of development is lowered, and "development efficiency" is increased under the Torrens system. This conclusion, however, is undercut by the fact that title insurance to indemnify against claims under the recording system is readily available at a reasonable cost, and because the exceptions to Torrens registration are large enough to make it a practical necessity to obtain title insurance for a development even if the developer possesses Torrens title.

F. Possessory title registration: An innovative variant on the Torrens system is to permit landowners to register their title for a nominal fee, but receive a certificate of title that is good only from that day forward. Any claims or interests affecting the property that predate the issuance of the certificate of title are fully preserved. The certificate is not initially of much value, but, over time, old claims or interests might disappear. When coupled with a statute of limitations as to old claims (patterned after the marketable-title acts), the certificate of title issued under a possessory title registration system would become conclusive after the elapse of the limitations period. This would eliminate the initial cost objection to Torrens registration but, by itself, does nothing to eliminate the problems of lack of comprehensiveness or risk of uncompensated recorder error. Minnesota is the only state to have adopted possessory title registration as a voluntary option.

IV. TITLE INSURANCE

A. Introduction: Title insurance is the most common form of title assurance in the United States. Title insurance involves the issuance of an insurance policy to a person — usually either a mortgage lender or a purchaser of property — by which the insurer warrants that title is as stated in the policy. The policy is a personal contract between the insurer and the person who buys the policy. Title insurers perform their own examination of the public land records in order to issue an insurance policy. They either employ lawyers to search the public records, or they maintain their own duplicate set of records, identical to that found in the recorder's office, but often supplemented by a tract index of their own creation.

B. Coverage: The scope of coverage is determined by the contract of insurance. The usual policy insures only that the title stated in the policy is a good record title. The policy does not insure against claims or interests that are not part of the record. Essentially, the insured has a claim under the policy only if someone else asserts a claim based on the public records inconsistent with the record title as stated in the policy.

1. Duty to disclose defects in title: Courts are beginning to impose on title insurers a duty to disclose anything they know about the parcel in question that is material or important, breach of which is actionable in tort.

★**Example:** Kosa acquired a parcel of land from Aiello under a deed that stated the total acreage of the tract was 12.486 acres, based on a survey done by Schilling. Walker Rogge agreed to purchase the tract from Kosa, after Kosa had shown Rogge a survey done by Price Walker that stated the tract consisted of 18.33 acres. The Kosa-to-Rogge contract stated that the acreage was 19 acres, more or less, and stipulated that the purchase price was to be reduced by $16,000 per acre if the tract was, in fact, smaller in area. The Kosa-to-Rogge deed referred to the Price

Walker survey but did not state the acreage. Rogge hired Chelsea Title to examine and insure title. Chelsea did so, issuing an insurance policy that excepted from its coverage "matters which could be disclosed by an accurate survey." At the time Chelsea issued the policy, it had in its files a copy of the Aiello-to-Kosa deed, stating the tracts's area to be 12.486 acres. In fact, the tract's acreage was 12.43 acres, close to the Schilling survey of 12.486 acres but significantly less than the Price Walker survey of 18.33 acres. Rogge sued Chelsea for damages on the title insurance policy and also for Chelsea's negligence in failing to disclose the acreage figure stated in the Aiello-to-Kosa deed. A trial court held that Chelsea was liable on its insurance contract because the quoted exception was too vague to apply to these facts, and that Chelsea had no liability in tort because it had not assumed a duty to search title and disclose the results of its title search. In *Walker Rogge, Inc. v. Chelsea Title & Guaranty Co.,* 116 N.J. 517 (1989), the New Jersey Supreme Court reversed on the first point, upheld the second finding, but remanded for consideration of a different tort issue. First, the contract exception was clear enough to exempt Chelsea from contractual liability for an acreage shortfall that an accurate survey would reveal. Second, there was substantial evidence to support the trial court's finding that Chelsea had undertaken a duty only to *insure* title, and that any *search* of title was for its own benefit and ancillary to its duty to insure. However, the court remanded for a determination of whether Chelsea had assumed a duty to assure Rogge of the correct acreage of the tract. Facts suggestive of that duty included the following: (1) Chelsea had twice before insured title to the tract and had in its files a copy of the Aiello-to-Kosa deed stating the area at 12.486 acres, and (2) Chelsea handled the closing at which the purchase price was based on the tract's acreage. Under these circumstances, perhaps Chelsea had a duty to reveal to Rogge what it knew (or should have known).

About half the states impose a duty on title insurers to disclose all defects uncovered by the insurer's title search. Thus, if a title insurer issues an insurance policy excluding "encroachments not of record" but discovers an actual, unrecorded encroachment, it has insured only good record title but still has an obligation to reveal the actual encroachment it has discovered.

2. **Marketable title and encumbrances:** Although title insurance policies typically insure against any loss caused by *defects in title,* or *liens* or *encumbrances upon title,* or *unmarketability of title,* courts limit the scope of this coverage to *title* rather than extending it to cover palpable diminutions of *value* that affect marketability but have no bearing on the clarity or certainty of ownership.

★**Example:** Lick Mill Apartments purchased and developed a portion of a 30-acre tract that had formerly been the site of chemical-processing plants and warehouses. Chicago Title insured title against defects, liens, encumbrances, and unmarketability. Prior to insuring title, Chicago Title hired Carroll to inspect the site, and Carroll reported the "presence of certain pipes, tanks, [and] pumps." When title was insured the records of various government agencies disclosed the "presence of hazardous substances" on the property, but it was not clear whether those records were inspected by or known to either Lick Mill or Chicago Title. After Lick Mill took title, it was required to expend considerable sums to remove and clean up the toxins on the site. Lick Mill then sought to recover those costs from Chicago Title, alleging that the toxins made title unmarketable and constituted an encumbrance on title. In *Lick Mill Creek Apartments v. Chicago Title Insurance Co.,* 231 Cal. App. 3d 1654 (1991), the California intermediate appeals court rejected these contentions. The court distinguished *unmarketable title* and *unmarketable land;* the former consists of a serious problem with the claim to ownership, and the latter consists of a serious problem with the physical condition or location of the property.

Lick Mill's *title* was impeccable, but the toxic wastes present on the land made the property unsaleable. As to encumbrances, while the toxic wastes did produce continuing liability of any owner to clean up the mess, that fact was rooted in the property's physical condition, not some continuing defect of the claim to ownership that is title. Note that in ***Lohmeyer v. Bower*** (Chapter 6), a present violation of a zoning law constituted unmarketable title sufficient to enable a buyer to rescind his purchase contract, but in ***Frimberger v. Anzellotti*** (Chapter 6), a present violation of a zoning law did not constitute unmarketable title for purposes of breach of the covenant of general warranty. As with ***Frimberger,*** the difference in result is due to the *ex post* or *ex ante* posture of the problem. When the deal is still inchoate (***Lohmeyer***), it makes sense to allow it to unravel, for that permits avoidance of damage before it hardens, but when it is done (***Frimberger*** and ***Lick Mill***), a finding of unmarketable title shifts costs, perhaps unfairly. Diligent investigation on Lick Mills's part would have enabled it to avoid the loss; shifting the loss to Chicago Title would greatly increase the scope of liability for title insurers, thus raising the cost of title insurance generally and probably imperiling the continuing existence of some insurers.

3. **Exclusions:** Policies typically contain specific exclusions from coverage, including such items as ***liens not on the record*** (e.g., mechanics' liens), ***off-record interests asserted by persons in possession*** (e.g., adverse possession), ***boundary disputes*** (e.g., encroachments or other boundary disputes not of record but which might be revealed by a survey), ***off-record easements or servitudes*** (e.g., implied easements or covenants or prescriptive easements), and ***government land-use regulations.***

4. **Measure of damages:** A title insurer is generally liable for the difference in value of the property with and without the insured-against defect, up to the maximum liability specified in the policy. This is true regardless of the amount paid for the property.

   Example: Jonah purchased Blackacre for $50,000 and obtained Titleco's insurance policy for $20,000 insuring good record title. It turns out that Watts, an adjacent landowner, has a record easement over Blackacre for access. If the value of Blackacre without the easement is $65,000, and the value of Blackacre with the easement is $40,000, Jonah has suffered $25,000 in damages but can only recover $20,000 (the policy limits), even though the diminution in value from Jonah's purchase price is only $10,000. This rule makes sense because Jonah is entitled to the full benefits of his excellent bargain.

Exam Tips *on*
ASSURING GOOD TITLE TO LAND

☞ Recording acts provide ample opportunity to create a complicated exam question. First, be certain you understand how each of the types of acts works, and recognize which is which — your professor may simply quote a statute and not tell you what it is. Second, be sure you understand what constitutes notice. Actual notice is easy; the problems arise with constructive and inquiry notice. Constructive notice is supplied by the chain of title from the record, and that raises the question of what constitutes the chain of title and what is in the record. States differ on these points; you need to be certain that you understand the policy arguments that surround these differences. Third, be sure you understand the scope of protection afforded by the acts. Note the shelter rule, which protects transferees from bona fide purchasers who are protected, even if the transferee might independently lack protection.

☛ A marketable-title-act problem can easily be combined with a recording act problem. The two types of acts perform different functions.

☛ Title insurance issues typically revolve around the scope of the insurance contract. While your professor may test on this, typically neither this nor registered title is likely to be a significant examination issue.

JUDICIAL CONTROL OF LAND USE: NUISANCE AND SUPPORT

ChapterScope

This chapter examines control of land use through the tort concept of nuisance, and various ways the judiciary can resolve these claims of nuisance. A related concept, lateral and subjacent support, is also discussed. Here are the most important points in this chapter.

- Nuisance is a relative concept. Nuisance consists of an intentional use of one's property that is unreasonable and substantially interferes with another person's use and enjoyment of their property, or an unintentional use that is negligent, reckless, or inherently dangerous and substantially interferes with another person's use and enjoyment of their property. However, none of this answers the question of which use should be preferred.

  - There are three views of when an intentional use is unreasonable. First, a use is unreasonable if the gravity of the harm it inflicts outweighs its social utility; second, a use is unreasonable if the harm inflicted is serious and the actor could compensate for this and similar harms without ceasing the activity; and, third, a use is unreasonable if the harm it inflicts exceeds some minimal threshold of discomfort that no one should be expected to endure.

- Because nuisance necessarily involves a weighing of the utility of two competing uses, courts have begun to experiment with the use of liability rules (which force the transfer of rights upon compensation) as well as property rules (which protect against forced transfer of rights). The result is four possible outcomes of nuisance suits, two of which use property rules and two which use liability rules.

  - Under either of the property rule outcomes, any later transfer of the right must be voluntary, and economically efficient transfers may be inhibited by high transaction costs.

    - No nuisance, no remedy.

    - Nuisance enjoined.

  - Under either of the liability rule outcomes, the judicial system forces a transfer of rights upon compensation to the other party. The justification for using liability rules instead of property rules is that this will produce a socially efficient outcome.

    - Nuisance permitted to continue upon payment of full compensation to affected property owners for the past and future damages

    - No nuisance, but the activity is enjoined upon payment of compensation to the enjoined user of the full costs of relocation

- Nuisances can be public or private. A public nuisance is a use that imposes harms on the entire public with no particularized harm on any private landowner.

I. THE SUBSTANCE OF NUISANCE

A. **The general principle:** An ancient common law maxim, *sic utere tuo ut alienum non laedas (one must use one's property so as not to injure another's property)* is the root of nuisance. Unfortunately, the maxim is not much help, because often one person's beneficial use is another person's injury and, in practice, some injuries to another's land are permitted and others not. It is more helpful to say that a person may not use his own land in an **unreasonable manner** that **substantially** lessens another person's **use and enjoyment** of his land. A nuisance may be **private** or **public.** A private nuisance involves interference with purely private rights to the use and enjoyment of land — usually one or more nearby landowners. A public nuisance involves interference with public rights — those held in common by everybody — but a public nuisance can also be a private nuisance.

B. **Private nuisances:** A private nuisance occurs when there is **substantial interference** with private rights to use and enjoy land, produced by **either** of the following:

- *Intentional and unreasonable* conduct, or

- *Unintentional* conduct that is either **negligent, reckless,** or so **inherently dangerous** that **strict liability** is imposed.

  ★**Example:** High Penn operated an oil refinery that emitted noxious odors several times each week, polluting the air for about a two-mile radius from the refinery. Along with many other people who owned land located within that radius, Morgan sued to enjoin the refinery's operations, alleging that the noxious odors made him sick and deprived him of use and enjoyment of his property. In *Morgan v. High Penn Oil Co.,* 238 N.C. 185 (1953), the North Carolina Supreme Court agreed, applying the hornbook rule that a use is a nuisance if it is *either **intentional and unreasonable** or **unintentionally produced by negligence, recklessness, or extremely dangerous activity.*** High Penn intended to operate the refinery and knew, or should have known, that its operation would produce the noxious odors, and the court assumed its use was unreasonable but did not explain quite why.

1. **Intentional conduct:** This is the most common form of nuisance. Intentional conduct is action that is known by the actor to interfere with another's use of land, but which is continued nevertheless. The focus here is upon whether the conduct is an **unreasonable interference** with another's land, but what is unreasonable? There are three views.

    a. **Balancing: Harm and social utility:** If the **gravity of the harm** *inflicted by the conduct outweighs its social utility* (unconstrained by nuisance law), the conduct is unreasonable. See *Restatement (Second) of Torts* §826(a). To measure the gravity of the harm, the *Restatement (Second) of Torts* suggests that courts should consider the **extent** of the harm, its **character,** the **social value** of the use, the **suitability of the use to the location,** and the **burden of avoiding the harm.** See *Restatement (Second) of Torts* §827 (1979). To measure the utility of the offending conduct, the *Restatement (Second) of Torts* suggests that courts should consider the **social value** of the conduct, its **suitability to the location,** and the **practical difficulty of preventing the harm.** See *Restatement (Second) of Torts* §828. The first *Restatement of Torts,* §827, distinguished between harm that damaged property and harm to personal comfort: "Where the invasion involves physical damage to tangible property, the gravity of the harm is ordinarily regarded as great even though the extent of the harm is relatively small. But where the invasion involves only personal discomfort and annoyance, the gravity of the harm is generally regarded as slight unless the invasion is substantial and continuing." That distinction is discarded by the *Restatement (Second) of Torts*, which applies its balancing formula globally. In practice, this multifaceted balancing test makes the issue of unreasonable use turn on the specific facts: "A nuisance may be merely the right thing in the wrong place — like a pig in the parlor instead of the barnyard." *Village of Euclid v. Ambler Realty Co.,* 272 U.S. 365 (1926). In theory, fault is not an issue — the most careful and prudent use is a nuisance if its harm outweighs its utility. In essence, this test gives judges the opportunity to assess the worth of competing uses and to decide which user should shoulder the costs inherent in two incompatible uses. This becomes quite indeterminate when you consider the possibility that any use inflicts some costs on others, and that the label "nuisance" simply becomes a way of allocating presumptive entitlement to any particular use. Perhaps for this reason the traditional remedies for nuisance have become considerably more sophisticated and capable of nuance, which suggests that some of the work of deciding what constitutes a nuisance has been transferred into the law of remedies for nuisance. See section II, below.

b. **Balancing: Uncompensated harm and ruinous liability:** A variation on balancing harm and social utility is contained in the *Restatement (Second) of Torts* §826(b), which holds that an intentional activity is unreasonable if it causes *serious harm* and *the actor could compensate for that and similar harm without going out of business.* This test becomes problematic only when the defendant would be forced out of business by compensating for the harm he causes, for in such circumstances this test would conclude that the activity is not unreasonable and thus not a nuisance. In essence, under those circumstances a court is asked to decide which is worse — uncompensated harm or forcing businesses to close. There are at least two reasons why an actor inflicting serious harm might be excused from liability because he can't afford to pay for the harm: (1) the injured party is able to avoid the harm at less cost than the compensation, and (2) the harm-inflicting activity generates positive externalities — benefits that the actor cannot capture and use to compensate the injured party but which outweigh the harm. The latter point takes you back to harm versus social utility. In theory, this test could be used globally, but its application inevitably becomes bound up in the remedies for nuisance. When the plaintiff seeks to enjoin a claimed nuisance, compensation is not a factor, and the general balancing of harm and social utility is applicable, but when the issue is whether a nuisance should continue upon payment of compensation to those harmed (see section II.D. below), this test becomes relevant.

c. **Substantial harm: The liability threshold:** A number of courts tacitly or explicitly ignore the balancing test if *substantial harm* is inflicted. In these jurisdictions, a nuisance exists if the injury it inflicts is severe enough to be above some maximum level of interference that a person can be expected to endure without redress — a "threshold of liability." An old Wisconsin case, *Pennoyer v. Allen,* 56 Wis. 502 (1883), is typical in defining substantial injury as "tangible" injury or a "discomfort perceptible to the senses of ordinary people."

Example: Dairyland Power's electrical generation plant spewed sulphur dioxide into the air, causing tangible but minor property damage to Jost's house and farm (e.g., rusty screens, inability to grow flowers or garden vegetables, and loss of about 5 percent of Jost's alfalfa crop). In *Jost v. Dairyland Power Cooperative,* 45 Wis. 2d 164 (1969), the Wisconsin Supreme Court ruled that the generation plant was a nuisance. The court invoked the principle, derived from the first *Restatement of Torts,* §827, that "where the invasion involves physical damage to tangible property, the gravity of the harm is ordinarily regarded as great even though the extent of the harm is relatively small." To permit a socially useful public utility to "deprive others of the full use of their property without compensation . . . would constitute the taking of property without due process of law." See also *Dolata v. Berthelet Fuel & Supply,* 254 Wis. 194 (1949), in which an admittedly socially and economically useful coal yard was enjoined as a nuisance because it caused substantial damage to an adjacent landowner. Note that although the court in **Morgan v. High Penn Oil Co.** did not state why the refinery's operation was unreasonable, a second look at the facts suggests that it was applying the *Jost* threshold invasion test.

2. **Unintentional conduct:** When an actor uses his land in a way that unintentionally injures another's use or enjoyment of land, the action is a nuisance if *either* the conduct is below the standard of care commonly required (i.e., it is negligent or reckless) *or* the **risk of harm** is so great that the conduct ought not be tolerated (i.e., it is inherently dangerous, like the unshielded storage of plutonium or large quantities of dynamite). Here the focus is entirely upon the actor's conduct — does it pose an unreasonable risk of harm either because it is careless or inherently dangerous?

3. **Substantial interference:** The alleged nuisance, whether intentional or not, must be a substantial impediment to the use and enjoyment of land. The average person is the standard measurement for substantial interference. See, e.g., **Morgan v. High Penn Oil Co.,** 238 N.C. 185 (1953); *Rose v. Chaikin,* 187 N.J. Super. 210 (1982).

   Example: An operator of a drive-in movie theater sued an adjacent amusement park, on the theory that the bright lights from the amusement park constituted a nuisance. Not so, said the Oregon Supreme Court in *Amphitheaters, Inc. v. Portland Meadows,* 184 Or. 336 (1948); the movie operator's use was "abnormally sensitive." But why should the theater operator's reliance on natural darkness be abnormal? Couldn't the introduction of vast amounts of artificial lighting be considered abnormal? A commonly accepted cultural baseline is required; here, in the midst of the electrified, urbanized industrial economy, the baseline was bright lights at night in an urban area.

   The necessity of using some cultural baseline produces mixed results when cultural attitudes vary or are in flux.

   Example: A halfway house for paroled criminals is established in a residential neighborhood, producing fear of criminal activity and a decline in property values. While one might think that the fear and declining values are indicators of a cultural baseline, courts divide on this issue. In *Arkansas Release Guidance Foundation v. Needler,* 252 Ark. 194 (1972), the Arkansas Supreme Court ruled that such a house was a nuisance, but in *Nickolson v. Connecticut Halfway House,* 153 Conn. 507 (1966), the Connecticut Supreme Court said it was not, even though the fear and the decline in values were present. In *Adkins v. Thomas Solvent Co.,* 440 Mich. 293 (1992), the Michigan Supreme Court ruled that a toxic waste dump did not constitute a nuisance where property values in the area had declined on the strength of well-publicized but unfounded fears of contamination.

C. **Public nuisances:** A public nuisance affects rights held in common by everybody — the public — rather than just private rights of land use held by landowners.

Example: A factory discharging pollutants into a publicly owned watershed, thereby contaminating the municipal water supply, is likely engaging in a public nuisance. Only the common right to potable water for the municipality is affected.

A pure public nuisance is rare — more commonly, a public nuisance is also a private nuisance.

Example: A factory discharging pollutants into a stream that supplies drinking water to downstream farmers as well as a municipality even further downstream is likely engaging in both a public and private nuisance.

The substantive test for a public nuisance is the same as for a private nuisance.

1. **Enforcement:** Public nuisances are normally abated by suits brought by public officials, but a *private citizen* may bring suit to abate a public nuisance if he has been *specially injured* by the nuisance. This means that the private plaintiff has suffered some particularized and personalized injury, but not necessarily in the use and enjoyment of land.

   Example: A factory discharges pollutants into the sea in a quantity sufficient to render the water unsafe for public bathing or fishing, thus creating a public nuisance. Jill, who owns no land, cultivates oysters in the tidal waters, and her oyster farming is ruined by the pollution. Jill may maintain suit to abate the public nuisance. She has suffered a particularized injury, one different from the injury inflicted on the public at large.

   This rule of special injury has been relaxed by statute or judicial decision in some states to permit a private person to sue as the representative of affected persons to abate environmental nuisances.

D. **Relationship to trespass:** Nuisance and trespass are closely related. Trespass involves a physical invasion of a person's land — an interference with his *exclusive right of possession.* By contrast, nuisance involves an interference with another person's right to *use and enjoy his land* and does not necessarily involve interference with the exclusive right of possession. Of course, there is some overlap: If a viscous sludge of animal waste from a hog farm crosses over the boundary to the neighbor's land, the neighbor can assert both trespass and nuisance. As well, the physical invasion that constitutes trespass can be microscopic.

   Example: Reynolds's aluminum plant emitted gases that poisoned Martin's cattle, and Martin prevailed on a trespass theory. On appeal, the Oregon Supreme Court, in *Martin v. Reynolds Metals Co.,* 221 Or. 86 (1959), affirmed, concluding that physical invasion occurred even when the invasion was by "invisible pieces of matter or by energy." Somewhat inexplicably, however, the court applied a balancing test to determine liability. By contrast, in *Wilson v. Interlake Steel Co.,* 32 Cal. 3d 229 (1982), the California Supreme Court ruled that noise alone, unaccompanied by physical property damage or other tangible invasion, did not support a trespass claim. Trespass, once proven, entitles the landowner to damages and an injunction regardless of his lack of any substantial injury. By contrast, a landowner in a nuisance action must prove significant injury in order to recover, as well as unreasonable interference, and (usually) that equity is in his favor. The remedy available to a successful plaintiff in a nuisance action may be an injunction, damages, or even an obligation to pay damages to a defendant as the price for an injunction. See section II, below.

II. REMEDIES: FOUR VIEWS OF NUISANCE

A. **Introduction: The economic theory of modern nuisance law:** The fundamental problem of nuisance law is that property uses are often incompatible. My beneficial use is your injury, and your beneficial use is my injury. If Eve operates a dairy farm on Blackacre, necessarily producing odors that interfere with Adam's outdoor tanning salon on Whiteacre, the two uses are incompatible. Each use interferes with the other—Eve's dairy farm interferes with Adam's tanning salon (the odors inhibit the spa patrons from tanning), and Adam's tanning salon interferes with Eve's dairy farm (by preventing Eve from maintaining a dairy farm in order to accommodate the spa patrons). Each use produces *externalities*—costs that are not imposed on the person producing them. Eve's dairy farm produces the cost (external to Eve) of inhibiting Adam's use as a tanning salon. Adam's tanning salon produces the cost (external to Adam) of preventing Eve's use as a dairy farm in order to accommodate Adam's tanning spa. Economic theorists argue that decisions are more efficient if all of the costs of the decision are internalized—borne by the decision maker. If Adam and Eve were a single unit, the relative costs of these incompatible uses would be weighed by the single decision maker, and the more economically desirable use would prevail. But Adam and Eve are not a single unit. Never mind, said Ronald Coase in his famous Coase Theorem. In a perfect world free of transaction costs, it doesn't matter which of Adam and Eve is entitled to continue their use, because the use right will end up in the hands of the person whose use is the more valuable.

Example: Suppose the damage to Eve from ceasing to use Blackacre as a dairy farm is $100,000, and the damage to Adam from ceasing to use Whiteacre as a tanning salon is $40,000. If the law gives Eve the use right, she will continue her dairy farming, because Adam will pay her no more than $39,999.99 to stop, and that sum is not enough to compensate her for the costs of stopping. But if the use right is given to Adam, he will sell that right to Eve for some price greater than $40,000 and less than $100,000, because both Adam and Eve will be better off by such a bargain. Similarly, if Adam suffered a greater damage than Eve from ceasing his activity, then the use right would end up in Adam's hands no matter where it was initially assigned. All of this, of course, assumes the absence of any transaction costs.

1. **Transaction costs—The gap between theory and reality:** We do not live in a perfect world free of transaction costs. The cost of moving the right from Adam to Eve or Eve to Adam is not zero; it is not even insignificant. Why? There are three standard answers.

    a. **Bilateral monopoly:** When there are only two persons involved in the transfer, there is an inherent bilateral monopoly problem. There is only one seller and only one buyer—dueling monopolies.

        Example: If Adam is given the use right, and Eve values it more highly, Adam has only one potential buyer: Eve. And Eve has only one source from which she can acquire the right she desires: Adam. They are forced to deal with only each other, if they are to deal at all. Adam is likely to want to extract as much of the potential gain of $60,000 ($100,000 – $40,000) as he can, but Eve has the same objective. They will haggle; they will bluster; they will hire lawyers to threaten more litigation and thus spend gains before acquiring them. In short, they will play negotiation games with each other, expending money and time as they do, thus making it harder to reach a deal and diminishing its value even if reached.

Paradoxically, some empirical research suggests that bilateral monopoly situations frequently do result in efficient outcomes, perhaps because people recognize in advance the prospect of wasteful haggling. See, e.g., Hoffman & Spitzer, *The Coase Theorem: Some Experimental Tests*, 25 J.L.&Econ. 73 (1982).

b. Free riders: When there are numerous parties to the negotiation, different problems emerge. One of them is caused by the human impulse to get a free ride at somebody else's expense.

Example: Suppose that, in addition to Adam, there were 99 other property owners, all using their property for uses incompatible with Eve's dairy farm. Suppose that a cessation of each of those additional uses would damage each affected property owner by $40,000. The total cost imposed by giving the use right to Eve would thus be $4,000,000 ($40,000 · 100), but suppose that Eve's use is not a nuisance, despite these disparate numbers. (Perhaps Eve was there first and the other people all "came to the nuisance" fully aware of the problem.) The rational response of Adam and his fellow landowners is to contribute something more than $1,000 apiece to amass a fund of more than $100,000 to purchase Eve's use right from her, but some landowners will not contribute, because they hope to receive the benefit of Eve's cessation of use without paying for it. The knowledge that this may happen will inhibit other landowners from making their contributions, because they dislike giving a free ride to someone else. Moreover, to complete the transfer, the contributing landowners will have to contribute the share of the free riders, and many of them may balk at this. Because there is no effective way to compel contribution, Eve's use right may not be purchased, even though it is clearly economically efficient to do so.

c. Holdouts: The mirror image to the free-rider problem is the problem of holdouts.

Example: Suppose that the damage to Adam of ceasing his use is only $500 (he can use Whiteacre as an exotic vegetable farm), and there is also damage to 99 other property owners (each in the amount of $500), or total damages of $50,000 (100 · $500). Now suppose that Eve's use is found to be a nuisance, and she is ordered to stop. It is efficient for Eve to purchase the use right vested in her 100 neighbors for some amount greater than $500 each and less than $1,000 each, but it does Eve no good to purchase the use right from 99 owners if even one refuses to sell. One owner is almost sure to hold out, because he will know that the marginal value of the last right is higher than $500 to $1,000. To see this, imagine that Eve has purchased 99 use rights for $600 each, or a total of $59,400. The last holdout will realize that Eve will rationally pay as much as another $40,599 to obtain the holdout's right. This simple fact is likely to spur holdouts. Of course, Eve can make her purchases conditional upon obtaining all rights, but that condition does not eliminate the incentive to hold out. Because Eve cannot compel everyone to sell on reasonable terms (e.g., three people may each demand $40,000), she may never be able to complete the transaction, and the right will stay with Adam and his cohorts, the inefficient outcome.

However, some empirical studies suggest that efficient results may occur by private bargaining even when there are as many as 40 parties involved, so the holdout problem may not be as intractable as it is often thought to be. See, e.g., Hoffman & Spitzer, *Experimental Tests of the Coase Theorem with Large Bargaining Groups*, 15 J.LEGAL STUD. 149 (1986).

2. **Who gets the initial entitlement?** Economic theory answers this by stating that the initial entitlement of land use should belong to the party whose use is the more valuable, but there are rival answers, too.

   a. **More valuable use:** The most efficient and economically logical answer is that the ***more valuable use*** should receive the initial entitlement, because this is the outcome that (but for transaction costs) would ultimately result. The prevailing balancing test for intentional and unreasonable use partially addresses these economic-efficiency concerns by assessing the relative social utility of competing uses and other issues of practicality.

   b. **First user:** Some would give the initial entitlement to the ***first user,*** on the theory that later users should adapt themselves to existing conditions. This approach is embodied in the ***"coming to the nuisance"*** doctrine, by which courts hold that those who knowingly acquire and use land in a manner incompatible with existing uses have voluntarily assumed the burden of what might be a nuisance were it to have been the late arrival. The "coming to the nuisance" cases typically involve new residents in rural areas who object to pre-existing rural uses. See, e.g., *Dill v. Excel Packing Co.,* 183 Kan. 513 (1958); *East St John's Shingle Co. v. City of Portland,* 195 Or. 505 (1952); *Gilbert v. Showerman,* 23 Mich. 448 (1871).

   c. **Disfavored uses:** Some would seek to identify uses that, however efficient or utile, are dangerous to public health or environmental preservation, and give the initial entitlement to the competing use. This approach suffers from the defect that it simply assumes that the dangers to public health or environmental preservation are always greater than the costs imposed by stopping the competing use, rather than relying on proof of that assertion, making this approach a simplistic version of the "more valuable user" approach.

   d. **Less valuable use:** Though inefficient and devoid of economic logic, some argue that the initial use entitlement should be given to the ***less valuable use,*** on the theory that this will accomplish a forced wealth transfer: The less valuable user will be spared the cost of cessation and may gain something from selling the use right to the more valuable user. This approach fails to explain why a wealth transfer should be forced. The less valuable user is not necessarily "deserving" of this gift, nor is the more valuable user necessarily "deserving" of this penalty.

3. **Economic and legal theory and remedies:** Economic theory tells us that either user — the "polluter" or the "receptor" of the pollution — can hold the initial entitlement. Legal theory holds that any property right can be protected by a ***liability rule*** or a ***property rule.*** A property interest protected by a property rule cannot be taken away from its owner involuntarily. A property interest protected by a liability rule can be taken away involuntarily but only upon payment of an award of damages. See Calabresi & Melamed, *Property Rules, Liability Rules, and Inalienability: One View of the Cathedral,* 85 Harv. L. Rev. 1089 (1972). These two theoretical insights, taken together, suggest that there are four possible outcomes to a nuisance suit:

   ■ *No Nuisance: The use continues without restraint.*

   ■ *Enjoin* the *nuisance* to stop it.

   ■ *Award damages* to landowners affected by a *nuisance,* but permit it to *continue.*

   ■ *Enjoin* the use (though maybe not a nuisance), and *award damages to the enjoined user.*

Example: Recall Adam's tanning spa and Eve's dairy farm. Think of Eve as the "polluter" — the creator of odors — and Adam as the "receptor" of those odors. The use right may be allocated to either party and, once allocated, may be protected by either a property rule or a liability rule. Seen graphically, there are four possible outcomes:

	Use Right in Receptor: Adam	**Use Right in Polluter: Eve**
Right protected by *Property Rule*	**Enjoin Eve:** Stop the nuisance	**No Nuisance:** Eve's use continues
Right protected by *Liability Rule*	**Damages to Adam:** Eve's use continues	**Enjoin Eve and Damages to Eve:** Adam's use continues

This pattern is in fact seen in the modern law of nuisance remedies. A court must ***allocate the right*** and *decide whether to protect that right by a* **property rule** *(injunction) or a* **liability rule** *(damages).*

B. No nuisance: Continue the activity: If a challenged activity is found not to be a nuisance, the use right is allocated to the challenged user and is implicitly protected by a property rule. Because it is not a nuisance, the challenged user cannot be forced to stop the use without his consent. The use will continue unless the challenged use is the less valuable one and transaction costs do not inhibit its transfer.

Example: Eve's dairy farm is found not to be a nuisance. She receives the use right and cannot be made to stop unless she agrees to, but if the cost to Adam of ceasing his use is $200,000, and the cessation cost to Eve is $100,000, the use right should voluntarily shift to Adam upon his payment to Eve of something between $100,000 and $200,000 (assuming modest transaction costs).

C. Nuisance: Enjoin and abate the activity: If a challenged activity is found to be a nuisance, and the challenger's use is protected by a property rule, the challenged activity will be enjoined, and it will thus stop. The challenger can continue his use at his pleasure. If the enjoined activity is the more valuable, the use right will likely be shifted to the enjoined user unless transaction costs prevent the transfer.

Example: Eve's dairy farm is found to be a nuisance, and she is enjoined from continuing her dairy farming. Adam's tanning use is protected by a property rule, but if the damage to Eve is $100,000, and the cost to Adam of ceasing to operate his tanning spa is $50,000, the use right should shift to Eve upon her payment to Adam of some price between $50,000 to $100,000 (assuming minimal or zero transaction costs).

★**Example:** Estancias Dallas constructed an apartment complex in Dallas adjacent to Schultz's residence. To save $40,000 Estancias located its central air conditioning unit about five feet from Schultz's lot line, 55 feet from his house, and 70 feet from his bedroom. The air conditioner was quite noisy ("the unit sounds like a jet plane or helicopter"), prevented Schultz from entertaining outdoors, and even interfered with indoor conversation and his sleep. To change the location of the unit would cost Estancias $150,000 to $200,000. The apartments could not be rented in sweltering Dallas without air conditioning. The value of Schultz's house was $25,000. In *Estancias Dallas Corp. v. Schultz,* 500 S.W.2d 217 (Tex. 1973), the Texas Court of Civil Appeals upheld a trial court's determination that the air conditioner was a nuisance and injunction of its further operation.

Why was it a nuisance? Surely, the gravity of the harm (the loss of the ***entire value*** of Schultz's house — $25,000) was outweighed by the social utility of the air conditioner (measured by the dollar cost of avoiding the harm — $40,000 at the outset, $150,000 to $200,000 after the injunction issued). Although the harm may have been serious, and Estancias could have compensated Schultz without ceasing business, that test is used when the plaintiff is seeking compensation. Without saying so, the Texas courts were applying the "threshold of harm" test exemplified by *Jost v. Dairyland Power Coop.* Although economic theory says that this result should have resulted in a shift of the use right from Schultz to Estancias upon payment of some amount between $25,000 and $150,000, that did not happen, which means that either Schultz was irrational, or transaction costs consumed the entire surplus, or that Schultz simply valued his peace and quiet in his long-time residence far more than an economic gain.

D. Nuisance: Pay damages and continue the activity: It is not possible to ignore the real-world presence of transaction costs. Thus, in situations where there are a large number of landowners affected by a more valuable use that is, on balance, a nuisance, the presence of holdout transaction costs (see section II.A.1.c, above) may prompt a court to protect the use right of the numerous landowners by a liability rule instead of a property rule. In short, the court may award damages to the affected landowners instead of enjoining the nuisance. The damages awarded are ***permanent damages*** — an amount sufficient to compensate now for all past and future injury that may be inflicted by continuation of the nuisance.

★**Example:** Atlantic Cement's factory produced dirt, smoke, noise, and vibration that substantially interfered with the use and enjoyment of land owned by a large number of neighbors. In ***Boomer v. Atlantic Cement Co.***, 26 N.Y.2d 219 (1970), the New York Court of Appeals upheld a trial court's finding that the factory was a nuisance and its award of damages instead of an injunction. The case was remanded for determination of the amount of permanent damages to be awarded for the "servitude" thus created over the affected land. The Court's rationale was partly the technological impossibility of abatement, coupled with recognition that the factory was the more valuable use (it produced positive externalities in the form of jobs and other economic benefits to the region) but that the holdout possibility might well frustrate a market transfer of the right if the factory were enjoined from further operation. In essence, the court applied the balancing formula that asks whether the defendant could compensate for all the serious harm it causes without ceasing business and concluded that Atlantic Cement could do so. Because we are not clairvoyant, there is the possibility of considerable error in ascertaining permanent damages — the present value of future injury that has not yet been inflicted — but if the damage award is not permanent, transaction costs (in the form of repeated litigation to determine future damages as incurred) will be high. An injunction is of dubious efficacy because of the nearly insurmountable transactions costs that would inhibit transfer of the use right from the affected homeowners to Atlantic Cement.

E. Nuisance or not: Enjoin the activity but award damages to the enjoined actor: Under some conditions, courts may enjoin an activity but require that the benefitted landowners compensate the enjoined actor for the lost use. Typically, this may occur when (1) the plaintiff asserts that his activity is the more valuable, (2) it is not clear either that (i) the challenged activity is a nuisance or, if it is, that (ii) equity favors an unadorned injunction, and (3) it is unlikely that the plaintiff is able or willing to acquire the use right in the market.

★**Example:** Spur operated a cattle feed lot in a rural part of Arizona. The feed lot necessarily gener-ated enormous quantities of manure, attracting clouds of insects and creating noxious odors, but nobody objected because there were no neighbors. Later, the Del Webb Corporation created Sun City, a retirement city, and expanded Sun City until it was sufficiently close to Spur's feed lot to make the two uses incompatible. In ***Spur Industries, Inc. v. Del E. Webb Development Co.***, 108 Ariz. 178 (1972), the Arizona Supreme Court enjoined Spur from further operation of the feed lot but required Del Webb to pay Spur "a reasonable amount of the cost of moving or shutting down." Equity required Del Webb to compensate Spur because Webb had come to the nuisance. The older common law view of nuisance (either nuisance and injunction, or no nuisance and no remedy) would have dealt with this by declaring Spur's feed lot to be no nuisance and denying any relief to Webb and the retirees it had induced to come to the nuisance. That is an unsatisfactory result, especially when the feed lot constituted a public nuisance on health grounds. The court's solution forced Webb to bear the cost of his having come to the nuisance. This remedy also forces the complaining user to "put his money where his mouth is." Because the plaintiff claims to have the more valuable use, he ought to be willing to shoulder some of the lesser cost of his adversary's cessation of use, particularly when he bears considerable responsibility for the use conflict. For this remedy to be effective, it is necessary to join all parties who are adversely affected by the use to be enjoined; otherwise, the free-rider problem can become insuperable.

III. SUPPORT RIGHTS

A. **Introduction:** Every landowner has the right to continued physical support of his land by abutting land. In essence, the natural topography may be altered only insofar as a neighbor's land is left with sufficient support. There are two types of support. ***Lateral support*** is the right to support from adjacent land — like the support supplied by a bookend to a row of books. ***Subjacent support*** is the right to support from underneath one's land — like the support supplied by the bookshelf to a row of books.

B. **Lateral support:** The scope of the right of lateral support is different for ***land itself*** and ***structures*** placed on the land.

   1. **Land itself:** A landowner who alters his land by removing the lateral support from his neighbor's land is strictly liable for any resulting damage to his neighbor's land. No matter how careful the alteration, if lateral support is removed, strict liability follows. The same principle applies to artificial supports, like retaining walls. Once an artificial support is substituted for natural support, the landowner and any successor in interest is obligated to keep the artificial support in place and effective.

   2. **Structures:** Most states hold that a landowner is liable for damage to structures from withdrawal of lateral support if either of two conditions is met: (1) the landowner was ***negligent,*** and the ***collapse would not have occurred but for the added weight of the structures,*** or (2) the ***collapse would have occurred whether or not the structures were there.*** If the withdrawal of lateral support is so extensive that the natural contours would have collapsed, the excavating landowner is strictly liable for all resulting injury to land or structures, but if the withdrawal of lateral support was not enough to cause the natural contours to collapse (i.e., the collapse was due to the added weight of the structures), the excavating landowner is liable only if he is negligent.

      a. **Minority rule:** Some jurisdictions hold that a landowner is strictly liable for removal of lateral support to adjacent buildings. This rule makes sense in dense urban locales, but probably not in rural locations. It is also justified on the ground that the second landowner to build can more easily avoid the costs of collapse, but this rule does give a boon to the first to build.

C. Subjacent support: The right of subjacent support is never an issue unless ownership has been split into two parts: (1) ownership of the surface, and (2) ownership of the right to mine under the surface. When this happens, the owner of the underground mineral rights is **strictly liable** for any damage caused to land or structures on the surface resulting from withdrawal of subjacent support.

Exam Tips on
JUDICIAL CONTROL OF LAND USE: NUISANCE AND SUPPORT

☞ Nuisance issues can easily be combined with other issues involving use, such as defeasible fees, servitudes, or quiet enjoyment by leasehold tenants.

☞ Even more than in some other areas, nuisance requires you to assess policy. Because either of two competing and incompatible uses can be a nuisance, you must have some theory to explain why the use you prefer should be protected. Economic theory may be useful to you, but other theories will work, too. Decide in advance which theory makes the most sense to you, apply it consistently and accurately to the facts, and be prepared to defend it and explain why other alternatives are less satisfactory.

☞ If economic theory is your preferred theory, be certain you understand the Coase Theorem and how transaction costs manifest themselves. If other theories suit your taste better, be able to explain why economic efficiency is not so important when resolving the problem of incompatible uses.

☞ Lateral and subjacent support are rarely tested.

CHAPTER 9

SERVITUDES: LAND USE LIMITS CREATED BY PRIVATE BARGAIN

ChapterScope

This chapter examines the various ways in which land use may be restricted by private agreement, focusing particularly upon easements, real covenants, and equitable servitudes. Here are the most important points in this chapter.

■ Easements are rights to use another's land. The right may be appurtenant to land ownership or purely personal ("in gross"). Personal rights to take things from another's land are called ***profits***. Negative easements (the right to prevent another person from using their own land in a certain way) do exist, but only in limited circumstances. Easements may be created by grant, estoppel, or prescription, or implied from prior use or necessity.

■ An easement by estoppel is a license to use land that has become irrevocable because the licensor has represented to the licensee that a certain use may be made of his land, and the licensee has relied to his detriment upon that promise. The license remains irrevocable so long as necessary to honor the reasonable expectations of the party who relied upon the promise.

■ An easement may be implied from prior use if one party has used a part of his property to benefit another part, later divides the property, and at the time of division, the use is apparent, reasonably necessary to the enjoyment of the dominant estate, and continuous thereafter.

■ An easement may be implied from necessity if one party owns land and later divides it in such a way that a parcel becomes landlocked—lacks access to a public road. An easement for access is then implied across the property owned (or formerly owned) by the grantor, connecting the landlocked parcel and a public road.

■ An easement by prescription occurs when a use is not permissive, continues for the relevant limitations period, and is conducted with the elements of adverse possession.

■ Easements appurtenant are transferable. Easements in gross are transferable if the parties so intend or are commercial in nature. The scope of an easement may not generally be enlarged beyond the original expectations of the parties, but sometimes courts make an exception if a new use imposes no additional burden on the servient estate.

■ Easements may be terminated by agreement, expiration, merger of the dominant and servient estates, abandonment, prescriptive use by the servient estate owner, or cessation of purpose.

■ Covenants are promises to use or not use one's own land in a certain way. As between the original parties, enforcement issues are purely contractual, but when certain elements are present, such promises may be enforced by or against successors in interest to the burdened or benefited estates in land. When damages are sought for enforcement of a covenant by or against a successor in interest, the covenant is called a ***real covenant***; when an injunction is sought for enforcement of a covenant by or against successors in interest, the covenant is called an ***equitable servitude***.

■ Real covenants can only be created by an enforceable written contract. The original contracting parties must intend that the burden and benefit of the restriction bind their successors in interest, and the substance of the covenant must **"touch and concern"** land use, rather than affect merely personal rights. Some jurisdictions require privity of estate between the original contracting parties (**"horizontal privity"**) in order to enforce the burden against a successor, but that rule is rapidly disappearing. Many jurisdictions require privity of estate between the original contracting party and his successors in interest (**"vertical privity"**) for either the burden or benefit to run to those successors. For the benefit to run, vertical privity means succession to "some interest"; for the burden to run, vertical privity means succession to the identical interest.

■ Equitable servitudes may be created by an enforceable written contract and, in some states, by implication from a common scheme of development undertaken by a single owner of property that is intended to be burdened by a common use restriction. For an equitable servitude to bind a successor in interest, the original use restriction must be intended to bind successors, the successor must take with notice of the restriction, and the substance of the restriction must touch and concern land use. Some commentators argue that the touch and concern is obsolete, and that its functions should be performed by rules governing termination or modification. Generally, an equitable servitude may not be enforced against a successor by someone who does not own land benefited by the restriction.

■ Real covenants and equitable servitudes may not be enforced when they are illegal or unconscionable, violate public policy, impair fundamental rights, or impose unreasonable restraints on alienation. The circumstances under which they may not be enforced is a developing area of law, partly because of the increasing use of restrictions in planned developments.

■ Real covenants and equitable servitudes may be terminated by agreement, merger, or changed circumstances that strip all benefits from the restriction. Courts generally protect equitable servitudes by a property rule (i.e., an injunction), without considering whether it might be more socially utile to protect such servitudes by a liability rule (i.e., damages).

I. INTRODUCTION

A. **The concept:** Neighbors often desire to make private agreements concerning use of their land and, because owners come and go, want those agreements to bind future owners or occupants. These agreements come in two varieties. First, one landowner may grant to another person the right to use his land for some specific purpose or in some manner. This type of agreement creates either an *easement* or *profit à prendre.* Both will be discussed in section II on easements. Second, one landowner may promise another landowner that she will use (or refrain from using) her land in a specified way. Depending on what remedy is sought for enforcement, these agreements create either a *real covenant* or an *equitable servitude.*

B. **Easements:** The principal issues surrounding easements are *creation, scope of the permitted use,* and *termination.* Easements are created by express grant, by equitable estoppel, by implication from prior use of an owner who divides land into separate parcels, by necessity resulting from an owner's division of land into separate parcels leaving one or more without access, and by prescription (the analogue to adverse possession). Issues of scope involve identifying the landowner (or person) who is entitled to use the easement, and deciding the proper intensity of permitted use. Easements may be terminated by abandonment, merger, release, actions inconsistent with the granted right and prejudicial to the burdened landowner, accidental destruction, prescription, or markedly changed circumstances.

C. **Covenants running with the land:** These promises concerning land use consist of *real covenants* (enforceable at law to recover damages for breach) and *equitable servitudes* (enforceable in equity by an injunction).

1. **Real covenants: Enforceable at law:** The principal issue concerning these covenants (created only by express agreement) is whether they may be enforced by or against subsequent owners of the land burdened or benefited by the promise. Often the sticking point in this inquiry is whether or not ***privity of estate*** exists. The traditional view is that *vertical privity*—privity of estate between the promisor and his assignee and between the promisee and his assignee—*must exist* for a real covenant to be enforceable by or against successors to the estate, although that view is under attack: The *Restatement (Third) of Property* (Servitudes) §5.2 proposes dispensing with privity for *negative covenants* (promises not to use land in some fashion) but retaining the concept for *affirmative covenants* (promises actively to use land in a certain way). The reason for seeking to enforce a real covenant is to obtain damages resulting from its breach.

2. **Equitable servitudes: Enforceable in equity:** These promises may be created by agreement or, in some states, by implication from a development scheme undertaken by a common owner. Privity is ***not*** required for these promises to be enforceable by or against successors to the estate, but the promise ***must be intended to bind successors,*** the successor ***must have notice*** of the promise, the nature of the promise ***must touch and concern*** use of the burdened land, and the promise ***must benefit neighboring land.*** Equitable servitudes are enforceable by an injunction and, in some cases, a lien.

II. EASEMENTS

A. Introduction

1. **Defined and distinguished from fee simple:** An easement is an interest in land that entitles the holder to use land owned or possessed by another person. It is not a freehold estate. An *easement* almost always gives its owner the right to ***use* another person's** land; a **freehold** (e.g., fee simple) gives its owner the right to ***exclusive possession of* one's own land.** In rare circumstances, an easement may give its owner the right to prevent another person from using their land in a certain way.

   a. **Ambiguous grants:** Some grants are none too clear about whether an easement or fee simple was intended, but if the interest conveyed is a limited area for a limited purpose, especially if there are no defined boundaries, an easement is the likely intention. Most courts employ a ***rebuttable presumption*** that an ambiguous grant conveys an ***easement.*** See, e.g., *Northpark Associates No. 2, Ltd. v. Homart Development Co.,* 262 Ga. 138 (1992); *Homan v. Hutchison,* 817 S.W.2d 944 (Mo. App. 1991); *Boucher v. Boyer,* 301 Md. 769 (1984); 2 Thompson on Real Property, §381, at 505 (1980 ed.). This presumption is supported by economic reasoning — it minimizes the transaction costs of uniting ownership of efficiently usable parcels. See Richard Posner, *Economic Analysis of the Law* 76 (4th ed., 1992).

★**Example:** In 1899, the Rutland-Canadian Railroad acquired a ribbon of land through Vermont as a "right of way" for its track. By 1970, the railroad's successor terminated service, and in 1975 it removed the tracks. In 1983, Congress enacted the Rails-to-Trails Act, which operated to transfer the railroad's interest in its right of way to Vermont public authorities for use as a public trail. In ***Preseault v. United States,*** 100 F.3d 1525 (Fed. Cir. 1996), the court of appeals affirmed a trial court's determination that the original interest was an easement because Vermont law stipulated that railroads acquiring rights of way acquired only the smallest interest in land necessary to accommodate their limited interest in creating a rail transport corridor. The difference between an easement or fee simple absolute was significant: A fee simple in the railroad would mean that the abandoned rail corridor remained the railroad's property and that it was validly conveyed to Vermont; an easement raised issues of whether it was abandoned (and thus title reverted entirely to the owner of the fee) or, if not, whether the public trail use was consistent with the scope of the easement for rail transport.

However, some courts presume that an ambiguous grant conveys the largest estate the grantor could convey — usually fee simple absolute. See, e.g., *Midland Valley R.R. v. Arrow Industrial Mfg. Co.,* 297 P.2d 410 (Okla. 1956).

2. **Types of easements:** There are two ways to classify easements — (1) *affirmative* or *negative* and (2) *appurtenant* or *in gross* — with the result that there are four basic types of easements: *affirmative appurtenant, negative appurtenant, affirmative in gross, and negative in gross.* To simplify, this discussion deals first with the distinction between easements appurtenant and in gross, then with the distinction between affirmative and negative easements.

   a. **Appurtenant and in gross:** Every easement must be either appurtenant or in gross.

      i. **Easement appurtenant:** An easement *appurtenant* is one that *benefits the owner of another parcel of land.* The benefited parcel is called the *dominant estate* (or *dominant tenement*), and the burdened parcel is called the *servient estate* (or *servient tenement*). An easement appurtenant passes with the dominant estate whenever the dominant estate is transferred to a new owner. The easement right is incidental to, or appurtenant to, the dominant estate.

      Example: Randall owns Blackacre, and Guy owns Whiteacre, an adjacent parcel. Guy grants an easement across Whiteacre from Blackacre for foot passage to and from the beach. The easement benefits whoever possesses Blackacre and is therefore appurtenant to Blackacre. If Randall sells Blackacre to Rodney, the easement passes also, and Rodney may enjoy the easement so long as he owns Blackacre.

      ii. **Easement in gross:** An easement that is designed to deliver a *personal benefit,* rather than to benefit a landowner, is an easement in gross. Easements in gross are not attached to, or appurtenant to, any parcel of land. They create a personal right to use the servient estate, but that personal right may be assigned if the parties so intended.

      Example: Refer to the prior example. Guy, owner of Whiteacre, grants "to Randall and his assigns the personal right to enter upon and cross Whiteacre for purposes of reaching the beach." An easement in gross is created in favor of Randall. If Randall sells Blackacre to Rodney without any assignment of this personal right, Rodney has no right to enter upon and cross Whiteacre, but if Randall assigns his easement in gross to Sally, she will have the right to cross Whiteacre. If Guy sells Whiteacre to Moira, Whiteacre continues to be burdened with the easement in gross in favor of Randall and his assigns.

Example: Roscoe, owner of Broadmeadow, grants to Power Corp. the right to string electrical transmission cables over a portion of Broadmeadow. Because Power Corp. does not own any property benefited by this grant, the easement must be in gross.

iii. **Ambiguous grants:** Courts prefer to construe ambiguous grants as creating easements appurtenant. This preference is partly historical, because England did not (and does not) recognize easements in gross, but it is mostly rooted in policy preferences. Easements appurtenant are easier to eliminate because the easement owner is easier to locate, they are more likely to create value, they and are more likely to be intended than an easement in gross.

Example: Suppose Guy, in the earlier example, conveyed "to Randall and his assigns the right to enter upon and cross Whiteacre for purposes of reaching the beach." This grant is ambiguous because it lacks the specific qualifier of the previous grant ("the *personal* right"). It will be construed as an easement appurtenant for three reasons: (1) Randall owns Blackacre, and the easement benefits the owner of Blackacre, raising a presumption that an easement appurtenant was intended; (2) If beach access across Whiteacre becomes useless, it is easier to eliminate the easement if the owner of Whiteacre can negotiate with the owner of Blackacre than if the owner of Whiteacre must locate Randall or some assignee (who may have no interest in asserting the easement and therefore is not easily located), and (3) An easement appurtenant creates value in Blackacre that probably more than offsets the burdens on Whiteacre, or the easement would not be created. If the burden on Whiteacre is $50, and the value to Blackacre is $100, Randall will pay more than $50 but less than $100 to obtain the easement. No matter how the difference between damage ($50) and added value ($100) is split between Guy and Randall, the easement, *if appurtenant,* will add $50 to the total value of Whiteacre and Blackacre, but if the easement is Randall's in gross, the only effect on land values will be to lower them by $50, the damage to Whiteacre produced by the easement.

b. **Affirmative and negative easements:** The overwhelming majority of easements are affirmative. Only a few types of negative easements may be created.

   i. **Affirmative easements:** As the name implies, an affirmative easement *permits a person to use the servient estate* in a specified manner.

   Example: Leroy owns Rockbottom, a farm situated between Hardscrabble, a farm owned by Lester, and a riverside dock used to ship farm produce. If Leroy grants Lester the right to cross Rockbottom for purposes of moving his farm produce to the riverside dock, an *affirmative easement appurtenant* has been created. Lester (or his successors in Hardscrabble, the dominant estate) will have the affirmative right to use Rockbottom (whether owned by Leroy or his successors) in the specified fashion. If Leroy had granted to Cyril, an urban fly fisherman, the right to cross Rockbottom to fish in the river, an *affirmative easement in gross* would have been created.

ii. **Negative easements:** A negative easement confers only the right to *prevent specified uses of the servient estate;* it confers *no right to use* the servient estate.

Example: Jonah, owner of Hillside, grants to Deborah, owner of Laurel Hollow, the right to prevent diversion of the flow from the irrigation ditch that crosses Hillside on its way to Laurel Hollow. This is a *negative easement appurtenant.* Laurel Hollow, the dominant estate, has no right to use Hillside, the servient estate, but does have a right to prevent Hillside from being used in a way that would divert the flow of water in the irrigation ditch.

Common law recognized only four negative easements, all appurtenant: (1) for light, (2) for air, (3) for subjacent or lateral support, and (4) for the continuing flow of artificial streams. By these easements, the owner of the servient estate could not block off his neighbor's light or air, or excavate to undermine his neighbor's structure or surface ground, or stop or divert irrigation ditches or aqueducts. Modern courts have analogized to these four by permitting negative easements for view (analogous to light and air) and for solar collection (a variation on light). It is sometimes claimed that negative easements are always appurtenant and that they may not be in gross. This was true at common law but is no longer correct.

iii. **Conservation easements:** Almost all states permit conservation easements, which do not benefit any dominant estate but are for the benefit of conservation organizations. The Uniform Conservation Easement Act is the principal statutory model for conservation easements. Conservation easements are perpetual, which raises concerns about the costs imposed on future generations by protecting property from future development, particularly when circumstances change. A tax incentive exists to create a conservation easement because the development value of the land is treated as a tax deductible charitable contribution in the year in which the easement is created. One important issue in conservation easements is whether the substance of the easement is within the scope of the statute. Typically, the statutes permit easements for conservation of natural resources and historic preservation.

Example: Lydia, owner of Flora Island, a nesting ground for terns, grants to the Audubon Society an easement to keep Flora Island "forever wild," as a habitat for nesting birds. This is a *negative easement in gross* and is permitted by the UCEA and other conservation easement statutes, but it would not be permitted under common law principles.

Example: Florence, owner of an historic home in Charleston, S.C., grants to the Charleston Historical Society an easement to preserve the exterior of her home and to prevent its occupancy by anyone who does not use it as his or her principal residence. The former easement is surely within the scope of the statute; the latter one probably is not. Its validity under common law probably depends on whether the Historical Society owns real property that is benefited by the easement.

Even if a negative easement is not recognized as valid, the same promise restricting land use may be enforced as a real covenant or equitable servitude. See sections III and IV, below.

3. **Profits à prendre:** A profit (as it is normally shortened) is the *right to take a natural resource or crop from the land of another.* Typical profits include the rights to take minerals (e.g., sand, gravel, ore), timber, fish, game, or crops. Common law courts preferred to construe profits as in gross rather than appurtenant, perhaps because in their origin many of these profits were vested in the landless. It makes economic sense to treat profits as in gross because the right conferred (e.g., to mine for copper ore) has substantial economic value by itself and thus is most efficiently utilized if it is easily transferable by itself, rather than as an adjunct to some unrelated property. For that reason, profits are freely assignable.

4. **Licenses:** A license is simply *permission* to enter the licensor's land. Licenses are ubiquitous (e.g., dinner guests, workers, and shoppers all have licenses), may be **oral or written,** and are *revocable* at any time unless the licensor makes the license irrevocable, either expressly or by his conduct.

   Example: Aldo tells his neighbor Fred that he may leave his canoe on Aldo's beach. Fred has a license to do so, but Aldo may revoke the license whenever he wishes.

   a. **License or easement in gross?** The same language may be construed as either a license or easement in gross. The consequential difference is that an easement may not be revoked and continues to bind successors to the servient estate who have notice of it, while a license is revocable and binds only the licensor so long as it remains alive.

      Example: If, in the prior example, Aldo's act were construed as creating an easement in gross in Fred, the easement would continue to inure to Fred's benefit if Aldo were to sell his beach front to Winnie after telling Winnie about Fred's right. Not so if it is a license. *Courts prefer to construe ambiguous cases as creating a license,* because easements in gross are often difficult to eliminate (e.g., Fred moves, leaving no forwarding address) and thus depress land values and make land less easily alienable.

   b. **Assignment:** Licenses are generally not assignable, but this rule is not invariable. Licenses are assignable if the parties so intend, and also if a license becomes irrevocable through operation of equitable estoppel, thus effectively becoming an easement appurtenant. See section II.A.4.c, below.

   c. **Irrevocable licenses:** Licenses may become irrevocable in three different ways.

      i. **Intention:** A license is irrevocable if the licensor expressly makes the license irrevocable.

      ii. **Equitable estoppel:** A license is irrevocable if equitable estoppel operates to make it so. If a licensor grants a license on which the licensee reasonably relies to make substantial improvements to property, equity requires that the licensor be estopped from revoking the license.

         ★**Example:** Holbrook permitted Taylor to use a roadway across his property in order for Taylor to reach his own property. With Holbrook's knowledge, and without any objection, Taylor used the access road to construct a substantial single-family residence. Holbrook later blocked the road with a steel cable strung taut across it. In *Holbrook v. Taylor,* 532 S.W.2d 763 (Ky. 1976), the Kentucky Supreme Court held that Holbrook was equitably estopped from revoking the license. See also *Shepard v. Purvine,* 196 Ore. 348 (1952); *Camp v. Milam,* 291 Ala. 12 (1973).

■ **Duration:** The traditional rule has been that a license made irrevocable through equitable estoppel continues to exist so long as is needed to prevent unjust enrichment, which generally meant that the license exists until the value of the reliance expenditures has been exhausted. Where valuable improvements have been made, this might well be at least as long as the useful life of the improvements, and some courts have hinted that such a license might last forever: "[T]he license will continue for so long a time as the nature of it calls for." *Stoner v. Zucker,* 148 Cal. 516 (1906). The *Restatement (Third) of Property*, however, treats such irrevocable licenses identically to easements unless the parties "intended or reasonably expected" that the license would remain irrevocable only until the reliance expenditures had been recovered. Because the creation of irrevocable licenses by equitable estoppel is by the actions of the parties, their intentions or expectations generally must be inferred from their actions.

■ **Easement compared:** An easement is of indefinite duration and can continue forever. An irrevocable license may last for a shorter period (e.g., one that expires when the value of the improvements has been fully recouped), but an irrevocable license might last as long as an easement (e.g., an irrevocable license for access, as in **Holbrook v. Taylor**). Thus, an irrevocable license is "similar in its essentials to an easement, . . . irrevocable to prevent the licensor from perpetrating a fraud upon the licensee." *Cooke v. Ramponi,* 38 Cal. 2d 282 (1952).

■ **Minority view — No estoppel:** A minority of jurisdictions reject application of equitable estoppel to oral licenses. The rationale for their view is that an irrevocable license is indistinguishable from an easement, and so the Statute of Frauds ought to apply to bar creation of irrevocable oral licenses. "The right . . . is essentially an easement and should be the subject of a [written] grant . . . It is no hardship . . . to secure an easement in perpetuity . . . or, such being refused, to [assess] the uncertainty implicit in the making of expenditures on the basis of a revocable license." **Henry v. Dalton,** 98 R.I. 150 (1959); *Crosdale v. Lanigan,* 129 N.Y. 604 (1892).

■ **Policy arguments:** The argument in *favor of irrevocability* based on estoppel is that it is unfair for the licensor to stand by and watch the licensee expend considerable money and effort in reliance on the license, then to rescind the license. The licensor is in the best position to prevent these reliance expenditures. The argument *against irrevocability* is that estoppel penalizes the "good neighbor" who fails to say no until the improvement is completed. The landowner who freely gives permission and is loathe to be a "bad guy" is the one who bears the cost of an irrevocable license imposed on his land. On this theory, the licensee should pay to the licensor the value of the irrevocable license (measured by the damage to the licensor's land resulting from irrevocability).

iii. **License "coupled with an interest":** When a license is tied together with some other legally recognized interest, the license is irrevocable until that other interest is vindicated.

Example: Dieter agrees to purchase from Parker a truckload of fertilizer, payment to be made only after Parker has delivered the fertilizer and spread it on Dieter's oat field. By virtue of the contract, Dieter has granted a license to Parker to enter upon Dieter's land, and that license is coupled with Parker's interest in performance of the contract, so it may not be revoked until Parker has had a reasonable opportunity to perform.

B. Creation of easements: Easements may be created by *grant,* by *estoppel* (though usually called an irrevocable license), by *implication* (in two different ways), and by *prescription* (the close cousin to adverse possession).

1. **Easements by grant:** Most easements are created expressly by a deed or other grant. Because an easement is an interest in land, its creation is subject to the Statute of Frauds, which requires a *writing signed by the grantor.* Of course, there are exceptions to the Statute of Frauds, which permit the creation of easements by estoppel, implication, and prescription.

   a. **By reservation:** Grantors sometimes convey land and, in the same deed, purport to "reserve" an easement in favor of the grantor or a third party.

      i. **In favor of grantor:** For archaic feudal reasons, early common law did not recognize easements reserved in favor of the grantor. Then common law judges invented the fiction that the grantee, by accepting the deed, had granted an easement back to the grantor. The modern upshot is that a reservation of an easement in favor of the grantor is valid. Common law distinguished between such a *reservation* (which created a *new easement*) and an *exception* (which passed title subject to a *pre-existing easement*). The distinction was important when easements could not be created in the grantor by reservation, but it is of no importance now.

      ii. **In favor of a third party:** Common law did not recognize the validity of easements purportedly reserved in favor of a third party because the fiction of a grant back to the grantor could not be extended to a third party, who was a stranger to the deed. The reasons for this refusal no longer exist, but the majority of modern courts continue to treat reserved easements in favor of a third party as void. See, e.g., *Estate of Thomson v. Wade,* 69 N.Y.2d 570 (1987). In such states, it is necessary to use two conveyances instead of one to create an easement in favor of a third party.

      Example: Carolyn, owner of Blackacre, wishes to convey Blackacre to Jake but reserve an easement for parking in favor of her neighbor, Liza. Carolyn must first convey Blackacre to Liza, who would then convey to Jake, reserving an easement in favor of herself.

      This rule is especially peculiar because a real covenant (which burdens land in much the same way as an easement) can be created in favor of a third party. A minority of modern courts have ruled that easements reserved in favor of a third party are valid.

      ★**Example:** McGuigan conveyed Lot 20 to Petersen by a deed that purported to reserve an easement for parking "during church hours" for the benefit of an adjacent church. Petersen conveyed Lot 20 to Willard under a deed that made no mention of the putative parking easement. After learning of the easement, Willard sought to quiet title in Lot 20. The trial court applied the majority view of easements reserved in favor of a third party and ruled that the McGuigan-to-Petersen deed was ineffective to create the parking easement. In *Willard v. First Church of Christ, Scientist,* 7 Cal. 3d 473 (1972), the California Supreme Court reversed, holding that the common law rule frustrates clear expressions of grantor intent and delivers windfall profits to people like Petersen (who presumably pay less for property burdened by an easement).

2. **Easements by estoppel:** An irrevocable license, the functional equivalent of an easement, can be created by estoppel. See section II.A.4.c.ii, above.

3. **Easements by implication:** Easements may be implied in law under two circumstances: (1) where property has been divided by a common owner and, prior to the division, one portion of the property has been used in an easement-like fashion for the benefit of another part of the property (implied from ***prior use***), and (2) where property has been divided by a common owner in such a manner that an easement for access is necessary (implied from ***necessity***).

   a. **Easements implied from prior use:** The problem is to identify when parties to a conveyance intend to create an easement without explicitly saying so. The following elements, which are often stated to be necessary to establishing an easement implied from prior use, are the principal factors that tend to establish an inference that the parties intended to create an easement:

   - **Common owner:** Prior to division, the ***quasi-servient estate*** and the ***quasi-dominant estate*** must be owned by the same person.

   - **Reasonable necessity:** The prior use must be ***reasonably necessary*** for the use and enjoyment of the "quasi-dominant estate."

   - **Continuous use:** The prior use must be ***continuous,*** not sporadic.

   - **Intended continuation:** The parties must ***intend,*** at the time of division, to continue the prior use.

   - **Existing use:** The prior use must be ***existing*** at the time of division, a requirement implied by the element of intended continuation.

   - **Apparent:** The prior use must be ***apparent,*** which does ***not*** necessarily mean that it is visible.

      i. **Common owner:** A person may devote part of her property to a use that benefits another part. There is no easement created while the property is owned by one person, but this prior use creates a so-called ***quasi-easement,*** an inchoate easement-in-waiting. When the common owner divides the property by selling one part to another person, an easement from prior use may be created. If the owner and grantor retains the quasi-servient estate (the burdened part), the implied easement is by ***implied grant.*** If the owner and grantor retains the quasi-dominant estate (the benefited part), the implied easement is by ***implied reservation.***

      Example: Brenda owns two lots adjacent to each other. She constructs a driveway over Lot 1 to her house on Lot 2. No easement is created, because Brenda cannot have an easement in her own property, but an inchoate quasi-easement exists. If Brenda sells Lot 2 to Richard, an easement by implied grant may be created: Brenda owns Lot 1, the servient estate, and Richard owns Lot 2, the dominant estate. If, instead, Brenda sells Lot 1 to Richard, an easement by implied reservation may be created: Richard owns Lot 1, the servient estate, and Brenda owns Lot 2, the dominant estate.

      ii. **Reasonable necessity:** The easement must be ***reasonably necessary for the owner of the dominant estate to use and enjoy her property.*** Reasonable necessity ensures that the easement was likely intended to continue after division. One corollary implication is that an easement implied from prior use can ***only be appurtenant.*** The term ***reasonable*** is capacious. Courts tend to find reasonable necessity if it would be costly or difficult to use the dominant estate without the easement, or if the price paid for either the dominant or servient estate reflects the existence of the easement. Most courts today require reasonable necessity for easements implied by grant and for easements implied by reservation.

★**Example:** Bailey owned three adjoining lots in Chanute, Kansas. She built a house on one of the lots and ran an underground sewer line across the other two lots to a municipal sewer. Later, she sold all three lots to separate owners under deeds making no mention of the sewer line. However, later owners built a house on each of the two vacant lots and connected the plumbing in those houses to the original Bailey sewer line. Van Sandt, the "downstream" owner, sued to enjoin Royster, an "upstream" owner, from continuing to use the Bailey sewer after he awoke to six inches of sewage in his basement, on the theory that no easement had ever been validly created across his property. In ***Van Sandt v. Royster,*** 148 Kan. 495 (1938), the Kansas Supreme Court upheld a trial court ruling that an easement by reservation implied from prior use had been validly created by Bailey when she conveyed title to each of the two "downstream" lots. The court rejected the older view that when an easement implied from prior use is created by implied reservation, ***strict necessity*** — absolute, indispensable necessity — is required. See, e.g., *Abbott v. Herring,* 97 App. Div. 2d 870 (N.Y. App. 1983); *Mitchell v. Castellaw,* 151 Tex. 56 (1952); *Winthrop v. Wadsworth,* 42 So. 2d 541 (Fla. 1949). The Kansas court rejected the logic underpinning the older view — that the grantor ought not be permitted impliedly to derogate from her grant — preferring to treat the "implied reservation" or "implied grant" character of the putative easement as but one element of a broader problem of determining the inferred intentions of the parties. Thus, if other elements tending to prove this inferential intention — especially apparent existing use — are present, it is hard to see why there should be a difference between reservation and grant. See also *Otero v. Pacheco,* 94 N.M. 524 (App. 1980); *Jack v. Hunt,* 200 Ore. 263 (1953).

iii. **Continuous use:** The use must be continuous, not sporadic. This element buttresses the fundamental concept that the use must be such that both parties ***intended for it to continue.*** Continuous use does not mean that it must be used constantly; rather, it means that the easement must be embodied in some ***permanent physical alteration.***

Example: An outdoor concrete staircase serving Parcel A, but located entirely on Parcel B, is permanent (and thus continuous) even though it is not in constant use.

iv. **Intended continuation:** This is the fundamental element, but the parties rarely provide express evidence of their intentions, or they would have memorialized the easement by express grant. Accordingly, many of the other elements — reasonable necessity, continuity, and apparent use — are proxies for this element. The price paid (which is also considered in deciding whether the claimed easement is reasonably necessary) is helpful to this issue, because parties who intend for a quasi-easement to continue are likely to settle on a price that reflects the value (and detriment) of the easement.

v. **Existing use at division:** The prior use must actually exist at the time of division. If it does not, there is surely no reason to think that the parties intended the continuation of a nonexisting use.

vi. **Apparent use:** The use must be apparent. This does ***not*** mean that the use must be visible. A prior use is apparent if it could be detected, or even inferred, from a reasonable inspection of the premises.

★**Example:** Refer back to the ***Van Sandt v. Royster*** example. Although Bailey's private sewer line, crossing the two lots she sold without reference to any easement, was underground, the Kansas Supreme Court in ***Van Sandt v. Royster,*** 148 Kan. 495 (1938), ruled that the sewer line was apparent because later buyers should have inferred the existence of some sewer by noting the existence and operation of plumbing fixtures, and could have employed a skilled plumber to detect the actual location of the sewer. See also *Romanchuk v. Plotkin,* 215 Minn. 156 (1943). But see *Campbell v. Great Miami Aerie No. 2309,* 15 Ohio St. 3d 79 (1984).

vi. **Scope:** The scope of the implied easement includes not only uses known or discoverable at the time of severance but also those uses that a party might reasonably have foreseen that the other party would have expected to be included in the implied easement.

Example: Etta owned two adjacent parcels. The north parcel contained a residence and farmland, the south parcel was exclusively farmland. At the time of severance, both parcels were used only for farming; the residence was unoccupied. Prior to severance, access to the north parcel for farming had been across the south parcel. At severance, an implied easement from prior use was created. Later, Stroda, the owner of the north parcel, sought to use the north parcel for residential purposes and contended that the implied easement included access for that purpose and for utilities necessary for residential occupation. Joice Holdings, owner of the south parcel, objected that the access easement was limited to agricultural uses. In *Stroda v. Joice Holdings*, 288 Kan. 718 (2009), the court held that it was reasonably foreseeable that dominant owner might expect to use the parcel for residential purposes. The presence of an unoccupied residence was enough to make the servient owner aware of this possible use.

viii. **Easements implied from a subdivision map:** When a common owner divides property under a deed that incorporates or refers to a map on which proposed streets or other rights of way are platted on the common owner's property, an easement in favor of the grantee with respect to the platted streets is implied even though there has been no prior use. The rationale for this deviation from the elements of easements implied from prior use is that the purchaser has relied on the future creation of the streets and paid accordingly. See 3 Powell, *The Law of Real Property* ¶409 (1992 ed.).

b. **Easements implied from necessity:** An easement is implied from necessity only when a common owner divides his property in such a way that one of the resulting parcels is left without access to a public roadway. An easement for right of way between the landlocked parcel and the public road across the owner's remaining parcel is then implied, either because the parties must have intended this result or because it is economically efficient and socially beneficial to create an easement for access. Easements by necessity are permitted only for right of way — ingress and egress between the landlocked parcel and a public road.

Example: Eunice owns Black Heart Ranch and divides it into two parcels, Sweetwater and Bitterroot. Sweetwater is bounded by a public road on the west, two ranches owned by neighbors on the north and south sides, and Bitterroot on the east. Bitterroot is bounded by

Sweetwater on the west and National Forest wilderness land on the remaining sides. An easement implied from necessity will burden Sweetwater for the benefit of Bitterroot, enabling the occupier of Bitterroot to cross Sweetwater to gain access to the public road.

    i. Common owner: An easement by necessity can be created *only* over property owned by the person who also owned the landlocked parcel and who divided the property to create the access problem. In cases of multiple division, an easement by necessity is created at the moment a parcel is landlocked, and thus the easement burdens the *last parcel* split off by the common owner — the parcel that completed the landlocking.

    ★**Example:** Hill owned a large parcel of land in Texas, which he sold in bits and pieces over time in the 1890s. One of those parcels was landlocked, and title to that parcel was eventually acquired by Othen, who habitually used a roadway crossing Rosier's land to reach a public road. To prevent erosion, Rosier built a levee that impounded water, making the roadway impassable at times. Othen sued Rosier to enjoin further interference with his right of way, which Othen contended was implied by necessity. In ***Othen v. Rosier,*** 148 Tex. 485 (1950), the Texas Supreme Court upheld a determination that no easement by necessity had been proven *across Rosier's land,* because there was no proof that when Hill, the common owner, had conveyed the Rosier property to Rosier's predecessor in interest it was *that conveyance that landlocked the Othen parcel.* Rather, it appeared that at the time Hill had conveyed the Rosier parcel, Hill owned other land (never identified by Othen) that was contiguous to both the Othen parcel and a public roadway. Othen had an easement implied by necessity across some property, but it wasn't across Rosier's property.

    One corollary is that an easement implied by necessity cannot burden property never owned by the common grantor who created the problem.

    ii. Necessity at severance — Not prior use: Necessity must exist at the moment the property is divided. No prior use is needed to establish an easement by necessity. The necessity of access is present the moment the parcel is landlocked, though the practical need may lie dormant for years.

    iii. Duration: An easement by necessity lasts as long as the necessity exists. If the necessity is removed (perhaps by creation of a new public road that provides access), the easement is terminated.

    iv. Location: Once the servient estate is identified, the owner of the servient estate is permitted to select a ***reasonably convenient location*** for the easement, on the theory that the servient estate owner can best minimize the damage to the servient estate.

4. Easements by prescription: Prescription is analogous to adverse possession. Easements are *not possessory interests,* so an easement cannot be acquired by adverse *possession,* but *adverse use* for a sufficient period of time can ripen into an *easement by prescription.* American courts ground prescription in the same policies that justify adverse possession. The archaic English fiction that a prescriptive use was pursuant to a grant, now lost, has been largely discarded by American courts. The English view pretended that prescription was really use by right; the American view frankly recognizes the adverse nature of prescriptive use. Easements by prescription may be appurtenant (as when one homeowner acquires a driveway easement over his neighbor's land) or in gross (as when repeated hunting or fishing create a prescriptive easement in gross in favor of the hunter or fisher).

a. **Elements of prescriptive use:** Virtually the same elements are needed to establish prescriptive use that are needed to establish adverse possession: (1) *adverse use under a claim of right* that is (2) *open and notorious* and (3) *continuous* for the prescriptive period. Note, however, that the *exclusive use* element is so altered from its meaning in adverse possession that it is **effectively not required.**

   i. **Prescriptive period:** The required prescriptive period is the same as the limitations period applicable for adverse possession. If the jurisdiction has a 20-year limitations period for adverse possession, the adverse use of another's land must continue for 20 years in order for an easement by prescription to be created.

   ii. **Adverse use under a claim of right:** The use of another's land must be *adverse* and *not with permission of the owner.* As with adverse possession, there is an *objective* and *subjective* version of this test. The objective version focuses on whether a neutral observer would think the use is under a claim of right and not permissive. The subjective version requires the adverse user to prove that she had a good faith belief that she had a right to use the land, and not just permission to do so.

   Example: A frequent problem is the common driveway. Suppose Mary and Al, neighbors, agree to split the cost of a driveway which both will use and which is located exactly on the property line. Under the objective version of adverse use, Mary and Al may each be using their neighbors' property in a permissive fashion, because they have permitted each other to use a driveway for which they have each paid half the cost. The result is different under the subjective test—both Mary and Al likely have a good faith belief that they are entitled to use the driveway. See, e.g., *Shanks v. Floom,* 162 Ohio St. 479 (1955). Contra: *Banach v. Lawera,* 330 Mich. 436 (1951).

   If a use is permissive, it can never ripen into a prescriptive right, no matter how long the use goes on. However, a permissive use can become adverse if the user does things that are inconsistent with mere permission and that give the owner notice of the user's claim of right.

   Example: Janet gives Bob permission to use a footpath through her rural wood for beach access. Bob then proceeds to widen the path, paves it with asphalt, and installs handrails. These acts are inconsistent with permission to use a rural footpath and ought to put Janet on notice that Bob claims a right to use the path that is independent of her permission. See, e.g., *Hester v. Sawyers,* 41 N.M. 497 (1937).

   Similarly, an adverse use can be rendered non-adverse if the owner of the burdened estate grants permission for the use.

   Example: Without permission, Evelyn walks her dog through Ricardo's wood twice daily, beating a worn path. Before the prescriptive period expires, Ricardo informs Evelyn that she has his permission to walk her dog in his wood. Evelyn's use, initially adverse, is now turned into a permissive, non-adverse use.

   Use of an easement by necessity *after it has terminated* is likely adverse and may ripen into an easement by prescription. Use of an easement by necessity is by right, and thus not prescriptive, but if the necessity ends, the easement by necessity terminates. Further use of the terminated easement is adverse, unless permission for the continued use is granted.

iii. **Open and notorious use:** To be open and notorious, the adverse use must be conducted so that the use may be discovered by any reasonable inspection. It may not be carried on in secret or carefully concealed.

iv. **Continuous use:** The element of continuous use is satisfied if the adverse user continually asserts her claim of right by making whatever use is consistent with the nature of the claimed easement, even if that use is periodic or episodic. It does ***not*** mean that the adverse user must use the property constantly.

> **Example:** Adam and Eve own adjacent waterfront lots in a summer home community. Each summer, Adam crosses Eve's lot whenever he wishes to go to the beach, sometimes several times a day, but sometimes only a few times a week. Adam beats down a clear footpath by his crossings and goes so far as to construct crude stone steps to the beach. Adam makes no use of the footpath during the fall, winter, and spring, when neither he nor Eve is there. This use involves a continual claim of right and adverse use that is consistent with the nature of the claimed easement — a footpath beach access during the summer period — and satisfies the continuous use element.

As with adverse possession, tacking is permitted, but occasional adverse use does not satisfy the continuous use element.

> **Example:** If Adam were to cross Eve's lot only a few times each summer, make no alterations to the lot, and otherwise use a public beach access, his use would be so occasional that it would not satisfy the continuous use element.

If the adverse use is interrupted, the prescriptive period starts over. Jurisdictions differ as to what constitutes interruption. Most states follow the adverse possession rule that only the owner's action of filing a lawsuit to stop the adverse use or physical prevention of the adverse use constitutes interruption. A minority hold that mere notice (a sign or letter) that tells the adverse user to stop is sufficient to interrupt the use. The minority view is a vestige of the "lost grant" theory of prescription: If prescription is founded on a fictional "lost grant," the owner's statement that there is no grant is sufficient to rebut the existence of the fictional lost grant.

v. **Exclusive use:** Many courts say that exclusive use must be shown to establish a prescriptive easement, but the meaning of exclusivity is so altered from adverse possession that, in effect, it is not required. For prescription purposes, exclusive use does not mean that the adverse user was the only user; rather, it means that the adverse user's claim "does not depend on a like right in others." *Page v. Bloom,* 223 Ill. App. 3d 18 (1991). In other words, exclusive use is shown simply by claiming an easement from ***one's own use,*** and not in common with the public or somebody else. Thus, even in the case of the common driveway, each neighbor's use is "exclusive" in this sense. See, e.g., *Causey v. Lanigan,* 208 Va. 587 (1968). Not all states are so liberal with the exclusivity element, however. Some states presume that when a putative easement is used in common with others, the use is permissive.

> ★**Example:** Refer to the ***Othen v. Rosier*** example, discussed under **easements implied by necessity**. Othen's alternative argument was that he had acquired an easement for right of way across Rosier's land by prescription, but the Texas courts rejected this claim because Othen used the roadway in common with Rosier.

b. Public prescriptive easements: Some jurisdictions permit the public at large to acquire prescriptive easements in private lands, so long as all the elements of prescription are satisfied. Other jurisdictions achieve the same result through *implied dedication, custom,* or the *public trust doctrine.* Some states reject all of these theories.

  i. Prescriptive easements in favor of the general public: The general rule is that the public at large can obtain a prescriptive easement in private property so long as the elements of prescriptive use are established. See, e.g., *Citizens of Brunswick County Taxpayers Assn. v. Holden Beach Enterprises, Inc.,* 329 N.C. 37 (1991); *Buttolph v. Erikkson,* 160 Vt. 618 (1993). However, most courts apply a rebuttable presumption that public use is permissive that and the use must be sufficiently widespread to be truly public. Use by the neighborhood alone may not be sufficiently public to create a public prescriptive easement. See, e.g., *Gore v. Blanchard,* 96 Vt. 234 (1922) (neighbors' use of a road to reach a pond for ice cutting was a mere "neighborly concession" and not "used for public purposes as a public way").

  ii. No public prescriptive easements: States that reject public prescriptive easements rely on one of two rationales. The older reason is rooted in the fictional "lost grant" — because the "public citizenry" could not receive a grant, there could not possibly have been such a grant, now lost; hence, no prescriptive easement in the public was possible. See, e.g., *Ivons-Nispel, Inc. v. Lowe,* 347 Mass. 760 (1964). The more modern objection is that the owner's cause of action (barred by elapse of the prescriptive period) can only run against specific persons, so the owner's cause of action to stop adverse use can never expire as against the entire public at large. See, e.g., *State ex rel. Haman v. Fox,* 100 Idaho 140 (1979). Some states have enacted statutes that permit owners to record and post notices that public use is by permission, thus negating any possible claim of public prescriptive right. See, e.g., Cal. Civ. Code §1009. Other states apply the requirement of exclusivity to the claim that a public prescriptive easement has been established. See *Sellentin v. Terkildsen,* 216 Neb. 284 (1984). If exclusivity is required, it is virtually impossible to prove, because no member of the public can be excluded. Some states simply reject the entire idea of a public prescriptive easement. *Miller v. Grossman Shoes, Inc.,* 186 Conn. 229 (1982).

  iii. Implied dedication: This theory is simply a pseudonym for a public prescriptive easement. The idea is that the owner *intends to dedicate* his property to *public use,* but the evidence of such intent is entirely inferred from (1) long-standing public use, and (2) the owner's failure to halt the use. See, e.g., *Gion v. City of Santa Cruz,* 2 Cal. 3d 29 (1970) (subsequently overturned by legislation).

  iv. Custom: Beach front property owners own the "dry sand" portion of the beach, because their title usually extends to the mean high-tide mark. Ancient common law held that the public acquired a customary right to use the dry sand portion of a beach if such public use had gone on so long that "the memory of man runneth not to the contrary." 1 W. Blackstone, Commentaries *67. That doctrine has been revived in at least four states: Florida, Hawaii, Oregon, and Texas. To establish this customary right, the public must prove *immemorial usage without interruption* that is *peaceable, reasonable, certain,* and *consistent with other customs.* See, e.g., *Public Access Shoreline Hawaii v. Hawaii County Planning Comm.,* 79 Haw. 425 (1995); *City of Daytona Beach v. Tona-Rama, Inc.,* 294 So. 2d 73 (Fla. 1974); *State ex rel. Thornton* *v. Hay,* 254 Or. 584 (1969); *Matcha v. Mattox,* 711 S.W.2d 95 (Tex. App. 1986). Idaho has embraced the doctrine in *dicta* but has not had occasion to apply it. *State ex rel. Haman v. Fox,* 100 Idaho 140 (1979). Claims of customary rights to private beaches have been considered and rejected elsewhere. See, e.g., *Bell v. Town of Wells,* 557 A.2d 168 (Me. 1989).

v. Public trust doctrine: Some states approach the issue of public beach access by invoking the public trust doctrine, under which the water and beach front below the mean high-tide mark is held by the state in ***public trust,*** to enable the public to use these tidal waters and lands for swimming, boating, fishing, and other common pursuits. This approach can be problematic because access to such public lands is often only through privately owned land.

★**Example:** In *Matthews v. Bay Head Improvement Assn.,* 95 N.J. 306 (1984), the New Jersey Supreme Court ruled that private beachfront landowners organized as a "quasipublic" entity must give the general public "access to and use of privately-owned dry sand areas as reasonably necessary." *Matthews* involved dry sand beaches that were owned by a non-profit corporation that controlled, either as fee owner or lessee, the dry sand portion of the beaches in Bay Head, N.J., and that restricted access to those dry sand beaches to residents of Bay Head and their guests. In a later New Jersey case, ***Raleigh Avenue Beach Ass'n v. Atlantis Beach Club, Inc.,*** 185 N.J. 40 (2005), the same court ruled that, under the principles announced by *Matthews,* a private beach club must permit the public to enter and use its private dry sand beach. The club was barred from charging any fees to transient users but was permitted to charge reasonable fees for its beach-maintenance services to those who remain on the beach for extended periods of time. In reaching this conclusion, the New Jersey court considered the relation of the dry sand to the foreshore, the extent and availability of public owned dry sand beaches in the area, the nature and extent of the public demand, and the usage of the dry sand by the owner. It is possible that this rule, as applied to privately owned dry sand beaches where the owners have not assumed "quasi-public" power, would amount to a taking of private property for which the Constitution requires just compensation. See Chapter 11.

In *Glass v. Goeckel,* 473 Mich. 667 (2005), owners of lakefront property to the water's edge sought to bar trespass across the dry shore of the lake on their property. The Michigan Supreme Court ruled that the public trust doctrine applied to protect the public's right to walk along the dry shore between the water's edge and the "ordinary high water mark," the point at which there is a distinct indication of the end of water action on the land. The dissenters thought that the public trust doctrine stopped at the water's edge, but would have defined the water's edge to end where wet sand gives way to dry sand.

c. Prescriptive easements not permitted: There are two types of easements that may not be acquired by prescription.

i. Negative easements: A negative easement may not be acquired by prescription because there is no cause of action that is cut off by elapse of the prescriptive period.

Example: Otto builds a solar collector on the roof of his home. Twenty years later, his neighbor, Patricia, builds a tall addition to her home, which completely blocks sunlight from falling on Otto's solar collector for nine months of each year. Otto has no prescriptive easement for sunlight. During the 20-year period when Otto's collector was soaking up sunshine, Patricia had no cause to action to stop him from doing so; thus, there is no right of Patricia's that is extinguished by elapse of time. Put another way, if Otto were to receive a prescriptive negative easement for sunlight, there would be nothing Patricia could do (short of blocking Otto's sunlight immediately) that would stop Otto from acquiring an interest in her property. Sound public policy would not encourage neighbors to cut off each other's light and air simply to avoid the possibility that a prescriptive easement might otherwise result. See, e.g., *Cohan v. Fleuroma, Inc.,* 42 App. Div. 2d 741 (N.Y. App. 1973); *Parker & Edgarton v. Foote,* 19 Wend. 309 (N.Y. 1838).

     ii. Easements upon public land: As with adverse possession, it is not generally possible to obtain a prescriptive easement in public land. This rule is, at bottom, another manifestation of the sovereign's prerogative. Also, sound public policy probably should not encourage people to use public land for purely private benefit and thus to acquire a private right at the expense of the general public.

C. Transfer of easements: The transferability of easements depends on the type of easement.

    1. Easements appurtenant: By their nature, easements appurtenant are transferable; they are a part of title to the freely transferable dominant estate.

    Example: Ingrid, owner of Blackacre, the dominant estate with respect to an easement for passage across Whiteacre, conveys her fee simple to Hendrik. The easement for passage that is appurtenant to Blackacre goes with the title. Similarly, if Hortense, owner of Whiteacre, conveys her fee simple to Emily, the burden of the easement passes along with title to Whiteacre.

    2. Easements in gross: Because the owner of an easement in gross is not nearly so easy to locate as the owner of an easement appurtenant, and thus a burden on land may persist long after its practical utility has ceased, courts tend to restrict transferability of easements in gross. The general rule today is that **commercial easements in gross are assignable,** and **noncommercial easements in gross are not assignable unless the parties intend to permit assignment.**

    ★**Example:** Frank and Rufus Miller owned a large tract of land on a creek in the Pocono Mountains. They dammed the creek to create Lake Naomi, and conveyed to Pocono Spring, a corporation they organized and controlled, the land underlying the lake surface. Pocono Spring granted to Frank Miller and "his heirs and assigns . . . the exclusive right to fish and boat" in the lake. A year later, Frank granted to Rufus Miller and his heirs and assigns a "one-fourth interest in and to the fishing, boating, and bathing rights . . . at, in, upon, and about Lake Naomi." Frank and Rufus then operated a boating and bathing business at Lake Naomi as partners until Rufus died. Frank Miller and Rufus Miller's estate then began granting licenses to others to use the lake, one of which (from Rufus's estate) was to the Lutheran Conference "to boat, bathe, and fish in the lake." Frank Miller sued the Lutheran Conference to enjoin their further use of Lake Naomi. Frank argued that (1) he never had any bathing rights, and so his purported conveyance of a one-quarter interest in them was a nullity, and (2) if he had had any bathing rights, they were in gross and thus neither divisible nor alienable. A trial court granted the injunction, which was affirmed in *Miller v. Lutheran Conference & Camp Assn.,* 331 Pa. 241 (1938). The court reasoned that Frank and Rufus, as partners, had acquired a bathing right by prescriptive use, and that the easement in gross so acquired, together with the easement in gross to fish and boat in Lake Naomi, was a commercial easement that was intended to be transferable. However, that did not end the case, for the court ruled that while the easements were transferable they were not divisible. For discussion of the indivisibility issue, see section II.D.5.b.iii, below.

Because a commercial easement primarily produces economic benefits, and a noncommercial easement primarily produces personal pleasure, courts reason that transferability of commercial easements is efficient and reflects the probable intentions of the parties, while rights granted for personal pleasure are likely to be the product of a personal relationship. Free assignment of commercial easements in gross advances the public convenience. The holders of these easements are mostly corporations, entities with perpetual existence, and thus are easily located, thus dampening fears of difficulty in eliminating easements by agreement. Also, corporations alter their existence by merger or acquisition, and it would be most inconvenient to wipe out, for example, utility easements, simply because one utility company acquired another.

Example: An easement in gross for underground utilities produces economic benefits, the social utility of which is enhanced by free transferability from one utility provider to another. An easement in gross for the right to meditate atop Mount Zen granted by Abbott Sensei, owner of Mount Zen, to Novice, a student of the Abbott, produces personal pleasure (and maybe enlightenment) but is surely rooted in the personal relationship between the two.

3. **Profits:** Profits have always been assignable. This might be due to the fact that, in their heyday, profits were valuable rights to the non-landowning laboring class of England, and common law courts recognized the exchange value of rights to take timber or game. But if profits may be freely assigned, why not easements in gross? Perhaps it is because profits are almost always commercial in nature.

D. **Scope of easements:** The scope of an easement involves two separate questions. How *extensively* and *intensively* may the *easement holder use the easement?* To what degree may the *owner of the servient estate use or interfere with the easement?*

1. **Parties' intentions control:** The overriding principle in determining scope of an easement is to identify and uphold the parties' intentions, but this is not always so easy because intentions frequently must be at least partly inferred. To do so, courts examine the following factors.

   ■ *How the easement was created* (i.e., whether by grant, implication, or prescription).

   ■ *How conditions have changed to affect the originally intended use.*

   ■ *What changes in use were reasonably foreseeable by the parties.*

   ■ *What changes are necessary to achieve the intended purpose of the easement.*

   ■ *Whether a changed use imposes an* **unreasonable burden** *on the servient estate.*

2. **How the easement was created**

   a. **Easements by grant:** The express language of the grant controls insofar as it may be dispositive, but extrinsic circumstances often must be consulted.

Example: An easement granted in 1870 in upper Michigan for "winter access to Horseshoe Pond for ice fishing" implied access by ski, sleigh, sled, or snowshoe in 1870, but it would not be unreasonable to interpret it today as including access by snow machine.

Example: In 1876, the owner of Blackacre conveyed an easement for right of way over Blackacre for the benefit of Whiteacre. The easement was used to transport animals to Whiteacre for slaughter and removal of their carcasses for sale. Around 1916, the slaughterhouse burned, and Whiteacre was converted to farming. The easement was then used for farm machinery and crop removal. By the 1950s, Whiteacre was used by the Kentucky Highway Department to store vehicles and equipment, which it moved in and out via the easement. In *Cameron v. Barton,* 272 S.W.2d 40 (Ky. 1954), the Kentucky Court of Appeals held that the easement "may be used in such a manner as is necessary in the proper and reasonable occupation and enjoyment of the dominant estate. As the passage of time creates new needs, and the uses of property change, a normal change in the manner of using [an easement] does not constitute a deviation from the original grant, and modern transportation uses are not restricted to ancient modes of travel."

   b. Easements by implication: The scope of implied easements depends on the reason for the implication.

      i. By prior use: Easements implied from prior use are construed the same way as easements by grant.

      Example: An agribusiness company constructed a roadway on its property to serve its lemon and avocado groves, then divided the property creating a roadway easement implied from prior use. The dominant estate was later acquired by a person who constructed a residence on the property. In *Fristoe v. Drapeau,* 35 Cal. 2d 5 (1950), the California Supreme Court ruled that even though the prior use that created the easement was agricultural, it was "within the reasonable contemplation of the parties" at the time of division that the easement could be used for residential purposes.

      ii. By necessity: The scope of an easement implied by necessity is exactly congruent with the necessity: no more, no less.

   c. Easements by prescription: Because prescriptive easements come about by a particular long-standing adverse use by ***one party alone,*** there is no reason to assume that any greater or different use was intended by the parties. Accordingly, courts are most reluctant to permit any expansion of the scope of prescriptive easements to accommodate changed future needs of the dominant estate. See, e.g., *Wright v. Horse Creek Ranches, Inc.,* 697 P.2d 384 (Colo. 1985), where a prescriptive roadway easement for ranching and hunting was not permitted to be used for providing access to a residential subdivision. Accord: *Aztec Ltd., Inc. v. Creekside Investment Co.,* 100 Idaho 566 (1979). Despite this general rule, some courts permit modest alteration of the scope of a prescriptive easement where the ***burden on the servient estate is moderate,*** and the ***alteration is consistent with the general pattern formed by the adverse use.*** See, e.g., *Glenn v. Poole,* 12 Mass. App. Ct. 292 (1981) (permitting a prescriptive roadway easement for hauling wood and gravel to be used for vehicle access to and from a garage and repair shop); *Farmer v. Kentucky Utilities Co.,* 642 S.W.2d 579 (Ky. 1982) (permitting the holder of a prescriptive easement for overhead passage of utility cables to clear brush and trees underneath).

3. **Change in location of easement:** If an easement specifies a specific location, or one has been agreed to by the parties' conduct, the location is permanently fixed unless the parties agree to a change.

Example: Harold, owner of a tract of ground including Long Lake and Whitechapel Pond, grants to Edgar an easement in gross "to fish in Whitechapel Pond." Edgar may not thereafter unilaterally change the easement to one permitting him to fish in Long Lake.

Example: Rosemary, owner of Blackacre (bounded on the west by a public forest, on the east by Big River, on the north by a public road, and on the south by Whiteacre), grants an easement appurtenant to Whiteacre for "passage across Blackacre to Big River." Over time, a well-beaten path is created across Blackacre from Whiteacre to Big River, thus fixing the location of this easement.

This rule does not prevent some modifications to the easement that impose no additional burden on the servient estate.

Example: Landowner granted Public Irrigation District an easement across his property for an irrigation ditch. District permitted a public school, at its expense, to place the ditch entirely underground in a concrete pipe, but in the identical location as the surface ditch. In *Abbott v. Nampa School District No. 131,* 119 Idaho 544 (1991), the Idaho Supreme Court held that, because no additional burden was imposed, District and the public school could place the ditch underground.

4. **Enlargement of the dominant estate:** An easement, however created, cannot be used for the benefit of land that is not the dominant estate. See, e.g., *S.S. Kresge Co. of Michigan v. Winkelman Realty Co.,* 260 Wis. 372 (1952); *Kanefsky v. Dratch Construction Co.,* 376 Pa. 188 (1954); *Penn Bowling Recreation Center, Inc. v. Hot Shoppes, Inc.,* 179 F.2d 64 (D.C. Cir. 1949). However, that rule does not always mean that the appropriate remedy for such misuse is to enjoin the violation.

★**Example:** Voss owned a wooded tract in a rural residential area of Washington overlooking the Hood Canal (Parcel A). Voss's Parcel A was burdened by an easement for right of way benefiting Parcel B. Brown purchased Parcel B and an adjacent Parcel C that was not benefited by the easement for access crossing Parcel A. Brown began to construct a residence that straddled the lot line between Parcels B and C, both of which Brown owned, and used the easement to bring in construction materials and personnel. Annoyed, Voss obstructed the easement and Brown sued to enforce the easement. Voss countersued to enjoin Brown from using the easement to benefit Parcel C, the nondominant estate. A trial court denied the injunction sought by Voss on the theory that Brown's use of the easement was reasonable, even though Brown was using it to benefit land that was not the dominant estate. The Washington intermediate appeals court reversed and issued the injunction, applying the traditional rule that an easement may not be used for the benefit of property to which the benefit is not appurtenant. In *Brown v. Voss,* 105 Wn. 2d 366 (1986), the Washington Supreme Court reversed, reasoning that although the appeals court was correct to conclude that any physical enlargement of the dominant estate is wrongful, an injunction should not issue because there was no evidence of irreparable harm to Voss from the enlargement: There was no increase in the volume or type of traffic or other increase in the burden placed on Voss's servient estate. Accordingly, the Washington Supreme Court sustained the trial court's award of $1 in damages to Voss. The usual remedy for using an easement for the benefit of a nondominant estate is an ***injunction*** to prevent the use, which leaves the parties free to reverse this outcome, if they wish, by private bargain. The approach taken by the Washington Supreme Court drags into court the private bargaining that would otherwise occur post-injunction, in the form of argument over the amount of damages and also over the relative equities of an injunction. Moreover, if damages only are awarded, the litigation might not be over, because the use of the nondominant estate now benefited by the easement might change, leading to further dispute. A foresighted drafter of the easement might have provided for automatic termination of the easement if the dominant estate owner uses it for the benefit of a nondominant estate.

5. **Division of an easement's benefit:** Different rules apply to division of the benefit of an easement appurtenant and an easement in gross, but both have the same objective — *preventing an unintended increase in the burden on the servient estate.*

   a. **Appurtenant easement: Division of the dominant estate:** The general rule is that a dominant estate may be divided and that each part of the divided estate is entitled to enjoy the easement, but this rule is subject to the important limit that the resulting increased burden on the servient estate must be within the original contemplation of the parties, a state of mind that is often necessarily inferred. Courts consider whether the division of the dominant estate is a "normal development," whether the division is foreseeable, and whether the burden on the servient estate is substantially increased.

   b. **Easements in gross and profits à prendre**

      i. **Nonexclusive easements:** The holder of a *nonexclusive* profit or easement in gross (one shared with the servient estate) may *not* divide it, because division would likely result in decreased utility of the use to the servient estate.

      Example: George, owner of Blackpool, grants Alexa the nonexclusive right to fish in Blackpool. If Alexa were permitted to subdivide the right, increased fishing pressure on Blackpool would result. This bright-line rule prevents that result and does not consider the relative burden of Alexa's division of her nonexclusive right into 2 or 1,000 users. The assumption embedded in the bright-line rule is that the more users, the higher the likelihood that each user will seek to catch as many fish as possible, because the cost of fewer fish will be borne by the other users. See, e.g., *Hinds v. Phillips Petroleum Co.,* 591 P.2d 697 (Okla. 1979); *Stanton v. T.L. Herbert & Sons,* 141 Tenn. 440 (1919).

      ii. **Exclusive easements in one person:** If a profit or easement in gross is *exclusive and vested in one person,* that person has the right to divide it, unless the easement or profit stipulates to the contrary. The rationale is that the risk of excessive use is borne by the easement or profit holder alone, and that person has it within their power to limit the risk by refraining entirely from division, so division ought not be objectionable.

      iii. **Exclusive easements in multiple persons: The "one stock" rule:** If a profit or easement in gross is *exclusive and vested in two or more persons,* the traditional rule is that division is permitted, *but the easement or profit must be used as a single unit.* This rule, derived from *Mountjoy's Case,* 1 Godbolt 17, 4 Leonard 147, Coke on Littleton 164b, 78 Eng. Rep. 11 (1583), holds that joint users may divide their easement or profit, but that the entire use must be conducted as a single unit. This rule prevents undue exploitation of resources by one user at the expense of his fellow users. A solo user of a right held by multiple people has the incentive to take as many fish or as much timber or coal as he can, because a disproportionate amount of the cost of exhaustion of the resource is borne by everyone else. By contrast, if the easement or profit must be worked together, there is no incentive to overexploit, because the cost of exhaustion of the resource is borne entirely by the easement or profit holders.

★**Example:** Frank and Rufus Miller jointly owned the right to fish, boat, and bathe in Lake Naomi. When Rufus's estate began to grant separate licenses to third parties for these purposes, Frank sought to enjoin the licensees from using Lake Naomi, partly on the ground that Rufus's estate lacked any legal authority to subdivide the rights by granting separate licenses. In *Miller v. Lutheran Conference & Camp Assn.*, 331 Pa.241 (1938), the Pennsylvania Supreme Court applied the rationale and principle of *Mountjoy's Case* when it decided that the boating, bathing, and fishing easement in gross held jointly by the Miller brothers could not be divided.

iv. **Exclusive easements in multiple persons: The "no increased burden" rule:** The one-stock rule, while still predominant, has been discarded by some courts in favor of a rule that permits division (or *apportionment* as it is sometimes called) if the *burden on the servient estate is not increased beyond what was initially contemplated.* See, e.g., *Centel Cable TV Co. of Ohio v. Cook,* 58 Ohio St. 2d 8 (1991); *Jolliff v. Hardin Cable Television Co.,* 26 Ohio St. 2d 103 (1971); *Cousins v. Alabama Power Co.,* 597 So. 2d 683 (1992); *Witteman v. Jack Barry Cable TV,* 183 Cal. App. 3d 1101 (1986).

6. **Use or interference by servient estate owner**

   a. **Use by servient estate owner:** Unless the easement grants an *exclusive* use right to the easement holder, the servient estate may use the easement to the extent that the use is *reasonable* and does not substantially interfere with the easement holder's use.

   Example: Landowner granted a nonexclusive easement to the city of Pasadena for the installation and maintenance of underground water mains along a five-foot-wide corridor, then granted California-Michigan Land & Water a similar easement along the same corridor. In *Pasadena v. California-Michigan Land & Water Co.,* 17 Cal. 2d 576 (1941), the California Supreme Court ruled that, because Landowner could use the easement so long as its use constituted no unreasonable interference with Pasadena's use, it was entitled to grant a competing easement to California-Michigan that was no more of an interference.

   b. **Interference by servient estate owner:** The servient estate owner may not *unreasonably interfere* with the easement holder's use of the easement. What constitutes an unreasonable interference is highly fact-specific.

   Example: Sakansky owned property on Main Street in Laconia, NH, that included an appurtenant easement for right of way, 18 feet wide, over Wein's property. Wein proposed to build a structure over the easement, leaving a passageway 18 feet wide and 8 feet high. To accommodate overheight vehicles, Wein proposed a new and more circuitous way over his property to Sakansky's dominant estate. In *Sakansky v. Wein,* 86 N.H. 337 (1933), the New Hampshire Supreme Court concluded that a "rule of reason" applied, that it was not reasonable to limit the headroom of the easement to 8 feet (even with the proposed alternative access), but that Wein was free to erect a structure over the easement so long as the headroom were reasonable.

   Example: Servient estate owner constructs speed bumps in an easement for right of way to slow down the traffic. If the speed of the traffic before the speed bumps was excessive, this is a reasonable interference. See, e.g., *Marsh v. Pullen,* 50 Or. App. 405 (1981). However, if the prior traffic was already slow, or if the speed bumps are exceedingly large, hazardous, or numerous, the interference might be unreasonable. See, e.g., *Beiser v. Hensic,* 655 S.W.2d 660 (Mo. App. 1983).

E. **Termination of easements: Easements are extinguished in five principal ways: (1)** *expiration,* **(2)** *merger,* **(3) some** *act of the easement holder,* **(4)** *complete cessation of purpose,* **or (5) some** *act of the servient estate owner.* **Once an easement is extinguished, it** *cannot be revived* **— it must be created anew in one of the ways easements are formed.**

1. **Expiration:** An easement created by grant may expire by its terms.

    Example: Fred grants Wilma an easement appurtenant for right of way for 25 years. The easement expires automatically at the end of 25 years. If Fred had granted Wilma the easement appurtenant "only until the city constructs a dedicated street that abuts Wilma's property," the easement would automatically expire on that event.

2. **Merger:** If the easement holder also acquires title to the servient estate, the easement is extinguished because an easement exists only in land owned by somebody else.

    ★**Example:** Refer back to the *Brown v. Voss* example. After the litigation was over, Brown defaulted on his purchase of Parcel B (the dominant estate), which was then sold to Voss, owner of Parcel A, the servient estate. At that moment, the easement burdening Parcel A and benefiting Parcel B was extinguished forever.

    Example: Frieda owns an easement in gross to fish in Shire Pond, located on Shingleshire. Later, when Frieda buys Shingleshire, the easement in gross is extinguished forever.

    The easement holder must acquire the ***entire servient estate*** for merger to extinguish the easement. If only part of the servient estate is acquired, and use of the easement still burdens the other part, the easement is not extinguished. See *Castle Associates v. Schwartz,* 63 App. Div. 2d 481 (N.Y. App. 1976). Note that these principles work in reverse, too. If the servient estate owner acquires the dominant estate, the easement is also extinguished forever.

3. **Actions of the easement holder:** The easement holder may do a number of things that will extinguish the easement.

    a. **Release:** The easement holder may release the easement, either unilaterally or as part of an agreement with the servient estate owner. Generally, a release must be written, because it affects an interest in real property and so is within the scope of the Statute of Frauds. An oral release is valid, through equitable estoppel, when the servient estate owner relies on it to his substantial detriment.

    b. **Abandonment:** An easement may be extinguished by abandonment if the easement holder manifests a ***clear and unequivocal intention to abandon*** the easement. Mere ***nonuse will not suffice*** to prove abandonment. Even if the easement is never used, it is not extinguished by lack of use and nothing more. See, e.g., *Lindsey v. Clark,* 193 Va. 522 (1952). Abandonment is established by ***acts of the easement holder*** that clearly and unequivocally establish **either a** *present intent to relinquish the easement* **or** *a purpose inconsistent with its future existence.*

    ★**Example:** The Vermont Railway owned a "right of way" easement for its rail line through Vermont. In 1970, it ceased operations over the portion of the line in dispute, using the tracks only to store railroad cars. In 1975, the Railway removed all of the tracks, switches, and other railroad equipment from the section in dispute. In the late 1980s, a trial judge ruled that the Railway had abandoned its easement in 1975, and that ruling was affirmed in *Preseault v. United States,* 100 F.3d 1525 (Fed. Cir. 1996). The easement holder's conduct manifesting an intent to abandon can be affirmative or negative.

Example: Railway, which owned an easement over Norton's land, removed its tracks and did not use the easement for ten years. The affirmative act of removal, coupled with nonuse, proved abandonment. *Norton v. Duluth Transfer Ry., 129 Minn. 126 (1915).*

Example: In 1955, Fagan granted an easement for access to Gull Lake over Lot 20 in favor of property owned by Hickerson's predecessor. In 1958, Fagan conveyed Lot 20 to Bender, who lacked knowledge of the easement. Bender built a house and other improvements that blocked the easement. Thirty years later, Hickerson sought to enforce the easement, which Bender claimed had been abandoned. In *Hickerson v. Bender,* 500 N.W.2d 169 (Minn. App. 1993), the Minnesota Court of Appeals agreed with Bender, ruling that the failure of the easement holders to object to Bender's blockage of the easement was "conduct clearly inconsistent" with continued use of the easement.

Don't assume it's easy to prove abandonment: "Far more decisions contain dictum about abandonment" than actually find abandonment; courts mostly "find that while the easement holder ceased to use the easement, he had no intention to abandon." R. Cunningham, et al., *The Law of Property* 465 (2d ed. 1993).

c. **Alteration of dominant estate:** If the *dominant estate owner alters the dominant estate so that the easement may no longer be used,* the easement is extinguished.

Example: The owner of Adirondack, a three-story office building, grants an easement appurtenant to Catskill, an abutting three-story office building, "for access from Catskill, the presently existing office building, in case of fire or other emergency across the roof of Adirondack and down the existing fire escape." The owner of Catskill demolishes it and builds a ten-story replacement. The easement is extinguished because its *particular purpose,* providing emergency access from the then-existing building, has been eliminated by the dominant estate owner's act of demolition. See, e.g., *Cotting v. Boston,* 201 Mass. 97 (1909). If the easement were not limited to this particular purpose — if, instead, it were "for access from any structure ever erected on the ground presently occupied by Catskill" — the destruction of Catskill would not affect the easement. Unless the easement's limited purpose is very explicit, courts tend to place a general construction upon the purpose of easements. See, e.g., *First Natl. Trust & Savings Bank v. Raphael,* 201 Va. 718 (1960).

4. **Cessation of purpose:** If the *purpose of an easement* has *completely ceased,* the easement is extinguished.

   a. **Easements by necessity:** An easement created by implication from necessity terminates when the necessity is eliminated, because its purpose has ceased.

   b. **Easements by estoppel:** An easement by estoppel (an irrevocable license) terminates in most jurisdictions when the licensee has reaped the full value of the expenditures made in reliance upon the license. At that point, its purpose has ceased to exist. See section II.A.4. c.ii, above.

c. Extrinsic changes that vitiate purpose: If acts of third parties completely vitiate the easement's purpose, the easement is extinguished.

Example: Leaman's property benefited from a right-of-way easement appurtenant (created by grant, not implied from necessity) across American Oil's property for access to a public road. When the public road was abandoned and another created, making the easement pointless (it turned into a dead-end), its purpose ceased. Though this change was entirely brought about by third parties (public authorities) and was not of the dominant estate owner's volition, nonetheless the easement terminated. *American Oil Co. v. Leaman,* 199 Va. 637 (1958).

d. Accidental destruction of the servient estate: If the servient estate is *accidentally destroyed* (i.e., not through the servient owner's intent), the easement is extinguished. This usually requires that the easement be *limited to use of a specific building.* If the easement extends to the ground itself, the destruction of a building will have no effect on the easement, but if the easement is just in the building (and not the land also), the easement terminates if the building is accidentally destroyed. See, e.g., *Cohen v. Adolph Kutner Co.,* 177 Cal. 592 (1918). Intentional destruction of the servient estate normally renders the servient owner liable for damages and does not extinguish the easement (see, e.g., *Rothschild v. Wolf,* 20 Cal. 2d 17 (1942)), but if a building is so obsolete and shabby that its continuation is uneconomic, its condition may be deemed "tantamount to [accidental] destruction," thus extinguishing the easement. See, e.g., *Walner v. City of Turlock,* 230 Cal. App. 2d 399 (1964).

5. Actions of the servient estate holder: There are two principal ways the owner of the servient estate can extinguish an easement.

a. Intentional destruction of servient estate: A minority of states hold that a servient owner's intentional destruction of a building burdened by an easement in the building alone (not the land) extinguishes the easement if continued operation of the servient building is economically disadvantageous. See, e.g., *Union Natl. Bank of Lowell v. Nesmith,* 238 Mass. 247 (1921). Most states reject this rule. See section II.E.4.d, above.

b. Prescription: A servient owner can extinguish an easement burdening the servient estate by adverse use sufficient to constitute prescription. The elements of adverse use are the same as for creation of an easement by prescription. See section II.B.4, above.

Example: Bender built a house and other improvements that blocked an easement for passage across his property to a lake. Thirty years later, Hickerson sought to enforce the easement. The easement had been extinguished by Bender's adverse use. *Hickerson v. Bender,* 500 N.W.2d 169 (Minn. App. 1993).

6. Changed circumstances in the surrounding area: The doctrine of *changed circumstances in the surrounding area,* which may extinguish a real covenant or equitable servitude, does *not generally apply to easements.*

Example: The Town of Brevard acquired an easement by grant for a garbage dump. The surrounding area changed, and the garbage dump became disagreeable. Nevertheless, the mere change in *surrounding circumstances,* while perhaps sufficient to extinguish a real covenant or equitable servitude, was not a valid reason to extinguish an easement by grant. *Waldrop v. Town of Brevard,* 233 N.C. 26 (1950).

Don't confuse this rule, which deals with changed circumstances in the *surrounding area,* with changed circumstances in the *dominant estate* or *servient estate.* Some changes in circumstances in the dominant estate or servient estate do in fact extinguish an easement (e.g., cessation of purpose or destruction of the servient estate). See, e.g., sections II.E.4 and II.E.5.a, above.

III. REAL COVENANTS

A. Introduction

1. **Real covenants defined:** A covenant is a promise and is generally the province of the law of contracts. A *real covenant* is a promise about land usage that **runs with an estate in land,** meaning that it **binds** *or* **benefits** *subsequent owners* of the estate. A real covenant may be **affirmative** or **negative.** A promise to *use land in a specified fashion* (e.g., to maintain a boxwood hedge) is affirmative; a promise *not to use land in a specified fashion* (e.g., no industrial use) is negative. Both types are enforceable.

2. **Benefit and burden:** A promise about land usage burdens some land and normally benefits other land.

   Example: Barbara, owner of Blackacre, promises Thomas, owner of Monteverdi, that she and her assigns will maintain forever a boxwood hedge on Blackacre that forms a border with Monteverdi. Blackacre bears the *burden* of this promise, and Monteverdi enjoys its *benefit.* (The nomenclature of dominant and servient estates is confined to easements.)

3. **"Runs with the land":** If one party breaches a covenant made with another person — even if it concerns land usage — the issues presented are purely a matter of contract law. Property law becomes involved only when a covenant about land use is sought to be enforced either by or against a successor to the *estate in the land* benefited or burdened by the covenant.

   Example: Refer to the prior example. If Barbara sells Blackacre to James and James rips out the hedge, Thomas may sue James for this breach of the covenant only if the burden of the covenant runs with the estate in Blackacre that James acquired from Barbara. Similarly, if Thomas sells Monteverdi to John and Barbara destroys the hedge, John may sue Barbara only if the benefit of the covenant runs with the estate in Monteverdi that John acquired from Thomas. Finally, if both Barbara and Thomas have sold to James and John, respectively, John may sue James for breach of the covenant only if both the burden and the benefit of the covenant run with their respective estates in land.

   The question of exactly when the burden or benefit runs is a complicated, technical subject addressed in sections III.B, C, D, and E, below. When you recall that a *real covenant* is defined as a covenant about land use that *runs with an estate in land,* you will realize that almost all the substance of this subject lies in the issue of when burdens or benefits, or both, run with **estates** in land. Although lawyers commonly speak of covenants "running with the land," that usage is mildly misleading: A real covenant runs with the **estate in land,** not the land itself. This distinction is important when considering whether *privity of estate* is present. See section III.D, below.

4. **Remedy available: Damages:** There are two principal remedies for breach of a promise — *money damages* or an *injunction* to compel performance of the promise. For

historical reasons, an award of damages is a ***legal remedy,*** and an injunction is an ***equitable remedy.*** Although virtually all American courts are combined courts of ***law*** and ***equity,*** it is still necessary to establish your client's entitlement to the remedy she seeks. If your client wants ***damages*** for breach of a covenant about land usage, she must prove that the covenant is an enforceable ***real covenant.*** If she cannot do that, the same promise might still be enforceable as an ***equitable servitude,*** but the only remedy then available for breach will be an injunction. See section IV, below. When you think ***damages,*** think ***real covenant;*** when you think ***real covenant,*** think ***damages.***

5. **Development of the real covenant:** English judges invented the ***real*** covenant to make bargains about land use last. Before real covenants were invented, only the immediate parties to a covenant were able to sue to enforce the covenant or were liable for its breach. This rule frustrated the efficient allocation of interests in land.

   Example: Morton leases Blackacre to Selwyn for a term of 15 years. Morton promises to build a new barn if the existing one ever burns down, and Selwyn promises to pay an annual rent of £50. Now, suppose Morton conveys his reversion in Blackacre to Algernon, and then the barn burns. Before real covenants, only Morton was liable for failure to rebuild the barn. Similarly, if Selwyn were to convey his leasehold to Edward, Edward would not be liable for rent.

   Because these rules inhibited the formation and transferability of leaseholds, English judges decided that covenants about land use attached themselves to the estates in land benefited or burdened by the covenant. Thus, successors to those estates could enforce the covenant or be liable for its breach. This rule developed from *Spencer's Case,* 5 Co. 16a, 77 Eng. Rep. 72 (K.B. 1583), in which the requirements for "running covenants" first began to be stated. By the nineteenth century, though, English judges confined real covenants to leaseholds, and they have kept them there. See *Keppell v. Bailey,* 39 Eng. Rep. 1042 (Ch. 1834). In America, real covenants may be created when a fee simple is transferred or even between neighbors with no transfer of title; the rule governing this point (which is rapidly disappearing) is called ***horizontal privity of estate.*** See section III.E.1, below.

6. **Covenant, not condition:** A real covenant is a ***promise*** concerning land use; it is ***not*** a ***condition*** of continued land use. Breach of a real covenant renders the violator liable for damages; breach of a condition causes forfeiture of the estate. Conditions concerning land use are the meat of defeasible fees. See Chapter 2.

7. **Compared to easements:** Affirmative easements confer rights to use another's land; real covenants do not. Real covenants are promises that land will be used, or not used, in specified ways. Negative easements, however, are very much like real covenants. A ***right*** to an unobstructed view over your neighbor's land (a negative easement) is functionally identical to a ***promise*** by your neighbor not to obstruct your view (a real covenant). While courts are reluctant to create negative easements (see section II.A.2.b.ii, above), they may well enforce the promise as a real covenant. Mostly, an interest claimed in another person's land that requires that person to refrain from some use will be construed as a covenant, enforceable against successors if the elements of a running real covenant are established.

8. **Compared to equitable servitudes:** An equitable servitude is a covenant about land use that is enforceable in equity against successors to the benefited or burdened estates in land. The rules concerning the running of equitable servitudes differ from the rules concerning the running of real covenants. See section IV, below.

B. Creation of real covenants: A real covenant can only be created by a written instrument. A deed signed only by the grantor suffices to create a real covenant on the part of the grantee, because the grantee is held to have made the deed his own by accepting it. Real covenants *may not be created by implication or prescription.*

C. Enforceability by or against successors: The elements necessary to enforce the *burden* of a real covenant against a successor to the burdened estate are more difficult to establish than the elements needed to claim the *benefit* of a real covenant by a successor to the benefited estate. The rationale is that, because the burden of a real covenant exposes the successor to liability that is potentially unlimited, this burden ought to be imposed only on those people who acquire the *identical estate* that was initially burdened. The elements necessary for the burden of a real covenant, or its benefit, or both, to run with the estate in land are as follows.

   1. Intent: The original parties must have **intended** *the burden (or benefit, or both) to run.* Almost always, this is satisfied by an explicit statement in the covenant that it binds "successors, heirs, and assigns." See section III.D, below.

   2. Horizontal privity: The older, but now largely discarded view, is that *horizontal privity — privity of estate* between the *original parties* — is required for the *burden* to run, but **not** for the *benefit* to run. Only a few relationships satisfy this technical term and concept, which is discussed fully at section III.E.1, below. All commentators and many courts reject this requirement altogether.

   3. Vertical privity: The traditional rule is that *vertical privity — privity of estate* between the *original promisor and the successor to the burdened estate* — is necessary for either the *burden* or *benefit* to run, but the definition of vertical privity is more easily met for benefits to run than for burdens to run. This technical concept is discussed fully at section III.E.2. below. The *Restatement (Third) of Property* (Servitudes) §5.2 rejects vertical privity in favor of treating *negative covenants* as binding on all future *owners or possessors* of the *burdened* and *benefited* properties, and creates entirely new rules for *affirmative covenants.* See section III.E.3, below.

   4. Touch and concern: The substance of the promise must *touch and concern* the burdened land and, in most states, the benefited land as well. It is commonly said of real covenants that if the benefit is in gross, the burden will not run. See section III.F, below.

D. "Running elements": Intent: The original parties to the covenant must intend for its burdens or benefits, or both, to run to successors to their respective estates in land. Courts look first to the covenant itself: Covenants typically state that they are intended to run or, what is the same thing, the parties promise on behalf of themselves, "their heirs, successors, or assigns." If a covenant is silent on this point, courts will examine all the surrounding circumstances (e.g., the covenant's purpose, conduct of the parties) to decide whether the parties intended to create a running covenant. Although old English law required that covenants dealing with things not yet in existence (e.g., a promise to build a structure) could not run unless the promisor had explicitly obligated his successors to perform the promise (see *Spencer's Case,* sections III.A.5, above and III.E.1, below), this rule has been abandoned nearly everywhere in America.

E. "Running elements": Privity of estate: Privity of estate exists in two dimensions. *Horizontal privity* refers to a relationship between the **original parties** to the covenant. *Vertical privity* refers to a relationship between one of the original parties and her successor to the estate in land owned by the original party. Traditionally, both horizontal and vertical privity were required for the burden of a real covenant to run, but only vertical privity was required for the benefit of a real covenant to run. Today, horizontal privity has been discarded by professors and many courts, but *not by all courts.*

1. **Horizontal privity:** Horizontal privity expresses a value judgment: It exists when the law deems the relationship between the estates in land owned by the original contracting parties to be sufficiently connected to permit the burden of the covenant to run. But what connection is sufficient? There are three views, none of which is mutually inconsistent with the others. Each developed from a different reading of *Spencer's Case,* where Elizabethan judges ruled that an original leasehold tenant's promise to build a wall on the premises could be enforced against a successor tenant because the original parties were in privity of estate. The court, however, didn't explain why.

   a. **Landlord-tenant view:** In 1834, two and one-half centuries after *Spencer's Case,* English judges finally held that horizontal privity was met *only if the original parties were landlord and tenant.* In England, horizontal privity is required and remains limited to covenants in leases. The burden of other covenants about land use are enforceable against successors, if at all, only as equitable servitudes. This view is no longer recognized in America, though some old cases did take this tight approach.

   b. **Mutual interests in the burdened estate:** Another view of *Spencer's Case* is that the parties had *mutual interests* in the burdened estate: The lessee had a leasehold, and the lessor had a reversion. On this view, *any* mutual interest *that exists at the time the covenant is created* would be sufficient to create horizontal privity. The requisite mutual interest could include a pre-existing easement or profit, or possessory and future interests in the same land, as well as a landlord-tenant relationship.

   Example: Adam owns Blackacre in fee simple and has a possibility of reverter in Whiteacre, which Eleanor owns in fee simple determinable ("so long as Whiteacre is used for animal husbandry"). Eleanor promises Adam, for herself and her assigns, that she will never again raise emus on Whiteacre. Horizontal privity is established, because both Adam and Eleanor have mutual interests in Whiteacre that preceded the covenant. If Eleanor should transfer her determinable fee to Mary Jane, who knows of the covenant, its burden will run with the estate Mary Jane acquired.

   Example: Oilco has the right to remove oil from Blackacre, owned by Isaac, who then then promises Oilco that he will not graze his sheep within 100 yards of each oil well drilled by Oilco on Blackacre. Horizontal privity is established: Both Oilco and Isaac had interests in Blackacre prior to execution of the covenant. See, e.g., *Flying Diamond Oil Corp. v. Newton Sheep Co.,* 776 P.2d 618 (Utah, 1989).

   Every American state that requires horizontal privity recognizes at least this form of horizontal privity. Some recognize only this form of horizontal privity. See, e.g., *Morse v. Aldrich,* 36 Mass. 449 (1837); *Whitinsville Plaza, Inc. v. Kotseas,* 378 Mass. 85 (1979).

   c. **Conveyances, or "instantaneous privity":** A third view of *Spencer's Case* is that the fact the promise was contained in a conveyance was what created horizontal privity. On this view, *any "connection of interest"* between the original contracting parties will do, whether or not that interest was mutual or in existence prior to the creation of the covenant. The most common such interest that suffices to create horizontal privity is a conveyance.

Example: Elmer divides Blackacre into two lots, retaining one and conveying the other to Juanita under a deed by which Juanita promises never to use the lot for commercial purposes. Horizontal privity is present. For that single, instantaneous moment when title passed from Elmer to Juanita, there was a "connection of interest" between their estates. It's like the passing of the baton in a relay race — privity exists at the moment of exchange. See, e.g., *Runyon v. Paley,* 331 N.C. 293 (1992).

The conveyance view is cumulative — mutual interests (including, of course, those of landlord and tenant) will suffice to create horizontal privity, but so will conveyances. This view is adopted by the original (1944) *Restatement of Property,* §534, but the *Restatement (Third) of Property* (Servitudes) (2000) flatly rejects any requirement of horizontal privity.

d. Applies to *burdens,* not *benefits:* In virtually every jurisdiction that requires horizontal privity, the requirement is applicable *only for the burden of a covenant to run* and is *not necessary* for the benefit of a covenant to run. See, e.g., *City of Reno v. Matley,* 79 Nev. 49 (1963); *165 Broadway Building v. City Investing Co.,* 120 F.2d 813 (2d Cir. 1941). But there is the inevitable exception. See, e.g., *Albright v. Fish,* 136 Vt. 387 (1978).

e. Horizontal privity abolished: About eight states have had occasion to abolish horizontal privity altogether, as does the *Restatement (Third) of Property* (Servitudes) §2.4. See *Orange & Rockland Util. v. Philwood Estates,* 52 N.Y.2d 253 (1981); *Gallagher v. Bell,* 69 Md. App. 199 (1986). Other states that have abolished horizontal privity include Illinois, Minnesota, Montana, New Mexico, and Pennsylvania. Still more have given broad hints that horizontal privity is on the way out, and many others have not had occasion to confront the issue. A moment's reflection will reveal that there is *no logical connection* between the relationship of the original parties' estates and the wholly separate question of whether the burden of a promise about land use ought to run with the estate in that land. Horizontal privity is simply a crude device to restrict the burdens of covenants from persisting into the future. If there are good reasons for doing so, they ought to be articulated and formulated into rules of law that restrict running covenants for those reasons.

2. Vertical privity: Vertical privity exists when the successor has acquired the burdened or benefited estate in land held by the original party to the covenant. It is *harder to establish vertical privity for the* **burden** *of a covenant than it is for the benefit of that covenant.*

a. Burden of a covenant: To establish vertical privity to enforce the burden of a covenant against a successor, it is necessary to prove that the successor acquired *the exact same estate in land* owned by the original contracting party. See *Restatement of Property* §535 (1944). If something less than the original promisor's estate is conveyed, the burden does not run.

Example: Paul purchases a fee simple absolute in Blackthorn from Phyllis, owner of adjacent Tumbleweed. In the deed, Paul promises for himself and his assigns that he will not use Blackthorn for industrial purposes, but he later leases Blackthorn to Ace Industries for use as a factory. Phyllis may not enforce the burden of the covenant against Ace because Ace did not succeed to the *identical estate* held by Paul, but Phyllis may sue Paul for breach of contract. See, e.g., *Old Dominion Iron & Steel Corp. v. Virginia Electric & Power Co.,* 215 Va. 658 (1975).

b. **Benefit of a covenant:** The benefit of a covenant will run to a successor of *some interest* in the benefited estate. See *Restatement of Property* §547 (1944). Just about any interest will do.

Example: Refer to the prior example. Suppose Paul had sold his fee simple absolute in Blackthorn to Ace, thus satisfying vertical privity for the burden. If Phyllis were to lease Tumbleweed to Jack for a ten-year term, Jack could sue Ace to enforce the real covenant and obtain damages because Jack succeeded to *some interest* of Phyllis in Tumbleweed. He need not acquire Phyllis's entire estate in order to reap the benefit of the original covenant. See, e.g., *Old Dominion Iron & Steel Corp. v. Virginia Electric & Power Co.*

c. **The problem of adverse possessors:** Land burdened or benefited by a covenant may later be acquired by adverse possession. Is the adverse possessor in vertical privity? *Restatement of Property* §547 (Illus. 3) (1944) took the position that an adverse possessor lacked vertical privity with respect to both the burden and benefit of a covenant. The *Restatement (Third) of Property* (Servitudes) §5.2 holds that the burdens of *negative* and *affirmative* covenants run to adverse possessors. Benefits of *affirmative* covenants run to adverse possessors who have acquired title, but adverse possessors who have not yet acquired title may only enforce *affirmative* covenants (1) to repair, maintain, or render services to the benefited property, or (2) that confer benefits that may be enjoyed by the possessor without diminishing the value of the covenant to the true owner and without materially increasing the burden of performance on the burdened party.

d. **The problem of third-party beneficiaries:** Two parties may enter into a covenant about land use that imposes mutual benefits and burdens but also explicitly benefits a third party's estate. Is the third-party beneficiary able to sue to enforce the benefit of the covenant?

★**Example:** Oboe purchases Lot 1 from Flute, under a deed that stipulates that Oboe, for himself and his assigns, agrees to use Lot 1 for residential purposes only, and which further states that the promise is for the benefit of Lot 2 (owned by Flute) and Lot 3 (owned by Cello, who purchased it from Flute prior to this transaction). Oboe builds a gas station on Lot 1. May Cello enforce the covenant at law? There is no vertical privity, because Cello has not succeeded to any interest of Flute *after the benefit was created.* See, e.g., *Runyon v. Paley.* But the *Restatement of Property* §541 (1944) provides that a covenant may be enforced by "such third persons as are also beneficiaries of the promise." Cases recognizing the ability of third-party beneficiaries to enforce covenants are almost always suits in equity, thus involving equitable servitudes, not real covenants. In **Neponsit Property Owners Assn. v. Emigrant Industrial Savings Bank,** 278 N.Y. 248 (1938), the New York Court of Appeals held that a homeowners' association that did not succeed to any estate of the benefited promisee was able to enforce the benefit of such a covenant on the theory that it was the corporate agent of the owners of benefited estates.

3. **The Third Restatement's alternative to vertical privity:** The *Restatement (Third) of Property*, Servitudes, jettisons the vertical privity concept as to both real covenants and equitable servitudes. Instead, it distinguishes between *negative* and *affirmative* covenants. A negative covenant is a *promise not to do an act*; an affirmative covenant is a *promise to do an act*. The characterization should turn on the substance of the matter rather than the verbal formulation. Thus, a promise "not to allow the trees to obstruct the view," though phrased negatively, requires some affirmative action to discharge its burden.

a. Negative covenants: Section 5.2 of the Third *Restatement (Third) of Property* treats negative promises like easements, imposing the burdens of such promises on all subsequent owners or possessors of the burdened estate, and extending the benefits of such promises to all subsequent owners or possessors of the benefited estate.

b. Affirmative covenants: The *Restatement (Third) of Property* creates separate rules for affirmative promises for *lessees*, holders of *life estates*, and *adverse possessors*. In addition, it treats the burdens and benefits of affirmative promises differently in each category.

    i. Lessees: A lessee is bound by an affirmative promise that **burdens** the leased estate *only* if it is a promise that can more reasonably be performed by the lessee-in-possession than the owner not in possession of the property. Lessees enjoy the **benefits** of affirmative promises that inure to the leased estate if they are promises (1) to repair, maintain, or render services to the benefited property, or (2) confer benefits that may be enjoyed by the possessor without diminishing the covenant's value to the lessor and without materially increasing the burden of performance on the burdened party.

    ii. Life estates: All of the **benefits** and **burdens** of affirmative covenants run to holders of **legal life estates** (those that are not beneficial interests under a trust), but a life tenant's liability for breach of an affirmative covenant cannot exceed the value of the life estate. *Restatement (Third) of Property*, Servitudes §5.4.

    iii. Adverse possessors: Adverse possessors who have acquired title get the benefit of affirmative covenants, but adverse possessors who have not yet acquired title may only enforce *affirmative* covenants (1) to repair, maintain, or render services to the benefited property, or (2) that confer benefits that may be enjoyed by the possessor without diminishing the value of the covenant to the true owner and without materially increasing the burden of performance on the burdened party.

    These rules do not have the force of law; they are merely the advice of the American Law Institute. Because the Restatements of the ALI are influential, these rules are likely to be adopted over time. At the moment, however, reports of the death of vertical privity are, as Mark Twain quipped of himself, greatly exaggerated.

F. "Running elements": Touch and concern the land: In order for either the benefit or burden of a real covenant to run to successors in interest, the substance of the covenant must **touch and concern** the benefited or burdened land. The same is true for equitable servitudes, and the meaning of **touch and concern** is the same for equitable servitudes and real covenants. Touch and concern originated as a way to control which covenants should be permitted to burden or benefit successors in interest, but modern commentary (particularly the *Restatement (Third) of Property*, Servitudes) is critical. The *Restatement (Third)* purports to discard touch and concern and asserts that the function of touch and concern can be fully performed by its doctrines governing termination of servitudes. Thus, the *Restatement (Third) of Property*, Servitudes, §3.1 holds that a servitude "is valid unless it is illegal or unconstitutional or violates public policy." The roster of such invalid servitudes includes, but is not limited to, servitudes that (1) are "arbitrary, spiteful, or capricious''; (2) "unreasonably" burden a "fundamental constitutional right"; (3) impose an "unreasonable restraint on alienation"; (4) impose an "unreasonable restraint on trade or competition"; and (5) are "unconscionable." However, because courts have not yet embraced the Third Restatement's approach, it is useful to canvass touch and concern.

1. **Essential meaning of touch and concern:** Judicial understanding of touch and concern has evolved. Early cases focused on whether the substance of the covenant delivered burdens and benefits that necessarily involved the *tangible use and enjoyment* of the land, but judicial and scholarly attention began to focus on the *effects* of the covenant.

   ★**Example:** As part of a planned development, the developer sold lots subject to a covenant to pay money annually to a homeowners' association for the purpose of maintaining private roads and sidewalks owned in common by all lot owners. In holding that the covenant touched and concerned the burdened estate, the New York Court of Appeals, in *Neponsit Property Owners' Assn. v. Emigrant Industrial Savings Bank,* 278 N.Y. 248 (1938), concluded that the covenant "affect[s] the legal relations — the advantages and the burdens — of the parties to the covenant, as owners of particular parcels of land and not merely as members of the community in general."

   To conduct this inquiry, courts have looked to the *effect of the covenant* — does it depress the value of the burdened land and increase the value of the benefited land? This approach uses *marketplace values* to determine what touches and concerns land. This approach may, in the end, be simply an attempt to determine which covenants are *sufficiently economically beneficial that they would be imposed by the present owners if they had the opportunity to negotiate between themselves free of transaction costs.*

   a. **The economic theory:** The law of servitudes is built on an implicit general presumption that servitudes reflect an efficient allocation of external costs associated with land use, and so should be enforced by and against the original promisors (and successors, if the other elements of running covenants are present).

   Example: Quikfat, a fast-food chain, proposes to build a store in a residential neighborhood. The presence of the store will damage surrounding residential values and will provide economic benefits to Quikfat. To simplify, say that the total benefit to Quikfat is $100,000 and that 100 neighbors will each suffer damage of $2,500. If each neighbor contributes $1,500 to purchase from Quikfat its promise not to build a fast-food store on the property, Quikfat will be better off (it will receive $150,000 to forego a benefit of $100,000), and each neighbor will be better off (by paying $1,500 to avoid a loss of $2,500). Creation of a servitude to secure this bargain is efficient. See, e.g., Ronald Coase, *The Problem of Social Cost,* 3 J. Law & Econ. 1 (1960). But neighbors won't pay unless they can be assured that the promise will endure, because they wish to forestall damage from Quikfat's use now and in the future. Hence, one function of "touch and concern" is to limit running covenants to those promises that are the **type of promise** *about land use to which* **future owners** *reasonably might agree.* From the above illustration, it should be clear that these promises are those that *deliver net social or economic benefits.* In the above example, the servitude produces net economic benefits of $150,000 ($250,000 of avoided costs minus $100,000 of foregone gain). See *Restatement of Property,* §537 (comment h) (1944) (Relationship between benefit and burden must have a "reasonable prospect of promoting land utilization as a whole").

2. **Negative covenants:** Negative covenants almost always touch and concern the burdened land, because their nature is to restrict land use. In nearly every case, they also deliver correlative benefits to other land.

Example: A promise given to neighbors in a residential community not to use Willowside for industrial purposes imposes burdens on Willowside but also generates correlative benefits to the surrounding residential land. The burden of the promise touches and concerns Willowside and the benefit of the promise touches and concerns the neighbors' land.

a. **Covenants against competition:** The burdens of covenants against competition generally touch and concern land, so long as they are reasonable in scope and duration. See, e.g., *Newcomb v. Congdon,* 160 App. Div. 2d 1192 (1990). The benefit of such covenants surely enhances the value of the benefited land, at least for the use insulated from competition, and so also touches and concerns the benefited land. See, e.g., *Whitinsville Plaza, Inc. v. Kotseas,* 378 Mass. 85 (1979). In *Davidson Bros., Inc. v. D. Katz & Sons, Inc.,* 274 N.J. Super. 159 (App. Div. 1994), a New Jersey appellate court invalidated a covenant that a building not be used as a grocery on the ground that it was contrary to "public policy" in that the surrounding community was poorly served by existing grocers.

3. **Affirmative covenants:** Courts are more reluctant to enforce affirmative covenants than negative covenants and sometimes use the touch-and-concern element to express this reluctance. Enforcement of affirmative covenants may require continuing judicial supervision and impose large (and sometimes crushing) obligations on successors to the covenant. An affirmative covenant that fails to address the economic external costs of land use is almost certainly one that does not touch and concern land.

Example: Kendall owned an ironworks and, in concert with other ironmongers, formed a corporation to operate a railroad and a lime quarry. On behalf of himself and his assigns, Kendall promised the corporation that his ironworks would purchase its requirements of lime from the quarry. Kendall sold the ironworks to Bailey, who refused to purchase lime from the quarry. In *Keppell v. Bailey,* 39 Eng. Rep. 1042 (Ch. 1834), the English Chancery court ruled that the burden of the covenant did not touch and concern the ironworks. Though it did not say so, it is evident that the covenant's purpose had nothing whatever to do with any external costs of using the land as an ironworks; it was a purely personal promise.

★**Example:** Stanley Stilwell sold a building lot to Caullett under a deed by which Stilwell reserved "the right to build or construct the original dwelling or building" on the lot. In ***Caullett v. Stanley Stilwell & Sons, Inc.,*** 67 N.J. Super. 111 (1961), the New Jersey court held that the covenant was unenforceable because it did not touch and concern Caullett's land. The promise did nothing to restrict land usage except in "the very incidental fashion" of precluding Caullett from construction unless Stilwell were to derive the builder's profit, making this "at best a personal arrangement . . . designed to [ensure] a profit" for Stilwell. There was no negative externality of Caullett's land use that the promise was designed to control.

As an alternative, occasionally a court will enforce an affirmative covenant (having concluded that the covenant touches and concerns) by creative remedies that resemble enforcement of a negative covenant.

Example: A developer constructed a golf course and a subdivision of 932 homes, each sold under an affirmative covenant of the developer that he would maintain the golf course for the benefit of the homeowners. The developer then sold the course to Oceanside Land Co., which allowed its condition to atrophy. The homeowners sought an injunction requiring Oceanside Land to repair and maintain the course. In *Oceanside Community Assn. v. Oceanside Land Co.,* 147 Cal. App. 3d 166 (1983), the court denied the injunction but granted the homeowners an equitable lien on the course in the amount of $9,320 each month the course was not properly maintained. Thus, the homeowners could foreclose on the course and acquire ownership if Oceanside Land failed to repair and maintain it, and Oceanside's financial exposure was limited to its investment in the land.

a. Covenants to provide utilities: These covenants generally touch and concern. See, e.g., *Choisser v. Eyman*, 22 Ariz. App. 587 (1974) (benefit of covenant to provide water); *Nicholson v. 300 Broadway Realty Corp.*, 7 N.Y.2d 240 (1959) (burden of covenant to provide steam heat). However, when such covenants are no longer useful, courts may construe their substance as not touching or concerning the burdened land. Recall that the *Restatement (Third) of Property*, Servitudes, §7.10, substitutes for touch and concern the doctrine that servitudes may be modified or terminated if changed circumstances make it "impossible as a practical matter to accomplish the purpose for which the servitude was created." Which doctrine should apply?

Example: Orchard Hill developed a tract of rural land for use as summer homes, and sold lots subject to a covenant that the purchaser and his successors would take and pay for water provided by Orchard Hill for six months of the year. Orchard Hill conveyed its interest to Eagle, and Gross acquired a lot from an original purchaser. Gross drilled his own well and then refused to take and pay for Eagle's water. In *Eagle Enterprises, Inc. v. Gross*, 39 N.Y.2d 505 (1976), the burden of the "take and pay" covenant was held not to touch and concern Gross's property, mostly because it had lost its utility to Gross, and its invalidation would not harm other lot owners who relied on seasonal water. Under the *Restatement (Third) of Property*, Servitudes, §7.10, the question would not be the initial validity of the covenant, but whether circumstances have sufficiently changed to make it impossible, as a practical matter, to accomplish the purpose of the servitude.

b. Covenants to pay money: The most common such covenant is one requiring payment of fees to a homeowners' association for the maintenance of common areas and facilities. These covenants are generally held to touch and concern land so long as the services produced by the payment enhance the value of the burdened land. This is virtually always the case when the payments maintain common streets, sidewalks, elevators, or other "essential" attributes of the development.

★**Example:** In *Neponsit Property Owners' Assn. v. Emigrant Industrial Savings Bank,* 278 N.Y. 248 (1938), the New York Court of Appeals held that a covenant to pay a fee to maintain common facilities touched and concerned the burdened property because the effect of the covenant was to impose burdens and advantages on estate holders in their unique capacity as landowners rather than as members of the general public.

There is some disagreement over whether covenants to pay for common recreational facilities touch and concern the burdened property. While the test is the same—Does it enhance value?—courts examine the following factors to determine this: Is the facility part of a ***common plan of development?*** Is the facility in ***close proximity*** to the burdened land? Is the facility ***open to common use of all burdened property owners?*** Most courts considering this issue have found that such covenants do touch and concern land. See, e.g., *Streams Sports Club, Ltd. v. Richmond*, 99 Ill. 2d 182 (1983); *Regency Homes Assn. v. Egermayer*, 243 Neb. 286 (1993); *Anthony v. Brea Glenbrook Club*, 58 Cal. App. 3d 506

(1976). But see *Chesapeake Ranch Club v. CRC Members,* 60 Md. App. 609 (1984) (recreational facility benefited community as a whole and did not enhance value of burdened lots).

4. **Benefit in gross:** The majority rule is summed up by an old saying, "If the benefit is in gross, the burden will not run." The rule comes from England, where easements in gross are not recognized. It was thus sensible for English courts to refuse to enforce the burden of a covenant against successors where the benefit was held in gross, because such a covenant is functionally identical to an easement in gross (particularly when the covenant is negative). See, e.g., *London County Council v. Allen,* [1914] 3 K.B. 642. American courts recognize easements in gross but still cling to the rule that "if the benefit is in gross, the burden won't run." See, e.g., *Chandler v. Smith,* 170 Cal. App. 2d 118 (1959); *Johnson v. State,* 27 Or. App. 581 (1976). *Restatement of Property* §537(a) (comment c), §543 (comment c) (1944). Contra: *Van Sant v. Rose,* 260 Ill 401 (1913). *Restatement (Third) of Property,* Servitudes, §2.6, comment d (2000), squarely rejects the majority rule, holding that the burden runs even if the benefit is in gross. See, e.g., *Eastling v. B.P. Products North America, Inc.,* 578 F.3d 831 (8th Cir. 2009) (applying Minnesota law and adopting the *Restatement (Third)* view because "we predict that the Minnesota Supreme Court would apply the [3d Restatement] principles").

   a. **Policy considerations:** Covenants with the benefit held in gross can be useful, as when landowners burden their property for historic preservation or environmental conservation purposes, and make a non-landowning enterprise (e.g., the National Trust for Historic Preservation or the Audubon Society) the beneficiary of the covenant. The burden-won't-run-if-the-benefit-is-in-gross rule might justify a rebuttable presumption that (1) the covenant was not designed to deal with externalities, and (2) there was no net benefit to land as a whole by the covenant, but those considerations do not justify a blanket prohibition against the running of the burden of a covenant whose benefit is held in gross.

5. **Burden in gross:** Though rarely encountered, it is possible for the benefit of a covenant to run with land, and the burden of the covenant to be in gross. Courts have not hesitated to permit such benefits to run. See, e.g., *Mueller v. Bankers Trust Co. of Muskegon,* 262 Mich. 53 (1933) (seller of land promised to build a bridge over creek on the land; subsequent purchaser permitted to enforce covenant, which touched and concerned the benefited land).

IV. EQUITABLE SERVITUDES

A. **Introduction:** An equitable servitude is a ***covenant about land use*** that will be enforced in equity (by an ***injunction***) against a successor to the burdened estate who acquired it with ***notice*** of the covenant. A covenant ***need not*** meet all the criteria of a real covenant to be enforceable as an equitable servitude. Covenants are more commonly enforced as equitable servitudes than as real covenants, because they are easier to enforce by or against successors, and most people prefer enforcement of a covenant by injunction than by damages for its breach.

   1. **Differences between real covenants and equitable servitudes:** A covenant about land use may be a real covenant, an equitable servitude, or both. There are four major differences between real covenants and equitable servitudes.

      a. **Remedy:** A real covenant is enforceable *at law by an award of* **money damages.** An equitable servitude is enforceable *in equity by an* **injunction.**

b. No privity needed: Neither horizontal nor vertical privity is needed for either the benefit or burden of an equitable servitude to run to successors in the burdened or benefited estates.

c. Creation: Equitable servitudes may be created by *implication* in many jurisdictions. A real covenant can only be created expressly and in writing.

2. **Origins of the equitable servitude:** The equitable servitude originated in ***Tulk v. Moxhay,*** 41 Eng. Rep. 1143 (Ch. 1848). Tulk sold Leicester Square to Elms, who promised for himself and his assigns not to build on Leicester Square. With knowledge of the covenant, Moxhay purchased Leicester Square from Elms and then proposed to build on the Square. Under English law, the burden of the covenant would not run, because horizontal privity was lacking (see section III.E.1.a), so Tulk sought and obtained an injunction. The Chancellor reasoned that it was highly unfair for Moxhay to purchase Leicester Square knowing of the covenant (and probably paying less because of its existence), only to ignore it with impunity. Because the covenant was intended to bind successors, its substance touched and concerned the land, and Moxhay had notice of it, it was enforceable in equity against Moxhay.

B. Creation: Because equitable servitudes are interests in land, the Statute of Frauds requires that they be created in a writing signed by the promisor, but acceptance of a deed containing a promise made by the grantee of the deed suffices even though the grantee does not sign the deed. There is, however, a ***major exception*** to this rule: Many states permit ***negative equitable servitudes*** (a promise to refrain from using one's land in a specified fashion) to be ***created by implication when there is a common scheme of residential development.***

1. **By implication from a common development scheme:** Many states will imply a ***negative equitable servitude*** where a real estate developer sells lots in a subdivision on the promise that all the lots will be burdened with the same use restriction (e.g., single-family residences only) and later fails to carry through on the promise to burden all lots.

   ★**Example:** In the 1890s, McLaughlin subdivided a tract of land in Detroit along Collingwood Avenue into building lots and started to sell them under deeds that restricted use to single-family residences. Later, McLaughlin sold some lots without those restrictions, including Lot 86, which eventually was acquired in 1910 by McLean. In the 1920s, as autos became more commonplace, McLean started to construct a gasoline filling station on Lot 86. His neighbors sought to enjoin this use as a violation of an implied negative equitable servitude. In ***Sanborn v. McLean,*** 233 Mich. 227 (1925), the Michigan Supreme Court agreed that an injunction was proper, reasoning that because the initial restrictions imposed by McLaughlin, the developer, were "for the benefit of the lands held by [McLaughlin] to carry out the scheme of a residential district," an implied reciprocal servitude burdened McLaughlin's retained property (including Lot 86), and that servitude was equitably enforceable against McLean, who was on inquiry notice from the "uniform residence character given the lots by the expensive dwellings thereon" that Lot 86 might be burdened by a covenant restricting it to residential use. See also *Mid-State Equip. Co., Inc. v. Bell,* 217 Va. 133 (1976).

   As in ***Sanborn,*** courts sometimes call the covenant so implied a ***reciprocal negative easement,*** although the term ***implied reciprocal covenant*** is more accurate. Whatever the label, it is (1) ***reciprocal*** (the common scheme contemplates covenants burdening all lots for reciprocal benefit), and (2) ***negative*** (it restricts land use rather than requiring affirmative acts or use). Although ***not*** an easement, it is in the nature of an easement because an equitable servitude is an interest in land. For an implied reciprocal covenant to be implied, the following elements must be present.

a. Common scheme of development: The development must be of uniform character and recognizable as such by purchasers. Otherwise, there is no basis for concluding that purchasers were relying on reciprocal covenants burdening everyone's use in order to produce a development of uniform character.

    i. When does the scheme begin? Courts vary considerably in their answers to this question. In general, the following four factors are often used to determine the existence of a common scheme: (1) *advertisements* mentioning the reciprocal covenants, (2) use of a *map showing the entire development* as a sales aid in conjunction with sales of burdened lots, (3) *representations* to buyers that all lots will be similarly burdened, and (4) *sale of a significant number of lots with a common use restriction.* At one extreme are courts that hold that the common scheme must exist at the very beginning of the project, before any sales have occurred. See, e.g., *Johnson v. Mt. Baker Park Presbyterian Church,* 113 Wash. 458 (1920). Many jurisdictions are more lenient. In *Sanborn v. McLean,* discussed above, 21 lots (out of a total of 98) were sold with single-family residential-use-only restrictions before the lot at issue in the case was sold without such a restriction, yet the court ruled that a common scheme had been created, notwithstanding the fact that, by the time the "common scheme" was completed, fewer than 60 percent of the total lots in the subdivision were burdened by reciprocal covenants. By contrast, in *Tindolph v. Schoenfeld Bros., Inc.,* 157 Wash. 605 (1930), restrictions imposed on 2 lots out of 23 were held insufficient to create a common scheme. See also *3 W Partners v. Bridges,* 651 A.2d 387 (Me. 1994) (no common plan when only 3 out of 67 lots were burdened).

    ii. No covenants on lots conveyed before the common scheme begins: If a developer conveys land without use covenants *before the common scheme begins,* no reciprocal covenant will be implied. The land is simply not part of the common scheme, and so there is no basis for finding an implied reciprocal covenant.

    Example: Developer buys Flatland, a 160-acre farm, and then sells Homestead, a 10-acre portion consisting of the house, barns, and adjacent pasture, without covenants restricting use. Later, Developer subdivides the remaining 150 acres into 300 lots, selling them as "residential-only lots — no farm animals permitted." MacDonald, the owner of Homestead, maintains a wide variety of farm animals on Homestead. While a common scheme may exist with respect to this 150-acre development, sufficient to create implied reciprocal covenants if necessary, no such covenant applies to Homestead. MacDonald can keep his farm animals so far as the law of servitudes is concerned.

b. Negative covenant: Courts will imply reciprocal covenants *only* when the substance of the covenant is **negative** — limiting the use that may be made of the property rather than requiring some positive act on the part of the owner of the burdened land.

2. No implied covenants: Some jurisdictions, notably California and Massachusetts, completely reject creation of equitable servitudes by implication. See, e.g., *Werner v. Graham,* 181 Cal. 174 (1919); *Sprague v. Kimball,* 213 Mass. 380 (1913). In California, even if use restrictions are recorded in the public records (e.g., in a subdivision map), they do not burden the lots described unless the deed specifically refers to the recorded restriction. *Riley v. Bear Creek Planning Comm.,* 17 Cal. 3d 500 (1976).

C. Enforceability by or against successors: As with real covenants, certain requirements must be met in order for the benefit or burden of an equitable servitude to run to successors to the original estate. These requirements are *not the same as for real covenants:* Some are identical, but there are also significant differences.

  1. Intent: This requirement is essentially the same as for real covenants. If the parties expressly or impliedly intended for the covenant to run to benefit or burden successors, the equitable servitude created by the covenant will run.

  2. Privity not required: Unlike real covenants, *neither horizontal nor vertical privity of estate is required* for either the burden or benefit of an equitable servitude to run.

  3. Notice: As with real covenants, a purchaser who pays real value for an estate and has *no notice* of the servitude at the time is *not bound* by the servitude. Notice can be *actual* or *constructive.* Constructive notice most often comes through the *record* — the public records of real estate titles — but can also be the product of circumstances that should trigger *inquiry* on the part of the buyer, inquiry that would reveal the servitude.

   a. Actual notice: Actual knowledge of the servitude is actual notice. This can happen by design (e.g., the seller tells the buyer, perhaps in person, by letter, or in the sale contract) or by accident (e.g., an otherwise ignorant buyer mentions his prospective use plans to a neighbor who reveals a copy of an unrecorded servitude on the property).

   b. Record notice: Every American jurisdiction (usually each county) maintains a public record of all transactions affecting title to real property. If a servitude is anywhere in the *chain of title* — the series of records that trace ownership back to some original title or before a specified point in history — the buyer has constructive notice of the servitude. Buyers are charged with knowledge of the contents of the chain of title because they ought to read it (or hire a professional to do so and report on it).

    i. Deeds from a common grantor *not* in the direct chain of title: States differ on whether a deed from a common grantor, but not in the *direct* chain of ownership, should be treated as in the *chain of title.*

    ★**Example:** In Massachusetts, a state that does not recognize implied reciprocal covenants, Gilmore subdivided a tract and imposed single-family residential use restrictions on several lots. In a deed to Guillette, Gilmore recited that the servitude created was thereby imposed on Gilmore's remaining lots. Later, Gilmore sold one of those lots to Daly without any servitude. Daly's direct chain of title went from himself to Gilmore to Gilmore's predecessor. No servitude was in any of those deeds. Nevertheless, in *Guillette v. Daly Dry Wall, Inc.,* 367 Mass. 355 (1975), the Massachusetts Supreme Judicial Court held that Gilmore's deed to Guillette was in Daly's chain of title. The effect of this rule is to require purchasers of property to search the records for all possible grants of *other property* owned by each grantor in the chain of title, on the possibility that there might be some servitude created in a deed outside the direct line of ownership. See also *Sanborn v. McLean,* 233 Mich. 227 (1925).

Most jurisdictions reject this latitudinarian view of the chain of title, on the ground that it imposes "intolerable" burdens on title searchers. See, e.g., *Buffalo Academy of the Sacred Heart v. Boehm Bros., Inc.,* 267 N.Y. 242 (1935); *Land Developers, Inc. v. Maxwell,* 537 S.W.2d 904 (Tenn. 1976).

c. Inquiry notice: A few courts have ruled that a purchaser should inquire about the existence of servitudes if the neighborhood exhibits a common character.

★**Example:** Recall the facts of ***Sanborn v. McLean.*** McLean's lot was free of any servitudes of record, but the Michigan Supreme Court thought that McLean should have inquired about restrictive covenants, and therefore had ***inquiry notice*** of the implied reciprocal covenant for residential use, because the neighborhood had a "strictly uniform residence character." But suppose that all the houses were two stories in height and had grass lawns edged by boxwood hedges. Should McLean have inquired about servitudes restricting use to two-story residences with grass lawns and boxwood hedges?

4. Touch and concern: As with real covenants, the traditional rule is that in order for either the benefit or burden of an equitable servitude to run to successors in interest, the substance of the covenant must ***touch and concern*** the benefited or burdened land. The meaning of ***touch and concern*** is the same for equitable servitudes and real covenants and was discussed in detail in section III.F, above. Recall also that the *Restatement (Third) of Property,* Servitudes, substitutes for the touch-and-concern requirement a general rule that all servitudes are initially valid except those that are illegal or unconstitutional or violate public policy, and permits modification or termination of servitudes when their purpose may no longer be accomplished due to changed circumstances.

D. Identifying the benefited land: Courts identify the benefited land by (1) ascertaining the intentions of the parties, and (2) determining whether the land intended to be benefited has actually received a benefit. This is easy if the covenant expressly states what land is intended to be benefited, but it poses some problems when courts must infer those intentions.

1. Land retained by the promisee: If the party imposing the covenant owns land adjacent to or near the burdened land, courts presume that the covenant was intended to benefit the retained land. See, e.g., *Grady v. Schmitz,* 16 Conn. App. 292 (1988). That presumption is rebuttable by proof that the promisee had no such intention. See, e.g., *Haldeman v. Teicholz,* 197 App. Div. 2d 223 (1994). So long as the retained land is in the immediate vicinity of the burdened land, courts will usually employ the presumption that the benefit attaches to the retained land. See, e.g., *Malley v. Hanna,* 65 N.Y.2d 289 (1985) (benefited land three lots away from the burdened land).

a. Promisee's assigns: The corollary to this principle is that if the promisee later conveys his retained and benefited land, the benefit runs to the assignee (assuming the other elements for a running benefit are present).

Example: Developer acquires St. John's Point and subdivides it into 10 lots. Developer sells Lot 1 to Carol under a deed restricting use to a single residence. The benefit of Carol's promise attaches to the nine lots Developer retains. Developer then sells the remaining nine lots, each burdened by the same covenant. Carol starts to construct a small hotel. Bret, owner of Lot 5, may enjoin Carol's hotel because he has succeeded to the benefit of Carol's promise. See, e.g., *Grange v. Korff,* 248 Iowa 118 (1956).

2. **Enforceability by third parties:** Sometimes the benefit of a covenant is sought to be enforced by a person who is neither a successor to the covenant nor a successor to land benefited by the covenant, but who was intended to be the beneficiary of the covenant. These situations are of two types: (1) the intended beneficiary is a ***prior purchaser*** of a lot in a subdivision developed by a common grantor, or (2) the intended beneficiary is a complete ***stranger to the chain of title*** — the beneficiary did not acquire his property from the person who imposed the covenant. Intended beneficiaries are generally, but not always, able to enforce a covenant. Note the curiosity that most states refuse to permit creation of easements in third parties (see section II.B.1.a.ii, above) but will permit third-party enforcement of real covenants and equitable servitudes.

   a. **Prior purchasers:** A prior purchaser of a subdivision lot burdened by covenants restricting use may enforce the benefit of the covenant, under one of three theories.

      i. **Through the title chain to the person imposing the covenant:** Some states insist that the prior purchaser and intended beneficiary have acquired title from the person imposing the covenant. In the case of a subdivision, this requirement is easily met, because the developer is that person.

         Example: Refer to the prior example. Suppose that Bret, owner of Lot 5, starts to construct a convenience store on his lot, and Carol, owner of Lot 1, wishes to enjoin that use. Does Carol enjoy the benefit of Bret's ***later covenant?*** Carol is not the successor to land that enjoyed this benefit at the time she acquired it, because she is the first purchaser in the subdivision. Nevertheless, she can trace her title to Developer, the person who imposed the covenant, and she was pretty clearly an intended beneficiary of Bret's covenant, so she may enforce its benefit. See, e.g., *Malley v. Hanna,* 65 N.Y.2d 289 (1985); *Brown v. Heirs of Fuller,* 347 A.2d 127 (Me. 1975).

         This insistence on a form of privity of estate prevents a covenant from being enforced by a stranger to the chain of title descending from the person imposing the covenant.

         Example: Suppose Developer, in the prior example, had inserted into Bret's covenant a statement that it was intended to benefit landowners in Cormorant Cove, an adjacent subdivision developed by somebody else. Evelyn, a Cormorant Cove landowner, would be unable to enforce the covenant because she could not trace her title to Developer, the party imposing the covenant.

      ii. **Unrestricted third-party beneficiary theory:** Some states follow the view, endorsed by *Restatement of Property* §541 (1944), that any intended third-party beneficiary can enforce the benefit of a covenant. Thus, in the prior example, Evelyn (an intended beneficiary) could enforce the covenant burdening Bret's land.

         Example: Barnes and Zamiarski, good friends, owned adjacent lots. Barnes conveyed his lot to Lewek under a deed restricting its use for the benefit of Zamiarski's lot. Kozial purchased the lot from Lewek and violated the restriction. In *Zamiarski v. Kozial,* 18 App. Div. 2d 297 (1963), New York's intermediate appellate court upheld an injunction of Kozial on the ground that Zamiarski's status as a third-party beneficiary of the Barnesto-Lewek covenant was sufficient, *by itself,* to permit Zamiarski to enforce the benefit of the covenant. See also *Nature Conservancy v. Congel,* 253 App. Div. 2d 248 (1985). But the New York Court of Appeals, in *Malley* *v. Hanna,* 65 N.Y.2d 289 (1985), takes a contrary view (requiring privity with the covenantee to enforce the benefit of the covenant), without mention of *Zamiarski.*

iii. **By implication from a common scheme:** This is the mirror image of implied reciprocal covenants. (See section IV.B.1, above.) The doctrine of implied reciprocal covenants creates ***burdens by implication.*** This doctrine is quite separate — it uses a common scheme of development to ***identify the property*** **benefited** *by covenants that* ***are*** **expressly created,** not produced by implication. Thus, a state that does not permit the creation of implied reciprocal covenants might still use the existence of a common scheme to identify the land benefited from express covenants in a subdivision.

Example: Shackelford subdivided Brier Neck into about 100 lots and sold them over a 16-year period as summer residential lots. Each lot was sold under a deed restricting use to a single dwelling. Later, a corner lot across the road from the entrance to Brier Neck was sold by Shackelford to Clark under the same restriction. Clark constructed an ice cream stand and grocery on the corner lot, and owners of lots in Brier Neck sought to enjoin Clark's commercial use. In *Snow v. Van Dam,* 291 Mass. 477 (1935), the Massachusetts Supreme Judicial Court used the existence of a common scheme (including the corner lot) to identify the benefited property — all the land within the common scheme. Because Massachusetts does not permit the ***creation*** of servitudes by implication from a common scheme, the common scheme was relevant only to ***determination of the benefited property.***

It may take more than two lots to create a common scheme sufficient to identify the benefited land.

Example: Lebold and Willett owned Lot 11 as co-owners. Lebold was the sole owner of a lot directly across the street from Lot 11, and Willett was the sole owner of the adjacent lot. Lebold sold his lot to Rodgers. Two years later, Lebold and Willett conveyed Lot 11 to Reimann, subject to a covenant restricting the location of structures on Lot 11. Reimann began construction of a dwelling not in conformity with the covenant, and Rodgers sought to enjoin the construction. In *Rodgers v. Reimann,* 227 Or. 62 (1961), the Oregon Supreme Court found the evidence insufficient to establish that the Lebold-Rodgers lot was the intended beneficiary of the covenant, whether via a common scheme or otherwise.

If the developer retains the right to modify or waive the use restrictions imposed by covenant, that may negate any implication that the covenants were intended for the benefit of lot buyers.

Example: Dickason subdivided a tract of land, conveying lots under deeds containing use restrictions that could be eliminated at any time by agreement between Dickason and the owner of the burdened lot to be freed from the covenant, without the consent of other lot owners. The retention of this power by Dickason, even though unexercised, negated any inference that other lot owners were the beneficiaries of the covenants. The reservation made the covenant "a personal covenant between the grantor and his individual grantees." *Suttle v. Bailey,* 68 N.M. 283 (1961). Other courts subject the exercise of a developer's reserved power to a rule of good faith, and thus inferentially hold that a developer's reservation does not necessarily negate intent to benefit lot buyers. See, e.g., *Moore v. Megginson,* 416 So. 2d 993 (Ala. 1982). Some states, notably California, reject the use of a common scheme altogether — either to create implied reciprocal covenants or to identify the property benefited by express covenants. In California, the scope of the benefit of a covenant is defined by its written text. See *Werner v. Graham,* 181 Cal. 174 (1919).

b. Complete strangers to the chain of title descending from the person imposing the covenant: A landowner who is *not part of a common scheme,* and who did *not acquire the land (immediately or remotely) from the person imposing the servitude,* may only enforce the benefit of a covenant if (1) the landowner is the *intended beneficiary,* and (2) the jurisdiction permits *any third-party beneficiary* to enforce the benefit of a covenant.

V. INTERPRETATION OF COVENANTS

A. General rule: Courts try to implement the intentions of the parties in creating the covenant, but the very terms used in a covenant are often ambiguous.

B. Building restriction or use restriction: Covenants may restrict certain *uses,* or they may restrict construction of certain types of *buildings.* The difference may be important.

Example: Aumiller purchased a lot under a covenant limiting "structures erected . . . to residential purposes." Aumiller, a building contractor, built a "model home" in multiple senses of the term — it was "entirely residential in appearance" but was used as a site at which Aumiller's customers could inspect his work product and negotiate home-building deals. A Pennsylvania appellate court applied a Pennsylvania policy disfavoring use restrictions and concluded that the covenant only limited the nature of the structure, not the use to which it was put. In Pennsylvania, use restrictions must "squarely address the use or manner of occupation of the property." *Groninger v. Aumiller,* 435 Pa. Super. 123 (1994), applying *Schulman v. Serrill,* 432 Pa. 206 (1968). Accord: *Patton v. Madison County,* 265 Mont. 362 (1994) (bed-and-breakfast use); *Jackson v. Williams,* 714 P.2d 1017 (Okla. 1985) (group-home use). Contra: *Fox v. Smidt,* 869 S.W.2d 904 (Mo. App. 1994).

C. Residential purposes: Many covenants limit use to "residential purposes." The content of this term is not self-evident, because people commonly use their residences for a variety of purposes.

1. Combined business and residential use: Some states take the view that any commercial or money-making enterprise, no matter how "domestic" it might be, is not residential. In *Metzner v. Wojdyla,* 125 Wn. 2d 445 (1994), the Washington Supreme Court enjoined Wojdyla's provision of day care for six children (including two of her own) in her own home, reasoning that the activity was commercial. In *Fick v. Weedon,* 244 Ill. App. 3d 413 (1984), a "bed and breakfast" was ruled to violate a residential-use-only covenant. But *Persson-Mokvist v. Anderson,* 942 P.2d 1154 (Alaska 1997), held that use as a "bed and breakfast" and for dog training was consistent with a residential-use-only covenant; *Stewart v. Jackson,* 635 N.E.2d 186 (Ind. App. 1984), held that day care for five children comported with a residential-use-only covenant. Uses that are clearly not residential are often tolerated so long as no structures result. See, e.g., *Fitzwilliam v. Wesley United Methodist Church,* 882 S.W.2d 343 (Mo. App. 1994) (church parking lot); *Bagko Development Co. v. Damitz,* 640 N.E.2d 67 (Ind. App. 1994) (Little League practice field). Such interpretations often hinge on a reading of the covenant as limiting use to those that are compatible with the architectural type and character of a single-family residence. See, e.g., *Deep East Texas Regional Mental Health & Mental Retardation Services* *v. Kinnear,* 877 S.W.2d 550 (Tex. Civ. App. 1994), holding that a group home for six mentally retarded people was consistent with a "single-family residence only" covenant.

2. **Group homes:** Most courts conclude that group homes for the handicapped, juvenile delinquents, or other groups do not constitute a violation of residential-use-only covenants because people do, in fact, live there.

   Example: The Community of Damien, a non-profit charity devoted to providing homes for people with terminal illnesses, leased a home in an Albuquerque residential subdivision, the use of which was restricted to "single-family residence purposes." Four residents moved in, each suffering from AIDS, and each needing some degree of nursing care. Neighbors sought to enjoin the use as a violation of the covenant. In *Hill v. Community of Damien of Molokai,* 121 N.M. 353 (1996), the New Mexico Supreme Court reversed a trial court's injunction, reasoning that because the Community provided the four residents "with a traditional family structure, setting, and atmosphere," and because the residents "use the home much as would any family with a disabled family member," the group home use was consistent with the covenant. See also *Double D Manor, Inc. v. Evergreen Meadows Homeowners' Assn.,* 773 P.2d 1046 (Colo. 1989). However, some courts have ruled that use as a "group home" violates the residential-use-only covenant. See, e.g., *Main Farms Homeowners' Assn. v. Worthington,* 121 Wn. 2d 810 (1993). Enforceability of these covenants, as so construed, may be barred by the federal Fair Housing Act, 42 USC §3604(f)(1), state statutes, or by judicial notions of public policy. See, e.g., *Hill v. Community of Damien of Molokai,* 121 N.M. 353 (1996); *Broadmoor San Clemente Homeowners' Assn. v. Nelson,* 25 Cal. App. 4th 1 (1994) (Fair Housing Act and state statute); *Crane Neck Assn. v. New York City/Long Island County Serv. Group,* 61 N.Y.2d 154 (1984) (public policy); *McMillan v. Iserman,* 120 Mich. App. 785 (1983) (public policy, alternative holding).

3. **What constitutes family?** Many residential-use-only covenants are phrased to limit use to "single-family residential use" or to a "single-family residence." This sparks the problem of defining "single family," particularly when the family is composed of unrelated individuals.

   Example: In *Hill v. Community of Damien of Molokai,* 121 N.M. 353 (1996), the New Mexico Supreme Court ruled that a group of four unrelated AIDS patients living together under the auspices of the Community of Damien were a family for purposes of the covenant because (1) they fit within the local zoning ordinance's definition of family, (2) "there is a strong public policy in favor of including small group homes within the definition of the term 'family,'" and (3) the residents possessed the "generic character of a relatively permanent functioning family unit."

   However, some courts conclude that group residences, involving unrelated persons, are not single-family residences. See, e.g., *Omega Corp. of Chesterfield v. Malloy,* 228 Va. 12 (1984). Once again, enforceability of these covenants as so construed might be barred by federal or state statutes or public policy.

D. **Racial restrictions:** An unpleasant fact about our national past is racial bias manifested by covenants restricting use and occupancy of property to white people. These covenants, while often still of record because they were created years ago, are ***not enforceable.*** The usual reason is that their enforcement is not constitutionally permitted.

   ★**Example:** Fitzgerald conveyed a residence in St. Louis to the Shelleys, who were of African ancestry. Kraemer sought to enjoin the Shelleys from occupying their new home because the property was burdened by a covenant restricting use and occupancy to persons "of the Caucasian race," and specifically barring ownership, use, or occupancy by "people of the Negro or Mongolian race." The Missouri courts enjoined the Shelleys from occupying the property and ordered that title be returned to Fitzgerald. In **Shelley v. Kraemer,** 334 U.S. 1 (1948), the U.S. Supreme Court reversed, holding that a state's refusal to permit a willing buyer and seller to transfer title to property because of the race of one of the parties was a violation of the equal protection clause of the Fourteenth Amendment.

Note that under the *Restatement (Third) of Property*, Servitudes, §3.1 a racially restrictive use covenant would be invalid even if it were not unconstitutional to enforce it.

E. **Architectural approval:** Covenants forbidding erection of any structure without first obtaining the approval of a designated "architectural review committee" are generally upheld so long as the architectural reviewers act reasonably and in good faith. See, e.g., *Rhue v. Cheyenne Homes, Inc.,* 168 Colo. 6 (1969).

VI. TERMINATION OF REAL COVENANTS AND EQUITABLE SERVITUDES

A. **Duration:** In general, a covenant endures for so long as the parties who created it intend it to endure. There is no blanket ban on perpetual covenants, although such covenants that limit use to an unreasonably narrow purpose may be treated as unenforceable restraints on alienation. In *Citibrook II v. Morgan's Foods of Missouri, Inc.*, 239 S.W. 3d 631 (Mo. App. 2007), a Missouri court ruled that a covenant limiting property to the operation of a Kentucky Fried Chicken franchise "forever" was of unreasonable duration.

B. **Merger:** If the same person acquires title to the burdened land and all of the benefited land the covenant — whether a real covenant or an equitable servitude — is extinguished by merger. It cannot be revived but must be created anew. See, e.g., *Pollock v. Ramirez,* 117 N.M. 187 (1994).

C. **Eminent domain:** Real covenants or equitable servitudes may be extinguished by eminent domain, which happens when the government takes the burdened land for a purpose inconsistent with the restrictive covenants. The majority of states require that the owner of benefited land be compensated for the loss of the benefit. The measure of that loss is the difference in value of the benefited land with the benefit and without the benefit. See, e.g., *Southern California Edison Co. v. Bourgerie,* 9 Cal. 3d 169 (1973). A few courts cling to the view that the benefit of a servitude is not an interest in land, and so compensation for its destruction is not required. This is a poorly reasoned view because it ignores the fact that the constitutional requirement of compensation applies to governmental takings of **all forms of property,** whether tangible or intangible. See, e.g., *Ruckelshaus v. Monsanto Co.,* 467 U.S. 986 (1984). Florida observes a unique rule: Compensation is required for takings of affirmative covenants but not for takings of negative covenants. Compare *Board of Public Instruction v. Town of Bay Harbor Islands,* 81 So. 2d 637 (Fla. 1955) (no compensation for government violation of a negative covenant) with *Palm Beach County v. Cove Club Investors, Ltd.,* 734 So. 2d 379 (Fla. 1999) (government required to pay monthly fees imposed by affirmative covenant on property taken by eminent domain).

D. Express waiver or release: If all the holders of the benefit of a covenant expressly *release* the covenant, it is extinguished. If all the benefit holders expressly waive the covenant to permit a specific nonconforming use, the covenant remains alive to bar other nonconforming uses. See, e.g., *Gibbs v. Kimbrell,* 311 S.C. 261 (App. 1993).

E. Expiration of the covenant: Covenants sometimes have a defined life span (e.g., "until Jan. 1, 2000" or "for the next 40 years"). When its defined life has expired, the covenant is extinguished.

F. Doctrines terminating equitable servitudes: Because equitable servitudes are enforceable in equity, the following equitable defenses, if proven, will effectively extinguish an equitable servitude by blocking its enforcement.

    1. Changed conditions within the affected area: A covenant will no longer be enforced in equity if conditions have so radically and thoroughly changed *within the area affected by a covenant* (usually a subdivision) that the covenant can no longer achieve its purpose.

    Example: When Shippan Point was subdivided in the 1910s, the lots were conveyed subject to a covenant limiting use to one single-family dwelling per lot. By the 1990s, 12 of the 25 lots in Shippan Point were in violation of the covenant. A Connecticut appellate court concluded that the covenant was no longer enforceable, due to these changed circumstances. *Shippan Point Assn. v. McManus,* 34 Conn. App. 209 (1994).

    Courts split on whether changed circumstances operate to extinguish the covenant entirely or merely bar its enforcement in equity. If the latter, a covenant unenforceable in equity might still be enforceable at law if the elements of a real covenant can be established. The modern trend is to extinguish covenants entirely when changed circumstances have been proven. See, e.g., *Hrisomalos v. Smith,* 600 N.E.2d 1363 (Ind. App. 1992). Some courts deal with widespread violations of covenants as evidence of abandonment, rather than as a subspecies of changed circumstances.

    2. Changed conditions in the surrounding area: Another common claim is that the nature and character of the *surrounding area* has so changed that it would now be inequitable to enforce the servitude. To succeed with this claim, it is necessary to establish that the extrinsic changes in the neighborhood have been so pervasive that *all of the benefited lots* have lost the benefit of the covenant at issue. Put another away, there is no point in enforcing the covenant any longer because its purpose can no longer be achieved.

    Example: Termination: Land in New York City in the early nineteenth century was burdened by residential-use-only covenants. As New York City grew northward, an elevated railroad was constructed amidst this land, making it most unpleasant for residential use. The covenant was held unenforceable in equity. *Trustees of Columbia College v. Thatcher,* 87 N.Y. 311 (1882).

    ★**Example: No termination:** In 1941, Western Land subdivided 40 acres of rural land southwest of Reno, burdening all of the lots with restrictive covenants limiting use to single-family dwellings. By 1969, Reno had grown up around the subdivision, bracketing it with high-traffic-volume boulevards. Western Land proposed to use a 3.5-acre undeveloped site at one of those busy intersections for a shopping center, but the homeowners sought and obtained a trial court injunction preventing Western Land from violating the covenant. In *Western Land Co. v. Truskolaski,* 88 Nev. 200 (1972), the Nevada Supreme Court upheld the injunction, reasoning that because the covenant continued to be of "real and substantial value to the residents of the subdivision," the doctrine of changed conditions did not operate to terminate the covenant.

Section 7.10 of the *Restatement (Third) of Property* (Servitudes) provides that covenants may be modified or terminated when change "makes it impossible as a practical matter to accomplish the purpose for which the servitude was created."

3. **Abandonment:** A servitude may be abandoned by widespread violation of the covenant without enforcement. If violations of a covenant are sufficiently numerous, and there has been no enforcement action taken, the covenant may be seen as abandoned. There are two competing tests of when abandonment by widespread violation has occurred: (1) the average person would reasonably conclude that the use restriction has been abandoned, or (2) the covenant's purpose has been so frustrated that enforcement would seriously impair the value of burdened lots without producing any substantial benefit.

Example: "Average person" test: Lots in Maple Hills were burdened by a covenant requiring the use of wood shingles on the roofs of all structures, but the Homeowners' Development Committee, which was required by another covenant to approve all construction, inadvertently misled owners to believe that the roofing covenant had been amended to permit tile roofs. Of the first 29 homes, only 8 had wood roofs. Of the 81 houses ultimately built in Maple Hills, 23 lacked wood-shingle roofs. A Utah appellate court concluded that the violations were so great that the average person would conclude that the covenant had been abandoned. *Fink v. Miller,* 896 P.2d 649 (Utah App. 1995).

Example: "Frustration of purpose" test: Property in Landen Farms, a "planned development" of about 2,000 residences, was burdened by use restrictions forbidding basketball hoops and backboards in the front driveway of any residence. Nevertheless, about 50 homes sported poles bearing a backboard and a hoop. An Ohio appellate court concluded that the covenant had been abandoned by non-enforcement, partly because the value lost by enforcement would be greater than any benefit produced, and partly because the purpose of a uniform aesthetic had been lost by non-enforcement. *Landen Farms Community Services Assn. v. Schube,* 78 Ohio App. 3d 231 (1992).

Some courts treat these factual patterns as simply another example of changed circumstances within the affected areas. See section VI.E.1, above. Other courts call these cases of *implied waiver* or *acquiescence.*

4. **Equitable estoppel:** If the party seeking to enforce a covenant has made knowingly false representations to a defendant ignorant of the true facts, intending and inducing the defendant's reliance on the misrepresentation, he will be estopped from enforcing the covenant. See, e.g., *Hohman v. Bartel,* 125 Or. App. 306 (1993).

5. **Laches:** The doctrine of laches — the unreasonable failure to assert a known equitable right, coupled with some prejudice to the defendant — will bar enforcement of an equitable servitude. The elapse of time necessary to establish laches, as well as sufficiency of the prejudice suffered by the defendant from non-enforcement, are matters within the reasonable discretion of the trial court.

6. **Unclean hands:** The equitable notion that a plaintiff must not be guilty of the conduct of which he complains may bar a person from enforcing a reciprocal servitude if guilty of the same violation.

   Example: Dick owns Blackacre, and Jane owns Whiteacre, each burdened with a covenant limiting use to residential purposes, imposed for mutual benefit. Dick builds a "self-storage" warehouse on Blackacre; Jane builds a competing warehouse on Whiteacre. Dick and Jane will be barred by unclean hands from enforcing the covenant against each other. However, if Dick merely were to rent out a room in his home on Blackacre, he would not be barred from enforcing the covenant against Jane. Trivial violations don't count for purposes of unclean hands. See, e.g., *Grady v. Schmitz,* 16 Conn. App. 292 (1988).

7. **Balance of hardships:** Even when injunctive relief is otherwise appropriate, a court may deny an injunction if the hardship imposed by the injunction is very large in relation to the benefits produced, but this principle is rarely invoked by courts in servitude cases, and it may be more theoretical than actual.

   ★**Example:** Rick subdivided 62 acres in 1946, restricting land use to single-family dwellings. West purchased a lot and built a house, but not many others followed suit. In 1959, Rick sought to sell 45 acres of the subdivision for industrial use, but West refused to release the covenant. In 1961, Rick agreed to sell 15 acres for development of a much-needed hospital. Although the court agreed that the site was a "desirable location" for a hospital, and implicitly that the social loss resulting from issuing an injunction was greater than the benefits produced, the court enjoined the proposed use. *Rick v. West,* 34 Misc. 2d 1002 (N.Y. Sup. 1962).

G. **Affirmative covenants to pay money — Perpetual burden?** Affirmative covenants to pay money (usually dues to a homeowners' association) may be enforced either by foreclosure of the equitable lien created by nonpayment or by suit to recover as money damages the unpaid dues. The latter remedy is, of course, an action at law to enforce the covenant as a real covenant, and equitable defenses will not usually apply. The burden of these covenants is personal and may not be easily avoided.

   ★**Example:** In 1969, MacKenzie purchased a lot in a residential development burdened by an affirmative covenant to pay homeowners' dues for various common purposes. In 1987, MacKenzie sought to sell the lot and learned that, because its soil would not percolate sufficiently to support a septic system, it was not lawful to build a residence on the lot. Believing the lot to be worthless, MacKenzie offered to give it to the homeowners' association, which refused to accept the gift. MacKenzie then stopped paying taxes, but nobody purchased it at a tax sale, and title remained in MacKenzie's name, although MacKenzie notified everyone with any practical interest in the lot that he was abandoning ownership of the lot. The homeowners' association sought and obtained a personal judgment against MacKenzie for the unpaid dues. On appeal, the Pennsylvania courts upheld the judgment, ruling that it was not possible to abandon title to real property held in fee simple absolute and thus that MacKenzie continued to be personally liable for the covenant to pay money. *Pocono Springs Civic Assn., Inc. v. MacKenzie,* 446 Pa. Super. 445 (1995).

   Section 7.12 of the *Restatement (Third) of Property* (Servitudes) provides that affirmative covenants to pay money for provision of services (other than as part of a homeowners' association) "may be modified or terminated if the obligation becomes excessive in relation to the cost of providing the services or facilities or to the value received by the burdened estate."

VII. COMMON INTEREST COMMUNITIES

A. **Introduction:** In recent decades, America has sprouted vast numbers of developments that are burdened with a myriad of restrictive-use covenants that purport to govern the behavior of the owners and occupiers in meticulous detail. Many, but not all, of these webs of covenants are contained in condominium developments. Among the covenants burdening these developments are those that permit a homeowners' association to impose additional use restrictions.

B. **Covenants recorded in the master deed:** A condominium development will have a recorded master deed in which the use restrictions that pertain to each unit are recited; thus, any purchaser of a condominium unit has constructive notice of such covenants. Courts divide as to the degree of deference to be given these covenants. Some states hold that these restrictions are "clothed with a very strong presumption of validity" and invalidated only when they are arbitrary, violate public policy, or interfere with the exercise of a fundamental constitutional right. See, e.g., *Hidden Harbour Estates v. Basso,* 393 So. 2d 637 (Fla. App. 1981); *Noble v. Murphy,* 34 Mass. App. Ct. 452 (1993). Other states think that such covenants should be generally enforceable unless they are ***unreasonable.***

★**Example:** The recorded master deed to Lakeside Village, a condominium development in Los Angeles, recited that no animals (including dogs and cats) "shall be kept in any unit." Nahrstedt purchased a unit and moved in with her three "noiseless" cats. The homeowners' association demanded their removal and assessed fines against Nahrstedt, who then sought to prevent the association from enforcing the covenant on the grounds that it was unreasonable. In ***Nahrstedt v. Lakeside Village Condominium Assn., Inc.,*** 8 Cal. 4th 361 (1994), the California Supreme Court concluded that the restriction was reasonable because it did not violate a "fundamental public policy," was not "wholly arbitrary," and did not "impose a burden . . . that far outweighs any benefit." Because the covenant was a recorded-use restriction of which Nahrstedt had constructive notice, it was "presumptively reasonable," the burden being placed on the challenger to demonstrate that the covenant's "effect on the project as a whole" (rather than on the individual homeowner) was unreasonable.

C. **Covenants imposed by homeowners' associations:** States that clothe original recorded covenants with a "strong presumption" of validity are not so deferential to covenants imposed by homeowners' associations after the owners have acquired title. Such covenants are valid if ***reasonable,*** a standard that is frankly designed to "fetter the discretion" of homeowners' associations and ensure that they will "enact rules and regulations that are reasonably related to the promotion of the health, happiness, and peace of mind" of the entire community of burdened homeowners. See *Hidden Harbour Estates v. Basso,* 393 So. 2d 637 (Fla. App. 1981); *Noble v. Murphy,* 34 Mass. App. Ct. 452 (1993). This standard has been applied to amendments imposing covenants barring registered sex offenders from residing within the community. See *Mulligan v. Panther Valley Property Owners Ass'n,* 766 A.2d 1186 (N.J. App. Div. 2001).

D. **Standard of review of actions taken by homeowners' associations:** As discussed below, the ***business judgment rule*** applies to the actions of directors of cooperative apartment corporations. Because condominium homeowners' associations are more recent, the law with respect to this issue is less developed. *Nahrstedt* suggests that "reasonableness" is the standard, but a later California decision says that the business judgment rule is the standard except when the issue is, as it was in *Nahrstedt,* the validity of an equitable servitude being enforced by the board. *Lamden* *v. La Jolla Shores Clubdominium Homeowners' Ass'n*, 21 Cal. 4th 249 (1999). See also *Riverside Park Condominium Unit Owners Ass'n v. Lucas*, 691 N.W.2d 862 (N.D. 2005).

E. **Cooperative apartments:** Condominiums are individually owned and financed separately from each other. Cooperative apartments are owned by a corporation; the individual apartments are occupied under long-term leases by people who acquire ownership of shares of stock in the apartment corporation and thus acquire the right to occupy the apartment. Because the nature of a cooperative apartment is that each owner-lessee is obligated for a portion of the entire cost of owning the building, and one owner's financial failure imposes immediate burdens on the others, the financial fate of cooperative apartment owners is far more interdependent than that of condominium owners. As a result, courts are willing to defer to the "business judgment" of the directors of the corporation and will permit the directors to deny ownership to anyone for any reason except violation of civil rights laws.

★**Example:** The board of directors of a cooperative apartment corporation terminated the tenancy of a tenant-shareholder because of his objectionable conduct. That conduct consisted of repeated false allegations directed toward another tenant, a physical altercation with that tenant, alterations to his apartment without obtaining required approvals, and the filing of numerous apparently vexatious lawsuits. The New York Court of Appeals reaffirmed that the business judgment rule was the operative standard to assess the validity of the board's action, and noted that to trigger any heightened judicial scrutiny, a plaintiff must show either that the board's actions (1) were *ultra vires*, (2) did not legitimately further the corporate purposes, or (3) were taken in bad faith. *40 West 67th Street Corp. v. Pullman*, 100 N.Y.2d 147 (2003).

Exam Tips *on*
SERVITUDES: LAND USE LIMITS CREATED BY PRIVATE BARGAIN

☛ Expect examination on these topics. This is a rich field, and it is in flux, so you need to understand the traditional rules and how they are breaking down. To be safe, you might analyze the problem presented under the traditional rules, but also note the differences between those rules and modern trends (which can easily produce a different outcome).

☛ Expect multiple issues concerning use rights and restrictions. Be certain you understand the various ways in which easements can be created. Use restrictions may manifest themselves as clear (or garbled) attempts to create a defeasible fee, through an agreement, or, in the case of an equitable servitude, by a scheme of common development. Be certain you understand the different requirements for benefits to run both in law (real covenants) and equity (equitable servitudes), and for burdens to run in law and in equity.

☛ The modern trend is to shift emphasis onto the circumstances governing termination, modification, and enforcement, by using new criteria to address those circumstances. Be sure you understand the factors involved and the policies behind their adoption. Be alert to the possibility of illegal restrictions, or those that unfairly and unduly burden fundamental rights. This is a loose and fuzzy area; justify your conclusions with well-reasoned policy arguments.

☞ Don't neglect the possibility that your professor may ask you to advise a developer, or a city, or a nonprofit conservation agency. Be prepared to think like a legal planner and counselor as well as like a litigator.

CHAPTER 10

PUBLIC CONTROL OF LAND USE: ZONING

ChapterScope ───────────────────────────────

This chapter examines zoning laws, the way in which we use the political process to control land use. Here are the most important points in this chapter.

- Zoning is usually done at the local level, pursuant to authority conferred by a state enabling act.

- Zoning must comply with the enabling act, the state and federal constitutions, and all other state or federal laws that limit zoning power.

- Zoning limits the use that may be made of property. Usually an area is zoned for a particular use.

- Some zoning laws are cumulative, meaning that in an area zoned for the least-favored use, all other uses are permitted, but in an area zoned for the most-favored use, only that use is permitted. Other laws are mutually exclusive. Zoning laws may address many other topics (e.g., density, aesthetics, or household composition).

- Zoning laws, when enacted, restrict or prohibit some prior lawful uses. To avoid challenges to the validity of the newly imposed regulation, zoning laws typically permit such nonconforming uses to continue for a limited period of time. If an owner discontinues the use, however, it may not be renewed.

- Zoning laws typically confer some discretion on a zoning board. Abuses of discretion can occur.

  - Variances permit otherwise prohibited uses or deviations from density or area controls. Variances are granted only to alleviate undue hardships not of the applicant's manufacture.

  - Exceptional uses are permitted by the zoning law under flexible criteria specified in the law.

  - Zoning amendments present the problem of spot zoning, an amendment that confers benefits on a discrete parcel without any public benefit, and often in disregard of the comprehensive use plan that zoning is supposed to implement.

  - Floating zones are uses that are not tethered to a specific area — the zoning board decides when the use becomes relevant and where it should be located.

  - Contract or conditional zoning involves a change in zoning conditioned upon imposition of a servitude restricting use that is designed to produce public benefits.

- Constitutional and statutory law impose limits on the zoning power. Zoning for aesthetic purposes is generally permitted, particularly when it upholds property values. When zoning restricts free speech it is presumed void, and the government has a heavy burden of justification. Zoning that restricts the ability of people related by blood or marriage to live together is presumptively void; zoning that restricts the ability of unrelated people to live together is presumptively valid under the federal constitution but not under some state constitutions.

■ Under some state constitutions, zoning that has the effect of making it impossible for people of low income to live in a community is invalid. These states impose an affirmative duty on local communities to adopt zoning laws that make housing accessible to people of all economic strata.

I. ZONING BASICS

A. Introduction: Zoning is the use of governmental power to regulate land use. Zoning laws divide a political jurisdiction into specific separate geographic areas and impose limits on the permissible uses of land within each area. Zoning has several legitimate objectives: (1) to *prevent incompatible uses* from occurring (thus reducing the need for nuisance law), (2) to *increase property values* generally by minimizing use conflicts (thus increasing the property tax base), and (3) to *channel development into patterns that may serve larger social goals* (e.g., reduce urban sprawl to conserve resources and reduce air pollution from auto commuting). Zoning is the use of public power to impose uniform results that might otherwise be accomplished in more piecemeal and selective fashion by private bargains (via servitudes) and nuisance law.

B. General constitutional validity: In general, zoning laws are constitutionally valid, even though they restrict the uses to which a landowner may devote his property (possibly to his economic detriment).

★**Example:** Euclid, Ohio, adopted a comprehensive zoning ordinance that restricted the permissible uses of property, limited the height of structures, and imposed minimum lot-size requirements for certain types of structures. In *Village of Euclid v. Ambler Realty Co.,* 272 U.S. 365 (1926), the Supreme Court upheld the validity of the law against a due process and equal protection challenge. The law's objective—minimizing land use conflicts to prevent nuisances from ever occurring—was a legitimate exercise of the state's inherent police power because its content was neither unreasonable nor arbitrary.

A valid law can, however, be applied to an individual in an unconstitutional manner. See *Nectow v. City of Cambridge,* 277 U.S. 183 (1928). A zoning law that so severely restricts use that no economically viable use is permitted is an unconstitutional taking of property without compensation. See *Lucas v. South Carolina Coastal Council,* 505 U.S. 1003 (1992), discussed in Chapter 11. Zoning ordinances that openly infringe constitutionally fundamental rights (e.g., free speech) or that employ suspect criteria (e.g., race) are presumptively unconstitutional. Zoning laws that lack such damning characteristics, however, are presumptively valid.

C. Statutory schemes: The point of zoning is to separate land uses and regulate the density of use within use districts. This can be done by *cumulative* zoning or *mutually exclusive* zoning.

1. Cumulative zoning: This type of zoning law identifies land use in a spectrum from "higher" to "lower." The least dense single-family residential use is the highest use, proceeding downward to more dense residential (e.g., apartments and other multiple-family dwellings), light commercial (e.g., a corner bookstore), heavy commercial (e.g., a supermarket or an office building), and industrial (e.g., a factory or power plant). The idea of cumulative zoning is that all uses at the level of the zoned district *and higher* will be permitted.

Example: A cumulative zoning law divides a city into four districts, labeled Single-Family Residential (SFR), Dense Residential (DR), Commercial (C), and Industrial (I). Only single-family residences will be permitted in SFR. Single-family residences and apartments will be permitted in DR. Those two uses plus commercial uses will be permitted in C, and all uses will be permitted in I.

2. **Mutually exclusive zoning:** This type of zoning law permits some uses and excludes all others within the zoned area.

   Example: A city's mutually exclusive zoning law divides the city into four districts: Industrial, Commercial, Dense Residential, and Single-Family Residential. Only the defined uses are permitted within each district, and all others are excluded. The result will be a city that has four separate monolithic use districts.

   Mutually exclusive zoning is most often used with respect to industrial or heavy commercial districts. Residential use is often barred in such districts, partly to dampen use conflicts, partly out of public health concerns, and partly to preserve space for industrial users. Zoning laws may be partly mutually exclusive and partly cumulative.

   Example: A city's zoning law divides the city into four districts: Single-Family Residential, Dense Residential, Commercial, and Industrial. Cumulative zoning applies to the first three classifications but not to Industrial. The result will be a monolithic industrial zone, mixed uses within the Commercial and Dense Residential classifications, and a monolithic single-family residential zone.

3. **Density zoning:** In addition to use regulation, zoning laws often seek to control the density of occupation within any given use district. This is usually done through a wide variety of limits on the size or height of structures, their location upon their site, and the functional uses created within the structure (e.g., limits on the number of bathrooms or bedrooms within a single-family structure). Density controls supplement use controls; they are not generally considered an alternative to use controls.

II. AUTHORIZATION FOR ZONING

A. **Enabling legislation:** Most zoning laws are adopted at the local level, although some states (e.g., Oregon) have enacted laws regulating land use statewide. The powers of local governments in relation to the government of the state in which they are located are controlled by the state constitution and state statutes. Usually, the power to adopt zoning laws is reserved to the state government. When this is the case, a state's legislature must enact legislation authorizing local governments to adopt zoning laws. Some state constitutions recognize a semi-autonomous status for certain cities and, in those states, a city with such status may have power to adopt zoning laws without express legislative authority from the state. In general, though, a local zoning law is void unless it is in conformity with the state's *enabling act* — the law authorizing localities to engage in zoning. Every state — even those with "home rule" cities — has enacted legislation authorizing localities to zone.

   1. **Defective enabling act:** Every state has its own constitutional law concerning the proper scope of a legislature's *delegation of legislative authority.* While legislatures may not simply hand over to someone else (e.g., the state's governor, or a city, or a private entity) unbounded discretion to legislate, they are generally permitted to delegate to administrative agencies,

cities, and other nonlegislative bodies the power to make rules that look exactly like laws, so long as that law-making power is exercised in conformity with clear standards in the authorizing legislation.

Example: The Standard State Zoning Enabling Act (which, with some modifications, is in effect in every state) empowers cities to: (1) "regulate and restrict the height, number of stories, and size of buildings and other structures, the percentage of lot that may be occupied, the size of yards, courts, and other open spaces, the density of population, and the location and use of buildings, structures, and land for trade, industry, residence, or other purposes"; (2) create use zones with differing regulations; and (3) modify zoning laws and grant variances when in the public interest to do so. The Standard Act also requires cities to (1) create a comprehensive plan designed to accomplish various public objectives specified in the Standard Act; (2) create procedures to establish, enforce, and alter zoning regulations; and (3) establish a zoning commission and an appeal mechanism for affected landowners. Because the limits on local discretion are clearly expressed in the Standard Act, it is not an unconstitutional delegation of legislative authority.

2. *Ultra vires* **local action:** If a local zoning law violates some express provision of the enabling act, or if it deals with matters not authorized by the enabling act, the law is void to that extent. It is *ultra vires* — beyond the authority given the locality under the zoning act.

   Example: The state of Nirvana has enacted the Standard Act. The city of Saint Cecilia, located in Nirvana, enacts a zoning law that prohibits the ownership of more than one motor vehicle by any individual. The law is *ultra vires:* While nothing in the Standard Act expressly forbids such local legislation, its subject matter — regulation of motor vehicle ownership — is beyond the scope of the powers granted Saint Cecilia under the Standard Act. The purported zoning law is not a regulation of land use. By contrast, a Saint Cecilia law forbidding the parking of more than one motor vehicle on any lot zoned single-family residential would be within the scope of Saint Cecilia's authority under the Standard Act.

B. **Comprehensive plan:** The Standard Act (the common enabling act) requires that zoning decisions be made "in accordance with" a comprehensive plan for land use in the locality, which is intended to be a general guide for overall development of a locality. Zoning laws are the specific means of implementing the vision of the comprehensive plan. The requirement of a comprehensive plan has received sporadic serious treatment. Unwritten plans have sufficed, or sometimes the zoning laws themselves were the plan. In some states the comprehensive plan is treated more seriously, hastened perhaps by enabling acts that require zoning to be consistent with a written and adopted comprehensive plan, but a persistent practical problem to the utility of a comprehensive plan is that no planner can accurately predict the future, nor control events that affect future land use.

   1. **Legal status of the comprehensive plan:** Generally, the plan itself is not binding but must be implemented by actual zoning ordinances. However, a few courts have held that, even without implementing law, local action violative of a comprehensive plan is void. See, e.g., *Baker v. City of Milwaukie,* 271 Or. 500 (1975). Even though a comprehensive plan may not, by itself, be binding law, it is an important legal benchmark to assess the validity of **discretionary action** by zoning officials under a zoning law. See section III, below.

III. STATUTORY DISCRETION AND RESTRAINT

A. Introduction: Communities are dynamic. Appropriate land usage should change as the underlying economic and social conditions dictate. Zoning responds to this fact in several ways: (1) tolerating the continued existence of land uses existing prior to adoption of the zoning law, (2) providing for amendment of the zoning law, and (3) conferring discretion on administrators in the application of the zoning statute. None of these mechanisms is without controversy.

B. Nonconforming uses: When zoning is introduced, some existing land uses will not be in conformity with the uses permitted under the new zoning law. These ***nonconforming uses*** are permitted to continue to exist because their immediate abatement would amount to either a taking of property without just compensation (see Chapter 11) or an unreasonable exercise of the zoning power. However, nonconforming uses may be, and often are, eliminated gradually.

    1. Forced phase-out: One mechanism to abate the nonconforming use is the forced phase-out. The zoning law (or zoning administrators, exercising discretion under the law) may specify a period after which the nonconforming use must cease. This so-called ***amortization period*** will vary, depending on the investment in the nonconforming use. The amortization period must be long enough to avoid a successful charge that the forced phase-out amounts to an uncompensated taking or denial of substantive due process.

        a. Majority rule: Valid if reasonable period: The majority view in American states is that forced phase-outs are valid so long as the amortization period is reasonable as to the affected nonconforming user. The general calculus of reasonableness "involves a process of weighing the public gain to be derived from a speedy removal of the nonconforming use against the private loss which removal of the use would entail." *Metromedia, Inc. v. City of San Diego,* 26 Cal. 3d 848 (1980). Every case, however, will turn on its own facts. Factors courts use to make this determination include the ***nature of the use,*** the ***character of the structure,*** the ***location, what portion of the user's total business is affected,*** the ***salvage value,*** the ***extent of depreciation*** of the use, and ***any monopoly or other advantage conferred on the user by reason of the foreclosure of similar and competing uses.*** See ***Art Neon Co. v. City and County of Denver,*** 488 F.2d 118 (10th Cir. 1973).

        b. Minority rule: Invalid per se: A minority of states hold that forced phase-outs are invalid. Some states conclude that localities lack statutory authority to impose forced phase-outs. See, e.g., *James J.F. Laughlin Agency, Inc. v. Town of West Hartford,* 166 Conn. 305 (1974). Other states conclude that forced phase-outs constitute an uncompensated taking of property, no matter what the length of the amortization period may be.

        ★**Example:** Moon Township, Pennsylvania adopted a zoning ordinance extensively regulating the location of stores vending pornography, the effect of which was to make illegal the store operated by PA Northwestern Distributors. The ordinance permitted Northwestern 90 days in which to cease operations. In ***PA Northwestern Distributors, Inc. v. Zoning Hearing Board,*** 526 Pa. 186 (1991), the Pennsylvania Supreme Court ruled that the "amortization and discontinuance of a lawful pre-existing nonconforming use is per se confiscatory and violative of the Pennsylvania Constitution." A concurring justice thought that the ordinance was void because the amortization period was unreasonable — it did not "provide adequate time for elimination of the non-conforming use."

2. **No expansion:** Typically, zoning ordinances stipulate that the nonconforming use may not be expanded beyond the precise boundaries of the existing use. Thus, a successful and growing business located as a nonconforming use will be forced to move to expand. A new occupant will be required to conform to the zoning law.

3. **Destruction or abandonment:** Another common provision is to stipulate that if the nonconforming use is destroyed or abandoned, permission to continue the nonconforming use terminates. Any replacement structure or new use must conform to the current zoning law. Abandonment usually requires proof that the user has voluntarily intended to abandon the nonconforming use, but some ordinances supplement abandonment with a bright-line rule that discontinuance of the nonconforming use for a specified period terminates permission for the use.

   Example: The community's zoning ordinance specified that discontinuance of a nonconforming use for two years terminated permission to continue the use. The owner of a warehouse that was a nonconforming use vacated the warehouse after it had agreed to sell the site to a residential developer. Nineteen months later, after the deal had failed to close, the warehouse owner moved some goods back in and installed a property manager. In *Toys 'R' Us v. Silva,* 89 N.Y.2d 411 (1996), the New York Court of Appeals ruled that even though the owner had resumed the nonconforming use before the two-year period had expired, the discontinuance was sufficiently substantial to cause loss of the right to continue the use.

C. **Administrative discretion: Variances, exceptions, amendments, spot zoning, and more:** Zoning laws, like all other exercises in central government planning, cannot deal with the incredible kaleidoscopic complexity of human nature. Accordingly, zoning laws attempt to respond to this by conferring discretion upon zoning administrators in the actual application of the law. The problems and possibilities of such devices are discussed in this section.

   1. **Variances:** Virtually every zoning law establishes a *zoning appeals board,* or *board of adjustment,* usually a group of people appointed by the local executive who are authorized to grant variances from the zoning law in the interest of alleviating *practical difficulties* or *unnecessary hardships.* The appeals board is typically assisted by, and relies upon, zoning officials in discharging this power to dispense with the law. Variances may be *area variances,* those awarded to alleviate siting problems (e.g., setback requirements or minimum yard area), or *use variances,* those permitting an otherwise prohibited use (e.g., a multiple-family residence in a single-family residential district). The theory of variances is that they should be granted when compliance with the law would impose such extreme burdens on the owner that application of the law might be unconstitutional or otherwise invalid. A variance is thus an administrative safety-valve to avoid judicial determinations that the zoning law is invalid as applied to the particular circumstances.

      a. **General standard for granting variances:** Almost every zoning law provides that a variance may be granted upon a showing that compliance with the zoning law would impose *undue hardship* on the applicant. This hardship must *neither be created by nor peculiar to the owner.*

         Example — No hardship: Aronson wished to add a porch on the back of his house to accommodate his invalid child. The porch would violate setback requirements but was well screened by shrubs and thus posed no visual intrusion on neighbors' privacy, nor would it lower property values. There was no other spot for the porch. A variance was denied: The invalid condition of Aronson's child, while a personal infirmity and perhaps a tragedy, was not a hardship within the meaning of variance law. *Aronson v. Board of Appeals of Stoneham,* 349 Mass. 593 (1965).

Example — Hardship: Commons owned a residential lot, 50 feet wide with a total area of 5,190 square feet, that had been created before the current zoning law, which required lots to be a minimum of 75 feet wide with an area of 7,500 square feet. Commons's builder proposed to construct a residence conforming to setback requirements that would be of the same value as existing homes. In the past, Commons had attempted to sell the lot to a neighbor and to acquire additional land adjacent to his lot, but both attempts had been unsuccessful. In ***Commons v. Westwood Zoning Board of Adjustment,*** 81 N.J. 597 (1980), the New Jersey Supreme Court reversed the denial of a variance, reasoning that "undue hardship" means that, absent a variance, the property may not effectively be used, a condition that Commons had established by his efforts to either sell the land to his neighbors or acquire additional adjacent land to conform to the ordinances's area requirements.

b. Alternate standards for granting variances: Because use variances generally have broader impact than area variances, the standard that must be met in order to grant a use variance is sometimes higher. One version of this is simply to impose a greater burden of proving the general standard when an applicant is seeking a use variance. See, e.g., *Hertzberg v. Zoning Board of Adjustment of Pittsburgh,* 554 Pa. 249 (1998). A different version is to impose the general standard — undue hardship — for use variances but to relax that standard for area variances. When relaxed, the standard for area variances is proof that compliance with the zoning law would impose ***practical difficulties*** on the owner. However, courts applying the "practical difficulties" seem to examine the same factors that are relevant to the undue hardship test. See, e.g., *Duncan v. Village of Middlefield,* 23 Ohio St. 3d 83 (1986).

2. Exceptional uses: Unlike variances, which are administrative deviations from the zoning law made in order to avoid judicial determinations that strict application of the zoning law is invalid, ***exceptional uses*** (also called ***exceptions,*** or ***conditional uses,*** or ***special uses***) are uses that are permitted by the zoning law but which might impose material external costs on neighbors. The standards set out in the zoning law governing an exception are rarely phrased in terms of external costs; usually the standard is something like "compatibility with existing uses," or "in furtherance of public health, safety, and general welfare." These standards may be sufficiently vague to raise concern about an impermissible delegation of legislative power.

Example: Brunswick, Maine's zoning law permitted apartment houses in "suburban residential" zones "only as an exception granted by" the zoning board. The zoning board refused to grant an exception for a 48-unit apartment complex proposed to be located in a suburban residential zone. The law permitted exceptions that did not "adversely affect the health, safety or general welfare of the public" and would not "alter the essential characteristics of the surrounding property," but the zoning board thought that the apartment complex would produce adverse effects and alter the essence of the surrounding property. In ***Cope v. Inhabitants of the Town of Brunswick,*** 464 A.2d 223 (Me. 1983), the Maine Supreme Court held that the zoning law was an impermissible delegation of legislative authority to the zoning board because the quoted standards "refer only to the same general considerations which the legislative body was required to address and resolve in enacting the ordinance." The court's view was that the ordinance embodied a determination "that an apartment building was generally suitable for location in a suburban residential zone" and that the quoted standards gave the zoning board no lawful "basis for determining that a particular location was unsuitable because of the existence of certain characteristics which rendered the general legislative determination inapplicable." However, to the extent that administrative discretion is reduced by specific and detailed criteria set forth in the zoning law (which must be met to be within an exception), the pitfalls exemplified by *Cope* can be avoided.

3. **Zoning amendments and spot zoning:** While enabling acts provide for amendment of zoning laws, this power may be abused. The usual problem is *spot zoning* — a zoning amendment that delivers special private benefits (and no public benefits) to a small, discrete parcel of land and is not in conformity with the comprehensive plan. One recurrent problem in this area is to decide on the degree of deference that courts should pay to such zoning amendments.

   a. **Presumptive deference:** The traditional approach is to presume (as with other legislation) that the zoning amendments are valid until the challenger has proven otherwise.

   Example: Rochester, Minnesota's City Council amended the city's zoning ordinance to rezone an acre-plus tract on the edge of the central business district from low-density residential use to high-density residential use, thus permitting Younge to construct a 49-unit condominium building. The site was bounded on two sides by multiple-unit apartment buildings and on the other two sides by lower-density residential use (a mix of single and multiple-family dwellings). The City Council concluded that the proposed use was compatible with the existing uses and that there was a need for more high-density housing in Rochester. A neighborhood group sought to invalidate the amendment on three grounds: (1) the amendment was "quasi-judicial" in character, and thus the courts should not presume its validity absent substantial documentary evidence supporting the change, (2) even if legislative, the amendment was "arbitrary and capricious because it was inconsistent with the city's land use plan," and (3) the amendment was invalid spot zoning. A trial court denied relief and, in *State v. City of Rochester,* 268 N.W.2d 885 (Minn. 1978), the Minnesota Supreme Court affirmed. Because amendments to zoning acts are in form legislative, and "a legislative body can best determine which zoning classifications best serve the public interest," there was no need to depart from the customary presumption of validity of legislation. The fact that the amendment was not consistent with Rochester's existing land use plan (it was later amended) was not, *by itself,* reason to void the amendment or to shift the burden of proof onto the city. Because there was ample evidence to show that the new use was compatible with existing uses and served the public need for more high-density housing, the amendment was reasonably related to the public health, safety, morals, and general welfare, and surely not arbitrary, capricious, or irrational. Because there was no proof that the rezoned property was "an island of nonconforming use," and no showing of any "substantial diminution" in property values due to the rezoning, there was no basis for characterizing the amendment as invalid spot zoning.

   The presumption of validity is the default position, but even the states that employ it will not defer uncritically to legislative judgment when *spot zoning* is established. A zoning amendment that delivers *special private benefits* to a *small, discrete parcel,* produces *little or no public benefits,* and is *inconsistent with the comprehensive use plan* is presumed to be invalid spot zoning. The burden then shifts to the government to prove that the changes wrought by the amendment bear a ***substantial relationship to the general welfare of the affected community.*** See, e.g., *Save Our Rural Environment v. Snohomish County,* 99 Wash. 2d 363 (1983).

b. Presumptive skepticism: Some states exhibit a generally skeptical attitude toward zoning amendments that apply to relatively small tracts, whether or not the other indicia of spot zoning are present. These states employ a variety of devices, considered below, to decide when judicial scrutiny should be sharply higher.

i. Legislative or judicial character? For a time, some states focused on the particular events pertinent to a zoning amendment in order to determine whether the action was more akin to a *legislative* or a *judicial* decision. The more the decision appeared to be adjudicative, the stronger the burden placed upon the municipality to prove a demonstrable public need for the change and that the property affected by the change is the most suitable property for the change. *Fasano v. Board of County Commissioners of Washington County,* 264 Or. 574 (1973), was the leading case. That approach was severely criticized, both conceptually and for the practical difficulties of implementation. Even Oregon, the originator of the approach, has retreated from it. See *Neuberger v. City of Portland,* 288 Or. 155 (1979).

ii. Correct original mistake or respond to changed conditions: Some jurisdictions require the government to prove that the zoning amendment is necessary either to (1) correct a mistake in the existing law, or (2) adapt to a substantial change in conditions affecting land use. See, e.g., *Greenblatt v. Toney Schloss Properties Corp.,* 235 Md. 9 (1964).

4. Floating zones: Some zoning laws provide for ***floating zones,*** a use designation not attached to any particular land until a landowner seeks to have his land designated as the recipient of the floating classification.

Example: Because it desires to encourage the responsible disposal of toxic wastes (e.g., motor oil, paints, or chemicals), the city of Ford Cove creates a floating zone, designated TWC, dedicated to toxic waste collection and shipment to a disposal facility. The floating zone specifies the criteria that any land must meet to receive the TWC designation: a site of at least half an acre, no residences, schools, office buildings, churches, or retail establishments within 1,000 yards, and drive-through vehicle access. The TWC designation does not attach to any land. Fred, owner of a one-acre lot surrounded by heavy industrial uses for over 1,000 yards in every direction, applies for the TWC designation. Fred's land is suitable to be rezoned TWC. The objection to floating zones is that they violate the comprehensive plan. The comprehensive plan is supposed to inform people about the future direction of land use, but a floating zone can conceivably land anywhere, thus undermining the predictive value of the plan. This objection loses some of its force if the criteria for its attachment to land are drawn with great specificity. Moreover, the discretion created by floating zones is no more than that exercised by granting variances and conditional uses. See, e.g., *Rodgers v. Village of Tarrytown,* 302 N.Y. 115 (1951) (upholding floating zones).

5. Conditional zoning: Sometimes a developer wishes to use land in a fashion not permitted by the zoning law, and requests rezoning in exchange for the creation of a servitude burdening the land that is intended to eliminate or dampen the negative externalities of the proposed use.

Example: A developer wishes to build townhouses on land zoned for "fully detached single-family residences." The developer offers to cluster the townhouses in a portion of the site shielded from view from neighbors, and covenant that the undeveloped portion of the site will remain undeveloped forever. Upon execution of the servitude, the land is rezoned. In essence, imposition of the servitude is the condition of rezoning.

a. Criticisms: Conditional zoning is criticized on several grounds. A good review of the following criticisms is contained in *Collard v. Incorporated Village of Flower Hill,* 52 N.Y.2d 594 (1981), in which the New York Court of Appeals upheld conditional zoning.

   i. Illegal spot zoning: Some say it is illegal spot zoning, but the servitude partially offsets the claim that an individual parcel is receiving a special benefit, thus suggesting that conditional zoning ought to be assessed by the same standards applicable to any zoning amendment.

   ii. Invalid disposal of the police power: This claim is that governments may not bargain away their legislative power, but the municipality is not precluded from changing the zoning use at some time in the future if public welfare so requires.

   iii. *Ultra vires:* Enabling acts typically do not expressly authorize the attachment of conditions to zoning amendments, but neither do they forbid the practice.

   iv. Waiver of restrictions: Some object that conditional zoning amounts to a waiver of governmental ability to restrict use of the affected land any further, an argument resting on the assumption that conditional zoning amounts to a binding contract between the landowner and the city preventing future zoning restrictions. Most courts reject this claim, reasoning that the only bargain is imposition of a servitude in exchange for an *immediate* rezoning, thus leaving the government free to change the zoning classification in the future.

6. Cluster zoning: The idea of cluster zoning is to zone a particular area for a particular use at a specified level of density of occupation, but confer upon zoning administrators discretion to decide exactly how that use and density will be achieved.

Example: The city of Grassy Point designates a particular area as single-family residential with no more than three such residences per acre. The city is then free to permit division of this area into three lots per acre, each with a single-family residence, or to permit the construction of 60 single-family townhouses on a 20-acre parcel, with the structures clustered on 8 acres and the remaining 12 acres devoted to common amenities, such as a swimming pool, tennis courts, park, and gardens.

Cluster zoning is usually not problematic, so long as it is in conformity with the comprehensive plan.

IV. LIMITS ON THE ZONING POWER

A. Introduction: States possess an inherent *police power* — the power to act to achieve the people's vision of public welfare, as communicated through their governmental agents — but that power is not unlimited. Exercise by a municipality of zoning power must conform to (1) the U.S. Constitution, (2) valid federal law preemptive of the local zoning law, (3) the relevant state constitution, and (4) state law, particularly the state's zoning enabling act and judicial doctrines developed to curb unreasonable and arbitrary exercises of the police power. This section focuses on the use of one or more of these sources of authority to limit the scope of zoning. Chapter 11 considers in more detail the general limitations imposed by the U.S. Constitution's takings clause on zoning and other regulations of property that are sufficiently invasive of property to be treated as *de facto* uncompensated takings of private property for public use.

B. Zoning for aesthetic objectives: The traditional, judicially created, rule was that the use of zoning to achieve aesthetic objectives was beyond the permissible scope of the police power. The traditional view embodied the idea that beauty is subjective, entirely in the eye of the beholder, and thus governments have no business imposing their aesthetic judgments on others. This view has, however, broken down; a substantial number of courts have upheld aesthetic land use regulations banning uses that result in *lower property values*. This view seems to be that if enough beholders have the same notion of beauty, it is objective enough to be enforced by law.

Example: The city of Rye, New York, enacted an ordinance banning clotheslines in front or side yards abutting streets. In *People v. Stover,* 12 N.Y.2d 462 (1962), the New York Court of Appeals concluded that it was a permissible exercise of the police power to legislate for aesthetic concerns and that the ordinance was reasonably related to those legitimate concerns, even though there was evidence that Rye might have been trying to squelch the Stovers' practice of protesting high municipal taxes by the odd means of stringing old clothes on a line in their front yard. See also *State v. Jones,* 305 N.C. 520 (1982) (upholding a regulation restricting use of land as an auto junkyard).

About 20 states permit regulations solely for aesthetic reasons; another 15 or so permit regulation for aesthetic reasons if coupled with other objectives; fewer than 10 have never addressed the issue; and only a half-dozen cling to the rule that aesthetic regulation is wholly outside the police power.

1. **Architectural review:** One of the principal applications of aesthetic zoning is the proliferation of architectural review controls. Typically, such a scheme conditions a land use permit of some kind (e.g., planning approval, building permit) on (1) the conformity of the proposed structure to the ***existing character*** of the neighborhood, and (2) the likelihood that the proposed structure will ***not*** cause ***substantial depreciation*** of neighboring property values.

   ★**Example:** The affluent St. Louis suburb of Ladue enacted an architectural review ordinance designed to preserve property values and maintain Ladue's conventional neo-colonial architectural aesthetic sensibilities. Stoyanoff proposed to build a pyramidal, flat-topped residence with triangular window and door openings arranged asymmetrically on the structure. The proposal was rejected, and Stoyanoff attacked the validity of the entire scheme as unauthorized by the enabling act, outside the scope of the police power if so authorized, and a violation of due process if within the otherwise permissible scope of the police power. In ***State ex rel. Stoyanoff v. Berkeley,*** 458 S.W. 2d 305 (Mo. 1970), the Missouri Supreme Court upheld the Ladue law, reasoning that architectural review is for the general welfare and thus authorized by the enabling act. The rejection of Stoyanoff's "monstrosity of grotesque design," as Ladue termed it, was reasonably related to preserving land values and the prevailing (if conventional) aesthetic sense of the community. The court emphasized the probable adverse effect of Stoyanoff's design on property values, an effect that, if true, is merely the market's expression of prevailing aesthetic sensibilities.

It is hardly a foregone conclusion that this trend toward permitting exercise of the police power in furtherance of aesthetics is a good thing. Some of the nation's leading architects have expressed the view that architectural review promotes trite mediocrity, going so far as to suggest that Frank Lloyd Wright would never have constructed anything if he had faced architectural review. Perhaps beauty really is wholly subjective; if so, aesthetic zoning may be inherently vague and capricious. Common law judges long dead would agree; most of their descendants currently occupying the bench do not. But not all judges of today embrace architectural review controls as valid; when the application of such review is so vague as to cause ordinary people to guess as to its meaning, it becomes an unconstitutional deprivation of property without due process.

★**Example:** Anderson, owner of a suitably zoned parcel on Gilman Boulevard in Issaquah, Washington, wished to construct a retail commercial building on the site, but under an Issaquah ordinance he needed the approval of his design by the Development Commission. The Commission was charged by the ordinance to approve designs "compatible" with neighboring structures, "harmon[ious]" in texture, lines, and masses," with "building components" of "appropriate proportions and relationship[s]," using "harmonious" colors, "harmonious" lighting, resulting in an "interesting project by use of complimentary details [and] functional orientation [that relates] the development to the site" and avoids "monotony." Anderson proposed an off-white stucco structure with a blue metal roof in "modern" style, featuring a façade of "large retail style windows." The Commission told Anderson the color was wrong and that the design was not "compatible with the image of Issaquah." Anderson then proposed a wood roof, a façade adorned with brick and painted "Cape Cod" gray with "Tahoe" blue trim. The Commission again balked, telling Anderson to "drive up and down Gilman and look at both good and bad examples." Anderson then modified the design to create larger roof overhangs, more brick, more trees and other landscaping, but the Commission told him that the building did not deliver the right "feeling," that it was not in harmony with the "certain feeling you get when you drive along Gilman Boulevard," and denied its approval. In *Anderson v. City of Issaquah,* 70 Wash. App. 64 (1993), a Washington appeals court ruled that the denial had deprived Anderson of due process because the statute, both as written and as applied, required persons of ordinary intelligence to "guess at its meaning and differ as to its application." *Connally v. General Construction Co.,* 269 U.S. 385 (1926).

2. **Aesthetic regulation and free speech:** In general, laws that regulate speech based on its *content* (e.g., "no political speech") are subject to *strict scrutiny,* which means that they are *presumptively void,* and the government has the burden of proving that the speech restriction is *necessary* to accomplish a *compelling government objective,* and laws that regulate speech in a *content-neutral* fashion (e.g., "No amplified speech in the park between midnight and 6 a.m.") are subjected to more relaxed scrutiny.

   a. **Zoning that is based on the content of speech:** Zoning laws sometimes classify on the basis of the content of speech; such laws are presumptively invalid and may be saved only if the government can overcome the burden of strict scrutiny.

   Example: The zoning law of the New Jersey borough of Mt. Ephraim prohibited "all live entertainment." The Court struck down the law as applied to an "adult bookstore" that permitted its customers to watch a live nude dancer through peepholes. The flat ban on live entertainment entirely suppressed whatever expression component there is to nude dancing so, as applied, it banned a form of expression — nude dancing — because of its content and without proof either that the ban was necessary to achieve a compelling interest or that the government's interest was indeed compelling. *Schad v. Borough of Mt. Ephraim,* 452 U.S. 61 (1981).

    i. The "secondary effects" exception: If a zoning law discriminates on the basis of speech content but does so to regulate the *secondary effects of speech* — consequences that are **not** *produced by the communicative impact of speech* — the law is presumptively valid and will generally be upheld.

    Example: Detroit adopted a zoning law that dispersed "adult theaters," cinemas displaying non-obscene pornography. The objective of the law was to eliminate the critical mass of seedy establishments that attracted "an undesirable quantity and quality of transients, adversely affect[ed] property values, cause[d] an increase in crime, . . . and encourage[d] residents and businesses to move elsewhere." In *Young v. American Mini-Theatres,* 427 U.S. 50 (1976), the U.S. Supreme Court upheld the law against a free speech challenge, reasoning that it was not designed to suppress speech on account of its sexual content, or expression of any particular viewpoint, but was intended to disperse a "low value" form of speech in order to mitigate the secondary, nonspeech effects empirically associated with it. See also *City of Renton v. Playtime Theatres,* 475 U.S. 41 (1986), in which the Court ruled that a zoning law that consolidated adult theaters and bookstores into about 5 percent of the land area of the city was a valid content-neutral regulation of the secondary effects of such speech.

b. Zoning that is neutral as to the content of speech: Zoning laws that regulate speech in a content-neutral fashion are invalid if they are *either* (1) broader than reasonably necessary to achieve a significant government purpose other than speech regulation, or (2) so restrictive that they fail to leave open ample alternative channels of communication.

    ★**Example:** In order to minimize "visual clutter," the affluent St. Louis suburb of Ladue banned all signs except "for sale" signs, business- or home-identification signs, and a few others, but certainly forbade Gilleo's 8½-by-11-inch window sign declaring, "For Peace in the Gulf." Even though Ladue's regulation was content-neutral (it was not attempting to regulate the message on signs), the U.S. Supreme Court in *City of Ladue v. Gilleo,* 512 U.S. 43 (1994), unanimously voided it because its "near-total prohibition" on signs failed to leave open enough alternative means of communication. Ladue's law banned an entire medium of communication. A narrower prohibition of signs — one that left open ample alternative channels of communication — would likely have been valid.

    Example: Los Angeles prohibited the posting of signs on public property. Roland Vincent, a political candidate, attached signs advertising his candidacy to utility poles. The city removed them, and Vincent's supporters attacked the validity of the ban. In *Members of the City Council of Los Angeles v. Taxpayers for Vincent,* 466 U.S. 789 (1984), the U.S. Supreme Court upheld the law, reasoning that it was content-neutral and that the ban left Vincent free to attach his signs to private property (e.g., distribute bumper stickers, rent space) and to use other low-cost substitute means to reach voters (e.g., distribute handbills).

C. Zoning that burdens religious exercise: Zoning laws can interfere with religious exercise, particularly with respect to the location of churches or other religious land uses.

1. Zoning and the free exercise of religion: Although generally applicable laws that impede religious conduct without the intent to do so are presumptively valid, *Employment Division,*

Dept of Human Resources of Oregon v. Smith, 494 U.S. 972 (1990), laws, including zoning laws, that prohibit acts only when engaged in for religious reasons, or because of the religious belief that they display, are invalid attempts to suppress the free exercise of religion.

Example: The city of Hialeah, Florida, prohibited the "ritual slaughter" of animals but exempted almost every such ritual killing except those engaged in for religious purposes. Hialeah is home to a large number of adherents to the Santeria religion, a sect that has as its central sacramental rite the ritual slaughter of an animal. Because the law had been carefully drawn to apply only to ritual slaughter of animals for religious purposes, it was found to be an invalid suppression of free exercise of religion. *Church of the Lukumi Babalu Aye v. City of Hialeah,* 508 U.S. 520 (1993).

2. **Zoning and the RLUIPA:** A federal law, the Religious Land Use and Institutionalized Persons Act of 2000, 114 Stat. 803 (2000), 42 U.S.C. §2000cc, requires all governments to justify individualized applications of land use regulations that impose substantial burdens on religious exercise by proving that the regulations are the least restrictive means of achieving a compelling government objective. RLUIPA also applies to state programs that receive federal funding and when the substantial burden imposed by a local land use regulation has a substantial effect on interstate or foreign commerce.

★**Example:** The land use regulations of Sutter County, California, sharply limited the location of churches, requiring a conditional use permit to be obtained to locate a church in residential or agricultural areas. The Guru Nanak Sikh Society sought a conditional use permit to locate a Sikh temple in a residential area. Although the Sikhs agreed to conform to all of the conditions proposed by the staff of the county planning commission, the commission denied the permit due to residents' fears of excessive traffic and noise. The Sikhs then located a more remote site and sought a permit for their temple on that location. Again the Sikhs agreed to conform to all proposed conditions. Although the planning commission approved the permit, the County Board of Supervisors denied it in order to preserve agricultural land for farming and to prevent "leapfrog" development. In *Guru Nanak Sikh Society of Yuba City v. County of Sutter,* 456 F. 3d 978 (9th Cir. 2006), the court first concluded that the denials were individualized applications of the land use regulations, and thus the RLUIPA was properly invoked. The court then decided that the denials constituted a substantial burden on the Sikh Society's religious exercise because the broad basis for the denials had the significantly oppressive effect of making it more likely that no Sikh temple would be approved anywhere in the county. The county had no compelling interest for the denials.

D. **Zoning and environmental protection:** When zoning laws are altered, the alterations may be subject to challenge for failure to comply with assessment of the environmental impact of the changes, as required by state laws mandating such assessment. The scope of environmental impact may be quite broad, extending not only to the physical environment but to existing patterns of population and community character. Nor may it be limited by geographic scope, as the impact on global climate change may also be required to be assessed.

★**Example:** New York City amended its zoning regulations to prohibit demolition of theaters in Manhattan's theater district and to grant those theaters the absolute right to transfer their air rights (the right to develop the space above the theater) to other nearby properties so long as they maintained theater operations. The amendments also provided for additional discretionary transfers of theater air rights. The amendments were claimed to have been adopted illegally due to an inadequate assessment of the environmental impact of the authorized transfers, as required by SEQRA, a state law. The city had determined that the authorized as-of-right transfers would not have a negative effect on transit, traffic, or air quality; would not displace area residents or businesses; and would only serve to accommodate otherwise anticipated development. The city made no similar determination about the future impact of possible discretionary transfers. In *Fisher v. Giuliani*, 720 N.Y.S.2d 50 (2001), the New York intermediate appeals court ruled that the city's assessment of the impact of the as-of-right air transfers complied with SEQRA, but that the city's failure to make a current assessment of the future impact of possible discretionary transfers did not comply with SEQRA. Accordingly, the discretionary transfer portion of the amendments was severed and voided.

E. Zoning controls of household composition: Zoning laws can interfere with important civil liberties concerning living arrangements, liberties protected by the federal and various state constitutions, or by federal and state law that is paramount to a local zoning ordinance.

    1. The fundamental liberty of family association: Under the U.S. Constitution's due process clauses, laws that substantially interfere with the constitutionally fundamental liberty of people to marry and associate together in traditional family relationships are presumptively void. To sustain their validity, the government must prove a close connection between the regulation and the government purpose for the regulation, and establish that the government interest in regulating is sufficiently important to merit the challenged regulation. This may or may not be *strict scrutiny* — the requirement that the government prove that the regulation is necessary to achieve a compelling government purpose; the U.S. Supreme Court has been deliberately vague about the standard of review it employs in these cases. In any case, zoning laws can easily interfere with these liberties by limiting use and occupation of residential property to people who bear some specified relationship with each other.

    Example: East Cleveland's zoning ordinance limited occupancy of dwellings to members of the same family and defined "family" so narrowly that it excluded a family unit consisting of Inez Moore, her son Dale, Dale's son Dale, Jr., and another grandson, John, who was a nephew of Dale and Dale, Jr.'s first cousin. In *Moore v. City of East Cleveland,* 431 U.S. 494 (1977), the U.S. Supreme Court applied a higher level of scrutiny because the zoning law substantially interfered with the right of members of the same extended family to arrange their living relationships. The Court said it "must examine carefully the importance of the governmental interests advanced and the extent to which they are served by the challenged regulation," and when it engaged in that examination it found that East Cleveland's ordinance cut deeply into the "institution of the family" — including the extended family — that is "deeply rooted in this Nation's history and tradition." So examined, East Cleveland's objective was insufficiently important to merit this regulation; its legitimate concerns — overcrowding, traffic and parking congestion, avoiding an undue burden on the public schools — were only "serve[d] marginally, at best" by the law.

        a. Unrelated persons: When does "family" begin? Zoning laws that substantially interfere with the ability of *unrelated persons* (persons not related by blood, marriage, or adoption) to live together are presumed valid and subject only to minimal scrutiny.

        ★**Example:** The village of Belle Terre's zoning law prohibited occupancy of dwellings by more than two unrelated persons. In *Village of Belle Terre v. Boraas,* 416 U.S. 1 (1974), the U.S. Supreme Court applied minimal scrutiny because the law did not substantially burden the deeply rooted liberty of related family members to arrange their living patterns. The Court's view was that the liberty of unrelated persons to live together in a group is simply not constitutionally fundamental. Because the law was rationally related to the legitimate governmental objectives of residential tranquility and low residential density, it was upheld. Justice Marshall dissented, arguing that the "choice of household companions . . . involves deeply personal considerations as to the kind and quality of intimate relationships within the home," and was a constitutionally fundamental liberty. Accordingly, Marshall thought that the zoning law "can withstand constitutional scrutiny only upon a clear showing [by the government] that the burden imposed is necessary to protect a compelling and substantial governmental interest."

    i. Unrelated persons and state constitutions: State constitutions can produce a different result. The highest courts of New York, New Jersey, California, and Michigan, at least, have construed their state constitutions to protect the right of unrelated people to live together. These courts regard the concept of family as more functional than biological or legal; if people associate together exhibiting the characteristics of permanence and intimacy that traditionally identify a unit as family, the association is a fundamental liberty interest under the relevant state constitution. See *McMinn v. Town of Oyster Bay,* 66 N.Y.2d 544 (1985); *New Jersey v. Baker,* 81 N.J. 99 (1979); *City of Santa Barbara v. Adamson,* 27 Cal. 2d 123 (1980); *Charter Township of Delta v. Dinolfo,* 419 Mich. 253 (1984). Some states interpret their state constitutions no more generously than the U.S. Supreme Court's position in **Belle Terre v. Boraas.** See, e.g., *City of Ladue v. Horn,* 720 S.W. 2d 745 (Mo. App. 1986).

2. Statutory limits on zoning controls of household composition: Federal and state laws prohibit housing discrimination against persons with handicaps, the most important such statute being the federal Fair Housing Act. The mandates of this law can collide with local zoning laws limiting occupancy by unrelated persons when handicapped people seek to live together in group homes for various therapeutic purposes.

    ★**Example:** While the federal Fair Housing Act (FHA) prohibits discrimination in housing against handicapped people, it exempts from that prohibition "reasonable local . . . restrictions regarding the number of occupants permitted to occupy a dwelling." 42 U.S.C. §3607(b)(1). The zoning code of Edmonds, Washington, limited occupancy of single-family dwellings to any number of people "related by genetics, adoption, or marriage, or a group of five or fewer [unrelated] persons." In **City of Edmonds v. Oxford House, Inc.,** 514 U.S. 725 (1995), the U.S. Supreme Court interpreted the FHA to exempt only "total occupancy limits," not occupancy limits based on the familial composition of the household. Because the Edmonds law permitted an unlimited number of related people to live together in a single-family dwelling, and capped occupancy of such structures only when unrelated persons live together, the Court ruled that the Edmonds law illegally discriminated against handicapped people when it was applied to bar occupancy by a group of 10 to 12 recovering alcoholics and drug addicts, living together under the auspices of Oxford House, a substance abuse treatment program.

F. Exclusionary zoning: All zoning is exclusionary in that it seeks to exclude unwanted *uses,* but sometimes zoning is used to exclude unwanted *people,* though perhaps not for constitutionally or statutorily forbidden reasons. A typical example is a zoning law that, in the interest of preserving open space, aesthetics, and high property values (with its corollary, a high tax base), requires a minimum lot size of two acres. The result is a landscape of expensive homes occupied almost entirely by affluent owners. The poor (often disproportionately composed of a racial minority) are excluded. However, excluding the poor, even if done intentionally, does not trigger any presumption of invalidity under the federal Constitution. See *James v. Valtierra,* 402 U.S. 137 (1971). The exclusion is rationally related to the legitimate objectives of preserving open space, aesthetics, and high property values and is thus valid under the federal Constitution. States, however, remain free to interpret their own constitutions and enabling acts to ban actions permitted under the federal Constitution.

★**Example:** The New Jersey township of Mount Laurel developed rapidly from 1950 to 1970. The zoning law in effect excluded all multi-family residential dwellings and mobile homes, and required minimum lot and dwelling sizes for single-family residences that were sufficiently large that low-income persons were effectively excluded from Mount Laurel. In *Southern Burlington County NAACP v. Township of Mount Laurel (Mount Laurel I),* 67 N.J. 151 (1975), the New Jersey Supreme Court ruled that the New Jersey constitution and the state's zoning enabling act both required that local zoning further the "general welfare," and that Mount Laurel's failure to accommodate the housing needs of poor people was contrary to the general welfare. The court's opinion was that a "developing community," one expanding in size and population and thus taking shape, could not adopt land use regulations that make it "physically and economically impossible to provide low and moderate income housing in the municipality," but must "make realistically possible the opportunity for an appropriate variety and choice of housing for all categories of people who may desire to live there." Mount Laurel's efforts to comply were found wanting in *Southern Burlington County NAACP v. Township of Mount Laurel (Mount Laurel II),* 92 N.J. 158 (1983), in which the court extended the duty identified in *Mount Laurel I* to *all* New Jersey *communities,* not just "developing" ones, increased the scope of that duty from simple removal of barriers to one requiring all communities to take active steps to accommodate its "fair share" of the poor, and introduced remedial devices to enable builders of low-income housing to construct such housing despite local refusal to permit construction. *Mount Laurel II* impelled the New Jersey legislature to enact a statute that created an administrative agency to enforce the "fair share" obligation of *Mount Laurel II.* The statute was upheld in *Hills Development Co. v. Bernards Township,* 103 N.J. 1 (1986).

The *Mount Laurel* approach remains a minority view. Most states hold that so long as a zoning law does not exclude people on a suspect basis (e.g., race), it need only be rationally related to a legitimate state interest to be valid. Thus, when minimum lot sizes are rationally related to legitimate local interests, they are upheld. See, e.g., *County Commissioners of Queen Anne County v. Miles,* 246 Md. 355 (1967); *Ketchel v. Bainbridge Township,* 52 Ohio St. 3d 239 (1990). Some economists, notably Charles Tiebout, argue that it is more efficient to let communities specialize in land use, so that people will have a choice of various types of communities in which to live. The *Mount Laurel* approach "produces great diversity *within* neighborhoods, but no diversity *between* neighborhoods, and thus may limit the variety of residential choices available to households." Ellickson & Tarlock, *Land Use Controls* 812 (1981). See also Tiebout, *A Pure Theory of Local Expenditures,* 64 J. Pol. Econ. 416 (1956). Massachusetts and Connecticut have enacted legislation that is designed to override local controls that operate to exclude low- or moderate-income residents. In Oregon, a state agency has authority to require localities to permit higher density housing when regional housing needs are unmet. Oregon, however, is one of the few states to have adopted a statewide land use plan. by the law.

1. **Growth controls:** Growth controls are either temporary stoppages (e.g., a building moratorium) or permanent limitations on the rate of new entrants (e.g., annual quotas for building permits). These techniques have generally been upheld as within the authority conferred by the enabling act and as constitutionally valid exercises of that power, rationally related to the

legitimate state interest of orderly growth. See, e.g., *Associated Home Builders v. City of Livermore,* 18 Cal. 3d 582 (1976) (building moratorium upheld); *Golden v. Planning Board of Ramapo,* 30 N.Y.2d 359 (1972) (timing controls upheld); *Construction Industry Assn. v. City of Petaluma,* 522 F.2d 897 (9th Cir. 1975) (annual building quota upheld).

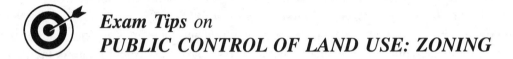

Exam Tips on
PUBLIC CONTROL OF LAND USE: ZONING

☛ This is an area where examination possibilities can take several distinctly different forms. Some professors emphasize the administrative process aspects of zoning, which focuses attention on the various devices that inject flexibility into the zoning process. Some professors are more interested in pursuing the limits on zoning, many of which are constitutional. Others may focus on the policy behind zoning, and raise questions about its wisdom and direction. Pay attention to these possibilities, and tailor your exam preparation to the emphasis your professor places on these materials.

☛ An administrative law focus on zoning is apt to emphasize the ways in which the process is vulnerable to abuse, or the ways in which the process can be used to reinforce values of democratic participation. Develop a good sense of the policy values underlying the administrative process.

☛ Constitutional limits on zoning represent a sliver of constitutional law. Make sure you understand what triggers the presumption of invalidity and what the government must prove to sustain such laws.

☛ Zoning produces a top-down approach to development, often characterized by monolithic uses, but the absence of zoning can produce a crazy quilt of shifting uses, responding to discrete economic events that may lack any pattern. If your professor wants you to engage zoning on this level, you will need to develop a coherent theory of why zoning is good or bad, and that may entail development of a theory of an ideal city, and how it may best be achieved, or some theory of human liberty and how zoning advances or retards your theory.

CHAPTER 11

TAKINGS: THE POWER OF EMINENT DOMAIN AND REGULATORY TAKINGS

ChapterScope

This chapter examines the government's eminent domain power, the power to take private property for public purposes, so long as just compensation is paid. The particular focus is upon regulatory takings, the point at which a government regulation of property becomes a taking requiring compensation. Here are the most important points in this chapter.

- The Takings Clause limits takings to those for public purposes and requires just compensation for all takings. The clause applies to all governments and protects all forms of property.

- The public-use requirement is satisfied so long as there is a conceivable public purpose for the taking.

- There are three principal *per se* tests that indicate when a regulatory taking has or has not occurred.

  - A taking occurs whenever a regulation permanently dispossesses an owner by stripping the owner of the right to exclude others.

  - A taking does not occur whenever a regulation does no more than duplicate the result under the prior applicable law of nuisance, even if the regulation deprives the owner of all economically viable use of the property, on the theory that the owner never had the right to use the property in such a fashion.

  - A taking occurs when a regulation deprives an owner of all economically viable use of the property, except when the regulation does no more than duplicate prior nuisance law.

- If the per se rules do not dispose of the case, a balancing test applies. The balancing test involves assessment of multiple factors: the degree to which the owner's investment-backed expectations are diminished, the nature of the government regulation, the breadth of the public benefits achieved, and the breadth of the impact of the regulation.

- Special rules apply when governments seek to impose conditions on issuance of land-use permits. If a condition, by itself, would be a taking, it is saved only if it bears a direct and essential nexus to a valid purpose underlying the land-use permit scheme to which it is attached. Even if the condition has such an essential nexus, the nature of the condition must be roughly proportional to the impact of the use on the validly regulated problem that the land-use scheme addresses.

- Compensation is required for regulations that constitute takings, no matter how long or short the regulation may endure.

I. INTRODUCTION

A. **The eminent domain power:** All governments in the United States have the power to take private property for public purposes, but that power (the *eminent domain* power) is limited by the U.S. Constitution, state constitutions, statutory law, and judicial decisions. The U.S. Constitution's Fifth Amendment provides that "private property [shall not] be taken for public use without just compensation." This is often called the "Takings Clause" or the "Eminent Domain Clause."

B. **All property protected:** The Constitution's Takings Clause protects **all property,** no matter whether it is tangible or intangible. See *Ruckelshaus v. Monsanto Co.,* 467 U.S. 986 (1984).

C. **Applies to all governments:** The Takings Clause applies to the states as well as the federal government. The substance of the Takings Clause is "incorporated" into the Fourteenth Amendment's Due Process Clause, which is applicable to the states. See *Chicago, Burlington & Quincy Ry. v. Chicago,* 166 U.S. 226 (1897). The Takings Clause surely applies to governmental action taken by the *legislative* or *executive* branches. There is more uncertainty about the degree to which *judicial* action might constitute a taking. See *Hughes v. Washington,* 389 U.S. 290 (1967); Thompson, *Judicial Takings,* 76 Va. L. Rev. 1449 (1990).

D. **The purposes of the Takings Clause:** The Takings Clause serves two important and related purposes.

   1. **Prevent forcible redistribution of property:** The Takings Clause *prevents forcible redistribution of property* by stipulating, through the *just compensation* requirement, that when governmental power is used to take private property, the public pays the property owner the value of the property taken.

   2. **Takings permitted only for public benefit:** The *public use* requirement of the Takings Clause was designed to *prevent any taking,* **whether or not compensated,** that forces a transfer of property from one private person to another with no public benefit in the forced transfer. Governmental power to take property may only be exercised for public benefit.

E. **The principal issues under the Takings Clause:** There are three principal issues that arise under the Takings Clause.

   1. **Public use:** Is a governmental taking of property for *public use?* Governments sometimes take private property and convey it to another private person in order to reap some alleged collateral public benefit. See section II, below.

   2. **Regulatory takings:** At what point does a governmental regulation of property (restricting its use, possession, or disposition) become so burdensome that it is a *de facto* taking of property, which triggers the constitutional requirement of just compensation? See section III, below.

   3. **Compensation:** It is well settled that the private property owner is entitled to the *fair market value* of the taken property — the price that a willing buyer and a willing seller would agree upon. Fair market value includes any *reasonable expectations* that a buyer may have about possible future uses (e.g., a change from cattle grazing to vineyard cultivation). An owner is not entitled to any additional value that is subjective and peculiar to the owner (e.g., the sentimental value of the family homestead). If there is no practical market for the property (e.g., it is a Gothic cathedral), any fair valuation method may be used. Common alternatives are capitalization of earnings and replacement value.

a. **Severance damages:** When only a portion of a private parcel is taken, the owner is entitled to *severance damages* — compensation for the resulting damage to the remaining portion. Severance damages are measured by a *before-and-after* rule — the owner must be paid the difference between the value of the entire parcel before taking and the value of the parcel the owner is left with after the taking. It does not matter that the value of property actually taken is less than this sum.

Example: Blackacre, a ten-acre tract, is worth $500,000 prior to condemnation of five acres for use as a public park. The condemned five-acre parcel, by itself, is worth $150,000. The remaining five-acre parcel is worth $200,000. Blackacre's owner is entitled to $300,000 in compensation ($500,000 – $200,000), *not* $150,000 (the value of the condemned portion considered in isolation).

b. **Effect of condemnation on value:** The fair market value due to a property owner is calculated without regard to the effect of condemnation itself on values. This can work to the advantage or disadvantage of property owners.

Example — Advantage: The government announces that it will condemn all property in a defined area for a new highway, but that the condemnation will not occur for three years. The market value of affected property will drop, because few people will wish to purchase a property that must be surrendered to the government in a few years. The government must pay the fair market value that existed *before* its market-depressing action.

Example — Disadvantage: The government announces that it will build a huge ground-control center for space probes in a certain city marked by economic depression and low property values, and that it will shortly condemn property for that purpose. In the weeks that follow the announcement and before the actual condemnation, speculators bid up the value of Blackacre, a parcel that is thought suitable for the center, from $100,000 to $200,000. When Blackacre is actually condemned, its owner is entitled to $100,000, not $200,000.

c. **Effect of condemnation on business located on the property:** Compensation is not generally required for damage to a business conducted on condemned property. The rationale for this rule is that damage to a business is merely incidental to the loss of the land itself. This rule also applies (absent specific statutory provision to the contrary) to the loss of business goodwill that results from condemnation.

F. **Constitutionally noncontroversial takings:** Most governmental takings of property are not constitutionally controversial. When a government condemns private property for a new public road, it is clearly doing so for public use and will admit that it is obligated to compensate the private landowners. The only issue is the amount of the compensation. Constitutional issues arise if the government denies that it has taken the property or if the taking is arguably not for public use.

II. THE PUBLIC USE REQUIREMENT

A. **Constitutional text:** The Constitution states " . . . nor shall private property be taken for *public use,* without just compensation."

1. **No takings except for "public use":** The near-universally accepted reading of the "public use" phrase is that it means that no governmental seizure of private property may occur, *even if just compensation is paid,* unless it is for a public use.

2. **The meaning of "public use":** A literal reading of the Constitution's text would limit governmental power to take private property to instances where the property will actually be used by the public (e.g., as a park, school, road, or military base). On this reading, seizures designed to produce some collateral public benefit are not permissible (e.g., a seizure of private property to convey it to a private corporation in order to construct a factory that will provide economic benefits to the community). In fact, the public-use limitation has virtually been eliminated by the Supreme Court's extreme deference to legislative judgments about what constitutes public use. So long as a taking is ***rationally related to any conceivable public purpose,*** the public-use requirement is satisfied. In essence, "public use" is whatever the legislature rationally thinks is conducive to "the public welfare."

★**Example:** New London, Connecticut, decided to condemn a number of private residential properties in the Fort Trumbull area of the city in order to assemble a 90-acre tract for an integrated redevelopment plan. Significant portions of the property were to be conveyed to private developers to construct (1) a "small urban village," consisting of shops, restaurants, and a waterfront hotel; (2) 80 new residences; (3) office and retail space; and (4) a marina, parking, and "water-dependent commercial uses." The Court had ruled in *Berman v. Parker*, 348 U.S. 26 (1954), that an "urban renewal" scheme in which blighted property was condemned and transferred to a private developer was a public use. In *Hawaii Housing Authority v. Midkiff*, 465 U.S. 1097 (1984), the Court had upheld as a public use the forced transfer of fee titles to long-term (e.g., 99 years) lessees of the ground on which their residences were located, given that only "22 landowners owned 72.5% of the fee simple titles" to land on Oahu, the most heavily populated Hawaiian island. Hawaii's desire to eliminate "the perceived social and economic evils" of this "land oligarchy" was "rationally related to a conceivable public purpose." Despite these precedents, the landowners contended that condemnation of non-blighted property for purely economic development purposes was not for a public purpose. In ***Kelo v. City of New London***, 125 S. Ct. 2655 (2005), the Court rejected that argument, concluding that so long as the condemnation was part of a "comprehensive development plan" that had been subjected to "thorough deliberation," the Court would defer to the judgment of government officials. In short, and with these additional caveats, the taking was rationally related to a conceivable public purpose. Justice Kennedy concurred because there was no clear evidence that this taking was primarily to benefit a private party, with only "incidental or pretextual public benefits." Justice O'Connor, joined by Rehnquist, Scalia, and Thomas, dissented. Justice O'Connor noted that the Court had upheld takings for later transfer to private persons only when the seizure was to cure a public harm. By contrast, the taking in ***Kelo*** involved only incidental public benefits and raised the possibility that anyone's property could be taken so long as the government could offer some plausible possibility that the new private user would make it more economically productive.

a. **State constitutional alternatives:** States are free to interpret their own constitutions independently, and so have the power to define the public-use limit upon takings differently from the U.S. Supreme Court.

Example: In *Poletown Neighborhood Council v, City of Detroit*, 410 Mich. 616 (1981), the Michigan Supreme Court upheld the condemnation of an entire viable residential neighborhood for transfer to General Motors as the site for an assembly plant. The court found sufficient public use in the intended purpose of "alleviating unemployment and revitalizing the economic base of the community." But the Michigan Supreme Court overruled *Poletown* in *County of Wayne v. Hathcock*, 471 Mich. 445 (2004), ruling that when property is taken for transfer to another private owner, public use is satisfied only when any of three tests is met: (1) the taking is *necessary* to accomplishment of the public purpose; (2) the property "remains subject to public oversight after transfer" (e.g., transfer to a publicly regulated utility); or (3) the condemnation itself (as distinguished from the later transfer) produces independent public benefits (e.g., condemnation of blighted property). The first test probes the *means* to the public end; the remaining two tests probe the sufficiency of those *ends*.

b. **Means v. ends analysis:** The traditional way to determine public use is to assess the ends of the condemnation. The Supreme Court used ends analysis when it stated in *Midkiff* that public use is satisfied if the condemnation is "rationally related to a *conceivable* public purpose." That form of inquiry was continued in **Kelo**, where the Court deferred to governmental judgment about the ends of the taking. Ends analysis need not be so deferential. Richard Epstein, in *Takings* (1985), argued that public use should be confined to the provision of "public goods" — items from which nobody can be excluded from consuming and the consumption of which by one person does not affect other people's ability to consume the good (e.g., a lighthouse) — and "quasi-public goods." Means analysis was advocated by Merrill in *The Economics of Public Use*, 72 Cornell L. Rev. 61 (1986). Merrill urged that forced transfers should occur only when transaction costs are sufficiently high to prevent voluntary transfers. The Michigan Supreme Court adopted a means test as one part of its *Hathcock* trilogy: Is the taking *necessary* to accomplish the public end?

3. **The relationship of public use and just compensation:** Because the compensation provided for a taking does not include the subjective value of the property to the owner (the personal value above its market value), or the potential gains above market value that might be reaped in a voluntary sale, the public-use requirement functions as a "property rule" to prevent absolutely those takings failing the public use test. But because the public-use test is so weak, this is not much of a barrier. Moreover, the property rule approach is susceptible to large errors. Courts are reluctant to deny to governments the eminent domain power, fearing that desirable public benefits would be lost because the transaction costs of proceeding through voluntary transfers are insurmountable; hence the weakness of the public-use test. But this reluctance to incur these errors of omission induces other errors of commission: A weak public-use test approves some projects of little or no public benefit and provides inadequate compensation. Here are two responses to this problem.

a. **Liability rule:** Courts could use a "liability rule" instead of a "property rule." Traditional fair market value compensation would be paid for takings for unquestioned public use (e.g., roads), but the compensation would increase to reflect subjective values and lost opportunity costs as the taking appears to edge closer to the precipice of a purely private-to-private forced transfer. The defect of this approach is its subjectivity, but its proponents argue that the errors that would occur under it would be of lesser magnitude than at present. See Krier & Serkin, *Public Ruses*, 2004 Mich St. L. Rev. 859.

b. **"Usings:"** Jed Rubenfeld, in *Usings*, 102 Yale L.J. 1077 (1993), argued that the Takings Clause was intended to prevent the government from making individuals mere instrumentalities of the state. To that end, he contended that the public-use requirement should mark the line between takings and mere regulation. When the government forces private property into state use, it has effected a taking. Thus, a regulation requiring property suitable for economic development to be kept forever wild is a conscription of that property for a state use: conservation. When the government does not conscript that property, but its policy ends could as well be served by destruction of the property, it has not taken the property. Thus, a requirement that cedar trees harboring a fungus destructive to economically valuable apple trees be destroyed is not a taking, because there is no state use of the property.

III. REGULATORY TAKINGS: HOW MUCH REGULATION OF PROPERTY IS TOO MUCH?

A. Introduction: At some point, government regulation of property becomes so extensive that it amounts to a *de facto* taking, even though the government denies that it is taking the property. But when? Everyone agrees that a seizure of title is a taking, but regulations may also interfere substantially with an owner's right to use, dispose, or possess property. In an early regulatory takings case, ***Pennsylvania Coal Co. v. Mahon,*** 260 U.S. 393 (1922), the Court declared that "while property may be regulated to a certain extent, if regulation goes too far it will be recognized as a taking." The Court has devised three categorical, or per se, rules and several balancing tests to determine when a regulation goes "too far" and becomes a taking.

B. The *per se* rules: One of the Court's categorical rules identifies a form of regulation that, *per se*, **does** **not** **constitute a taking.** The other two categorical rules identify when a taking **has occurred.**

1. Permanent dispossession: When a government regulation *permanently dispossesses* an owner of her property, the regulation is a taking.

    a. Real property: As applied to real property, a taking has occurred if a regulation produces a **permanent** *physical occupation* of all or a part of the property. Temporary occupations are not per se takings.

    ★**Example:** New York required landlords to permit cable television operators to install cable facilities on their property. Loretto, a landlord, claimed that the forced cable installation was a taking of her property, even though the physical occupation consisted entirely of a half-inch-diameter coaxial cable along the roof and descending to the apartments within, together with associated small directional taps and junction boxes for the cable, most or all of which were on the roof of the building. In ***Loretto v. Teleprompter Manhattan CATV Corp.,*** 458 U.S. 419 (1982), the U.S. Supreme Court agreed, ruling that a "permanent physical occupation authorized by government is a taking without regard to the public interests that it may serve." The Court reasoned that the permanent loss of the ability to exclude others was especially destructive of property expectations — "the character of the invasion is qualitatively more intrusive than perhaps any other category of property regulation."

    b. Personal property: A taking has occurred when governments, by regulation, confiscate personal property.

    Example: Florida law provided that the interest earned on private funds deposited into court in interpleader cases must be turned over to the state. In *Webb's Fabulous Pharmacies v. Beckwith,* 449 U.S. 155 (1980), the U.S. Supreme Court ruled that a taking had occurred because the property owner had been permanently dispossessed.

    c. Physical *invasion* distinguished: A physical invasion of property by the government that is not permanent, and that does not permanently deprive the landowner of the right to exclude others, is not a per se taking but must be assessed under the balancing process that applies to claims of regulatory takings that cannot be disposed of under the categorical rules. However, when government action strips all utility from an owner's possession, the action may be treated as a government invasion of property that constructively dispossesses the owner.

Example: Government aircraft continually flew over Causby's land at low altitude, thus making his property virtually unusable. In *United States v. Causby,* 328 U.S. 256 (1946), the U.S. Supreme Court held that a taking had occurred, because Causby's loss was "as complete as if the United States had entered upon the surface of the land and taken exclusive possession of it."

2. **Nuisance abatement:** If a government regulates property to *abate activities that are common law nuisances,* there is **no taking,** even though the regulations might bar all economically viable uses of the property. The theory is that ownership of the property never included the right to inflict nuisances, so nothing has been taken by forbidding what was never lawful.

   a. **Origins:** This categorical rule originated in cases that sought to distinguish between regulations designed to prevent harmful (or noxious) uses and those designed to reap a public benefit. Only the latter were said to be takings.

   ★**Example:** In the 1890s, Hadacheck acquired rural land outside of Los Angeles that was ideal for brick-making because of the extent and fine quality of the clay deposits. Hadacheck invested heavily in machinery and equipment and developed a thriving brick business. Eventually, the city grew out to his brickyard and kiln, and Los Angeles enacted an ordinance forbidding his continued operations, on the grounds that the continued activity was annoying and inconvenient to his newly arrived residential neighbors. Because the ordinance allowed Hadacheck to remove his clay (but not to make bricks), there was no taking, said the U.S. Supreme Court in *Hadacheck v. Sebastian,* 239 U.S. 394 (1915). The Court never expressly declared that Hadacheck's brickyard was a nuisance, but was persuaded that Los Angeles was seeking to regulate a "noxious" use, even if it might be lawful. The concept of permissible regulation to address noxious-but-lawful uses was extended in *Miller v. Schoene,* 276 U.S. 272 (1928), in which the Court upheld a Virginia law that mandated uncompensated forcible destruction of red cedar trees harboring cedar rust fungus, a killer of apple trees.

   In these cases, the Court thought that the cedar trees were harmful to apple trees, and the brickyard was harmful to residential neighbors, but it is equally true to say that the cedar trees were destroyed to reap the public benefit of a continued apple industry, or that the brickyard was quashed to reap the public benefit of residential tranquility. The problem with this approach is the unstable, and ultimately indeterminate, distinction between harm and benefit.

   Example: Suppose a government bans billboards on private land abutting public highways. As Frank Michelman, in *Property, Utility, and Fairness,* 80 Harv. L. Rev. 1165, asks: Does the regulation prevent "the 'harms' of roadside blight and distraction, or [secure] the 'benefits' of safety and amenity?" Michelman asserts that for this distinction to work, "we [must] establish a benchmark of 'neutral' conduct," which distinguishes between regulations that seize public benefits (compensation required) and those that control private harms inflicted on the public (no compensation required).

b. **Contemporary statement:** The modern approach to cut the Gordian knot of harm-or-benefit is to use the common law of nuisance, as it exists in a state prior to the imposition of a regulation that is claimed to be a nuisance-abatement measure, as the benchmark. The only regulations that fall within this rule are those designed to stop common law nuisances, as determined by an *objectively reasonable application* of the precedents pertinent to nuisance.

★**Example:** South Carolina prohibited *any* development of Lucas's beachfront lots on the Isle of Palms in order to protect its ecologically fragile barrier islands. The South Carolina Supreme Court ruled that the legislation was not a taking, but in *Lucas v. South Carolina Coastal Council,* 505 U.S. 1003 (1992), the U.S. Supreme Court reversed and remanded the case to determine whether the law simply abated a common law nuisance. Regulation of private property is no taking if the regulations "do no more than duplicate the result [obtainable by private parties] . . . under the State's law of private nuisance, or by the State under its complementary power to abate [public] nuisances." Even if a regulation forbids the only economically viable use of the property, it does not "proscribe a productive use that was previously permissible under relevant property and nuisance principles." A government desire to "prevent harm" is not, by itself, enough to trigger per se validity because "the distinction between 'harm-preventing' and 'benefit-conferring' is . . . in the eye of the beholder." On remand, the South Carolina courts ruled that the uses prohibited by the law were not common law nuisances. After *Lucas,* regulations that address "harms," but which are *not* common law nuisances, are evaluated under the balancing tests. There is no per se insulation of such regulations from the Takings Clause.

3. **Loss of all economically viable use:** If a government regulation leaves the owner with *no economically viable use* of his property, and the regulation does **not** *abate a common law nuisance,* a taking has occurred. There are two rationales for this rule: (1) the severity of such regulations impeach the usual assumption that government regulation of property is for the advantage of everyone, including affected property owners, and (2) the effect of these regulations is to achieve public benefits by imposing the costs of such benefits *entirely upon affected property owners.*

Example: Refer to the *Lucas v. South Carolina Coastal Council* example. South Carolina's Beachfront Management Act, as applied to Lucas's lots on Isle of Palms, a barrier island near Charleston, forbade the construction of "any permanent habitable structures." Assuming that this rendered the property "valueless," as the trial court had concluded, the U.S. Supreme Court in *Lucas v. South Carolina Coastal Council,* 505 U.S. 1003 (1992), held that a regulation that deprives a landowner of all economically viable uses is a per se taking, unless the loss of all economically viable use results entirely from abatement of a common law nuisance (which would make the regulation a per se non-taking). The Court justified the rule partly because "total deprivation of beneficial use is, from the landowner's point of view, the equivalent of a physical appropriation," and partly because such regulations "carry with them a heightened risk that private property is being pressed into some form of public service under the guise of mitigating serious public harm."

a. **Partial destruction — "Conceptual severance":** The "loss of all economically viable use" rule applies only to a regulation that strips the owner of all economically viable use of the *entire* property. If a regulation operates to deprive the owner of all economically viable use of only *part* of his property, the question of whether or not the regulation is a taking will be decided by the balancing tests. ***Tahoe-Sierra Preservation Council, Inc. v. Tahoe Regional Planning Agency,*** 535 U.S. 302 (2002).

> **Example:** Suppose a newly imposed regulation requires a landowner to leave 90 acres of a single 100-acre tract in its natural state forever. In ***Lucas,*** the Court admitted that "it is unclear whether we would analyze the situation as one in which the owner has been deprived of all economically beneficial use of the burdened portion of the tract, or as one in which the owner has suffered a mere diminution in value of the tract as a whole." Without deciding the issue, the ***Lucas*** Court suggested that the answer "may lie in how the owner's reasonable expectations have been shaped by the State's law of property — i.e., whether and to what degree the State's law has accorded legal recognition and protection to the particular interest in land with respect to which the takings claimant alleges a diminution in (or elimination of) value." In ***Tahoe-Sierra,*** the Court applied the balancing test to a multi-year moratorium on *all* development. Taken together, ***Lucas*** and ***Tahoe-Sierra*** suggest that if the hypothetical 100-acre tract were split into two separate titles — one of 10 acres, still usable after the regulation, and the other of 90 acres, with no economic value left after the regulation — the ***Lucas*** loss-of-all-economically-viable-use rule would govern the 90-acre parcel, but if the 100-acre parcel were a single title. the ***Lucas*** rule would not apply.

C. Balancing public benefits and private costs: If the per se rules do not resolve the issue of whether a regulation is a taking, courts weigh the public benefits achieved by the regulation against the private costs imposed. A regulation is not a taking if it ***substantially advances a legitimate state objective.*** To determine whether this test has been met, at least the following conditions must exist: (1) ***public benefits from the regulation must outweigh the private costs of the regulation,*** (2) the regulation must ***not be arbitrary,*** and (3) the property owner must be permitted to ***earn a reasonable return*** *on investment* in the property.

1. **Origins:** Regulatory takings law effectively originated with ***Pennsylvania Coal Co. v. Mahon,*** 260 U.S. 393 (1922), and its significance and meaning have been debated ever since. Pennsylvania's Kohler Act prohibited underground coal mining that would cause surface subsidence, but only where the surface and the underground coal were owned by two different people. Mahon, owner of the surface, had expressly assumed the risk of subsidence when he purchased his property, but he invoked the Kohler Act to restrain the owner of the underground coal, Pennsylvania Coal Company, from further underground mining. In ***Mahon,*** the Court recognized that "property may be regulated to a certain extent" but added that "if regulation goes too far it will be recognized as a taking." The Court voided the Kohler Act because it went "too far" — it destroyed the economic viability of Pennsylvania Coal's property, the underground coal the Kohler Act required to be left in place. The law made "it commercially impracticable to mine . . . coal," a result with "very nearly the same effect for constitutional purposes as appropriating or destroying" the right to mine coal. Justice Brandeis dissented on the ground that the Kohler Act prohibited a "noxious use" and that the diminution in value was not absolute — the appropriate measure should not be the decline in value "of the coal alone, but . . . the value of the whole property."

   a. **"Average reciprocity of advantage":** In his dissent in ***Mahon,*** Justice Brandeis charged that the Court was creating a rule that regulations in aid of public safety must display "'an average reciprocity of advantage' as between the owner of the property restricted and the rest of the community" in order to be valid without compensation. The concept of "average reciprocity of advantage" suggests that a regulation must bestow some public benefits (and, perhaps, that some of those benefits must be enjoyed by the affected landowner). Brandeis denied that "average reciprocity of advantage" was *necessary* to a regulation's validity, but did concede that was "an important consideration." This concept comes back in the ***Penn Central*** multifactor test, in the form of evaluation of the nature or character of the regulation, and also figures in some academic perspectives on takings. See, e.g., section III.F.4, below.

b. **Application of *Mahon* balancing: Conceptual severance:** The balancing calculus that ***Mahon*** employed was mostly to assess whether the diminution in value attributable to the regulation was so much that the regulation's effect was practically indistinguishable from an appropriation or destruction. In order to reach this conclusion, the Court conceived of the coal required to be left in place as a distinct property interest, but Justice Brandeis argued that the appropriate measure was the effect the regulation had on the *entire* property interest held by Pennsylvania Coal. Years later, in *Keystone Bituminous Coal Assn. v. De Benedictis,* 480 U.S. 470 (1987), the Supreme Court adopted Justice Brandeis's approach to uphold the validity of a later Pennsylvania law, the Subsidence Act, which required coal miners to leave sufficient coal in place to support the surface. The Court distinguished the Subsidence Act from the Kohler Act on two grounds: (1) the coal forcibly left in place to support the surface did "not constitute a separate segment of property for takings law purposes," and (2) the miners had "not come close to . . . proving that they have been denied the economically viable use of [their] property" because the coal left in place was only a small fraction of the entire coal deposit owned by them.

2. **Contemporary statement:** The principal modern case developing the balancing approach is ***Transp. Co. v. New York City,*** 438 U.S. 104 (1978), in which the Supreme Court upheld New York City's Landmarks Preservation law. As applied to Penn Central, the law prevented Penn Central from building an office tower over Grand Central Station but left Penn Central with the economic return from the terminal building and "transferable development rights" — the right to develop other properties in the vicinity owned by Penn Central more intensively than New York's zoning law would otherwise allow. The Court admitted that the balancing test was an "essentially ad hoc, factual inquir[y]" that turned on a number of factors: (1) the nature of the government regulation (the more akin to a physical invasion, the more likely a taking; the more it merely "adjust[s] the benefits and burdens of economic life to promote the common good," the more likely it is not a taking); (2) the reasonable expectations of the property owner (the stronger the "investment-backed expectations" and the more thoroughly frustrated they are by the regulation, the more likely there is a taking); (3) the degree to which the regulation is designed to stop uses that cause "substantial individualized harm" but are not common law nuisances; and (4) the degree to which the regulation enables the government actually to use the property for "uniquely public functions." The Landmarks Law posed no threat of physical invasion, left Penn Central with the ability to earn a "reasonable return" on its "investment-backed expectations," and did not raise issues of government use.

a. **Application of *Penn Central* balancing: "Investment-backed expectations":** The concept of investment-backed expectations has proven to be enigmatic. First, it is related to conceptual severance: The phrase might refer to an interest in a distinct property interest (e.g., Pennsylvania Coal's interest in its "support estate," a property interest totally wiped out by the Kohler Act), or it might mean a financial interest in a larger estate that is much diminished, though not totally eliminated (e.g., the diminution in value to coal miners of the

Subsidence Act upheld in **Keystone**). Second, the phrase is suggestive of inherent limits: If either "investment" or reasonable "expectations" are lacking, there might be no protected interest at all.

★**Example:** From 1959 to 1978, SGI, a Rhode Island corporation, owned a 20-acre parcel that was mostly a salt marsh wetland. During that period, various new regulations were adopted that effectively barred development of the wetland, but permitted construction of one large residence on an upland portion of the property. Upon dissolution of SGI in 1978, title to the parcel passed to Palazzolo, the sole shareholder of SGI, who sought approval to develop the parcel more intensively. Upon denial of his plans, Palazzolo brought suit, contending that Rhode Island had taken his property. The Rhode Island Supreme Court ruled that the use restrictions in place in 1978, when Palazzolo had acquired title, were part of the "background title" he had acquired, and thus he could not assert that they constituted a taking. In **Palazzolo v. Rhode Island,** 533 U.S. 606 (2001), the U.S. Supreme Court reversed that ruling, reasoning that such a rule would immunize extreme and unreasonable regulations against future attack, would be capricious (e.g., older owners or those with the will and means to hold property for a long time could challenge regulations, but younger owners or those who have recently arrived in a locality and acquired property could not), and would deny to in-place owners the ability to transfer to others the same title they had. The Rhode Island Supreme Court also ruled that the use regulations did not deprive Palazzolo of all economically viable use of his land, because he could still build a large residence. On that point, the U.S. Supreme Court affirmed. Palazzolo argued that the upland portion (on which he was permitted to build the residence) was a separate parcel and that he had been stripped of all economically viable use in the wetlands, but because he had not made that argument in the lower courts, the U.S. Supreme Court declined to address it. The Court concluded that the regulation did not deny to Palazzolo all economically viable use of his property but remanded the case for a determination of whether, under the **Penn Central** test, the regulations constituted a taking. Justice O'Connor concurred, suggesting that regulations in place at the time an owner acquires property are relevant to the **Penn Central** issue of the owner's reasonable investment-backed expectations.

b. **Application of *Penn Central* balancing: "Parcel as a whole":** The problem of conceptual severance can occur in several different dimensions. Although it is usually thought of as a physical or geographic problem (e.g., can a 100-acre parcel be conceptually split if only 90 acres are subjected to regulations that bar all economically viable use?), it can also be a functional problem (e.g., loss of the right to possess, or to use, or dispose), or a temporal problem. Suppose a government bars all economically viable use of the entirety of a parcel, but only for a limited period of time. An incomplete answer was provided in *First English Evangelical Lutheran Church of Glendale v. County of Los Angeles*, 482 U.S. 304 (1987), in which the Court ruled that *if a regulation constitutes a taking,* compensation is required from the moment the regulation is first effective, even if it is later rescinded. *First English* thus held that regulatory takings, however short their duration, require compensation, but the case did not decide whether a temporary loss of all economically viable use constitutes a taking.

Example: An interstate regional agency controlling land use in the Lake Tahoe basin adopted a moratorium on any development of certain properties in the basin. The moratorium was intended to halt all development until a land-use plan could be put into effect that permitted development in a manner that would not contribute to the continued degradation of the water purity of Lake Tahoe. Affected property owners asserted that the moratorium denied them all economically viable use of their property and, under *First English*, they were entitled to compensation for the duration of the moratorium. Not so, said the Supreme Court in ***Tahoe-Sierra Preservation Council, Inc. v. Tahoe Regional Planning Agency***, 535 U.S. 302 (2002). Justice Stevens, writing for the majority, declared that the effect of the regulation on the value of the parcel must be considered with respect to the "parcel as a whole" and that it was improper to sever the time the fee simple absolute title was subject to a moratorium from its otherwise infinite duration. If the moratorium had been a *permanent* ban on development that resulted in loss of all economically viable use, it would have been a taking, but this ban was merely temporary. Left unanswered were such questions as: How long must a "temporary" moratorium last before it becomes "permanent"? (5 years? 10 years? 30? 100? 1,000?) If conceptual severance is improper for temporal losses of all economically viable use, why is it proper for permanent losses of only one function, as in *Loretto*?

D. **Exactions: Conditional burdens:** Governments frequently regulate land use by requiring landowners to obtain a permit for the use. A typical example is a building permit. The regulation requiring a building permit is not problematic, so long as the condition of obtaining the permit is compliance with reasonable health and safety standards or the like. Problems occur when the government imposes as a condition to the obtaining of a building or other use permit some condition that could not independently be imposed without compensating the landowner. In essence, the question becomes: May the state condition the grant of a building permit on the landowner's consent to what would otherwise be an uncompensated taking? There are two dimensions to this problem.

1. **"Essential nexus":** The first issue may be framed by a question: Is a condition that, *standing alone,* is a taking rendered valid and **not a taking** if it is **substantially related** to the purposes of a valid land-use regulation (e.g., a building permit requirement)? If a government may validly forbid someone from building an unsafe structure, it must validly be able to attach conditions to issuance of a building permit that advance the purpose of ensuring safety (e.g., no flammable materials may be used in the structure); but the government may not validly attach conditions to issuance of a building permit that are unrelated to the purpose of enhancing safety (e.g., erection of a flagpole from which the city flag must be flown daily). A *condition that would be a taking, if imposed in isolation, is* **not a taking** when attached as a condition of issuance of a land use permit under an otherwise valid regulation *only if the government can prove* the condition is **substantially related** to the **government's valid regulatory objective.** This requirement is sometimes described as an **essential nexus** between the legitimate regulatory interest and the condition, so that the condition advances the state's reason for limiting development in the first place.

★**Example:** Nollan owned a beachfront lot along the Southern California coast on which was a dilapidated cottage. Nollan's lot extended to the mean high-tide mark along the beach, a point some distance seaward of a concrete retaining wall on his lot. He sought approval from the California Coastal Commission for permission to demolish the structure and construct a new, somewhat larger, residence consistent in size and design with the neighboring houses. Pre-existing regulations of the Coastal Commission forbade construction on Nollan's site if the structure would impede public access to the public portion of the beach (seaward of the mean high-tide mark) or would promote congestion on the beach. The Commission refused to grant Nollan a permit unless he consented to a recorded easement that would permit unrestricted public use of Nollan's beachfront lying between his retaining wall and the mean high-tide mark. Nollan refused and brought suit, contending that the easement condition was a taking. In *Nollan v. California Coastal Commission,* 483 U.S. 825 (1987), the U.S. Supreme Court agreed with Nollan. The Court assumed that the underlying regulation—prohibition of beachfront construction when it impedes public beach access or promotes beach congestion—was valid (although it did not so decide), but concluded that the condition imposed for a permit to build—Nollan's grant of a permanent right to the public to use the private beach portion of his lot—"utterly fail[ed] to further the end advanced as the justification for the prohibition." The Coastal Commission had failed to prove that the easement-for-public-access condition **substantially advanced** the purposes of the pre-existing regulations of coastal construction; thus the easement condition was simply "an out-and-out plan of extortion."

2. **"Rough proportionality":** The second issue posed by the problem of exactions, or conditional burdens, is whether the government can impose a condition to a land use permit that is disproportionate to the impact of the proposed use on the activity that the government sought to regulate in the first place. Even if a condition that would be a taking if imposed in isolation is valid because it satisfies the ***essential nexus*** test, it *is a taking unless the government proves that the nature and scope of the condition* are **roughly proportional** to the impact of the proposed development on matters that the underlying regulation addresses.

★**Example:** Dolan wished to expand her plumbing and electrical supply store in Tigard, Oregon, in a fashion that was consistent with the city's zoning law. The site fronted a street and backed up against Fanno Creek. Although a portion of the site was within the 100-year flood plain of Fanno Creek, none of the proposed new construction was within that flood plain. The city conditioned a building permit upon Dolan's agreement to dedicate to public use (for storm drainage) the entire portion of her lot within Fanno Creek's flood plain and to "dedicate an additional 15-foot strip of land adjacent to the flood plain as a pedestrian [and] bicycle pathway." The city denied Dolan's request for a variance exempting her from these conditions, after concluding that it was "reasonable to assume that customers and employees of the future uses of the site could utilize a pedestrian [and] bicycle pathway adjacent to this development for their transportation and recreational needs," that the pathway "could offset some [auto] traffic [and alleviate] traffic congestion," and that "increased storm water flow from [Dolan's] property to an already strained creek and drainage basin can only add to the public need to manage the stream channel and flood plain for drainage purposes." Dolan sued, claiming that the required dedications of her property constituted takings. In *Dolan v. City of Tigard,* 512 U.S. 374 (1994), the U.S. Supreme Court agreed. First, it concluded that the conditions satisfied the "essential nexus" test of *Nollan* because "the prevention of flooding . . . and the reduction of traffic congestion" were legitimate public purposes of the underlying regulation and the required dedications were substantially related to those purposes. However, the city had failed to prove that either required dedication was even "roughly proportional" to the impact of Dolan's development on the legitimate public purposes of preventing flooding and reducing traffic congestion. While a ban on development within the flood plain was valid, the city was unable to prove "why a public greenway, as opposed to a private one, was required in the interest of flood control." While the Court had "no doubt that the city was correct in finding that [Dolan's development] will increase [auto] traffic," it had "not met its burden of demonstrating that the additional number of vehicle and bicycle trips generated by [Dolan's development] reasonably relate to the city's requirement for a dedication of the pedestrian [and] bicycle pathway easement."

The "rough proportionality" test applies *only to exactions;* it does not apply to ordinary land-use regulations, the underlying regulations to which exacting conditions are attached. See *City of Monterey v. Del Monte Dunes,* 526 U.S. 687 (1999).

3. **Summary:** The *essential nexus* and *rough proportionality tests* are cumulative, not alternatives. Each test must be satisfied for an exaction to be valid without compensation. If a condition is a taking by itself, the condition *cum* regulation is a taking unless the government can prove (1) the condition is **substantially related** to the **government's valid regulatory objective,** and (2) the nature and scope of the condition are **roughly proportional** to the impact of the proposed development. The logical order of analysis is, first, to establish that the condition would be a taking if imposed independently; second, to prove that such a condition satisfies the essential nexus test; and, third, to show that such a condition exacts concessions that are roughly proportional to the development's impact.

Example — "Essential nexus": The city of Esmeralda imposes a building permit system in order to limit development because Esmeralda's city-owned electrical utility is unable to increase substantially its power production, and no other sources of electricity are available. Cassie applies for a building permit to enlarge her house and is told that a building permit will be issued only if she deeds a strip in front of her house to Esmeralda for a public pedestrian path. The condition — donation of a portion of her property to the city — is clearly a taking when considered in isolation. It is not saved because it is imposed as a condition to an otherwise valid building permit scheme because the condition — dedication of the bicycle path — is wholly unrelated to the reason for limiting development — conservation of scarce electrical power. See **Nollan v. California Coastal Commission,** 483 U.S. 825 (1987).

Example — "Rough proportionality": Now suppose that the city of Esmeralda offers Cassie a building permit on the condition that she install a windmill to generate electricity and that the electricity generated be sent into the city's power grid. The condition likely satisfies the essential nexus test because the condition is directly related to the reason for the development limit. Suppose that Cassie's proposed addition will add 100 kilowatts monthly to the demand on the city electrical utility and that the windmill will likely generate 110 kilowatts each month. The condition is roughly proportional to the electrical energy impact of Cassie's proposed development. See **Dolan v. City of Tigard,** 512 U.S. 374 (1994).

Some criticize these tests as adding little protection against overreaching regulations and discouraging "mutually beneficial land use deals and generating vast inefficiencies." See Fennell, *Hard Bargains and Real Steals: Land Use Exactions Revisited,* 86 Iowa L. Rev. 1 (2000).

E. **Remedies:** Once a regulation is found to be a taking, the affected property owner has several remedies.

1. **Injunctive and declaratory relief:** Enforcement of a regulation that is a taking will be enjoined, and the regulation will be declared to be a taking. If the government wishes to proceed with the regulation, it must pay just compensation.

2. **Damages:** A regulation may take effect immediately, but it takes some time for it to be determined to be a taking. Because injunctive and declaratory relief provide no redress for an "interim taking," the affected property owner is entitled to damages for the loss of his property during the period a regulatory taking was in effect. *First English Evangelical Lutheran Church of Glendale v. County of Los Angeles*, 482 U.S. 304 (1987). Suits for damages raise a number of procedural and choice-of-law issues.

   a. **Measure of damages:** For interim takings, the fairest measure may be the market rate of return on the difference between the fair market value of the affected property burdened by a regulation that constitutes a taking and its fair market value free of the regulation, over the time the regulatory taking is in effect.

   b. **Duration of an interim taking:** Generally, the taking occurs when the regulation becomes effective. One corollary is that statutes of limitation upon actions to recover for injuries to property also begin to run from that date.

   c. **Choice of forum:** The constitutional claim that a regulation constitutes a taking is not perfected until the affected landowner has exhausted his or her remedies in state court. To the extent that a state court decides issues or claims under federal law, the doctrines of issue and claim preclusion may bar later litigation of these claims in federal court.

   d. **Choice of law:** Although most regulatory takings claims must first be brought in state court, in order to allow the state an opportunity to pay compensation if the regulation is a taking, that rule does not apply if the regulation or taking is *not for a legitimate public purpose*. In such cases (e.g., the taking is not for a public use), the affected landowner may seek damages under 42 U.S.C. §1983, which permits damages actions to be brought for deprivation of constitutional rights under color of state law. Jury trials are permitted in §1983 actions, which may not always be the case with respect to state court inverse condemnation proceedings.

F. **Academic theories about regulatory takings:** There is a vast literature on takings. Summarized here are the main points of some of the more influential commentators.

1. **Joseph Sax:** Sax, a law professor at U.C. Berkeley, argues that when governments act as "sovereigns" — to resolve disputes about land use — there should be no compensation requirement, but when governments act as "entrepreneurs" — performing functions that are functionally indistinguishable from private economic activity — there should be compensation. Sax, *Takings and the Police Power,* 74 Yale L.J. 36 (1964). Sax also asserts that no compensation should be required when a government acts to control external costs of land use, but should pay compensation when its regulations do not address such externalities. Sax, *Takings, Private Property and Public Rights,* 81 Yale L.J. 149 (1971).

2. **Frank Michelman:** Michelman, a law professor at Harvard, offers an abstract utilitarian calculus to determine when compensation should be paid with respect to any given regulation: "[C]ompensation should be paid whenever demoralization costs exceed settlement costs, [and demoralization costs are less than the efficiency gains from the regulation], and not otherwise." To understand this, you must comprehend Michelman's definitions. *Efficiency gains* are the excess of benefits over losses attributable to a measure, measured by the market price people would pay to gain the benefits or avoid the losses. *Demoralization costs* are the sum of (1) the money that would have to be paid to people "to offset disutilities" that result from the realization that no compensation will be paid, and (2) the "present capitalized dollar value of

lost future production caused by demoralization" resulting from failure to compensate. *Settlement costs* are a monetized version of the transaction costs necessary to avoid demoralization: "[T]he dollar value of the time, effort, and resources which would be required in order to reach compensation settlements adequate to avoid demoralization costs." Michelman defends utilitarian refusal to compensate on combined grounds of altruism and distributive fairness — an uncompensated loser "ought to . . . appreciate [that lack of compensation] holds forth a lesser long term risk to people like him than [any alternative]." Exactly *why* this is so is less clear. Michelman, Property, *Utility, and Fairness: Comments on the Ethical Foundations of "Just Compensation" Law,* 80 Harv. L. Rev. 1165 (1967).

3. **Bruce Ackerman:** Ackerman, a Yale law professor, eschews dense abstraction about property in favor of colloquial, lay, understandings of property. At bottom, Ackerman's view is the prosaic observation that, if the government takes physical possession of property away from its owner, compensation is required (see *Loretto* and the per se taking rule that applies to permanent dispossession), but if regulations diminish the value of property, no compensation is required unless the diminution is so severe that it would be a "bad joke" to claim that the property owner is left with something of value. However, humor, like beauty, is subjective. Ackerman's threshold of "bad jokes" might be lower than that of many others; Ackerman does not make clear how the courts are to determine which "bad joke" threshold is constitutionally required. Ackerman, *Private Property and the Constitution* (1977).

4. **Richard Epstein:** Epstein, a University of Chicago law professor, argues that regulations that redistribute wealth are presumptive takings. Some may be saved by the fact that they confer *implicit in-kind compensation,* an updated version of "average reciprocity of advantage." See Justice Brandeis's dissent in **Mahon,** section III.C.1.a, above. Others may be valid because they do no more than control common law nuisances, a view explicitly embraced by the Court in **Lucas.** Epstein's conclusions are sweeping; much of the social welfare state (which is premised on the assumption that the use of political power to redistribute wealth among the people is valid) would be constitutionally suspect under his view of the scope of the Takings Clause. Many people reject Epstein's view because they don't like the conclusions it produces; nevertheless, Epstein poses a basic question: If the Takings Clause was intended to prevent governments from redistributing property for public benefit without compensating the losers of their property, why is it permissible to use the regulatory state pervasively to do just that? Epstein, *Takings* (1985).

5. **Jed Rubenfeld:** Rubenfeld, another Yale law professor, argues that a compensable taking occurs when a regulation enables the government actually to *use* the property in question. Without *public use,* there would be no compensable taking. He grounds this view in a theory that the function of the Takings Clause is to prevent people from being forced to become instrumentalities of the state. The government's purpose in regulating becomes of paramount importance: If the government's purpose would be served equally by regulation or destruction of the property, "no use-value of the thing is being exploited," and no compensation is needed. Only if the government's regulatory purpose cannot be achieved except by enlisting the property in the service of the state would compensation be required. Rubenfeld, *Usings,* 102 Yale L.J. 1077 (1993).

6. **William Fischel:** Fischel, a Dartmouth economist, thinks that the legislative process is adequate to protect against overreaching government regulation, except when that process is distorted. Courts are good at overseeing process, so Fischel argues that courts ought to examine

regulatory takings claims mostly to see whether insiders are using their political muscle to extract gains from outsiders, people who can't protect themselves either by *exit* (leaving the jurisdiction) or *voice* (voting). The risk of this exploitation is highest when the regulated property is land (it can't be taken out of the jurisdiction) and the political unit imposing the land use regulation is small in population and area. These small towns and suburbs are especially apt to impose restrictive zoning and other regulations designed to keep property values high and taxes low, mostly at the expense of builders, owners of fallow land, and would-be residents. Fischel posits that governments with large populations and area are less susceptible to this insider-versus-outsider warfare, and more susceptible to special-interest-group capture. His conclusion is that courts should defer to regulations imposed by large governments but exercise careful scrutiny of land-use regulations by small governments. Is it so clear that large government susceptibility to interest-group capture is not a process failure that should merit close judicial scrutiny of regulations that ensue from such governments? Fischel, *Regulatory Takings: Law, Economics, and Politics* (1995).

Exam Tips on *TAKINGS: THE POWER OF EMINENT DOMAIN AND REGULATORY TAKINGS*

☞ Regulatory takings are easily combined with zoning and nuisance.

☞ The most difficult part of applying the loss-of-all-economically-viable-use test is to decide what constitutes the property to which the regulation applies. Pay particular attention to the fee titles to which the regulation applies and when they were created. It is far less likely that courts will recognize separate property interests when those interests are created by developers for the instrumental purpose of coming within this rule.

☞ Remember that to apply the per se "nontaking" rule of nuisance replication, you must necessarily apply nuisance law.

☞ The balancing test is ad hoc, so use the facts with care and imagination if you are required to apply this test. This is a multifactor test, and you must assess the relative importance of the various factors in light of the particular facts.

Essay Exam Questions

QUESTION 1: Henry, a reclusive art collector, lived in a townhouse adjacent to a studio occupied by Horst Sprockets, a post-modern artist. Sprockets would frequently throw up his window in the dead of night, screaming, "It means nothing!" and then hurl paintings out the window into a public street. Henry would frequently get out of bed, go out into the street. and collect these paintings. Virtually every morning after these midnight outbursts, Sprockets would go outside and collect all the paintings he could find, taking them back into his studio, but he made no other effort to find his paintings. This pattern continued for the ten-year period, 1970 to 1980, in which Sprockets and Henry lived next door to each other. In 1980, Sprockets died, bequeathing "all of my paintings that I own at my death" to the Museum of Interminable Indeterminacy (MII), the pre-eminent art gallery for post-modernist graphic art.

In 2002, Henry hired Sotheby's to auction his "valuable collection of 132 paintings and mixed-media works by the important German post-modernist Horst Sprockets." The MII has sued Henry, contending that it owns Henry's entire Sprockets collection. Please indicate the likely resolution of this dispute and the reasons for your conclusion. In doing so, please ignore any issues of copyright law.

QUESTION 2: Archibald, an elderly lawyer still actively practicing law as a partner of the law firm of Archibald & Zedd, drafted his own will, the pertinent parts of which follow:

> I devise my country estate, Blackacre, to my son Alfred for his life, then to his widow for her life, and then to my issue who survive Alfred, and if none so survive, to the issue of my sister Abigail, who should survive Alfred and his widow. I devise Park Place, the building currently occupied by my law firm, Archibald & Zedd, as its offices, to my law partners for their lives, and after the death of all of them, to such of their children as may reach the age of 21 for the remainder of their lives, and then in fee simple absolute to my grandchildren. The rest and residue of my estate I devise to my youngest brother, Reginald, but if he should ever reside in California, to my sister-in-law Frieda only for so long as the Chicago Cubs fail to win the World Series and, if they ever do so succeed, then in fee simple absolute to my favorite bartender, Henri, who tends bar nightly at the Philosopher's Club.

Archibald died shortly after his will was validly executed. He was survived by his brothers, Ferdinand, age 74, and Reginald, age 64; his sister, Abigail, age 67, and her two children, Tony, age 43, and Mariko, age 40; his sisters-in-law, Frieda, age 72 and married to Ferdinand, and Rebecca, age 65 and married to Reginald; and his children, Alfred, age 47 and married to Iris, age 52, and Gordon, age 45 and unmarried. Archibald was also survived by the partners of Archibald & Zedd: Frederick, age 62 and the father of two children (ages 30 and 28); Thomas, age 51 and the father of one 22-year-old child; Jane, age 49 and the mother of two children (ages 20 and 17); and Terry, age 42 and childless.

Please identify who owns Blackacre, Park Place, and the "rest and residue" of Archibald's estate. If you are able to identify any property that comprises a portion of the rest and residue of Archibald's estate, please do so.

QUESTION 3: In 1972, Aura purchased a 200-acre tract, Nirvana, in a remote rural area in the hopes of living with minimal impact upon the Earth. She immediately moved into a tipi on the western edge of her acreage, built a house by hand of materials indigenous to the site, but soon learned that her wood-burning fireplace was inadequate to keep the house warm. Aura found a geothermal spring on the eastern edge of her property and constructed a buried pipeline to carry scalding hot water to her house, where it circulated in radiators, heating her home to a comfortable temperature. Aura's access to her home was by way of a visible footpath she had worn down, running from her home across the adjacent Turner-Fonda Ranch to a public highway. From there she hitchhiked. Aura used the footpath at least twice each week, ignoring the ranch's "No Trespassing" signs.

In 1990, desiring to create a community of like-minded low-impact travelers upon the Earth, Aura divided Nirvana into three parcels. Lots 1 and 3 divided Nirvana in half on a north-south axis, extending about two-thirds of Nirvana's depth. The only public road runs along the southern edge of Lots 1 and 3. Lot 2, the back third of Nirvana, is bounded by Lots 1 and 3, the Turner-Fonda Ranch, the Ponderosa Ranch, and United States Forest Service land. In 1991, Aura conveyed Lot 3 by a deed that stated: "to Kayak and Rolf, a married couple, and their heirs, as co-tenants with right of survivorship, if Lot 3 is used only in a 'minimal impact' manner, and Aura, Kayak, and Rolf agree, on behalf of themselves, their heirs, successors, and assigns, that "minimal impact" means that motor vehicles will never be permitted on Nirvana, nor will any meat or tobacco ever be consumed on Nirvana."

In 1992, Aura conveyed Lot 2 "to Rainbow and his heirs, subject to existing encumbrances." The following year, Rainbow conveyed Lot 2 to Willow and Aspen, as "tenants by the entirety." Willow and Aspen were two women who, earlier in the year, had publicly proclaimed their lifelong commitment to each other by signing a "commitment contract" that specified that all of their assets thereafter acquired would be "shared equally." Rainbow told Willow and Aspen that he was selling out because he was "tired of living next door to a crazy eco-freak who wanted to run his life and control use of his property."

Problems emerged almost immediately. Willow and Aspen brought in building materials by a four-wheel-drive "sport-utility vehicle" (SUV) over the footpath formerly used solely by Aura and a few ranch hands. Willow constantly smoked large black Cuban cigars and was fond of grilling steaks outside. The mixture of cigar smoke and aroma of burning flesh wafted onto Aura's lot and produced nausea and headaches in Aura.

In 1997, matters came to a head. In January, Kayak and Rolf diverted all the flow from the geothermal spring to their hot tub. In February, Rolf died in the hot tub. In March, Aspen moved out, telling Willow she could no longer stand the constant cigar smoke. Willow replied, "Come back anytime, but I can't give up my stogies." In April, the Turner-Fonda Ranch erected a large fence, blocking the footpath. Willow immediately demanded that Aura permit her to drive her SUV over Lot 1 to reach the road. Aura refused. Willow then purchased Rolf's interest in Lot 3 from Rolf's estate, by quitclaim deed, and created a road over Lot 3, which she used for her SUV.

The jurisdiction in which Nirvana is located has a ten-year statute of limitations for actions to recover possession of real property.

Please analyze the rights and obligations of the parties involved.

QUESTION 4:   On January 1, 1985, Helen leased Blackacre to Albert for a term of years, expiring December 31, 1994, under a written lease signed by both of them. In the lease, Albert agreed to pay rent of $36,000 each year, payable in monthly installments of $3,000, and to pay any amount by which the real property taxes exceed $5,000 in any year. Helen promised to keep Blackacre in good repair. Blackacre consisted of a single warehouse, in which were located some offices. Blackacre is located in an area that is zoned by the city "for commercial or industrial use only."

In 1986, Albert assigned his interest in the Blackacre lease to Althea, who promptly converted the warehouse into two "artist loft spaces," which she advertised as "suitable for an artist's studio and residence." Althea then entered into identical subleases for the lofts with Mike and Vaughan. Each sublease expired December 31, 1994, obligated the tenant to pay rent of $2,000 per month, and incorporated by reference "all terms of the lease between Albert and Helen, dated January 1, 1985, which are not inconsistent with this sublease." Mike and Vaughan moved all of their possessions into their respective units.

In 1987, Helen conveyed and assigned her interest in Blackacre to Melvin. In 1988, both Mike and Vaughan complained to Althea of leaky plumbing, lack of heat, broken windows, and inoperable electrical wiring in the lofts. On September 1, 1988, both Mike and Vaughan vacated their lofts, leaving a note for Althea that they were "terminating the lease because of the atrocious living conditions." Althea advertised for new tenants and engaged the services of a rental broker but had no success. On January 1, 1989, Althea notified Melvin that she was vacating Blackacre and treating the lease as terminated. The 1989 property taxes for Blackacre are $10,000. Melvin has paid $5,000 of those taxes; the remainder is due and unpaid.

Discuss the rights and obligations of the parties.

QUESTION 5: In January 1990, Albert, the true owner and actual possessor of Blackacre, conveyed Blackacre by quitclaim deed to Muriel in receipt of $10,000. In July of 1990, Albert conveyed Blackacre by special warranty deed to Vernon, who paid $10,000 to Albert and knew nothing about the prior deed to Muriel. In August 1990, Muriel took possession of Blackacre, recorded her deed, and conveyed Blackacre by general warranty deed to Jane, who paid Muriel $15,000. In September 1990, Vernon recorded his deed. In October 1990, after learning of Vernon's recording, Jane recorded her deed and took possession of Blackacre, which is located in a jurisdiction that has enacted the following statute: "Every conveyance of real property is void as against any subsequent purchaser of the same property, or any part thereof, in good faith and for a valuable consideration, whose conveyance is first duly recorded."

QUESTION 6: Brownacre is located in a state that has enacted the following statute: "Every conveyance or mortgage of real property is void as against any subsequent purchaser or mortgagee of the same property in good faith and for a valuable consideration, whose conveyance or mortgage is first duly recorded." Harold, the owner of Brownacre, borrows $10,000 from First Bank and gives First Bank a mortgage to Brownacre in order to secure repayment of the loan. First Bank fails to record the mortgage. Harold then borrows $14,000 from Segundo Finance, and after telling Segundo of the prior mortgage in favor of First Bank, gives Segundo a mortgage to Brownacre. Segundo Finance promptly records the mortgage. Harold then borrows $5,000 from Third-Rate Credit and gives Third-Rate a mortgage to Brownacre. Third-Rate has no notice of First Bank's mortgage, and Third-Rate records its mortgage. An adjacent chemical plant begins to leak toxic polychlorinatedbiphenyls (PCBs), and the value of Brownacre plummets. Harold defaults on all the mortgages. After the foreclosure sale, there is $20,000 to distribute among First Bank, Segundo Finance, and Third-Rate Credit. How much should each creditor receive and why?

Essay Exam Answers

SAMPLE ANSWER TO QUESTION 1:

The paintings were created by Sprockets and thus, whether by Locke's labor theory or the principle of first possession or recognized rights of a creator to his creation, they are Sprockets's paintings when created. However, Sprockets may have abandoned them by flinging them out of the window in the dead of night. His midnight actions suggest that he voluntarily relinquished any claim of ownership to the paintings, but his regular actions of the following morning suggest the contrary. Perhaps he abandoned them for the period from midnight until the early morning, when he changed his mind and took possession of them once again as a finder.

If abandonment occurred when Sprockets hurled them out of the window, Henry became their owner by finding them and taking possession. The state, as owner of the public street, has no viable claim as the owner of the *locus in quo* because the paintings are surely neither mislaid nor lost, they are not imbedded in the soil, they do not constitute "treasure trove," and there is no employee or other servant-type relationship between the state and Sprockets.

If abandonment did not occur, Sprockets remains the true owner. However, Henry has possessed the paintings for at least 20 years. A typical New Jersey-style jurisdiction has a six-year statute limitations for recovery of personal property, commencing when Sprockets either knew or should have known by exercising due diligence, who had his paintings. Perhaps Sprockets was so exhausted by his midnight outbursts that he never observed Henry gathering up the paintings in the night, but he certainly knew that his paintings were disappearing from the street. Is it reasonable for a painter who wanted to recover his paintings not to inquire of his neighbors or to make other inquiries as to their whereabouts? Surely not. Henry is the likely owner of those paintings that Henry has possessed for longer than six years. Sotheby's can auction away and deliver clear title to the purchasers.

On the other hand, if the jurisdiction applies traditional adverse possession principles, the limitations period may not have run against the MII, Sprockets's successor (assuming, again, no abandonment). Nor may the elements of adverse possession be present. While Henry had actual possession, it is not likely that his possession was open and notorious. The difficulty of ever proving open and notorious possession of chattels argues against the use of the traditional real property–based adverse possession principles and use of the New Jersey approach of focusing upon the true owner's efforts to learn the facts that would enable the true owner to recover the property.

SAMPLE ANSWER TO QUESTION 2:

There are three components to Archie's will: Blackacre, Park Place, and the residual estate.

Blackacre:

Alfred has a presently possessory life estate.

Alfred's widow has a contingent remainder in a life estate, which is valid under the Rule Against Perpetuities because the identity of Alfred's widow (the only contingency) will be known at Alfred's death, thus making Alfred the validating life for the widow's contingent remainder. Alfred will either have a widow (thus vesting in her at the moment of Alfred's death) or he will have none (thus causing the contingent remainder to fail to vest).

Archie's "issue who survive Alfred" have a contingent remainder in a fee simple absolute. The interest is valid under the rule against perpetuities because the identity of these people will be known at Alfred's death — either at that moment there will be living lineal descendants of Archie (thus vesting in those people) or there will not be any such people (and the interest will fail to vest). Alfred is again the validating life.

The "issue of Abigail who survive Alfred and his widow" appear to have an alternative contingent remainder in fee simple absolute. This interest violates the Rule Against Perpetuities and so is destroyed. The first contingency—that Archie have no issue who survive Alfred—will vest or fail in timely fashion as explained immediately above. It is this contingency that makes this contingent remainder an alternative contingent remainder. The second contingency—the identity of the people who are lineal descendants of Abigail at the time both Alfred and his widow have died—may vest too remotely. Here's how: Gordon could die, never having begotten children. All of Alfred's children could die. Abigail could die, and, after having produced one grandchild of Abigail, Xenia (born after Archie's death), so could both of Abigail's children. Alfred's present wife could die and 20, years later he could marry Lolita, an 18-year-old born after Archie's death. Alfred then dies without having produced any more children. Some time later (say, 60 years) Lolita dies, survived by Xenia, the only descendant of Abigail. Too late: the vesting would occur more than 21 years after the expiration of any relevant life in being.

The destruction of this last contingent remainder means that there will be left a reversion in Archie. This reversion would exist even if the Rule Against Perpetuities had not destroyed the last contingent remainder. To see this, note that in the remote vesting scenario above, there would be no issue of Alfred surviving him. If Lolita should then renounce her life estate, the following contingent remainder (even if valid) would not become possessory, so possession would revert to the grantor. This being the case, the reversion was not created by operation of law after Archie's death but was an interest in Blackacre that was owned by Archie at the time of his will. Because it does not pass via this grant, it must pass via his residuary clause. Reversions, of course, are vested at creation and thus valid under the Rule Against Perpetuities.

Park Place:

The devise to Archie's law partners for their lives creates a possessory life estate in Frederick, Thomas, Jane, and Terry, the people who answer the description of being Archie's law partners at his death.

The devise to "such of the children of my law partners who reach age 21" for their lives creates a vested remainder subject to partial divestment in a life estate in the presently living children of Frederick and Thomas (all of whom have reached age 21) and a contingent remainder in a life estate in Jane's presently living children and any unknown children of Archie's law partners. The interest is valid under the Rule Against Perpetuities because the identity of all of these people will be known not later than 21 years after the death of all of Frederick, Thomas, Jane, and Terry, the closed class of Archie's law partners. Twenty-one years after all of them have died, they will either have children who have reached the age of 21 (thus vesting in that group) or they will not (and the interest will fail to vest). The closed class of Frederick, Thomas, Jane, and Terry constitute collective validating lives.

The devise to Archie's grandchildren creates a contingent remainder in fee simple absolute that is valid under the Rule Against Perpetuities. The identity of Archie's grandchildren will be definitively known at the death of all of Archie's children, and the class of Archie's children is a closed class inasmuch as this interest is created at Archie's death. The closed class of Archie's children constitutes the collective validating lives.

Residual Estate:

Reginald receives a fee simple subject to an executory limitation in Archie's residual estate, which consists of Archie's reversion in Blackacre and perhaps other, unknown property.

Frieda receives an executory interest in a fee simple subject to an executory limitation (at least before the Rule Against Perpetuities is applied). The divesting condition applicable to Reginald's estate (which must occur for Frieda's executory interest to become possessory) is Reginald's move to California. Because this condition will occur, if at all, during Reginald's life, Frieda's executory interest is valid under the Rule Against Perpetuities. Reginald is the validating life.

Henri appears to receive an executory interest in fee simple absolute. However, the interest is void under the Rule Against Perpetuities because the divesting condition—the Chicago Cubs winning the World Series—may never occur or may occur hundreds of years from now.

The destruction of Henri's interest leaves Frieda with an executory interest in a fee simple determinable and creates a possibility of reverter in Archie's intestate heirs, who would appear to be his children, Alfred and Gordon. The possibility of reverter is in Archie's heirs (Alfred and Gordon) because the interest is created by operation of the Rule Against Perpetuities after Archie's death, and thus Archie had not retained this interest at his death, so it could not pass by will. However, this possibility of reverter, while valid under the Rule Against Perpetuities, may be destroyed by statute after a specified period of time (often 20 or 30 years) if the jurisdiction has enacted such legislation. If such a statute exists, Alfred and Gordon must hope that Uncle Reginald will move to California within the statutory period and that the Chicago Cubs will win the World Series during that same period. If so, their possibility of reverter will ripen into a fee simple absolute, which they will own as equal tenants in common.

SAMPLE ANSWER TO QUESTION 3:

The various servitudes and other interests in land created by these events are as follows.

1. Prescriptive easement:

Aura must have acquired fee simple absolute in Nirvana in 1972, because there is no indication to the contrary. She started to use the footpath immediately after moving onto Nirvana, apparently without permission. (She ignored the "No Trespassing" signs.) Her usage has likely ripened into a prescriptive easement. Her use was actual, open and notorious (she wore down a "visible" footpath), continuous ("at least twice a week" with no indication of any interruption). Was it exclusive? If the jurisdiction applies the sensible rule that "exclusivity" means only that the general public is excluded, this element is met, because at least until the arrival of Willow and Aspen in 1993, Aura "and a few ranch hands" were the sole users. But if the Texas rule (see *Othen v. Rosier*) applies, Aura's use may not be exclusive because she was not the *sole* user. In any case, usage by "a few ranch hands" and the implied toleration by those hands of Aura's use does not constitute permission for Aura's use from the owner of the Turner-Fonda Ranch. Under the objective test of "hostility," Aura's use is exactly what a "true owner" of an easement for foot travel would do. If the jurisdiction applies the aggressive trespass standard, her use would also be "hostile," since she ignored the "No Trespassing" signs. Only if the jurisdiction applies the "good faith" standard would Aura lack "hostility." The majority rule is said to be the objective test, though some academics claim that good faith is the *sub rosa* majority rule. The better rule is the objective test, because it avoids subjective state-of-mind inquiry. The prescriptive period is likely to be the same as the limitations period applicable to claims for recovery of possession—10 years—so Aura's use ripened into a prescriptive easement in 1982. The easement is appurtenant, since Aura's use was entirely in connection with her ownership of Nirvana. The servient estate is the Turner-Fonda Ranch, and the dominant estate is Nirvana.

　　a. Scope of the easement: Does the benefit of the prescriptive easement attach to Lots 2 and 3, once Aura has divided Nirvana? Normally, the scope of an easement depends on what the parties intended, but this rule is of no help when the easement is by prescription. The scope of the easement ought to depend on whether the division of Nirvana imposes a substantially increased burden on the ranch. The additional use of four more people as pedestrians is modest, although it does represent a four-fold increase in quantity. However, the use made by Willow and Aspen — vehicle access — is much more burdensome and destructive. This use may be enjoined by the Turner-Fonda Ranch as beyond the scope of the prescriptive easement, but the Turner-Fonda Ranch is not entitled to block the footpath entirely, preventing Aura, Kayak, or even Willow from using the path as a footpath.

2. Title to Lot 3:

There are two issues concerning the initial title to Lot 3.

   a. Joint tenants or tenants in common: The usual presumption is that title is as tenants in common, but the deed explicitly recites a "right of survivorship." Moreover, Kayak and Rolf are a married couple, which may indicate some intention to create joint tenancy. Joint tenancy is most common among married couples, as a cheap and easy method to avoid probate. Without knowing more, this issue can be reasonably resolved either way, though the married status of Kayak and Rolf argues in favor of rebutting the tenancy in common presumption and finding a joint tenancy.

   b. Fee simple determinable or servitude: The deed conveys Lot 3 "if" it is used only in a "minimal impact manner," defined negatively to exclude motor vehicles, meat, or tobacco use. The word "if" might suggest a limitation on the duration of the grant, and hence fee simple determinable, but it also suggests that the grant is conditional upon the grantees' promise to abide by the use restrictions, and hence a use covenant is created. Because forfeitures are generally to be avoided in cases of ambiguity, it is better to conclude that a covenant, rather than a determinable limitation, was created.

3. Easement reserved by implication from prior use:

When Aura started piping scalding hot water from the spring to her house, she created a "quasi-easement." When she sold Lot 3 did she impliedly reserve an easement in her favor for the piped water? It was in use at the time, but was it apparent or reasonably necessary? The pipeline was buried and, unlike the buried sewer in *Van Sandt,* there are no surface indications on Lot 3 of the existence of the pipeline. This is not very apparent. Is the easement necessary? If the jurisdiction adheres to strict necessity in cases of implied easements reserved in favor of the grantor, it may not be strictly necessary. However imperfect her wood-burning fireplace, it provides some heat; Aura can install a more efficient wood stove, or maybe she can use more technologically advanced methods of heating. These arguments are useful, but of lesser force, even if the jurisdiction adheres to reasonable necessity. Aura probably does not have an implied easement for the pipeline. This easement has not ripened into one by prescription because only six years have elapsed from the sale and, in any case, Aura's use is not open and notorious. Cf. *Marengo Cave.*

4. Reciprocal covenant?

The conveyance from Aura to Kayak and Rolf raises the issue of whether a reciprocal covenant was created, either impliedly or by express agreement.

   a. Implied from common scheme: Aura intends to create a "minimal impact" community on Nirvana, and the initial deed reflects a version of that vision. Is a single deed enough to create a common scheme? In a development of three rural lots of roughly 67 acres each, one of which is to be retained by the developer, the single deed represents half the development. This is probably enough, when taken together with Aura's intentions and her joinder with Kayak and Rolf in promising to keep Nirvana "minimal impact." However, the jurisdiction may not recognize the creation of implied reciprocal covenants, in part because this doctrine makes it difficult for a later purchaser to detect its existence.

b. By express agreement: Aura has agreed with Kayak and Rolf to confine Nirvana to "minimal impact" uses. This agreement is made at a time when Aura owns Lot 1 and 2, so it is clear that she intended to burden both Lots 1 and 2 with this use servitude and did so via the agreement.

5. Rainbow's title to Lot 2:

Rainbow acquires fee simple absolute "subject to existing servitudes." This is probably adequate notice — to him of the existence of the "minimal impact" covenant. At the very least, it puts him on inquiry notice — a few questions to Aura and the whole scheme will be revealed, if Aura has not already done so, which is more likely the case. Thus, Rainbow takes with notice. Moreover, some jurisdictions regard all deeds from a common grantor as within the chain of title. Under that rule, Rainbow would have constructive notice of the Aura-to-Kayak-and-Rolf deed; in those rejecting this rule, he would not have constructive notice from the record.

6. Willow's and Aspen's title to Lot 2:

a. Form of co-ownership: Although the deed recites that Willow and Aspen take title as tenants by the entirety, they are not married (even in Vermont, a state that recognizes civil unions between same-sex partners, it is doubtful that a "commitment contract" would suffice to constitute civil union). Their title is presumed to be as tenants in common. The evidence in favor of joint tenancy is meager — practically the only evidence is the fact that tenancy by the entirety contains a right of survivorship — but given the fact that Willow and Aspen are a committed same-sex couple it appears highly likely that Willow and Aspen are attempting to replicate marital property rights to the extent that they are able to do so. Thus, joint tenancy ought to be preferred simply because it is reasonably clear that they intended to create a survivorship right.

b. Does the covenant run with the estate? Assuming that the "minimal impact" covenant was created by express agreement or by implication from a common scheme, will it run at law or in equity?

i. Law: The original parties surely intended for the burden to run — the agreement purported to bind successors, and the common scheme was surely designed for the same purpose. Horizontal privity is not present if the jurisdiction adheres to the restrictive Massachusetts rule of mutual interests, but this is the minority rule, so the jurisdiction probably recognizes horizontal privity when the relationship between the original parties is that of grantor and grantee. Vertical privity is surely satisfied. Rainbow acquired fee simple absolute from Aura and conveyed the same estate to Willow and Aspen. Willow and Aspen probably have notice — Rainbow's deed is explicitly subject to existing servitudes, and Rainbow informs Willow and Aspen that Aura is asserting some control over use of his land, which ought to be enough to trigger a duty to inquire. The most uncertain issue is whether the use covenant "touches and concerns" the land. The ban on motor vehicles probably does — the presence or absence of motor vehicles affects the relations of the Nirvana residents as landowners and has an effect on land values, although that effect is probably subjective. To most people, the vehicle covenant depresses the value of both parcels. Whether or not the vehicle covenant touches and concerns, the meat-and-tobacco covenant is much more problematic. These activities are legal, and they have little impact on land values or on the relations of landowners as landowners. Nor are they the type of promise that landowners might create to control externalities of land use. They probably do not touch and concern the land and thus do not run with the estate acquired by Willow and Aspen.

ii. Equity: Intent is present, and perhaps notice, but the same touch-and-concern problems as discussed above may prevent the covenant from running as an equitable servitude, at least as to the meat-and-tobacco covenants.

   c. **Easement implied by necessity:** When Aura conveyed to Rainbow, did she create an implied grant of an easement for access by necessity? Aura was the owner of Nirvana who created the landlocked situation, but before the division Aura had secured the footpath easement by prescriptive use, and that footpath leads directly onto Lot 2. There is no necessity unless vehicular access is deemed necessary, and the parties have agreed not to permit vehicles (assuming the no-vehicles covenant runs). If the rationale for access easements implied by necessity is that the implication is needed to complete an imperfectly expressed bargain, there should be no implied easement, but if the rationale for such easements is the perceived public benefit in ensuring that all property has culturally ordinary access (i.e., by vehicle), then an implied easement is required. Of course, if the no-vehicles covenant is unenforceable, then an easement for vehicle access is indeed necessary and thus implied. The benefit of that appurtenant easement passed with the estate Rainbow transferred to Willow and Aspen.

   d. **Easement reserved by implication from prior use:** Aura's access to Lot 1 is by the footpath, which cuts across a corner of Lot 2. This easement, upon division, is apparent, in use, and reasonably permanent, but is it necessary? It is surely not strictly necessary, if the jurisdiction adheres to that view, because she could make the longer walk down Lot 1 to the road. It may be reasonably necessary, since it is the more direct route, and the one that she has maintained for 20 years or more. Because the theory behind these implied easements is to create them where there is evidence of the parties' intentions, this is a good case for finding reasonable necessity. The parties apparently intended to perpetuate the footpath, since Aura, Willow, and Aspen each used it after division.

The present rights and obligations of the parties are as follows.

Turner-Fonda Ranch: The Ranch is obligated to remove the obstruction of the footpath and can be compelled to do so by injunction sought by any of Aura, Willow, or Aspen. The Ranch has a claim for damages against Willow and Aspen for their trespass, consisting of driving their vehicle over the footpath, if the statute of limitations applicable to trespass claims permits.

Aura: Aura must permit vehicle access across Lot 1 in favor of Lot 2 if the no-vehicles covenant does not "touch and concern" the land, but if it does, she may deny such access and either enjoin Willow from using her vehicle on Lot 2 or Lot 3 or recover damages. Aura may insist upon continuing footpath access across Lot 2 should Willow or Aspen contest that right. Aura may have a claim for nuisance against Willow stemming from the cigar and meat odors, but she is probably unduly sensitive to them, and so no nuisance likely exists. On the merits of the nuisance claim, the social utility of meat and tobacco usage, while probably not high, is probably not outweighed by the gravity of the harm inflicted. Aura probably has no recourse against Kayak and Rolf's estate for their diversion of the hot water, since it is unlikely that an implied easement from prior use was created.

Aspen: Aspen is jointly liable with Willow for the trespass upon the Ranch. Aspen may have a claim against Willow for half the fair rental value of Lot 2 if (1) she has been ousted by Willow, or (2) the jurisdiction does not require ouster to trigger such liability. Willow has not denied Aspen permission to enter Lot 2; indeed, she invites her to come. The problem, of course, is the cigar smoke. Is cigar usage so obnoxious and offensive as to constitute ouster? Maybe in a small apartment, but probably not in the context of 60 acres. The jurisdiction may adhere to the minority rule that no ouster is needed, since that rule has much to be said for it — it encourages negotiation between parties and avoids litigation over ouster, but does inhibit productive use by one co-owner without consent of the others.

Willow: Willow is jointly liable with Aspen for the trespass upon the Ranch. She is probably not liable for nuisance. Willow's rights and obligations, with respect to her creation of a road across Lot 3, depend upon whether she owns any interest in Lot 3. If Kayak and Rolf owned as joint tenants (which is the preferred outcome), then Willow has purchased nothing from Rolf's estate, and Willow is a trespasser liable to Kayak for damages. If Kayak and Rolf were tenants in common, then Willow owns a half interest in Lot 3 as a tenant in common with Kayak, but Willow is still liable to Kayak for breaching the no-vehicles covenant (and also to Aura) and (possibly, depending on unknown facts) for waste if the location of the road permanently impaired the land value.

Kayak: If Kayak is a tenant in common with Willow, she is liable to Aura in law and equity for breach of the no-vehicles covenant, though she will be able to recover from Willow. If Kayak is the sole owner of Lot 3, she may pursue a trespass claim against Willow. Kayak probably has no liability concerning the hot water pipe.

Rolf: Rolf doesn't care any more, but his estate has no liability to Willow for breach of one or more deed covenants of title, since the deed to Rolf's interest in Lot 3 (if any) was a quitclaim deed, which contains no covenants of title.

SAMPLE ANSWER TO QUESTION 4:

There are three major issues presented: (1) Is Althea liable to Melvin for unpaid rent or taxes? (2) Are Mike and Vaughan liable to Melvin for unpaid rent or taxes? (3) Are Mike and Vaughan liable to Althea for unpaid rent or taxes?

1. Althea's liability to Melvin:

Althea's liability depends on whether she is in either privity of contract or privity of estate with Melvin.

Privity of contract: Privity between Althea and Melvin hinges on whether Albert assigned his interest to Althea and she assumed the lease. (An assignment from Helen to Melvin, also needed, is stipulated in the facts.) Althea did not expressly assume the lease, and although an assumption might be inferred from Althea's conduct, the prevailing view is that an assumption will not be found unless it is made expressly.

Privity of estate: Privity of estate between Althea and Melvin hinges on whether Althea has subleased or assigned her interest to Mike and Vaughan. (Helen has assigned her interest to Melvin, which transfers to Melvin the estate formerly held by Helen.) If Althea has subleased to Mike and Vaughan, her privity of estate with Melvin (standing in Helen's shoes) continues, and Althea is liable for rent. If Althea has assigned her lease to Mike and Vaughan, then privity of estate is destroyed, and Althea has no liability on this theory for any unpaid rent after the date of the assignments.

The argument for assignment is that although the transactions with Mike and Vaughan are denominated subleases, they expire at the moment of expiration of the master lease. Because Althea lacks any reversionary interest, the transactions are functionally assignments.

The argument for a sublease is that even though Althea failed to retain any reversion in the subleases, the difference in rent and use of the term "sublease" is an indication that Althea intended to keep a reversionary interest necessary to earn the sublease profits. It is in Althea's economic interest to owe Melvin $3,000 per month in rent and collect $4,000 per month in rent from Mike and Vaughan. Nonetheless, many courts (perhaps most) will treat Althea's failure to retain a reversion, coupled with the entry into possession of Mike and Vaughan, as an assignment that places Mike and Vaughan in privity of estate with Melvin and extinguishing the intervening purported leasehold through merger.

Assuming that Althea has subleased, and thus is in privity of estate with Melvin, she has either abandoned the lease or has been constructively evicted. Althea has been constructively evicted if Melvin's failure to discharge his duty of repair so deprived Althea of the enjoyment of the property that the leased premises were rendered unsuitable for the purposes for which they were intended. But the intended purposes of the premises were not residential (indeed, that use is illegal). Nevertheless, the problems (no electricity, no heat, broken windows, inoperable plumbing) would appear to make the premises unsuitable for most commercial purposes. If so, the lease is terminated, and Althea has no further liability. If there is no constructive eviction, Althea has abandoned, and Melvin may either accept her offer of surrender of the lease (thus terminating the lease) or may leave the premises vacant and continue to hold Althea liable for the rent. Because the lease to Althea is commercial, Melvin probably does not have to seek out new tenants on behalf of Althea.

Althea's defenses: If Althea is in privity of estate with Melvin, and she has not been constructively evicted, she may assert as a defense to her liability for rent or taxes that Melvin has breached the covenant of repair. The covenant runs with the estate, and Melvin acquired Helen's entire estate. There are several subsidiary issues. Are the covenants to repair and to pay rent mutually dependent? Courts are more apt to view residential leases through the contract lens and thus regard lease covenants as mutually dependent, but this lease is commercial. Courts are less willing to do so with respect to commercial leases, and unless the lease specifically makes the covenants dependent, Althea may not be able to suspend rent payments to Melvin. However, Althea will be entitled to recover damages from Melvin's breach of the duty to repair. These damages are limited to the cost of repair, rather than the lost profits to Althea that might be a consequence of Melvin's failure to repair.

Althea has no ability to assert breach of the implied warranty of habitability, since she is a commercial user. If anyone can assert this claim, it's Mike and Vaughan.

Althea's liability on the tax covenant: As with the rent covenant, Althea's liability for taxes depends on whether there is privity of either contract or estate with Melvin. Assuming privity of estate, the only additional issue is whether the covenant to pay taxes runs with the estate. Does its substance touch and concern the estate burdened? Property taxes are a burden of landownership; while the covenant is an affirmative obligation to pay money, the payment is inextricably linked to the land itself. Even though the promise is for the benefit of the landowner, it is one that shares the burdens of land occupation and so touches and concerns the burdened leasehold. Althea has the same defenses to this covenant as to the covenant to pay rent.

2. Mike's and Vaughan's liability to Melvin:

Mike and Vaughan are liable to Melvin only if either privity of contract or privity of estate is present between them. Mike and Vaughan are in privity of contract with Melvin only if the "sublease" with Althea was really an assignment (which it probably is, given Althea's failure to reserve a reversion) and they assumed the master lease. Their "subleases" did obligate them to perform all of the covenants of the master lease, and that may be enough to constitute assumption, on the theory that Melvin was the intended third-party beneficiary of that promise.

It won't matter too much whether privity of contract is present, because privity of estate almost surely is present. The purported subleases are very likely to be seen as assignments, thus creating privity of estate between Mike and Vaughan and Melvin. If the agreements are truly subleases, there is no privity of estate with Melvin, because there was no promise to pay the rents directly to Melvin.

Assuming that Mike and Vaughan are in privity of estate with Melvin, the issue arises whether they have abandoned or been constructively evicted. Melvin's failure to repair is the cause of their problems, and the substance of the problems are sufficiently severe that it seems likely that Mike and Vaughan have lost all beneficial use of the property for the purposes they intended to devote the leasehold toward. Of course, those purposes are partly residential and thus illegal, but even the commercial use as an artist studio would seem to be virtually impossible to achieve. They have probably been constructively evicted, which would have terminated the lease. If not, they have abandoned, and Melvin has the same options as described with Althea.

Mike and Vaughan have the same defenses that Althea has to liability for either the rent or tax covenants. But, in addition, it may be that once the residential use was established, Melvin acquiesced to the residential use and is in breach of the warranty of habitability. If so, by leaving, Mike and Vaughan have elected to terminate the lease and may also be able to recover their relocation costs.

3. Mike's and Vaughan's liability to Althea:

Liability on the part of Mike and Vaughan to Althea depends on whether the "subleases" are really subleases or whether they are assignments. If the subleases are assignments, the purported subleases have been extinguished by merger. Mike and Vaughan then have no liability to Althea for anything, but they are liable to Melvin in accordance with the master lease. If the "subleases" really are subleases, then Mike and Vaughan are in privity of contract and privity of estate with Althea, but only as to the terms of the subleases. As discussed above, the purported subleases are most likely assignments, so Mike and Vaughan probably are not liable to Althea.

Assuming that Mike and Vaughan are in privity of contract and estate with Althea on the subleases, Mike and Vaughan have either been constructively evicted or abandoned. Constructive eviction is pretty clear here, since Althea rented the spaces for residential habitation, the landlord's duty to repair was incorporated by reference in the subleases, and Althea's failure to keep the premises in good repair deprived Mike and Vaughan of virtually all utility to the premises. Moreover, the warranty of habitability is surely implied into these subleases, since the purpose of Mike's and Vaughan's occupation was partly residential. Even though the residential occupation is illegal, the policy underlying the implied warranty of habitability is to provide minimum residential living standards, and this policy seems applicable to any living arrangements. Mike and Vaughan have terminated the lease but still may recover their relocation costs from Althea.

In the unlikely event that Mike and Vaughan have not been constructively evicted and have abandoned, it appears that Althea has discharged her duty to mitigate damages by seeking to relet the premises.

SAMPLE ANSWER TO QUESTION 5:

Jane prevails over Vernon, because Jane purchased from Muriel, who recorded before Vernon, and Jane obtains the shelter of Muriel's recording before Vernon. At the time Jane purchased from Muriel, Muriel had recorded her deed from Albert, which was prior to the time that Vernon, a subsequent purchaser without notice, recorded. Thus, even though Vernon records before Jane, it does not matter; Jane stands in the position of Muriel, whose claim is superior to that of Vernon. Because Jane is asserting Muriel's title, Jane's notice is irrelevant. This is an application of the "shelter rule," which is rooted in the idea that for Muriel to have the full benefit of her prior recording, she must be able to convey that benefit for value. For that to occur, her purchaser (Jane) must receive what Muriel had.

Vernon may recover $10,000 from Albert for breach of the deed covenants. By special warranty deed, Albert has promised Vernon that he, Albert, has taken no action contrary to the six deed covenants contained in the deed. But Albert has breached three covenants: (1) seisin, because at the time Albert conveyed to Vernon he no longer owned Blackacre; (2) right to convey, because having parted with title to Blackacre Albert no longer had a right to convey it; and (3) general warranty, because Jane (through Muriel) has a paramount title. Quiet enjoyment isn't breached, because Vernon never had possession; future assurances isn't breached because there is nothing further Albert could have done to perfect title in Vernon; encumbrances isn't breached because the property is not encumbered — it's a relative title problem.

SAMPLE ANSWER TO QUESTION 6:

This is a "circular priority" problem. First Bank is prior to Segundo, since Segundo has notice of First Bank's mortgage, but it is junior to Third-Rate, since Third-Rate recorded first and had no notice of First Bank's lien. Segundo is ahead of Third-Rate, since Third-Rate had constructive notice, but it is behind First Bank. And Third-Rate is ahead of First Bank but behind Segundo. Just about the only rationale that serves to cut this Gordian knot is to deliver to each party his reasonable expectations. Segundo expects to be in second position (behind First Bank's $10,000 lien), so give Segundo the $10,000 that would be left if First Bank were prior to Segundo. Third-Rate expects to be junior only to Segundo's $14,000, so give Third- Rate its full $5,000. (There is $6,000 left after deducting $14,000 from the $20,000 available.) What's left goes to First Bank, since First Bank cannot expect to have priority over anyone, given its failure to record. So, First Bank should get $5,000; Segundo $10,000; Third-Rate $5,000.

Multiple-Choice Questions

1. George leased Blackacre for 5 years from Elvis. During that term, the state took title to Blackacre by eminent domain. Which of the following statements is correct concerning George's rights as a lessee of Blackacre?

   I. George may continue to occupy Blackacre for the balance of his term unless the state specifically condemned his leasehold.

   II. George has no further obligation to pay rent for the balance of the lease term.

   III. George is entitled to a share of the condemnation award based on the value of the unexpired term of the leasehold less rent that would have become due during that term.

   (A) I only.

   (B) II only.

   (C) III only.

   (D) II and III only.

2. In 1980, without Bertram's permission, Adele moved onto Bertram's realty and constructed a dwelling in which she has lived since then openly, notoriously, and continuously. In 1987, Bertram died intestate. Bertram's sole heir was his 6-year-old son, Garth, whose legal guardian was his aunt, Florence, Bertram's sister. In 1990, Florence became aware of Adele's occupation of Garth's realty. In 1998, Florence, on behalf of Garth, sued Adele to eject her and recover possession of Garth's realty. Adele's defense was that she had acquired title by adverse possession. The jurisdiction adheres to the "objective" view of hostility and requires that all suits to recover possession of realty be filed within 15 years after the cause of action accrues, except that if, at the time the cause of action accrues, the holder of the cause of action is disabled by reason of being a minor, a prisoner, or insane, the action may be filed within 10 years after the disability is removed. Has Adele become the owner of the realty by reason of adverse possession?

   (A) No, because the limitations period did not begin to run until 1999, when Garth reached age 18, the age of majority, and the limitations period will not expire until 2009.

   (B) No, because while the limitations period began to run in 1987, when Garth inherited the realty, the limitations period will not expire until 2002, 15 years later, and Florence filed suit on Garth's behalf in 1998.

   (C) No, because the limitations period began to run in 1990, when Florence first became aware of Adele's occupation of the realty, and the period will not expire until 2005.

   (D) Yes, because the limitations period began to run in 1980, when Adele first occupied the realty, and the period expired in 1995.

   (E) No, because while the limitations period expired in 1995 Adele did not occupy with the requisite elements of adverse possession.

3. Alan owned two adjacent parcels of realty, Blackacre and Whiteacre. The northern boundary of Blackacre is the southern boundary of Whiteacre. A dirt road crossed both parcels, providing access to a river that flowed along the southern boundary of Blackacre. Alan sold Whiteacre to Henri under a grant deed that conveyed an easement for access to the river along the dirt road.

Later, Alan divided Blackacre in half. He retained the southern portion and conveyed the northern portion to Chet. The deed to Chet did not mention any easement for river access across Alan's retained parcel. However, at the closing Alan told Chet he was welcome to use the dirt road to reach the river. During the next 12 years Henri and Chet used the road frequently to gain access to the river. Chet fished in the river and caught enough fish that he purchased a used home freezer for $25 at a yard sale, which he used to store his catch. Because the dirt road had eroded badly and was increasingly difficult to use, Henri graded and graveled the road. When Henri asked Chet to contribute to the cost of grading and graveling the dirt road, Chet refused on the ground that he did not hold the benefit of an easement across Alan's property. In the jurisdiction adverse use of another's realty for 10 years is sufficient to acquire an easement by prescription. The jurisdiction also provides, by statute, that all holders of the benefit of an easement must share equally the expenses of maintaining the easement. If Henri asserts a claim against Chet under the above statute, Henri's most effective argument would be that Chet held an easement by

   (A) dedication.

   (B) implication.

   (C) express reservation.

   (D) grant.

   (E) estoppel.

4. George owned two contiguous parcels, Grassacre and Timberacre. A water well was located on Grassacre. George sold Timberacre to Bill under a grant deed that conveyed an easement for access to the well on Grassacre. Later, George divided Grassacre, conveying to Eunice a portion of Grassacre that did not include the well. The deed to Eunice did not mention any easement for access to the well on George's retained portion of Grassacre, but George did tell Eunice that she was

welcome to use the well to obtain water for herself and her livestock. During the next 11 years Bill and Eunice each regularly drew water from the well. Because the well pump and casing failed while George was vacationing in South Africa, Bill replaced the pump and well casing at a considerable cost to himself. In doing so, Bill installed a much better and more powerful pump and a higher quality and longer lasting well casing. When George returned he was in a surly mood because of the cost of these improvements to the well and told Eunice she could no longer use the well. If Eunice's only claim is that she has acquired an easement by prescription across George's property, which of the following would be George's best argument in response to that claim?

   (A) Eunice has been using the road with George's permission.

   (B) The material alteration of the condition of the well terminated any prescriptive use right that Eunice had obtained.

   (C) The deed from George to Eunice made no mention of any easement for access to the well on George's property.

   (D) Because Bill improved the road at his expense, Eunice will be required to establish by prescription a right to use Bill's improvements and she has not yet done so.

Questions 5 and 6 are based on the following facts.

Hector, owner of a large farm, Blackacre, in fee simple absolute, conveyed Blackacre by deed "to Virgil for life, then to Dante and his heirs so long as Blackacre remains a farm, and if it ceases to be a farm, to Homer and his heirs." Virgil took possession of Blackacre and then conveyed "all my right, title, and interest in Blackacre to Beatrice for her life." Beatrice took possession of Blackacre and turned it into a gaudy amusement park. Upon learning of this, Virgil died of shock.

5. Assume for this question only that the jurisdiction applies all the common law rules applicable to possessory estates and future interests. Who is entitled to possession of Blackacre?

   (A) Beatrice, because her life estate has not yet expired.

   (B) Dante, because the divesting condition did not occur by reason of Dante's actions.

   (C) Hector, because his possibility of reverter created by operation of law automatically became a reversion, which is now possessory.

   (D) Virgil's heirs, for the remainder of Beatrice's life, because Beatrice's actions divested her of possession.

   (E) Homer, because Virgil's life estate has expired, terminating Beatrice's life estate, and Dante's remainder has been completely divested in favor of Homer.

6. Assume for this question only that the jurisdiction applies all of the modern reform doctrines applicable to possessory estates and future interests. Who is entitled to possession of Blackacre?

   (A) Beatrice, because her life estate has not yet expired.

   (B) Dante, because the divesting condition did not occur by reason of Dante's actions.

   (C) Hector, because his possibility of reverter created by operation of law automatically became a reversion, which is now possessory.

   (D) Virgil's heirs, for the remainder of Beatrice's life, because Beatrice's actions divested her of possession.

   (E) Homer, because Virgil's life estate has expired, terminating Beatrice's life

estate, and Dante's remainder has been completely divested in favor of Homer.

Questions 7 and 8 are based on the following facts.

In a jurisdiction adhering to the common law concerning possessory estates and future interests, Giles executed a deed to Greenacre, a parcel of real estate he owned in fee simple absolute, "to Franklin University, for so long as the property shall be used as a dormitory for undergraduate students at Franklin University, but if Franklin University shall ever admit students solely on the basis of race, to Jefferson University for so long as the property shall be used as a dormitory for undergraduate students at Jefferson University." Franklin University and Jefferson University were both charitable institutions devoted to post-secondary education. They were physically contiguous and Greenacre lay on the boundary line between the two universities.

7. Immediately after the deed was executed and delivered, Giles's interest in Greenacre is best described as

   (A) a valid reversion.

   (B) a valid possibility of reverter.

   (C) a valid right of re-entry (or power of termination).

   (D) void under the common law rule against perpetuities.

8. Immediately after the deed was executed and delivered, Jefferson University's interest in Greenacre is best described as a

   (A) valid contingent remainder.

   (B) valid executory interest.

   (C) void contingent remainder.

   (D) void executory interest.

9. Samuel, owner of Blackacre in fee simple absolute, devised Blackacre "to my daughter, Liz, for life, then to my

granddaughter, Lily, and her heirs."
Blackacre consisted of a house and barn, a
cleared, level, fenced pasture of 40 acres
and 80 acres of dense woods surrounding
the pasture. Liz moved into the house.
Samuel had taken great pride in his race
horses, which he had bred and pastured at
Blackacre, but under Samuel's will the
race horses had all been sold. Liz had no
interest in animal husbandry. Instead, Liz
decided to plant the pasture with young fir
trees, which she intended to harvest and
sell as Christmas trees. Lily, a devoted
horsewoman who hoped to revive Blackacre as a horse breeding farm, objected
and sought an injunction to prevent Liz
from implementing her Christmas tree
plan. In response to Lily's request for an
injunction, a court will probably find for

(A) Liz, because as a life tenant she has
the right to use Blackacre in any way
she desires so long as she does not
destroy the house or barn.

(B) Lily, because Liz's proposed use is
affirmative waste per se.

(C) Lily, because Liz's proposed use is
inconsistent with Samuel's intent that
Blackacre be preserved as a horse farm.

(D) Liz, if the planting of Christmas trees
is a reasonable use of the pasture.

10. Arnold, Beatrice, and Clayton acquired
title to Hundred Acres as joint tenants.
Arnold occupied Hundred Acres and began
to plant and harvest row crops, which produced a substantial profit to Arnold. Beatrice and Clayton lived in a distant location
and never visited Hundred Acres although
they were aware of Arnold's occupation.
Arnold became ill and died, leaving a will
that devised his entire estate to Clayton.
Which of the following most accurately
states the proportional interests that Beatrice and Clayton would hold as a result of
these events?

(A) Clayton and Beatrice would be tenants
in common with equal interests in
Hundred Acres.

(B) Clayton and Beatrice would be joint
tenants with equal interests in Hundred Acres.

(C) Clayton and Beatrice would be tenants
in common, with Clayton holding a
two-thirds interest and Beatrice holding a one-third interest in Hundred
Acres.

(D) Clayton and Beatrice would be joint
tenants, with Clayton holding a
two-thirds interest and Beatrice holding a one-third interest in Hundred
Acres.

11. Amy, Bob, and Charles acquired title to
Centurion Farm as joint tenants. Amy
occupied Centurion Farm and used the
entire farm to breed and raise cattle and
hogs, which activity was highly profitable
to Amy. Bob and Charles never set foot on
Centurion Farm although they were aware
of Amy's occupation of the farm. Bob sold
his interest in Centurion Farm to Zeke by a
valid grant deed. Which of the following
statements accurately describes the relationships between the parties that result
from these events?

(A) Amy, Charles, and Zeke hold equal
shares in Centurion Farm as joint tenants.

(B) Amy, Charles, and Zeke hold equal
shares in Centurion Farm as tenants in
common.

(C) Amy, Charles, and Zeke hold equal
shares in Centurion Farm as tenants in
common, but Amy and Charles have
survivorship rights as to each other's
interest in Centurion Farm.

(D) Amy and Charles hold equal shares of
a two-thirds interest in Centurion
Farm as joint tenants, and Zeke holds

a one-third interest in Centurion Farm as a tenant in common.

12. Allen, Barbara, and Cedric acquired title to City Square as joint tenants. Allen occupied City Square and rented it out to third party tenants, collecting and keeping the rents. Barbara and Cedric each lived in Tokyo and never viewed City Square, although they were aware of Allen's occupation. Allen borrowed $50,000 from Creditcorp, secured by a mortgage of City Square granted to Creditcorp by Allen. Unfortunately, Allen suddenly died, leaving a will by which he devised his entire estate to Zara. Which of the following statements most accurately describes the relationships between the parties that result from these events?

(A) Creditcorp's mortgage is extinguished and Barbara and Cedric own equal interests in City Square as joint tenants.

(B) Creditcorp's mortgage is valid and may be enforced by Creditcorp against the entirety of City Square, including the two-thirds interest in City Square owned in equal portions by Cedric and Barbara as joint tenants and the one-third interest owned by Zara as a tenant in common.

(C) Creditcorp's mortgage is valid and may be enforced by Creditcorp against the one-third interest in City Square owned by Zara, but not against the two-thirds interest in City Square owned in equal portions by Cedric and Barbara as joint tenants.

(D) Creditcorp's mortgage is extinguished, Zara owns a one-third interest in City Square as a tenant in common, and Cedric and Barbara own equal portions of a two-thirds interest in City Square as joint tenants.

13. Alex, Betty, and Clive acquired title to Skyview as joint tenants. Alex occupied Skyview and turned it into a Christmas tree farm, selling the trees for a considerable profit to him. Although Betty and Clive were aware of Alex's actions they said nothing to Alex and never visited Skyview. Three years later, Clive conveyed his interest in Skyview by quitclaim deed to Zelda. If Zelda asserts a claim against Alex for a share of the profits that result from Alex's Christmas tree farming operations, which of the following would be Alex's most effective argument in defense against Zelda's claim?

(A) A quitclaim deed is not sufficient to convey a joint tenant's interest in real property.

(B) A quitclaim deed conveys only the interest held by the grantor without deed warranties of any kind.

(C) A quitclaim deed is not sufficient to convey the grantor's right of survivorship in a joint tenancy.

(D) Zelda has no right to share in the farm profits because she is not a joint tenant with Alex.

14. Albert, Brenda, and Calvin acquired title to Lonely Dell as joint tenants. Albert occupied Lonely Dell and built greenhouses in which he grew roses for sale to wholesale floral markets, earning a tidy profit in the process. Neither Brenda nor Calvin took any interest in Lonely Dell. Three years later Brenda conveyed her interest in Lonely Dell by grant deed to Nick. A month later Nick visited Lonely Dell and told Albert he wanted to take possession of one-third of Lonely Dell. Albert shouted at him: "Get lost; I've got the whole place under cultivation. There's no room for you and I won't permit you on this place." Fearing for his safety, Nick left and has not returned. Which of the following would be Nick's best argument in support of a claim against Albert for the fair rental value of Lonely Dell?

(A) Because Nick is a tenant in common he is absolutely entitled to partition of Lonely Dell.

(B) Albert is making a sufficient profit from his farming operations to afford a fair rental payment to his co-owner Nick.

(C) Albert has ousted Nick from Lonely Dell and is thus liable to Nick for the fair rental value of Nick's interest in Lonely Dell.

(D) The fair rental value of Lonely Dell is the appropriate measure of the damages suffered by Nick from Albert's threatening speech and truculent attitude.

15. Several years ago, Toby, owner of Oak Hill in fee simple absolute, conveyed his interest in Oak Hill to Greg, a realtor, by warranty deed. Greg immediately resold Oak Hill to Fred, his partner and fellow realtor, without recording the deed Greg had received from Toby. Fred recorded the deed he received from Greg and, a year later, sold Oak Hill to Betty, who recorded her deed. A year after that, Toby delivered a deed to Oak Hill to Ruth in exchange for fair value. Ruth recorded her deed immediately. The jurisdiction has a statute that provides that no conveyance of real property is effective against a subsequent purchaser for value without notice unless it shall have been recorded. The official records of deeds are maintained only by means of a grantor-grantee index. If Ruth asserts that her title is superior to Betty's, and sues Betty to quiet title in Oak Hill, which of the following would be Ruth's most effective argument?

(A) The deed from Greg to Fred was outside the chain of title.

(B) Greg lacked power to convey any interest in Oak Hill.

(C) Toby committed intentional misrepresentation in the sale of Oak Hill to Ruth and that stripped Toby of any power to deliver good title to Oak Hill.

(D) As Greg's partner, Fred had constructive notice that Greg had not recorded his deed from Toby.

16. In January Owen executed a will by which he devised Mill Pond "to my sister Ophelia for life, then in equal shares to Ophelia's children." At that time, Ophelia had two children, Louise and Ethel. Six months later Louise and Ethel were killed in a terrorist bombing. Owen died soon after. Ten years later Ophelia executed and delivered to Oliver a deed conveying "all my right, title, and interest" in Mill Pond. A year later, Ophelia died without a will, leaving as her sole survivor her 6-year-old son, Edgar. Which of the following correctly describes Edgar's interest in Mill Pond immediately *before* Ophelia's death?

(A) Vested remainder subject to complete divestment.

(B) Contingent remainder.

(C) Vested remainder subject to partial divestment.

(D) Vested remainder subject to complete divestment and partial divestment.

(E) Executory interest.

(F) No valid interest.

17. On February 1, 2009, Anne borrowed $50,000 from Clarke, signing a note secured by a mortgage on Hillcrest, her vineyard. On June 1, 2009, Anne entered into a valid written contract by which she agreed to sell Hillcrest to Lester. The contract contained a provision by which Anne

promised to deliver to Lester title to Hill-crest free from encumbrances on or before August 7, 2009. On August 6, 2009, Anne executed and delivered to Lester a general warranty deed. On August 10, 2009, Clarke recorded his mortgage to Hillcrest. On August 15, 2009, Lester recorded his deed. A statute in the jurisdiction provides: "In the event of conflicting claims to the same real property, the interest which shall first have been recorded shall have prior-ity." On August 20, 2009, Anne used the proceeds of the sale to Lester to pay her debt to Clarke in full, receiving in exchange a satisfaction and release of mortgage, which Anne immediately recorded. If Lester sues Anne for breach of the covenant against encumbrances, to which of the following is Lester entitled?

(A) Rescission of the deed, because the covenant against encumbrances was breached at the time the deed was delivered.

(B) Damages for breach of contract, because the covenant against encum-brances was breached at the time the contract was made.

(C) Nominal damages only, because Lester sustained no actual damages as a result of the existence of Clarke's mortgage and Anne's breach of the covenant against encumbrances.

(D) Nothing, because there was no breach of the covenant against encumbrances.

18. On February 10, 2008, Alix borrowed $150,000 from Damon, signing a note secured by a mortgage on Seven Maples. On June 15, 2008, Alix entered into a valid written contract by which she agreed to sell Seven Maples to Leroy. The contract contained a provision by which Alix prom-ised to deliver to Leroy title to Seven Maples free from encumbrances on or before August 30, 2008. On August 15, 2008, Alix executed and delivered to Leroy a general warranty deed to Seven Maples. On September 10, 2008, Damon recorded his mortgage to Seven Maples. On September 15, 2008, Leroy recorded his deed to Seven Maples. A statute in the jurisdiction provides: "In the event of con-flicting claims to the same real property, the interest which shall first have been recorded shall have priority." Although Alix received the full value of Seven Maples from Leroy, she did not pay Damon her debt. On January 3, 2010, Leroy conveyed his entire interest in Seven Maples to Quentin under a general war-ranty deed. Damon instituted foreclosure proceedings in February 2010. In April 2010 Quentin paid Alix's debt to Damon in full and obtained a satisfaction and release of the mortgage. The jurisdiction has a statute requiring that actions founded on breach of any covenant contained in a deed be brought within one year from the date of delivery of the deed. If Quentin sues Alix on May 1, 2010, for breach of the covenant against encumbrances, which of the following would be Alix's *least* effective argument in defense?

(A) Quentin has an adequate remedy against Leroy.

(B) An action for breach of the covenant against encumbrances can only be brought by the immediate grantee of the deed in which the covenant is con-tained.

(C) Quentin had constructive notice of the mortgage.

(D) Quentin's claim against Alix is barred by the statute of limitations.

19. The Brick Building, a historic office build-ing designed by a famous nineteenth-century architect, was listed as an Historical Landmark by the Historical Preservation Society, a nonprofit charitable corporation. Cindy, owner of the Brick Building in fee simple absolute, entered

into a lease of Brick Building to Guido for a 10-year term, ending January 1, 2010. The lease stipulated that the annual rental was $120,000, payable at the rate of $10,000 per month. Under the lease Guido promised to keep the premises in good repair, to make no alterations inconsistent with the Brick Building's historic character, and to make an annual contribution of $5,000 to the Historical Preservation Society. Guido also promised in the lease that he would not assign or sublet his interest in the Brick Building without Cindy's prior consent. Guido took possession of the Brick Building and, after having obtained Cindy's consent, subleased one-fourth of the Brick Building to Eve for a 5-year term for an annual rent of $30,000, payable at the rate of $2,500 per month. Then Guido asked Cindy for consent to lease the remainder of the building to Henry for a term ending January 1, 2010, for an annual rent of $120,000, payable at the rate of $10,000 per month. Although Henry was extremely wealthy and possessed an impeccable reputation, Cindy refused to consent, citing the fact that Henry had unsuccessfully led a campaign to urge the city to condemn the Brick Building and turn it into a civic museum. Guido entered into the lease with Henry anyway and Henry and Eve took possession of the Brick Building. Cindy then sued Guido, seeking damages and recovery of possession of the Brick Building, on the ground that Guido had breached the lease and was no longer entitled to possession, even though all parties are current on the rent payments. The jurisdiction's Supreme Court is in the vanguard of discarding older conceptions of landlord-tenant law and adopting new and modern policies and rules on these issues. Which of the following is Guido's **best** argument in defense?

(A) Cindy's consent to the sublease to Eve should be treated as a continuing con-

sent to all further assignments or subleases made by Guido.

(B) Because Guido is no longer in possession of any portion of the Brick Building he is no longer in privity of estate with Cindy and thus Cindy's claim is made against the wrong party.

(C) Guido has not breached the lease by leasing to Henry without Cindy's consent because Cindy's refusal to consent to the lease to Henry was unreasonable.

(D) Guido has not breached the lease because he is current with the rent payments.

20. The Granite Building is another historic office building designed by a famous nineteenth-century architect and listed as a Historical Landmark by the Historical Preservation Society, a nonprofit charitable corporation. Carolyn, owner of the Granite Building in fee simple absolute, entered into a lease of the Granite Building to Gordon for a 10-year term, ending January 1, 2015. The lease stipulated that the annual rental was $120,000, payable at the rate of $10,000 per month. Under the lease Gordon promised to keep the premises in good repair, to make no alterations inconsistent with the Granite Building's historic character, and to make an annual contribution of $5,000 to the Historical Preservation Society. Gordon also promised in the lease that he would not assign or sublet his interest in the Granite Building without Carolyn's prior consent. After having obtained Carolyn's consent, Gordon leased the entire Granite Building to Hubert for a term ending January 1, 2015, under an instrument by which Hubert promised Gordon that he would perform all of Gordon's obligations under the lease between Gordon and Carolyn. A year later and after having obtained Carolyn's consent, Hubert assigned all of his interest in the Granite Building to

Alice, who took possession for 6 months, at which point (with Carolyn's consent) she assigned her entire interest in the Granite Building to Peter. During their time of possession, each of Gordon, Hubert, and Alice fully performed all of the lease covenants. Peter, however, has failed to pay the rent for 2 months, has altered the Granite Building to compromise its historic integrity, and has absolutely refused to pay any money to the Historical Preservation Society. The jurisdiction permits intended third party beneficiaries of contracts to enforce them. Which of the following statements most accurately summarizes the rights and obligations of the parties?

(A) Carolyn may recover damages consisting of unpaid rent and the cost of restoring the Granite Building to its historic character from Gordon, Hubert, Alice, and Peter, or any of them, and the Historical Preservation Society may recover the unpaid annual contribution of $5,000 from Gordon, Hubert, Alice, and Peter, or any of them.

(B) Carolyn may recover damages consisting of unpaid rent and the cost of restoring the Granite Building to its historic character from Gordon, Hubert, and Peter, or any of them, and the Historical Preservation Society may recover the unpaid annual contribution of $5,000 from Gordon, Hubert, and Peter, or any of them.

(C) Carolyn may recover damages consisting of unpaid rent and the cost of restoring the Granite Building to its historic character from Gordon, Hubert, and Peter, or any of them, and the Historical Preservation Society may recover the unpaid annual contribution of $5,000 from Gordon and Hubert, or either of them.

(D) Carolyn may recover damages consisting of unpaid rent and the cost of restoring the Granite Building to its historic character from Gordon, Hubert, and Peter, or any of them, and the Historical Preservation Society may recover the unpaid annual contribution of $5,000 from Peter only.

(E) Carolyn may recover damages consisting of unpaid rent and the cost of restoring the Granite Building to its historic character from Gordon and Peter, or either of them, and the Historical Preservation Society may recover the unpaid annual contribution of $5,000 from Peter only.

21. Sean owned a tract of land which he legally subdivided into 30 lots. His first sale was Lot 1, which he sold to Lila under a deed that contained no use restrictions of any kind. Then Sean sold Lots 2 through 10 to Andrew, a speculator in real estate, under duly recorded deeds that limited the use of each lot to one single-family residence of not less than 2,000 square feet living area. Sean then sold Lots 11 through 20 to separate purchasers. None of the deeds contained any restrictions on use. Before any construction began, Andrew sold Lot 2, immediately adjacent to Lot 1, to Sally, under a general warranty deed that contained no mention of any restrictions. Sean then sold Lots 21 through 30 by deeds that contained the identical restriction in the deeds to Andrew. Sally began construction of a tiny two-room cottage of 750 square feet in area, and Lila has sued to enjoin its construction. Which of the following would be Sally's best argument in defense?

(A) The deed from Andrew to Sally did not mention any use restrictions.

(B) The deed from Sean to Lila did not mention any use restrictions on Lot 2.

(C) When Lila purchased Lot 1 she was not aware of any actual or intended use restrictions on any lots in the subdivision.

(D) Sally lacked notice of the use restriction burdening Lot 2.

22. Sam owned a tract of land which he legally subdivided into 20 lots. His first sale was Lot 1, which he sold to Lois under a deed that contained no use restrictions of any kind. Then Sam sold Lots 2 through 10 to Alissa, a speculator in real estate, under duly recorded deeds that limited the use of each lot to one single-family residence of not less than 2,000 square feet living area. Sam then sold Lots 11 through 15 to separate purchasers. None of the deeds contained any restrictions on use. Before any construction began, Alissa sold Lot 2, immediately adjacent to Lot 1, to Sandra, under a general warranty deed that contained no mention of any restrictions. Sam then sold Lots 16 through 20 by deeds that contained the identical restriction in the deeds to Alissa. Sam had advertised his subdivision as "Highland Acres, a residential community." When bargaining with Lois prior to her purchase, Sam had told Lois that his "vision was of a community with one nice single-family residence on each lot." Lois had replied that she "couldn't care less about a residential community" and stated that she would buy Lot 1 only if it came "free of all use restrictions." After her purchase of Lot 1, Lois began construction of a retail convenience store on Lot 1. Sandra has filed suit seeking an injunction prohibiting Lois from constructing anything on Lot 1 other than a single-family residence of not less than 2,000 square feet. Is Sandra entitled to an injunction?

(A) Yes, on the theory of implied reciprocal servitudes.

(B) Yes, on the theory of equitable estoppel.

(C) No, because Lois's deed contained no use restrictions.

(D) No, because Lot 1 is not part of the property subject to implied reciprocal servitudes.

23. Otto owned a tract of land, the eastern boundary of which was a public road. The property commanded a fine view of a mountain peak to the west. Otto divided the tract into two lots, A and B. Lot A fronted the road and Lot B was landlocked. When Otto sold Lot A to Virgil he reserved in the deed an easement "for vehicle and pedestrian access" across an identified strip of Lot A. Otto constructed a roadway across the easement strip while Virgil built a home on Lot A oriented to capture the view of the mountain peak. Later, Otto sold Lot B to Horace under a deed that also conveyed the access easement to Horace. A few months after purchasing Lot B, Horace began construction of a home on Lot B. Horace conveyed to Power & Light, a utility, a license to set power poles on the easement over Lot A and to run electrical transmission lines along those poles, for the purpose of bringing electrical service to Lot B. If Virgil seeks to enjoin Power & Light from erecting power poles on or stringing power lines over Lot A, the court should find for

(A) Virgil, because an appurtenant easement is not alienable.

(B) Virgil, because Power & Light's proposed use is outside the scope of the easement.

(C) Horace, because an appurtenant easement is divisible for purposes incidental to its contemplated use.

(D) Horace, because every appurtenant easement contains and includes an easement in gross.

24. Oscar owned a tract of land, the eastern boundary of which was a public road. The property commanded a fine view of a mountain range to the west. Oscar divided the tract into two lots, A and B. Lot A fronted the road. Lot B was landlocked. When Oscar sold Lot A to Miriam he touted the view as "exceptional" and reserved in the deed an easement "for vehicle and pedestrian access" across an identified strip of Lot A. Oscar constructed a roadway across the easement strip while Miriam built a home on Lot A oriented to capture the view of the mountain range. Later, Oscar sold Lot B to Helen under a deed that also conveyed the access easement to Helen. A few months after purchasing Lot B, Helen began construction of a home on Lot B that is sufficiently large that it will completely block Miriam's view of the mountain range from her home. If Miriam seeks to enjoin Helen's construction in a manner that will block her view, the court should find for

    (A) Miriam, because Miriam's home was built first.

    (B) Miriam because the size of Helen's intended home will interfere with Miriam's implied easement for light, air, and view.

    (C) Helen, because Miriam has no right to an undisturbed view of the mountain range.

    (D) Helen, unless he was aware of Miriam's view when he purchased Lot B.

25. Ralston, record owner of Blackacre, entered into a valid written contract with Newbury for the sale of Blackacre. The contract obliged Ralston to deliver marketable title at the closing. Prior to the closing Newbury learned that Peters had been in possession of Blackacre for a period longer than the limitations period applicable to adverse possession and that Peters's occupation had not been by Ralston's permission. At the closing Newbury refused to accept the deed tendered by Ralston on the ground that Ralston's title was not marketable. Newbury declared that he was rescinding the contract and demanded a return of his deposit. Ralston refused to return the deposit and demanded that Newbury accept the deed and pay the balance of the purchase price. In litigation between Ralston and Newbury, who will win?

    (A) Ralston, unless Peters is successful in an action to quiet title to Blackacre.

    (B) Ralston, if he was ready, willing, and able to furnish Peters with a policy of title insurance which specifically insured against claims of adverse possessors.

    (C) Newbury, but only if Peters has complied with all the requirements for acquiring title by adverse possession.

    (D) Newbury, if there is reasonable doubt about whether Ralston still has title due to Peters's adverse possession.

26. On January 15, Horton, owner of Stony Point in fee simple absolute, delivered a deed to Stony Point to Ingram, who paid $5,000 cash and executed a note for $20,000 for the balance of the purchase price, secured by a mortgage on Stony Point. Neither the deed nor the mortgage was recorded. On May 1, Horton entered into a contract to sell Stony Point to Lewis and, on May 31, Horton delivered a deed to Stony Point in exchange for receipt of $25,000 cash from Lewis. Ingram made no payments on the note and, after Horton threatened to foreclose, in October Ingram executed and delivered to Horton a deed to Stony Point. In November, Lewis learned of these facts and filed suit against Horton to quiet title to Stony Point. The court should find for

(A) Lewis, because Horton is estopped from denying Lewis's title to Stony Point.

(B) Lewis, if Horton committed a fraud upon Lewis in the sale of Stony Point to Lewis.

(C) Horton, unless Lewis recorded the deed to Stony Point he received from Horton.

(D) Horton, because at the time of his conveyance to Lewis, Horton did not hold title to Stony Point.

Questions 27 through 30 are based on the following facts.

Polk owned Blackacre and Whiteacre, adjacent parcels of realty. On January 15, Polk died testate. Under her will Polk devised Blackacre "to Wildlife Foundation for so long as Blackacre is used solely for wildlife habitat, and if it is ever devoted to any other purpose, then to Garfield University." Polk devised Whiteacre "to Ned, my nephew, for life, then to Nell, my niece, and her heirs, but if Whiteacre should ever be used for any purpose other than farming, to Garfield University." Wildlife Foundation and Garfield University are each charitable organizations.

27. Garfield University has a valid future interest in

(A) Blackacre only.

(B) Whiteacre only.

(C) Blackacre and Whiteacre.

(D) Neither Blackacre nor Whiteacre.

28. After application of the rule against perpetuities the interest in Blackacre held by Wildlife Foundation is best described as a

(A) fee simple subject to an executory limitation.

(B) fee simple determinable.

(C) fee simple absolute.

(D) fee simple subject to a condition subsequent.

29. After application of the rule against perpetuities the interest in Whiteacre held by Nell is best described as a

(A) vested remainder in a fee simple subject to an executory limitation.

(B) vested remainder in a fee simple determinable.

(C) vested remainder in a fee simple absolute.

(D) vested remainder in a fee simple subject to a condition subsequent.

30. Assuming that Garfield University's interest in Whiteacre is valid, it is best described as a

(A) vested remainder subject to divestment upon a condition subsequent.

(B) contingent remainder.

(C) shifting executory interest.

(D) springing executory interest.

Answers to Multiple-Choice Questions

1. D When a government takes title by eminent domain it takes all interests in the property, whether presently possessory or future. Thus, the state took Elvis's fee simple absolute, consisting of George's presently possessory leasehold and Elvis's reversion, and failure specifically to condemn the leasehold is irrelevant. Statement I is wrong. Because George's leasehold was taken by government action, and thus he lost the right to possession, he is excused from any further obligation to pay rent. Statement II is correct. George's leasehold is an interest in property and, once taken by eminent domain, the takings clause of the Constitution requires that George receive 'just compensation" for his loss. Here, the government has taken Elvis's reversion and George's leasehold so the condemnation award must be apportioned between them. The value of the remaining term of the leasehold is the measure of George's loss, but because he is excused from rent for the balance of that term the rent that he would otherwise be obliged to pay must be deducted from that value. Statement III is correct. Thus, **D** is the only correct answer.

2. D A cause of action to recover possession of real estate accrues when the wrongful occupation first occurs. That was in 1980, when Adele occupied Bertram's realty. When Bertram died his son, Garth, inherited the realty and his father's cause of action to recover possession of the realty. Thus, **B** is wrong. Bertram, the holder of the cause of action *at the time the cause of action accrued,* was not disabled at that time. Garth's disability, age, does not matter. Thus, **A** is wrong. Because a cause of action to recover realty accrues when the wrongful occupation occurs, not when the rightful possessor learns of the occupation, **C** is wrong. Because Adele actually occupied the realty and did so openly, notoriously, continuously, she would appear to have occupied in the manner in which a true owner would occupy, thus satisfying the objective version of hostility. Thus, **E** is wrong.

3. B When Alan divided Blackacre it is possible that an easement for river access via the dirt road access was impliedly created in favor of Chet. An easement implied from prior use occurs when an owner conveys a portion of his land after he has used one portion of the land for the benefit of the other portion, and such use is apparent at the time of conveyance, continuous, and reasonably necessary to the enjoyment of the parcel benefited. Because Alan owned Blackacre and each of these elements could be present here **B** is the most effective argument. Note that there are not enough facts given to decide with certainty that an easement was implied from prior use, but this argument is the only one that has any real possibility of success. An easement by dedication is for public purposes and there is no indication that Alan ever sought to create a public right in the dirt road, so **A** is wrong. An easement by express reservation occurs when the grantor expressly reserves in the deed a right to use the conveyed land in some specified manner. Here, Alan reserved no use rights in Chet's property, so **C** is wrong. Similarly, because Alan's deed to Chet made no mention of a right of river access across Alan's retained land, there was no easement by grant, so **D** is wrong. Although Alan did grant a license to Chet and that license could become irrevocable by equitable estoppel, thus creating what is often termed an easement by estoppel, there is no indication that Chet substantially relied to his detriment on Alan's promise to allow Chet to use the dirt road. Purchase of a $25 home freezer is probably not a sufficiently large investment to support equitable estoppel. While E could be an effective argument, on these facts it appears far less efficacious than **B**.

4. A An easement by prescription may be established only by *adverse use*; if the use is by *permission* of the landowner it is not adverse and no prescriptive use right can be acquired by the user. George gave permission to Eunice and thus Eunice's use of the well has always been permissive. If Eunice had acquired a prescriptive easement the improvement of the well would have no effect on the continuation of her prescriptive easement, so **B** is wrong. The fact that the deed from George to Eunice made no mention of any easement is irrelevant to the question of whether Eunice has acquired an easement by adverse use, not by grant, so **C** is wrong. Bill's improvement of the well gives him no greater interest in Bill's property, although he does acquire (by virtue of the statute) a right to recover a *pro rata* share of the costs of the improvement from other easement owners (which will include Eunice if she has a prescriptive easement). Thus, while Eunice may be liable to Bill for her share of the maintenance costs, she does not have to perfect any use rights as against Bill, so **D** is wrong.

5. **C** Hector initially created a life estate in Virgil, followed by a vested remainder in Dante subject to complete divestment in favor of the executory interest created in Homer. However, the executory interest in Homer is void under the rule against perpetuities because the uncertainty of whether Blackacre will cease to be used as a farm could continue for centuries, long after the death of all lives in being at the creation of that executory interest plus 21 years. The fact that Blackacre ceases to be used as a farm within the lifetime of Virgil is irrelevant to the common law perpetuities rule, which determines the validity of interests in property by assessing the *possibility* of prolonged uncertainty at the moment of creation, not by reference to subsequent events. Homer's interest is removed, leaving a vested remainder in Dante subject to complete divestment in favor of Hector, the grantor. This is because Dante's remainder, once possessory, would exist only "so long as Blackacre remains a farm," leaving an unstated possibility of reverter in Hector. This possibility of reverter was not created by Hector's grant, but arose by operation of law, the result of the application of the rule against perpetuities to Homer's executory interest. Hector's possibility of reverter automatically stripped Dante of his right to future possession when Beatrice turned Blackacre into an amusement park. Because that was while Virgil's life estate was still in existence and Dante's interest was a remainder, the result was that Dante's remainder lapsed and Hector's possibility of reverter became a reversion. When Virgil died, that terminated his life estate and Beatrice's life estate *pur autre vie* (which was dependent on Virgil's continued life), thus making Hector's reversion possessory.

    The other answers are wrong. **A** is wrong because Beatrice's life estate expired on Virgil's death; her life estate was for the shorter of her life or Virgil's life. **B** is wrong because the condition divesting Dante does not indicate that the change in use must occur by Dante's actions. **D** is wrong; Virgil's heirs acquire no interest in Blackacre because Virgil's interest, a life estate, is not capable of inheritance — it dies with Virgil. **E** is wrong because Homer's executory interest is destroyed by the rule against perpetuities.

6. **E** The relevant reform doctrine that changes the answer is "wait and see." Under "wait and see" the validity of future interests under the rule against perpetuities is determined, not by *possibilities* at the time the interest is created, but by reference to actual events. Wait and see validates a contingent future interest if the uncertainty as to ownership is actually resolved by later events occurring within the perpetuities period. Here, the divesting condition (the change in use of Blackacre from a farm to an amusement park) has actually occurred within the lives of Virgil, Dante, and Homer, all lives in being on the effective date of the conveyance creating Homer's executory interest. Thus, Homer's executory interest is valid and, because the divesting condition has occurred, Homer has divested Dante. When Virgil dies, terminating his life estate (and Beatrice's life estate, which is measured by Virgil's life), Homer is entitled to possession.

7. **B** Giles has created a fee simple determinable in Franklin University ("so long as . . . used as a dormitory") which creates a possibility of reverter in Giles. But Giles has also made Franklin's fee simple determinable subject to an executory interest in Jefferson University ("but if Franklin

. . . shall ever admit students solely on the basis of race"). Jefferson's executory interest is in a fee simple determinable ("so long as . . . used as a dormitory") and that creates a possibility of reverter in Giles.

Giles does not have a reversion because a reversion is a future interest in a grantor that is certain to become possessory as soon as a prior possessory estate (e.g., a life estate or a leasehold) exhausts itself and inevitably expires. Giles's interest is not certain to become possessory because it is impossible to know if Franklin University will stop using the property as a dormitory or will start practicing racial discrimination in its admissions, and whether, in that latter event, Jefferson University will cease to use the property as a dormitory. Thus, **A** is wrong.

Giles does not have a right of re-entry (or power of termination) because the grant conditions the possessory right on an express condition, rather than conveying possession and attaching a condition after the fact. This is the difference between a qualified grant ("so long as'' or "until") and an unqualified grant followed by a condition ("to A, but if . . ." or "to A, provided, however . . ."). Thus, **C** is wrong.

The interest retained by Giles is immune from destruction under the rule against perpetuities, for no very good reason. The common law conceived of possibilities of reverter and powers of termination as vested upon creation because they represented an interest that the grantor had retained, despite the fact that the grantor's right to possession can remain uncertain for an indefinite period, much longer than that permitted under the rule against perpetuities.

8. **B** As described in the answer to question 7, Franklin has a fee simple determinable that is also subject to an executory limitation. Jefferson's interest becomes possessory only by divesting the possessory interest of Franklin (which will occur only if Franklin starts to admit students on the basis of race alone) and future interests that divest a possessory interest or a vested future interest are executory interests. Jefferson's executory interest is contingent — its right to possession is dependent on uncertain events — and that uncertainty (will Franklin start to admit students on the basis of race alone?) may persist for long after the perpetuities period of a life in being at the creation of the interest plus 21 years. Thus, Jefferson's executory interest would ordinarily violate the rule against perpetuities but the rule exempts from destruction interests in a charity that follow another charity's interest. Here, both Jefferson and Franklin are charitable institutions and Jefferson's interest follows Franklin's interest, so Jefferson's executory interest is valid. As a result, **D** is incorrect.

Answers **A** and **C** are wrong because a remainder is a future interest that will automatically become possessory upon the natural expiration of the prior estate.

9. **D** A life tenant does not have the right to use real property in any way she desires so long as the structures are not destroyed. Rather, a life tenant generally may not make changes to the property that materially diminishes its value. Thus, **A** is wrong because it is too broad a statement of the life tenant's rights.

Planting of Christmas trees might be affirmative waste if it substantially reduces the value of the farm. It is possible that the Christmas tree planting might increase the farm's value because there is a stream of future income that may be derived from the Christmas trees, and that value may well offset whatever drop in value is attributable to the lost pasture. On these facts it is impossible to be certain, but it is certain that Liz's proposal is not waste per se. **B** is wrong.

Most American courts no longer hold to the idea that ameliorative waste — a change in the property that increases its value — is actionable waste. However, such beneficial changes can be waste if it is clear that the grantor intended that the asset be preserved in its original form for the remainderman. Here, however, there is no evidence that Samuel intended that Blackacre be preserved as a horse farm for Lily. Indeed, Samuel's testamentary direction that his horses be sold is some evidence, however slim, to the contrary. **C** is wrong.

On these facts it appears that Liz's use is probably reasonable, and surely if she can prove its reasonableness her proposed planting of Christmas trees is not waste. **D** is correct.

10. B The distinctive characteristic of the joint tenancy is the right of survivorship, which means that a joint tenant's interest expires at his death and cannot be transferred by will or through intestate succession. Thus, Arnold's will is ineffective to pass any interest in Hundred Acres from Arnold to Clayton. Arnold's interest in Hundred Acres terminates at his death, leaving Clayton and Beatrice with equal ownership of Hundred Acres as joint tenants. Their fractional interest increases to one-half apiece from one-third because Arnold's interest simply vanishes with his death. In a sense, his interest is equally divided between Clayton and Beatrice. Answers **A** and **C** are wrong because Arnold's will is ineffective to sever the joint tenancy. Arnold's will can only dispose of property he owns at his death, but at his death he owns no interest in Hundred Acres. Answer **D** is wrong because Arnold's will cannot transfer his interest and thus augment Clayton's share.

11. D Bob's sale of his interest in Centurion Farm operated to sever the joint tenancy as to his interest, but not as to the interests of Amy and Charles. Thus, Zeke, the successor to Bob's interest, holds a one-third interest as a tenant in common with Amy and Charles, but Amy and Charles's joint tenancy continues as to their two-thirds interest in Centurion Farm. Answer **A** is wrong because Zeke is a tenant in common; **B** is wrong because only Zeke holds as a tenant in common; and **C** is wrong because there are no survivorship rights that attach to a tenancy in common and, in any case, Amy and Charles continue to be joint tenants as to their respective interests.

12. A The mortgage of City Square, executed only by Allen, one joint tenant acting alone, does not sever the joint tenancy because a mortgage is a security device that operates to pledge the mortgagor's interest in the mortgaged property as collateral to secure the repayment of the loan made by the mortgagee. Even states that view mortgages as transfers of title recognize that the transfer of title is conditional and only for security purposes. Accordingly, the better reasoned view is that a mortgage by one joint tenant does not sever the joint tenancy. Thus, Allen could only mortgage his own interest and that interest died with him. At that point the mortgage is extinguished. A creditor takes the risk of this loss if he accepts a mortgage from only one joint tenant. Because Allen's interest cannot be transferred by will Barbara and Cedric own equal interests as joint tenants. Answers **B** and **C** are wrong because (1) Zara owns no interest in City Square and (2) the mortgage does not survive Allen's death. Answer **C** would be correct only if the mortgage operated to sever the joint tenancy. Answer **D** is wrong because (1) Zara owns no interest in City Square and, (2) in the event the mortgage is seen to sever the joint tenancy, Creditcorp's mortgage would not be extinguished.

13. B A quitclaim deed conveys whatever interest in the subject property owned by the grantor and contains no deed warranties. The significance of this to these facts is that ordinarily an owner of property is not liable to his co-owners for profits earned from a business conducted on the property. Thus, while the deed transferred all of Clive's interest in Skyview to Zelda, making her a tenant in common as to one-third of the property, Clive never had any interest in Alex's Christmas tree farming profits. Answer **A** is wrong because a quitclaim deed is sufficient to transfer a joint tenant's interest in realty. Answer **C** is a correct statement of law but is wrong because the right of survivorship is of no relevance to any claim for a share of Alex's Christmas tree farming profits. Answer

D is wrong because Zelda's lack of entitlement to a share in Alex's farm profits has nothing to do with her status as a tenant in common rather than a joint tenant.

14. **C** Each co-owner is entitled to possession. Because Albert denied Nick's right to possession he ousted Nick, thus triggering an obligation on Albert's part to pay Nick the fair rental value of Nick's interest in Lonely Dell. Some jurisdictions do not require ouster as a prerequisite for this obligation; in such jurisdictions Albert would be liable to Nick even if he had never denied Nick possession. Even in those jurisdictions, answer **C** is better than the alternatives. Answer **A** is a correct statement of law but is wrong because Nick's entitlement to partition has no relevance to the question of whether Nick is entitled to rent from Albert. Answer **B** is wrong because the profitability of Albert's rose-growing business is legally irrelevant to the question of whether Nick is entitled to rent from Albert. Answer **D** is wrong because even if Albert committed a tort the fair rental value of Lonely Dell is not relevant to determination of such tort damages.

15. **A** A recorded deed that cannot be discovered by a reasonable search of the chain of title is not within the chain of title. Because the title index is entirely by grantor-grantee a reasonable searcher would find no evidence of any transfer of title from Toby to Greg, but would find evidence of a transfer of title from Toby to Ruth. As far as the chain of title reveals, Toby transferred title once, to Ruth. For purposes of determining priorities under a recording statute, a deed recorded outside the chain of title is treated as if it were unrecorded. Thus, the Greg-to-Fred deed and the subsequent deed of Fred to Betty are outside the chain of title and treated as unrecorded. Neither deed is effective against Ruth, who took without notice. Answer **B** is wrong because Toby's original deed to Greg conveyed his interest in Oak Hill to Greg and thus gave Greg power to convey an interest in Oak Hill, but because of Greg's failure to record he left Toby with power to convey an interest to someone else. Answer **C** is wrong because, although Toby may have committed fraud, that does not affect the relative rights of Betty and Ruth. Answer **D** is wrong because even if Fred knew that Greg had not recorded his deed such notice is irrelevant to the question of whether Ruth had such notice.

16. **C** The interests created by Owen's will do not become effective until Owen's death. At that moment, Ophelia had a life estate in Mill Pond and her then nonexistent children (Louise and Ethel had each died prior to Owen's death) had a contingent remainder because the remainder is in a class of people who cannot be ascertained. Four years later when Edgar was born to Ophelia, Edgar acquired a vested interest because his identity was established and there was no condition precedent to his right to take possession after the expiration of Ophelia's life estate. However, his vested remainder was subject to partial divestment in favor of other children of Ophelia, should any be born to her.

Answers **A** and **D** are wrong because there was no condition subsequent which, if it occurred, would take away Edgar's right to possession after the expiration of Ophelia's life estate. Answer **B** is wrong because Edgar's identity was known and there was no condition precedent to his right to possession after the expiration of Ophelia's life estate. Answer **E** is wrong because Edgar's interest will not divest another vested estate. Answer **F** is wrong because Edgar does have an interest in Mill Pond, as described above, and that interest is valid under the rule against perpetuities because the uncertainty as to the ownership of the remainder will be eliminated at Ophelia's death, and Ophelia was a life in being at Owen's death, the moment the interest was created. At Ophelia's death we will know the identities of all her children who were born after Owen's death.

17. **C** The covenant against encumbrances, included within a general warranty deed, is the grantor's promise that the title delivered under the deed is free from liens. Anne breached the covenant

because when she delivered the deed there was such a lien, the mortgage to Clarke. However, Anne's prompt satisfaction of the mortgage eliminated that lien, thus preventing any real damages to Lester, but Lester can recover whatever nominal damages he suffered. Answer **A** is wrong because the appropriate remedy for breach of the covenant is a suit for damages, not rescission. Answer **B** is wrong because the covenant was contained in the deed and was not breached until the deed was delivered; the contractual promise was merged into the deed and was not breached at the time the contract was made. Answer **D** is wrong because Anne did breach the covenant.

18. **A** The fact that Quentin has an adequate remedy against Leroy for Leroy's breach of the covenant is not a defense to a valid claim that Quentin may have against Alix. Answer **B** is wrong because it might be an effective defense; many states hold that the covenant against encumbrances may only be asserted by the grantee of the deed containing the covenant. Answer **C** is wrong because the mortgage was recorded well before Quentin acquired title and thus Quentin had constructive notice of its existence, which is likely to be an effective defense. Answer **D** is wrong because Quentin's claim is, indeed, likely to be time-barred.

19. **C** The modern trend is to imply into commercial leases a condition that consent to transfer of a lessee's interest may be withheld only on commercially reasonable grounds. While this rule is still a minority rule, in a jurisdiction in the vanguard of adopting modern landlord-tenant rules would probably have adopted this principle. Cindy's refusal to consent is not commercially reasonable: Henry is financially sound and of impeccable reputation; Cindy's objection appears to be rooted in a personal pique. Answer **A** is the next best answer but is likely wrong because the rule in *Dumpor's Case,* which holds that consent, once given, is continuing unless the landlord expressly reserves the right to withhold future consents, is an artifact of an older conception of leaseholds as conveyances, rather than the bundle of contract rights that tends to inform modern notions of leaseholds. Accordingly, the rule in *Dumpor's Case* is uncommonly observed today, especially in a "vanguard" state. Answer **B** is wrong because (1) Guido does remain in privity of estate with respect to the subleased portion of the Brick Building, and (2) even if there were no privity of estate between Guido and Cindy, Guido would remain liable for contractual damages, if any exist. Answer **D** is wrong because the lease could have been breached by some failure other than failure to pay rent.

20. **C** Carolyn and Gordon were originally in privity of estate and privity of contract. When Gordon leased to Hubert he effected an assignment of his interest because he leased the entire remaining portion of his right to possession to Hubert. As a result Gordon was no longer in privity of estate with Carolyn but remained in privity of contract with Carolyn because Carolyn has not released him from the lease obligations. Moreover, Gordon is liable to the Historical Preservation Society because it is a third party beneficiary of the contribution covenant. Thus, Gordon is liable for all the lease covenants Peter breached. Hubert became in privity of estate with Carolyn for the duration of his possession of the Granite Building and, by reason of his promise to perform Gordon's lease obligations, became in privity of contract with Carolyn by reason of Carolyn's ability to enforce that assumption agreement as an intended third party beneficiary and with the Historical Preservation Society as a third party beneficiary of the contribution covenant in the original lease. When Hubert assigned to Alice he was no longer in privity of estate with Carolyn but remained liable in contract because of the assumption agreement. Thus, Hubert is liable for all the covenants Peter breached. Alice was in privity of contract with Carolyn only during the 6 months she was in possession of the Granite Building. None of the breaches of the lease covenants occurred during her time of possession and, because she is no longer in privity of estate with Carolyn nor in privity

of contract with her (she did not assume the lease) she has no liability to Carolyn. Peter is in privity of estate with Carolyn but not privity of contract. He is liable for breach of those lease covenants the burden of which runs with the estate in land that he possesses. Three lease covenants are it issue: the rent covenant, the no alterations covenant, and the contribution to the Historical Preservation Society covenant. All of the elements necessary for the burden of the first two covenants to run are present: The covenants are intended to bind the leasehold possessor, horizontal privity between Gordon and Carolyn is present (if necessary in the jurisdiction), vertical privity between Gordon and Peter is present (Peter has an estate of the same duration and nature as Gordon), and the substance of the covenants touches and concerns the land because rent is essential to continued occupancy and the no alterations covenant concerns land use, is designed to control a negative externality, and will increase the value of the benefited estate and decrease the value of the burdened estate. However, the third covenant — the contribution covenant — does not run with the burdened estate. First, even though the jurisdiction recognized third party beneficiary enforcement of contracts, it may not permit third party beneficiaries of real covenants to enforce them, especially when the third party owns no benefited estate. Second, and even more important, the substance of the covenant probably does not touch and concern the burdened estate; it is more akin to a purely personal promise, such as a tenant's promise to take a photo of the landlord's sister each year on her birthday.

Answer **A** is wrong because Alice has no liability and Peter may not be liable to the Historical Preservation Society. Answers **B** and **D** are wrong because Peter is probably not liable to the Historical Preservation Society. Answer **D** is wrong for the additional reason that Gordon and Hubert are liable to the Historical Preservation Society. Answer **E** is wrong because Carolyn may recover damages from Hubert as well as Peter, and the Historical Preservation Society may recover from Gordon and Hubert but not Peter.

21. **C** When Sean conveyed Lot 2 he had no interest in Lot 1, having already conveyed it to Lila. A use restriction contained in a deed cannot usually be enforced to benefit land not owned by grantor at the time of the conveyance, but if Lila, the prior purchaser, was aware of such intended restrictions and relied upon them in purchasing Lot 1 she might be able to enforce the restrictions. Here, however, there is no evidence of any such reliance. Answer **A** is wrong because the use restriction burdening Lot 2 is in the chain of title that runs to Sally and thus burdens Lot 2 even though her immediate deed from Andrew makes no mention of the restriction. Sally will have a claim against Andrew for breach of the deed covenant against encumbrances contained in the warranty deed, but that is no help to her defense against Lila. Answer **B** is wrong because Lila could enforce the restrictions on Lot 2 without any mention of them in her deed from Sean if she knew of them and relied on them in purchasing Lot 1. Because that is not the case here, the failure to mention the use restrictions on Lot 2 in the deed to Lila is irrelevant to the problem. Answer **D** is wrong because Sally had constructive notice of the use restriction because the use restriction was in her chain of title.

22. **D** Although Sam indicated an intent to create a subdivision limited to a single-family residence on each lot he did not communicate to Lois his intent to burden lots with such use restrictions and acquiesced to Lois's demand that she take title free of all use restrictions. It is significant that Lot 1 was the first sale. The first tangible manifestation of Sam's intent to create a planned community with all lots subject to implied reciprocal servitudes was Sam's sale to Alissa, suggesting that the scope of the common development subject to implied reciprocal servitudes is limited to Lots 2 through 20. Answer **A** is wrong for the foregoing reasons, but would be correct if Sam's sales pitch was adequate to establish his intent to create a common development scheme burdened by the covenant. Answer **B** is wrong because equitable estoppel is entirely irrelevant to these facts. Answer

C is wrong because if there was a valid common development scheme creating implied reciprocal servitudes it would not matter that Lois's deed contained no use restrictions.

23. **B** The easement was for vehicle and pedestrian access. Utility service, however beneficial, is an entirely different use. Answer **A** is wrong because appurtenant easements are freely alienable and pass with the title to the property to which they are appurtenant. Answer **C** is a generally correct statement of law but is wrong because the purpose for which the division has been made — utility service — is not incidental to the originally contemplated use of the easement. Answer **D** is wrong because it is both a wrong statement of law and irrelevant to these facts.

24. **C** Absent very unusual and special circumstances there is no right to continue to enjoy one's view. Answer **A** is wrong because prior construction does not confer any negative easement for view. Similarly, Answer **B** is wrong because there is no implied easement for light, air, and view in the absence of highly unusual circumstances not present here. Answer **D** is wrong because notice of a prior view does not prevent a later purchaser from lawfully obstructing the view.

25. **D** Marketable title is a title that is free of *reasonable* doubt, not every doubt, but if the doubt is very remote and improbable it is insufficient to impair marketable title. If there is reasonable doubt that Ralston still has title, Ralston's title is not marketable. Answer **A** is wrong because Ralston lacks marketable title if there is a reasonable *possibility* that Peters will succeed in a quiet title action. Answer **B** is wrong because a title insurance policy insures against economic loss due to defective title. While it may be an acceptable substitute for marketable title, Newbury is entitled to market-able title, not a substitute. Answer **C** is wrong because it is not necessary that Newbury establish that Peters is certain to have title by adverse possession, only that there exists reasonable doubt on that score.

26. **A** The doctrine of estoppel by deed, or after-acquired title, holds that a person who conveys realty in which he has no interest is estopped from denying the validity of the conveyance if he later acquires title to the property. Answer **B** is wrong because fraud does nothing to pass title, although Horton is liable for damages that are the proximate result of his fraud. Answer **C** is wrong because record-ing statutes help determine the priority of conflicting claims among multiple grantees, but do not address the claims of a grantee as against his grantor. Answer **D** is wrong, because estoppel by deed addresses this problem.

27. **A** As to Blackacre, Polk's will created in Wildlife Foundation a fee simple subject to an executory limitation, and an executory interest in Garfield University. Although the uncertainty as to whether Garfield's executory interest will ever become possessory may remain for a period longer than the perpetuities period, the interest is not destroyed by the rule against perpetuities because it divests an interest held by another charity. As to Whiteacre Polk's will created a life estate in Ned, a vested remainder in fee simple subject to an executory limitation in Nell, and an executory interest in Garfield University. However, the executory interest in Garfield is void under the rule against perpetuities because the uncertainty as to whether Whiteacre will ever be used for nonagricultural purposes may not be resolved for hundreds of years, long after the expiration of the perpetuities period. There is no charity-to-charity exemption to save Garfield's interest in Whiteacre.

28. **A** As explained in the answer to Question 27, the rule against perpetuities does not destroy Garfield's executory interest because a contingent future interest in a charity that follows an interest in another charity is exempt from the rule. Accordingly, Wildlife Foundation owns a fee simple subject to the executory limitation in Garfield University. Answer **B** is wrong because a fee simple determinable describes a fee that, upon occurrence of the condition specified, will automatically be terminated

and re-vest possession in the *grantor.* Answer **C** is wrong because the fee simple owned by Wildlife Foundation may be divested. Answer **D** is wrong because a fee simple subject to a condition subsequent describes a fee that, upon occurrence of the condition specified, will be subject to termination if the *grantor* acts to exercise his right to re-enter and re-take possession.

29. C As explained in the answer to Question 27, the rule against perpetuities destroys the executory interest in Garfield University. Accordingly, Garfield's interest and the divesting condition associated with it are excised from Polk's devise. That leaves Nell with a vested remainder in a fee simple absolute. It is a vested remainder because possession will occur immediately upon expiration of Ned's life estate, we know Nell's identity, and there is no condition precedent to her right to possession other than the expiration of the preceding estate. It is a fee simple absolute because the rule against perpetuities eliminates the entire clause after the grant to Nell and her heirs ("but if . . . to Garfield University"). The words "and her heirs," of course, are words of limitation, describing the duration of the estate. In medieval England those words meant that the estate was capable of inheritance, meaning fee simple absolute. Today, the words "and her heirs" are simply old-fashioned and unnecessary "legalese" that describes fee simple absolute. Answer **A** is wrong because Garfield's executory interest is void. Answer **B** is wrong because the elimination of the entire divesting clause leaves no possibility of reverter in Polk's heirs. Answer **D** is wrong because the elimination of the entire divesting clause leaves no right of re-entry in Polk's heirs.

30. C Garfield's interest, if valid, is an executory interest because it becomes possessory, if at all, by divesting another vested interest. It is a shifting executory interest because it will become possessory, if at all, by divesting a vested interest of another transferee from the grantor, Polk. Answer **D** is wrong because a springing executory interest divests the grantor after some time has elapsed from the moment the interest is created. Answers **A** and **B** are wrong because Garfield's interest is not a remainder. Although a remainder comes into possession at the expiration of the prior estate (and Garfield's interest will become possessory when the defeasible fee expires due to the use of Whiteacre for nonagricultural uses) it is also true that a remainder cannot follow a vested fee simple, so it is not a remainder. Answer **B** is wrong for the further reason that a remainder is contingent either because the identity of its owner is unknown or there is an express condition precedent to possession that is something other than the expiration of the prior estate. Here, the only contingency attached to Garfield's right of possession is that Whiteacre not be used for agricultural purposes, and that condition also defines the end of the prior estate.

Table of Cases

Cases listed in italics are ones that appear as principal cases in Dukeminier/Krier/Alexander/Schill: Property, Seventh Edition, 2010. The outline's major discussion of a Dukeminier/Krier/Alexander/Schill case occurs on the page or pages listed in italics

Abbott v. Herring 237
Abbott v. Nampa Sch. Dist. No. 131 247
Abramowitz, Estate of 26
Adkins v. Thomas Solvent Co. 218
Adrian v. Rabinowitz 128
Albert M. Greenfield & Co., Inc. v. Kolea 140
Albright v. Fish 257
Albro v. Allen 90
Alexander v. Andrews 204
Allen v. Gordon 94
American Book Co. v. Yeshiva Univ. Dev. Found. 136
American Oil Co. v. Leaman 252
Amphitheaters, Inc. v. Portland Meadows 218
Anderson v. City of Issaquah *290*
Anderson v. Gouldberg 6, 11
Anderson Drive-In Theatre v. Kirkpatrick 149
Angle v. Slayton 204
Anthony v. Brea Glenbrook Club 262
Arkansas Release Guidance Found. v. Needler 218
Armory v. Delamirie *10*
Armstrong v. Maybee 138
Aronson v. Board of Appeals of Stoneham 285
Art Neon Co. v. City & County of Denver 283
Associated Home Builders v. City of Livermore 296
Austin Hill Country Realty v. Palisades Plaza, Inc. 146
Ayer v. Philadelphia & Boston Face Brick Co. 203
Aztec Ltd. v. Creekside Inv. Co. 246

Bagko Dev. Co. v. Damitz 270
Baker v. City of Milwaukie 282
Baker v. Weedon *39, 40*
Baliles v. Cities Serv. Co. 166
Ballard v. Alaska Theater Co. 156
Banach v. Lawera 240
Barash v. Pennsylvania Terminal Real Estate Corp. 147

Barnard v. Monongahela Natural Gas Co. 7
Barr v. Eason 103
Barton v. Mitchell Co. 148
Bean v. Walker *191*
Becker v. IRM Corp. 155
Beiser v. Hensic 250
Bell v. Town of Wells 243
Belle Terre, Vill. of v. Boraas 293, 294
Berg v. Wiley *143*
Berman v. Parker 300
Berzito v. Gambino 151
Bianchi v. Lorenz 180
Blackett v. Olanoff 147, 148
Blackwell v. Del Bosco 149
Board of Educ. of Minneapolis v. Hughes *176, 202*
Board of Pub. Instruction v. Town of Bay Harbor Islands 272
Bocchini v. Gorn Mgmt. Co. 147
Boomer v. Atlantic Cement Co. *224*
Borelli v. Brusseau 108
Boucher v. Boyer 229
Brant v. Hargrove 92
Braswell v. Braswell 71
Bridges v. Hawksworth 13
Broadmoor San Clemente Homeowners' Ass'n v. Nelson 271
Broadway Nat'l Bank v. Adams *51, 68*
Brown v. Heirs of Fuller 268
Brown v. Lober *181*
Brown v. Southall Realty Co. 139, 149
Brown v. Voss *247, 250*
Brown, In re Marriage of 110
Brunswick-Balke Collender Co. v. Seattle Brewing & Malting Co. 140
Bryant v. Willison Real Estate Co. 175
Buffalo Acad. of the Sacred Heart v. Boehm Bros., Inc. 202, 267
Building Monitoring Sys., Inc. v. Paxton 153
Burgess v. French 173

Bushmiller v. Schiller 166
Butler v. Haley Greystone Corp. 209
Buttolph v. Erikkson 242

Cameron v. Barton 246
Camp v. Milam 233
Campbell v. Great Miami Aerie No. 2309 238
Cappaert v. Junker 155
Cardona v. Eden Realty Co. 155
Carma Dev. v. Marathon Dev. Cal., Inc. 136
Castle Assocs. v. Schwartz 250
Caulfield v. Improved Risk Mutuals, Inc. 175
Caullett v. Stanley Stilwell & Sons, Inc. 261
Causby; United States v. 303
Causey v. Lanigan 241
Centel Cable TV Co. of Ohio v. Cook 249
Chambers v. North River Line 138
Chandler v. Smith 263
Charles E. Burt, Inc. v. Seven
    Grand Corp. 147, 149
Charter Township of Delta v. Dinolfo 294
Cheney Bros. v. Doris Silk Corp. *7*
Chesapeake Ranch Club v.
    CRC Members 263
Chicago Bd. of Realtors, Inc. v.
    City of Chicago *157*
Chicago, Burlington & Quincy Ry. v.
    Chicago 298
Chillemi v. Chillemi 185
Choisser v. Eyman 262
Church of the Lukumi Babalu Aye v. City of
    Hialeah 292
Citibrook II v. Morgan's Foods of
    Missouri, Inc. 272
Citizens of Brunswick County Taxpayers Ass'n v.
    Holden Beach Enters., Inc. 242
City of. *See name of city*
Clark v. Maloney 11
Coe v. Clay 128
Cohan v. Fleuroma, Inc. 244
Cohen v. Adolph Kutner Co. 252
Cohn, In re 25
Collard v. Incorporated Vill. of Flower
    Hill 288
Columbus-Am. Discovery Group v. Atlantic
    Mut. Ins. Co. 10
Commons v. Westwood Zoning Bd. of
    Adjustment 285

Commonwealth v. Fremont Investment &
    Loan *192*
Commonwealth Bldg. Corp. v. Hirschfield 124
Conklin v. Davi 167
Connally v. General Constr. Co. 290
Construction Indus. Ass'n v. City of
    Petaluma 296
Cook v. Cook 111
Cooke v. Ramponi 234
Cooper v. Leverhulme 76
Cope v. Inhabitants of the Town of
    Brunswick 285, 286
Cotting v. Boston 251
County Comm'rs of Queen Anne County v.
    Miles 295
County of Wayne v. Hathcock 300
Cousins v. Alabama Power Co. 249
Covington v. Murray 97
Craft; United States v. 97
Crane Neck Ass'n v. New York City/Long Island
    County Serv. Group 271
Crechale & Polles, Inc. v. Smith 125
Crosdale v. Lanigan 234

Daniels v. Anderson *204*
Danielson v. Roberts 11, 12
David Props., Inc. v. Selk 125
Davidow v. Inwood N. Prof'l Group 150
Davidson Bros., Inc. v. D. Katz &
    Sons, Inc. 261
Davis v. Tazewell Place Assocs. 173
Davis v. Vidal 134
Day v. Clark 204
Daytona Beach, City of, v. Tona-Rama, Inc. 242
Deep E. Tex. Reg'l Mental Health & Mental
    Retardation Servs. v. Kinnear 270–271
Delfino v. Vealencis *99*
Delta, Charter Township of v. Dinolfo 294
Dickhut v. Norton 153
Dill v. Excel Packing Co. 222
Dolan v. City of Tigard *309, 310*
Dolata v. Berthelet Fuel & Supply 218
Double D Manor, Inc. v. Evergreen Meadows
    Homeowners' Ass'n 271
Duke of Norfolk's Case 72
Dumpor's Case 137
Duncan v. Vassaur 93
Duncan v. Village of Middlefield 285

Dunlap v. Bullard 134
Dwyer v. Skyline Apartments, Inc. 155
Dyar v. Martinez 198

Eagle Enters., Inc. v. Gross 262
Eastling v. B.P. Products North America, Inc. 263
East St. John's Shingle Co. v.
  City of Portland 222
Easton v. Strassburger 172
Echo Consulting Servs., Inc. v. North Conway
  Bank 149
Edmonds, City of, v. Oxford House, Inc. *294*
Edwards v. Habib 153
Elam, In re Marriage of 110
Elkus v. Elkus *106*
Employment Div., Dep't of Human Res. of Or. v.
  Smith 291–292
Erickson v. Sinykin 11
Ernst v. Conditt *134*
Estancias Dallas Corp. v. Schultz *223*
Estate of. *See name of estate holder*
Euclid, Vill. of, v. Ambler Realty Co. *217, 280*

Farmer v. Kentucky Utils. Co. 246
Fasano v. Board of County Comm'rs of Wash.
  County 287
Favorite v. Miller 10, 11
Fick v. Weedon 270
Fidelity Fed. Sav. & Loan Ass'n v. De La
  Cuesta 189
1500 Lincoln Ave.; United States v. 97
Fink v. Miller 274
First Am. Nat'l Bank of Nashville v.
  Chicken Sys. of Am., Inc. 132
First English Evangelical Lutheran Church of
  Glenside v. County of Los Angeles 307, 311
First Fed. Sav. Bank v. Key Mkts., Inc. 136
First Nat'l Trust & Sav. Bank v. Raphael 251
Fisher v. Giuliani *293*
Fitzwilliam v. Wesley United Methodist
  Church 270
Flying Diamond Oil Corp. v. Newton Sheep
  Co. 256
40 West 67th Street Corp. v. Pullman *277*
Fox v. Smidt 270
Franklin v. Anna Nat'l Bank of Anna 94
Frimberger v. Anzellotti *180, 213*
Fristoe v. Drapeau 246

Gabel v. Drewrys Ltd. U.S.A., Inc. 201
Gallagher v. Bell 257
Ganz v. Clark 127
Garner v. Gerrish *123*
Gazzolo v. Chambers 128
Gemma v. Gemma 110
Ghen v. Rich *5*
Gibbs v. Kimbrell 273
Gilbert v. Showerman 222
Gilkinson v. Third Ave. R.R. Co. 26
Gion v. City of Santa Cruz 242
Giordano v. Miller 137
Glass v. Goeckel 243
Glenn v. Poole 246
Goddard v. Winchell 12
Golden v. Planning Bd. of Ramapo 296
Gore v. Blanchard 242
Gower v. Waters 143
Grady v. Schmitz *267, 275*
Graham, In re Marriage of *106*
Grange v. Korff 267
Greenblatt v. Toney Schloss Props. Corp. 287
Groninger v. Aumiller 270
Gruen v. Gruen *27*
Guillette v. Daly Dry Wall, Inc. *202, 266*
Gulstine, Estate of 109
*Guru Nanak Sikh Society of Yuba City v.
  County of Sutter* *292*

Haberstick v. Gundaker Real Estate, Inc. 172
Hadacheck v. Sebastian *303*
Haldeman v. Teicholz 267
Hamaker v. Blanchard 11
Haman, State ex rel., v. Fox 242, 243
Hamel v. Gootkin 92
Hammonds v. Central Ky. Natural Gas Co. 7
Haner v. Bruce 198
Hannah v. Peel *12, 13*
Hannan v. Dusch *127, 128*
Harms v. Sprague *92*
Harper v. Paradise *206*
Harris v. Griffin 190
Hartman Ranch Co. v. Associated Oil Co. 134
Hatch v. Riggs Nat'l Bank 72
Hawaii Hous. Auth. v. Midkiff 300
Hawkinson v. Johnston 144
Heinzman v. Howard 175
Henrioulle v. Marin Ventures, Inc. 155

Henry v. Dalton 234
Herpolsheimer v. Christopher 128
Herter v. Mullen 123
Hertzberg v. Zoning Bd. of Adjustment of
    Pittsburgh 285
Hester v. Sawyers 240
Hewitt v. Hewitt 111
Hickerson v. Bender 251, 252
Hickey v. Green 165
Hidden Harbour Estates v. Basso 276
Hilder v. St. Peter *150, 151, 152*
Hill v. Community of Damien of Molokai 271
Hills Dev. Co. v. Bernards Township 295
Hinds v. Phillips Petroleum Co. 248
Hochstein v. Romero 198
Hocks v. Jeremiah 26
Hoffman v. Newell 97
Hohman v. Bartel 274
Holbrook v. Taylor *233, 234*
Holy Props. v. Kenneth Cole Prods., Inc. 145
Homan v. Hutchinson 229
Howard D. Johnson Co. v. Parkside
    Dev. Corp. 206
Howard v. Kunto *18*
Hrisomalos v. Smith 273
Hughes v. Washington 298
Hurley v. City of Niagara Falls 13

Ink v. City of Canton *48*
International News Serv. v. Associated Press *7*
Irvin L. Young Found., Inc. v. Damrell 92
Ivons-Nispel, Inc. v. Lowe 242

Jaber v. Miller 134
Jack v. Hunt 237
Jack Spring, Inc. v. Little 143
Jackson v. Williams 270
Jacque v. Steenberg Homes, Inc. 9
James v. Valtierra 295
James J.F. Laughlin Agency, Inc. v. Town of
    W. Hartford 283
Javins v. First Nat'l Realty Corp. 150
Jee v. Audley 79
Jensen v. Schreck 190
Jinks v. Edwards 128
Johnson v. Amstutz 69
Johnson v. Davis *172*
Johnson v. Hendrickson 99

Johnson v. M'Intosh *4*
Johnson v. Mt. Baker Park Presbyterian
    Church 265
Johnson v. Scandia Assocs., Inc. 155
Johnson v. State 263
Joiner v. Haley 155
Jolliff v. Hardin Cable Television Co. 249
Jones v. Alfred H. Mayer Co. 157
Jones v. Lee *169*
Jones; State v. 289
Jordan v. Nickell 144
Jordan v. Talbot 143
Jost v. Dairyland Power
    Coop. 217, 218, 224
Julian v. Christopher 136

Kanefsky v. Dratch Constr. Co. 247
Kanter v. Safran 144
Kassan v. Stout 143
Keeble v. Hickeringill *5*
Kelly v. Neville 40
Kelo v. City of New London *300, 301*
Kendall v. Ernest Pestana, Inc. *136*
Keppell v. Bailey 254, 261
Ketchel v. Bainbridge Township 295
Keystone Bituminous Coal Ass'n v. De
    Benedictis 306, 307
Kilbourne v. Forester 125
Kimbrough v. Reed 41
King v. Moorehead 150
King v. Reynolds 128
Kline v. Burns 151
Kline v. 1500 Mass. Ave. Apt. Corp. 154
Krieger v. Helmsley-Spear, Inc. 136
Kutzin v. Pirnie *170*

Ladue, City of, v. Gilleo *291*
Ladue, City of, v. Horn 294
Lamden v. La Jolla Shores Clubdominium
    Homeowners' Assn 277
Land Developers, Inc. v. Maxwell 267
Landen Farms Cmty. Servs. Ass'n v. Schube 274
LaSara Grain v. First Nat'l Bank of
    Mercedes 173
Leach v. Gunnarson 179
Lee; United States v. 98
Lempke v. Dagenais *173, 174*
Lennon v. U.S. Theatre Corp. 145

Lewis v. Searles 38
Lewis v. Superior Court 205
Licari v. Blackwelder 163
*Lick Mill Creek Apartments v. Chicago
    Title Ins. Co.* 212, 213
Lindsey v. Clark 250
Lingsch v. Savage 172
Lohmeyer v. Bower 168, 180, 213
London County Council v. Allen 263
*Loretto v. Teleprompter Manhattan
    CATV Corp.* 302, 308, 312
*Lucas v. South Carolina Coastal
    Council* 280, 304, 305, 312
Luthi v. Evans 198

Mahoney v. Mahoney 107
Mahoney v. Middleton 204
*Mahrenholz v. County Bd. of Sch.
    Trustees* 43, 46, 47
Main Farms Homeowners' Ass'n v.
    Worthington 271
Malley v. Hanna 267, 268–269
Maloy v. Stuttgart Mem'l Hosp. 95
Mamalis v. Bornovas 93
Mann v. Bradley 93
Mannillo v. Gorski 15
Marengo Cave Co. v. Ross 15
Marini v. Ireland 151
Marriage of. *See name of party*
Marsh v. Pullen 250
Martin v. Reynolds Metals Co. 219
Marvin v. Marvin 111
Massey v. Prothero 103
Matcha v. Mattox 243
Matthews v. Bay Head Improvement Ass'n 243
McAvoy v. Medina 13
McCurdy v. McCurdy 109
McCutcheon v. United Homes Corp. 155
McEneaney v. Chestnut Hill Realty Corp. 172
McGuire v. City of Jersey City 146
McIntyre v. Scarbrough 41
McMillan v. Iserman 271
McMinn v. Town of Oyster Bay 294
Melms v. Pabst Brewing Co. 41
Members of City Council of Los Angeles v.
    Taxpayers for Vincent 291
Merchants Row Corp. v. Merchants
    Row, Inc. 136
Mercury Inv. Co. v. F.W. Woolworth Co. 129

Messersmith v. Smith 200
Metromedia, Inc. v. City of San Diego 283
Metropolitan Nat'l Bank v. United States 199
Metzner v. Wojdyla 270
Michalski v. Michalski 100
Mid-State Equip. Co., Inc. v. Bell 264
Midland Valley R.R. v. Arrow Indus.
    Mfg. Co. 230
Miles v. Shauntee 149
Miller v. Green 207
Miller v. Grossman Shoes, Inc. 242
*Miller v. Lutheran Conference &
    Camp Ass'n* 244, 249
Miller v. Schoene 303
Mills v. Damson Oil Co. 199
Mississippi State Dep't of Pub. Welfare v.
    Howie 126
Mister Donut of Am., Inc. v. Kemp 206
Mitchell v. Castellaw 237
Monterey, City of, v. Del Monte Dunes 310
Moore v. City of E. Cleveland 293
Moore v. Megginson 269
Moore v. Regents of Univ. of Cal. 8
Morgan v. High Penn Oil Co. 216, 218
Morone v. Morone 112
Morris v. Albright 35
Morse v. Aldrich 256
Morse v. Curtis 204
*Mountain Brow Lodge No. 82, Indep.
    Order of Odd Fellows v. Toscano* 47
Mountjoy's Case 248, 249
Mueller v. Bankers Trust Co. of Muskegon 263
Mulligan v. Panther Valley Property
    Owners Ass'n 276
Murphy v. Financial Dev. Corp. 189
Murphy v. Hendrix 149

Nahrstedt v. Lakeside Vill. Condo.
    Ass'n, Inc. 113, 276
National Bellas Hess, Inc. v. Kalis 120
Nature Conservancy v. Congel 268
Nectow v. City of Cambridge 280
McMinn v. Town of Oyster Bay 294
*Neponsit Property Owners Ass'n v. Emigrant
    Indus. Sav. Bank* 258, 260, 262
Neuberger v. City of Portland 287
New Jersey v. Baker 294
Newcomb v. Congdon 261
Newells v. Carter 16
Newman v. Bost 25–26

Newman v. Hinky-Dinky Omaha
  Lincoln, Inc. 136
Newton County v. Davison 95
Nicholson v. 300 Broadway Realty Corp. 262
Nickolson v. Connecticut Halfway House 218
Noble v. Murphy 276
Nogarr; People v. 92
Nollan v. California Coastal Comm'n *309, 310*
Northpark Assocs. No. 2, Ltd. v.
  Homart Dev. Co. 229
Norton v. Duluth Transfer Ry. 251
Nystrom v. Cabada 172

O'Brien v. O'Brien 106
O'Callaghan v. Waller & Beckwith
  Realty Co. 155
Oceanside Cmty. Ass'n v. Oceanside
  Land Co. 261
Ogilvie v. Idaho Bank & Trust Co. 92
O'Keeffe v. Snyder 22
Old Dominion Iron & Steel Corp. v.
  Virginia Elec. & Power Co. 257, 258
Omega Corp. of Chesterfield v. Malloy 271
165 Broadway Bldg. v. City Investing Co. 257
Orange & Rockland Util. v. Philwood
  Estates 257
O'Reilly v. Frye 123
Orr v. Byers *199*
Otero v. Pacheco 237
Othen v. Rosier *239, 241*

PA Nw. Distribs., Inc. v. Zoning Hearing
  Bd. 283
Page v. Bloom 241
Pagelsdorf v. Safeco Ins. Co. 155
Paine v. Meller 169, 175
Palazzolo v. Rhode Island *307*
Palm Beach County v. Cove Club
  Investors, Ltd. 272
Palm Springs, City of, v. Living Desert
  Reserve 49
Paradine v. Jane 139
Parise v. Citizens Nat'l Bank 191
Parker & Edgarton v. Foote 244
Parkhurst's Estate, In re 26
Pasadena v. California-Michigan Land &
  Water Co. 249
Patton v. Madison County 270

Payne v. TK Auto Wholesalers 11
Penn Bowling Recreation Ctr., Inc. v. Hot
  Shoppes, Inc. 247
*Penn Cent. Transp. Co. v. City of
  New York* *306, 307*
Pennell v. City of San Jose 157
Pennoyer v. Allen 217
Pennsylvania Coal Co. v. Mahon *302, 305, 312*
People v. Nogarr 92
People v. Stover 289
Pernell v. Southall Realty 143
Persson-Mokvist v. Anderson 270
Peterson v. Superior Court (Paribas) 155
P.H. Inv. v. Oliver 152
Pierson v. Post *4, 6*
*Pocono Springs Civic Ass'n, Inc. v.
  MacKenzie* *275*
Poletown Neighborhood Council v. City of
  Detroit 300
Pollock v. Ramirez 272
Porter v. Porter 93
Posner v. Davis 172
Preble v. Maine Cent. R.R. Co. 16, 17
Preseault v. United States *230, 251*
Pross v. Excelsior Cleaning & Dyeing Co. 138
Public Access Shoreline Haw. v. Hawaii County
  Planning Comm'n 242

*Raleigh Ave. Beach Ass'n v. Atlantis
  Beach Club, Inc.* *243*
Redarowicz v. Ohlendorf 174
Reed v. King 172
Regency Homes Ass'n v. Egermayer 262
Reno, City of, v. Matley 257
Renton, City of, v. Playtime Theatres 291
Reste Realty Corp. v. Cooper *148*
Rhue v. Cheyenne Homes, Inc. 272
Rick v. West *275*
Riddle v. Harmon *89, 91*
Riley v. Bear Creek Planning Comm. 266
Riley v. Griffin 177
Riverside Park Condominium Unit Owners
  Ass'n v. Lucas 277
Robroy Land Co. v. Prather 80
Rochester, City of; State v. 286
Rockafellor v. Gray *181, 182*
Rodgers v. Reimann 269
Rodgers v. Village of Tarrytown 287
Rogers v. Yellowstone Park Co. 110

Romanchuk v. Plotkin 238
Rose v. Chaikin 218
Rosengrant v. Rosengrant *183*
Rothschild v. Wolf 252
Ruckelshaus v. Monsanto Co. 272, 298
Rucker v. Wynn 144
Rumiche Corp. v. Eisenreich 138
Runyon v. Paley 257, 258

Sabo v. Horvath 203
Sakansky v. Wein 249
Sanborn v. McLean *207, 264, 265, 266, 267*
Sanderson v. Saxon 90
Santa Barbara, City of, v. Adamson 294
Sargent v. Ross 155
Save Our Rural Env't v. Snohomish County 287
Sawada v. Endo *97*
Schad v. Borough of Mt. Ephraim 291
Schley v. Couch 12
Schulman v. Serrill 270
Schwenn v. Kaye 182
Sellentin v. Terkildsen 242
Sensenbrenner v. Rust, Orling & Neale 173
Shack; State v. 9
Shanks v. Floom 240
Shapiro v. Sutherland 172
Shelley v. Kraemer *272*
Shelley's Case. *See* Wolfe v. Shelley
Shepard v. Purvine 233
Shippan Point Ass'n v. McManus 273
Shorter v. Shelton 143
Skendzel v. Marshall 191
Slavin v. Rent Control Bd. of Brookline 136
Smiley v. Van Winkle 135
Smith v. Chanel, Inc. 7
Smith v. McEnany 147
Smith's Transfer & Storage Co. v. Hawkins 120
Snider v. Deban 128
Snow v. Van Dam 269
Snyder v. Ambrose 146
Snyder v. Lovercheck 173
Sommer v. Kridel *145, 146*
Sondin v. Bernstein 93
South Staffordshire Water Co. v. Sharman 12
Southern Burlington County NAACP v. Township
    of Mount Laurel (Mount Laurel I) *295*
Southern Burlington County NAACP v. Township
    of Mount Laurel (Mount Laurel II) 295

Southern Cal. Edison Co. v. Bourgerie 272
Spencer's Case 254, 255, 256
Spiller v. Mackereth *101*
Sprague v. Kimball 265
Spur Indus., Inc. v. Del E. Webb Dev. Co. *225*
S.S. Kresge Co. of Mich. v. Winkelman
    Realty Co. 247
Stambovsky v. Ackley *172*
Standard Live Stock Co. v. Pentz 127
Stanton v. T.L. Herbert & Sons 248
State v. *See name of other party*
State ex rel. Haman v. Fox 242, 243
State ex rel. Stoyanoff v. Berkeley *289*
State ex rel. Thornton v. Hay 242–243
Stephens & Co. v. Albers 6
Stewart v. AmSouth Mortgage Co., Inc. 91
Stewart v. Jackson 270
Stoner v. Zucker 234
Stover; People v. 289
Stoyanoff, State ex rel., v. Berkeley *289*
Strauch v. Charles Apartments Co. 155
Strawn v. Canuso 172
Streams Sports Club, Ltd. v. Richmond 262
Stroda v. Joice Holdings 238
Suttle v. Bailey 269
Swartzbaugh v. Sampson *103*
Sweeney v. Sweeney *183, 184*
Sylva Shops Ltd. P'ship v. Hibbard 146
Symphony Space, Inc. v. Pergola
    Props., Inc. *79, 80*

Tahoe-Sierra Preservation Council, Inc. v.
    Tahoe Reg'l Planning Agency *305, 308*
Tefft v. Munson 203
Tenhet v. Boswell 93, 94
Thomas v. Johnson 93
Thompson v. Baxter 123
Thompson, Estate of, v. O'Tool 126
Thomson, Estate of, v. Wade 235
Thornton, State ex rel., v. Hay 242-243
3 W Partners v. Bridges 265
Tillinghast v. Bradford 68
Tindall v. Yeats 93
Tindolph v. Schoenfeld Bros., Inc. 265
Toledo Trust Co. v. Simmons 11
Townsend v. Singleton 124
Toys 'R' Us v. Silva 284
Trustees of Columbia Coll. v. Thatcher 273

Tulk v. Moxhay *264*

Union Bond & Trust Co. v. Blue Creek
   Redwood Co. 191
Union Gas & Oil v. Fyffe 7
Union Nat'l Bank of Lowell v. Nesmith 252
United States Nat'l Bank of Or. v.
   Homeland, Inc. 145
United States v. *See name of other party*

Van Sandt v. Royster *237, 238*
Van Sant v. Rose 263
Van Valkenburgh v. Lutz *14*
Varnum v. Brien *112*
Village of Belle Terre v. Boraas *293, 294*
Village of Euclid v. Ambler Realty Co. *217, 280*
Violi, Estate of 93

Waldorff Ins. & Bonding, Inc. v. Eglin Nat'l
   Bank *206*
Waldrop v. Town of Brevard 252
Walker v. Ireton 165, 166
Walker Rogge, Inc. v. Chelsea Title & Guar. Co. ... *212*
Walner v. City of Turlock 252
Ward v. Mattuschek 164
Wardlow v. Pozzi 93

Warshawsky v. American Auto. Prods. Co. 140
Washington Hydroculture, Inc. v. Payne 138
Wayne, County of, v. Hathcock 300
Webb v. Russell 135
Webb's Fabulous Pharmacies v. Beckwith 302
Werner v. Graham 265, 270
Wesson v. Leone Enters., Inc. 149
Westbrook v. Gleason 204
Western Land Co. v. Truskolaski *273*
White v. Brown *38*
White v. Samsung Elecs. Am., Inc. *8*
Whitinsville Plaza, Inc. v. Kotseas 256, 261
Whorton v. Dillingham *111*
Willard v. First Church of Christ, Scientist *235*
Wilson v. Interlake Steel Co. 219
The Winkfield 24
Winthrop v. Wadsworth 237
Witteman v. Jack Barry Cable TV 249
Wolfe v. Shelley (Shelley's Case) 70
Woodrick v. Wood *42*
Woods v. Garnett 204
Woodward v. Commissioner of Soc. Sec. 62
Wright v. Horse Creek Ranches, Inc. 246
Young v. American Mini-Theatres 291

Zamiarski v. Kozial 268
Zimmer v. Sundell 202
Zimmerman v. Marsh 100

Subject Matter Index

Abandonment, 9–10, 17
  Of easements, 250
  Nonconforming use and, 284
  Servitudes and, 274
  Tenant, 144–146
Acceptance of Gift, 26–27
Accession, 23
Actual and Exclusive Possession, 14
Adverse Possession, 13–23
  By accession, 23
  Continuity of, 17–19
  By co-owners, 22, 103
  Covenants and, 258
  Easement by, 239
  Elements of, 14–19
  Extent of property acquired by, 19–20
  Of personal property, 22
  By tenants, 21–22
Agency, 26
Alienability, 33, 46
  Of contingent interests, 64
  Of freehold estates, 50–51
  Of life estate, 38
  Possession rights, 96–97
  Restraints on, 47, 50–51
  Survivorship rights, 96–97
Animals, 4, 6
Antenuptial Agreements. See Prenuptial Agreements
Apartments. See Cooperative Apartment Corporations
Architectural Review, 272, 289–290
"As is" Sales, 173

Bailments, 24
Bank Accounts, 94–95
Benefit of the Bargain, 205
Benefits, Internalization of, 2–3
Body, Human, 8–9
Boundary Disputes, 15, 17, 23
Business Judgment Rule, 276, 277

Cause of Action, Accrual of, 20–21
Chain of Title, 4, 202, 207, 266
  Strangers to, 268, 270
Charities, 78
Chattels, 156. See also Personal
      Property
Chose in Action, 26

Civil Rights Act, 157–158
Civil Unions. See Marriage; Same-Sex Couples
Class Closing Rules, 76–77
Cohabitants, 111–113
Color of Title, 14, 17
  Entry and, 19–20
Common Interest Communities, 276–277
Common Law, 20
  Fee simple in, 32
  Lease holdovers, 126
  Marital interests under, 104–108
  Marriage, 111
Community Property, 85, 95, 108–111
Concurrent Ownership, 14, 85–114
  Forms of, 86–98
  Marital interests. See Marital Interests
  Partition of property, 99–100
  Rights and obligations of co-owners, 98–104
Condemnation. See Regulatory Takings
Condominiums, 86, 113–114, 277
Conduct
  Intentional, 216–218
  Unintentional, 218
Consideration, 24
Constructive possession, 12, 19–20
Contracts
  Binding, 164
  Breach of, 168–170
  Default, 168–169
  Installment sale, 171, 190–191
  Leaseholds as, 118–119
  Marriage, 111–112
  Obligations under, 166–168
  Oral, 165
  Privity of, 129, 131–132, 133
  Rescission, 169
  Revocation of, 166
  Of sale, 161, 162–176
  Title insurance, 211–213
Conveyance, 34
  Invalid, 200
Cooperative Apartment Corporations, 86, 114, 277
Co-owners. See also Concurrent
      Ownership
  Adverse possession by, 22
Co-parceny, 86, 98
Copyright, 7–8

Covenants, 227–228, 229
  Affirmative, 258, 261–263
  Dependent, 149
  Duration, 272
  Equitable servitudes, 227, 228, 229, 263–270
    Enforceability of, 266–267, 268–270
    Identification of benefited land, 267–270
    Negative, 265
    Real covenants distinguished, 255, 263–264
  Future, 181–182
  In general warranty deed, 177–178
  Homeowners' associations imposition of, 275, 276
  Implied, 207
  Interpretation of, 270–272
  Negative, 258, 259, 260–261
  To pay money, 275
  Present, 179–181
  Racial restrictions, 271–272
  Real covenants, 227, 228, 229, 253–263
    Easements distinguished, 254
    Equitable servitudes distinguished, 254, 263–264
  Termination of, 228, 272–275
    Changed conditions, 273–274
    Expiration, 273
  Of title, 179–182
  Touch and concern doctrine, 228, 255, 259–263
  Use, 48
Creditors, 111, 201
Curtesy, 105
Cy pres Doctrine, 81–82

Damages
  For breach of contract, 169–171
  Liquidated, 141, 170–171
  Mitigating, 145–146
  Money, 263
  For nuisance, 224–225
  Personal injury, 110
  Punitive, 152
  For regulatory takings, 311
  Severance, 299
  For warranty breach, 182
Death
  Deed delivery and, 183–184
  Spouse's rights upon, 107, 111
Debts, 111, 201
Declaratory Relief, 310
Deeds, 161, 176–186
  Covenants in, 276
  Defective, 17

  Delivery of, 183–186
  General warranty deed, 177–178
  Of gift, 25
  Prior, 204
  Quitclaim, 178, 207
  Recording of. *See* Recording Acts; Recording System
  Special warranty deed, 178
  Of trust, 162, 190
  Wild, 201–202
Defeasible Fee, 31, 32, 42–50
  Dower interest in, 105
  Rule Against Perpetuities and, 77–78
  Valuation of, 48
Defense of Marriage Act (DOMA), 112
Delivery, 25–26
  Of deed, 183–186
  Of possession, 126–129
Demise, Power to, 127
Dependent Covenants, 149
Destruction, Right of, 9
Detainer, Unlawful, 142–143
Devise, 33
Discrimination, Prohibition of, 157–159, 271–272, 280
Disposal. *See* Disposition
Disposition, 3, 9. *See also* Transfers
Dispossession, Permanent, 302–303
Division, Equitable, 13
Divorce, 85, 86, 106–107, 111
Doctrine, Legal, 5
DOMA (Defense of Marriage Act), 112
Domestic Partners, 112
Donees, 26
Dower, 104–105, 107

Easements, 119, 228–229, 229–253
  Affirmative, 231–232, 254
  Appurtenant, 227, 230, 244, 248
  Conservation, 232
  Creation of, 235–244, 245–246
    By estoppel, 235
    By grant, 235, 245–246
    By implication, 236–239, 246
    By prescription, 239–244, 246
  Division of, 248–249
  Exclusive, 248–249
  In gross, 230–231, 244–245, 248–249
  Implied, 227, 238–239
  Licenses, 233–234

Location change, 247
Merger of, 250
Negative, 227, 231, 232, 243–244
By prescription, 227
Prescriptive, 18
Profit à prendre. *See* Profit à Prendre
Public prescriptive, 242–243
Real covenants distinguished, 255
Reservation of, 235
Scope of, 238, 245–250
Termination of, 227, 250–253
Transfers of, 244–245
Types of, 230–233
Upon public land, 244
Use of, 249–250
Efficiency, 2, 5
Ejectment, 119, 143
Eminent Domain, 140, 297–313. *See also* Regulatory
    Takings
Covenants extinguished by, 272
Takings clause, 298–299
Enfeoff, 64
Entry
Color of title and, 19–20
Re-entry rights, 29, 134, 142
Right of, 44, 54, 57, 77
Statutory destruction of, 77–78
Environmental Protection
Zoning and, 292–293
Equitable Distribution Statutes, 106
Equitable Servitudes. *See* Covenants
Escheat, 31, 34
Escrow, 184, 185
Estate
Conveyance of, 33
Determinable, 56, 58
Dominant, 230
Alteration of, 251
Division of, 248
Enlargement of, 247–248
Duration of, 31, 32
Escheat of, 34
Freehold. *See* Freehold Estates
Leasehold. *See* Leasehold Estates
Life. *See* Life Estate
Possessory, 30
Privity of, 18, 129, 132–133, 181, 229, 255–258
Servient, 230, 252
Estoppel
Deed delivery by, 185–186

Easements by, 235
Equitable, 23, 165, 233, 274
Eviction, 124, 142
Constructive, 146, 147–149
Retaliatory, 153
Exactions, 308–310
Exception, 235
Exclusion, Right of, 6, 9
Exclusivity, 7
Executory Interests, 29, 35, 46, 49, 53, 54,
    64–66
Rule Against Perpetuities and, 77–78
Shifting, 54, 64, 66
Springing, 54, 64, 66, 184
Externalities, 2

Fair Housing Act, 158, 294
Fairness, 5
Family, 271, 293–294
Fee Simple, 31, 32–33
Absolute, 22, 29, 32–33, 42
Conditional, 34, 36
Determinable, 29, 42–43
Easements distinguished, 229
Subject to condition subsequent, 42, 43–45
Subject to executory limitation, 42, 49–50
Fee Tail, 30, 31, 34–36
Modern equivalent, 36
Feme Covert, 95, 104
Feme Sole, 95, 104
Feoffee, 64
Feudalism, 30–31
Fiduciary Duty, 101, 103
Brokers, 162–163
Fiduciary Relationship, 171
Financing Devices, 186–192
Finders of Lost Property, 9–13
Fixtures, 156
Forfeiture, 31, 50
Fraud, 209
Free Speech, 290–291
Freehold Estates, 29–51
Alienability of, 50–51
Defeasible fees. *See* Defeasible Fee
Fee simple. *See* Fee Simple
Fee tail. *See* Fee Tail
Feudal origins of, 30–31
Life estate. *See* Life Estate
Future Interests, 21, 30, 53–83
Contingent, 72

Grantees, 58–66
Grantor-retained, 55–58
Restatement (Third) of Property, proposed
          changes, 66–67
Reversions as, 33
Statutory destruction of, 78
Types of, 54
Validity of, 73, 75–77

Gas, 7
Gifts
    Acceptance of, 26–27
    Causa mortis, 24
    Class, 61
    Inter vivos, 24
Good Faith, 166
    In accession, 23
    In adverse possession, 15–16
Group Homes, 271
Growth Controls, 295–296

Habitability, 149–153
Harm, 216–218
Holdovers, 123–124, 126
Homeowners' Associations, 262–263,
          275, 276
    Covenants imposed by, 276
    Standard of review of actions taken by,
          276–277

Inheritance, 33–34
Injunctions, 263, 310
Installment Sale Contracts, 171, 190–191
Intellectual Property, 7–8
Intent, Gifts and, 24, 25
Interests
    Contingent, 53, 63–64
    Executory. *See* Executory Interests
    Future. *See* Future Interests
    Marital. *See* Marital Interests
    Mutual, 256
    Vested, 53–54, 74–75
        Uncertainty in, 73
Interference, Substantial, 216, 218
Intestacy, 33

Joint Tenancy, 85, 86, 87–95
    Four unities of, 85, 88–89
    Severance of, 90–94
Judgment, Confession of, 141

Knowledge, Actual, 15

Labor Theory, 2
Laches, 46, 274
Land Use
    Covenants re. *See* Covenants
    Judicial control of, 215–226
    Permits, 297
    Public control of. *See* Zoning
Landlords. *See also* Leasehold
          Estates
    Obligations of, 118, 146–156
    Remedies, 117–118, 125–126, 129, 141–146
    Self-help, 143–144
    Tort liability of, 153–156
Law
    Common. *See* Common Law
    Statutory. *See* Statutory Law
Lawyers, 163
Leasehold Estates, 30, 31, 117–159
    Assignments, 117, 129–132, 133–136
    Delivery of possession, 126–129
    Fixtures, 156
    Holdovers, 123–124, 126
    Illegal uses, 138–139
    Joint tenancies and, 92–93
    Landlord's obligations, 118, 146–156
    Landlord's remedies, 117–118, 125–126, 129,
          141–146
    Nature of, 118–119
    Periodic tenancy, 117
    Social regulation of, 156–159
    Subleases, 117, 129, 132–133
    Tenancy at will, 117
    Tenant's obligations, 117, 137–140
    Tenant's remedies, 118, 128, 146–156
    Term of, 119–120
    Term of years, 117
    Termination of, 144
    Transfer, what constitutes, 137
    Types of, 117, 119–126
Legal Doctrine, 5
Lending Practices, 191–192
Licenses, 119, 233–234
Lienholders, 21
Liens, 200
Life Estate, 22, 29, 31, 36–42
    Alienation restraints, 50
    Equitable, 39–40, 50
    Fee simple split, 33

Legal, 39–40
In personal property, 40
Waste, 40–42
Limited Access Property, 3
Locus in Quo, 11
Loss, Risk of, 174–176
Lost Property, 9, 10–13

Maine Doctrine, 17
Marital Interests, 85–86, 104–113
Common law re, 104–107
Community property, 85, 95, 108–111
Death and, 107
Divorce and, 106–107
Separate property, 85, 109–110
Spousal elective share, 105, 107
Tenancy by the entirety, 95–98
Unmarried cohabitants, 111–113
Marketability Rules, 68–83
Marriage, 31
Common law, 111
Contracts, 111–112
Same-sex, 86, 112–113
Substitutes, 112
Merger, 69, 70, 178–179
Covenants extinguished by, 272
Of easements, 250
Minerals, 15
Misappropriation, 7
Mislaid Property, 10, 13
Mortgages, 162, 186–190
Cotenants' responsibilities for, 102
Deceptive lending practices, 191–192
Joint tenancies and, 91–92
Mortgage lenders, 163
Mortgagees as purchasers, 201
Types of, 187–188
Unfair lending practices, 191–192

Natural Law Theories, 2
Necessity, 236, 236–237, 238–239
Negligence, 153
Notice, 199
Actual, 201
Constructive, 201–207
Inquiry, 205–207, 267
Of occupation, 15
Record, 201–205, 266
Notice Acts, 196–197
Novation, 131
Nuisance, 119, 215–226

Abating, 223, 303–304
Avoiding, 139
Coming to, 222
Economic theory of, 220-224
Private, 215, 216–218
Public, 215, 216
Remedies, 220–225
Trespass and, 219

Occupation, 15–16
Oil and Gas, 7
Open and Notorious Possession, 14–15, 241
Ouster, 19, 101
Ownership
Accounting for costs of, 102–103
Concurrent. *See* Concurrent Ownership
Co-owners, 22
Disclaimers of, 16–17
Duration of, 32
Possession and, 2, 24
Uncertainty about. *See* Rule Against
Perpetuities
Partition, 99–100
Patent, 7
Pensions, 110
Periodic Tenancy, 117, 119, 120–122
Perpetuities. *See* Rule Against Perpetuities
Personal Image, 8
Personal Property, 23–27
Adverse possession of, 22
Bailments, 24
Gifts of, 24–27
Life estate in, 40
Seizure of, 146
Taking by regulation, 302
Tenancy by the entirety and, 98
Police Power, 288
Possession, 3–23. *See also* Estate
Actual, 14, 127–129
Adverse. *See* Adverse Possession
Capture and, 4
By conquest, 4
Constructive, 12, 19
Continuous, 17–18
By creation, 7
Custom re, 5
Delivery and, 24–25
Delivery of, 126–129
Discovery and, 4
Entitlement to, 142
Exclusive, 14, 100–101

First, 6
Future right to. *See* Future Interests
Inquiry and, 206–207
Leasehold estates and, 117
Legal right to, 126–127
Obligation to take, 129
Open and notorious, 14–15, 241
Ownership and, 2, 24
Recovery of, 45–46
Rights, 96–97
Tacking, 18–19
Unlawful, 117
Unowned things, 4–9
Wrongful, 124

Possessors, Prior, 6
Prenuptial Agreements, 107
Privity
    In adverse possession, 18
    Of contract, 129, 131–132, 133
    Equitable servitudes and, 264, 266
    Of estate, 18, 129, 132–133, 181, 229, 255–258
    Horizontal, 228, 255, 256–257
    Vertical, 228, 255, 256, 257–258
Productivity, 5, 7
Professional Skills and Credentials, 106–107
Profit à Prendre, 119, 228, 233
    Division of, 248–249
    Transfer of, 245
Property
    Concept and definition of, 1–2
    Customs re, 3
    Improvements to, 103
    Legal protection of, 1–2, 3
    Limited access, 3
    Marital. *See* Marital Interests
    Personal. *See* Personal Property
    Real. *See* Real Property
    Redistribution of, 298
    Repairs to, 102–103
    Social contingency and, 1
    Theories of, 2–3
Property Rights
    Abandonment, 9–10
    In body, 8–9
    Disposition, 3, 9
    Exclusion, 6, 9
    Intangible, 7
    Lost property, 9–13
    Mislaid property, 9, 10
    Personal image, 8

Policy and, 5
Possession, 3–4, 9
Use, 3, 9
Wives, 104–105
Property Rules, 5
Property Values, 289
Public Records, 209
Public Trust Doctrine, 242, 243

Quiet Enjoyment, 146–149, 181
Quiet Title Actions, 22
Quitclaim Deeds, 178, 207

Race Acts, 196
Race-notice Acts, 197
Real Property, 30
    Invasion of, 302–303
    Support rights, 225
Recording Acts, 193, 194, 197–198
    Protection afforded by, 200–201
Recording System, 194–196
    Instruments, 198–200
    Title registration contrasted, 208–211
Redemption, 187
Re-entry, Right of, 29, 134, 142
Registration, 194
Regulatory Takings, 297–313. *See also* Eminent
        Domain
    Academic theories re, 311–313
    Arbitrariness prohibited, 305
    Compensation for, 297, 299, 301–302, 311–313
    Conditional burdens
        Essential nexus, 308–309, 310
        Rough proportionality, 309–310
    Legitimate state objective in, 305–308
    Public use requirement, 297, 298, 299–302, 312
    Remedies, 310–311
    Use permits, 308–310
    By use regulation/restriction, 302–313
    What constitutes, 302–313
Releases, 131
    Of covenants, 273
    Of easements, 250
Religion, Free Exercise of, 291–292
Religious Land Use and Institutionalized Persons Act
        of 2000 (RLUIPA), 292
Remainders, 21, 34, 36, 53–54, 58–64
    Contingent, 53, 56, 58, 62–64
    Destructibility of, 68, 69–70. *See also* Rule
                Against Perpetuities
    Marketability rules, 68–83

Vested, 53, 55, 58, 59–62
    Complete divestment, subject to, 53
    Indefeasibly vested, 53
    Partial divestment, subject to, 53
Rents, 100–102. *See also* Leasehold
        Estates
    Acceleration, 141
    Double, 135
    Payment of, 137
    Rent control, 156–157
Reservation of Easement, 235
Resources, Common, 7
Restitution, 204–205
Return on Investment, 305
Reversions, 33, 34, 36, 54, 55–56
    Leasehold estates, 132
Reverter, Possibility of, 42, 43, 56–57, 77
    Statutory destruction of, 77–78
RLUIPA. *See* Religious Land Use and
        Institutionalized Persons Act of 2000
        (RLUIPA)
Rule Against Perpetuities, 36, 46, 54, 68, 72–83
    Commercial transactions, 79–80
    Measuring lives, 75–77
    Possibilities vs. probabilities, 78–79
    Validating lives, 75–77
Rule in Shelley's Case, 68, 70–71, 72
Rule of Convenience, 61–62, 76–77

Sale. *See* Transfers
Same-Sex Couples, 112–113
Security Deposits, 141
Seisin, 30
Separate Property, 85, 109–110
Servitudes, 48, 227–278
    Covenants. *See* Covenants
    Easements. *See* Easements
    Equitable. *See* Covenants
Sex, Determination re, 113
Shelley's Case. See Rule in Shelley's Case
Shelter Rule, 200–201
Speech, Freedom of, 290–291
Spendthrift Trust, 50, 68
Spousal Contracts, 108
Statute of Frauds, 163–166
Statute of Uses, 65–66
Statutes, Modification by, 13
Statutes of Limitations
    Adverse possession, 13
    Covenant breach, 180
    Tolling, 19, 20

Statutory Law, 20
    Modification by statute, 13
Substantial Interference, 216, 218
Support Rights, 225
Survivorship Rights, 87, 94

Takings, Regulatory. *See* Regulatory Takings
Taxes
    Cotenants' responsibilities for, 102
    Death, 31
    Liens, 97–98
    Payment of, 19
Tenancy
    In common, 85, 86–87
    By the entirety, 85, 86, 95–98
    In partnership, 86, 98
    Periodic, 119, 120–122
    At sufferance, 123–126
    At will, 119, 122–123
Tenants
    Adverse possession by, 21–22
    In chief, 30
    In demesne, 30
    Obligations of, 117, 137–140
    In possession, 31
    Remedies, 118, 128, 146–156
Termination, Power of, 29, 44, 53, 56, 57–58
Title
    Abandoned property, 9–10
    Adverse possessor, 22
    After-acquired, 182, 202–203
    Assuring good, 193–214
    Chain of. *See* Chain of Title
    Color of, 14, 17, 19–20
    Covenants of, 179–182
    Defective, 167–168
    Equitable, 174–175, 185
    Forfeiture, 44–45
    Intent to transfer, 24
    Marketable, 167, 193, 207–208, 212–213
    Quiet title actions, 22
    Record, 203–204
    Recording of, 194–201
    Registration, 193, 194, 208–211
    Relative, 6, 9, 10
    Transfers in Torrens system, 209. *See also*
        Transfers
    Warranties of, 171, 177–178, 194
    Worthier, 68, 71–72
Title Insurance, 193, 194, 211–213
Title Searching, 195–196

Torrens System, 208–211
Tort Liability, 153–156
Tract Index, 207
Trade Secrets, 7
Transfers, 161–192
    "As is" sales, 173
    Closings, 163
    Contracts of sale, 161, 162–176
    Deeds, 176–186
    Of defeasible fee, 45
    Disclosure duties, 171–173
    Of easements, 244–245
    Of fee simple determinable, 43
    Of fee simple subject to condition subsequent, 44
    Financing devices, 186–192
    Of leasehold interest, 135–137
    By mortgagor, 188
    Of possibility of reverter, 57
    Of rights, 215
    Title, 24, 209
Treasure Trove, 12
Trespass, 119
    Aggressive, 16
    Nuisance and, 219
Trespassers, 9–11
Trusts, 26, 67–68
    Advantages, 68
    Basics, 67–68
    Beneficiaries, 67
    Deeds of, 162, 190
    Perpetual, 82–83
    Public, 242, 243
    Revocation, 72
    Spendthrift, 50, 68

UMPA (Uniform Marital Property Act), 108
Unclean Hands, 275
Unfair Competition Law, 7
Uniform Conservation Easement Act, 232
Uniform Marital Property Act (UMPA), 108
Uniform Statutory Rule Against Perpetuities
    (USRAP), 54, 80, 81, 82–83
Use
    Adverse, 240
    Apparent, 238
    Competing, 215
    Conditions on, 254
    Continuous, 237, 241
    Covenants, 48
    Disfavored, 222

    Of easements, 249–250
    Economically viable, 304–305
    Enjoining, 222–223, 224–225
    Exceptional, 279, 285–286
    Exclusive, 3, 241
    Illegal, 138–139
    Incompatible, 219–220, 280
    Of land. *See* Land Use
    Nonconforming, 283–284
    Open and notorious, 241
    Permits, 308–310
    Prescriptive, 239–242
    Prior, 236
    Public, 297, 298, 299–302, 312
    Residential purposes, 270–271
    Restrictions, 270, 302–313
    Social utility, 216–217
    Value of, 219–223
    Zoning and. *See* Zoning
USRAP (Uniform Statutory Rule Against
    Perpetuities), 54, 80, 81, 82–83
Utilitarian Theories, 2
Utility, 2

Variances, 279, 284–285

Wait-and-see Statutes, 80–81
Wardship, 31
Warranties
    Habitability, 149–153
    Quality, 173–174
    Title, 171, 177–178, 194
Waste, 2
    Avoiding, 138
    Life estate, 40–42
Winkfield Doctrine, 24
Women
    Married, 95, 104
    Single, 95, 104
Worthier Title, Doctrine of, 68, 71–72

Zoning, 168, 279–296
    Aesthetic objectives, 289–291
    Amendments, 286–287
    Authorization for, 279, 281–282
        Comprehensive land use plan, 282
        Enabling legislation, 281–282
    Cluster, 288
    Conditional, 279, 287–288
    Contract, 279

Cumulative, 280–281
Density, 281
Environmental protection and, 292–293
Exceptional uses, 279, 285–286
Exclusionary, 294–296
Floating, 279, 287
Household composition and, 293–294

Limits on power for, 279, 288–296
Mutually exclusive, 280, 281
Nonconforming uses, 283–284
Religious exercise and, 291–292
Spot, 279, 286–287
Statutory discretion and restraint re, 279, 283–288
Variances, 279, 284–285